The Worlds Cause Lawyers Make

The Worlds
Cause Lawyers Make

Structure and Agency in Legal Practice

Edited by

AUSTIN SARAT

STUART SCHEINGOLD

STANFORD LAW AND POLITICS

An imprint of Stanford University Press · Stanford, California 2005

Stanford University Press
Stanford, California
© 2005 by the Board of Trustees of the
Leland Stanford Junior University

Library of Congress Cataloging-in-Publication Data

The worlds cause lawyers make : structure and agency in legal
practice / edited by Austin Sarat and Stuart Scheingold.
    p. cm.
Includes bibliographical references (p.   ) and index.
ISBN 0-8047-5228-1 (cloth : alk. paper) —
ISBN 0-8047-5229-x (pbk. : alk. paper)
    1. Cause lawyers. 2. Public interest law. 3. Practice of law—
Moral and ethical aspects. 4. Practice of law—Political aspects. I.
Sarat, Austin. I. Scheingold, Stuart A.
K118.P82W67 2005
340'.115—dc22

                                                        2005000745

Printed in the United States of America on acid-free, archival-
quality paper

Original Printing 2005
Last figure below indicates year of this printing:
14   13   12   11   10   09   08   07   06   05

Typeset at Stanford University Press in 10/13 Minion

To Stephanie, Lauren, Emily, and Mr. B (AS)

To Bill C., Dick K., Jerry L., Don S., Bill G., and Len C.
Brothers lost, Brothers found (SS)

Acknowledgments

This project has been, from its inception, a genuine collaboration, first between the two editors, and then among all of the participants. We are grateful to the extraordinary group of scholars who assembled to pool their efforts to understand cause lawyering for their energy, interest, and insight. We would like to thank Terrence Halliday, formerly chair of the Working Group on the Comparative Study of the Legal Profession, for his continuing encouragement. We are particularly grateful to the Département de sciences sociales de l'Ecole Normale Supérieure de Cachan and the Groupe d'Analyse des Politiques Publiques (CNRS), and especially Professors Jacques Commaille and Patrice Duran for making possible the conference at which the essays collected in this book were first presented. For their generous financial support we gratefully acknowledge the GIP–Mission de recherche Droit et Justice, the journal Droit et Société, the Mission Scientifique des Universités (MSU), the Centre National de la Recherche Scientifique (CNRS), the Ecole Normale Supérieure de Cachan, and the Office of the Dean of the Faculty at Amherst College. Finally, a special word of thanks to Liora Israël for her energetic commitment to, and work on behalf of, this project.

Contents

Contributors   xi

Introduction: The Dynamics of Cause Lawyering—Constraints
and Opportunities   1
AUSTIN SARAT AND STUART SCHEINGOLD

Section I. Causes and the Lawyers Who Serve Them: How Do
Causes Make Their Lawyers and Lawyers Make Their Causes?

1. Corporate Responsibility and the South African Drug Wars:
   Outline of a New Frontier for Cause Lawyers   37
   RONEN SHAMIR

2. A Political-Professional Commitment? French Workers' and
   Unions' Lawyers as Cause Lawyers   63
   LAURENT WILLEMEZ

3. Professional Identity and Political Commitment among Lawyers
   for Conservative Causes   83
   ANN SOUTHWORTH

4. Economic Libertarians, Property, and Institutions: Linking Activism,
   Ideas, and Identities among Property Rights Advocates   112
   LAURA HATCHER

5. From Cause Lawyering to Resistance: French Communist Lawyers
   in the Shadow of History (1929–1945)   147
   LIORA ISRAËL

Section II: Making a Practice: Balancing Professionalism
and Activism

6. Supporting a Cause, Developing a Movement, and Consolidating
   a Practice: Cause Lawyers and Sexual Orientation Litigation in
   Vermont   171
   SCOTT BARCLAY AND ANNA-MARIA MARSHALL

7. Exploring the Sources of Cause and Career Correspondence
   among Cause Lawyers   203
   LYNN C. JONES

8. Dilemmas of "Progressive" Lawyering: Empowerment and
   Hierarchy   239
   COREY S. SHDAIMAH

9. Negotiating Cause Lawyering Potential in the Early Years of
   Corporate Practice   274
   DOUGLAS THOMSON

Section III. Strategy and Social Capital

10. Cause Lawyers and Judicial Community in Israel: Legal Change
    in a Diffuse, Normative Community   307
    PATRICIA J. WOODS

11. Transgressive Cause Lawyering in the Developing World:
    The Case of India   349
    JAYANTH K. KRISHNAN

12. Cause Lawyering for Collective Justice: A Case Study of the *Amparo
    Colectivo* in Argentina   383
    STEPHEN MEILI

13. Asylum Law Practice in the United Kingdom after the Human
    Rights Act   410
    RICHARD J. MAIMAN

14. ATLA Shrugged: Why Personal Injury Lawyers Are Not Public
    Defenders of Their Own Causes   425
    MICHAEL MCCANN AND WILLIAM HALTOM

Afterword: In the End, or the Cause of Law   463
PETER FITZPATRICK

Index   471

Contributors

SCOTT BARCLAY, Political Science, SUNY, Albany

PETER FITZPATRICK, Law, Birkbeck College, University of London

WILLIAM HALTOM, Political Science, University of Puget Sound

LAURA HATCHER, Political Science and Legal Studies, University of Wisconsin, Madison

LIORA ISRAËL, Ecole Normale Superieure de Canchan, France

LYNN C. JONES, Criminal Justice, Northern Arizona University

JAYANTH KRISHNAN, Law, William Mitchell School of Law

RICHARD J. MAIMAN, Political Science, University of Southern Maine and University of Sussex

ANNA-MARIA MARSHALL, Political Science, University of Illinois

MICHAEL MCCANN, Political Science, University of Washington

STEPHEN MEILI, Law, University of Wisconsin

AUSTIN SARAT, Law, Jurisprudence and Social Thought and Political Science, Amherst College

STUART SCHEINGOLD, Political Science, University of Washington

RONEN SHAMIR, Sociology, Tel-Aviv University

COREY S. SHDAIMAH, Social Work, Bryn Mawr College

ANN SOUTHWORTH, Law, Case Western Reserve University

DOUGLAS THOMSON, Criminal Justice, Chicago State University

LAURENT WILLEMEZ, Sociology, Université de Poitiers, France

PATRICIA J. WOODS, Jewish Studies and Political Science, University of Florida

The Worlds Cause Lawyers Make

The Dynamics of Cause Lawyering

Constraints and Opportunities

AUSTIN SARAT AND STUART SCHEINGOLD

> History is a story of events and not forces or ideas with predictable courses.
> —Hannah Arendt, *The Human Condition*, p. 252

Introduction

Cause lawyering is a distinctive, if not unique, style of legal practice. A heterogeneous category, encompassing lawyers who devote their entire professional lives to a single cause as well as lawyers who are less closely identified with any cause (Hilbink 2003), it is characterized, in the United States and elsewhere, by its difference from conventional, client-centered advocacy (see Simon 1978). The classic, lawyer "as hired gun" approach treats legal professionalism as a set of technical skills available to the highest bidder (Fried 1976; Silver and Cross 2000). As a result, moral and/or political commitment, the defining attributes of cause lawyers, are for most of their peers relegated to the margins of their professional lives (see Simon 1984, 1998). Lawyering, in this conception, is neither a domain for moral or political advocacy nor a place to express a lawyer's beliefs about the way society should be organized, disputes resolved, and values expressed.

For cause lawyers such objectives move from the margins to the center of their professional lives (Sarat 1998). Lawyering is attractive precisely because it is a deeply moral or political activity, a kind of work that encourages pursuit of the right, the good, or the just. Cause lawyers have something to believe in and bring their beliefs to bear in their work lives (Scheingold and Sarat 2004). In this sense they are neither alienated from their work nor anxious about the separation of role from person. Causes offer lawyers the chance to enlist in a partisan pursuit of the good while refusing completely to commodify their professional skills.

This kind of legal practice was pioneered in the United States and has been exported and marketed abroad along with American notions of rights and ideas about the need for an autonomous legal order (see Dezalay and Garth 2002). Yet cause lawyering also has indigenous roots and is locally adapted in many different parts of the world (for examples see Meili 1998; Shamir and Chinski 1998; Sterret 1998; Kidder and Miyazawa 1993). Cause lawyering is, in short, shaped and transformed by legal, professional, and political traditions very different from the United States and by social contexts in which the development of the rule of law would in itself be a substantial achievement. Where it is simply imposed on a local context, it tends not to flourish (Morag-Levine 2001).

Whether here or abroad, cause lawyering exists within a distinctive set of constraints and opens up an equally distinctive set of possibilities. How cause lawyers adapt to those constraints and take advantage of those possibilities is the subject of this book. In the chapters that follow, contributors describe how cause lawyers deal with constraints imposed by the causes/movements with which they are affiliated, the practice settings in which they work, and/or the strategic resources made available to them by their broader legal/political environment. But they also discuss the way lawyers help to fashion those movements, practice settings, and environments in their work as innovators, inventors, and agents of change. It is in this spirit that we title this book *The Worlds Cause Lawyers Make: Structure and Agency in Legal Practice* and that the contributors have examined the mutually constitutive relationship among the social, political, and legal worlds in which cause lawyers operate and which they help to construct.

In two previous edited collections we explored respectively the relations of cause lawyers and the organized legal profession and the way cause lawyering is shaped by, and shapes, processes of political change associated with globalization and democratization. In the first, *Cause Lawyering: Political Commitments and Professional Responsibilities* (Sarat and Scheingold 1998a), we argued that legal professions everywhere both need and, at the same time, are threatened by cause lawyering. They need lawyers who commit themselves and their legal skills to furthering a vision of the good society because this "moral activism" puts a humane face on lawyering and provides an appealing alternative to the value-neutral, "hired gun" imagery that often dogs the legal profession (Sarat and Scheingold 1998b).

Yet cause lawyering is everywhere a deviant strain within the legal profession. Morally activist lawyers share with their clients responsibility for the ends they are promoting in their representation. In so doing, lawyers elevate the profession's moral posture beyond a crude instrumentalism in which they sell their services without regard to the ends to which those services are put (Scheingold and Sarat 2004). Cause lawyers thus reconnect law and morality, making tangible the idea that lawyering is a "public profession," one whose contribution to society goes beyond the aggregation, assembling, and deployment of technical skills.

In the United States, cause lawyering has been able to gain and maintain a foothold as a consequence of efforts made by the organized bar to protect the profession's own social capital.[1] Hostility to cause lawyering has historically been an expression of the institutional interests of the legal profession—and specifically of its links to corporate wealth and its stake in social and professional stratification. Today the organized profession is no longer quite so hostile to cause lawyering (Sarat 2001). This is due not so much to a change of heart but to the profession's continuing efforts to enhance its reputation by capitalizing on the public resonance of an inclusive understanding of rights and justice—ideals with which cause lawyering, but not the profession as a whole, is identified. It has been, albeit to a limited extent, incorporated into the bar's definition of civic professionalism. This accommodation to cause lawyering represents an acknowledgment not only of the profession's compact with the public but also of its own integrity and its constitutive links to the ideals of liberal democracy—including equal justice under law (Scheingold and Sarat 2004; Halliday 1998).

But cause lawyers also threaten the profession by destabilizing the dominant understanding of lawyering. In many countries lawyers are, to varying degrees, pledged to principles of "partisanship" and "nonaccountability" which require that they advocate their clients' causes regardless of their own personal beliefs. By rejecting nonaccountability, if not partisanship, cause lawyers establish a point from which to criticize the dominant understanding from inside the profession itself. They denaturalize and politicize that understanding. Cause lawyering exposes the fact that it is contingent, and constructed, and, in so doing, raises the political question of whose interests the dominant understanding serves. The result threatens ongoing professional projects and puts at risk the political immunity of the legal profession and the legal process.

Our second edited collection, *Cause Lawyering and the State in a Global Era* (Sarat and Scheingold 2001), spoke to a gap in the scholarly literature on the legal profession. Rarely had that literature taken the connection of lawyers and the formation and transformation of states as its subject. Although state transformation and globalization clearly influence, and are influenced by, law and lawyers, with a few notable exceptions, researchers tend to ignore these interdependencies (see Halliday and Karpik 1997). Instead, as Halliday (1998: 3) puts it, most research on lawyers focuses "on the internal organization and behavior of legal professions, overwhelmingly attends to single countries, and within national studies; it is the economic organization and behavior of professions, especially the market for legal services, that has captured most scholarly attention."

Similarly, the literature on state transformation and globalization, again with a few important exceptions (Trubek et al. 1994; Santos 1995; Keck and Sikkink 1997), ignores law and lawyers almost entirely and tends to treat the rule of law as something of a black box. The result is that not only are lawyers neglected but so too is the wealth of research that de-centers law and documents its pervasive presence and constitutive power as social practice throughout civil society, culture, politics, and the economy (McCann 1994: 6–9). *Cause Lawyering and the State in a Global Era* responded to that situation by connecting research on one kind of lawyering, cause lawyering, to the analysis of the state and state transformation in a global era.

Since those books were published, the study of cause lawyering has grown dramatically as a field of research in sociolegal studies and in research on the legal profession (see Hilbink 2003). This book, *The Worlds Cause Lawyers Make: Structure and Agency in Legal Practice*, adds to that growing body of research by turning from the macrosociological and political questions that animated our previous volumes to the connections of lawyers and causes, the settings in which cause lawyers practice, and the ways they marshal social capital and make strategic decisions. At each turn, we note constraints, the givens that shape what cause lawyers do and what cause lawyering can be, while also attending to the dynamic interactions of cause lawyers and the legal, professional, and political contexts in which they operate. Thus we take a constructivist view of cause lawyering,[2] analyzing what cause lawyers do in their day-to-day work, how they do it, and what difference it makes. We describe how they maneuver within a structure of constraints and how they improvise, invent, and create. We are interested in the ways in which cause lawyers fabricate their legal and professional contexts as well as the way those contexts constrain their professional lives.

Structure and Agency

Another way of describing our goal is to say that this book looks at cause lawyering as a form of human action in a field of institutional possibilities and, in so doing, begins the work of locating it in regard to what might be called the "structure-agency" problematic.[3] Structure refers to the social institutions, patterns of behavior, or ways of thinking that shape human behavior, and agency is the ability of humans to act with conscious intention. Structures both enable and constrain agency, even as they are the results of agentic action (Hay 1995). We will argue that because of the idealism that gives meaning to the work of cause lawyers and because of the way that meaning is refracted through political, professional, and market prisms, cause lawyering provides an especially rich and resonant terrain for inquiring about issues of structure and agency.

The structure-agency debate has at its base the fundamental question: Are we free to act as we please, or are we shaped and governed by social forces beyond our immediate control? (Ritzer 1992). Structuralists are interested in the specific conditions which produce human actions or behavior. For them, it is crucial to recognize the explicit and implicit, the recognized and taken-for-granted, ways in which our actions and behaviors are *produced*. Structuralists insist that the task of social analysis is to explore the reasons for behavior according to the structure/context in which it takes place (Hay 1995). They call our attention to institutions and their practices, to the forces of history, to demographics, such as class, race, and gender, as they work themselves out in situated action. They deny that the human actor is the ultimate social reality. For structuralists, then, as Marx observed, "men make their own history, but not under circumstances of their own choosing" (as cited in Marcuse 1964: 48).

Critics have identified three primary problems with structuralism (see Archer 1988). First, there is the problem of attributing too much power or influence to too few structures, for example, class in the Marxist tradition and neglecting the plurality of structural influences, which open up spaces of contestation, contingency, and choice. Second, there is the problem of change. Structuralism identifies and attends to repetitive patterns of behavior and action and, as a result, cannot explain how or why changes occur (Taylor 1993). Finally, critics charge that structuralist accounts underestimate the reflexivity and autonomy of human actions. They tend to concentrate on the individual's position in a social hierarchy and do not deal with the ambiguity and ambivalence of human experience.

Agency analysis responds to these criticisms by emphasizing plurality, fluidity, and possibility (Taylor 1993). It portrays individuals as operating with relative freedom in a world in which social forces make things available to the repertoire of human choice. It describes social power as fragmented/pluralized so that no single structure of power can control our actions and emphasizes the volitional character of human action, with individuals deciding what to do from a range of available options (Archer 1988). The agency approach sometimes insists on a methodological individualism and argues that the only reality we can grasp is the deeds/actions of individuals. Moreover, because individuals are aware of their options, choices, and motives, scholars should take seriously accounts and explanations provided by actors themselves rather than dismissing them as epiphenomenal or ideological.

Today, few stand rigidly on one or another side of the structure-agency debate, and important theorizing has opened up ways of talking about structure and agency in social life that are less binary and oppositional. For example, Giddens's (1984) "structuration theory" combines agency and structure approaches. He argues that structure and agency are "mutually dependent and internally related. Structure only exists through agency and agents have 'rules and resources'... which will facilitate or constrain their actions" (cited in McAnulla, n.d.: 3). In Giddens's theory actors are situated, but not inert. Giddens emphasizes reflexivity and assumes a high degree of self-awareness on the part of social actors while also recognizing the influence of structures, contexts, and constraints.[4]

In sociolegal studies, Ewick and Silbey (1998) have provided one of the most important formulations of the dynamic life of structure and agency. According to their work (1998: 39), "the individual and social structure ... (are) mutually defining. Within this framework," they continue, "consciousness is understood to be part of a reciprocal process in which the meanings given by individuals to their world become patterned, stabilized, and objectified. These meanings, once institutionalized, become part of the material and discursive systems that limit and constrain future meaning making."

They further argue that social life, through its patterns and organization, offers up specific, and limited, opportunities for "thought and action" (Ewick and Silbey 1998: 39). Social difference and temporality matter in shaping the kinds of opportunities that will be available for any individuals. What Sewell (1992) calls "schemas" define the realm of the possible and desirable, imaginable and unimaginable, in any place and at any time. But they are loosely rather than tightly organized; schemas can be altered, though not dispensed with. They can be the subject of resistance, contextual adaptation, and borrowing. They can be used differently in different settings, and those setting-specific differences, in turn, can be used to critique schemas found or used elsewhere in society. As Ewick and Silbey (1998: 40) note, "By applying schemas from one setting in another, people are able to make familiar what may be new and strange; moreover, they can appropriate the legitimacy attached to the familiar to authorize what is unconventional." It is our contention that cause lawyers provide wonderful examples of this borrowing and appropriation, applying the schemas of lawyering and legal professionalism to political action and reciprocally recoding politics as law.

But there is more to social life than cultural codes and values, what Sewell

(1992: 2) calls "fundamental tools for thought." Societies generate resources and material endowments and distribute them in nonrandom ways. These resources and endowments in turn provide greater opportunities for some social actors, expanding the range of the possible. Their absence constrains others, making the world seem more fixed and immutable than it otherwise would be. Schemas require resources in order to be translated into action; resources without cultural codes to direct their use are of little value. This differential distribution of values and material conditions accounts for the stability of social life over time, but also helps explain how, if not why, change occurs. "The possibilities of invoking schemas in a variety of settings," Ewick and Silbey (1998: 41) contend, "open up the potential for generating new resources and thus the ability to challenge or revise cultural meanings or the distribution of resources."

Their argument helps explain how social structure can appear "external and coercive" while not being separate from individual and collective patterns of thought and action (Ewick and Silbey 1998: 41). "Human agency and structure," Sewell (1992: 4) observes, "far from being opposed, in fact presuppose each other." Structures both constrain social action and are open to innovation. Structures are not "immutable constraints"; they are instead "ongoing processes" which establish the "expectations, limits, and contingencies" to which human action is accountable (Ewick and Silbey 1998: 41, 42). Individuals must, if they are to be at all efficacious, deal with these expectations, limits, and contingencies, taking them on, taking them seriously, as the raw material out of which anything new must be fashioned. Yet, through action guided by imagination, individuals can, and do, bring about new possibilities of being in the world.

Considering Structure and Agency in Three Domains of Cause Lawyering

Studies of lawyers and the legal profession are relative latecomers to the structure-agency debate. Where legal profession scholars attend to it they tend to focus either on the structures which constrain legal practice, giving it its shape and organization (e.g., Heinz and Laumann 1982), the ways lawyers act collectively to create favorable conditions within which they can market their services (Abel 1981), or how they contribute to the development of particular types of political institutions (Halliday and Karpik 1997). Others have analyzed structural transformations in different practice settings (compare Galanter and Paley 1991 and Seron 1992). Still others, emphasizing agency, look at the play of ideology in the legal profession (Gordon 1984) and the microdynamics of lawyer-client interactions (see Sarat and Felstiner 1995).

Legal profession scholars have generally not drawn on the kind of work done by Ewick and Silbey (1998) to combine structure-agency analysis. They have explored neither the ways in which law and professional norms define the field within which lawyers work nor how they rework both. One important exception is found in the work of Nelson and Trubek (1992a: 22). Borrowing from Bourdieu's (1977) theory of practice, they develop "an analytic framework that integrates studies of structural and organizational changes with studies of the reactions and perceptions of the actors involved in the changing systems . . . (and accepts) that the actions of lawyers reflect choices that are neither totally unconstrained nor totally determined structurally." Their framework "unites political economy and phenomenology" and suggests that professional ideals are partly "formed within the workplace and partly are designed, consciously or unconsciously, by lawyers for the promotion of their economic, power, and status goals. Thus lawyers' 'ideals' carry within themselves heavy traces of . . . structure."

In addition, Halliday (1999) has advanced a theory of the relationship between lawyer professionalism and political liberalism that combines structure and agency approaches. He argues (1999: 1016) that "a theory of professional action, like the general theory of action, must incorporate a *motivational theory of action*." But it must also attend to what he calls (1999: 1017) the "*institutional structure of politics*." Halliday (1999) points out, in particular, that in the research so far carried out on cause lawyers there has been little explicit attention given to the play of constraints and opportunities, to the ways cause lawyers deal with the worlds they inherit and yet make space within those worlds for new possibilities.[5] He advocates (1999: 1054–55) an agenda of research that attends to "the interplay of jurisdictional control, status politics, (and) economic benefit" alongside "ideological, aesthetic, altruistic, and civic motivations" in the worlds of cause lawyers.

Following Nelson and Trubek's (1992a) and Halliday's (1999) suggestions, *The Worlds Cause Lawyers Make: Structure and Agency in Legal Practice* describes the ways cause lawyers work in, and on, a field of constraints generated by the complex intersections of legality, professionalism, and politics. We see cause lawyers as operating within a relatively distinctive "arena" of practice. According to Nelson and Trubek (1992b: 179), "Conceptions of lawyer professionalism reflect 'the arenas' in which they are produced, that is the particular institutional settings in which groups construct, explicitly or implicitly, models of the law and of lawyering. The arenas perspective allows for the possibility that different groups will develop different versions of the professional ideal in response to a variety of political, ideological, and situational concerns."

Legality, professionalism, and politics are the general structural components that shape cause lawyering. Each consists of a historically specific set of cultural schemas and resources that define the limits of the possible. But they also provide the material with which cause lawyers can and do work. Law, professionalism, and politics are mixed and remixed in distinctive combinations by lawyers in different societies, in different historical periods, serving different causes, and working in different practice settings. How they think and what they do in their everyday work helps to produce, reproduce, and transform the schemas and resources made available to them by their legal, professional, and political worlds.

As we see their work, cause lawyers operate within a set of taken-for-granted assumptions about the boundaries between law and politics, about the meaning of professionalism, and about the place of politics in law and the learned professions. In addition, they work with, and against, prevailing conceptions of how legal practices can and should be organized, and what lawyers, qua lawyers, can and should do. Because they exist in a marginalized position in regard to the professional project of organized legal professions, they have greater room to maneuver than those who hew to the conventional version of law practice.

By their difference they help give meaning to the professional mainstream even as they innovate, invent, and transgress. By and through their actions, they construct and transform the boundary between law and politics, fabricating political action with legal tools and legal action that responds to political necessity. They construct the causes and movements they serve even as their relation to those causes shapes what they can do and how they can do it. At the same time, it is important to acknowledge, as we will detail below, that the ideals that drive cause lawyers undergo their own transformations out of the welter of personal, political, and professional circumstance that constitute the praxis of cause lawyering. As they carve out their own ways of practicing law, cause lawyers carry forward traditional understandings of lawyer work even as they reshape them. They use social capital and professional skill to define strategies, sometimes operating well within those understandings, sometimes pushing to, and beyond, their limits.

To open up analysis of structure and agency in the work of cause lawyers we focus on three different, though related, domains—lawyer relations with causes, their practice settings, and strategic decision-making. These domains do not exhaust the range of possibilities. They do, however, provide a way of beginning to map the play of constraints and opportunities in the work of cause lawyers.

Cause as Constraint and Opportunity

Causes are, at one and the same time, the givens with which their lawyers work as well as the tangible product of that work. They exist in the form of abstract moral or political ideals or are embodied in organizations, institutions, and social movements. For our purposes, a cause becomes a movement when it provides the basis for "a sustained series of interactions between power holders and persons successfully claiming to speak on behalf of a constituency lacking formal representation, in the course of which those persons make publicly visible demands for changes in the distribution or exercise of power, and back those demands with public demonstrations of support" (Tilly 1992: 306).[6]

Cause lawyers may be motivated by an identification with a cause or movement, or they may operate at greater or lesser distance from it. In any case, causes constrain lawyers in various ways, for example, by setting their agendas, dictating strategic considerations, and/or offering distinctive sets of incentive and rewards. Nevertheless, as Shamir and Chinski (1998: 231) note:

> a "cause" is not an objective fact "out there." A cause, rather, is a socially constructed concept that evolves. . . . The assumed social type of a lawyer for a cause may misleadingly signify an unproblematic acceptance of the cause as a reified fact that one simply promotes through legal means. Yet . . . it is in the very act of legal representation that a cause . . . is asserted or defused, comprehended or dissolved, recognized or silenced. Cause lawyers, in short, are not simply carriers of a cause but are at the same time its producers: those who shape it, name it, and voice it.[7]

Although scholars sometimes warn of lawyer domination of movements, patterns of interaction generally are more complex and multidimensional than such scholars recognize (Silverstein 1996). During the earliest phases of organizational and agenda formation lawyers help define the realm of the possible, offering advice about the relative efficacy of legal versus political strategies. With their help marginalized groups can "capitalize on the perceptions of entitlement associated with (legal) rights to initiate and to nurture political mobilization" (Scheingold 1974: 131). They contribute to what McCann (2004: 10) calls "'rights consciousness raising'" by providing a vocabulary drawing on "legal discourses to 'name' and to challenge existing social wrongs or injustices." And, as McCann (2004: 10) suggests, there has been a "sort of 'contagion effect' generated by rights litigation over the last forty years in the United States . . . , by legal rights mobilization increasingly in other regions such as the European Union . . . , and by human rights advocacy around the world."

Lawyers do ideological work for their causes, devising new legal arguments, instruments, or remedies uniquely designed for them. This ideological work contributes to the development of a cause or serves as leverage in political contests even when chances of success in the legal arena are remote (McCann 2004: 20–21). Yet there is no guarantee that lawyers working for a cause or with a movement will offer distinct advantages. Rights are, in some cases, tremendously significant, but lawyers are themselves often the most skeptical about the capacity of rights-based legal action to effect change. As McCann (2004: 21) observes, "Legal mobilization does not inherently disempower or empower citizens. How law (and therefore lawyers) matters depends on the complex, often changing dynamics of context in which struggles occur. Legal relations, institutions, and norms tend to be double-edged, at once upholding the larger infrastructure of the status quo while providing many opportunities for episodic challenges and transformations in that ruling order." Lawyers serve and construct causes at various times in the life history of those causes or movements, doing various tasks, producing uncertain and not always beneficial results.

Constraints and Opportunities Associated with Different Practice Settings

Cause lawyering is more than an ideology, a story lawyers can tell themselves about how their work comports with their beliefs; it is more than an abstract moral or political commitment, and more than a relationship, close or distant, to a social movement. It is a way of doing things that takes money, time, and strategic ingenuity. Practice sites help shape cause lawyering by providing different opportunities while imposing different costs. They make certain strategic decisions possible, while foreclosing others. They provide the arenas in which lawyers are challenged to animate their work with their own political and moral commitments. And it is in the course of a practice conceived for other purposes that lawyers may come to cause lawyering. "Lawyers for a cause," Shamir and Chinski (1998: 230–31) observe, "are not necessarily those who consciously and deliberately orient their professional lives toward promoting that cause. It is in the course of engaging in various professional practices that the possibility of becoming or functioning as a lawyer for a cause is realized." Thus a second domain in which to observe the play of structure and agency in the work of cause lawyers is the setting in which they practice. As Nelson and Trubek (1992b: 205) put it, "The legal workplace is an arena of professionalism in the sense that the specific organizational contexts in which lawyers work produce and reflect particular visions of professional ideals."

The play of opportunity and constraint in the work of cause lawyers depends on conditions at the practice site, whether pro bono programs in corporate firms, salaried practice in public and private agencies, or small firms, and on how those conditions fit with the broader political ethos. Pro bono programs in *corporate firms* offer the most limited opportunities for cause lawyers while entailing the greatest constraints. In return for a more than comfortable income, the time open for cause lawyering is very confined, as is the choice of causes and the means to pursue them. In terms of risk and reward, *salaried practice* constitutes the moderate middle in that full-time cause lawyering and a stable and adequate income are assured, but the agenda—that is the means and ends of cause lawyering—is determined by the priorities of the organization providing the salary. In contrast to the other two practice sites, *small-firm* cause lawyering is a high-stakes game. It is a tremendously important (and under-studied) setting for cause lawyering. Private practitioners make crucial contributions in common law and especially in civil law countries. They have maximum freedom to choose causes, colleagues, tactics, and strategy, but in a setting that tends to be volatile and insecure.

In any case, for each cause lawyer the search for a practice setting that provides sufficient opportunity for individuality, creativity, and agency, while reconciling political beliefs and the demands of legal work, is a personal quest. Cause lawyers "adopt distinct visions of their job as lawyers: how they behave in and out of court, their relationship with clients, how they behave in terms of legal ethics, and how they organize their practices" (Hilbink 2003: 9). In some cases, their objectives are pragmatic and particular: an alternative to the stifling prospect of life as a hired gun. Any worthwhile cause becomes, in effect, a port in the storm—chosen without much reflection and with no ideological or programmatic strings attached. In other instances, their choices reflect serious dedication to a particular objective and/or to some broader ideal (Sarat 1998). Thus, abortion rights may be pursued as ends in themselves and/or as one element of a feminist political agenda. Similarly, support for tort reform may be based on objections to excessive jury awards and/or may be a sign of commitment to the property rights movement. The defining attribute of cause lawyering is not how beliefs are reconciled with the demands of practice but rather the simple imperative that they must be reconciled.[8]

Opportunities and Constraints in Fashioning Strategy

What lawyers can do to serve their cause is shaped by a variety of factors, for example, the goals of the cause or movement, the resources that it can make available or that lawyers can mobilize, the possibilities at the practice site, the lawyer's own experience, skills, and understandings, the lawyer's social capital and networks, the nature of existing social, political, and legal arrangements, and so forth. Merely listing such factors is a reminder that strategic decision-making operates in a highly structured and constrained environment. Yet here, as in their relations with the causes they serve and their practice settings, cause lawyers have opportunities to exercise their imaginations, their will, and their creativity.

Do they take advantage of existing possibilities of redress or market new legal devices? Do they operate below the radar screen of publicity and public notice or in a high-profile, attention-getting manner? Do they work in accordance with existing legal and professional norms or engage in transgressive practices? Do they seek to build social capital or networks with existing power holders or assume an oppositional, outsider posture? The answers to each of these questions depend as much on the agency of particular lawyers as on the constraints they face.

The major strategic question confronting cause lawyers in the United States is whether to engage legally or politically (Scheingold 2001). Legal engagement, what might be termed rule of law cause lawyering, means giving priority to the courts and litigation—whether through class actions, amicus briefs, or by raising legal and constitutional issues in connection with the representation of particular clients. Constitutional litigation, the bedrock of American cause lawyering, provides institutional access, legitimacy, and bargaining leverage. All of these advantages are, however, most readily available in connection with liberal democratic objectives. It is fair to say that so long as cause lawyers work within the parameters of liberal democracy, they have the access necessary to make headway both legally and politically. Although success in litigation and in the political arena do not go hand in hand, the access that is available for liberal democratic cause lawyering has proven useful as a political resource for those willing to move between legal arenas.

On the other hand, cause lawyers whose beliefs are at odds with liberal democracy face the daunting challenge of deploying the institutions and instruments of liberal democracy against itself. Not surprisingly those who challenge core premises of liberal democracy—irrespective of whether that challenge comes from the left or the right—are generally deprived of the opportunities afforded by constitutional litigation. They are therefore not only much more dependent on political mobilization but must also mobilize *against* the law and *against* the grain of mainstream politics. This latter point must, however, be qualified. There are times and places when mainstream conceptions have expanded beyond liberal democracy—as seems to be the case these days with respect to the religious right and was so earlier with respect to social democratic goals and values. Generally speaking, however, lawyers who choose transformative strategies ordinarily face the no-win choice of succumbing to the immediate but ultimately unsatisfactory rewards of liberal democracy or becoming, in effect, *lost-cause* lawyers (Sarat 1998).

More overtly, political cause lawyering functions in multiple venues: ranging from lobbying, through political mobilization and organization to street demonstrations and civil disobedience (McCann and Silverstein 1998). Where lawyers do not depend on litigation, they have to "find a network of allies from a variety of domains, i.e. they must mobilize social capital. That is a long and subtle process of creating understandings, mutual dependence, loyalty, trust, etc."[9] The politicization of cause lawyering also can involve participation in social movements as activists supporting direct political action. To engage politically entails overt identification with, and commitment to, the political agenda of one side in conflicts over constitutional rights, welfare and environmental policies, electoral arrangements, and the like. In pursuing an openly political path, cause lawyers, in effect, declare their solidarity with their clients and the causes they jointly pursue.

Choosing political strategies tests and probably violates the nethermost boundaries of mainstream professionalism, and this ordinarily means running into substantial structural obstacles. Moreover, insofar as the public associates cause lawyering with causes deemed "radical or subversive," cause lawyers put the profession's social capital at risk. It is, thus, one thing for cause lawyers to use even the most innovative strategies to vindicate widely accepted rights and quite another to become advocates in political struggles that challenge the state or the deeply rooted values from which its legitimacy is derived. But whether and how cause lawyers operate on the strategic terrain defined by legality, professionalism, and politics is, in every case, the result of choices within a framework of constraint, agentic behavior within a pattern set by cultural schema and material resources. Here, as elsewhere, attention both to structure and agency is necessary in order to understand the worlds that cause lawyers can, and do, make.

Overview of the Book

Each of the contributors to this book was charged to prepare an empirical case study of cause lawyering and to explore the framework of opportunities and/or constraints in the work of the lawyers they studied. They were asked to take the issue of structure-agency as at least a background framework, or jumping off point, for their work. The contributors took this charge seriously, though each of them gave it their distinctive signature. Because we regarded our work as a starting point for the study of structure and agency in the work of cause lawyers, they were neither offered a common resolution to the structure-agency problematic nor asked to theorize about it. Instead they were to provide data on which such theorizing subsequently might be built. The contexts and examples they chose in which to discharge this task are as varied as their approach to it, ranging over many different national contexts, causes, and several different historical periods. As a result, what follows is as rich in the diversity of its engagement with the structure-agency problematic as it is consistent in providing insight into it.

The Worlds Cause Lawyers Make: Structure and Agency in Legal Practice is organized into three major sections, each of which explores one of the three domains noted above. We begin with "Causes and the Lawyers Who Serve Them: How Do Causes Make Their Lawyers and Lawyers Make Their Causes?" The chapters in this section take up the constraints and opportunities which causes present to their lawyers. In what ways do lawyers identify with those causes? How do causes fit into their identity narratives? How do they negotiate their commitments to profession and cause? Where are the significant points of tension in that negotiation?

Because cause lawyers are often important players in social movements this section assesses how they construct and constrain the movements with which they are associated. How do they operate in the context of their relations with activists? What contributions do they make to articulating movement goals and to the development of strategies? Do they legalize movements or take into their own work the more political orientation of the movements they serve?

We begin with Ronen Shamir's "Corporate Responsibility and the South African Drug Wars: Outline of a New Frontier for Cause Lawyers." In his chapter, Shamir looks at work lawyers recently have done on behalf of the corporate social responsibility (CSR) movement. He focuses particularly on what politically activist nongovernmental organizations (NGOs) and their lawyers did in the fight for legally defined and enforceable CSR standards. He shows a complex pattern of constraints imposed by those NGOs on their lawyers and yet identifies many instances in which lawyer agency mattered.

In the specific example that Shamir provides, the South African government, AIDS activists, and local and international NGOs fought a very public legal battle against foreign pharmaceutical manufacturers in South African courts. Their overarching goal was to redefine the concept of social responsibility from a voluntary practice to a legal duty and thus compel the compulsory licensing of low-cost, generic AIDS medications. They framed the issue before the courts in terms of public health, right to life, and the duty of the state to provide for

the medical well-being of its citizens. The most important organization pushing these arguments was the Treatment Action Campaign (TAC), an organization founded in 1998. Its goals defined the agenda for the lawyers who worked
with it, and it had a combined legal and political strategy right from the start. It
sought to ensure "equal access and equal treatment of people with HIV/AIDS,
[and] to campaign for affordable and quality access to health care" through the
combined efforts of litigation, lobbying, advocacy, and mass mobilization.

Shamir's account illustrates how TAC collaborated successfully with a number of other NGOs in different aspects of this campaign. TAC's broad collaborative efforts highlight much of what is strategically innovative about cause
lawyering on nascent global issues. As Shamir writes, "The approach that seeks
to devise new regulatory structures binding on Multinational Corporations was
actualized in South Africa by lawyers and NGOs who deployed interactive networks of exchange and coordination, and generated considerable resources in
terms of personnel, expertise, practical know-how, and information." Shamir's
research shows lawyers to have been crucial innovators in the movement for
CSR in the global community. By introducing a "new moral language" in the
South African courts, the choices and actions of cause lawyers, Shamir claims,
have been crucial in a "transcendence of the public/private divide . . . and the effort to create a conceptual umbrella that covers labor, civil rights, and environmental issues."

In the next chapter, Laurent Willemez takes up Shamir's interest in docu-
menting the contributions lawyers make to social movements, this time focusing on French labor lawyers. Willemez takes up what is perceived to be a problem for lawyers working with, and for, political movements, namely the
commonly accepted conflict between a cause lawyer's professional and ideological commitments. Movement work demands, he suggests, strong ideological
affiliation while professionalism demands distance and detachment from the
goals of the movement. Here Willemez documents the play of two different
structures of constraints on the work that cause lawyers do.

Before Willemez examines these constraints, he briefly addresses some of the
problems, as well as the merits, of "importing" an American concept—cause
lawyering—into a French context. While he acknowledges that structural differences in the legal system and unionism lead to distinct understandings of the
nature of the legal profession in France, he argues that the cause lawyering concept is useful for analyzing "ties between law and politics." Cause lawyering
analysis focuses on how attorney activism shapes political and social movements at various levels.

Yet the distinctive context of the French legal system matters. French labor lawyers tend to be relatively low on the legal profession's status hierarchy. Because of this, rather than seeing themselves as rebels, they want to be considered lawyers in the most traditional French sense. Thus the lawyers Willemez interviewed all refused to acknowledge any conceptual distinction between political and legal action. Willemez describes them as self-proclaimed "guardians of tradition" who acknowledge the constraints and obligations of their profession as much as their ideological commitments. They claim to be pursuing a kind of lawyering based on a French custom of "independence, liberty, and disinterest in financial gains." Cause lawyering in the French traditional context could thus actually be called "true lawyering," the modern descendant of a long tradition of political lawyering. Willemez claims that the emergence of cause lawyers serving social movements responds to the late nineteenth-century decline of lawyers in the legislative and executive branches. This decline, he argues, led them to engage politically elsewhere, in this case for the cause of labor.

This intermingling of motivations is further compounded by the practice setting of French labor lawyers, which nurtures interdependence between the lawyers and the unions. Labor lawyers' practical needs to build and maintain a clientele inform their behavior vis-à-vis the movements they serve and thus can interfere with the independence part of the "true lawyer" ideal. On the flip side, unions need lawyers to be lawyers, taking advantage of distinctive legal skills to push labor issues in the courts by setting precedents and building new conceptions of rights and new legal remedies. Ultimately, then, the cause constrains, even as it enlists, lawyer activism. Ideological commitment without legal skill and credibility in the legal arena is less valuable than an ideological commitment given shape by legal and professional traditions.

Ann Southworth's chapter takes up the tension between ideological commitment and professional identity among lawyers working on behalf of conservative and libertarian causes in the United States. Southworth describes the self-perceived identities of these lawyers, and the relationship between their own identity and the ideological dimensions of their work. Does commitment to a cause constrain and shape professional motivations in distinctive ways? Do cause lawyers carry a particular professional burden that other lawyers do not have to shoulder?

She begins by addressing the question of whether or not conservative and libertarian lawyers can be appropriately classified "cause lawyers," a type of lawyering pioneered on the left. She argues that the widely accepted core elements of cause lawyering are not necessarily ideologically defined. Southworth's research reveals interesting differences among her subjects, however, as to the degree of "self-conscious commitment to the cause." Here lawyer agency matters as lawyers create their own distinctive identity narratives and their own ways of relating to the causes with which they identify themselves.

Although lawyers for business interests mostly agreed ideologically with the legal arguments they made on behalf of their clients, they "generally rejected the idea that they were cause lawyers, while lawyers for religious conservative, libertarian, order maintenance, and mediator groups frequently embraced that characterization of their work." They exemplified what Hilbink (2003: 8) calls a "proceduralist" view of cause lawyering. For business lawyers, the cause imposed few constraints and created few conflicts with their professional role; for other conservative cause lawyers, the constraints of serving a cause seemed more significant and the conflicts somewhat more vexing. Lawyers for religious and libertarian causes most adamantly rejected Simon's (1978) "principle of neutrality." Embracing a core aspect of cause lawyering, libertarians and religious conservatives expressed a deeply felt belief that they are "morally accountable for the positions they take on behalf of their clients."

Southworth also discusses the impact that the lawyers' professional surroundings have had on the evolution of their motivations. Many of the libertarians fit the classic mold of a cause lawyer who endeavors to build a career out of preexisting, deeply held political convictions. Others, however, as Shamir and Chinski (1998) might have predicted, did not take such deliberate routes to work on behalf of conservative causes. Some describe a growing conservatism in their personal convictions which, over time, informed their professional decisions as lawyers. Others, who began in different professions, or originally took a particular legal position for mostly practical reasons, later came to apply their conservative beliefs more directly to their professional lives. These lawyers were ideologically influenced by their work and came later to influence the causes for which they work.

The next chapter, by Laura Hatcher, continues Southworth's effort to trace the reciprocal influence of cause on lawyer and lawyer on cause again in the context of conservative cause lawyers in the United States. Hatcher focuses on the work that lawyers have done to fashion the property rights movement and its constitutive ideology. Unlike Southworth, Hatcher finds a motivation-focused analysis too restrictive for discussing the development of conservative cause lawyering and the influence of lawyers in and on social movements. Cause lawyering research instead should examine the tension between political ideology and professionalism that Willemez explores in the context of "institutional spaces and during particular professional practices."

Hatcher also insists on the need to examine relations of causes and their lawyers over time, with an eye toward historical continuities and discontinuities. The specific professional practices Hatcher looks at have taken place over the last 100 years in the legal academy and nonprofit, conservative law firms. Thus Hatcher begins her discussion of lawyers who serve the property rights movement with a historical survey of laissez-faire ideology in United States law. That ideology, Hatcher contends, can be described as a set of ideas concerning "the importance of the individual, free competition, and the state's appropriate role in economic regulation." Some of the foremost conservative thinkers of the nineteenth century worked very hard to translate these economic ideas into constitutional arguments and legal devices, thus giving life to a sort of "laissez-faire jurisprudence." Hatcher's chapter shows lawyers as ideological innovators, offering opportunities for movement activity by marketing new legal ideas. Their work, she contends, contributed immeasurably to the Supreme Court's early twentieth-century acceptance of the theory that the state should not interfere with the economic rights of individuals.

Alongside their ideological work, the development of the property rights movement has also been supported by a careful, institutional process of professionalization among lawyers. She explains how nineteenth-century bar associations (organized by the most conservative lawyers) provided an elitist organizational setting within which lawyers could regulate their profession. Right-wing activists today, Hatcher argues, also attend to this professionalism process. Her work thus highlights institutional manifestations of unity and division across the ideological spectrum of the right wing.

At the same time, Hatcher highlights agency by noting differences among conservative cause lawyers in their conceptions of how to advance common ideological goals. These conflicting viewpoints are reflected in both conservative legal institutions, like the Pacific Law Foundation and the Institute for Justice, and organizations such as the Federalist Society. In her view they serve "a special function as power in the form of money, grants, as well as ideas, flows through them into the legal practices of various conservative lawyers, including property rights advocates."

Liora Israël concludes the first section by taking up Hatcher's call for an examination of relations between lawyers and movements in historical context. Her chapter analyzes the ideological activism of French communist lawyers immediately preceding and during World War II. Unlike Willemez's or Southworth's interview-based arguments about the personal and professional motivations of contemporary cause lawyers, Israël employs a methodology more appropriate for a historical analysis, focusing on "types and contexts of action" to analyze the *Association Juridique Internationale* (AJI) and the extent to which its members in 1930s and 1940s France can be classified cause lawyers.

Founded in 1925 by Marcel Willard, the AJI was built on Lenin's concept of justice, whereby a good militant will use a court of law as a stage for propaganda. "Good lawyering" for the communist cause could thus theoretically entail defending political ideals before the court at the expense of one's own client. However, practically speaking, there were limitations on the AJI's ability to carry out the Leninist ideal. Israël's discussion of the activities of the AJI in the prewar years sheds light on both the limitations and the achievements of lawyers promoting their causes. She focuses particularly on the progress the AJI was able to make as a *direct result* of its lawyers' "double commitment to their profession and to their party." Her work again highlights tensions between ideological commitment and professional responsibilities, this time by examining cause lawyers serving a radical left movement.

As the Nazi occupation of France grew near, communist lawyers had to develop new tactics to keep their cause alive. During this period, they continued defending the party ideology on a rhetorical platform of liberal rights. However, Israël notes how a shrinking of public space and the refusal to open judicial proceedings to the press were deeply damaging to their goals. Beginning in 1940, communist lawyers faced total repression by the occupying Nazi forces, yet they remained influential as key players in the Resistance movement between 1940 and 1944.

Their involvement in that movement had both practical and intellectual dimensions. Lawyers involved in the Resistance used their access to closed court sessions and judicial files to try to intimidate repressive judges, modify legal procedures, and, in so doing, to undermine the power of the Vichy regime. Further, like the conservative cause lawyers that Hatcher describes, AJI lawyers continued to do ideological work for their movement, legitimizing the Resistance as an alternative to the Vichy regime and smoothing the transition to the post–World War II Gaullist government.

Israël concludes that consideration of French communist lawyers provides historical evidence that cause lawyers are able to apply professional skills in the service of political movements even under extreme conditions. Operating within multiple layers of constraint, their strategies mattered, both for those movements and for the society in which they worked. In her view, cause lawyers can be effective in political mobilization. This is particularly well illustrated, she claims, by the wartime work of former AJI lawyers, who demonstrated "how legal competence could be used in clandestine and dangerous situations, when the defense of a cause could require its denial in front of the Court."

The chapters in the next section of the book, "Making a Practice: Balancing Professionalism and Activism," examine the daily world of legal work. They ask whether particular kinds of practice and organizations of practice are more conducive to cause lawyering than others. They describe how different kinds of cause lawyers construct their practices. In addition, chapters in Section II speak to the perennial problem of maintaining commitment to cause lawyering, exploring how cause lawyers strive to create working conditions that are supportive of their political values. Each attends to the complex intersections of activist commitment and the organization of work.

The chapters in this section also chronicle the efforts of cause lawyers in disparate settings to stake out their own terrain and in the process to find a tenable position within the legal profession. In some instances they counterpoise their own vision of lawyering for a cause against the conventional commitment to client service. They may do so either to defend and legitimate their enterprise in the face of external opposition or to articulate and reinforce coherence and *esprit* among their cause lawyering cohort.

More often, as these chapters show, cause lawyers are too taken up with the day-to-day struggle of maintaining their practices and pursuing their political objectives to devote much energy to staking out professional terrain. This section illustrates the complex and varied relationship between cause lawyering and the practice of law as well as the way cause lawyering destabilizes boundaries between law and politics. And, throughout, these chapters stress the local and contextual quality of cause lawyering. Thus they explore the great diversity of styles and substance in the kind of work that is encompassed by the term cause lawyering.

Scott Barclay and Anna-Maria Marshall begin by providing an example of cause lawyering in private practice. Their chapter highlights the significant contributions private practitioners make to social movements while describing the limitations they face in trying to do cause-oriented work. To illustrate these contributions and limits, Barclay and Marshall discuss Susan Murray and Beth Robinson, two private practice lawyers in Vermont who litigated *Baker v. State*, the landmark case that declared it unconstitutional to deprive homosexual Vermonters of the benefits of marriage. Murray and Robinson's work litigating, lobbying, and organizing on behalf of homosexual rights qualifies them both for the title cause lawyer. However, their position working in a traditional law firm, as private practice attorneys, sets them apart from the familiar conception of public interest, altruistically motivated cause lawyers.

Though Murray and Robinson, like lawyers serving Israeli Bedouins described by Shamir and Chinski (1998), did not begin their careers intending to be legal activists for the homosexual community, they slowly emerged over the course of time as leaders in the movement, and highly effective ones at that. In an overview of the two lawyers' career paths, Barclay and Marshall show how their role was based "not just on their political commitment and their community activism, but also on their law firm's existing client base and enthusiasm for public service." These factors led them to develop a gay-friendly legal practice, within the context of a large firm, Lamgrock, Sperry and Wool, which handles both private and corporate clientele. Through work they did (estate planning, custody disputes, adoption agreements, etc.) on behalf of paying gay, lesbian, and bisexual clients, Murray and Robinson came to understand the fundamentally unequal legal treatment of homosexuals. Here political commitment emerged from day-to-day work representing clients within the frame of the profession's conventional understanding. In this sense, private practice provided an opportunity for a kind of social learning. As these lawyers did what counted as traditional legal, fee paying work, they came to see its limitations in addressing the needs of their clients. This led them to consider new avenues for, and a new definition of, their legal work.

Both lawyers became actively involved in efforts to reform the law both on a legislative front and through litigation. It was this type of work that paved the way toward *Baker v. State*. Barclay and Marshall argue that the approach Murray and Robinson took in their advocacy "challenged the image of a cause lawyer as an erudite professional, committed exclusively to legal strategies." Yet they say that Murray and Robinson were able to effectively balance their professional and activist commitments, using the flexibility provided by a private practice setting and the social capital built up through their success as conventional lawyers as advantages in their cause lawyering work, advantages they were able to pass on to the social movement, ultimately making them more effective cause lawyers.

Like Willemez, Southworth, and Barclay and Marshall, Lynn Jones's chapter again takes as its point of orientation the tension between cause lawyers' professional and activist identities, focusing in particular on the "structural locations" of cause lawyers' work (legal centers, movement organizations, activist networks, and law firms) as factors helping to explain how those tensions get worked out. According to Jones, "it is important to explore the conditions under which cause lawyers work, because it may be that cause and client advocacy are not in conflict." Her findings suggest that certain cause lawyers are able to construct professional identities based on their work setting and support networks, which minimize conflict with their activist pursuits.

Jones considers a diverse array of lawyers working on behalf of many different movements or causes. She divides lawyers into two categories: "core cause lawyers" (self-identified and colleague-identified lawyers *primarily* concerned with their activist work) and "marginal cause lawyers" (committed to activism, but giving precedence to neither their traditional nor cause lawyering activities).[10] She notes that both core and marginal cause lawyers tend to shift between a variety of work settings for reasons that range from political, to financial, to institutional. However, core cause lawyers tend to be found in public interest centers and law school clinics, while marginal lawyers can be found in a wider variety of professional environments. To help explain the tensions and compatibility between lawyers' professional and activist identities, Jones devotes the majority of her chapter to discussing the opportunities and constraints associated with different degrees of activism in these various professional settings.

Jones finds that, in certain contexts, cause lawyers might not even behave much like lawyers, preferring instead to contribute more generally to a cause, through organizational or rhetorical skills. However, that same lawyer, at another time or in another setting, could take on more of a leadership role, perhaps shaping the direction of a social movement through litigation. This difference occurs because, as Jones argues, different organizational and professional settings shape the different types of cause lawyer roles individuals adopt.

Core cause lawyers generally forgo opportunities for greater prestige, better professional reputation, and more financial compensation by choosing the professional settings they do. At the same time, the settings in which core cause lawyers practice help them "secure a position in the subculture within the profession." This helps, in turn, to encourage an alternative professional identity—one not so incompatible with their activist pursuits. By contrast, marginal cause lawyers experience significantly more difficulty, mainly because their "activist and professional subcultures do not overlap, are not as developed, or are in conflict."

Following the research of Barclay and Marshall and Jones, the next two chapters emphasize the significance of practice sites in offering opportunities and imposing constraints on what cause lawyers do and on whether they are able to persist in their cause lawyering commitments over the course of their careers. Corey Shdaimah is particularly interested in exploring possibilities for new and different kinds of relations between lawyers and clients in what she calls traditional public interest, salaried practice settings where "left activist lawyers engaged primarily in client representation." Shdaimah considers theories of client empowerment and disempowerment in order to better understand how the social capital of clients informs the strategic choices of cause lawyers, and in turn how strategy can affect the lives and social capital of individual clients. The clients and lawyers Shdaimah studied at Northeast Legal Services (NELS) were dealing with problems having to do with public housing, child custody, social security disability insurance, consumer bankruptcy, and predatory lending.

Sociological theories, Shdaimah notes, identify a number of mechanisms people use to distinguish lay people from professionals, thus classifying professionalism as a structure of hierarchy. This hierarchy challenges the values of progressive lawyering, which emphasize "autonomy or client decision-making, collaboration, and the more amorphous elements of respect and dignity." Often cause lawyering turns out to be progressive in its ends, but conventional in its attachments to the perks and prestige of the professional hierarchy. Thus, Shdaimah suggests, the possibilities for a healthy accommodation are not limitless as lawyers and clients orient themselves to the complexities of combining activist goals with professional expertise and commitments.

She offers the interactions of NELS lawyers and clients as one place to examine how the possibilities get played out. Starting with the idea that progressive lawyers should facilitate client autonomy, the lawyers Shdaimah interviewed spoke of their own fears of undermining that autonomy and inadvertently manipulating client decisions simply by virtue of their more powerful, professional position. On the other hand, clients she interviewed admitted to their own reluctance to proactively embrace independence and autonomy. They did not report feeling manipulated or disempowered by their attorney's leadership in decision-making. Indeed, while compromising client autonomy, the exercise of power by attorneys generally expanded the legal options available to a client. Here the ends of progressive lawyering were pursued in ways that were well within the norms of the mainstream legal profession.

A similar pattern of accommodation occurs with respect to attorney-client collaboration—lawyers are more skilled and knowledgeable in law, but clients have situational knowledge assets. Theories of progressive lawyering, however, assume that clients want to, and should, collaborate. However, Shdaimah's interviews indicate that clients are less prone to want collaboration in the most straightforward sense (in making legal procedural and strategic decisions). NELS clients recognize the greater social capital their lawyers possess and wish to use it to advance their legal cause.

NELS lawyers are a distinctive kind of cause lawyers, working in a practice setting preoccupied primarily with making service to individual clients their cause. Nonetheless, even here, in a public interest, salaried law practice explicitly oriented toward protecting the independence and autonomy of clients and encouraging collaboration, professional hierarchy did not disappear. Redefining the cause could not itself alleviate the tension between progressive lawyering theory and practice.

Douglas Thomson concludes this section by analyzing constraints and opportunities which different practice settings provide in determining the persistence of what he calls "public interest law commitment." His discussion is based
upon interviews with fifteen recent law school graduates. Thomson calls his interviewees "public interest law persisters" (PILPs)—lawyers who, regardless of
professional surrounding, expressed affinity for cause lawyering. Although each
of these lawyers had displayed a strong commitment to public interest law
while in law school, they chose different initial career paths, some practicing
public interest law right away, and others joining corporate firms. Thomson analyzes the strategies these young lawyers employed and revisions in their expectations made to maintain their interest in public interest law despite institutionalized impediments along their desired career path.

PILPs who work in public interest law from the start find, not surprisingly, a
much richer professional community to support their interest and reported
high overall satisfaction with their work. In contrast, PILPs who initially took
corporate positions needed to develop internal coping strategies to sustain their
interest in more explicitly public interest oriented work. For example, Thomson describes how some "construct nuanced understandings and preferences
among the work available," avoiding the least public interest-like work. One
PILP, who decided initially to work in the private sector, specifically chose a
small law firm over a large one to gain litigation experience which he knew
would be useful to him in the public advocacy work he hoped to do in the future.

Thomson's interviews reveal that PILPs in large firms face a number of obstacles that their public sector peers do not. Thomson contends that these obstacles present significant challenges to maintaining a continuing aspiration to
be cause lawyers. Although law firm practices "do undercut prospects for efficacious cause lawyering to emerge," Thomson argues, at the same time "the
firms continue to play a potential role in making the possible imaginable." That
is to say, the opportunities for pro bono work in corporate law firms sustain the
imaginations of PILPs and fund their work, thus helping to keep a vision of
cause lawyering alive in a setting which is generally thought to be least conducive to it.

The chapters in the third and last section of the book, "Strategy and Social
Capital," suggest that the strategic decisions that cause lawyers make are deeply
intertwined with the social capital they are able to mobilize. Thus cause lawyers
often seek to mobilize networks, build alliances, and develop relations with
powerful actors as part of the work they do. Where they are able to do so, their
strategies are less oppositional than where they have no access to such social
capital. In these chapters we see cause lawyers continuously trying to innovate

within the frame of the legal order, inventing and marketing new devices and remedies, pushing the limits of existing procedures, forging strategic decisions out of the materials and possibilities found in their political and legal environments.

Patricia Woods's chapter is especially valuable in drawing out these connections. She examines cause lawyering on behalf of forces in Israel challenging religious powers in the state and pushing for a legal system firmly grounded in secular principles of rights. Their strategy has been to mobilize social capital and work within the state (as "insiders" focused especially on the High Court of Justice—HCJ), in pushing political and legal reform. According to Woods, the Israeli example is useful for addressing the more general question of agency in cause lawyer strategy. In this case, Israeli cause lawyers helped shape and change the direction of major social norms, though their activities tended to alienate the religious community, thanks to "their participation in a normative socio-professional community surrounding the HCJ justices."

Once a community made up exclusively of political and social elites, Israel's judicial community is now comprised of "HCJ justices, legal scholars, government lawyers, cause lawyers for major social movement organizations, clerks and interns for government bodies."

In the late 1960s, what was a modest Court began to show signs of change, moving away from strict legal positivism, and signaling an openness to new judicial norms. As Woods recounts, cause lawyers adjusted their strategies accordingly. Professional and social relations arising from the small size of the country, few law schools, etc., created a "feedback loop" within the judicial community marked by "diffuse, informal and formal legal interaction, debate and conflict." A shared a commitment to the rule of law as a device to resist religious fundamentalism affords cause lawyers access; their "participation in such diffuse, normative communities will allow them access to the debates through which the norms of those communities develop and change."

Further, interactions within the community, Woods argues, sparked cause lawyers to bring politicized cases before the HCJ, which, in turn, "contributed to increasing that institution's political salience." Moreover, collective and individual strategies of the movements surrounding the HCJ contributed to raising the political stakes surrounding its work. All of this, she observes, shows how cause lawyer strategy can, given the right conditions, be built from the inside of existing networks of legal, professional, and political power.

The importance of social capital in shaping strategic possibilities and opening up avenues for inventiveness is also emphasized in the chapter by Jayanth Krishnan. In his discussion of Indian cause lawyers, Krishnan describes how social capital opens up possibilities for "transgressive" cause lawyering which expands "generally accepted professional standards of legal practice . . . to their limits and beyond." Amassing professional status is very important in Indian courts and affords lawyers greater liberty to push the legal, professional, and political envelope.

The common model of Indian lawyering challenges American notions of cause lawyering and its strategic decision-making. First and foremost, Indian lawyers are neither involved in nonlitigation-related activities such as mobilization, negotiation, advising, and strategizing with activists, nor, as in the Israeli model, in an informal community fostering new and shared understandings of law. Nonetheless, many demonstrate "transformative interests and values" thanks to an education rich with the discourse of liberal democracy, feminism, environmentalism, and civil rights.

Cause lawyers in India are tied, in ways that neither their American nor their Israeli counterparts are, to a rigid hierarchy of courts. Lawyers, based on their professional standing, argue all of their cases at one or another level of the court system. Perhaps not surprisingly, Krishnan finds that lawyers at lower court levels have the greatest difficulty in engaging in transgressive behavior. These lawyers lack the professional capital that earns them respect and financial stability necessary to support such risk taking. High Court and Supreme Court lawyers, on the other hand, are both freer to pursue causes in their work and to act transgressively. These lawyers have more professional flexibility, financial stability, and social capital, all of which allow them to take more risks. Yet because they depend for their livelihood on fee paying, wealthy, conservative clients, their freedom to pursue the most aggressive forms of cause lawyering is limited by their fear of offending those whose money keeps them in practice. Thus their social capital provides both opportunity and constraint in what seems by now a familiar pattern in which cause lawyers find themselves enmeshed.

This pattern is also in play in the work of the cause lawyers discussed in Stephen Meili's chapter. His research focuses on cause lawyers in Argentina who work on class action suits under a nascent law known as the "amparo colectivo." It considers the dynamics of cause lawyering in a postauthoritarian political context, and how this context affects the motivations, strategies, and self-perceptions of cause lawyers.

The "amparo colectivo" became Argentinean law in 1994 as part of a wave of constitutional reforms in which cause lawyers played a major role. Their success in creating this new legal device in a postauthoritarian political environment "gives . . . [them] a significant stake not only in the legitimacy and vitality of the rights they are championing, but also the entire judicial system that they have entrusted to protect those rights." Successful legal inventiveness drew Argentinean cause lawyers into the state, tempering their strategic calculations even as it became apparent that the "amparo colectivo" would have little success mobilizing mass political action or social movements among the Argentine people.

Cause lawyers continue to try to make the "amparo colectivo" as effective a legal tool as they can, to root out corruption and abuse, bolster confidence in the Argentinean legal system, and thus consolidate democracy and rule of law. For attorneys in a postauthoritarian society like Argentina, the constraints of law, profession, and politics are numerous. Yet at one and the same time, cause lawyers challenge the state with the rights-based grievances of their clients and promote the legitimacy and integrity of the state they are challenging. This creates a hierarchy of concerns that heavily informs their legal practice. According to Meili, this hierarchy was largely responsible for the complete dearth of class action suits following the Argentinean banking crisis and the imposition of withdrawal restrictions known as the "corralito." Although both private lawyers and class action cause lawyers had an interest in defending the access rights of Argentinean citizens to their own money, only private lawyers pursued legal redress. Thus, paradoxically, "the corralito experience suggests that cause lawyers may have a stronger interest in the integrity of the state and its institutions than noncause lawyers." Allegiance to the state, in turn, decreases the aggressiveness, rights-assertion, and transgressive behavior of cause lawyers.

Following on Meili's analysis of the significance of a new law in shaping the work of cause lawyers in Argentina, Richard Maiman takes up the status and efficacy of cause lawyering in the United Kingdom since the 1998 adoption of the Human Rights Act. That act introduced new provisions into British law guaranteeing such rights as due process, freedom of association, and privacy of family life. Moreover, compared with the judiciary's traditional impotence vis-à-vis the British Parliament, it broadened judicial power to check policies of the government, providing a seemingly important new resource for cause lawyers. Yet Maiman claims that judges have been reluctant to "assume a more expansive role in defining rights." "To what extent," he asks, "will [judges] be facilitated in doing so by aggressive legal advocacy?"

His chapter tries to answer this question by looking at the strategies of British cause lawyers and their successes and failures in promoting aggressive, rights-based jurisprudence under the Human Rights Act. In Maiman's words "The Human Rights Act steers a rather tortuous course between the conflicting principles of fundamental law and popular sovereignty." It is a "super statute," but, in practice, the judiciary can nullify only governmental acts short of Parliamentary legislation which are found to be incompatible with it. Although judges may issue a "Declaration of Incompatibility," ultimate authority remains vested in the Parliament. Further, lacking an autonomous oversight agency to monitor government compliance with the act, lawyers find themselves relying on, but yet having limited opportunities for, "strategic litigation" which might impact policy in a meaningful way.

To illustrate the challenges British cause lawyers face in defending the statutory provisions of the Human Rights Act, Maiman focuses on immigration/asylum law. This has been a highly contentious area of law in the United Kingdom since it committed itself through the 1951 Geneva Convention "to grant political asylum to refugees who can demonstrate a well-founded fear of persecution in their countries of origin, based on nationality, race, ethnicity, religion, political opinion, or social grouping." It was a sudden surge in asylum requests in 1999, however, that set in motion a concerted government effort to limit asylum cases and discourage immigration. In spite of their strategic ingenuity in using the Human Rights Act, cause lawyers were able to do little to resist this effort.

Enthusiasm about the statutory changes, and a desire to "make hay" in the courts, was not sufficient for truly effective cause lawyering. Much to their disappointment, nearly every lawyer Maiman interviewed reported encountering continued judicial resistance to rights-based arguments. A "frightened government, scrambling to retain power" imposed substantial barriers to their efforts, leading Maiman to conclude that "there is little reason to expect that lawyers working on behalf of asylum seekers will play more than a marginal role in the unfolding drama."

A different drama takes center stage in the last chapter of this book, the drama surrounding efforts to change the tort system in the United States. It discusses the role of the Association of Trial Lawyers of America (ATLA) in the tort reform debate. Though personal injury lawyers do not necessarily evoke an immediate association with cause lawyering, Michael McCann and William Haltom argue that those lawyers, in fact, generally aim to serve such larger social values as "access to justice, rule of law, civil rights and democratic accountability" through their work. They support this contention with testimonial evidence from lawyers and organizational leaders at ATLA, who display cause-oriented, activist motivations for their work.

Since the 1960s, tort lawyers have made considerable progress in the courtroom, advancing the cause of public interest law. In recent years, however, thanks to a politically motivated critique of the so-called litigation explosion, ATLA's lawyers have been compelled to fight a more explicitly political battle in defense of their cause. Curiously, they have refrained from joining that battle publicly, preferring to engage in what McCann and Haltom call "insider stealth tactics."

Instead of investing time and resources in a public relations war, tort lawyers have concentrated on building political "insider influence" and forging coalitions. Through campaign contributions and alliance building, ATLA has won the support of many public officials. Other factors contributing to ATLA's reticence to leap into the public debate have less to do with inducements and more to do with constraints. First, legal constraints often preclude full public disclosure of case details, thus limiting ATLA's freedom to expose corporate wrongdoing in a public defense of litigation. Second, cynicism about trial lawyers has become so deeply ingrained that it seems futile to try an image makeover that may not ultimately produce any tangible results for their cause. Third, the paradox between zealous client advocacy and cause-oriented altruism drives a wedge between lawyers' professional interests and defense of their ideological commitments. Finally, ideological and strategic differences of opinion among trial lawyers have prevented the development of any coherent public defense.

Although McCann and Haltom concede that ATLA's insider defense against tort reform has been successful thus far, they conclude their chapter by outlining several "potentially costly implications" of its strategy. They point out, for example, that campaign finance reform laws may limit ATLA's future ability to secure the necessary insider political influence. Further, ATLA's silence in the public debate has allowed the tort-reform camp to win the "hearts and minds" of the public, the people whose opinions matter most in the jury box. Ultimately ATLA's well-developed preference for backroom tactics over the public declaration of its moral and political vision suggests that the plaintiffs' bar is unlikely "to be a force for either advancing new substantive policy agendas or new forms of democratic politics in contemporary U.S. society." Here short-term victories may end up turning into long-term defeats.

Victory becoming defeat, constraint becoming opportunity, private practice becoming public commitment, these are but a few of the paradoxes which *The Worlds Cause Lawyers Make: Structure and Agency in Legal Practice* unearths. This book illustrates the promise of an approach which brings the structure-agency problematic front and center in scholarship on the legal profession generally and cause lawyering in particular. It begins to suggest ways of thinking about cause lawyering work in domains—relations with movements, practice settings, strategic decision-making—which are variously constituted by the intersections of legality, professionalism, and politics. It attends to some of the crucial "antinomies" of cause lawyering, for example, "between the necessity of a relatively autonomous legal system for the preservation of certain rights, and the resistance of such a system to the extension of other rights; between the ambiguities of professionalism as an ideal and an interest; between the tension of law and morality, of the bright line between professional neutrality and moral commitment" (Halliday 1999: 1016). In the end, it reveals the frustration as well as the persistence, the tangle of loyalties as well as of competing claims, and the ingenuity in the face of defeat that has been, and likely will be, an ongoing feature in the worlds in which cause lawyers now work and the worlds these political lawyers are likely, in the near term, to be able to bring into being.

Notes

1. Unfortunately, available research does not shed much light on the way cause lawyering interacts with the organized legal profession in other nations. For partial exceptions, see Lev (1998) and Boon (2001).

2. For an elaboration of such a view in the context of a broader analysis of lawyer professionalism, see Nelson and Trubek (1992b: 185). In the context of previous research on cause lawyering the work of Shamir and Chinski (1998) has been particularly important in advancing a constructivist perspective.

3. On structure and agency generally, see Bourdieu (1977), Giddens (1984, 1991), Swidler (1986), Sewell (1992).

4. For a useful critique of Giddens's approach, see Stones (1991).

5. Scheingold and Sarat (2004) use the opportunity and constraint model to analyze cause lawyering in relation to the organized bar, legal education, practice settings, and the institutions of American liberal democracy.

6. McCann (2004: 8) suggests the need for a broader perspective on social movements. In his view, social movements aim for a broader scope of social and political transformation than do most more conventional political activities. Although social movements may press for tangible short-term goals within the existing structure of relations, they are animated by more radical aspirational visions of a different, better society. Second, social movements often employ a wide range of tactics, as do parties and interest groups, but they are far more prone to rely on communicative strategies of information disclosure and media campaigns as well as disruptive "symbolic" tactics such as protests, marches, strikes, and the like that halt or upset ongoing social practices. Third, social movements tend to develop from core constituencies of nonelites whose social position reflects relatively low degrees of wealth, prestige, or political clout. Although movements may find leadership or alliance among elites and powerful organizations, the core "indigenous population" of social movements tends to be "the nonpowerful, the nonwealthy and the nonfamous."

7. Hilbink (2003: 8) observes, "lawyers also reveal distinct visions of the cause for which they work. The cause may be conceived of in procedural or substantive terms, it may incorporate different understandings of strategy and audience as well as varied views on how strategies and goals are determined."

8. For a detailed analysis of this phenomenon, see Scheingold and Sarat 2004: chapter 4.

9. We are grateful to Richard Abel for pointing this out to us.

10. Hilbink (2003: 8) offers a different way of categorizing cause lawyers. He identifies three types which he calls "proceduralist," "elite/vanguard," and "grassroots."

References

Abel, Richard. 1981. "Why Does the American Bar Association Promulgate Ethical Rules?" *Texas Law Review* 59: 639.

Archer, Margaret. 1988. *Culture and Agency: The Place of Culture in Social Theory*. Cambridge: Cambridge University Press.

Arendt, Hannah. 1958. *The Human Condition*. Chicago: University of Chicago Press.

Boon, Andrew. 2001. "Cause Lawyers in a Cold Climate: The Impact(s) of Globalization on the United Kingdom," in *Cause Lawyering and the State in a Global Era*, ed. Austin Sarat and Stuart Scheingold. New York: Oxford University Press.

Bourdieu, Pierre. 1977. *Outline of a Theory of Practice*, trans. Richard Nice. New York: Cambridge University Press.

Dezalay, Yves, and Bryant Garth. 2002. *The Internationalization of Palace Wars: Lawyers, Economists, and the Contest to Transform Latin American States*. Chicago: University of Chicago Press.

Ewick, Patricia, and Susan Silbey. 1998. *The Common Place of Law: Stories from Everyday Life*. Chicago: University of Chicago Press.

Fried, Charles. 1976. "The Lawyer as Friend: The Moral Foundations of the Lawyer-Client Relation." *Yale Law Journal* 85: 1060.

Galanter, Marc, and Thomas Paley. 1991. *Tournament of Lawyers: The Transformation of the Big Law Firm*. Chicago: University of Chicago Press.

Giddens, Anthony. 1984. The *Constitution of Society: Outline of the Theory of Structuration*. Berkeley: University of California Press.

———. 1991. *Modernity and Self-Identity: Self and Society in the Late Modern Age*. Stanford, Calif.: Stanford University Press.

Gordon, Robert. 1984. "Critical Legal Histories." *Stanford Law Review* 36: 57.

Halliday, Terence. 1998. "Lawyers as Institution-Builders: Constructing Markets, States, Civil Society and Community," in *Crossing Boundaries: Traditions and Transformations in Law and Society Research*, ed. Austin Sarat et al. Evanston, Ill.: Northwestern University Press.

———. 1999. "Politics and Civic Professionalism: Legal Elites and Cause Lawyers." *Law and Social Inquiry* 24: 1013.

Halliday, Terence, and Lucien Karpik, eds. 1997. *Lawyers and the Rise of Western Political Liberalism*. New York: Oxford University Press.

Hay, Colin. 1995. "Structure and Agency," in *Theory and Methods in Political Science*, ed. David Marsh and Gerry Stoker. New York: St. Martin's Press.

Heinz, John, and Edward Laumann. 1982. *Chicago Lawyers: The Social Structure of the Bar*. New York: Russell Sage Foundation.

Hilbink, Thomas. 2004. "You Know the Type . . . Categories of Cause Lawyering." *Law and Social Inquiry* 29: 657.

Keck, Margeret, and Kathryn Sikkink. 1997. *Activists Without Borders: Transnational Advocacy Networks in International Politics*. Ithaca, N.Y.: Cornell University Press.

Kidder, Robert, and Setsuo Miyazawa. 1993. "Long-Term Strategies in Japanese Environmental Litigation." *Law and Social Inquiry* 18: 605.

Lev, Daniel. 1998. "Lawyers' Causes in Indonesia and Malaysia," in *Cause Lawyering: Political Commitments and Professional Responsibilities*, ed. Austin Sarat and Stuart Scheingold. New York: Oxford University Press.

Marcuse, Herbert. 1964. *One Dimensional Man: Studies in the Ideology of Advanced Industrial Society*. Boston: Beacon Press.

McAnulla, Stuart. n.d. "The Structure-Agency Debate and Its Historiographical Utility." Retrieved from http://www.psa.ac.uk/cps/1998/mcanulla.pdf.

McCann, Michael W. 1994. *Rights at Work: Pay Equity Reform and the Politics of Legal Mobilization*. Chicago: University of Chicago Press.

———. 2004. Law and Social Movements," in *The Blackwell Companion to Law and Society*, ed. Austin Sarat. London: Blackwell Publishing.

McCann, Michael, and Helena Silverstein. 1998. "Rethinking Law's Allurements: A Relational Analysis of Social Movement Lawyers in the United States," in *Cause Lawyering: Political Commitments and Professional Responsibilities*, ed. Austin Sarat and Stuart Scheingold. New York: Oxford University Press.

Meili, Stephen. 1998. "Cause Lawyering and Social Movements: A Comparative Perspective on Democratic Change in Argentina and Brazil," in *Cause Lawyering: Political Commitments and Professional Responsibilities*, ed. Austin Sarat and Stuart Scheingold. New York: Oxford University Press.

Morag-Levine, Noga. 2001. "The Politics of Imported Rights: Transplantation and Transformation in an Israeli Environmental Cause-Lawyering Organization," in *Cause Lawyering and the State in a Global Era*, ed. Austin Sarat and Stuart Scheingold. New York: Oxford University Press.

Nelson, Robert, and David Trubek. 1992a. "Introduction: New Problems and New Paradigms in Studies of the Legal Profession," in *Lawyers' Ideals/Lawyers' Practices: Transformations in the American Legal Profession*, ed. Robert Nelson, David Trubek, and Rayman Solomon. Ithaca, N.Y.: Cornell University Press.

———. 1992b. "Arenas of Professionalism: Professional Ideologies in Context," in *Lawyers' Ideals/Lawyers' Practices: Transformations in the American Legal Profession*, ed. Robert Nelson, David Trubek, and Rayman Solomon. Ithaca, N.Y.: Cornell University Press.

Ritzer, George, ed. 1992. *Metatheorizing: 6 Key Issues in Sociological Theory*. London: Sage Publications.

Santos, Boaventura de Sousa. 1995. *Toward a New Common Sense: Law, Science and Politics in the Paradigmatic Transformation*. New York: Routledge.

Sarat, Austin. 1998. "Between (the Presence of) Violence and (the Possibility of) Justice: Lawyering Against Capital Punishment," in *Cause Lawyering: Political Commitments and Professional Responsibilities*, ed. Austin Sarat and Stuart Scheingold. New York: Oxford University Press.

———. 2001. "State Transformation and the Struggle for Symbolic Capital: Cause Lawyers, the Organized Bar, and Capital Punishment in the United States," in *Cause Lawyering and the State in a Global Era*, ed. Austin Sarat and Stuart Scheingold. New York: Oxford University Press.

Sarat, Austin, and William L. F. Felstiner. 1995. *Divorce Lawyers and Their Clients: Power and Meaning in the Legal Process*. New York: Oxford University Press.

Sarat, Austin, and Stuart Scheingold. 1998a. *Cause Lawyering: Political Commitments and Professional Responsibilities*. New York: Oxford University Press.

———. 1998b. "Cause Lawyering and the Reproduction of Professional Authority: An Introduction," in *Cause Lawyering: Political Commitments and Professional Responsibilities*, ed. Austin Sarat and Stuart Scheingold. New York: Oxford University Press.

————, eds. 2001. *Cause Lawyering and the State in a Global Era*. New York: Oxford University Press.

Scheingold, Stuart. 1974. *The Politics of Rights: Lawyers, Public Policy, and Political Change*. New Haven, Conn.: Yale University Press.

————. 2001. "Cause Lawyering and Democracy in Transnational Perspective, A Postscript," in *Cause Lawyering and the State in a Global Era*, ed. Austin Sarat and Stuart Scheingold. New York: Oxford University Press.

Scheingold, Stuart, and Austin Sarat. 2004. *Something to Believe In: Professionalism Politics, and Cause Lawyers*. Stanford, Calif.: Stanford University Press.

Seron, Carroll. 1992. "Managing Entrepreneurial Legal Services: The Transformation of Small Firm Practice," in *Lawyers' Ideals/Lawyers' Practices: Transformations in the American Legal Profession*, ed. Robert Nelson, David Trubek, and Rayman Solomon. Ithaca, N.Y.: Cornell University Press.

Sewell, William. 1992. "A Theory of Structure: Duality, Agency, and Transformation." *American Journal of Sociology* 98: 1.

Shamir, Ronen, and Sara Chinski. 1998. "Destruction of Houses and Construction of a Cause: Lawyers and Bedouins in Israeli Courts," in *Cause Lawyering: Political Commitments and Professional Responsibilities*, ed. Austin Sarat and Stuart Scheingold. New York: Oxford University Press.

Silver, Charles, and Frank B. Cross. 2000. "What's Not to Like About Being a Lawyer?: A Life of Counsel and Controversy." *Yale Law Journal* 109: 1443.

Silverstein, Helena. 1996. *Unleashing Rights: Law, Meaning, and the Animal Rights Movement*. Ann Arbor: University of Michigan Press.

Simon, William. 1978. "The Ideology of Advocacy." *Wisconsin Law Review*, p. 30.

————. 1984. "Visions of Practice in Legal Thought." *Stanford Law Review* 36: 469.

————. 1998. *The Practice of Justice: A Theory of Lawyers' Ethics*. Cambridge: Harvard University Press.

Sterett, Susan. 1998. "Caring About Individual Cases: Immigration Lawyering in Britain," in *Cause Lawyering: Political Commitments and Professional Responsibilities*, ed. Austin Sarat and Stuart Scheingold. New York: Oxford University Press.

Stones, Rob. 1991. "Strategic Context Analysis: A New Research Strategy for Structuration Theory." *Sociology* 25: 685.

Swidler, Ann. 1986. "Culture in Action: Symbols and Strategies." *American Sociological Review* 51: 273.

Taylor, Michael. 1993. "Structure, Culture, and Action in the Explanation of Social Change," in *Politics and Rationality*, ed. William James Booth, Patrick James, and Hudson Meadwell. Cambridge: Cambridge University Press.

Tilly, Charles. 1992. "Social Movements and National Politics," in *Statemaking and Social Movements*, ed. Charles Bright and Susan Harding. Ann Arbor: University of Michigan Press.

Trubek, David M., Yves Dezalay, Ruth Buchanan, and John R. Davis. 1994. "Global Restructuring and the Law: Studies of the Internationalization of Legal Fields and the Creation of Transnational Arenas." *Case Western Reserve Law Review* 44: 407–98.

Causes and the Lawyers Who Serve Them

*How Do Causes Make Their Lawyers and
Lawyers Make Their Causes?*

Corporate Responsibility and the South African Drug Wars

Outline of a New Frontier for Cause Lawyers

RONEN SHAMIR

Introduction

Multinational corporations (MNCs) are increasingly expected to display social responsibility and to improve their social, rather than economic, performance regarding their employees and ever widening circles of stakeholders. Accordingly, MNCs have also become increasingly vulnerable to criticisms implicating them in a variety of human rights abuses, environmental disasters, infrastructure neglect, health hazards, and unfair labor practices that occur mainly in and around their operations in the global South (Sethi 2002). Corporate giants of various types experience the heat of consumer boycotts, bad press, demonstrations, and public shaming campaigns that address their misconduct or lack of adequate response to a variety of perceived social wrongs. On the legal front, attempts are under way to invoke legal means and to develop legal instruments for enforcing corporate liability in developing countries, while various initiatives press for new regulatory frameworks that will substitute for national jurisdictions that are unwilling or unable to tame corporate behavior (Held 2002; Hertz 2001).

In response, and in order to defend their reputation and please consumers and investors, more and more corporations speak the language of social responsibility and corporate citizenship (Dickerson 2002). Shaped through the push and pull of public expectations and corporate response, a whole field of action thus emerges. Designated in this chapter as the field of corporate social responsibility (CSR), it is host to multiple social actors and to a variety of pro-grams and initiatives. National, international, and regional bodies, nonprofit organizations, business-sponsored civic groups, commercial entrepreneurs, business consultants, and corporate executives, among others, act in the field and try to install their own versions of what CSR is. One important locus of the CSR field is the business school, where ideas of "corporate citizenship" are be-ing packaged for MBA students as scientific tools for enhanced corporate suc-cess. The old academic interest in philanthropy and charity moves from reli-gious studies departments to the business school, and the old field of business ethics—heretofore marginal to business studies—enjoys a late blooming as no-tions such as transparency and accountability are incorporated into the general conceptual package of social responsibility.

In tandem with business education, a whole commercial market develops around shaping, assessing, and advising on the desired dimensions of business social responsibility. Accounting firms, for example, embark upon the CSR bandwagon, developing special expertise in "social auditing" and offering their commercial services to interested corporations. A new breed of strategic con-sultants is also operating in the field. With a typical background in public rela-tions, these experts now sell strategic CSR models, advise corporations on how to develop CSR campaigns, and offer follow-up reports and impact assessment studies. Nowhere are the benefits of the CSR market more felt than in the in-dustries of public relations and advertising. Here, a new line of "social brand-ing" strategies is already in full swing (Klein 1999). Copywriters and graphic de-signers are now trained in the new art of associating products and services with "morally good" notions like saving the planet, educating the poor, reaching out to communities, and preparing children for life in the global village. Law firms also begin to appreciate the new business opportunities this field seems to be offering. For example, lawyers advise on how to frame mission statements, so-cial compacts, and codes of conduct in ways that would not implicate corpora-tions with contractual obligations they are not ready to assume, while others, operating as adversaries, seek new ways to impose corporate accountability for potential or actual wrongdoing.

All in all, the CSR field may be defined as the social universe where ongoing negotiations over the very meaning and scope of the term social responsibility take place. The field may be best grasped as representing a dynamic continuum of such meanings, where at one end of the spectrum are concepts of CSR that tend to define it mainly in terms of organized philanthropy while at the other end are concepts of CSR which tend to define it in terms of enforceable and formal regulation. In between, the field is suffused with numerous alternative conceptions, most of which tend to rely on private regulation and corporate self-regulation, with varying degrees of external controls in respect to questions such as monitoring, enforcement, and sanctioning. Therefore, the CSR field is currently a major site where crucial debates about the privatization of social responsibilities and, moreover, crucial debates concerning the trajectory and nature of global regulatory regimes, take place (DeWinter 2001).

In this chapter I seek to raise some preliminary questions concerning the actual and potential role of cause lawyers in the field of CSR. Specifically, I wish to offer an exploratory framework for investigating the role of cause lawyering in transforming CSR into an enforceable, legally sanctioned regime of duties, obligations, and liabilities in diverse areas such as welfare, employment, and human rights. In what follows, I look in detail into one case study, namely the legal dispute that emerged in South Africa between some of the world's most formidable pharmaceutical giants and the South African government. I use the case to illustrate and analyze the relationship between activist lawyers, nongovernmental organizations, and the state in order to examine the conditions necessary for successful legal advocacy on behalf of groups demanding an enforceable regime of CSR. However, the case I analyze is unique in many respects, and I thus also use it as a reference point for considering other potential situations and models that may be available for lawyers who take part in shaping the CSR field.

Cost Does Matter I: Pharmaceuticals and
the South African AIDS Crisis

In 1997, in an attempt to respond to a widespread AIDS crisis, the South African government introduced amendments to the South African Medicines and Related Substances Control Act No. 101 of 1965. The amendments included an empowering provision, which vested the minister of health with discretion to prescribe conditions for the supply of more affordable medicines to the public, notwithstanding anything to the contrary contained in the Patents Act of 1978. The amendments were introduced on the basis of data showing a catastrophic AIDS-related death rate of 120,000 people annually, with more than 4.5 million South Africans then infected with the HIV virus and 1,700 more people infected every day, 200 babies among them.

The social theory behind the amendments was that the high cost of AIDS/HIV drugs—protected by patent rights held by major pharmaceutical companies—put them beyond the reach of many infected people relying on public health services.[1] The government of South African could not afford the task of subsidizing those drugs to its needy population, and given that five of the leading pharmaceutical multinational corporations involved in the production of AIDS/HIV drugs had global sales tripling South Africa's entire national budget, they had to share in the distributive burden. Accordingly, the amendments were designed to push the cost of drugs to affordable levels by allowing the South African government to buy, import, or license the production of cheaper versions of patented medicines. The amendments were introduced on the premise that the 1994 constitution of South Africa guaranteed the social right to health care as a binding obligation of the government.

In 1998, the Pharmaceutical Manufacturers' Association (PMA) of South Africa, acting on behalf of 40 of the world's largest pharmaceutical companies (e.g., Bayer, Bristol-Myers, Glaxo-Wellcome, Merck, Pfizer, and Hoffman-La Roche), challenged the constitutionality of the Amendment Act at the High Court of South Africa (case 4183/98). The most important dispute involved Section 15c of the act that provided authority for fast-track *compulsory licensing of medicines* and authorized parallel imports. The PMA challenged the constitutionality of the act on three principal grounds. First, the act was challenged as an unconstitutional infringement upon the property rights of the pharmaceutical companies. Second, it was challenged as an unconstitutional delegation of powers to the executive branch of the state. Third, it was challenged as an unconstitutional infringement upon the freedom of occupation, since the law stipulated that health care professionals should advise patients on the availability of cheaper drugs. However, at stake were more than patent rights in South Africa. Underlying the dispute was a struggle over the interpretation of the TRIPS (Agreement on Trade Related Aspects of Intellectual Property Rights) agreement and over the ability of other developing countries to follow the South African example.

The legal, economic, and political resources the PMA brought to the case were considerable. The PMA retained the legal services of D. M. Kisch Inc., the largest and most reputable firm in South Africa dealing with patents, trademarks, and intellectual property rights. The firm was comprised of 18 senior partners (Directors), all of whom had degrees in fields such as chemistry, biochemistry, electronic engineering, mechanical engineering, physics, and metallurgy alongside their legal degrees. Some of the partners also had been public prosecutors in the 1980s in South Africa. The lawyer who assumed the case on behalf of D. M. Kisch was Nico Vermaak, who submitted the PMA brief to the High Court. Vermaak had been admitted as an attorney of the High Court of

South Africa in 1980, specialized in patents in fields relating to the pharmaceutical industry, and had experience in cases involving the intersection of patent rights with constitutional and administrative law.

In addition, the PMA also retained the services of Fanie Cilliers, who had been described in the South African press as South Africa's best litigation lawyer.[2] Cilliers is known as a highly competent lawyer with a sharp eye for minute and technical aspects of the law, although with little reflexive consideration for the extra-legal aspects of the cases he handles.

Outside the court, the pharmaceutical companies launched a public relations campaign designed to disengage the dispute from the question of cost and to ground it in principled constitutional questions. A document titled "Talking Points on the South African Case," distributed among pharmaceutical executives, stated that the dispute was "over the constitutionality of the legislative means chosen by the government, not about the desire of all parties to improve access to quality medicines for HIV/AIDS and other diseases."[3] The attempt to portray the dispute as a mere "matter of domestic legal constitutional issues" was vigorously pursued by PMA's attorneys and was key to their overall strategy of a forecasted legal success. As we shall see below, when this attempt finally collapsed, the PMA abruptly withdrew from the case.

Two principal measures were undertaken by the pharmaceutical companies in order to substantiate their position. First, they advocated the theory that the plight of AIDS patients in South Africa had not been due to the cost of drugs but rather due to South Africa's poorly maintained distributive infrastructure. The problem of access to drugs, according to this theory, had to do with an infrastructure marred with inefficiency and corruption. The "Talking Points" document stated that reduced costs of drugs obtained by compulsory licensing and parallel trade "have not proven to be effective tools in increasing access to medicine and health care in developing countries." At the same time, the document stated that "despite having access to cheap, high quality medicines, the State loses around 50% of all its stock to theft, fraud and mismanagement at State facilities."[4] The state's public health sector, and not the pharmaceutical companies, in other words, was to blame for the crisis.

Second, some of the companies launched a "social responsibility" campaign, announcing sharp cuts in the cost of several AIDS-related drugs. For example, two days after the opening of the trial, Merck Inc. announced that it was lowering its prices for the company's two antiretroviral medicines used to treat HIV infections. "At these new prices," the notice said, "Merck will not profit from the sale of these medicines in the developing world." Merck announced that its goal was to "spur efforts to accelerate access to these life-saving medications" and that it was Merck's third major initiative in less than a year regarding access to HIV/AIDS in Africa.[5] Likewise, Pfizer Inc. announced that it was offering to give away Diflucan, an expensive AIDS drug, to poor South Africans as part of its policy of responding to the "unmet medical need" in South Africa.[6]

Other developments outside South Africa were also relevant, thickening the net of actors involved in the case. One of the early arguments of the pharmaceutical companies was that the South African law was not only unconstitutional, but also in violation of TRIPS, which is an agreement entered to by all members of the World Trade Organization. The agreement stipulates, among other things, that all member states should bring their domestic patent and intellectual property rights laws in accordance with the principles of TRIPS until 2005. Specifically, the pharmaceutical companies argued that parallel imports were illegal under Article 28 (exclusive rights of patent owners to import a patented product into a country) and Article 31 (compulsory licensing) of TRIPS.

Prompted by the strong lobby of PharMA (the American Pharmaceutical Manufacturers Association), as well as by major pharmaceutical companies, the U.S. government adopted the view that the South African law was in violation of TRIPS and subjected South Africa to trade pressures.[7] Later in 1998, the office of the United States Trade Representatives (USTR) put South Africa on a Special 301 Watch list due to the provisions of the South African Medicines Act, which authorized parallel imports and empowered the government to abrogate patent rights. Subsequently, the White House announced that four items, for which South Africa had requested preferential tariff treatment, would be held in abeyance pending adequate progress on intellectual property rights protection in South Africa. The U.S. Department of State followed suit and sent a report to the U.S. Congress, titled, "US Government efforts to negotiate the repeal, termination or withdrawal of Article 15(c) of the South African Medicines and Related Substances Act of 1965." According to the report, "all relevant agencies of the U.S. Government . . . have been engaged in an assiduous, concerted campaign to persuade the Government of South Africa (SAG) to withdraw or modify the provisions of Article 15(c) that we believe are inconsistent with South Africa's obligations and commitments under the WTO Agreement on Trade Related Aspects of Intellectual Property Rights (TRIPS)."[8]

The South African government came under pressure from the European Commission as well. Leon Brittan, vice president of the European Commission, wrote a letter to then Vice President Thabo Mvuyelwa Mbeki, claiming that South Africa was in violation of TRIPS and that the legislation would "negatively affect the interests of the European pharmaceutical industry."[9] Other se-

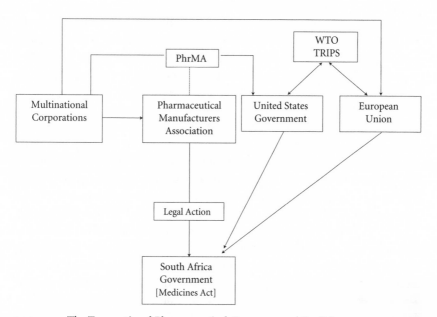

F I G . 1.1. The Transnational Pharmaceutical-Governmental Coalition

nior European officials joined the campaign and complained to the South African government that its amended Medicines Act jeopardized the patent rights of the pharmaceutical industry. Thus, the South African government had been subjected to legal, economic, and diplomatic pressures from both the pharmaceutical industry and the representatives of the United States and the European Union (see Figure 1.1).

The Slow Rise and the Fast Fall of the PMA Case

The case of the PMA against the government of South Africa in the matter of the constitutionality of the amendments introduced into the Medicines and Related Substances Control Act was scheduled to open on March 5, 2001, nearly three years after PMA initiated proceedings. On February 16, 2001, the court was asked to allow the Treatment Action Campaign (TAC)—a nonprofit organization—to be admitted to the case as a "friend of the court" (amicus curiae). The interest of TAC in the case was explained to the court in a "founding affidavit" submitted by Theodora Steele, a member of the executive committee of TAC. Prior to this formal request, on January 26, 2001, TAC approached the parties, asking for their consent to admit TAC as a "friend of the court." The South African government granted permission, but PMA's attorney replied that the requested intervention was not required because "the issues before the Court are of a constitutional nature and do not relate, in any way, particularly to access to Aids medication."[10]

Asked to be admitted by the court, TAC's "founding affidavit" explained the background for its request. It explained that TAC was a voluntary nonprofit association founded in 1998 by Zackie Achmat, a well-known AIDS activist in South Africa. The objectives of TAC—established in the wake of the new legislation and the opposition of the PMA—were to promote legislation to ensure equal access and equal treatment of people with HIV/AID, to campaign for affordable and quality access to health care, and to invoke litigation, lobbying, advocacy, and mobilization in order to fight all forms of discrimination relating to treatment of HIV/AIDS.

TAC also explained its former out-of-court involvement with the issue at stake, the broad national and international support it enjoyed in pursuing the matter, and the resources and information it could bring to the court's attention, thus helping it to see the broad context of the dispute. On the merits, the essential position of TAC had been articulated in the "founding affidavit" as follows:

> It is my contention, and that of the TAC, that the ability of many persons with HIV to purchase and take medicines that treat HIV and its attendant illnesses, has a profound and inseparable bearing on their constitutional rights to human dignity and life and access to health care. In this respect people with HIV are directly dependent on the State's ability to fulfill its constitutional duty to bring about the progressive realization of their rights of access to health care services. . . .
>
> The TAC has a direct interest in supporting reasonable legislative and other measures, taken by the state, to improve access to health care services and to promote the achievement of equality. The TAC believes that Medicines and Related Substances Control Amendment Act (90 of 1997) represents an attempt by the respondents to perform their constitutional obligations diligently and without delay, and that the HIV/AIDS epidemic creates a unique and historically unparalleled necessity to ensure that this is done with the minimum of delay.
>
> The TAC is concerned that the rights of its members are being directly threatened by the action of the applicants.

In short, the TAC wanted to break out of the strict constitutional questions raised by the PMA and to introduce a legal argument that the PMA tried to avoid, namely that the limitation of patent rights could be justified in the name of a greater public good. This legal argument, and especially the rich documentation that TAC gathered in its support, did not constitute the heart of the respondents' brief presented to the court by the attorney general of South Africa. This latter brief, unlike TAC's, mainly responded to PMA's contention that the amendments were unconstitutional because they delegated too much discretionary powers to the health minister (a "delegation doctrine" argument) and because the amendments were so broad as to allow for too wide a discretion (a "void for vagueness" argument).

Thus, the first issue before the court—when it convened on March 5, 2001, to hear oral arguments in the case after nearly three years of delays and postponements—was to decide whether to admit TAC's amicus curiae brief. The attorneys of the PMA, well aware of the linkage between "cost" and "rights" that TAC had established, fought hard to convince the court not to admit TAC. Attorney Cilliers of PMA continued the line adopted by D. M. Kisch that the TAC should not be allowed to seize on an opportunity in a related matter to have a hearing in its own issue raised in its own affidavits but not raised as an issue in the proceedings as it is already before the Court. Cilliers tried to raise some procedural arguments, first contending that TAC filed their request too late. He then moved to substance, arguing that TAC would add nothing to the government's case because the court case was neither about access to medication for HIV or AIDS patients nor about cheaper AIDS drugs but rather about the constitutionality of certain sections of the act. When these failed, Cilliers asked for a four-month postponement, arguing that TAC introduced new legal arguments and new data that would have required a long period of study by the PMA.

During these first two days of the hearings, thousands of demonstrators gathered outside the court and next to the U.S. embassy in Pretoria, calling upon the drug companies to withdraw their lawsuit. Inside the court, attorneys for TAC convinced Judge Bernard Ngoepe who handled the case that public health and access to drugs were part of the issue at stake. Justice Ngoepe set April 18, 2001, for the next hearing, ruled that TAC could be admitted as a friend of the court, and allowed the PMA more time to study the new materials. The admission of TAC thus promised to turn the case into a wide and open discussion about South Africa's AIDS crisis and the responsibility of the private market in its endurance.

Subsequently, on April 17, 2001, TAC presented the court with legal "heads of argument." These were accompanied by a large number of factual, conceptual, and scientific affidavits as well as accounts of persons with AIDS, testifying about their plight and the relevance of cost to that plight. The brief was more than fifty pages long and was by far more thorough—on strict legal and constitutional grounds—than the government's brief. The heart of the argument was that according to South Africa's postapartheid constitutional law, courts must interpret legislation along the spirit and objects of the Bill of Rights and that at stake in the present case were not only rights to property but also rights to life, dignity, and access to health care services. Specifically, TAC argued that Section 27 of the constitution that established the social right to access to health care services put the state under a positive duty to adapt measures to meet this end. TAC linked such particular provisions with the general principles of respect to human dignity and with a right to life, grounding both in South African law and international law (e.g., Universal Declaration of Human Rights and the International Convention on Economic, Social and Cultural Rights 1996).

Of specific interest for the purposes of this chapter was the suggestion of TAC that the state's duty to provide access to cheap drugs had to be accommodated by the market, thus implicitly pushing the question of "social responsibility" from being a voluntary practice into a legal duty. As aforementioned, the pharmaceutical companies accompanied their legal challenge with various campaigns in the course of which they voluntarily lowered the cost of some drugs. The PMA did not shy away from pointing at these campaigns—in their formal brief—as proof that they did not shirk their social duties toward the public. In its own brief, the TAC referred to this argument, suggesting that such voluntary practices could not suffice:

> Indeed, the suggestion by [PMA] that somehow significance should be placed, for constitutional purposes, (as opposed to moral or ethical obligations) on the donations made by various members of the PMA, misconceives the right to dignity. It demeans those who are poor and unable to afford medicines and relegates them to the role of supplicants dependent upon the largesse of the wealthy and the powerful. The State cannot discharge its constitutional obligations by relying on the charity of others. (3.23 TAC brief)

The ultimate purpose of the brief, then, was to reframe the dispute as a "right to health" case and, within this context, to establish a direct link between South Africa's AIDS crisis and the high cost of drugs incurred on the needy due to the pharmaceutical industry's economic leverage. In articulating and presenting its position on the matter, the TAC firmly sided with the South African government, in fact becoming a powerful ally that decisively changed the balance of power between the two formal parties.

On April 18, 2001, news was spreading about the intention of the PMA to withdraw its legal action.[11] On April 19, on the first day of hearings, Attorney Cilliers for PMA dramatically announced that "by the consent of all parties, we would simply ask your lordship to note that the application is withdrawn." In the settlement announced by the government and the drug firms, the government agreed to consult the industry before making decisions on parallel imports of patented drugs and the generic substitution of key medicines. The drug companies also announced that "the applicants recognize and reaffirm that South Africa may enact national laws or regulations . . . or adopt measures necessary to protect public health and broaden access to medicines in accordance with the South African Constitution and TRIPS (agreement on Trade Related Aspects of Intellectual Property Rights)."[12] The pharmaceutical industry, in short, backed from its earlier position, thus ending a three-year legal struggle and making the headlines all over the world.

In order to understand this dramatic turn of events, the TAC initiative has to be put in a broader context, demonstrating how NGOs are becoming major players in global politics.

Cost Does Matter II: NGOs and the South African AIDS Crisis

The ability of the TAC to rely on substantial intellectual and political resources, in effect turning itself into a more crucial party than the government of South Africa, was due to the fact that it was part of a broader coalition of organizations and persons across the globe. TAC, as aforementioned, was established in 1998 by Zackie Achmat, then the director of South Africa's National Coalition for Gay and Lesbian Equality, himself diagnosed with HIV. Achmat, reputed to be an excellent organizer and a highly committed activist, established TAC with the active support of a number of local and international organizations. Among these organizations, the connection of TAC with the Aids Law Project (ALP), and the backing it received from it, was probably the most decisive. The ALP operates as a research and resource center specializing in the social, legal, and human rights issues relevant to AIDS. ALP focuses on framing AIDS-related issues in terms of human rights, and its mission is to initiate legal action on matters of public importance, to refer people in need to relevant legal services and to use research to develop law, policies, and "best practice" recommendations on questions such as AIDS and employment, AIDS and pregnancy, AIDS and development, and AIDS and women. The ALP is also a collaborating center of the United Nations Joint Program on AIDS (UNAIDS) and a partner of the Canadian HIV/AIDS Legal Network (CHALN). The project was initiated by Judge Edwin Cameron, an HIV positive, in 1993.

The AIDS Law Project, in turn, is part of the reputed Center for Applied Legal Studies (CALS), which operates at Wits (Witwaterstand) University in Johannesburg. CALS was founded in the late 1970s with a focus on human rights and a mandate for research, public interest litigation, and training for law reform work largely in issues relating to the apartheid regime. As such, CALS has a tradition of hosting first-rate human rights experts experienced with law-related activism. Consequently, members of CALS took an active part in formulating the interim constitution during the transition years and in shaping the 1994 constitution and other relevant postapartheid legislation. CALS is also behind the *South Africa Journal of Human Rights* (*SAJHR*), the leading law journal on these issues in South Africa. It is through CALS and its affiliated ALP that the Treatment Action Campaign gained access to highly professional legal representation.

Three lawyers were at the forefront of the legal work performed on behalf of TAC: Matthew Shaskelson, Gilbert Marcus, and Mark Heyward. Matthew Shaskelson is an attorney who heads the Constitutional Project of CALS, with considerable record of involvement in key cases and legal matters pertaining to human and civil rights and a wide variety of constitutional questions. Shaskelson was also a member of the labor relations committee in charge of articulating the constitutional framework for this subject and published articles at the *SAJHR* (dealing with rent boycotts, 1987; dealing with property rights in the interim period, 1995). With Richard Spitz, he also published a book on the transition period, focusing on the work of constitutional committees and constitutional law. Matthew Shaskelson is the son of Arthur Shaskelson, currently president of South Africa's Constitutional Court and formerly highly active in human rights and antiapartheid law-related activism. Shaskelson's constitutional decisions were broadly cited in the brief submitted to the court by the lawyers for TAC. Together with Gilbert Marcus, Shaskelson submitted the brief on behalf of TAC.

Gilbert Marcus is a veteran antiapartheid lawyer and a highly reputable litigator. Like Shaskelson, Marcus also has a record in representing gay and lesbian rights as well as in free-speech-related matters. In 1998, he was involved in striking down the old sodomy law, challenged by Zackie Achmat's National Coalition for Gay and Lesbian Equality. Marcus, a private practitioner, is on the editorial board *SAJHR* (to which Arthur Shaskelson is patron), served as a private counsel to Nelson Mandela and has a record of filling in for the general attorney's office where high expertise and legal skills on principled issues had been called for.

Mark Heyward is the head lawyer for the AIDS Law Project of CALS. Heyward was the immediate link tying TAC to the resources and expertise of CALS and was instrumental in educating the TAC about the legal aspects of the case (see his July 1999 lecture to TAC delegation on "Background to Issues Surrounding Compulsory Licensing and Parallel Imports of Essential Drugs"). Beyond his affiliation with the AIDS Law Project, Heyward also held a position as an executive committee member and deputy chairperson of the AIDS Consortium National Committee of TAC. In this latter capacity, Heywood took part in TAC's most crucial meetings with both the government's representatives and the pharmaceutical companies' executives. Heyward outlined some of the legal arguments contained in TAC amicus already in May 2000, when appearing in the public hearings of the South African parliamentary Portfolio Committee on Health. In this context, he argued:

> The South African government needs to use South Africa's moral legitimacy to challenge the pricing practices of pharmaceutical companies—and the economic policies of industrialized countries that have contributed to the collapse of almost all public health facilities in the vast majority of African countries. Government also needs to reassess its use of available resources. Hugh sums of money are spent on submarines despite the massive need for HIV testing and treatment.[13]

The three lawyers, Shaskelson, Marcus, and Heyward, orchestrated an in and out of court legal campaign that substantially overrode the resources and capabilities that the South African attorney general could summon; and it was their direct involvement that finally persuaded PMA to withdraw the legal action. However the TAC did not focus on a legal struggle taken in isolation from other forms of activism. TAC has formulated what it labeled as a "multidimensional" process designed to force the pharmaceutical companies to reduce the prices of drugs and to withdraw their legal action. TAC organized demonstrations and picketing outside the premises of pharmaceutical companies, PMA, and the U.S. embassy. It held negotiations with the pharmaceutical companies' senior executives and meetings with government agencies, parliamentary commissions, and civil society organizations. It mobilized petitions, marches, mass protests, and symbolic acts of civil disobedience (see TAC's "founding affidavit" for a detailed and chronological list of activities). For example, TAC's chairperson, Zackie Achmat, made headlines in October 2000 when he assumed responsibility for smuggling a generic HIV-related drug (Biozole) into South Africa in order to publicize the difference between its price [1.49 SA Rand] and the price of Pfizer Inc. patented original (Fluconazole, sold for 100 SA Rand) (also see the September 6, 2000, cover story of Achmat as Man of the Week, www.time.com).

The above-mentioned forms of protest were carried outside South Africa as well. In July, 2000 a "Global march for access to HIV/AIDS treatment," led by the TAC, and cohosted by the HealthGAP Coalition of the United States attracted endorsement of over 250 organizations from outside South Africa (see "founding affidavit"). On March 5, 2001 (the first day of the trial), TAC called for an international day of action. This day of action included a protest march

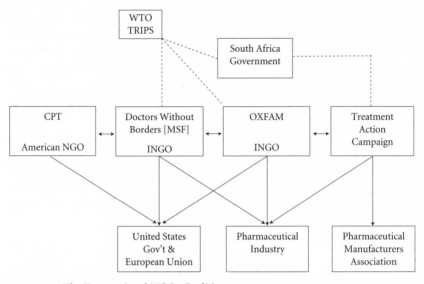

FIG. 1.2. The Transnational NGOs Coalition

in Sydney, Australia, picketing the WTO headquarters in Vancouver, Canada, demonstrations outside the premises of drug companies in Denmark, and numerous acts of protest which were orchestrated by hundreds of nonprofit organizations in the UK, Brazil, Italy, Germany, France, Thailand, the United States, and the Philippines. On April 19, 2001, when PMA withdrew their case, TAC published a joint press release with Oxfam and Medicins Sans Frontieres (see below), acknowledging the contribution of the global network that supported TAC: "We have been encouraged and strengthened by the support we've received from around the world, and we are especially grateful to the 260,000 concerned citizens and 140 organizations from 130 countries who signed the global 'Drop the Case' petition" (www.acessmd-msf.org).

It is often hard to distinguish who did what and who initiated what around the South African case, as Internet exchange of documents and calls for action blurred sources and originals. However, two major international nongovernmental organizations (INGOs) were key to the globalization of the South African dispute: Medicins Sans Frontieres (operating in the United States under the name "Doctors Without Borders"), and Oxfam. Additionally, in the United States, Ralph Nader's Consumer Project on Technology (CPT) became highly instrumental in lobbying against the pharmaceutical industry and advocating the cause of TAC (see Figure 1.2).

Medicins Sans Frontieres (MSF) is an international humanitarian medical aid organization that was founded in 1971 by a group of physicians. Its core assumption is that health care needs supersede national borders. Accordingly, the purpose of MSF is to deliver emergency aid to victims of armed conflict, epidemics, and natural and man-made disasters, and to others who lack health care due to social or geographical isolation. MSF has permanent offices in eighteen countries and each year, more than 2,000 volunteer doctors, nurses, other medical professionals, logistics experts, water/sanitation engineers, and administrators join 15,000 locally hired staff to provide medical aid in more than eighty countries.

As aforementioned, MSF won the 1999 Nobel Prize for its activities. MSF integrates its commitment to providing medical care with an advocacy approach which emphasizes the duty of "Bearing Witness and Speaking Out": speaking out against human rights abuses and violations of humanitarian law that its teams witness while providing medical relief. Specifically, the mission is now defined by MSF as "rebellious humanitarianism," namely that it does not see its mission merely in terms of "doing good" when called upon to do so in cases of humanitarian emergencies or disasters. Rather, rebellious humanitarianism means political engagement in the sense of taking an active role in the actual definition or redefinition of situations *as* disastrous or catastrophic, in the sense of defining situations in terms of human rights abuses, and in the sense of defining situations in terms of those who are responsible.

It was precisely that rebellious humanitarianism which has prompted the involvement of MSF with TAC. Annexed to the TAC amicus was an affidavit by Dr. Eric Goemaere of MSF. In this affidavit, Goemaere described the operation of the MSF's HIV/AIDS clinics in the Western Cape:

> These clinics are among the few in the Western Cape dedicated to the provision of treatment for people with HIV/AIDS. The clinics also dispense free treatment for the opportunistic infections that are common in people with HIV/AIDS. As a result, on a daily basis, people with HIV/AIDS who cannot afford the high cost of medicines visit the MSF clinics. The need is such that even patients with little income will pay hefty sums to travel from the surrounding areas in the hopes of receiving treatment in the MSF clinics.
>
> At the moment our doctors and nurses are able to provide the medicines necessary for the treatment of opportunistic infections, the complications that arise as a result of the damage HIV causes to the immune system.
>
> However, the medical indication for many of the patients visiting the MSF clinics is antiretroviral therapy, which directly inhibits HIV from replicating and so can prevent the development of opportunistic infections. Our doctors and nurses cannot provide out patients with the anti-retroviral therapy because the high price of these drugs makes this an unsustainable option (once begun, antiretroviral therapy is life-long).
>
> Thus as a result of the high price of medicines, our doctors and nurses are regularly unable to offer the antiretroviral treatment needed by our patients.[14]

MSF's support for TAC went far beyond the affidavit. MSF was vocal along-side TAC in insisting that voluntary demonstrations of business social respon-sibility should be transformed into mandatory obligations. A case in point con-cerned Pfizer Inc., the patented producer of Flucanazole (used by HIV/AIDS patients to treat cryptococcal meningitis, a frequently fatal fungal infection of the brain). In 2000, MSF and TAC lobbied Pfizer to reduce the price of the drug or issue a voluntary license allowing a local producer to produce it at a much lower cost. Pfizer responded by announcing its intentions to deliver the drug free of charge to some needy patients. MSF welcomed the news from Pfizer but cautioned that a donation is not a long-term solution for saving the lives of people with AIDS. Rather, it called on pharmaceutical companies "to use mech-anisms other than charity to make life-saving drugs available, namely by lower-ing prices or issuing voluntary licenses for importing or producing generic ver-sions locally."[15]

MSF's major contribution concerned the pressures it exerted on the Euro-pean Commission to reverse its original position, siding with the pharmaceuti-cal industry and claiming that the South African law violated TRIPS. MSF brought the issue of cost to the forefront of the debates about access to health care in launching its Campaign for Access to Essential Medicines in late 1999. The campaign was designed to create a global resource center studying and monitoring drug prices, patent rights, pharmaceutical practices, and the activ-ities of global governance institutions. Launched at Brussels and followed by a joint conference with the American Consumer Project Technology organiza-tion in Amsterdam in November 1999, MSF organized to exert pressure on the European Union's representatives in Seattle in December 1999. In particular, the MSF's Access Campaign focused on meetings and study sessions with the Eu-ropean Commissioner for Trade Pascal Lamy, introducing their interpretation of TRIPS and lobbying for a change of policy. As a result of these meetings and other lobbying efforts, MSF announced that the commissioner adopted general policy guidelines in respect to the access issue. Dr. Morten Rostrup, the presi-dent of MSF, published an open letter to Commissioner Pascal Lamy (Trade) of the European Commission, asking him "to officially withdraw the letter of the Commission of 23 March 1998 and inform President Mbeki of South Africa about this decision. We also ask you to explicitly express support for South Africa's right to use TRIPS-legal measures to address public health concerns."[16] A similar open letter was sent to Lamy by MSF in the Netherlands and the other twenty-one Dutch NGOs. Repeating MSF's letter almost word by word, the Dutch NGOs also urged Lamy to explicitly and formally state the commission's support for South Africa's position and expressed the "hope the Commission will decide on this step before the court case opens on March 5."[17] A similar letter was sent by Nicolas de Torrente, executive director of MSF, to President George W. Bush, and to seven heads of pharmaceutical companies on the eve of the trial.[18]

Concurrent activities had been undertaken by Oxfam International, particularly by Oxfam UK. Oxfam was founded in the UK in 1942 as a relief organization, and developed during the 1950s as an organization providing relief to famine victims. Oxfam International (OI) is a confederation of twelve autonomous nongovernmental organizations, committed to fighting poverty and promoting social justice around the world. Oxfam aligned itself with TAC and MSF and launched a Cut the Cost Campaign focusing on the cost of medicines in general and AIDS/HIV drugs in particular, emphasizing the moral duty of private companies to assume a fair share of the burden associated with access to health services.

A substantial part of Oxfam's contribution to the struggle was evident on the Internet. Oxfam regularly published position papers, policy recommendations, and involved itself in a rapid distribution of information and news concerning the South African case, the TRIPS agreement, and the role of rich countries in interpreting WTO's rules. The Cut the Cost Campaign was part of an overall perception that Oxfam developed in respect to the social consequences of globalization. Thus, for example, in its May 2000 "White Paper on globalization" which was submitted to the British government, Oxfam detailed a "process of globalization that is redistributing wealth and opportunity in the wrong direction, from the poor to the rich. This is morally indefensible, economically inefficient, and socially unsustainable."[19] While most of the analysis focused on the role that rich countries and global institutions should play in reducing the growing inequality between rich and poor, Oxfam also addressed duties that should be imposed on private market actors. For example, Oxfam also referred to the multilateral framework, already advocated by the French and German governments, under which private sector creditors will be required to contribute to debt relief in cases where debt sustainability threatens to undermine recovery.

In this context, Oxfam articulated a clear position in respect to corporate responsibility to communities, workers, consumers, and the environment, calling for a regulatory process whereby heretofore-voluntary practices would become enforceable standards. Oxfam published the e-mail addresses of key policymakers in the British government and of executives in the pharmaceutical industry and urged its subscribers to send them messages of protest. The pressure Oxfam exerted on the pharmaceutical industry was precisely of the type that

sought to transform the industry's long-standing tradition of publicizing its social responsibility actions into a binding duty at times of crisis. For example,
Oxfam urged its subscribers to write Jean-Pierre Garnier, GlaxoSmithKline's
chief executive officer (one of Britain's biggest pharmaceutical companies) and
to demand Glaxo's withdrawal from the South African case. Further, Oxfam
urged its subscribers to ask Garnier to develop a "clear policy" on how Glaxo
would meet his own stated commitment to "maximize affordable access to
medicines in the developing world."

The CPT was a lead player in launching the campaign against the pharmaceutical companies in the United States. The CPT is a Washington-based nonprofit consumer organization created by consumer advocate Ralph Nader, and
part of Nader's Center for Responsive Law. The director of CPT is James Love,
a health economist who is one of the United States' leading experts on compulsory licensing for AIDS drugs. Love is also a member of MSF's Working Group
on Research and Development for Drugs for Neglected Diseases. In the United
States, and in cooperation with Doctors Without Borders (the American
branch of MSF), Love became the main engine behind the organization's involvement in the South African case. The involvement of the CPT in counter-
ing the industry-administration position on the matter had been marked by
first-rate levels of expertise that matched, if not eventually surpassed, the data
that served as the basis for the industry's policy preferences.

As aforementioned, the United States (Clinton-Gore) administration
adopted the industry's view that "South Africa has become a 'test case' for those
who oppose the U.S. government's long-standing commitment to improve the
terms of protection for all forms of American intellectual property, including
pharmaceutical patents." In July 1997, as pressures mounted, the CPT wrote vice
president Gore concerning the United States' policy toward South Africa pharmaceutical policies, presenting essential data and asking him to reconsider and
reverse the American position in the matter. Love also gave testimony to the
South African parliamentary Portfolio Committee on Health in Cape Town.
Love presented a thorough analysis of the new legislation and its relation to
TRIPS, providing judicial interpretations of specific articles of TRIPS related to
parallel imports and compulsory licensing, as well as exact comparative data on
the cost of patented and generic drugs in various countries. CPT also launched
an Internet resource center, containing all the documents relating to the case,
position papers, open letters, research findings, and a rich library containing all
the major documents, press releases, and activities published and sponsored by
the TAC, Oxfam, MSF, and other involved NGOs. In April 1999, Ralph Nader
and James Love again wrote Vice President Gore, asking for a reversal of U.S.

policy on South Africa's Medicines Act and on parallel import and compulsory licensing in general. This letter is an excellent example of both the unequivocal rhetoric the CPT employed in this case and the resources that it was able to gather in order to affect a policy change. It is therefore cited below at some length:

> We are writing to express our outrage that you have used your office to pressure the South African government to repeal its statutory authority for providing for compulsory licensing of patents for essential medicines. . . .
>
> As Chairman of the United States/South Africa Binational Commission (BNC), you have engaged in an astonishing array of bullying tactics to prevent South Africa from implementing policies, legal under the rules of the WTO, that are designed to expand access to HIV/AIDS drugs. . . .
>
> We are attaching several documents. Appendix A is a report prepared by the United States Department of State and provided to the House Committees on Ways and Means, Appropriations and International Relations, on February 5, 1999. Appendix B is a copy of Article 31 of the WTO/TRIPS agreement, which sets out the rules under which nations can use compulsory licensing of patents to achieve public interest objectives. Appendix C is a four page section from a 1999 World Health Organization (WHO) report that explains how compulsory licensing of essential medicines is done under the WTO/TRIPS agreement. Appendix D is a copy of the presentation to the Executive Board of the World Health Assembly by Peter Goosen, Charge d' Affairs at the South African Permanent Mission in Geneva. Appendix E is a background paper on compulsory licensing prepared by the Consumer Project on Technology (CPT) for a March 26, 1999 meeting in Geneva on compulsory licensing. Appendix F is a US government position paper on compulsory licensing that was presented by Lois Boland from the US Patent and Trademark Office. Appendix G is a presentation by Adrian Otten, the Director of the Intellectual Property Division for the World Trade Organization (WTO), for a meeting of the World Health Assembly's ad hoc working group on the Revised Drug Strategy, held in Geneva on October 13, 1998. Taken together, these documents provide a chilling account of the US government's abuse of its superpower status. . . .
>
> The fact that compulsory licensing is legal under international trade law and under the TRIPS agreement is acknowledged by US officials in other settings, such as when they are in the presence of informed persons. For example, in a March 26, 1999 meeting in Geneva on compulsory licensing, US PTO official Lois Boland acknowledged that countries have the right to use compulsory licensing under international law and under the WTO/TRIPS agreement. But she added: "The fact that [the current US] view is not reflected in the TRIPs agreement, in the multilateral context, is fully acknowledged. In our bilateral discussions, we continue to regard the TRIPs agreement as an agreement that establishes minimum standards for protection and, in certain situations, we may, and often do, ask for commitments that go beyond those found in the TRIPs agreement." This is the key point. The US is seeking something more than what is required by the TRIPS. The US government's bullying of

South Africa has been justified to poorly informed reporters and Members of Congress as if it was simply a matter of getting South Africans to abide by international law. . . .

Today we are asking that you reverse US policy toward South Africa. We ask that you instruct Secretary Madeleine Albright, Under Secretary Stuart Eizenstat at the Department of State, Secretary William Daley at the Department of Commerce, United States Trade Representative Charlene Barshefsky, Stuart Nightingale at the US Food and Drug Administration and others to stop their opposition to South African policies on compulsory licensing and parallel imports of pharmaceutical drugs. We and the HIV/AIDS and public health communities who are increasingly concerned about this issue await your response.

Sincerely,

Ralph Nader
James Love Director Consumer Project on Technology[20]

The above letter was more or less replicated a few months later, when CPT and MSF organized a joint letter of protest to Gore signed by 307 health experts and concerned nonprofit organizations.[21] Throughout this period, the American press reported that Gore's presidential campaign trail was systematically disrupted by AIDS activists, led by "Nader consumer groups."[22] Finally, CPT directly contributed to the South African legal action when James Love filed an affidavit as part of the TAC amicus brief. This exceptionally informed affidavit provided the court with a series of studies and fourteen tables dealing with the cost of drugs and a variety of issues relating to the commercial practices of the pharmaceutical industry and the effect of practices such as parallel imports and compulsory licensing upon prices.

In sum, CPT developed a detailed and well-documented brief, arguing that the South African amendments were within the framework of the WTO's TRIPS agreement, which allowed government to overcome patent rights under certain conditions. Advocating the idea that "cost mattered," the position advocated by the CPT and impressed upon administration officials and members of Congress had been that the industry's arguments were wrong and that compulsory licensing would have had a positive effect on public health. This position was particularly crucial at hearings on the U.S. Role in Combating the Global HIV/AIDS Epidemic held in the summer of 1999 by the Government Reform Subcommittee on Criminal Justice, Drug Policy and Human Resources. In these hearings, the position advocated by the CPT began to receive wide attention and recognition, as more and more witnesses and members of Congress shaped opinions in favor of the South African government.

The results of the lobbying efforts led by CPT began to show toward the end of 1999. James Love published an action summary on the Internet, reporting that Gore began to soften his position in the hope of easing up pressures and shaking off protesters.[23] On December 1, 1999, the U.S. government finally dropped South Africa from its "301 Watch List," a clear sign of a government change in policy.

Thus, when the case opened in April 2001, the American and European political backing that the PMA enjoyed in the early stages of the dispute had no loner been there. Instead, the campaign orchestrated by NGOs created a worldwide image crisis that badly hurt the reputation of pharmaceutical companies as socially responsible and one that indicated that the PMA was on its way to losing the legal action as well. The decision of the PMA to finally pull out of the case was thus taken in an attempt to avoid a precedent-setting judicial decision in the matter and in an attempt to rehabilitate the public image of the industry. However, it seems that the South African case illustrates that the emergence of global social norms by way of struggles "in the shadow of the law" is no less significant than actual judicial decisions. Global law, in this case at least, had been shaped through a complex process of negotiations—in and out of court—by corporations, governments, and NGOs with results that will affect any future policy concerning access to affordable medicines.

Discussion

Underlying the South African dispute was the attempt of an industry to preserve a boundary separating *legally protected* business interests from *voluntary* practices of social responsibility. This boundary was undermined by the legal strategy adopted in this case and by a supporting network of economists, physicians, health experts, and activists. The case illustrates the role lawyers may play in shaping the CSR field and in pushing it away from the corporate-inspired notion that CSR should remain voluntary and unenforceable.[24] Working together with other experts and cooperating with social movements and voluntary associations, a new global frontier of cause lawyering may thus be crystallizing, directing lawyers toward a renewed focus on corporate practices in general and on the need to legalize, in one way or another, the CSR field.

However, the South African case has unique characteristics. First, the legal dispute was not initiated by cause lawyers. Rather, cause lawyers have been put into action due to the readiness of the South African government to legalize a regime of corporate social responsibility by introducing a redistributive law that sought to change the unequal share of corporations in assuming health care responsibilities. Cause lawyers in this case enjoyed governmental support and, moreover, relied on an already existing legislation. Yet at other countries, and possibly more often, cause lawyers may find themselves confronting a poor-government–rich-corporation alliance. It is often the case that "irresponsible" corporate practices are performed with the consent or cooperation of the host government. Sometimes, it is the host government or its agents who directly engage in wrongdoing (e.g., violation of human rights) from which the corporation directly or indirectly benefits. In such cases cause lawyers, to the extent that they pursue legal action in the host country, operate in a hostile environment.

Second, the cause lawyers active in the South African case operated within the framework of an autonomous legal system whose courts, procedures, and judges were equipped and able to handle such a complex dispute. Within this context, the lawyers who acted in this case did so on behalf of a resourceful and experienced legal center that provided the means and ways for developing a successful legal campaign. However, the legal systems of many impoverished countries are not sufficiently developed, or insufficiently autonomous, to handle such disputes. In such countries, typically, the very availability of cause lawyers is also scarce, and those who do operate lack necessary resources.

Third, the South African cause lawyers were aligned with a broader advocacy network that included both local and international organizations, and which was able to deploy a multitude of nonlegal tactics that exerted ongoing pressure on the pharmaceutical companies. Although in the South African case such coalitions mobilized cause lawyers in the host country, in other cases such coalitions have to mobilize cause lawyers outside the host country, where laws and courts may facilitate a more or less effective litigation.

In other words, all or some of the above-mentioned conditions for a successful legal campaign are typically absent in other contexts where corporations are expected to comply with various standards of responsibility. In such cases, it seems that a preliminary crucial step is to move litigation from the often ill-adapted legal systems of impoverished or hostile host countries to countries where the political and legal infrastructure allows for greater emphasis on the responsibility of corporations. This ability is dependent upon the existence of a conscious public attentive to corporate wrongdoing and on the ability of lawyers and other activists to develop global connections that bring them in touch with wrongdoing in "hidden" corners of the globe.

For example, lawyers in the United States are currently trying to reactivate a dormant eighteenth-century law (1789 Alien Tort Claims Act, ATCA) in order to sue multinational corporations like Coca-Cola, ExxonMobil, Shell, and Unocal for violations of human rights that allegedly took place in countries like Colombia, Indonesia, and Nigeria (Brown Chomsky 2002; Shamir 2004). Consider the identity of ATCA plaintiffs. In many ATCA cases, indigenous, poor, and oppressed people are able to advance a claim only because they are aided, funded, and represented by institutional players elsewhere. In the case against Unocal, Burmese farmers were represented by lawyers of EarthRights International, the New York–based Center for Constitutional Rights, and two commercial law firms specializing in civil right cases and class action suits. In the case against Texaco, members of three indigenous tribes from Ecuador were aided by a wide coalition: An Ecuadorian lawyer working in the United States initiated the case and was joined by an American commercial law firm specializing in class action lawsuits, a group of law professors from Boston, the Massachusetts Environmental Law Society, Earth Justice International, and Amazon Watch. In the case against Shell in Nigeria, family members of Ken Sero-Wiwa were represented by the New York–based Center for Constitutional Rights and aided by EarthRights International. In the case against Coca-Cola, the Colombian Union Sinaltrainal was aided and represented by the American United Steel Workers Union and by the International Labor Rights Fund. The International Labor Rights Fund also assumed representation in a case against Exxon-Mobil in Indonesia. ATCA cases thus blur the lines between public interest lawyers and private lawyers, nonprofit organizations and commercial law firms, labor unions and civil rights groups, and environmental concerns and class action interests. Such coalitions are needed not only in order to be more effective, but also in order to jointly develop a new "moral" language. The transcendence of the public/private divide, the various types of expertise that are brought to bear upon the issues at stake, the creation of ad hoc legal coalitions, and the effort to create a conceptual umbrella that covers labor, civil rights, and environmental issues are all elements in the new frontier of cause lawyering that the focus on CSR opens up.

Still, a transnational organization of lawyers, able to monitor corporate wrongdoing on a global scale and, moreover, able to take strategic decisions concerning the form and locale of litigation, is yet to be realized. Moreover, so far I have discussed the new frontier only insofar as it concerned the prospects of successful litigation. However, the new frontier for cause lawyers may also include other types of legal action. First, cause lawyers may become more fully engaged with legislative and regulative efforts at the national and international levels, working at institutional settings such as the European Union, the World Bank, the World Trade Organization and at various branches of the United Nations.

Second, cause lawyers who shift their attention to CSR may play crucial roles in the development of corporate self-regulation schemes that may nonetheless become more binding than they are today. The fundamental stance that may be assumed here is succinctly summarized in Oxfam's "White Paper on globalization," which asserts that

> As public consciousness about the power and impact of TNCs has increased, corporations have responded by proclaiming their attachment to ethical standards, preferably as expressed through non-enforceable codes of conduct. . . .
>
> At their best, voluntary codes of conduct can act as a guide to corporate practice and set standards for others to follow. . . . At their worst, they are little more than a public relations exercise. But the deeper point is that corporate behavior is too important for poverty reduction to be left in the field of voluntary codes and standards defined by the corporate sector itself. . . . What is needed is a set of verifiable and enforceable guidelines covering all aspects of corporate activity.[25]

Along these lines, innovative cause lawyers may have an important role to play in transforming codes of conduct, with or without corporate cooperation, into more obligatory instruments. For example, such a transformation may rely on the development of new legal doctrines that would treat codes of conduct as a binding corporate "promise," not unlike the handling of governmental promises in doctrinal administrative law.

In sum, the field of corporate social responsibility opens up a plethora of opportunities for new and creative forms of cause lawyering at both the national and the transnational levels. The extent to which these opportunities will be realized and further perfected (in both the organizational and conceptual sense), however, is still unclear.

Notes

1. In India, the generic industry produces cheaper drugs and forces decreased in prices of brand names. An IMF economist has noted that drug prices in Malaysia, where patent protection existed, are up to 760% higher than in India. The HIV treatment Zidovudine (AZT), produced by Glaxo Wellcome, costs $239 in the United States while the same drug costs $48 in India.

2. Leading human rights lawyer George Bizos has written an account of inquests into the deaths of people who died in detention under apartheid, and referred to Cilliers as an eminent senior counsel who frequently defended the police at such inquests.

3. Merck internal document, March 6, 2001.

4. Ibid.

5. Merck Press Release March 7, 2001, www.merck.com.

6. Associated Press release, April 3rd, 2000. In: Associated Press Archive, www.newslibrary.com.

7. On May 20, 1997, Aldrage B. Cooper, Jr., a vice president of Johnson and Johnson

(J&J) wrote U.S. Secretary of Commerce William Daley, asking that the U.S. government oppose South African legislative provisions that would permit parallel imports of pharmaceuticals. On February 23, 1998, Pharmaceutical Research and Manufacturers of America (PhRMA) asked USTR to designate South Africa as a Priority Foreign country under the Special 301 Review. Bristol-Myers Squibb Inc. also complained to USTR, asking that South Africa be "designated a priority foreign country" under Special 301. The complaint focused on the decision of South Africa to permit registration of a generic from of Paclitaxel (BMS brand name Taxol).

8. May 1, 1998, June 30, 1998. CPT documents. In: http://lists.essential.org/info-policy-notes/msg00013.html

9. http://lists.essential.org/1999/pharmpolicy/msg00342.html. Accessed March 23, 1998.

10. See Appendix AA7, TAC founding affidavit.

11. The Guardian revealed that GlaxcoSmithKline, Bristol-Myers-Squibb, and Merck broke ranks with the other companies, with Merck in particular "deeply uncomfortable" about the legal action and urgently looking for a way out. "Firms Split Over Deal in Cheap Drugs Lawsuit," *The Guardian*, April 18, 2001.

12. *New York Times* editorial, April 20, 2001.

13. "Argument for an Expanded Access Plan to all Aspects of HIV/AIDS Care and Treatment." www.mrc.ac.za/aids/june2000/hivaccess.htm.

14. Appendix AA4, TAC founding affidavit.

15. See letter of May 10, 2000, from MSF to Pfizer and follow-up announcements in www.acessmed-msf.org.

16. Letter of February 12, 2001. www.accessmed-msf.org.

17. www.cptech.org/ip/health/sa/22ngos.html.

18. Letter of April 17, 2001, CPT archives. In: http://lists.essential.org/info-policy-notes/msg00013.html.

19. www.oxfam.org.uk/policy/papers/global/global1a.htm#Section1.

20. www.cptech.org/ip/health/sa/2gore.html.

21. Letter of August 1, 1999, CPT archival documents. In: http://lists.essential.org/info-policy-notes/msg00013.html.

22. "AIDS Activists Dog Gore A 2nd Day," *Washington Post*, June 18, 1999.

23. "E-DRUG: Gore Hopes New AIDS Pact Will Help Shake Off Protesters." August 12, 1999, www.healthnet.org/programs/e-drug-hma/e-drug.199908/msg00049.html.

24. So far, attempts to move CSR into the enforceable domain of law seem to have made little headway. For example, the European Commission recently rejected proposals to adopt a regulatory approach to corporate social responsibility (CSR) in its July 2001 White Paper on the subject. The EC emphasized the "voluntary nature of CSR," and clarified that the EC did not intend to impose responsible behavior on companies by regulation or directive. It rejected mandatory social and environmental reporting, said it will not introduce compulsory social labeling of products, and rejected proposal for European regulation requiring pension funds in member states to disclose any socially responsible investment policies they may have.

25. www.oxfam.org.uk/policy/papers/global/global2.htm.

References

Brown Chomsky, Judith. 2002. "Fighting for Justice Abroad Through Litigation at Home: Multinationals in U.S. Courts." Paper presented at the 2002 meeting of the Law and Society Association, Vancouver, Canada.

DeWinter, Rebecca. 2001. "The Anti-Sweatshop Movement: Constructing Corporate Moral Agency in the Global Apparel Industry." *Ethics & International Affairs* 15: 99–115.

Dickerson, Clair Moore. 2002. "Human Rights: The Emerging Norm of Corporate Social Responsibility." *Tulane Law Review* 76: 1431–60.

Held, David. 2002. "Globalization, Corporate Practice and Cosmopolitan Social Standards." *Contemporary Political Theory* 1: 59–78.

Hertz, Noreena. 2001. *The Silent Takeover.* London: Random House.

Klein, Naomi. 1999. *No Logo: Taking Aim at the Brand Bullies.* New York: Picador.

Shamir, Ronen. 2004. "Between Self-Regulation and the Alien Tort Claims Act: On the Contested Concept of Corporate Social Responsibility." *Law and Society Review* 38, no. 4: 635–64.

Sethi, S. Prakash. 2002. "Corporate Codes of Conduct and the Success of Globalization." *Ethics and International Affairs* 16: 89–106.

CHAPTER TWO

A Political-Professional Commitment?

French Workers' and Unions' Lawyers as Cause Lawyers

LAURENT WILLEMEZ

The expression "cause lawyering" doesn't exist yet in France, either in the scientific literature (legal and sociological[1]) or in the literature for professionals and practitioners. Introducing this U.S. concept to the French socio-legal landscape, I hope to address some of the special links between French law and politics. But such a process of importation needs to be epistemologically careful. Cause lawyering has to be put in its national and social context.

Labor law has existed in France (under a variety of names) since the beginning of the twentieth century. From the very beginning, some attorneys helped (and worked for) workers' unions and socialist parties (what was called in France the "mouvement ouvrier"), advising their leaders about judicial strategies and representing them in court.[2] Nowadays, many lawyers specialize in labor law (also called "social law"), but few of them defend and represent only workers and labor unions. Such lawyers have both a political and a professional commitment. They qualify, according to Sarat and Scheingold's definition, as cause lawyers—lawyers who "challenge established conceptions of professionalism with efforts to decommodify, politicize and socialize legal practice."[3]

As many cause lawyering scholars have shown, engaged lawyers experience many difficulties in assuming both roles, precisely because the legitimacy of each is based on different principles. Indeed, one part of the definition of activism or political engagement is the pursuit of an "ethic of conviction"[4]; "professional power" is, for its part, based on the institutionalization of "formal knowledge," and more precisely social recognition of such institutionalization.[5]

TABLE 2.1

Background Information on Interviewees

No.	Location	Sex	Age	Activity type[a]	Father's profession
1	Paris suburb	Male	62	Associé	Businessman
2	Paris	Male	55	Associé	?
3	Paris	Male	35	Collaborateur	?
4	Paris	Female	40	Solo	Worker
5	Paris	Male	52	Associé	Physician
6	Paris	Male	75	Associé	?
7	Angers	Male	52	Associé	?
8	Poitiers	Female	53	Associé	Carpenter
9	Poitiers	Female	45	Associé	Small banker
10	Amiens	Male	58	Associé	?
11	Paris	Female	40	Solo	Shopkeeper
12	Paris	Female	54	Associé	Attorney
13	Lille	Female	41	Solo	Small corporation's manager[b]
14	Lille	Male	51	Associé	Teacher
15	Lille	Male	51	Associé	Physical therapist

[a] In France, the status of *collaborateur* is very specific: theoretically, it is used of newcomers into the profession, who work simultaneously for two sorts of clientele: the clientele of the "boss" (who is a partner—with the status of *associé* or an individual) and his or her own clientele. After a few years, the second clientele becomes more important and the attorney can found his or her own firm. Actually, a general trend of the profession is the lengthening of the duration of *collaboration*, so that many *collaborateurs* can be seen as hidden salaried attorneys.

[b] Her mother is a labor inspector (*inspecteur du travail*), a state officer in charge of controlling actual implementation of labor law in corporations.

Thus it is logical that a lawyer involved in contrasting activities should experience a sense of contradiction, from both within and without; one goal of the study of such lawyers should be to understand how they "accommodate to the political and professional contradictions that are intrinsic to left-activist legal practice."[6]

However, attorneys who specialize in defending workers don't seem to feel these contradictions. Rather, they claim the position of "go-betweens," and most of them do not feel any conflict between belonging to the legal field on the one hand and to the political or activist field on the other.[7] To explain this, it can be shown that cause lawyering for such attorneys is a "way of salvation," to use Max Weber's phrase.[8] That is, they continue to be what they have been: traditional lawyers on the one hand (far removed from corporate lawyering) and activists with traditional or current beliefs on the other. Thus their conception of lawyering and their political engagement are often fulfilled through cause lawyering, principally because such law practice allows them to continue to live in a certain form of what Weber would term "enchantment" allowed by their profession and political commitment.

Such an approach leads to some important theoretical and methodological points. Theoretically, first, cause lawyering cannot be considered only in idealistic terms, which would view cause lawyers as "altruistic" people, "lawyering for the good," whose goal is turned "to achieve greater social justice."[9] An alternative theoretical approach is that such lawyers are interested in practicing labor law in an activist way. Thus analysis of cause lawyering allows us to follow a theoretical line proposed by Pierre Bourdieu in his sociology of interest[10]: showing interests that have been concealed within apparently altruistic and pro bono activities doesn't mean that people are cynical or self-conscious about their interests. The second consequence of such an approach is methodological. To pursue a sociological analysis of workers' lawyers and, at the same time, contribute to the effort to define cause lawyering, it is necessary for the investigation to go in several directions. It has to take into account the objective social positions of people—their actual practice of lawyering, their social and political background, and their economic situation—as well as their mental and cognitive orientations.[11]

In pursuit of those objectives I conducted a series of semi-structured interviews. Fifteen lawyers, who specialized in defending and representing workers and unions, were interviewed in Paris and in several large towns. The interviews lasted between one and two hours; they were taped (one excepted) and transcribed.

1. Questions of Importation

I begin by attending to the importation of a U.S. notion into the French landscape of legal and political sociology. Indeed, as has already been noted, the expression "cause lawyering" doesn't exist in France; this paper, then, is an attempt at importation and conceptual translation. It is a contribution of French sociology to the study of cause lawyering.[12]

Forgetting Conditions of Production of a Concept

Importing a concept like "cause lawyering" into an academic tradition different from the one in which it was created does not necessarily mean acceptance of "symbolic imperialism." It is true that in the context of American hegemony in the social sciences, and specifically in socio-legal studies, importing the concept could be seen as resignation to the domination of U.S. intellectual products. Thus Bourdieu and Wacquant suggest we should be very critical of people, called "smugglers," who "propose and propagate, often sincerely, American cultural products" and of "American cultural institutions which accompany and often organize—even without explicit consultation—the process of collective conversion to the new symbolic Mecca."[13]

One danger of such importation lies in the consecration of the concept, ignoring the different contexts that allowed scholars to create it. As Austin Sarat[14] has explained, the concept of cause lawyering emerged in a specific context, namely the evolution of the Law and Society movement in the United States. In this context U.S. socio-legal scholars became increasingly interested in studying the legal professions and less interested in the political side of lawyering. Studying cause lawyering could be considered a way of restarting a project whose subject is at the intersection of law, political science, and political commitment. Such a blending of political and scientific engagement fits very well with the recent history of scholarship on cause lawyering. It is unusual in France, where the epistemological split between the social sciences and the social world is quite deep.

French socio-legal studies, called legal sociology, are very different from their American counterpart. They originated in law schools, as a sub-product of legal studies. Nowadays, socio-legal studies have been taken over by newcomers from sociology and political science.[15] But it remains difficult, for example, to propose courses in legal sociology in faculties of sociology. Thus for two main reasons—differences in the conception of political and academic engagement, and differences in the history of legal sociology—the importation of U.S. socio-legal concepts by French academics must be done carefully and thoughtfully.

Lastly, trying to import a foreign concept into a national sociology raises the huge question of comparison. In my case, differences in legal systems and in the structures of unionism complicate the analysis. For instance, the social role of lawyers is very different in France and in the United States, to such an extent that in the French language, the word "lawyer" can be hard to translate. In France the idea of a single concept of "lawyering" describing, under a single rubric, attorneys, law teachers, and other legal professionals is unthinkable.

A Careful and Useful Importation

Despite such challenges, cause lawyering still seems a useful construct with which to study the professional and political situation of French union lawyers. This concept reshapes ties between law and politics. Recently some French scholars have newly considered the place of law in the social and political order. Employing Bourdieu's sociology, they have focused on actors and social groups that use the authority of law as a political tool. Moreover, these scholars have shown how law can be considered a field (in a Bourdieuian sense) where actors compete to define the scope of law.[16] The concept of cause lawyering can be attached to this sociological tradition. It can be used to reintroduce to the political sociology of legal actors a Weberian sociology of the professions—that is, a sociology of professional activities in practice settings.

Cause lawyering is also a useful contribution to a constructivist tradition within the law and society movement. Cause lawyers can be considered as those actors who are able to "transform" conflicts into legal and political disputes.[17] They also bridge the gap between law and social movements. This last fact is crucial in understanding the role of attorneys in the French labor movement.[18]

2. Cause Lawyering as a Condition for the Possibility of a Traditional Conception of Professional Engagement

Taken as a whole, workers' attorneys share a traditional conception of lawyering, with respect to their social status and their occupational position.

A Weak Position Beyond a Certain Diversity

Workers' attorneys occupy a fairly weak position within the profession as a whole: they all work in very small firms, often as sole practitioners; their style of activity is much more litigation-oriented (emphasizing small-scale litigation, for example, before a *conseil des prud'hommes*—see Table 2.2) than that of other kinds of lawyers. They tend to come from disadvantaged backgrounds, and their social trajectory is based on achievement rather than on ascription, to use categories from American sociology of stratification. Within a profession that is increasingly divided and unequal, workers' lawyers who declare themselves to be politically engaged belong to a marginal segment of the profession.[19]

Consider, for example, a small firm in a town in southwestern France. This firm specializes in defending workers. It is composed of only three attorneys. Both partners, founders of the firm, are women. Because they work in a middle-size town, they cannot make their living solely from labor law. While their revenue is a bit higher than the national average, they are very dependent on funding from legal aid (*aide juridictionnelle*), which produces around 40 percent of the firm's revenue. Both of the partners had upwardly mobile, working-class parents.

Along with the homogeneity of social positions among workers' lawyers, there is also a certain diversity. Some have managed better than others to make a living from their political work. Others are not able to be what they consider

TABLE 2.2

Methods of Litigation for Workers' Lawyers: Labor Relations Board (Conseil des Prud'hommes), Civil and Criminal Court (Tribunal de Grande Instance)

---

1) In France, the *conseil des prud'hommes* is a very special institution. Its courts are formed by four *conseillers* (two representing employers and two representing workers), who are not professional magistrates but are elected by all French workers and management and judge in the name of the Republic. All the personal disputes involving labor (except questions referred by the criminal courts, such as accidents at work) are judged by the *conseil des prud'hommes*. Workers can defend themselves alone or can be represented by a union's legal specialist (called *défenseur syndical*) or by an attorney. The procedure is brief and informal, and the defense pleadings are brief (and it is above all an oral procedure). If there is an appeal against a judgment, the court of appeal (*cour d'appel*) is composed of professional magistrates. Then, the last appeal takes place before a *cour de cassation* (which is the Court of Final Appeal) and establishes precedents (*jurisprudence*).

2) In case of mass layoffs, a law of January 1993 allows workers' councils to litigate before a *tribunal de grande instance*. If the council representatives think that the procedure of collective redundancy is not correct, they are allowed to call a lawyer who would intervene formally and would complain before civil courts.

3) Finally, in the case of an accident at work, when employers are accused of having prevented union representatives from doing their job or when unions' constituents are attacked by employers (for example during a strike), the competent jurisdiction is the criminal court.

---

real cause lawyers. To survive they have to widen their realm of activity, for example litigating with (and not against) employers, or being divorce attorneys (which in France seems to be the most common type of litigation). The low social position of such attorneys can be easily understood when one remembers that the market for labor law, as for other realms of law, is quite limited in France. Moreover, unions tend rely on just a few attorneys.

One forty-year-old Parisian female lawyer I interviewed has a case load in which she spends about 60 percent of her time defending workers, with divorce litigation as her second major activity. She also has to serve as legal counsel for a workers' council.[20] Such activities have to do with general law (property law, divorce law, consumer protection law, etc.) but very rarely with labor law.[21]

Another lawyer, a woman practicing in Lille, a large city in northern France explained: "Today, I'm working alone with a secretary... with a clientele which... is not very remunerative, because it is based on legal aid... And I'm not a native of this region, without reliable contacts who would provide me... a steady practice."[22] Thus this attorney also specializes in family law (that is, divorce law) and provides paid legal counsel for women's associations.

In contrast, other workers' attorneys didn't seem to have difficulties finding a clientele, because they had been supported by unions or because of their social origin. This allows them to specialize in worker defense. As will be seen below, their social position has huge implications for their conception of engaged lawyering.

A Traditional Conception of Lawyering

Notwithstanding their diversity, workers' attorneys share a common conception of their profession and of their practice. They want to maintain the traditional image of French lawyering, and consider themselves its guardians. This conception of lawyering is based on a few fundamental principles: independence, liberty, disinterest in financial gains, respect for ethical rules.[23] Thus one attorney explained that when he chooses young *collaborateurs*, "there must be a certain... I am waiting for... some ethics, a certain behavior toward our function, toward our clients... he must have the same cast of mind [as mine]; it is not essentially the profit motive."[24]

Désintéressement is a key issue. Karpik shows how this "rhetoric of generosity" was invented within the profession at the end of seventeenth century by some leaders in order to find a place in the social space between merchants and political power. Karpik treats this ethical rule as a "strategy," and then as a collective identity.[25] For workers' and unions' attorneys, *désintéressement* is both a strategy and an ethical ideal. Thus many of the lawyers interviewed strongly rejected any other form of lawyering, such as lawyering driven primarily by the profit motive. Attorneys who specialize in corporate law, tax law, or commercial law provide the perfect counter-example to workers' lawyers, because they are not independent and because they only want to earn money, putting aside their convictions and ethical responsibilities. A forty-two-year-old woman insists on the difference between corporate attorneys and her conception of lawyering: "You will see, the practices of workers' lawyers are very small, small. We don't have any international structure, we don't have any national structure. It's another world . . . It remains a very small practice. It is a choice as well. Elsewhere, we couldn't have the same liberty to speak and to choose."[26]

Another example is drawn from an interview with an attorney well known in the profession and in the unions. He showed a book to the interviewer, *Cabinets d'avocats en France: les acteurs du droit des affaires en France*,[27] and said about it: "For me, the analysis is wrong. It is a sort of... market vision. . . . It is something dealing with market and corporation."[28]

Workers' lawyers see themselves as gatekeepers of "true" lawyering, but their discourse often sounds like a lamentation about its disappearance and the increasingly widespread presence of corporate lawyering, with its departures from the traditions of the French legal professions. As an examination of actual changes in the profession would show, such fears are often ungrounded. Indeed, the transformation of the French bar is quite progressive and is located primarily in just a few business towns (Paris, Nanterre—a suburb of Paris— Lyon, Strasbourg, Bordeaux, and Nice). Elsewhere, traditional patterns of the profession still remain. Nonetheless, lawyers I interviewed felt that the way they practice (and the profession they love) is disappearing.[29]

This conception of their profession is linked to their social position. They belong to a marginalized segment of the bar and think of themselves as the only "true" attorneys—as the last bastion of respect for the traditions of the French bar. This outlook gives them a certain feeling of moral superiority and helps justify their choice of practice. But to fully understand these positions, it is necessary to attend to the political side of their activity. In their lives and in their work, workers' lawyers always combine law and politics.

3. Cause Lawyering as a Condition for the Possibility of Loyalty

Fusing law and politics is the first definition of cause lawyering. This approach is quite well known in France, where attorneys have always been closely linked to political action.[30] This linkage between political and professional engagement turns out to be another way for workers' and union attorneys to claim their place in the tradition of the French legal profession. Moreover, such engaged professional practice allows people to be loyal to traditional beliefs, despite appearances to the contrary.

Cause Lawyering as Political Lawyering

Workers' attorneys can be seen as the successors to a large number of French lawyers who have taken part in political action. Indeed, from the end of the nineteenth century, a slow decline in the legislative and executive power of lawyers led them to invest in new forms of engagement—such as defense of the middle class[31] and participation in the judicial strategies of workers' unions and, thereafter, in resisting the Germans and in the anti-colonial wars.[32] Since the 1970s, many attorneys have been engaged in a variety of social movements or interest groups.[33]

Many lawyers for workers and unions see themselves as contributing to the old spirit of lawyers' political engagement and define themselves as militants. Many refuse to acknowledge a divide between political and legal action.

Evidence for the claim of a link with politics can be seen in an interview with a fifty-seven-year-old man. On the walls of his waiting room were many press articles about victories against management. As one client waiting to see this lawyer put it: "We know where we are." On the walls of the attorney's room were also a few slogans from May 1968, union posters, and a picture of Che Guevara. At the end of the interview, he said, as if he were pleading: "I always practiced engaged law. . . . Labor law is not neutral. You are on one side or the other. As for our firm, we are on the side of the workers. . . . Law is a wonderful way to change the world."[34]

When another lawyer was asked about her tie to politics, she answered: "Explain politics? But it came naturally, because the firm opened in 1974... in '74, there were many social movements, students were engaged, lawyers were engaged... There isn't any break between the profession and militancy."[35]

But if a political definition of themselves and of their activity is common to most of the lawyers I interviewed, there is no single definition of "militancy" or of "politics." The younger and the less well established attorneys see their engagement as a "humanistic" one, much more than an actual political one. Their conception of workers' lawyering is rather broad: to defend the "weaker" against the "stronger."

Consider, for example, the explanation of a forty-year-old woman in Paris of why she became a labor lawyer. After talking about her career path, she said: "The workers' status has always... I have always been preoccupied by their weakness... When I became an attorney, it was in part in order to defend the weaker against the stronger. Indeed, labor law is from the outset a law in which you find one side weaker and another side stronger—linked together by this subordination between them."[36]

A Stage in a Constituent's Career

Moreover, workers' lawyering is for some of the engaged attorneys a condition of their loyalty to traditional beliefs. Many of the lawyers interviewed who were more than fifty years old were leftist militants in the 1970's (one was Maoist) or members of the Communist Party. Older lawyers were engaged in opposition to the Algerian War. When they relate their life-histories, their lawyering appears to them to be a normal step in their career of engagement.[37]

A fifty-three-year-old woman attorney in a western French town told me that having attended law school at the very beginning of the seventies, she committed herself to the women's liberation movement, far-left associations, and workers' unions and a student union. When she decided to become a lawyer, she was not at all interested in law or in the legal profession.[38]

Another lawyer related a life-history beginning with youthful opposition to the Algerian War and including involvement with far-left movements. In 1967, this lawyer became a leader of the UJC-ML (*Union des Jeunes Communistes Marxistes-Léninistes*), which was a Maoist movement. In 1968–70, he organized anti–Vietnam War committees. In 1973, he became a member of the Paris bar and then left Paris for one of its suburbs. Thanks to his ties with some unions, he built a firm specializing in the representation of unions and workers, and in 1985 he was elected leader of the bar (*bâtonnier*) in Versailles.[39]

In a study of militants active between 1968 and 1975, Isabelle Sommier found that many former 1968 militants found refuge in what she called "escapism"— that is, an "attempt to exorcize an embarrassing past" and a refusal to undertake new political engagement.[40] In contrast, workers' lawyers explain how their legal engagement is driven by their political commitment, and they relate a linear trajectory, which is quite unusual for militants of the 1970's.[41]

Some of the best known workers' lawyers now have a comfortable income and have adopted a bourgeois way of life. Nor do they have much contact with the working class. Illustrative of this contradiction is the case of an attorney whose firm is located in a suburb but who explains very seriously that the location is "in the underbelly of the beast"—that is, the underbelly of capitalism. He implicitly says that he has adopted a Maoist strategy in his choice of location.[42] He located his firm in a suburb close to Nanterre, where many large corporations have their registered headquarters and their central workers' councils. Yet he portrays himself, like other workers' lawyers, as not having changed—as still being faithful to old beliefs and old commitments.

Such judgments, however, overlook the circumstances that are often preconditions of commitment to political lawyering. As one lawyer explained his own diminishing political engagement: "When I began my professional activity [at the beginning of the 1970's], I had two different fields: labor law and housing law. My main principle was never to represent a boss or a house-owner. It was clear. I had chosen my side. Then, after a certain time, when you settle down… your family, your children… I said to myself: I must provide for my family… And it is true that for about seven to eight years, I have been agreeing to work for employers."[43]

In other words, as one's family responsibilities increase it becomes more and more difficult for some lawyers to live solely for and from political engagement. Those who are able to do so—that is, practice cause lawyering in a fulfilling way—tend to be associated with unions. For others, like the attorney quoted above, it is necessary to broaden their client base, and that often means representing "the other side." To understand how this works, it is necessary to consider in more detail how labor law is actually practiced.

4. Cause Lawyering as a Practice: Creating Social Capital and Building New Legal Categories

Analysis of the practice settings of lawyers representing workers reveals the mutual interdependence among lawyers and union leaders and militants.

Unions provide clientele to attorneys, yet attorneys translate the cause they defend into legal and judicial categories—contributing to a "rising in generality," that is, a cause's taking on a general rather than a particular significance.[44]

Labor Lawyers and Unions: Building and Maintenance of Clientele

Workers' lawyers have two sorts of clients: unions and individual workers. Major cases are brought to them by organizations that exist at different levels of unionism, particularly *confédérations, fédérations, unions départementales* (see Table 2.3) and workers' councils (*comités d'entreprise*).

For many years, unions have built networks and enduring relationships with lawyers who have become their regular attorneys. By sending workers to such attorneys, unions provide clients that are essential if these attorneys are to be fully engaged—that is, if they are to confine their labor law practices to exclusive representation of workers. For these lawyers, political commitment and professional engagement cannot be separated from the material benefits that are derived from their practice.

Different sorts of relationships exist between unions and workers' attorneys. Some lawyers are historically linked to unions and tend to monopolize legal representation of the unions and their members—preventing other attorneys, and principally newer firms, from gaining access to this client base. Older lawyers, who are the main figures in this kind of cause lawyering, lead a leftist

TABLE 2.3

Some Aspects of Union Organization in France

First, French unions are divided into five main kinds of organizations, each with its own legal office:
 —CGT (Confédération générale du Travail), the most important union, historically linked to the Communist Party
 —CFDT (Confédération française et démocratique du Travail), a leftist union but has regularly negotiated with managers' associations
 —FO-CGT (Force Ouvrière), which is mainly present in the civil service
 —CFTC (Confédération française des Travailleurs chrétiens), distinguishable as a Christian union
 —CGC (Confédération générale des cadres), managers' and executives' union.

Second, unions are organized with two additional categories:
 —Constituents who share the same occupation are also gathered into *fédérations*, which have some autonomy from the *confédération*. Some *fédérations* are well known: for example, the CGT *fédération* of printing (called FILPAC—Fédération de l'Imprimerie, du Livre et du Papier-Carton) and the CFDT *fédération* of chemistry and energy (FCE). These federations sometimes have their own legal service.
 —Constituents are also organized on a territorial basis, in *départements* (territory divisions), called *unions départementales*. They do not have legal services, but there are some militants who specialize in law, and above all in *prud'hommes*.

lawyers' union, Syndicat des Avocats de France, and have come to monopolize the field of union defense and representation.

One example is provided by a very famous firm in Paris. The present leader inherited the firm and his union clientele from his father. The firm is very closely linked to the CGT [Confédération générale du Travail; see Table 2.3], and this preferential relationship has existed for more than fifty years.

Another attorney explained his practice by noting: "Our firm has been working with the CFDT (Confédération française et démocratique du Travail) since 1973. . . . If we have regular connections with CFDT people or with clients sent by CFDT, we often ask in vain for a strong relationship, strategies to follow, and mutual expectations."[45]

A last example is a workers and union firm in a town in northern France. The firm was established in the early 1970's. All of the CGT's local unions work with this firm. Accordingly, other attorneys who aspire to cause lawyering must somehow overcome the obstacle of being largely excluded from the client base provided by union representation.[46]

Thus attorneys who are younger and do not have a traditional union's practice face many difficulties in attempting to build a practice which would allow them to live from and for cause lawyering. They do not have the social capital traditional cause lawyers have. Indeed, the relationship between such traditional workers' attorneys and unions can be seen as depending on the activation and maintenance of a social capital—that is, the "whole actual or potential resources that are bound to ownership of a sustained network of more or less institutionalized relationship" (Bourdieu 1980: 2–4). These relationships are, according to Bourdieu , founded on "exchanges that are inseparably material and symbolic" (ibid.).

To the extent that they are dependent on such social capital, French cause lawyers confront ethical and moral contradictions. Ethically, they want to see themselves as independent liberal professionals whose legitimacy is based on freedom and individualism. Morally, they are considered "organic intellectuals" (Gramsci 1983) engaged in "radical practice" in solidarity with unions.[47] This engagement with, and dependence on, unionism is intrinsic to the older generation and takes shape in what is called "collective" litigation—that is, the struggle. This dependence on unions directly contradicts the ethical ideal of independence. Indeed, there is evidence that the leaders of legal committees within unions are highly critical of attorneys and even cynical toward them, considering them to be legal tools in their hands.

For a newer generation of union attorneys, the contradiction is moral—rooted in their difficulty building client networks. Several of them give legal consultations which are organized by the union. But they must earn additional income by serving a few clients for whom they will litigate. This leads to more limited engagement with cause lawyering.

Creating Categories and Reframing Socio-Legal Disputes

In contemporary French society, law plays an increasingly important role. As a result, unions often have to reframe their action and their conception of labor in legal terms and categories. In such circumstances, lawyering has pervasive utility.

Analyzing the actual situation of contemporary French unionism can be very useful in understanding the importance of law and legal professionals.[48] First, the crisis of unions and of union activism led them to transform their mode of struggle. More and more, unions are becoming institutions which provide services, including legal aid. Second, the relationship between the State, management organizations, and worker unions has been changing for about ten years. Collective bargaining has been increasing, and management organizations have been strengthening their skills, above all their legal skills. In these new conditions, law is a major tool, which is regularly deployed. Law has become a new means of legitimization. Law provides a new frame for all public policies—and more specifically for social and labor policies. Union organizations have to respond to such challenges by conforming to the new rules of the game, even if they would not have chosen them.

In this context, cause lawyering is a major resource for worker unions. One of the major activities of political lawyering is to create new legal categories, through which old definitions and representations of reality are transformed.[49] Such engaged lawyers produce a discourse through which labor problems, difficulties with management, even the class struggle, become legal questions to which legal answers can be given. The social reality of work is thus transformed into a legal and judicial reality.[50] Cause lawyers who were interviewed for this research took on a major role in the activity of legalizing labor questions. Among the many tools cause lawyers use to bring labor problems within the scope of the law, two are particularly important.

One tool for such discursive and social transformation lies in what is called in France *jurisprudence* work—that is, the use of precedents by judges and attorneys. A concrete analysis of such work allows us to see how lawyers deploy precedents in their pleadings in order to show that a present case can be linked to earlier judicial decisions. Thus much of the everyday work of lawyers is taken up with reading legal literature (and often scholarly literature) in order to locate precedents which could be useful for the present case. Obviously, it is the attorneys for workers who monopolize this work. At the same time, these cause lawyers are well versed in the daily reality of workplace practices—which allows them to define relevant precedents. This kind of work can entail collective action by lawyers. Some lawyers have organized meetings where they shared their knowledge about legal texts and judgments. Such cooperative endeavors among legal specialists working on behalf of unions typify the conception of legal action as collective and activist work.

But there is another important kind of cause lawyering activity. Michael Mc-Cann has demonstrated in his research on pay equity claims that for activists and for workers litigation is a way of appropriating new rights and new claims.[51] For attorneys, one way to claim such new rights is to build new legal categories which can transform old "oppressions" into legal offenses.[52] Litigation about "moral harassment" is a good example of this process. In French law, what is called in northern Europe "mobbing" did not exist until the end of the 1990's, when unions' legal specialists, law teachers, and labor lawyers introduced it. Every one of the lawyers interviewed for this research worked on such cases. "Moral harassment" is a way of defining longstanding practices by management—namely moral pressure, abuse of power, and so on.[53] These familiar aspects of the relationship between workers and management are being redefined by cause lawyers as offenses. One attorney in Paris explained the situation as follows:[54] "We can," she said, "invoke article 1134 of the Civil Code... In that case, the bosses are purple with rage, because for twenty-five years they threw freedom of contract in our faces. But now we use article 1134, saying: the principle of loyalty is an essential principle within the working contract, and so an employer who harasses his employee is guilty of disloyalty. . . . We have turned the gun on them."[55]

Thus legal action, and especially litigation, are building new ways of defining work, and attorneys are the main actors in this process of redefinition. Two important tools are used: precedents and the building of new categories. When they employ these tools, cause lawyers can be seen as legal inventors.

Conclusion

Two conclusions can be drawn from this qualitative investigation into workers' cause lawyers:

1. On the one hand, cause lawyering can be seen as political lawyering. As with all political activity, it is impossible to reduce commitment to altruism or to disinterested activity. On the contrary, workers' lawyers must live from, and not simply for, activism. This does not mean that they are not motivated by ide-

ological belief. If one major recent gain in political sociology has been to link interests and beliefs, then the analysis of cause lawyering needs to take this sort of approach.

2. On the other hand, there is a danger that cause lawyering can lead to putting too much reliance on the law, as if law could solve everything and be an omnibus means of fighting against injustice. As McCann usefully reminds us, legal action is only one of the tools for social action that are available to social movements.

Notes

Special thanks go to Stuart Scheingold and to John Feneron at Stanford University Press for helping put this paper into correct English.

1. Until Liora Israël's paper (Israël 2001) and a volume of the French political science journal *Politix* in 2003.

2. For a history of such tradition, see Vauchez and Willemez (2002).

3. Sarat and Scheingold (1998: 7).

4. In German, *Gesinnungsethik*, which is opposed to *Verantwortungsethik* (Weber 1919).

5. Freidson (1986).

6. Sarat and Scheingold (1998: 119).

7. What is called here "political" is not directly linked to the field of political competition for leadership or to political parties; thus unionism is considered political action, though in France unions have made many efforts to stay far away from politics in the strict sense of the term.

8. Weber (1919). In France, one of the major contributions of Pierre Bourdieu was the application of Weber's notions of sociology of religions to other social activities and other fields. It thus became possible to show, without any religious connotation, how people are looking for something like "salvation," even outside of religious contexts.

9. This definition of cause lawyering can be found in the text of Carrie Menkel-Meadow's radical paper (1998). But this idealistic vision of cause lawyering is one of the possible directions followed.

10. See, for example, in French, Bourdieu (1994).

11. "There exists a correspondence between social structures and mental structures, between objective divisions of social world and visions and divisions that people implement. . . . The two approaches, which can be considered 'structuralist' and 'constructivist,' are logically inseparable. . . . Analysis of structures and of 'social mechanisms' only gains its whole explicative strength and its descriptive truth because it includes the results of the analysis of perceptions' and actions' schemes that people [agents] implement in their judgments and activities" (Bourdieu 1989: 7–8; translated by me).

12. The use of the concept for understanding non-U.S. situations has always been an important part of cause lawyering studies, as can be seen from a survey of the tables of contents of earlier books on the subject: see Sarat and Scheingold (1998, 2001).

13. Bourdieu and Wacquant (1998: 113; translated by me).

14. In his introduction to the cause lawyering meeting at Cachan, France, in October 2003. The following lines must be read as a reconstruction of an intellectual history by a French scholar and do not represent the views of the organizers of the cause lawyering project.

15. See, for example, Commaille (1994) and Lacroix (1985) for two different traditions.

16. Public law and, moreover, constitutional law have been analyzed by François (1993). But Dezalay remains the main "translator" of Bourdieuian sociology in the socio-legal field; see, e.g., Dezalay and Garth (1999).

17. The term "cause lawyering" was translated at the beginning of the 1990's by *Politix*, a new political science journal.

18. As proposed, for example, in the United States by Burstein (1991) and McCann (1994).

19. Studies of the present state of the profession are very few; see, however, Karpik (1999); Vauchez and Willemez (2002), Boigeol and Willemez (2005).

20. In France, the activities of workers' councils have to do not only with their offical role but with activities concerning workers (organization of holidays, canteen lunches, and entertainment).

21. Interview, September 11, 2002.

22. Interview, September 20, 2002: "Donc aujourd'hui je fonctionne toute seule avec une secrétaire… Avec une clientèle qui était pas… qui est assez fragile puisqu'elle est fondée sur beaucoup d'aide juridictionnelle… Moi, je suis quelqu'un qui est pas du tout de la région avec aucune relation qui puisse me drainer… une clientèle assurée."

23. Karpik (2001); for a general description of ethical rules, see Damien and Hamelin (2000). In reality, of course, the attorneys who were interviewed talked much about money and about the necessity of owning a practice: in this regard at least, Karpik's book can be seen as a bit idealistic about lawyers (for more about this idealistic point of view, see my Ph.D. dissertation on French lawyers in the nineteenth century, Willemez 2000).

24. Interview, February 22, 2002: "la loyauté dans la manière de… faire, de travailler. Il faut une certaine… j'en attends… une certaine éthique, un certain comportement par rapport à notre fonction, à nos clients… il faut que ce soit la même forme d'esprit, c'est pas essentiellement un but lucratif."

25. Karpik (1989: 737–39).

26. Interview, October 12, 2000: "Vous allez voir, les cabinets de droit du travail pour les salariés sont de tout petits cabinets. Tout petit. On n'a pas de structure internationale, on n'a pas de structure nationale. C'est un autre monde … Ca reste de tout petits cabinets. Mais c'est aussi un refus. On pourrait pas avoir la même liberté de parole, de choix, d'orientation."

27. This is the French version of "the Pritchard," a well-known list of corporate lawyering publications, put out by *Legalease*.

28. Interview, September 1, 2000: "Pour moi, c'est une fausse analyse. C'est une sorte de vision… du marché … C'est un peu un truc de marché, de marché-entreprise."

29. Vauchez and Willemez (2002).

30. Le Béguec (1994)

31. See Israël, this volume.

32. In recent years, French scholars have been investigating the place of lawyers in social movements and interest groups: see, for instance, Agrikoliansky (2002) and Israël (2003) on human rights and civil liberties, Mouchard (2002) on the unemployed and poor, and Willemez (2003) on unions.

33. Halliday and Karpik (1997).

34. Interview, September 1, 2000: "J'ai toujours fait du droit engagé. . . . Le droit du travail n'est pas neutre. On est dans un camp ou dans un autre. Nous, en ce qui nous concerne, on est dans le camp des travailleurs. . . . Le droit, c'est un moyen absolument extraordinaire pour changer le monde."

35. Interview, February 20, 2002: "Expliquer le politique? Mais ça s'est fait naturellement, parce que le cabinet s'est ouvert en 1974... c'était le social, il y a des étudiants qui militent, il y a des avocats qui militent... il y a pas de coupure entre la profession et la militance, ça va avec."

36. Interview, September 11, 2002: "C'est vrai que le statut des salariés m'a toujours... leur fragilité m'avait toujours préoccupée... Quand je suis devenue avocate, c'était un peu pour défendre les faibles contre les forts. Effectivement, le droit du travail, c'est un droit dans lequel il y a *a priori* d'un côté les forts, de l'autre côté les faibles, avec le lien de subordination." The "link of subordination" is a French legal category which defines the link between the employer and the worker in a working contract (*contrat de travail*).

37. Engagement can be seen as a career, if one uses interactionist sociology (Becker 1963). Some French scholars who specialize in social movements or political parties use this perspective: see for instance Fillieule (2001).

38. Interview, February 20, 2002.

39. This life-history is based on an interview (September 1, 2000), but also on a book about May 1968 (Hamon and Rotman 1987).

40. See Sommier (1998: 220–23); Mauger (1994).

41. Regarding changes in commitment, see Snow and Machalek (1984). For instances of conversion from unionism or far-leftist politics to humanitarianism or the writing of novels, see Collovald, Lechien, Rozier, and Willemez (2002); Collovald and Neveu (2001).

42. After May 1968, some far-leftist students in France (and sometimes the most brilliant of them) chose to disseminate far-leftist propaganda in factories and so became workers (concealing their educational background); some of them are still workers today.

43. Interview, October 18, 2000: "Moi, quand j'ai commencé mon activité professionnelle, j'avais deux champs d'activité importants: droit du travail et droit locatif. J'avais pour principes de ne jamais plaider pour un patron et de ne jamais plaider pour un propriétaire, c'était clair, j'avais choisi mon camp. Et puis, à partir d'un certain temps, quand vous vous installez, avec les charges qui augmentent, famille, enfants, je me dis: 'c'est bien, mais il faut que je fasse vivre tout le monde', et c'est vrai que depuis... mettons 7–8 ans, j'ai accepté de plaider employeurs aux prud'hommes."

44. The French sociologist Luc Boltanski showed how one of the distinctive features of representational activity is to transform a particular dispute or conflict into a general cause (Boltanski 1990).

45. "Notre cabinet travaille avec la CFDT depuis 1973. . . . Si nous avons des contacts réguliers avec des personnes de la CFDT ou envoyées par la CFDT, nous réclamons souvent en vain des relations suivies sur les dossiers en cours, les stratégies à mener, et les attentes que nous pouvons avoir les un des autres" ("documents préparatoires à la réunion du mercredi 27 juin avec la commission juridique de la CFDT"—no year given, written between 1999 and 2001).

46. Interview, September 7, 2002, with a respondent from the huge firm, now in practice by herself.

47. To follow Scheingold's analysis (1988).

48. See Vauchez and Willemez 2002.

49. In this way, it is interesting to combine two approaches of American sociology: first an approach based on "framing theories" (Snow and Benford 2000), and second an approach based on "social problems": in France, the sociologist D. Cefaï has proposed such a combination (Cefaï 2001).

50. For an analysis of such transformation of social problems into legal problems, see Gusfield (1963).

51. McCann (1994: 65–68).

52. It can be shown that cause lawyers do not necessarily create or fabricate the causes they defend, but rather reframe them in new words and new categories.

53. The double origin of "moral harassment" is interesting: first it was a psychiatric definition and second a development based on aspects of sexual harassment.

54. The situation changed in 2001, when the law recognized "moral harassment" as an offense.

55. Interview, October 12, 2000: "On peut invoquer l'article 1134 du code civil... Alors là, les patrons sont un peu verts qu'on utilise cet article, parce que pendant 25 ans, ils nous l'ont mis entre les dents: c'est-à-dire la liberté du contrat, le contrat qui fait force de loi entre les parties, etc. Mais maintenant que nous nous servons de l'article 1134 en disant: le principe de loyauté est un principe essentiel au contrat de travail, et donc un employeur qui harcèle son salarié se rend coupable de loyauté... on a retourné l'arme contre eux."

References

Agrikoliansky, Eric. 2002. *La Ligue française des droits de l'hommes et du citoyen depuis 1945: sociologie d'un engagement civique.* Paris: L'Harmattan.

Becker, Howard. 1963. *Outsiders.* Chicago: University of Chicago Press.

Boigeol, Anne, and Laurent Willemez. 2005. "Fighting for Monopoly: Unification, Differentiation and Representation of the French Bar," in *Organization and Resistance: Legal Professions Confront a Changing World*, ed. Bill Felstiner. Oxford: Hart Publishing.

Boltanski, Luc. 1990. *L'amour et la justice comme compétences: trois essais de sociologie de l'action.* Paris: Metailié.

Bourdieu, Pierre. 1980. "Le capital social: Notes provisoires." *Actes de la recherche en sciences sociales,* January, pp. 2–4. Trans. as "The Forms of Capital," in *Handbook of Theory and Research for the Sociology of Education* (New York: Greenwood Press, 1986), pp. 241–58.

———. 1989. *La Noblesse d'Etat: grandes écoles et esprit de corps.* Paris: Minuit.

———. 1994. "Un acte désintéressé est-il possible ?" in *Raisons pratiques,* 149–67. Paris: Seuil.

Bourdieu, Pierre, and Loïc Wacquant. 1998. "Sur les ruses de la raison impérialiste." *Actes de la recherche en sciences sociales* 121–22: 110–18.

Burstein, Paul. 1991. "Legal Mobilization as a Social Movement Tactic: The Struggle for Equal Employment Opportunity. *American Journal of Sociology,* 96, no. 5: 1201–25.

Cefaï, Daniel. 2001. "Les cadres de l'action collective: définitions et problèmes," in Daniel Cefaï and Trom, *Les formes de l'action collective: mobilisations dans les arènes publiques,* 99–134. Paris: Editions de l'EHESS.

Collovald, Annie, and Erik Neveu. 2001. "La critique politique du néo-polar," in *Juger la politique,* ed. Jean-Louis Briquet and Philippe Garraud, 193–215. Rennes: Presses Universitaires de Rennes.

Collovald, Annie, Marie-Hélène Lechien, Sabine Rozier, and Laurent Willemez. 2002. *L'Humanitaire ou le management des dévouements: enquête sur un militantisme de solidarité internationale en faveur du Tiers-Monde.* Rennes: Presses Universitaires de Rennes.

Commaille, Jacques. 1994. *L'esprit sociologique des lois.* Paris: Presses Universitaires de France.

Damien, André, and Jacques Hamelin. 2000. *Les règles et les usages de la nouvelle profession d'avocat.* Paris: Dalloz.

Dezalay, Yves, and Brian Garth. 1999. *Global Palace Wars: Lawyers, Economists and the Creative Destruction of the State.*

Fillieule, Olivier. 2001. "Propositions pour une analyse processuelle de l'engagement individuel." *Revue française de science politique* 51, nos. 1–2: 199–217.

François, Bastien. 1996. *Naissance d'une constitution: la Vè République.* Paris: Presses de Sciences-po.

Freidson, Eliot. 1986. *Professional Powers: A Study of Institutionalization of Formal Knowledge.* Chicago: University of Chicago Press.

Gramsci, Antonio. 1983. *Cahiers de Prison.* Paris: Gallimard.

Gusfield, Joseph. 1963. *Symbolic Crusade.* Urbana: University of Illinois Press.

Halliday, Terence, and Lucien Karpik. 1997. "Politics Matter: A Comparative Theory of Lawyers in the Making of Political Liberalism," in *Lawyers and the Rise of Western Political Liberalism,* ed. T. Halliday and L. Karpik. Oxford: Clarendon Press.

Hamon, Hervé, and Patrick Rotman. 1987. *Génération.* Paris: Seuil.

Israël, Liora. 2001. "Usage militants du droit dans l'arène judiciaire: le *cause lawyering.*" *Droits et Société* 49.

————. 2003. "Faire émerger le droit des étrangers en le contestant, ou l'histoire para-doxale des premières années du GISTI." *Politix* 62: 115–44.

Karpik, Lucien. 1989. "Le désintéressement." *Annales ESC* 3 (May–June): 733–51.

————. 1999. "Avocats: renouveau et crise." *Justice* 1: 67–82.

————. 2001. *French Lawyers: A Study in Collective Action (1274–1994)*. New York: Oxford University Press. (French edition 1995.)

Lacroix, Bernard. 1985. "Ordre politique et ordre social: objectivisme, objectivation et analyse politique," in Jean Leca and Madeleine Grawitz, *Traité de science politique*, 1: 469–565. Paris: Presses Universitaires de France.

Le Béguec, Gilles. 1994. "Le jeune barreau parisien au début des années 20," in *Avocats et barreaux en France (1910–1930)*, ed. Gilles Le Béguec. Nancy: Presses Universitaires de Nancy.

McCann, Michael. 1994. *Rights at Work: Pay Equity Reform and the Politics of Legal Mobilization*. Chicago: University of Chicago Press.

Mauger, Gérard. 1994. "Gauchisme, contre-culture et néo-libéralisme," in Centre Universitaire de Recherches Administratives et Politiques de Picardie (CURAPP), *L'identité politique*. Paris: Presses Universitaires de France.

Menkel-Meadow, Carrie. 1998. "The Causes of Cause Lawyering," in Sarat and Scheingold (1998): 31–68.

Mouchard, Daniel. 2002. "Les mobilisations des 'sans' dans la France contemporaine: l'émergence d'un 'radicalisme auto-limité'?" *Revue française de science politique* 52, no. 4: 425–47.

Sarat, Austin, and Stuart Scheingold, eds. 1998. *Cause Lawyering: Political Commitments and Professional Responsibilities*. New York: Oxford University Press.

————. 2001. *Cause Lawyering and the State in a Global Era*. New York: Oxford University Press.

Scheingold, Stuart. 1988. "Radical Lawyers and Socialists Ideals." *Journal of Law and Society* 15, no. 1: 122–38.

Snow, D., and R. D. Benford. 2000. "Framing Processes and Social Movement: An Overview and Assessment." *Annual Review of Sociology* 26: 611–39.

Snow, D., and R. Machalek. 1984. "The Sociology of Conversion." *Annual Review of Sociology* 10.

Sommier, Isabelle. 1998. *La violence politique et son deuil: l'après 68 en France et en Italie*. Rennes: Presses Universitaires de Rennes.

Vauchez, Antoine, and Laurent Willemez. 2002. *Contribution à la connaissance statistique de la profession d'avocat*. Rapport pour le Conseil national des Barreaux.

Weber, Max. 1919. *Politik als Beruf*, in *Gesammelte Politische Schriften*. UTB, 1988.

Willemez, Laurent. 2000. "Des avocats en politique (1848–1880): contribution à une socio-histoire de la profession politique en France." Thèse de doctorat en science politique, Université Paris I.

————. 2003. "Quand les syndicats de saisissent du droit: invention et redéfinition d'un rôle." *Sociétés contemporaines* 52: 17–38.

CHAPTER THREE

Professional Identity and Political Commitment among Lawyers for Conservative Causes

ANN SOUTHWORTH

A substantial literature has developed around the idea that there is something distinctive and laudable about lawyers who seek to further a particular vision of the good society. Lawyer activists, or "cause lawyers," pose a challenge to the "hired-gun" model of the lawyer's role—the view that lawyers are morally unaccountable for the work they pursue on behalf of clients. Yet little empirical research thus far has focused on the professional ideologies of lawyers who serve causes (Halliday 1999; but see Menkel-Meadow 1998; Scheingold and Bloom 1998). Do all such lawyers feel personally committed to the causes they serve? Are there differences in degrees of commitment by types of causes pursued? Do lawyers' views about the worthiness of their causes change over time? This chapter draws on interviews with lawyers for conservative and libertarian causes to consider whether and to what extent they believe in the goals they seek to advance.

Defining "cause lawyers" and distinguishing them from "conventional" lawyers has proven to be problematic. Sarat and Scheingold (1998) have argued for defining cause lawyers by bracketing a range within a continuum of lawyer activism. At one end are lawyers who regard service to causes they believe in as an appealing but secondary aspect of service to clients. In practice, these lawyers may be difficult to distinguish from conventional lawyers, who are said to take no responsibility for the ends they promote.[1] At the other end of the range are lawyers who place causes ahead of clients and make substantial financial sacrifices to pursue those ends. Between these poles are lawyers whose motivations include elements of moral activism and more conventional professional ideals and concerns.

This chapter examines how lawyers for conservative and libertarian causes view the causes they serve and their roles in furthering those causes.[2] Reversing the typical order of inquiry for studies of cause lawyers, the research from which this chapter draws identifies lawyers who serve conservative and libertarian causes and then examines their professional ideologies to determine whether and to what extent they identify with those causes. Lawyers included in this study expressed varying views about their moral accountability. Some were fervent believers while others appeared only mildly committed to their clients' ends. Several lawyers seemed sufficiently detached from the causes they served to fall altogether outside the definition of cause lawyer.

Like Jones's chapter in this volume, this one considers how lawyers' identities vary by work setting. However, it does not attempt to explain the processes associated with identity formation or to measure activism by objective criteria.[3] The focus here is primarily on lawyers' self-perceptions. It draws primarily from lawyers' own accounts of their career histories and participation in service to causes.

This chapter adopts Sarat and Scheingold's (1998) concept of a continuum as a way to describe the variety of professional identities of lawyers for conservative and libertarian causes. The conventional professional model approximates the norms of most lawyers who pursued the interests of business clients from positions in law firms and trade associations. The activist model characterizes the views of most of the lawyers who worked in advocacy organizations, think tanks, and academia. However, the interviews also revealed examples of lawyers in private firms who appeared strongly devoted to the causes they served and lawyers employed by nonprofit organizations who indicated that their motivations included factors other than ideological commitment. Many of the lawyers who appeared to identify most strongly with causes worked in small private firms. Moreover, most lawyers fit neither the cause lawyer nor the conventional professional model perfectly; their accounts of their own motivations for undertaking work for causes cited both ideological and pragmatic considerations. Furthermore, lawyers often reported that their professional orientations had changed over time and that their commitment to causes sometimes evolved *through* their work.

Can Lawyers for Conservative and Libertarian Causes Be "Cause Lawyers"?

It may be necessary at the outset to defend the claim that some lawyers for conservative causes might be "cause lawyers." Most of the scholarly literature on advocates for political causes has focused on left-liberal causes (e.g., Handler et al. 1978; Tushnet 1987; Davis 1993; Olson 1984; Silverstein 1996; McCann 1994; Milner 1986; but see den Dulk 2001; Epstein 1985; Hatcher 2001; O'Connor and Epstein 1983). The term "cause lawyer" was coined by scholars who were sympathetic to causes of the left to describe lawyers who served those causes, and some have questioned whether the label applies to lawyers who serve causes of the right. In her essay on the motivation and commitment of cause lawyers, Menkel-Meadow posed a series of skeptical questions about whether lawyers for conservative causes were cause lawyers:

> What does it mean to have a cause, and must that cause be located on the left to liberal side of the political spectrum? How, for example, do we define the cause lawyering of the Right to Work Foundation, the Mountain States Defense Fund, the Pacific [Legal] Foundation, Right to Life, and others committed to causes that we who "founded" the public interest movement find abhorrent? (Menkel-Meadow 1998: 34) (footnotes omitted)

In two previous edited collections on cause lawyers, not one essay focused on lawyers for conservative causes, and only one other piece (Hatcher) in this volume does so. Sharp disagreements about the applicability of the term to lawyers for conservative causes have occupied panels of scholars convened to discuss cause lawyers. Nevertheless, Sarat and Scheingold have cautiously endorsed the view that the term applies across ideologies.[4]

Answering whether conservative lawyers should be treated as "cause lawyers" is complicated by the difficulty of defining the concept's boundaries as applied to causes of the left, but there is some consensus around several core elements. One is that lawyers must be engaged in advocacy that challenges prevailing distributions of power and resources (e.g., Sarat and Scheingold 1998: 13; Menkel-Meadow 1998: 37).[5] The design of this research (described below) ensured that all lawyers interviewed served client organizations that sought objectives that would significantly change prevailing distributions of power and resources. Without exception, these organizations tied their missions to some vision of a substantially different social order, although some sought primarily to undo changes they blamed on activist lawyers of the left. Another element sometimes included in the cause lawyer concept is self-conscious commitment to the cause (e.g., Scheingold and Bloom). Assessing whether and how strongly lawyers identified with the causes they served is the focus of the remainder of this chapter.[6]

If "cause lawyer" is viewed as an analytic category, then, it theoretically could include lawyers whose moral activism embraces goals of the political right. Lawyers in this study differ from their liberal counterparts in particular ways that might suggest that they should be viewed as a different breed. Certainly, their political values and public policy objectives are different and generally at odds with those of the lawyers who have been the subjects of most of the existing cause lawyer literature.[7] Clement Vose (1972: 334–36) has asserted that backgrounds and life experiences sometimes explain lawyers' decisions to devote themselves to causes,[8] and the backgrounds and defining experiences for conservative and libertarian cause lawyers distinguish them from many of their left counterparts. Their inspiration frequently came from leading figures of conservative, libertarian, and religious activism, such as Barry Goldwater, Stanton Evans, William Buckley, Ayn Rand, Milton Friedman, James Dobson, Francis Schaeffer, and Richard John Neuhaus rather than from Ralph Nader, Edgar Cahn, or Cesar Chavez. Their preferred alternative bar associations were the Federalist Society and the Christian Legal Society rather than the National Lawyers' Guild. Nevertheless, lawyers for conservative and libertarian causes are sufficiently similar in function to their liberal counterparts to be studied as part of the same general phenomenon: lawyers who reject the hired-gun model in favor of a more politically engaged approach to their work.

Research Design

This chapter draws primarily from semistructured interviews conducted in 2001 and 2002 with seventy-two lawyers for conservative and libertarian nonprofit organizations. The interviews lasted from fifty minutes to four hours, and they focused primarily on lawyers' backgrounds, career histories, and present work.

The interviews are part of a larger empirical project about lawyers for conservative causes, some aspects of which I am pursuing with John Heinz[9] and Tony Paik.[10] Our research adopts a broad definition of "conservative" to include diverse constituencies of the American conservative alliance: nationalists, religious populists, libertarians, and business interests. These constituencies frequently disagree with one another, but they have formed a successful and enduring coalition in American politics since the late 1960s (Himmelstein 1990; Hodgson 1996; McGirr 2001).

We defined the set of organizations and lawyers to study by selecting seventeen "issue events"—legislative events involving issues that were important to different conservative constituencies from 1995 through 1998. We then searched online archives for articles about these legislative controversies and identified all nongovernmental nonprofit organizations that appeared on the conservative side of the issues. This method produced the names of eighty-one organizations. Using a variety of public sources, we identified 1,300 lawyers who had served these organizations in any capacity.

To identify lawyers to interview, I compiled a list of some of the most prominent lawyers associated with organizations identified through the issue-events method. I supplemented that list with other prominent lawyers for organizations that appeared in two already compiled lists of conservative groups: the Conservative Directory, published by RightGuide.com, and The Heritage Foundation's list of "U.S. Policy Organizations" (Wagner, Hilboldt, and Korsvall 2000: 681).[11] The seventy-two lawyers interviewed included representatives of all the major conservative constituencies, with some variation in practice setting, geographic location, age, and gender.[12] They served conservative and libertarian organizations in various roles. Some were employed full time as officers or counsel. Some served on boards of directors, or as outside counsel on litigation and other legal matters. Others served as scholars or consultants. Many of the lawyers interviewed were primary organizers of the groups they represented.

This research adopts a functional definition of "conservative cause lawyer" for purposes of selecting lawyers to interview. It includes lawyers who serve organizations that pursue conservative causes, whatever the lawyers' reasons for doing so. Political commitment is at the heart of most definitions of "cause lawyer" and is the subject of this chapter. However, this research treats professional identity as an issue to be explored in interviews and not one that can be assumed from lawyers' practice settings, types of clients served, causes pursued, or strategies employed. The design posits that lawyers' motivations for serving causes sometimes may be mixed; lawyers may pursue work for reasons that include both ideological elements and more crass or mundane concerns. As Laurent Willemez observes in his examination of French employees' and union lawyers in this volume, ideological commitment is not the same as altruism; Bourdieu's (1990) sociology of interest shows how ideology and interest reinforce one another. Moreover, lawyers whose purposes are less than pure may sometimes contribute greatly to social causes (Shamir and Chinsky 1998).

The functional definition employed here does not even require lawyers to see themselves as conservative. In interviews, many libertarian lawyers objected to that characterization of their positions and took strong exception to being lumped together with social conservatives and advocates for corporate interests. Several lawyers who worked on abortion and religious liberty issues claimed to be working in the liberal activist tradition on behalf of groups long neglected by the ACLU and other civil liberties groups. Other Christian activists indicated that their guiding philosophy was more Christian than conservative. Some lawyers for business organizations did not view themselves as conservatives at all; rather, they saw themselves as nonideological pragmatists. One of the tasks of this research is to identify similarities, differences, and relationships among lawyers for these diverse and sometimes sparring constituencies of the conservative coalition (Heinz, Paik, and Southworth 2003).

The seventy-two lawyers interviewed included sixteen who worked for conservative religious groups, nine for organizations that opposed abortion, twenty for libertarian groups, eleven for organizations devoted primarily to business interests, and four for affirmative action opponents. Four lawyers worked for "order maintenance" groups—organizations devoted to fighting crime and preserving the established cultural order—and eight served "mediator" organizations—organizations that sought to appeal to diverse conservative constituencies. The practice settings in which these lawyers worked were: thirty-five in advocacy organizations or public interest law firms, five in think tanks, eight in universities, four in trade associations, thirteen in small firms or solo practice, and seven in large law firms. The office locations of lawyers interviewed were: twenty-nine in Washington, D.C.; thirteen in Virginia; two in New York; ten in California; four in Arizona; nine in Illinois; and five in other Midwestern states. Six of the lawyers were in their thirties; twenty-seven in their forties; twenty-four in their fifties; ten in their sixties; four in their seventies; and one in his eighties. Sixty-eight of the lawyers were men and four were women.[13]

Professional Identity by Types of Causes Served

There are significant ideological divisions among the lawyers interviewed, but the most striking differences in terms of professional identity were those between the lawyers for business interests, who served primarily in large firms and trade groups, and lawyers for other causes, who worked primarily in advocacy organizations, think tanks, universities, and small firms.[14] Lawyers for business interests generally rejected the idea that they were cause lawyers, while lawyers for religious conservative, libertarian, order maintenance, and mediator groups frequently embraced that characterization of their work. Lawyers for business interests appeared to agree with the positions they advocated on behalf of clients, but most did not view the work as an expression of personal political commitment. Lawyers in other practice settings, serving the other conservative and libertarian constituencies, generally appeared to be more personally engaged and committed to political goals. Nevertheless, even these lawyers also frequently indicated that factors other than ideological commitment had influenced their careers.

Lawyers in large firms and trade associations who pursued conservative causes for hire on behalf of paying clients generally seemed not to view themselves as activists. Still, they did not describe themselves quite in terms of what William Simon (1978: 36–38) has described as the "principle of neutrality"—the view that lawyers should remain detached from their clients' ends and hold themselves unaccountable for the clients' purposes. Most of them indicated that they were comfortable with the causes they served. A lawyer who represents large religious institutions for fees noted that he had an "affinity" for religion and religious institutions and that he saw himself as a "liaison between their insular world and the dangerous one out there."[15] Another lawyer in a large firm said of his regulatory practice: "I'm very comfortable ideologically being on this side of the aisle, on this side of the divide in private practice. . . . I won't say I'd never handled a case that I didn't agree with ideologically, but, by and large, since I'm skeptical of government regulation, I'm very comfortable fighting off [agency] action, which frequently I think goes beyond what it should under the statute."[16] Another lawyer who had been a strong advocate for tort reform well before he began to practice law noted with delight that his clients "pay me to do what I wanted to do anyway."[17] A lawyer active on the management side of labor issues said that even in his "raging liberal days" he had always "looked askance at the unions." They were, as he saw it, on the wrong side of the issues he really cared about—civil rights and the Vietnam War. In addition, he "always [had believed] that if somebody doesn't like working somewhere they just go somewhere else."[18] Another lawyer who handled punitive damages appeals in a large firm said:

> I really do believe that what I'm doing is in the public interest. I feel as if the pendulum has swung far too far in favor of the plaintiffs' bar and that they are doing things that are injurious to the well-being of our country. That certain activities are no longer available, or easily available because of the fear of liability. That insurance premiums or the price of products have gone up unduly because of excessive liability. . . . So, when one thinks of public interest law, one doesn't typically think of, well-heeled lawyers in fancy suits working at large law firms. But I do. I think that a lot of what we do is beneficial to the long-term economic health and happiness of this country.[19]

These lawyers' expressions of comfort with their roles are consistent with Robert Nelson's (1988: 12) findings about large firm lawyers: that "on questions of law and policy related to their own practice [large firm lawyers] strongly identify with positions favorable to clients."

Nevertheless, these business lawyers generally indicated that they viewed the organizations they served as clients rather than vehicles for personal political expression. One lawyer, who described himself as a "dyed-in-the-wool moderate" who was "not ideological at all" noted: "I really think there is a distinction between groups like us that fall within the conservative camp because of the interests of the clients we serve and those who are pushing an ideological agenda."[20] A lawyer who represented a group that sought to make English the official language of the federal government said that he had taken the case because he was asked to do so by a group that retained him as appellate counsel: "It didn't mean anything more to me than being just another client that needed representation, and had that been an ultra-liberal, radical cause, I don't think I would have approached it any differently."[21] He had not considered the political implications of the representation until a Hispanic associate in his office confronted him about it: "[T]he first time I realized that this case had political overtones was when she asked me what the hell I was doing representing [this advocacy group]. . . . I told her what I told you, that it was just like another client."[22] A lawyer who serves as counsel to a business advocacy organization said that he cares about the issue on which he is active "because that's what clients pay me to care about."[23] Another large firm lawyer who had handled many high-profile regulatory matters said that there were "lots of these issues where I would be glad to be on the other side." He observed that he often was not "wrapped up personally" in the position he was taking.[24] These accounts by business lawyers, indicating that they did not feel morally accountable for their work for clients, are compatible with David Luban's (1990: 1016) assertion that "[t]he true haven of the standard conception . . . is large-firm practice."

These lawyers for business interests styled themselves as political moderates who could work across political lines and who would not allow conflict in their professional roles to become personal. Several of them said that they often voted for Democrats.[25] Some emphasized that they enjoyed friendly relationships with their opponents. One lawyer observed: "Oddly enough, sometimes it's easier to be friends with the other side because you just kind of know your role. You gotta put on your battle gear and . . . take shots at each other and go have a beer afterwards."[26] Another reported that he had "a very good rapport" with his legislative opponents who "do a great job representing their clients," and he noted with dismay that one opponent—a lawyer with a consumer advocacy group—once had refused to shake his hand.[27] Another lawyer said:

> I'm a very practical person. I have a lot of tentacles out into various organizations. We are affiliated with a lot of other organizations. . . . I'm looking at what the solution is. How do you fix the thing? . . . Unlike the Federalist Society and the Taxpayers Union and some of these other groups, or if you would want to, on the other side, Joan Claybrook's group and Ralph Naders', [which] coalesce large groups of like-minded organizations, I was very much focused on doing my job—on the pragmatic approach of what we're doing, how we get from A to B and what we get done.[28]

Eight of the lawyers who appeared to identify most strongly with the causes they served were in solo or small firm practices where they mixed paid and unpaid work.[29] One of these lawyers indicated that he spends 50 percent of his professional time on uncompensated work, all of which dovetails with his commitment to "faith-based" approaches to social problems.[30] He runs a conservative public interest law foundation, serves on boards of numerous state and national organizations, and is heavily involved in the Republican Party and the conservative movement. Another lawyer said that he spends significant amounts of time on uncompensated activities such as "testifying to the House Judiciary Committee . . . or testifying on some civil rights measure, or on the flag burning amendment—something I'm doing, [because I believe in the cause], not because somebody is paying me to do it."[31] He explained that "the main reason" he left a large firm to pursue a more politically oriented practice was that he "didn't really care from anything other than a professional standpoint how the disputes I was working on were resolved."[32] Another lawyer in a small practice had run for the U.S. Senate, played central roles in the passage of state referenda, litigated dozens of high-profile cases, and served on boards of numerous libertarian organizations.[33] He had negotiated up front with his firm for the "opportunity to do things on my own that I believed in" and to "discuss my extreme classical liberal libertarian views" in the press.[34] Another lawyer who helped establish several religious groups and served at a high level in the Reagan administration worked in a small firm that serves churches and not-for-profit Christian groups and attracts like-minded Christian evangelicals.[35] It appears, then, as Scheingold and Bloom (1998: 236) found in their research on left activist practice and as Heinz et al. (2005) found in their study of social and political values in the Chicago bar, that small firms may afford lawyers greater freedom to select work consistent with their political commitments than large law firms do.

Many of the lawyers who worked for causes other than business interests appeared to be passionately committed to the causes they served. Some religious conservatives invoked religious "calling" to explain their activism.[36] A lawyer who was active on abortion issues, for example, said that he believed that he "was called by the highest power to do justice and serve our fellow men and women" and that, while "secular people" often think of that as a "social change orientation, it was a much larger position for us."[37] Another said of his decision to become a lawyer: "A lot of prayer went into it. As a Christian person it was important to me . . . that I do things that seem to me to be in the service of God."[38] Three Christian evangelical lawyers who had left private practice to work full time for religious advocacy groups described their decisions in religious terms.[39] One said: "The idols in my life were money and prestige and people being proud of me and having a fancy job and making money. And I had always heard in church the claims that God makes about himself and that he is worthy of worship and devotion of one's life to him and started thinking: 'Maybe you're suppose to take that seriously.'"[40] Another recounted how becoming a born-again Christian led him to conclude that "[T]his change in my life, acknowledging, recognizing that I'm a Christian, should have something to do with how I spend the better part of my day, what my job is, what my career is, what my vocation is, what my calling is."[41] For many of these lawyers, religion appeared to strongly influence the political goals to which they devoted their services.[42]

Lawyers for libertarian groups typically described their commitments in more political terms, but they, too, offered earnest and ambitious accounts of their purposes. A lawyer who had been tortured as a prisoner of war in Vietnam saw the right to self-defense (and thus the right to own guns) as "a natural right of a human being by virtue of his birth."[43] A lawyer who focused on "economic liberty" issues said that he wanted "to make some real changes in the world" by vindicating constitutional rights through lawsuits.[44] Another said that his experience working as a geologist before attending law school showed him that government bureaucrats "need to be fought."[45] A lawyer who had pursued First Amendment cases for the past fifteen years said that "preserving the right to speak freely—that's what it's still about for me."[46] One lawyer described his "passionate commitment" to the libertarian vision—"to allow, to empower individuals to live their lives to the fullest in terms of applying their talents, their abilities without government coercion."[47] A lawyer who worked for a group that opposes affirmative action said emphatically: "It's wrong to discriminate against African-Americans. It's wrong to discriminate against other groups, too, on the basis of race."[48]

Some lawyers for religious and libertarian groups described themselves as champions of vulnerable groups or individuals. Abortion opponents, for example, viewed themselves as protectors of unborn children, and religious liberties advocates claimed that they were asserting the rights of religious people to express their views in an oppressively secular (and morally corrupt) public domain. One lawyer described his decision to devote himself to opposing abortion: "We felt we had to use our small tools to confront the age and confront the culture and protect the innocent as best we could."[49] A lawyer who spent years "keeping people who were home schooling out of jail" later brought equal access cases challenging government officials who determined that "everybody can have their meetings in our public school or this government auditorium except religious groups."[50] An attorney whose organization assists in prosecuting pornography cases asserted that local governments were "outgunned" by the industry and that his organization was established to "help level the playing field."[51] Several libertarians identified their constituency as disadvantaged minorities thwarted in their entrepreneurial ambitions by burdensome regulation (cf. Hatcher, this volume).[52] Another libertarian lawyer described himself as a champion of consumers harmed by misguided regulation—for example, the FDA's slow approval process for new drugs that might save lives, and the National Highway Transportation Safety Administration's fuel emissions standards, which encourage Detroit to produce smaller (and less safe) automobiles.[53] The counsel for an organization dedicated to "restoring balance" to the criminal justice system said that he viewed his constituency as innocent crime victims.[54] Another lawyer regarded himself as an advocate for average American citizens, who deserved a "simpler, fairer, flatter, more visible" tax system.[55] Opponents of affirmative action asserted that they were challenging employment and educational admissions processes that systematically disadvantage poor and working-class white males. An advocate for a group that opposes compulsory union membership trembled as he described how his client crossed a picket line and was beaten unconscious by union members. He said that his role was to "stick up for" workers against people who "use their power to mess around with people's lives."[56]

Some lawyers in religious and libertarian groups indicated that they were more interested in developing favorable law than in serving individual clients. Several described strategies for building favorable precedent[57] and the difficulty of planning and executing litigation campaigns.[58] Activism for these lawyers sometimes took the form of recruiting clients through whom they would pursue the cause.[59]

Like the left activists described in Jones's chapter in this volume, many lawyers for libertarian and social conservative groups emphasized that it was important to them to pursue work they believed in. One abortion opponent reported that he had disliked his elite law school because most of his classmates were selling out to make money, but he was thrilled to discover an anti-abortion advocacy group: "[f]inally I . . . saw something to do in law that I would enjoy, that I would believe in."[60] Another said of his decision to join a libertarian advocacy organization rather than a large law firm: "I knew I would do something I believed in which is more fun than working on cases because someone is paying you to."[61] A lawyer who quit his job with a private firm to join a think tank noted how "liberating" it was to pursue one's own causes; "to gear up for battle and to do that about something you strongly believe in is fantastic, really intense."[62] Another said of his career choices that it was important to him "that what I did professionally would at least be consistent with my libertarian beliefs."[63] An attorney who had joined a firm in which many of his clients were nonprofit Christian organizations reported that "many of his prayers had been answered" because his professional work and his interest in serving Christian groups "were meshing together rather nicely."[64] An academic said of the many requests he received for representation on constitutional matters, "if it's not a case going in the direction I want to go, I turn it down."[65] A lawyer in a small firm who mixed paid with unpaid work said that he did not compartmentalize his life except as he was required to do so by professional ethics: "I see the pieces of my life forming a coherent whole. . . . I see a connection between my religious beliefs, my political involvement, the kinds of cases I work on, my appetites for other types of civic involvement. There is a coherent fabric to my life."[66] Another small firm lawyer said that working to further his political beliefs was "where I find my satisfaction in law."[67]

Several lawyers for libertarian and religious organizations described incidents that had offended their political sensibilities and prompted them to leave their jobs. One lawyer resigned from a large law firm when it denied his request to handle a controversial U.S. Supreme Court brief.[68] Another lawyer was fired from his job with an advocacy organization when he refused to dismiss a lawsuit that threatened the financial interests of a board member's friend.[69] An attorney who now works for a libertarian organization left his law firm when a client asked him to pursue government protection for the industry—a position that conflicted with his libertarian commitments.[70] A lawyer who now works for a Christian organization resigned from his law firm after his partners asked him to stop representing an anti-abortion group pro bono and to cease praying at the office.[71] Another lawyer left private practice to establish a religious liberties group around the time he began "seeing some things [he] really didn't like" from his primary client.[72]

Lawyers for religious and libertarian advocacy organizations rejected the conventional model's claim that lawyers are morally unaccountable for their service to clients. For these lawyers, decisions about what clients and causes to serve were personal. A lawyer who directs a Christian law group asserted that conventional professional ideals are "all a game to escape responsibility."[73] A lawyer active on abortion issues who learned that I had a young daughter leaned toward me and asked, "Wouldn't you want to know if your daughter was about to have an abortion?"[74] Several lawyers questioned the integrity of lawyers who took positions contrary to their own. A lawyer who fights pornography said that he could respect lawyers who disagreed with him about whether and how to regulate pornography but not those who denied that pornography causes harm; he asserted that anyone who took that position "either has to be a fool or a damn liar."[75] Another lawyer said that the ACLU has good lawyers who, he conceded, "may even be sincere in their beliefs," but he asserted that their positions on child pornography were outrageous.[76] An opponent of affirmative action said: "[I]f there were any justice in the world, all these people would be disbarred that were involved in propagating these myths and lies [about differential admissions standards in universities]."[77]

Although lawyers in advocacy organizations, thinks tanks, and academia generally appeared to be more politically committed to their work than their counterparts in large firms and trade associations, some described mixed motivations for accepting their current jobs and some expressed rather conventional professional orientations.[78] A lawyer who took a position with a large religious advocacy organization had absolutely no experience with those issues before taking the job and was not particularly drawn to the organization's agenda: "What drew me to the job was to find something as different as I could from what I was doing"—litigating for a large federal agency.[79] Another lawyer for the same organization said that he was an agnostic.[80] A lawyer who took a position with a libertarian advocacy organization upon graduating from law school said that she "liked what [the organization] was doing" but that she also wanted to be near her extended family, who lived in the area.[81] Just as many lawyers for liberal causes obtain nonpecuniary benefits from public interest work (Komesar and Weisbrod 1978: 87–89), some lawyers employed by conservative and libertarian advocacy groups indicated that they liked their jobs because the positions offered greater responsibility than conventional practice did,[82] provided more intellectually engaging work,[83] and called for hours that were more compatible with family commitments and other types of civic involvement.[84] A general counsel for a large religious organization observed: "I remind myself and I tell my clients that I am their lawyer. It doesn't matter, it shouldn't matter to them whether I agree or disagree with them. . . . They pay me to advise them, I give them advice and they decide."[85] A lawyer who worked for an organization that opposes affirmative action said that he believed in the organization's goals, but he had added, "I don't think any of this stuff is the be all and end all of the universe."[86]

Practice settings and types of causes served, then, appear to bear some relation to the professional identities of the lawyers. The processes that produce such variation are not well understood and will not be explored here. It is worth noting, however, that lawyers probably seek to work in organizations in which they expect to feel comfortable, that institutions, in turn, recruit lawyers who they believe will further their missions, and that lawyers' professional identities are strongly influenced by the constraints and opportunities of the institutions in which they practice. Large law firms attract lawyers who are comfortable serving corporate clients and other moneyed interests. The clients of large law firms demand technical expertise and committed advocacy from their lawyers, and they also may expect their lawyers to sympathize with the institutional arrangements that maintain "their clients' favorable position in society" (Nelson 1988: 243). However, corporate clients and the firms that serve them also derive value from the ideals of lawyer independence and neutral partisanship, which allow lawyers to claim distance from their client's ends (Simon 1978). The center-right politics and mainstream professional ideology of these organizations suit their clients' needs and preferences well, just as they are uncomfortable environments for lawyers who do not share those political views and professional norms (cf. Wilkins 2004: 1586–89). Advocacy organizations and think tanks—particularly those that pursue primarily symbolic interests—sell messages about how public policy must change to accomplish some public good. They need and attract salaried lawyers who strongly identify with the organizations' agendas—not advocates who might take the opposite side of the issue tomorrow. Solo practices and small firms generally are better able than large firms to accommodate lawyers who seek to develop practices reflecting their political commitments. Lawyers in such practices have large numbers of clients and generally are less dependent on any particular client than lawyers in large firms (Heinz et al. 2005). Moreover, their clients are more likely to be "one-shotters" who have little long-term influence over the lawyers' practices (ibid.). The publicity and political connections that lawyers cultivate through their work for causes may help them build their reputations and generate business. More flexible institutional arrangements and smaller likelihood of disqualifying conflicts of interest also may help explain why small firms attract lawyers who wish to pursue causes consistent with their values.

The Making (and Unmaking) of Lawyer Activism

The prototypical cause lawyer selects law as a profession, or chooses a particular area of practice, in order to advance a predefined social or political agenda (Bisharat 1998: 477); their activism and their causes are simply given. But individuals' commitments to groups and identities sometimes emerge and transform over time (Spears et al. 1999; Turner 1999). Social identity sometimes changes through participation in collective action (McAdam 1989; Drury and Reicher 2000), and participation in social activism often deepens participants' commitment to causes (McAdam 1989). Lawyers' professional norms develop in the workplace and reflect the "arenas" in which those values evolve (Nelson and Trubek 1992; cf. Bellow 1977). This section considers lawyers' own accounts of how their professional identities and political commitments changed over time.

A few lawyers fit the profile of the classic cause lawyer, who decides at an early age to devote his or her professional life to particular political ends. A libertarian lawyer said that he attended law school "To do exactly what I'm doing right now; . . . I knew I wanted to do constitutional law and I wanted to defend individual liberty."[87] He decided to attend a state university to avoid incurring debts that might interfere with that plan, and he "never stepped foot in the placement office."[88] A lawyer who was tortured in Vietnam went to law school "to serve a system which would not permit that behavior."[89] A libertarian asserted that changing social policy "was all I was really interested in doing career-wise" and that he was inspired to attend law school by the constitutional law class he took as an undergraduate: "[E]verything just came together for me, especially reading cases like *Brown v. Board of Education*. I thought, 'This is how you change the world—not through politics but through law.'"[90] Another said that he became a lawyer to "to make environmental regulations more reasonable."[91] One conservative reported that he went to law school to advance the goal of "getting the courts back in a business that they had been out of since 1937"—"policing the boundaries of the congressional authority and the Constitution."[92] An opponent of affirmative action explained: "I . . . always have thought it would be right if I could have a career [through which] I could advance the conservative cause."[93]

Most lawyers, however, described much less direct and deliberate routes to their current work on behalf of conservative and libertarian causes. Many said that they attended law school without a clear sense of why they were there or what they would do with their legal education. Several were involved in conservative or libertarian politics before they attended law school, but few reported that they attended law school to prepare to further political or social change through law. Some, in fact, expressed distaste for liberal activist lawyers who defined the "traditional" public interest movement, although many of them, particularly those who helped to found the earliest conservative public interest organizations, had defined themselves against left-wing lawyer activism. Of those lawyers who reported that pursuing social or political change was a reason for attending law school, many recalled that they had envisioned being involved in causes of the left.[94] Lawyers for religious groups frequently reported that they had hoped that becoming a lawyer would enable them to help people.[95] Few, however, indicated that they had imagined the types of activist practices in which they later became engaged, perhaps because most evangelical Christian legal advocacy organizations are relatively new (den Dulk 2001).

Many said that they had not become involved in the causes they now serve until late in their careers. The general counsel for an antipornography group worked for a large insurance company for twenty-seven years after graduating from law school.[96] Another lawyer worked for a poverty law clinic after graduating from law school before deciding that he wanted "to go into some type of Christian work."[97] A libertarian ran a business for twenty-five years before going to law school.[98] Several Christian lawyers were in private firms when they experienced religious epiphanies that triggered their flight to activist practices.[99] A lawyer who eventually devoted himself to fighting abortion full time was not involved in the issue for the first thirteen years of practice.[100]

Some said that they were not even conservatives when they graduated from law school. A lawyer who now works for a trade association described himself as a McGovern Democrat when he took his first job as a legislative aide after law school, but he underwent a gradual shift that eventually led him to work for a moderate Republican.[101] This change also coincided with increasing financial responsibility for his family: "I didn't want to work for anybody there [who] would make me gag, but I really was mostly interested in the work, and, with a family, I was getting very career oriented and really not ideological at all."[102] A lawyer who said she was "insufferably self-righteous about how liberal I was" early in her career described a series of experiences that led her to redefine her political commitments.[103] Although she was sympathetic to the political goals of campus activism in the 1960s, she was uncomfortable with the "strategy of destruction" that characterized some of that work. She later began reading books that challenged her assumption that "government is the answer to poverty and government is the answer to injustice and . . . everybody else is wicked and government is good."[104] Later in her career, she found herself at odds with feminists who thought that gender should play a more prominent role in how she defined herself. Eventually, she said, "Things just converged and I began to think of myself more as a conservative."[105] A lawyer who had gone to Mississippi after law school to fight segregation and who was active in Democratic politics in the 1970s concluded that he could not seek an appointment in the Carter administration because he no longer believed in the policies it sought to implement.[106] A prosecutor of obscenity who had always thought of himself as a liberal and who had always voted for Democrats began paying closer attention to "judicial appointments and how they would affect my life as a prosecutor."[107] A lawyer active in causes of the left was dismayed when the ACLU adopted a pro-choice position, and he later helped to establish and lead an anti-abortion education and advocacy group.[108] Several property rights lawyers said that they had viewed themselves as liberal Democrats until the Democratic Party ran away from them in the 1970s.[109] These accounts of the transformation of lawyers' professional ideals are consistent with a literature on the conservative influence of professional socialization (Granfield 1992; Stover and Erlanger 1989). They also may reflect a rightward shift in public opinion and growing disaffection with legal activism during the early years of these lawyers' careers (Galanter 2002).

Two lawyers indicated that their political values had become *less* conservative in recent years. One lawyer said he had been raised in a conservative Mormon household but now was repelled by causes of the religious right. He worked in a small firm representing mostly business interests:

> [My background] formed a very conservative person. And I was rather proud of that . . . as a new lawyer. And as time went on my views changed and attitudes changed. And now, I would just hate to think of myself as being grouped with some of the more conservative lawyers in the country that espouse some of these right-wing—or especially religious right-wing—causes, because they trouble me a great deal. I just don't see myself as that type of person or in that group.[110]

Another lawyer who had held a high-level political appointment in the Reagan administration indicated that his conservative commitments had moderated somewhat in recent years.[111]

Many lawyers indicated that their commitment to the causes they now serve evolved over time *through* their work for those causes. The president of an anti-abortion group said that he first became interested in the issue in college when he read about *Roe v. Wade* and concluded that it was flawed jurisprudentially, but his interest later "evolved from a more legalistic view to more of a cultural commitment."[112] Another lawyer said that he had enjoyed constitutional issues in law school and during his Supreme Court clerkship, but that his political commitments had developed more recently "as I've gotten deeper into these issues that I found I care very much about."[113] A lawyer who works for a Christian evangelical group began prosecuting pornography cases to gain trial experience; "I wasn't particularly religious. I got into these cases, not because I had a passion for the work, but because I just wanted the jury trials."[114] At first, he tried to distance himself from some of the evangelical Christians associated with the fight against pornography, but years later, after he had become a well-known pornography prosecutor, he became an evangelical Christian himself.[115] Another lawyer said, "I would never have thought in a hundred million years that [pornography] would have been my issue."[116] In 1973, when he was a law student volunteering in a prosecutor's office, his boss asked him to parse the U.S. Supreme Court's new obscenity decisions in *Miller v. California*.[117] He was assigned responsibility for answering dozens of defense motions challenging the constitutionality of obscenity prosecutions under the new standard. After graduating from law school, he quickly became the office expert on obscenity. He said that at first he viewed such work in conventional professional terms; it was simply part of the prosecutor's obligation to enforce the law. Over time, however, he became convinced that pornography had harmful social consequences, and he is now among the most prominent advocates for regulating Internet pornography. A lawyer who served as in-house counsel to a large religious organization said that the organization's agenda had almost nothing to do with his decision to take the job, but "the more I learned about it, the more that I read, the more I become a part of it and am responsible for achieving it, the more I identify with it."[118]

Several lawyers emphasized the absence of deliberation in the paths that led to their current positions. A lawyer who was active on religious liberty issues observed that he had not anticipated such a career when he went to law school: "People who are ten years old and fifteen years old . . . come up to me and say, 'I'm inspired by you' and 'What steps did you take to get here?' And I feel like I just sort of fell into this. . . . I'm embarrassed to say there was no orderly way or conscious, deliberate way that I moved into this."[119] Another abortion opponent said that he had no intention of pursuing causes when he went to law school:

> I had some pretty strong political opinions at the time; I had a strong sense of right and wrong. But at the time, I did not connect going to law school with those feelings and beliefs. Later on, they sort of merged. But at the time—at the age of twenty-one—my interests in life were pretty simple, really. I just enjoyed eating and I enjoyed drinking beer, traveling . . . I didn't have a huge social or political agenda.[120]

A lawyer who was the litigation director for an advocacy organization said that he had taken the position in part because his search for an academic job was not going well: "It was . . . very fortuitous that I came into this position. . . . I would like to tell you that I had a brilliant plan, which I executed with clarity and vision, but, unfortunately, I did not."[121] Some of these lawyers, then, became lawyers for causes without self-consciously embarking on such a course; their current positions may say as much about where they found career opportunities as they do about their political commitments.

Finally, although this chapter emphasizes how lawyers identify with and are influenced by causes, the interviews demonstrate that lawyers also influence the causes they serve. As Shamir and Chinksy (1998: 231) have noted, lawyers "are not simply carriers of a cause but are at the same time its producers: those who shape it, name it, and voice it."[122] The interviews are filled with stories about how lawyers have helped to define causes—for example, how they have helped give "tort reform" its name, linked free enterprise theories to the interests of disadvantaged minorities, and recast the culture wars as matters of federalism. They have established new organizations to pursue these agendas and often served as their principal advisors and spokespeople.[123] These lawyers, then, often were primary architects of their causes, and their identification with those causes likely increased as they shaped them to their own visions.

Conclusion

This research demonstrates that at least some lawyers who serve conservative causes challenge conventional models of professionalism in ways that are similar to their counterparts on the left; they "commit themselves and their legal skills to furthering a vision of the good society" (Sarat and Scheingold 1998: 3). Some lawyers in this study—mostly lawyers in trade associations and large private firms who serve business clients—did not regard themselves as activists at all; they viewed their roles in more conventional professional terms. These lawyers identified with their clients' positions but did not feel personally invested in them. For others, personal and professional commitments were the same, and service to causes came before service to clients. However, most lawyers described their professional choices in complex terms that fit neither the conventional nor the cause lawyer model neatly. Moreover, lawyers' political and professional orientations sometimes changed over time, and they often were dynamic participants in defining the causes they served. The variety of motivations and political commitments described by lawyers in these interviews suggests that cause lawyering is better understood as a spectrum of lawyer activism than as a distinctly specified concept, and that locating any particular lawyer on that spectrum sometimes requires identifying when in his or her perhaps complex career history professional identity should be assessed.

Notes

1. Murray Schwartz (1978: 671) and David Luban (1988: 20) have argued that the hired-gun model is the "standard conception of the lawyer's role"—that moral unaccountability is a basic element of the predominant professional ideology (Schwartz 1978: 671–73: Luban 1988: xx). Other commentators have agreed with this assessment (e.g., Simon 1978: 36; Wolfram 1986: 580; Abel 1989: 247; Wasserstrom 1975: 4). However, the empirical foundation for that claim is weak. Although there is substantial evidence that lawyers in large corporate firms do not independently evaluate the social and political consequences of their clients' goals (Kagan and Rosen 1985; Nelson 1985: 436) and rarely decline work on the ground that it conflicts with their personal values (Heinz et al. 2005; Nelson 1988: 254–56), lawyers in other practice types exercise more autonomy in selecting clients (Heinz et al. 2005). Moreover, lawyers' political values generally are closely aligned with their clients' interests (ibid.). It is unclear whether this correlation reflects lawyer self-selection, firms' selective recruitment of lawyers, power relationships between lawyers and clients, or "mutually-reinforcing processes" (ibid.), but if lawyers agree with the positions they take on behalf of clients, they are not hired guns in the sense in which that term ordinarily is used.

The ABA's Model Rules of Professional Conduct assert that a "lawyer's representation of a client . . . does not constitute an endorsement of the client's political, economic, social or moral views or activities" (Rule 1.2(b)). However, Ted Schneyer (1984) has noted that the professional codes contain contradictory language, some parts of which do not square with the "standard conception.".

2. Individual accounts are notoriously unreliable sources for objective factual reports (Snow and Machalek 1984: 175); they often say more about how the teller wishes to be perceived than about actual behavior or motivation (cf. Scott and Lyman 1968). Such accounts, however, provide compelling evidence of how individuals perceive their roles and explain their actions (Hunt and Benford 1994: 489; Engel and Munger 1996). Thus, while interviews with conservative and libertarian lawyers may not generate reliable evidence of their actual behavior and motivation, they may help us understand how these lawyers view their relationships with clients and whether they hold themselves morally accountable for the clients and causes they represent.

3. Scheingold and Bloom (1998) also use objective criteria—the types of strategies that lawyers employ—to define activism or "transgressiveness," but I am skeptical about the suggestion that lawyers who engage in political strategies are more ideologically committed to the causes they serve than are lawyers who employ more conventional legal strategies. Hired guns may be no less likely than ideologically committed lawyers to use all available means to pursue their clients' ends, including legislative and administrative advocacy, media work, and grassroots mobilizing.

4. "In this volume we are excluding 'right-wing' lawyers from our consideration of cause lawyering. We do so because, at least until very recently in the United States, moral activism was almost entirely associated with lawyering for progressive causes. It is too soon in the development of conservative cause lawyering to provide a reliable assessment: however, the increasing prominence of right-wing cause lawyering suggests that it is now an important focus for research" (Sarat and Scheingold 1998: 25).

5. Sarat and Scheingold (1998: 13) state: "The objective of the attorneys we characterize as cause lawyers is to deploy their legal skills to challenge prevailing distributions of political, social, economic, and/or legal values and resources." Menkel-Meadow (1998: 37) defines cause lawyering as "any activity that seeks to use law-related means or seeks to change law or regulations to achieve greater social justice—both for particular individuals . . . and for disadvantaged groups."

6. Some scholars suggest that financial sacrifice might also be required. Sarat and Scheingold (1998: 5), for example, ask: "Must cause lawyering be somehow unremunerative?" and Menkel-Meadow (1998: 34) asks: "Does the location of work in a profit-making setting affect how we view the work?" However, that factor seems to function primarily as a measure of ideological commitment. The commitment of a lawyer who is highly compensated may be more suspect than that of the lawyer who receives little pay. Assessing in any particular case whether a lawyer made financial sacrifices to pursue cause-oriented work requires reference to the range of alternatives that lawyer faced as he navigated his career—information that is difficult to gather and assess.

This research did not gather income data, but some lawyers reported that they received little financial compensation for their work. Several lawyers for religious organizations worked in extremely modest surroundings, and one who was active on abortion and religious liberties issues asserted that he and another respondent were the lowest paid members of their elite law school class.

7. There was some overlap. For example, lawyers for one economic liberty group occasionally work with local National Association for the Advancement of Colored People (NAACP) and poverty law groups to challenge the use of eminent domain power on behalf of business interests and to overturn regulations that they contend impede minority entrepreneurial enterprises. Religious liberties groups sometimes find themselves on the same side as the ACLU. A lawyer whose organization fights pornography said that they occasionally work with feminist groups, although "feminists are confused about the subject" (interview, February 2001). A libertarian lawyer who was active on school voucher litigation drew inspiration from Berkeley Professor John Coons "who was writing from the left on school choice" (interview, March 2001).

8. In his study of constitutional litigation, Clement Vose (1972: 334) asserted that "the types of cases a lawyer handles, the kinds of clients he represents, and his conception of counsel's role are strongly influenced by the experiences and beliefs associated with his nonlawyer characteristics."

9. American Bar Foundation, Northwestern University.

10. University of Iowa, Department of Sociology.

11. I defined prominence primarily in terms of the lawyers' positions within the organizations and/or my subjective assessment of how well known they were in the field.

12. Seven of the lawyers I sought to interview did not return my calls. I was unable to schedule interviews with another sixteen lawyers who were willing to meet with me. Three lawyers had moved to other jobs.

13. Women comprise a small percentage of lawyers who serve conservative causes (Heinz, Paik, and Southworth 2003: 18–20) and even fewer of the most prominent of these lawyers.

14. These differences, in turn, probably corresponded with substantial differences in

income and social background. Lawyers for business interests generally worked in nicely furnished office buildings in Washington, D.C. Many of them worked for large well-known law firms and presumably earned handsome salaries. They generally had attended more elite law schools and came from more privileged social backgrounds, as indicated by their father's occupation, than lawyers for religious conservative, law and order, and libertarian groups. However, lawyers for the mediator organizations had more elite educational credentials and social backgrounds than any other group of lawyers interviewed, including the lawyers for business interests.

15. Interview (January 2001).

16. Interview (June 2001).

17. Interview (March 2001). Another lawyer said that he believed that his advocacy for tort reform furthered good public policy: "My personal interest in this is trying to draw that balance between making sure that the victim gets adequate compensation [while] . . . still allow[ing] people to be able to get affordable insurance and access to health care" (interview, June 2001).

18. Interview (June 2001).

19. Interview (September 2002).

20. Interview (June 2001).

21. Interview (January 2002).

22. Id.

23. Interview (June 2001).

24. Interview (September 2002).

25. Interview (September 2002); Interview (September 2002).

26. Interview (June 2001).

27. Interview (June 2001).

28. Id.

29. Interview (February 2001); Interview (March 2001); Interview (June 2001); Interview (October 2001); Interview (January 2002); Interview (February 2002); Interview (March 2002); Interview (September 2002).

30. Interview (February 2001).

31. Interview (June 2001).

32. Id.

33. Interview (September 2002).

34. Id.

35. Interview (October 2001).

36. Kevin den Dulk (2001) provides a much more extensive discussion of how the meaning of causes served by evangelical attorneys is bound up with their religious worldviews and how religious ideas have shaped evangelical public interest advocacy.

37. Interview (March 2001).

38. Interview (April 2002).

39. See also interview (March 2001) (A lawyer who had left practice for the seminary expecting to become a pastor concluded that God had given him a collection of gifts that prepared him to serve as general counsel for this religious group).

40. Interview (October 2001).

41. Interview (September 2001).

42. For articles considering how religion might influence professional identity, see Levinson (1993); Allegretti (1998).

43. Interview (October 2001).

44. Interview (March 2001).

45. Interview (March 2002) ("A lot of environmental rules and regulations were being driven by the mindset that whatever touches the land is bad, and somehow inherently environmentally wrong. I didn't agree with that, and I thought that there are a lot of lawyers out there using environmental laws to stop projects. I thought it might be nice to be a lawyer who uses the law to help support good environmentally sound projects").

46. Interview (April 2002).

47. Interview (September 2002).

48. Interview (June 2001).

49. Interview (March 2001).

50. Interview (November 2001).

51. Interview (October 2001).

52. Interview (March 2001); Interview (March 2001); Interview (March 2001); Interview (April 2001); Interview (November 2001).

53. Interview (June 2001).

54. Interview (March 2002).

55. Interview (October 2001).

56. Interview (October 2001).

57. E.g., Interview (April 2001) (respondents convened scholars to develop litigation blueprint); Interview (October 2001) ("I am pushing for us to start looking for some places to take up Second Amendment cases"); Interview (November 2001) ("We could cherry pick a little bit on the kind of cases we were doing. . . . We were able to develop a much larger . . . overall game plan"); Interview (March 2002) (respondent had been working to "build our body of case law" and reported that when the group is asked to represent someone who is "really not interested in pursuing the law, we suggest they go somewhere else, because we really want to move the law forward in the area"); Interview (September 2002) ("We were looking . . . to come up with . . . intellectually, interesting cases and move the law in certain directions").

58. Interview (March 2001) ("You can't always do as much as you want to develop the law . . . because there have to be clients whose cases would move the law in that direction); Interview (March 2001) (describing the difficulty of ensuring that the wrong cases do not go up on appeal and of finding ways to tee up cases that will present issues in a favorable way); Interview (April 2001) ("We've tried to work out an overall litigation strategy. . . . It turns out that that's a very difficult thing to do because the litigations seem to have a life of their own").

E.g., Interview (January 2001) (I "started to think about who would be a good client" for this case); Interview (February 2001) ("Right now I'm fishing for a Commerce Power case"); Interview (March 2001) ("One of the great things about the [organization] is the ability to be entrepreneurial and to go out and find cases and find areas that you think are in need of litigation"); Interview (March 2001) (respondent contacted a man he had read about in the newspaper and offered to represent him); Interview (June 2001) ("Every one of [our] cases is produced by a network that you just have to have in place and that you have to work on. . . . [Y]ou can't just open your doors and hope the cases come in. . . . It's not like trolling for clients, but you have to have a reputation"); Interview (September 2002) (organization wanted to work "with groups that would provide us with plaintiffs").

Lawyers for causes of the left have drawn some criticism for pursuing causes through clients. See, e.g., Hegland (1971) (arguing that public interest lawyers sometimes use clients as "tickets" for cause-oriented litigation and that lawyers become unaccountable when they represent interests rather than clients); see also Bell (1976) (arguing that NAACP Legal Defense and Education Fund attorneys failed to represent the interests of African-American parents who were dissatisfied with the results of integration); cf. *NAACP v. Button*, 371 U.S. 415, 448–70 (1963) (Harlan, J., dissenting) (warning about ideological conflicts between civil rights lawyers and their clients).

59. Interview (April 2001).
60. Interview (April 2001).
61. Interview (June 2001).
62. Interview (June 2001).
63. Interview (March 2001).
64. Interview (September 2002).
65. Interview (January 2002).
66. Interview (September 2002).
67. Interview (September 2002).
68. Interview (April 2001).
69. Interview (June 2001).
70. Interview (September 2001).
71. Interview (December 2001).
72. Interview (September 2001).
73. Interview (March 2001).
74. Interview (February 2001).
75. Interview (February 2001).
76. Interview (September 2002).
77. Interview (October 2001).
78. Interview (June 2001).
79. Interview (March 2001).
80. Interview (March 2002).
81. E.g., Interview (April 2001) ("I took the job because I thought it would be intellectually interesting. . . . I would have a lot more responsibility for cases than I would ever have, even as a partner, in a private firm, and that they would be cases that would get a lot of public interest—notice"); Interview (October 2001) ("I went into public interest practice because I believed in the cause and wanted to advance it, and I stayed because I found that I have responsibility for handling major cases that I could never have had, or would have been a little difficult to have, had I been in private practice. I've already done four cases in the United States Supreme Court. Very few attorneys in private practice get to do that").

82. Interview (February 2001); Interview (June 2001); Interview (June 2001); Interview (October 2001); Interview (October 2001).

83. One lawyer had left private practice to teach and handle freelance work for think tanks because he had custody of his son and liked having "flexibility to basically be with my son" (Interview, October 2001). Another left a high-level political position in the Justice Department when President Clinton took office and accepted a job with an advocacy organization where he could have some flexibility and avoid travel (interview, June 2001). A lawyer in a religious liberties organization said that his group "tr[ies] to make sure that family is not sacrificed on the altar of the job" (interview, April 2001). Another lawyer had his young son at the office when I arrived for the interview (interview, April 2002). Two lawyers indicated that they liked the flexibility of their positions with nonprofit groups because they "home schooled" their children (interview, February 2001; interview, November 2001).

84. Interview (April 2001).

85. Interview (June 2001).

86. One respondent noted that if you want to work for religious organizations and get paid for it, you have to have the right mix of pro bono and fee generating cases. Interview (January 2001).

87. Interview (March 2001).

88. Id.

89. Interview (October 2001).

90. Interview (March 2001).

91. Interview (March 2002).

92. Interview (September 2002).

93. E.g., Interview (June 2001).

94. E.g., Interview (February 2001) (remembers being inspired by Robert Kennedy and motivated by the desire to make the world a better place); Interview (March 2001) ("I was concerned about the plight of the poor"); Interview (April 2001) (went to law school to participate in "fighting segregation"); Interview (October 2001) ("I felt really strongly about . . . things like prison reform"); Interview (January 2002) (had served in the domestic Peace Corp, taught in a desegregated school in Louisiana just before going to law school, and hoped that it would be possible to use his law degree to further social and political change); Interview (April 2002) (described himself as a 1960s activist who went to law school "to change the system"); Interview (September 2002) (remembers his "desire to use the law to make changes in the world"; spent a night in jail during summer after first year of law school in connection with Chicago Freedom Movement); Interview (September 2002) (during law school, respondent represented radicals who took over university buildings); Cf. Interview (January 2001) (wanted to change the world but did not think that law school would directly help him accomplish that); Interview (April 2002) (respondent was "anything but conservative" when she attended law school").

95. E.g., Interview (January 2001) (never dreamed of becoming a public interest lawyer but saw law as a profession in which one could do some good); Interview (February 2001) (went to law school without any particular social or political agenda, but "buried in my soul was a desire to do something good with my life"); Interview (February 2001) (decision to attend law school "was stimulated in my mind by a concept that,

as an attorney, you can do more good than one can as a lay person"); Interview (March 2001) ("The idea of helping people, particularly the poor . . . representing their rights in court was quite appealing to me"); Interview (June 2001) (in law school, respondent became interested in doing legal services work for the poor, and in second and third years of law school he worked in legal aid program); Interview (October 2001) ("I really wanted to help people"); Interview (April 2002) (went to law school because he wanted to help people); cf. Interview (January 2002) ("I decided to attend law school primarily from my study of the prophets in the Old Testament and their concern with social justice").

96. Interview (February 2001).

97. Interview (February 2001).

98. Interview (June 2001).

99. E.g., Interview (September 2001) (described a pivotal moment when he went to visit the national headquarters of a Christian organization while on a business trip to defend the deposition of a client he knew was in the wrong); Interview (October 2001) (was driving down the highway considering his career when "the radio . . . all of sudden locks onto this . . . Christian station and . . . one of Jim Dobson's *Focus on the Family* shows had started, and the topic of the show was 'Where are the Christian lawyers?'").

100. Interview (February 2002).

101. Interview (June 2001).

102. Id.

103. Interview (April 2002).

104. Id.

105. Id.

106. Interview (April 2001).

107. Interview (October 2001).

108. Interview (January 2001).

109. Interview (September 2002); Interview (September 2002).

110. Interview (January 2002).

111. Interview (February 2002).

112. Interview (February 2001).

113. Interview (June 2001).

114. Interview (December 2001).

115. Id.

116. Interview (October 2001).

117. *Miller v. California*, 413 U.S. 15 (1973). *Miller* established a three-part test for determining whether state statutes designed to regulate obscene materials are constitutional.

118. Interview (June 2001).

119. Interview (November 2001).

120. Interview (December 2001).

121. Interview (April 2001).

122. Kevin den Dulk (2001: 166) has shown how evangelicals' beliefs about "the na-

ture and limits of state power, the authority and integrity of the institutional church, and the primacy of individual salvation" influenced the course of evangelical legal advocacy.

123.   I consider some of those themes in another paper (Southworth 2005).

References

Abel, Richard L. 1989. *American Lawyers*. Oxford: Oxford University Press.

Allegretti, Joseph. 1998. "Lawyers, Clients, and Covenant: A Religious Perspective on Legal Practice and Ethics." *Fordham Law Review* 66: 1101.

Bell, Derrick A. 1976. "Serving Two Masters: Integration Ideals and Client Interests in School Desegregation Litigation." *Yale Law Journal* 85: 470.

Bellow, Gary. 1977. "Turning Solutions Into Problems." *NLADA Briefcase* 34: 106, 108.

Bisharat, George. 1998. "Attorneys for the People, Attorneys for the Land," in *Cause Lawyering: Political Commitments and Professional Responsibilities*, ed. A. Sarat and S. Scheingold. Oxford: Oxford University Press.

Bourdieu, Pierre. 1990. *The Logic of Practice*. Stanford, California: Stanford University Press.

Davis, Martha F. 1993. *Brutal Need: Lawyers and the Welfare Rights Movement 1960–73*. New Haven, Conn.: Yale University Press.

den Dulk, Kevin. 2001. "Prophets in Caesar's Courts: The Role of Ideas in Catholic and Evangelical Rights Advocacy." Doctoral dissertation. Madison: University of Wisconsin.

Drury, John, and Steve Reicher. 2000. "Collective Action and Psychological Change: The Emergence of New Social Identities." *British Journal of Social Psychology* 39: 579–604.

Engel, David M., and Frank W. Munger. 1996. "Rights, Remembrance, and the Reconciliation of Difference." *Law and Society Review* 30: 7.

Epstein, Lee. 1985. *Conservatives in Court*. Knoxville: University of Tennessee Press.

Galanter, Marc. 2002. "The Turn Against Law: The Recoil Against Expanding Accountability," *Texas Law Review* 81: 285.

Granfield, Robert. 1992. *Making Elite Lawyers: Visions of Law at Harvard and Beyond*. New York: Routledge.

Halliday, Terence C. 1999. "Lawyers and Politics and Civic Professionalism: Legal Elites and Cause Lawyers," *Law & Social Inquiry* 24: 1013.

Handler, Joel et al. 1978. *Lawyers and the Pursuit of Legal Rights*. New York: Academic Press.

Hatcher, Laura J. 2001. "Translating Ideology into Activism." Draft prepared for the Law and Society Association annual meeting.

Hegland, Kenney. 1971. "Beyond Enthusiasm and Commitment." *Arizona Law Review* 13: 805.

Heinz, John P., with Monique R. Payne. 2005. "Divided Opinions," in *Urban Lawyers: The New Social Structure of the Bar*, ed. J. Heinz et al. Chicago: University of Chicago Press.

Heinz, John, Anthony Paik, and Ann Southworth. 2003. "Lawyers for Conservative Causes: Clients, Ideology and Social Distance." *Law and Society Review* 37: 5.

Himmelstein, Jerome L. 1990. *To the Right: The Transformation of American Conservatism* Berkeley: University of California Press.

Hodgson, Godfrey. 1996. *The World Turned Right Side Up: A History of the Conservative Ascendancy in America.* New York: Houghton Mifflin.

Hunt, Scott A., and Robert D. Benford. 1994. "Identity Talk in the Peace and Justice Movement." *Journal Contemporary Ethnography* 22: 488.

Kagan, Robert A., and Robert E. Rosen. 1985. "On the Social Significance of Large Law Firm Practice." *Stanford Law Review* 37: 399.

Komesar, Neil K., and Burton A. Weisbrod. 1978. "The Public Interest Law Firm: A Behavioral Analysis," in *Public Interest Law: An Economic and Institutional Analysis*, ed. B. Weisbrod et al. Berkeley: University of California Press.

Levinson, Sanford. 1993. "Identifying the Jewish Lawyer: Reflections on the Construction of Professional Identity." *Cardozo Law Review* 14: 1577.

Luban, David. 1988. *Lawyers and Justice: An Ethical Study.* Princeton, N.J.: Princeton University Press.

Luban, David. 1990. "Partisanship, Betrayal, and Autonomy in the Lawyer-Client Relationship: A Reply to Stephen Ellmann," *Columbia Law Review* 90: 1004.

McAdam, D. 1989. "The Biographical Consequences of Activism." *American Society Review* 54: 744–60.

McCann, Michael W. 1994. *Rights at Work: Pay Equity Reform and the Politics of Legal Mobilization.* Chicago: University of Chicago Press.

McGirr, Lisa. 2001. *Suburban Warriors: The Origins of the New American Right.* Princeton, N.J.: Princeton University Press.

Menkel-Meadow, Carrie. 1998. "The Causes of Cause Lawyering: Toward an Understanding of the Motivation and Commitment of Social Justice Lawyers," in *Cause Lawyering: Political Commitments and Professional Responsibilities*, ed. A. Sarat and S. Scheingold. New York: Oxford University Press.

Milner, Neal. 1986. "Dilemmas of Legal Mobilization: Ideologies and Strategies of Mental Patient Liberation Groups." *Law and Policy*, 8: 105–29.

Nelson, Robert L. 1985. "Ideology, Practice, and Professional Autonomy: Social Values and Client-Relationships in the Large Law Firm." *Stanford Law Review* 37: 503.

Nelson, Robert L. 1988. *Partners With Power: The Social Transformation of the Large Law Firm.* Berkeley: University of California Press.

Nelson, Robert L., and David M. Trubek. 1992. "Arenas of Professionalism: The Professional Ideologies of Lawyers in Context," in *Lawyers' Ideals/Lawyers' Practices: Transformations in the American Legal Profession*, ed. Robert L. Nelson et al. Ithaca and London: Cornell University Press.

O'Connor, Karen, and Lee Epstein. 1983. "The Rise of Conservative Interest Group Litigation." *Journal of Politics* 45: 478–89.

Olson, Susan M. 1984. *Clients and Lawyers: Securing the Rights of Disabled Persons.* Westport, CT: Greenwood Press.

Sarat, Austin, and Stuart Scheingold. 1998. *Cause Lawyering: Political Commitments and Professional Responsibilities.* Oxford: Oxford University Press.

Scheingold, Stuart, and Anne Bloom. 1998. "Transgressive Cause Lawyering: Practice Sites and the Politicization of the Professional." *International Journal of the Legal Profession* 5: 209–53.

Schneyer, Ted. 1984. "Moral Philosophy's Standard Misconception of Legal Ethics." *Wisconsin Law Review* 1984: 1529.

Schwartz, Murray. 1978. "The Professionalism and Accountability of Lawyers." *California Law Review* 66: 669.

Scott, Marvin B., and Stanford M. Lyman. 1968. "Accounts." *American Sociological Review* 33: 46.

Shamir, Ronen, and Sara Chinsky. 1998. "Destruction of Houses and Construction of a Cause: Lawyers and Bedouins in the Israeli Courts," in *Cause Lawyering: Political Commitments and Professional Responsibilities*, ed. A. Sarat and S. Scheingold. New York: Oxford University Press.

Silverstein, Helena. 1996. *Unleashing Rights: Law, Meaning, and the Animal Rights Movement.* Ann Arbor: University of Michigan Press.

Simon, William. 1978. "The Ideology of Advocacy: Procedural Justice and Professional Ethics." *Wisconsin Law Review* 1978: 29.

Snow, David A., and Richard Machalek. 1984. "The Sociology of Conversion." *Annual Review Sociology* 10: 367–80.

Southworth, Ann. 2005. "Conservative Lawyers and the Contest Over the Meaning of 'Public Interest Law,'" *U.C.L.A. Law Rev.* 52 (forthcoming).

Spears, Russell, Bertjan Doosje and Naomi Ellemers. 1999. "Commitment and the Context of Social Perception," in *Social Identity: Context, Commitment, Content*, ed. Naomi Ellemers et al. Oxford: Blackwell.

Stover, Robert, and Howard Erlanger. 1989. *Making It and Breaking It: The Fate of Public Interest Commitment During Law School.* Chicago: University of Illinois Press.

Turner, John. 1999. "Some Current Issues in Research on Social Identity and Self-categorization Theories," in *Social Identity: Context, Commitment, Content*, ed. Naomi Ellemers et al. Oxford: Blackwell.

Tushnet, Mark. 1987. *The NAACP's Legal Strategy Against Segregated Education, 1925–1950.* Chapel Hill, NC: University of North Carolina Press.

Vose, Clement E. 1972. *Constitutional Change: Amendment Politics and Supreme Court Litigation Since 1900.* Lexington, Mass.: Lexington Books.

Wagner, Bridgett G., John E. Hilboldt, and Eric T. Korsvall. 2000. *Policy Experts 2000: A Guide to Public Policy Experts and Organizations.* Washington, D.C.: Heritage Foundation.

Wasserstrom, Richard. 1975. "Lawyers as Professionals: Some Moral Issues." *Human Rights* 5: 1.

Wilkins, David B. 2004. "From 'Separate Is Inherently Unequal' to 'Diversity Is Good for Business': The Rise of Market-Based Diversity Arguments and the Fate of the Black Corporate Bar." *Harvard Law Review* 117: 1548.

Wolfram, Charles. 1986. *Modern Legal Ethics.* Eagan, Minn.: West Group.

CHAPTER FOUR

Economic Libertarians, Property, and Institutions

Linking Activism, Ideas, and Identities among Property Rights Advocates

LAURA HATCHER

Introduction

Over the past three decades, much ink has been spilt in attempts to assess the efficacy of lawyers working on behalf of political ideas. Much of this work was received with skepticism as social change either did not occur quickly enough or was postponed owing to changing political conditions. According to this skeptical view, lawyers' work on behalf of progressive causes may actually be ineffective in the long run because it reinforces institutions and norms and thereby stymies more radical transformation (Brigham 1987; McCann 1986; Rosenberg 1991; Scheingold 1974). More recently, some scholars have revised their position, citing research suggesting that much of this critical assessment was based upon overly broad generalizations about lawyers or unsophisticated understandings of the way litigation and law are related to legal consciousness and the formation of political interests (for example, Brigham 1996; McCann 1994; McCann and Silverstein 1998). Following this reassessment of lawyering and lawyers' relationships to movements and social change, recent scholarship has broadened the scope of investigation to include other settings in which lawyers use their professional skills to advance political transformation.[1]

As studies of the settings, types of lawyers, and variations in strategies and tactics have broadened in scope, scholars have also grown concerned that right-wing, conservative, and Christian right lawyers might be included in this research. Beginning in the 1970s in the United States, a growing number of non-profit organizations devoted to advocating right-wing causes have appeared.

Although these organizations have not been completely ignored in research concerning lawyering and social change, they also have not received the scrutiny that progressive or left-oriented organizations have had. Much of this work, to date, studies lawyers within organizational settings and presents us with a map of what right-wing legal advocacy looks like (see, for example, Heinz, Paik, and Southworth 2003, as well as Southworth in this volume). However, understanding the settings and locations of right-wing advocacy is just the beginning. As Ann Southworth suggests in her work on conservative lawyers in this volume, we need to understand how identities, commitments, and motivations among lawyers have shaped this terrain. In a similar vein, but with a heavy focus on the way in which professional activities and institutions provide spaces for their work and the formation of ideology, this chapter presents a picture of one particular group of right-wing legal advocates, those I term "property rights advocates." These are lawyers specifically concerned with the structure of property relations in U.S. society who are often connected to movements termed "green backlash." Their work goes well beyond antienvironmental litigation and instead focuses on increased, civil rights–style protection of private property rights. Environmental regulations are often the most obvious place to begin such a discussion, as these advocates have worked steadily and seen success in litigation opposed to various forms of environmental and land use regulations. Yet their work really concerns an issue that is at the heart of the liberalism that informs the U.S. constitutional system: the use of property as a means of checking state power.

Property rights advocates frequently have held positions in the Ronald Reagan or George H. Bush administrations; a few very important legal academics are involved in this movement, and the law review and law school settings are often locations where they develop their ideas. They are, or have been, active with the Federalist Society at some time or another as can be seen by a look through the proceedings of the Federalist Society meetings over the last two decades. Finally, the notion of private property they advance is very similar to one advanced by conservatives in the late nineteenth century on behalf of corporate clients, with two very important differences: rather than mobilizing the doctrine of substantive due process to assist them, these activists utilize the takings clause of the Fifth Amendment; and the contemporary movement generally champions the individual farmer, rancher, or property owner who is faced with some sort of economic loss due to environmental or land use regulations.[2] These activists are well aware of their connection to nineteenth-century laissez-faire ideology, and at times make use of it to explain their reliance upon the takings clause as a more effective protection of individual liberty than substantive due process (because it can be found "literally" in the text of the Constitution rather than requiring judges to discover it through interpretive methods).

These activists are not simply in nonprofit legal foundations. Their work takes them into other institutional settings, and so my research describes the way those spaces and their work as lawyers are connected. As Liora Israël argues in her chapter in this volume, in which archival material is crucial, a sociopolitical analysis that does not rely upon the motivations of lawyers places the locations of their work and the types of actions they take at the center of the investigation. Indeed, I agree with Israël's argument that definitions of "cause lawyer" that rely on motivations tend to create analytical difficulties when we shift to studies of lawyers outside of liberal American lawyers working in nonprofit law firms. Although interviews of cause lawyers whose motivation is the focus of investigation have yielded remarkable insights concerning the connection between the work of lawyers in advancing their political goals and their reasons for their involvement in a type of lawyering that is quite politically motivated, such work also requires a specificity with regard to when the interview takes place that makes analysis of lawyering on behalf of political change over a long period of time difficult. To put it bluntly, a lawyer's motivation for doing his or her work may change over time or be misremembered. When we are studying movements that have been active for decades and may even be rooted in work done over a century ago, such discussions fail to help us understand how to conceptualize the category "cause lawyer" and build it into a theory of lawyering and social change.

Moreover, while identity is important in the discussion below, it is identity as it takes shape in specific institutional spaces and during particular professional practices, rather than identity as it is shaped by motivations or a raised consciousness. The importance of the judiciary and judicial decision making, both as a legitimizing mechanism for the work of these lawyers and also as a source for empowering their critique, is part of the backdrop in this work, as are their connections to the legal academy. And, as Israël argues, these institutional settings and the relationships lawyers have to them can be key factors in understanding what the social science categories "cause lawyer" or "cause lawyering" can contribute to our understanding of lawyering more generally as well as lawyers' roles in social change. However, in this chapter, the role of the legal profession—as an institution within U.S. society—as well as its work to advance capitalism in various periods plays an important role in establishing the context for the current work done by property rights advocates. Their relationship to legal theory is also important as it often gives a normative foundation to work. Not only have they learned strategies and tactics by watching left-oriented groups, such as the Legal Defense Fund (NAACP LDF), and the American Civil Liberties Union (ACLU), they have also learned from the mistakes of their forerunners and built upon the ideas of nineteenth-century jurisprudence. We see that the version of legal ideology discussed here has taken over a century to bring to its current stage of development.

Thus, the research here seeks to answer the question of how ideas and professional practices have created right-wing legal theories associated with economic libertarians. These ideologies, currently being advanced by groups such as the Pacific Legal Foundation and the Institute for Justice, are shaping U.S. constitutional law and the politics of environmental regulation as well as energy policy. To understand how these ideologies have developed, I examine the professional practices in locations where these lawyers develop ideas, learn legal strategies, and implement them in their work. Elsewhere, I have included grassroots mobilizations and the judicial selection process in my analysis (Hatcher 2002); however, in this chapter, I consider the legal academy and conservative nonprofit law firms. In order to understand the long-term growth of these ideologies, I begin with a historical survey of the development of laissez-faire ideology in U.S. law.

For the historical portion of this study, I have relied upon a reading of various secondary and some primary sources discussing the development of the legal profession, the development of doctrinal shifts in constitutional law during a period when the Supreme Court was particularly concerned with economic liberties, and sociological works examining the makeup of the bar. For the other elements of the study, I utilize content analysis of various types of movement literature: newsletters and other materials sent to me through U.S. mail as well as by e-mail from the Pacific Legal Foundation, the Institute for Justice, the Federalist Society, and various other conservative and libertarian organizations; various materials provided on Web sites by these and other legal foundations and think tanks; monographs, magazine articles; and various law review articles and symposia written by important individuals in conservative legal activism, such as Judge Richard Posner, Richard Epstein, and others who are not involved in right-wing activism, but are actively engaged in dialogue with the legal thinkers who have influenced conservative legal thought. The latter materials include both scholarly work and writings that are intended to reach a broader public. Along with this, *amicus* briefs as well as case law have provided insights into the workings of property rights advocacy and changes occurring in U.S. constitutional law.

In addition, I attended for observation purposes two of the national student meetings of the Federalist Society. My study of the Federalist Society has also involved a review of the symposia proceedings for their national meetings, which are published in the *Harvard Journal of Law and Public Policy*. Other symposia proceedings have contributed to an analysis of arguments and ideas in the law and economics movement. Finally, newspaper articles from newspapers of record (particularly the *New York Times* and *Washington Post*) have also been collected concerning the Federalist Society, law and economics, or property rights activism over the last twenty years. This last set of data is not exhaustive, but has been helpful in determining when key events occurred.

Rather than understanding lawyers in terms of their personal worldviews and thinking of ideology in terms of personal beliefs, the work here draws on the notion that ideology is a set of practices giving shape and contour to social life.[3] Whether left or right, lawyers as active participants in a professional terrain learn to behave in ways expected of them as participants in an adversarial process. The practices that are part of a realist legal culture form an ideology that is, itself, important to take into account in studying lawyers who actively litigate for some type of social change. But it is also important to be mindful of how these practices inform the attitudes and understandings of those who oppose social change or oppose a direction of change advocated by others. Property rights advocates, who are part of the latter two categories, behave according to the practices of their profession, changing strategies as they face new opportunities and challenges. Liberal legalism has been a part of these practices at least since the "glory days" of the Warren Court (Kalman 1996). The linkage between liberal legalism and liberal politics grew out of the seeming success of the NAACP's litigation campaign in *Brown v. Board of Education*, which declared school segregation unconstitutional. The reliance on the courts, particularly the Supreme Court, by activist lawyers since then has been scrutinized and discussed at great length (Brigham 1987; McCann 1994; Rosenberg 1991). The use of the courts by conservatives and economic libertarians, however, still requires further evaluation, particularly as it relates to liberal legalism.

Property rights advocates are explicitly connected to key institutions of power in the United States, particularly capitalism, the federal government, and the legal academy. Although there are other movements with strong advocates in these locations, the way in which property rights advocates are connected to organizations such as the Federalist Society and intellectual movements, such as the law and economics movement, is worthy of much closer scrutiny. Although conservatives have been working on behalf of conservative causes since the time of the U.S. founding (Jameson 1926), today's activists at times take on the practices and tactics often identified as part of more progressive lawyering. Although all conservative legal activism is not tied to the advocacy of property rights, a core group of conservatives, involved with the Federalist Society and the founders of some of the first conservative nonprofit organizations, began their legal activism in the realm of private property rights. In some respects, then, these right-wing lawyers were the beginning of a move made in part because they believed that progressive public interest lawyering, contrary to scholarly assessments, was highly effective in projecting a particular understanding of the "public interest." Through a brief study of their history, I find that this early work encompassed several sites where pressure was and still is placed on state institutions in the hopes of creating political, legal, and at times, broader social change. However, to truly understand the ideas empowering much of their work, I also discuss the role of "academic safe havens" in producing legal ideology. Thus, the Federalist Society and the conservative branch of the law and economics movement become a part of this analysis.

Conservatives, Law, and Property: A Historical Perspective

In order to reconnect conservatives to capitalism and regulatory issues, I place contemporary conservative property rights claims in the context of historical developments in legal activism. The purpose of this historical comparison is to gain an understanding of how changes in state and society shape the activities of lawyers working on behalf of property rights. By weaving together literatures on the laissez-faire movement, the rise of the legal profession, and the development of activist lawyering in nonprofit organizations, I intend to draw attention to some of the characteristics that make this activism possible in certain social and political contexts and suggest ways in which the relationship among ideas, practices, and ideologies can be developed further to enrich analysis of today's political scene. Therefore, we begin this discussion with work on behalf of property rights that occurred over a hundred years ago.

The Heart of Laissez-Faire

Lawyers of the last half of the past century were focused on encouraging economic growth, clearly believing that it and the ability of individuals to own property were the only ways to ensure individual liberty. They displayed a remarkable ability to translate economic theory as well as political and legal philosophy into legal terms and constitutional devices for their own ends. As Twiss (1942) argues in *Lawyers and the Constitution; How Laissez Faire Came to the Supreme Court*, laissez-faire lawyers were able to develop a constitutional doctrine of economic liberty that, although not lasting in its strongest form for a very long time, did have an impact on society during that period and certainly is still available as a tradition within constitutional law on which today's property rights advocates are able to draw (Twiss 1942: 4).

What I refer to as "the" laissez-faire tradition is actually a set of arguments concerning the importance of the individual, free competition, and the state's appropriate role in economic regulation. Not all lawyers who can be identified as "laissez-faire" in their ideology were in full agreement on every point. However, certain legal thinkers were extremely influential in shaping the various positions of the period. One such individual was Thomas M. Cooley who published a highly influential work in 1868 titled *A Treatise on the Constitutional Limitations which Rest Upon the Legislative Powers of the States of the American Union*. The ideas embodied in this work, along with the powerful position held by its author as a judge on the Michigan Supreme Court, gave laissez-faire a theoretical framework that, coupled with the passage of the Fourteenth Amendment, grounded the legal thinking of lawyers who represented business interests.

Cooley's position on police power and economic regulation was rooted in his understanding of property, which he explains in detail in *General Principles of Constitutional Law* (1880). There he argued that the Constitution is clear in that the Fifth Amendment constrains the federal government from depriving individuals of property without compensation, and that the Fourteenth Amendment supplements the Fifth by providing that no state can take property without due process of the law. But more importantly, his understanding of what property is provides the basis for what is protected in these two constitutional provisions: "Whatever a man produces by the labor of his hand or his brain, whatever he obtains in exchange for something of his own, and whatever is given to him in the law will protect him in the use, enjoyment and disposition of" (315). He argues that property is that which is recognized as property in the law, and that the law can withdraw the "attribute of property, and then any one may be at liberty to destroy it" (315). His source for much of this is Jeremy Bentham's *Principles of the Civil Code*.

Furthermore, Cooley felt very strongly that all "class legislation" was undemocratic. In essence, he argued that any legislation that seemed to favor one class over another was unconstitutional, whether it was favoring the rich over the poor or the poor over the rich.[4] This notion of equality before the law was very much a part of the legal landscape by the 1880s. One can hear it echoed in the majority opinions in important cases such as those known as the Civil Rights Cases and, later, in *Plessy v. Ferguson*. It required that the government exercise a peculiar kind of neutrality where economic issues were involved, refraining from interfering on anyone's behalf regardless of the merit of their claims or the issues of social justice that develop when economic activities are structured in particular ways. Moving these ideas into the law, however, took well over a decade and required talented and highly skilled lawyers.

Twiss (1942) traces this process in his book, arguing that the bar is a "great propaganda machine" that barrages the judiciary with "words, phrases, symbols and creeds weighty by the predominantly verbal nature of legalism" (261). He explains that the lack of legal precedent for these views challenged laissez-faire lawyers and that the intimate relationship between ideas and crafting legal arguments is an activity requiring a great deal of finesse, particularly when the lawyer urges a position that is not represented in current precedent: "By developing constitutional devices and forms of words [lawyers] were able to gain entrance to the judicial mind, whereas the direct assertion of laissez faire doctrine was generally unsuccessful. The Supreme Court maintained its virtue inviolate against direct assault but yielded to the subtle, seductive persuasion of phrases uttered in its own cabalistic tongue" (254).

Twiss suggests that the fine art of persuasion was very much alive in the nineteenth century, as lawyers' pocketbooks, social standings, and clients all benefited from the development of laissez-faire jurisprudence. The skill of these lawyers was very high indeed; they were quite often among the best lawyers in the profession and they often wore multiple hats in their public lives. Besides being lawyers, they were also businessmen and politicians, and many helped organize the bar associations in their states or were leaders in pushing for the adoption of the Langdellian case law method in a newly structured law curriculum.[5] Such men included John Archibald Campbell, who served on the U.S. Supreme Court from 1853 through 1861 before setting up private practice in New Orleans, and William M. Evarts, who, besides serving as the U.S. attorney general, secretary of state, Republican senator for New York, and president of bar associations, also lawyered on behalf of large railroad corporations.

Campbell has a special place in this story. Not only were his arguments in the *Slaughter-House Cases* critical in the late nineteenth century to the development of laissez-faire legal theory, but economic libertarians use these arguments today when promoting their interpretation of the Fourteenth Amendment. Campbell, a southerner, had been a justice of the U.S. Supreme Court up until 1861 when he stepped down as the Civil War began. Though an ardent supporter of states' rights, in the *Slaughter-House Cases*, he found himself arguing against a state statute and arguing that the Constitution, particularly the Thirteenth and Fourteenth Amendments, required the federal court to curb Louisiana's regulatory powers. His arguments rested in part on the importance of understanding that the "citizens" referred to in the Fourteenth Amendment were all of the citizens of the United States and not only the former slaves. Campbell's argument was at least in part an argument against redistribution of wealth by the government (Connor 1920). Though the U.S. Supreme Court ultimately rejected this claim on the basis that the Civil War Amendments were intended to protect the newly freed slaves, Campbell's argument has been resurrected in recent years as a means for protecting small business owners and other individuals against various types of regulatory actions and as an argument against contemporary redistributive policies. Today, the Institute for Justice makes this claim the most strongly.

However, in 1873, the U.S. Supreme Court was unwilling to agree with this argument. Justice Samuel Miller, writing for the majority, found instead that any business that served the public interest could be regulated. Justice Field, dissenting, suggested that individuals have an "inalienable" right to pursue their occupations. Like Campbell, Field read the Fourteenth Amendment to extend beyond the former slaves and provide protection against state interference to all citizens as they went about their various activities. Field's position with regard to economic interests was grounded in an understanding of the importance of private property strikingly similar to the positions asserted by Cooley and other constitutional theorists of the period. Today's economic libertarians recall Field's and Campbell's positions with the same respect given to lone voices in a wilderness, and they want the precedent in *The Slaughter-House Cases* overturned because they see it as the chief stumbling block in economic liberties today.[6]

Campbell's argument and the arguments made by J. Stephen Field provided another attorney, William Evarts, known as the "prince of the American Bar," strong grounds on which to build work on behalf of corporate clients in cases such as *Munn v. Illinois* (1877). Evarts was known as an especially charismatic and persuasive orator (Dyer 1933; Twiss 1942). Yet Evarts's significance may have as much to do with his other professional activities as with his arguments in courtrooms. He was deeply involved in changes being made to the legal curriculum as well as the mobilization of bar associations.

It is no coincidence that the ability to make particular types of arguments became a critical aspect of legal education in this period. Although it would be incorrect to say that laissez-faire lawyers were alone within the legal profession in working to reshape legal education, Robert Gordon (1983) has reminded us of the important relationship that developed between law schools and the law firm at the end of the nineteenth century. Law schools became an important training ground for lawyers in "legal science," an ideological activity in which

lawyers attempted to regularize legal decision making and argument by a theoretical framework. The importance of this activity for liberal thought, as Gordon explains:

> lies in the realm of personal and property rights, which define how far one may go in
> exercising one's liberty and where one must stop to avoid infringing upon that of
> others. The state is instituted to define and enforce rights; its medium of rights-def-
> inition is law, which both facilitates liberty as freedom of action and protects liberty
> as security, including security against the state itself. (82–83)

The laissez-faire lawyers of the period hoped to convince judges that the law
required them to strike down legislation not conforming to their theory that
the state should not interfere with the economic rights of individuals. This theory, through argumentation and careful legal analysis, became part of the jurisprudence of the Supreme Court, despite the Court's initial resistance to the
position. But both the initial resistance and its later adoption can be understood as aspects of the legal process—not merely judges who had decided to
"switch sides" or whose politics became the only means by which they decided
their cases. Rather, through the manipulation of the principles of reasoned argument, laissez-faire lawyers were able to gain legal ground (Cushman 1998;
Gillman 1993).

There were, of course, other things happening in the period that enabled the
adoption of these views. Bar associations, often organized by the most conservative lawyers, were developed to maintain the ethnic and class makeup of the
bar. The importance of what a legal professional ought to be was a hot topic in
this period, as the bar went through a process wherein legal practice was given
a heightened status in society (Larson 1977). Associations, such as the Association of the Bar of the City of New York (ABCNY) were organized throughout
the United States. In Michael Powell's 1988 study of the ABCNY, which included
William Evarts as one of its most preeminent members, New York lawyers utilized strict entrance requirements for their own association and advocated for
greater entrance requirements for the bar more generally during the late nineteenth century. Much of this was tied to their own sense of upward mobility
and the belief that if the profession became overrun by "undesirables," it would
not be distinctive enough to provide upward mobility to its practitioners (Powell 1988: 34–35). This suggests that for conservative lawyers, political and economic interests and their legal theories were informing one another in ways
that shaped their ideology.

The restrictive membership requirements for the ABCNY also provided
lawyers with a safe haven where they could discuss their ideas and a platform
from which to argue for their worldview. By excluding diverse opinions or in-

terests, the lawyers were able to find a consensus based upon similar under-standings of the world. This provided a focus on particular aspects of the legal landscape that, as Powell demonstrates, has been difficult for the ABCNY to maintain in the twentieth century with a more diverse membership. The lawyers were able to claim a high level of expertise, and though Powell argues that they were unsuccessful in many ways on the state and local levels, their ability to influence national level policy was remarkable. By regulating the pro-fession, they were able to legitimate the autonomy and special privilege of the legal profession; gain an honored place in society; and offer a means for distin-guishing between various types of lawyers, thereby stratifying the profession and placing themselves on top. These lawyers included many of the same indi-viduals working on behalf of the railroads and other corporate interests, and so they also had powerful connections to business and society. Through their var-ious activities they were able to change the legal landscape over the course of the last two decades of the nineteenth century.

Lawyers at the time were aided by their ability to be autonomous from the state through the development of lawyering as a "profession," while simultane-ously being allied with the state (Halliday and Karpik 1997). As Halliday and Karpik (1997) have explained, their autonomy within the legal profession al-lowed them to struggle with the state when it took a form they did not support, while providing them with some of the tools for that struggle. Their connection to the state, through the judicial process, and their relationships with judges also enabled them to achieve their goals while others continued to struggle. They achieved this interesting relationship through a conscious and concerted effort to professionalize their work—to bring it to a status that is above that of other work and is therefore seen as more valuable (Gordon 1983; Halliday and Karpik 1997; Larson 1977; Powell 1988). Today's right-wing activists are able to use many of the same means to advance their position, though changes in soci-ety and the growth of the legal profession have made it necessary for them to blend old and new strategies.

Those new strategies include lawyering in nonprofit legal foundations and law firms. This form of lawyering appears to have developed in the very late nineteenth century and throughout the twentieth, coinciding with the democ-ratization process, the rise of legal realism, and the growth of the legal profes-sion itself. At its inception, it was connected to the lawyers discussed above, who, concerned with the status of immigrants entering this country, established organizations that later became the models for public interest lawyering (Auer-bach 1975). We often connect such activities in the United States to groups such as the NAACP and the ACLU. However, their strategies became the basis for other groups, including conservatives responding to what they perceived to be a very powerful means of influencing the public's views about what is in its best interest.

Conservatives and the Construction of an
"Alternative" Public Interest

The broader conservative movement, comprised of more than just the legal activists discussed here, diminished to some extent during the Progressive Era, but began to gain ground once again in the United States after World War II. The Cold War, along with a swiftly changing economy that brought with it many societal changes, provided the basis for the development of a conservative movement that gained momentum throughout the 1960s and swept the political scene in the 1980s. An aspect of this movement that is both very interesting and not very well understood is its ability to hold various viewpoints together in a tension that itself seems very productive. Differences among conservatives, in fact, are often lost in discussions about conservative politics. Although the Christian right remains distinguishable in many ways from more secular aspects of the movement, it seems to blend into the conservative landscape. Yet these very deeply felt differences of opinion are alive and well and are shaping the political landscape in the United States today.

In the 1940s and 1950s, the differences among the economic libertarians and the "traditional" conservatives were so deep that speaking of *a* conservative movement was difficult. "Economic libertarians" or "libertarians" refers to groups who advance the idea that individual liberty must be closely guarded against state infringement. Often there is a natural rights caste to their positions, though not always. As discussed below, Judge Richard Posner describes himself as a "pragmatic economic libertarian" who does not seem particularly interested in the tenets of natural law and natural right in his work. However, a more idealistic approach, such as that advanced by Richard Epstein of the University of Chicago, seems to lean toward a natural right in property as a protection against governmental infringement of individual rights. "Traditional conservatives," or sometimes "Burkean conservatives," are often linked to Catholic political theory or a version of liberalism that places a much stronger emphasis on the importance of the political community and political processes for the protection and development of individuals. There is, within this community, a range of conservative thinkers. It should be noted, however, that none of these categories explicitly include the Christian right, a fact that is important to keep in mind both in discussing the conservative movement as it emerged in the mid-twentieth century and the movement of conservative lawyers we have in contemporary U.S. politics. In fact, within these discussions concerning property rights and economic liberties, it is rare to find Christian right lawyers despite their high visibility in litigation concerning social issues.

Beginning in the mid-1950s, what conservative historian George Nash refers to as "the great fusion" took place. This was a sort of rapprochement among various actors on the right side of the political spectrum (Nash 1996). In today's political scene, the Federalist Society is an excellent example of a conservative organization that enables a balance between various actors by providing a place where some conservatives come together and argue their differing positions with very little involvement from "liberals" and progressives.[7] But when the first conservative nonprofit legal foundation, the Pacific Legal Foundation, came on the scene in the early 1970s, scholars who were aware of its presence did not discuss the distinctions within the right and potential conflicts in conservative legal ideology. The distinctions, however, become glaringly apparent with closer scrutiny. Indeed, today's economic libertarians have become stronger politically and increasingly vocal in demanding recognition for their legal theory. One example of a conservative organization that is both identifiably "libertarian" and becoming increasingly prominent nationally is the Institute for Justice. However, before turning to them, a brief review of the early stages of right-wing legal foundations seems in order. Here, the Pacific Legal Foundation is an excellent point of departure as its history is representative of these roots.

The Pacific Legal Foundation

The Pacific Legal Foundation (PLF) is important for several reasons. It represents the beginning of nonprofit law firms devoted to right-wing causes and remains one of the most active conservative groups. It has worked in the area of property rights protection for nearly three decades, and recently has expanded its scope in terms of both particular strategies and moving into more areas of law. Property rights advocates use multiple strategies to accomplish their goals. The shifts in the PLF's strategies and tactics over time are indicative of the development of conservative legal activism. Case sponsorship was not a part of their strategies until changes in the judiciary created a hospitable environment for them (Smith 1993). Although they do react to "liberal," or more progressive, legal activism, they do not simply combat one ideology with another, but rather engage and work with various ideologies to produce particular ends. Legal maneuvering is part of their professional activities. With regard to conservative lawyering, the ideology of liberal legalism mingles with conservative politics to produce their particular brand of lawyering.

In 1973, the PLF was founded in California, during the governorship of Ronald Reagan by two members of his administration, Ronald Zumbrun and Raymond Momboisse (Aron 1989; Epstein 1985; O'Connor and Epstein 1989).[8] They, along with the California State Chamber of Commerce and other Reagan staffers, including Edwin Meese, hoped to provide a conservative answer to liberal activity by providing the courts with an alternative view of the public interest which would "combat" the liberals' use of the courts (Aron 1989; L. Epstein 1985). According to the PLF, its founders wanted "to preserve the basic freedoms set out by the U.S. Constitution and to reverse the growing trend toward greater government control and influence into American lives. [The founders of the PLF] also saw an increasingly politicized judiciary tending more and more to *make* laws rather than to interpret them" (PLF 1998). Rather than advocating specific causes, the PLF's goal was to address legal issues in California with particular attention to the legality of environmental impact reports. Over time, however, the PLF's strategies expanded to include litigating precedent-setting cases, legal research, public outreach, monitoring government administrative proceedings, preparation of legal briefs and oral arguments, moot court sessions, on-site meetings, and other related activities. Its fundraising apparatus and organization are impressive: with offices located in six states, its 2001 budget revenues exceeded $8,667,012, with 36.74 percent coming from individual donors, 36.52 percent from grants, 11.41 percent from corporate contributors, and the remaining coming through other forms of income (PLF Annual Report 2002: 6).

The PLF litigates cases throughout the country. In 2001, they were involved in 204 cases, sponsoring some while filing as *amici* in most of them (PLF Annual Report 2002: 4–5). If a case is one the PLF would like to see brought before the Supreme Court, the PLF assists the plaintiff by petitioning the Supreme Court for *writ of certiorari*. However, their primary litigation strategy remains the *amicus* brief. Through a process of monitoring cases around the country, the PLF files as *amici* in cases reaching federal appellate or state Supreme Court review (Kendall and Lord 1998; O'Connor and Epstein 1983). The PLF claims its work has impacted many areas of law, including land use, endangered species, agricultural development, public finance and taxation, education, welfare, public contracting and employment, energy development, national defense, and tort liability. The list suggests the degree to which the PLF's litigation activity has expanded well beyond its initial narrow scope. Yet it remains focused on economic interests. This is a result of the PLF's belief that economic liberty remains at the heart of individual freedom (PLF 1998).

The PLF was just the beginning. After opening for business, as Lee Epstein reports, its leadership contemplated the possibility of a wider conservative legal

movement. The PLF commissioned a study to determine the need and poten-
tial efficacy of such a movement, and as a result of the study, the National Legal
Center for the Public Interest (NLCPI) opened in 1975 (L. Epstein 1985: 125–26).
The NLCPI was instrumental in establishing a group of public interest law
foundations throughout the United States including organizations such as the
Mountain States Legal Foundation and the Southeastern Legal Foundation.
Other groups were also established in the same era, though they were not affiliated with the NLCPI, including the Washington Legal Foundation (Aron 1989;
L. Epstein 1985). Today, over a dozen conservative and economic libertarian organizations form a nationwide network of nonprofit organizations litigating
"in the public interest" on behalf of property interests as well as in other issue
areas. However, not all conservatives see the world in quite the same way, and as
the legal foundations proliferated, they also drew the criticism of some who felt
that economic liberties were not being defended as strongly as they should be
in the highly regulated society in which we live. As discussed below, the Institute for Justice was begun in order to establish yet another version of public interest groups, one grounded in libertarian principles and disinclined to accept
pragmatic answers to regulatory issues.

The Institute for Justice

William Mellor and Clint Bolick, both of whom formerly held positions in
President Reagan's administration, founded the Institute for Justice (IJ) in 1991.
The IJ claims to be the only true libertarian law group and proclaims itself the
best defender of civil rights and liberties throughout the political spectrum. It
is not directly affiliated with other conservative legal foundations, though it was
begun with the help of a grant from the Landmark Legal Foundation. According to IJ, Mellor and Bolick decided to start the organization out of a growing
concern that other conservatives were not working hard enough to protect economic liberties. Their goal at that time was to work to change the structure of
civil rights, to "reclaim the moral high ground" from the left (Mellor and Bolick 1991). Today, IJ plays an increasingly important role in litigation concerning
the Fifth Amendment's takings clause and conservative litigation more generally. Its goal, as stated in its literature, is to "[a]dvance a rule of law in which individuals control their destinies as free and responsible members of society" (IJ
2001). This is strikingly similar to the desires for a regularized legal process
where outcomes are predictable that was so salient among laissez-faire lawyers
in the previous century and seems to be a characteristic of liberal legal theory.
The IJ's strategies for attaining this goal include holding Policy Activist Seminars for practicing lawyers and educational programs for law students. In 2001,

their budget exceeded $2 million and revenues exceeded $5 million. IJ is active in areas including civil rights, economic liberties (claimed as civil rights), interracial adoption, mandatory community service, private property protection, welfare reform, and school choice (IJ 2001).

IJ openly advocates judicial activism, maintaining that the inconsistent record of the legislative and executive branches in protecting essential rights and liberties requires the judiciary to "serve as the bulwark of liberty." An underlying assumption is that the judicial branch must thwart any legislative action that contradicts the Constitution. As the IJ explains, "Unlike the executive and legislative branches, where the political dynamic makes any victory for liberty tenuous, courts can provide dramatic and lasting results. Yet courts cannot fulfill this vital role unless presented with skillfully argued cases guided by a long-term philosophically and tactically consistent strategy" (IJ 2001).

Litigation, then, is fundamental to IJ's strategy and the importance of argumentation is key here. Moreover, like the lawyers of 100 years ago, they emphasize having a theory that guides which cases they should take and which arguments they will make.

Their long-term goal is to overturn the 1873 *Slaughter-House Cases* and "restore judicial protection for economic liberty" (IJ 2001). In their analysis of the *Slaughter-House Cases*, the Institute for Justice maintain that this "relic" of constitutional law endangers "some of our most vital liberties—especially the right to earn an honest living—completely unprotected" (ibid.). They argue that one legacy of this case is that "the 'right' to a welfare check" receives greater protection than the "right to earn an honest living" (ibid., emphasis IJ's). In particular, these activists are concerned that the *Slaughter-House Cases* struck a "death blow" to the privileges and immunities clause, and that in the 120 years since the decision, that clause "has not been invoked to limit or strike down a single economic regulation, giving tragic prescience to the observation in Justice Field's *Slaughter-House* dissent that the majority opinion meant that the clause "was a vain and idle enactment which accomplished nothing" (ibid., citing 83 U.S. 96).

Ultimately, then, the IJ seeks to resurrect the privileges and immunities clause to protect economic liberties. They make it very clear that their goal is not to return to the days of substantive due process. IJ argues that using other constitutional privileges (such as the equal protection clause) is unsatisfactory in part because those provisions were never intended for use in economic regulation. However, they recognize that this is not an easy argument to make in court, and so while they frequently make a claim in their briefs regarding the privileges and immunities clause, they also argue cases on the basis of due process, equal protection, and the takings clause (ibid.).

Among their strategies, the IJ sponsors cases as well as pursuing various other means for achieving their ends. Such strategies include an active grass-roots campaign in areas of the country where they are litigating, hoping to "build public support and foster an ethos of economic liberty" (IJ 2001). Part of this includes a media strategy that IJ claims has been so successful in helping to win in state legislatures that it has robbed IJ of its ability to bring strong arguments regarding the privileges and immunities clause to court. Mellor explains, in his part of the joint speech made with Clint Bolick, that this is because legislators are responding to the vitality of IJ's activism (Mellor and Bolick 1991: 3). IJ also creates "nontraditional alliances" that "cut across racial, economic and ideological grounds," citing a case in Denver in which it allied itself with the NAACP (IJ 2001).

The IJ also files *amicus* briefs in major Supreme Court cases. An excellent example of this activity comes from IJ's work in takings cases. Richard Epstein, a University of Chicago Law School professor, is a frequent co-author of these briefs.[9] His scholarly work undergirds much of this group's property theory. He maintains that all transactions between the state and individuals should be treated as transactions between private individuals. Therefore, he argues, the constitutional test to determine whether a taking falls under Fifth Amendment protection is quite simple: "Would the government action be treated as a taking of private property if it had been performed by some private individual?" If so, then the taking must be compensated or deemed unconstitutional (R. Epstein 1985). Epstein's briefs are sometimes published and the Institute makes many of their legal documents available online as well. Through disseminating their ideas in these forms, their theories of property and the individual are presented to a wide audience of legal academics and lawyers.

Other conservative groups, including the PLF, maintain litigation strategies and view them as important to achieving their goals; they appear to understand the role of judges and courts in rather different ways. The PLF has not always advocated judge-made law, but instead argued that judges should show restraint and act as interpreters of the laws legislators make. This tends toward a more traditional conservative theory of judicial decision making. The PLF advocates a "common-sense policy" that charts a middle road between "laissez-faire anarchy and micromanaged, command and control, bureaucratic tyranny" (Best 1997: 1). The rights of citizens should always be placed ahead of the rules and regulations of bureaucracy, and judges should base their decisions upon what legislators require in the language of the statutes rather than their personal opinion. Judges are to be restrained, and the laws they interpret are to be grounded in common sense (Best 1997). Moreover, the law itself should be based upon principles that balance the interests of all the parties involved. The PLF's position makes the legislature the arena for much political debate, deferring to elected legislators to know what is in the best interests of the people, and desiring referenda and ballot initiatives from the people to provide legislators with direction. This position is similar to "reasoned elaboration," identified with some forms of sociological jurisprudence, though it has a populist twist in relying on popular democracy in some instances. It is most often maintained by many conservatives, who believe it is the best means of protecting citizens from the tyranny of judges while also maintaining the judiciary's legitimacy. The judge remains an active participant, but policy cannot be set by judges.[10]

IJ, on the other hand, views the judge as a pro-active participant in the law-making process, reviewing and striking down any legislation that is unconstitutional. Eschewing the approach that considers the "felt needs of the times" as important in judicial decision making, it wants judges to review legislation in light of the literal language of the Constitution. This perspective assumes that not only is the state to be severely limited, but also that the majority will mandate action that is not constitutionally sound. The IJ operates as if the courts were the ultimate defenders of personal freedom. This contrasts with the more procedural understanding of legal decision making advocated by other conservatives. In this respect, the PLF and others like them are reminiscent of the earliest legal realists, who were concerned that the courts would lose their place in the political system if judges were too activist (Kalman 1986).

This is one of the more important aspects of conservative activism, that is, the way in which the different understandings of appropriate judicial roles manifest themselves among various positions. Indeed, the difference in the areas of law in which each organization is active may be partly shaped by the different perspectives concerning appropriate judging. The highly idealistic IJ, perceiving a more dramatic role, tends to litigate in many more areas of law. This suggests the depth of their belief in the judiciary as the protector of personal liberties. Thus, while both groups have adopted strategies informed by liberal legalism, IJ's position tends to be more reminiscent of the belief that Stuart Scheingold refers to as "the myth of rights" (Scheingold 1974: 39–61).

Among conservatives working to advance property rights, the ideology underpinning beliefs concerning the roles of judges and lawyers as well as the "public interest" is largely the same today as it was in the nineteenth century, despite other shifts in the social context. Thus, their arguments are strikingly similar in both periods. But with the rise of the public interest law practice in the twentieth century, today's lawyers make one tactical move that sets them apart from their nineteenth-century predecessors: they do not openly work on behalf of large corporations as the laissez-faire lawyers of the last century did, but rather position themselves as seeking justice for the "little guy"—quite often, small businesses and private property owners fighting state regulations. The advent of the public interest lawyer in society, then, provides these lawyers with a legal form that advances their ideology while appearing to work on behalf of disadvantaged individuals. This results in an odd mixture of ideals and language from both centuries. In order to produce this mixture and find a balance within conflicting viewpoints, conservative lawyers have formed spaces within the legal academy to develop their theories. These I term "safe havens" because they were created as part of a critique of the supposed liberalism of the legal academy and as a means of providing conservative law students with support for their work. However, they take on a special function as power in the form of money, grants, and ideas flows through them into the legal practices of various conservative lawyers, including property rights advocates. In the next section I will discuss two such safe havens: the Federalist Society and the law and economics movement.

Intellectuals, Property Rights, and the Creation of Safe Havens

As Kalman (1996) explains, in the late 1970s and early 1980s, concerns about the lack of conservatives in the legal academy led conservative legalists to call for the creation of spaces that would encourage and support law students interested in pursuing conservative jurisprudence (77–78). Quickly thereafter, the Federalist Society took shape as a debating society at Yale Law School, the University of Chicago School of Law, and Harvard Law School, and within a few years, chapters sprang up throughout the country (Carter 2001). Predating the federalists by over a decade but also an important place for conservative legal scholars and their students was the development of the law and economics movement (Kalman 1996: 79; Minda 1995: 83). This group's greatest contributors have been at the University of Chicago, but it also had strong proponents at other institutions, including more liberal theorists such as Guido Calabresi, who at that time was the Dean of Yale Law School.[11]

Although both law and economics and the Federalist Society have been linked to conservative political agendas, the law and economics movement, in contrast to the Federalist Society, is most often considered an "academic movement" within the legal academy. It is not intended to be a debating society but is rather a group of legal academics and practitioners seeking to understand the way in which the economic analysis of law can enable sound judicial interpretation. Nor does the law and economics movement have an organizational structure that includes boards of directors, law school chapters, or practice groups designed to enable more effective lawyering, as does the Federalist Society. Yet these scholars hold conferences, maintain journals, and provide like-minded lawyers and other scholars with a place to develop their ideas. There are significant differences in organizational and structural elements; for our purposes here the most important aspect of both groups and their relationship to one another is the way they function as spaces where legal ideology can be formed by conservative lawyers and scholars.

By focusing our attention here, we can see the importance of professional competition in the creation of legal ideologies while exploring the way in which ideas are developed before being implemented through legal advocacy. But also quite importantly, we can discover legal realism serving as a backdrop for much of what occurs in these safe havens. The engagement with legal realism, I argue, serves to re-create it as well as enables the production of conservative forms of legal ideology. These engagements around legal realism and the working out of conservative legal ideology demonstrate the empirical reality that ideologies are constantly undergoing reproduction and transformation (Harrington 1994: 61). Moreover, we can see that the conditions within the legal academy and within this movement of property rights advocates produce certain idioms. It is their potential for elaboration that enables transformation and sustenance for conservative lawyers as these legal ideologies take shape (Harrington 1994).

Epstein and Posner: Law, Economics, and Utility

In the 1970s, Richard Epstein, now active with the IJ while serving on the faculty at the University of Chicago School of Law, spent time examining the economic analysis of law, particularly with reference to strict liability in tort law. His work eventually led him to critique the concept of utilitarianism as used by Judge Posner and some of the other scholars in the law and economics movement (R. Epstein 1985, 1979). Epstein's critique, along with those made by Ronald Dworkin (1978), led to Posner's distinction between philosophical utilitarianism and economic utilitarianism that also enabled his separation of "normative" and "positive" theory. At the same time that Epstein was engaging with Posner on these issues, he was working out a property theory and an interpretation of the takings clause of the Fifth Amendment that has become critical to many of the rights claims made by lawyers in libertarian cases. This work was eventually set out in Epstein's full-length monograph, *Takings: Private Property and the Power of Eminent Domain* in 1985.

Epstein's critique of utilitarianism and wealth maximization was grounded in his interest in developing a theory of takings that would require compensation by the government for nearly all takings and severely limit eminent domain powers. He views taxation as a form of taking as well as land use restrictions and zoning generally associated with this area of law. He argues that utilitarianism, when applied to takings issues, would bring about "perverse" results because of the "leaps of faith required" (R. Epstein 1985: 200). This is largely because a utilitarian analysis would require "perfect knowledge" on the part of the state in order to determine what form of compensation would be required. Thus, Epstein says:

> The conclusion here seems odd, if not perverse, because the general assumption is that the eminent domain clause protects only individual rights, leaving to the political branches of government the unique power to decide the utilitarian question of whether to proceed. The conceptual point raises serious questions about the state's power to initiate programs. Nonetheless, the conclusion seems inescapable on formal grounds. The only way to compensate net losers is through tax revenues, but these too are takings of private property requiring compensation. (R. Epstein 1985: 200)

Epstein sees this perversity as occurring largely because the state cannot be trusted to make the correct calculations and protect individual rights since ultimately it would always work to protect its own interests. A fervent believer that judges should be the defenders of individual liberty, he is also a fervent believer that the political branches will always seek to empower themselves (through taxes and takings, for example) at the cost of individual liberty.

The more interesting and perhaps, for this discussion, the more important angle in Epstein's argument has to do with the appropriate relationship between the individual and the state. He argued from an almost Hobbesian perspective regarding the state of nature, seeing it as a place where all war against all in a self-interested contest to obtain the greatest amount of wealth. He said that in this state of nature there were two major failures: the first was to protect against private aggression; and the second was that individuals would not voluntarily work to create the centralized power to combat private aggression (R. Epstein 1985: 5). Thus, the state was created to rectify both of these problems— but this is really the only purpose of the state. Its work is not to redistribute income or ensure that distributive justice will be done. Instead, says Epstein, anytime the state acts in a way that, had it been a private individual its action would be considered a private aggression, the state should be held responsible just as a private individual would be held responsible. In essence, this is an expansion of tort law such that the state would have to compensate for any type of public use of private property even as individuals infringing on the rights of another individual would be required to provide compensation for the action.

Ultimately, Epstein's argument rests on a natural rights theory found in liberal political theory for its foundation of legal interpretation.

Posner took exception to much of Epstein's argument, particularly when the language of rights was introduced. Posner (1993) argues in *The Problems of Jurisprudence,* in an extensive discussion of Epstein's work, that the line between regulation and redistribution is "too uncertain to support the structure of permissions and prohibitions that Epstein erects on it" (344). Posner went on to explain that there were times when we might see rich people hurting (i.e., "harm") poor people and determine that redistribution would be the best form of redress for this situation: "Then redistributive measures would be a method of correcting negative externalities" (344). But perhaps Judge Posner's most stinging criticism in a community seeking more democratic jurisprudence is that Epstein's theory would, when taken to its final conclusion, prove to be antidemocratic:

> the approach would encounter the objection that it is anti-democratic, because it greatly curtails the scope of democratic decision making. The people get to choose the administrators, but not, for the most part, the policies; those are prescribed by libertarian theory. I do not wish to seem misty-eyed about democracy . . . the precise extent to which the democratic principle should be allowed to prevail over competing political principles is highly contestable . . . a pragmatist will demand that the libertarian demonstrate that the risks entailed by such a curtailment are acceptable. (345)

Such a demonstration would, of course, require empirical evidence. Ultimately it is Posner's desire for this empirical evidence that leads to his rejection of Epstein's theory on the grounds that it would be impossible to know what is or is not "natural"—*as an empirical matter. It, too, is a matter of philosophical reasoning* and philosophy is no basis for constitutional theory (Posner 1997: 345).

The disagreement here is over what is truly conservative and what is truly the best form of democratic government. It turns on an epistemological debate: How do we know what the law is? Do we find it through philosophical inquiry into natural rights? Or do we find it through the precise evaluation performed through objective criteria? Yet, throughout this debate, there is no doubt that either individual is libertarian at heart. Indeed, unlike the strident comments Posner often makes concerning liberal and progressive legal theorists, with Epstein he is rigorous yet respectful. He introduces Epstein with a discussion of his brilliance. Epstein, when he took over the *Journal of Legal Studies,* wrote a preface to the first volume under his editorship honoring Judge Posner. This is not the sort of discussion Posner had with progressive law and economics scholar Professor Robin Paul Malloy, who in law reviews and a debate critiqued Posner's theories as lacking morality (Malloy 1994a, 1994b; Posner 1994). There, Posner's attitude was openly hostile. Posner and Epstein, by contrast, through their treatment of each other's works, regard each other as fellow conservatives while simultaneously distinguishing their separate positions. They are, according to each other, libertarians of different stripes. Epstein is much less likely to accept certain types of regulations and redistributions. Posner, however, suggests that he can see regulations and redistributions might be necessary if they maximize a society's wealth. Whether he really would find them acceptable is, I think, open to question. But his position suggests he can conceive of a wide array of possibilities. Just as the law and economics movement provided a space where conservatives could debate with one another and constitute one another's identities, the Federalist Society as discussed below provides all of this as well as a means of instructing lawyers in better legal practice.

The Federalist Society: Critiquing and Changing the Legal Academy

As the story of the founding of the Federalist Society is told, Steve Calabresi, nephew of Judge Guido Calabresi (at that time dean of the Yale Law School) and now a law professor at Northwestern University School of Law, was sitting with his class at Yale Law School one day when he and his classmates were asked how many people voted for President Reagan. According to Calabresi, only two in a class of eighty-eight raised their hands. At that moment, Calabresi claims, he realized that conservatives did not have a place to meet, support one another, and develop their ideas. As he told the *American Bar Association Journal*, "I think some others in that room had voted for him, and I realized we needed an organization to at least encourage others to come forward" (as cited in Carter 2001: 47). Indeed, the lack of a conservative presence in law schools had been noted even by liberals. Laura Kalman (1995) quotes Alan Freeman as stating that he had his "first authentic right-wing student in about 1974, and felt sorry for him in his loneliness and alienation" (77). And, as already stated, conservatives were and have continued to be deeply concerned with the liberal legal academy, particularly as they blame it for many of the difficulties they see society facing today. Judge Robert Bork, at the first national meeting of the Federalist Society, stated the position quite succinctly: "The Court responds to the press and law school faculties. The personnel of the media are heavily left-liberal. Their values are quite egalitarian and permissive. Law school faculties tend to have the same politics and values. So if there are new constitutional values they will be the values of that class" (Associated Press 1982).

Founded in 1982 by five law students, the Federalist Society attracted the most important conservative law scholars, judges, and lawyers to their national meetings. Their mission statement explicitly states their goal as reforming the current legal order: "We are committed to the principles that the state exists to preserve freedom, that the separation of governmental powers is central to our Constitution, and that it is emphatically the province and the duty of the judiciary to say what the law is, not what it should be. The Society seeks to promote awareness of these principles and to further their application through its activities" (Federalist Society 2001a).

The Society seeks to provide a forum for "legal experts of opposing views to interact with members of the legal profession, the judiciary, law students, academics, and the architects of public policy" (Federalist Society 2001a). Today's Federalist Society has a membership of more than 5,000 law students and 20,000 legal professionals. It holds national symposiums twice a year and maintains student, lawyer, and faculty divisions in addition to fifteen practice groups in various areas of law.[12] The 145 individual student chapters around the country hold meetings in which featured speakers discuss their views and interact with students.

The national lawyers' conventions, which began in 1986, feature speakers from various parts of the political spectrum, including the leading lights in the conservative movement such as Judge Frank Easterbrook, Edwin Meese, and speakers from "opposing viewpoints" such as Nadine Strossen and Laurence Tribe. Speakers attend the meetings of the individual practice groups and discuss issues directly related to those areas of law. They also feature plenary panels in which judicial decision making and salient political and legal issues are debated among panelists from conservative, right libertarian, and "liberal" positions.

Very shortly after its establishment, luminaries no less prominent than President Ronald Reagan and Attorney General Edwin Meese were among the speakers at Federalist Society meetings, encouraging the development of the organization while also allowing their political views to be aired. By 1985, just three years after the organization was created, Edwin Meese used its meetings as a forum for critiquing the U.S. Supreme Court justices. Having recently opened a debate with the justices in which he said they were engaging in "chameleon jurisprudence, changing color and form in each era," Attorney General Meese maintained that "This approach to jurisprudence has led to some remarkable and tragic consequences" (as cited in Shenon 1985: 11). His use of the meeting as a platform for a critique of the judiciary has been repeated dozens of times over the last two decades. These speakers also brought support and encouragement with them. In 1987, President Reagan, speaking at a meeting in Washington D.C., told the 500 participants, "Your work is having an impact" (as cited in Taylor 1987: 18). From its inception, the arguments among conservatives have been heated. For example, at this same meeting, Judge Bork suggested that it was too late to turn back New Deal policies. This suggestion was not well received by his audience and sparked a heated discussion, but the debate caused him to remark later that "We didn't used to have things like this," referring to the activity of debating ideas with other conservatives and being criticized by them (as cited in Taylor 1987: 18).

Noteworthy is the fact that the formation of the Federalist Society was student led and while it involved key faculty at Yale, Harvard, and the University of Chicago, it was organized by law students for law students. The national student symposiums were the first meetings the Society held, and they continue to be strongly attended today. Speakers here, too, include the biggest names in the business, with Laurence Tribe and other liberal lawyers making appearances on select panels in addition to Judge Posner, Judge Easterbrook, Richard Epstein, Lino Graglia, and various other important conservative legal theorists. As the founding members moved into their professional careers, the Federalist Society expanded. Indeed, the organization appears to have developed into a professional organization as its founding members developed from law students to key players in the Washington legal scene. Such former members include Gale Norton, Spencer Abraham (a founding member), as well as a large number of individuals working in the Justice Department and former Supreme Court clerks.

The Society is very action-oriented. The practice groups have the continued training of legal professionals at the heart of their activity. The law school debates have the training and development of future lawyers in mind. And the newest division for faculty has the further development of their ideas and careers as an important goal. Ideas are clearly important to the Federalist Society, but so is the ability to activate those ideas. That "reform" is a part of their mission statement is noteworthy. It suggests that these conservatives believe they can activate the theories they develop together and implement them to change the judiciary into what they believe it ought to be—and thereby change the tenor of U.S. politics. The issue, however, is what will this look like? How will the judiciary operate if the members are able to implement their ideas?

In their mission statement, the Federalist Society states that it is "emphatically the duty of the judiciary to say what the law is, not what it should be" (Federalist Society 2001a). Given the source of the statement, it would be easy to associate it with the advocacy of original intent. Yet in making this connection, there is a risk of overemphasizing originalism as the only domain of the conservative, missing what a truly conservative jurisprudence would be. As Keith Whittington has pointed out, originalism is readily connected to conservative political views:

> because so many of its modern defenders are also identifiable conservatives. This easy identification has developed in part because of a failure of imagination as to what a truly "conservative" judicial policy might be, despite the existence of various academic exemplars. A truly conservative approach to judicial interpretation would focus not only a relatively neutral methodology such as originalism but would embrace a more explicitly substantive vision of constitutional meaning that brought it into line with conservative policy making. (Whittington 1999: 167)

An interesting aspect of the Federalist Society is that, because of its desire to bring together conservatives and right libertarians, there is considerable disagreement within the membership as to what "the law" is and where to find it. That is, the substantive constitutional meaning remains contested among property rights advocates. Although some adhere to original intent and are very concerned with what the Founding Fathers thought about constitutional matters, right libertarians tend to be much less concerned with intent and instead ground their theories of legal decision making in textualism. Richard Posner, who claims to be a pragmatic economic libertarian, and other advocates of law and economics ground their theories, as has been discussed above, in efficiency and wealth maximization. These, however, are theories of jurisprudence and do not necessarily provide conservatives more generally with the substantive meaning of the Constitution. To state this in a way that social scientists can relate to, they are arguing over method rather than research findings.

Since many conservatives agree that the state exists to protect the individual and therefore the state should be as small as possible with a free market leading to free people, it is easy to see these differences as very small ones. Although this might not seem very important, it can mean more statist approaches among traditional conservatives that directly conflict with a right libertarian antistatist approach. Although these difference are not always fully appreciated, members of the Federalist Society are well aware of them, and they can become quite heated in debates where issues of authority come into play in determining who understands "the law" the best.

Again we perceive a search for a foundation to ground legal interpretation among these conservative legal theorists, and the legal realism that conservatives fear is part of the liberalism of the legal academy provides a foil in their arguments and once again constitutes these politics. Right libertarians, such as Richard Epstein, view the language of the Constitution as the final authority concerning what is or is not constitutional. However, other conservatives, such as Judge Robert Bork, look to original intent as their groundwork (as cited in Whittington 1999: 167).[13] Neither Posner nor Epstein think that the Founding Fathers' intentions are particularly important when interpreting constitutional law, preferring instead to ground interpretation of the Constitution in theories of utility maximization or Natural Law.

Conclusions: Shifting Strategies in Shifting Contexts

Conservative legal activism did not spontaneously erupt on the political scene in the 1970s and 1980s. Rather, this activism appears to be part of conservatism and right-wing activity that stretches far back into our history. One issue investigated here is the connection property rights advocates have to the history of laissez-faire and its development as an ideology underpinning nineteenth-century jurisprudence—not only during the Lochner era in Supreme Court history, but also through the development of professional bar associations, changes in law school curriculum, and the development of the legal profession in its modern form.[14] My argument is that these last developments were part of the ideological construction of laissez-faire along with the legal academy, and they serve to shape some of the ideas fueling today's conservative legal activism and legal ideology.

When turning attention to the late nineteenth century in U.S. law, it is often the case that the first thing one thinks of is the events leading up to what is known as the Lochner era. In the way this narrative is usually constructed, activists are found in the labor movement at the state level and they attempt to expand regulations to protect workers from exploitative business practices. As this story runs, these activists contend with a conservative judiciary that, particularly with regard to the U.S. Supreme Court, sees its chief purpose as the protection of economic liberties. The interpretations of why the Lochner era came to be and how to understand its culmination are many (Cushman 1998; Gillman 1993; Kens 1998). Yet, quite often, these stories underanalyze the importance of how the judiciary *became* conservative. For this, it is important to go back further, to the years following the Civil War when the United States was undergoing a fast and in many ways brutal industrialization process. During these years, the bar was also undergoing a transformation that would have lasting consequences for law in society. Although it is true that one can go back to before the Civil War to begin a discussion of the rise of laissez-faire lawyers, their activity during the Reconstruction is especially intriguing given the larger goals of this analysis. They were, in many ways, setting the pattern for conservative legal advocacy as it has emerged in more recent times.[15]

The shape of this pattern and the practices that constitute it provide the ideological basis for laissez-faire claims even as they produce that ideology (Harrington 1994). Laissez-faire lawyers of the previous century and their contemporary counterparts are "knowing participants" in the legal culture, whose knowledge involves a communal understanding of the language of the law (Brigham 1987). Thus, their understanding of what are effective strategies and how best to achieve their ends is informed by their status as active participants in a professional terrain—a terrain including a particular language bounded by the rules of appropriate behavior and the possibilities for influencing judges. In the late nineteenth century, this professional terrain was developing with the rise of professions and the desire for expertise. However, laissez-faire lawyers also were part of that professionalization, working on its behalf in the hopes that it would provide them with a means by which they could see their goals attained. These lawyers developed the grammar in which their twentieth-century counterparts are schooled and speak with ease and appropriate etiquette. In both periods, lawyers can be seen working with ideologies, and through this work, constructing it within an awareness of their particular audience (Harrington 1994). As Benjamin Twiss (1942) pointed out in his study of laissez-faire lawyers, they understand the landscape within which they work because they are part of it, and they choose to use language and other types of practices that will empower them and legitimize their claims before judges and legislators.

Other scholars have demonstrated that the legal activism we saw in the late nineteenth century occurred as the state addressed social issues arising during industrialization (Kolko 1963; Paul 1960; Twiss 1942). The relationship between this transformation and changes in capitalism is an important part of the story (Gordon 1983; Miller 1968). Other scholars have demonstrated that as the market economy took shape, lawyers working on behalf of corporate interests attempted to persuade the courts toward laissez-faire jurisprudence. The acceptance of many laissez-faire ideas served as the backdrop for scholarly understandings of progressivism, with the progressives coming onto the scene during a period of increased conflict in the hopes of reforming a system where capitalism was running amuck (Gillman 1993; Gillman and Clayton 1999; Skowronek 1982). Further, because nineteenth-century laissez-faire lawyers' tactics and strategies are very similar but not identical to today's conservative and libertarian legal activists, studying them provides suggestions for ways we can understand today's legal activism and the ways in which changes in society, political institutions, and the legal profession give it shape.

Once we move to the last half of the twentieth century we find that in both contexts, the state is attempting to adapt to shifts in capitalism and the economy. In the late twentieth century, some of these changes result in a reaction to the changing structure of property relations occurring through environmental law. Increased environmental protections during the Cold War and an increased concern regarding pollution have had the effect of changing relations between landowners, their land, and the state. Conservatives, always concerned with the connection between property and liberty, have mobilized in order to strengthen the due compensation requirement of the takings clause. Against this backdrop and in discussions among lawyers concerning correct interpretation of the property guarantees in the Fifth Amendment, issues arise regarding the rule of law and the appropriate role of the legal profession. The point here is that conservatives are active in both periods in part as a reaction to what they see as expanding regulations that would encroach on individual liberty; and, in both periods we find disagreements among conservatives concerning the role of the state in protecting economic liberties. The state does not utilize *the same* strategies in both periods, nor do property relations change in the same way; rather, the simple fact that the regulation of property itself changes seems to mobilize these lawyers. And, in both periods, the movements to retrench property rights also seem to spill over into issues concerning the legal profession and judges.

Like their nineteenth-century counterparts, the right-wing activists I describe rely on the importance of private property and the clear distinction between the public and private spheres to ground their arguments. Individual liberty is seen as a means for ensuring upward economic and social mobility. Equality is defined as the law's neutrality to social differences. And, like their nineteenth-century counterparts, they also see the courts as a place to go when others are interfering with individual liberties—others, including the government in the form of environmental and land use policies. How best to understand the work of these lawyers, I would argue, should remain an open question until more studies have been done that consider them from various epistemological positions. Within discussions about cause lawyers and cause lawyering, right-wing activity is not always understood to fit in the literature. Whether we distinguish "cause lawyering" and "cause lawyers" for analytical purposes, the lawyers discussed here fit uneasily within a literature that has long been about progressive and liberal lawyers working on behalf of underprivileged or disempowered clients. Yet it is precisely the tension that inclusion of right-wing lawyers creates that may be productive and enable a fuller understanding of what these categories describe. Their work and the settings in which they operate may provide contrasts as well as draw attention to the way similarities can inform our understandings of the links lawyers have to social change, especially in a world where neoliberalism and global capitalism are increasingly linked to lawyers (Shamir, this volume). By comparing the work of lawyers from various political and normative positions—and in this I do not mean simply trying to understand motivation and identity issues, but rather the way motivation, identity, and institutions become connected in their work—we can develop a much richer understanding of the changing forms of legal practice and their relationship to political and social transformation.

Notes

This work is based upon my dissertation entitled "Conservative Cause Advocacy: The Multiple Sites of Conservative Legal Ideology" (Amherst, Mass.: University of Massachusetts, 2002). Besides owing a great debt of gratitude to the contributors and editors of this volume for their suggestions, I would also like to express my gratitude to Farid Benavides, John Brigham, Laura Donaldson, Alec Ewald, Sheldon Goldman, Christine Harrington, Rhys Livingstone, Aaron Lorenz, Erika Marquez, and Janet Rifkin for their support and help in reading drafts of various forms of this work.

1. Some of the best work of this type can be found in the previous two cause lawyering volumes (Sarat and Scheingold 1998, 2001).

2. The takings clause requires just compensation for any property taken by the government. However, what constitutes a "taking" has recently become a very important issue as more forms of property proliferate in U.S. culture than existed at the time the Fifth Amendment was written. Moreover, the issue of what "just compensation" means has long been alive and well in constitutional jurisprudence, though it tends to be a more contested issue in periods when there are changes to capitalism, for example, through the transformation from a more agrarian-based economy to the industrialized form at the end of the nineteenth century and more recently, the move to protect the environment and regulate land, which has placed a great deal of pressure on the notion of "just compensation" as questions concerning the economic interests involved in land development have been raised in cases such as *Nollan v. California Coastal Commission* and, quite recently, *Palazzolo v. Rhode Island*.

3. There is an extensive literature on this, including the work of Karl Klare (1979), Alan Hunt (1985), and Isaac Balbus (1976) in sociology of law. The discussion here draws heavily on Brigham (1996) and Harrington (1994) as they apply these ideas to the way in which ideology shapes political interests and legal practices.

4. For insightful discussions of Cooley, see Kens (1998) and Twiss (1942).

5. On the social and professional backgrounds of lawyers in the period, see Twiss

(1942) and Paul (1960), and just after the turn of the century, see Miller (1951); for discussions of the development of bar associations and the roles of elite lawyers, see Powell (1988), Halliday (1987), and Warren (1966). Through a process of cross-checking for names of lawyers in these and the various works cited in this chapter, I was able to locate many of the same individuals documented as working in various arenas of public life.

6. See the discussion of the *Slaughter-House Cases* at the Institute for Justice's Web page at www.ij.org. Further discussion of this case and its symbolic importance follows in the next section of this chapter.

7. As part of my research, I attended the student meeting of the Federalist Society held at Harvard Law School in March 2000. Liberals and progressives do attend these meetings, though they are few and far between. However, the variation among conservatives was remarkable, even to someone who has lived in Utah and Idaho for a large amount of her life. Their willingness to engage in debates over theoretical issues was also remarkable, though there was a not surprising tendency to deploy straw men and denigrate positions that could not be identified as "conservative." Of course, the same is often true of liberals and progressives when they discuss ideas that are conservative. Indeed, in listening to various conversations where liberals and conservatives attempt to speak with one another, I am often reminded of Lyotard's notion of a differend, where the ability to communicate is frustrated because the parties are using what amounts to two different languages (Lyotard 1988). Although I deal in more detail with the Federalist Society in other work, space limitations require the focus to remain on the right libertarian group, the Institute for Justice.

8. Momboisse served as assistant attorney general in then Governor Reagan's administration, and in that capacity had litigated on behalf of welfare reforms challenged by liberal public interest groups. Similarly Zumbrun advised the Department of Welfare under Reagan, and lobbied on its behalf in a state House heavily opposed to Reagan's reforms.

9. Epstein fits quite nicely into the tradition of lawyers who wear several hats. In addition to writing books and law review articles, he is also active in litigation, appears as a consultant on various news shows, and was at one time considered for a judicial appointment by President Reagan.

10. This position may be changing. Shortly after the 2000 presidential election, the PLF seemed to move away from this position toward something closer to the IJ's. However, at the time this was written, the data remained inconclusive. Whether the shift was related to the changes in the political context, organizational issues, or the perceived ability to win with a stronger form of private property rights claims remains an open question.

11. Calabresi was the dean of Yale Law School and now serves as a judge for the U.S. Court of Appeals, 2nd Circuit. He is the uncle of Stephen Calabresi, one of the founders of the Federalist Society.

12. Those practice groups include areas of law such as administrative law and regulation; professional responsibility; intellectual property; financial service and e-commerce; international and national security law; labor and employment law.

13. Whittington describes three such exemplars: Richard Epstein, Richard Posner,

and Hadley Arkes. I am inclined to agree with Whittington's analysis here and would like
to suggest that the same can be said to be true for liberal or progressive jurisprudence.
However, one reason it does not happen is related to the apolitical politics described in
the judicial selection chapter. Professor Whittington's views were recently cited with approval by Randy Barnet of Boston University School of Law at the 2002 National Student
Symposium of the Federalist Society. At the meeting, he was the only political scientist
discussed and it was with explicit reference to his work on originalism.

14.   In particular, see Paul (1960) and Twiss (1942). Other work done by sociologists
and historians in this same historical period that explores some of the same themes includes Halliday and Karpik (1997), Powell (1988), and Warren (1966).

15.   One is reminded of Charles Tilly's (1995) discussion of the repertoire of activism
that enables activists to gain ground as long as that repertoire has salience within the society (see also Tarrow [1998]).

References

Aron, Nan. 1989. *With Liberty and Justice for All: Public Interest in the 1980s and Beyond.*
Boulder, Colo.: Westview Press.

Associated Press. 1982. "Federal Judge Assails Supreme Court Ruling." *New York Times*
(April 27): Section A.

Auerbach, Jerold S. 1975. *Unequal Justice: Lawyers and Social Change in Modern America.*
New York: Oxford University Press.

Balbus, Isaac. 1976. *The Dialectics of Legal Repression: Black Rebels Before the American
Criminal Courts.* New Brunswick: Transaction Books.

Best, Robert K. 1997. "A Common Sense Policy to Protect the Environment." *Monograph
Series,* Issue MS–4, Pacific Legal Foundation Web page, www.pacificlegal.org/mn-
grph4.htm (retrieved August 1997).

Brigham, John. 1987. *The Cult of the Court.* Philadelphia: Temple University Press.

———. 1996. *The Constitution of Interests: Beyond the Politics of Rights.* New York: New
York University Press.

Carter, Terry. 2001. "The In Crowd: Conservatives Who Sought Refuge in the Federalist
Society Gain Clout." *ABA Journal* September: 46.

Connor, William. 1920. *John Archibald Campbell: Associate Justice of the United States
Supreme Court, 1853-1861. Boston and New York: Houghton Mifflin Company.*

Cooley, Thomas M. 1972. *A Treatise on the Constitutional Limitations which Rest Upon the
Legislative Powers of the States of the American Union.* New York: DeCapo Press.

———. 1880. *The General Principles of Constitutional Law in the United States of America.* Boston: Little, Brown.

Cushman, Barry. 1998. *Rethinking the New Deal Court: The Structure of a Constitutional
Revolution.* Oxford and New York: Oxford University Press.

Dworkin, Ronald. 1978. *Taking Rights Seriously.* Cambridge: Harvard University Press.

Dyer, Brainerd. 1933. *The Public Career of William Evarts.* Berkeley: University of California Press.

Epstein, Lee. 1985. *Conservatives in Court.* Knoxville: University of Tennessee Press.

Epstein, Richard. 1979. "Nuisance Law: Corrective Justice and Its Utilitarian Constraints." *Journal of Legal Studies* 8: 49.

———. 1985. *Takings: Private Power and the Power of Eminent Domain.* Cambridge: Harvard University Press.

Federalist Society. 2001a. "Mission Statement." Federalist Society Web pagewww.fed-soc.org (retrieved April 15, 2001).

———. 2001b. "Our Background." Federalist Society Web page www.fed-soc.org (retrieved April 15, 2001).

Gillman, Howard. 1993. *The Constitution Besieged: The Rise and Demise of Lochner Era Police Powers Jurisprudence.* Durham, N.C.: Duke University Press.

Gillman, Howard, and Cornell Clayton, eds. 1999. *The Supreme Court in American Politics: New Institutionalist Perspectives.* Lawrence: University Press of Kansas.

Gordon, Robert. 1983. "Legal Thought and Legal Practice in the Age of American Enterprise, 1870–1920," in *Professions and Professional Ideologies in America,* ed. Gerald L. Geison. Chapel Hill: University of North Carolina Press.

Halliday, Terence. 1987. *Beyond Monopoly: Lawyers, State Crises, and Professional Empowerment.* Chicago: University of Chicago Press.

Halliday, Terence, and Lucian Karpik. 1997. *Lawyers and the Rise of Western Political Liberalism.* Oxford and New York: Clarendon Press.

Harrington, Christine. 1994. "Outlining a Theory of Practice," in *Lawyers in a Postmodern World: Translation and Transgression,* ed. Maureen Cain and Christine B. Harrington. New York: New York University Press.

Hatcher, Laura. 2002. *Conservative Cause Advocacy: Mapping the Cites of Conservative Legal Activism.* Amherst, Mass.: University of Massachusetts.

Heinz, John, Anthony Paik, and Ann Southworth. 2003. "Lawyers for Conservative Causes: Clients, Ideology and Social Distance." *Law and Society Review* 37, no. 1: 5 .

Hunt, Alan. 1985. "The Ideology of Law: Advances and Problems in Recent Applications of the Concept of Ideology to the Analysis of Law." *Law and Society Review* 19, no. 1: 11.

Institute for Justice. 2001. Institute for Justice website. www.ij.org. Retrieved August 2001.

Jameson, J. Franklin. 1926. *The American Revolution Considered as a Social Movement.* Cambridge: Harvard University Press.

Kalman, Laura. 1986. *Legal Realism at Yale, 1927–1960.* Chapel Hill: University of North Carolina Press.

———. 1996. *The Strange Career of Legal Realism.* New Haven, Conn.: Yale University Press.

Kendall, David T., and Charles P. Lord. 1998. "The Takings Project: A Critical Analysis and Assessment of the Progress So Far." *Environmental Affairs* 25: 509.

Kens, Paul. 1998. *Lochner v. New York: Economic Regulation on Trial.* Lawrence: University Press of Kansas.

Klare, Karl. 1979. "Law Making as Praxis." *Telos* 40: 123.

Kolko, Gabriel. 1963. *The Triumph of Conservatism: A Reinterpretation of American History, 1900–1916.* New York: Free Press.

Larson, Magli Saffarti. 1977. *The Rise of Profesionalism: A Sociological Analysis.* Berkeley: University of California Press.

Lyotard, Jean-Francois. 1988. *The Differend: Phrases in Dispute.* Minneapolis: University of Minnesota Press.

Malloy, Robin Paul. 1994a. "Law and Economics Is Moral," in *Adam Smith and the Philosophy of Law and Economics*, ed. Robin Paul Malloy and Jerry Evinsky. Boston: Kluwer Academic.

———. 1994b. "Rebuttal Response to Posner," in *Adam Smith and the Philosophy of Law and Economics*, ed. Robin Paul Malloy and Jerry Evinsky. Boston: Kluwer Academic.

McCann, Michael W. 1986. *Taking Reform Seriously: Perspectives on Public Interest Liberalism.* Ithaca, N.Y.: Cornell University Press.

———. 1994. *Rights at Work: Pay Equity Reform and the Politics of Legal Mobilization.* Chicago: University of Chicago Press.

McCann, Michael W., and Helena Silverstein. 1999. "Rethinking Law's 'Allurements': A Relational Analysis of Social Movement Lawyers in the United States,"in *Cause Lawyering: Political Commitments and Professional Responsibilities*, ed. Stuart Scheingold and Austin Sarat. Oxford and London: Oxford University Press.

Mellor, William H., and Clint Bolick. 1991. "The Quest for Justice: Natural Right and the Future of Public Interest Law." Heritage Lecture 342. Speech made before the Heritage Foundation, September 10, 1991, published on the Institute for Justice's website, www.ij.org, downloaded in March 2001.

Minda, Gary. 1995. *Postmodern Legal Movements: Law and Jurisprudence at Century's End.* New York: New York University Press.

Miller, Arthur Selwyn. 1968. *The Supreme Court and American Capitalism.* New York: Free Press.

Miller, William. 1951. "American Lawyers in Business and Politics: Their Social Backgrounds and Early Training." *Yale Law Journal* 60: 66.

Nash, George H. 1996. *The Conservative Intellectual Movement in America Since 1945.* New York: Basic Books.

O'Connor, Karen, and Lee Epstein. 1983. "The Rise of Conservative Interest Group Litigation." *Journal of Politics* 45: 479.

———. 1989. *Public Interest Profiles: Institutional Profiles.* New York: Greenwood Press.

Pacific Legal Foundation. 1998. Web page www.pacificlegal.org (retrieved December 30).

Pacific Legal Foundation. 2001. "Annual Report," *Guide Post* 28, no. 1.

Paul, Arnold. 1960. *Conservative Crisis and the Rule of Law: Attitudes of Bar and Bench, 1887–1895.* Ithaca, N.Y.: Cornell University Press.

Posner, Richard. 1993. *The Problems of Jurisprudence.* Cambridge: Harvard University Press.

Posner, Richard. 1994. "The Limits of Science in Legal Discourse," in *Adam Smith and the Philosophy of Law and Economics*, ed. Robin Paul Malloy and Jerry Evinsky. Boston: Kluwer Academic.

———. 1997. "Against Constitutional Theory." *New York University Law Review* 73, no. 1: 1.

Powell, Michael. 1988. *From Patrician to Professional Elite: The Transformation of the New York City Bar Association.* New York: Russell Sage Foundation.

Rosenberg, Gerald. 1991. *The Hollow Hope: Can Courts Bring Social Change?* Chicago and London: University of Chicago Press.

Scheingold, Stuart. 1974. *The Politics of Rights: Lawyers, Public Policy and Political Change.* New Haven, Conn.: Yale University Press.

Scheingold, Stuart, and Austin Sarat, eds. 1998. *Cause Lawyering: Political Commitments and Professional Responsibilities.* Oxford: Oxford University Press.

———, eds. 2001. *Cause Lawyering and the State in a Global Era.* Oxford: Oxford University Press.

Shenon, Philip. 1985. "Meese Says Some Judges Practice 'Chameleon Jurisprudence'." *New York Times* (November 16): Section 1.

Skowronek, Stephen. 1982. *Building a New American State: The Expansion of National Administrative Capacities, 1877–1920.* Cambridge: Cambridge University Press.

Smith, Christopher E. 1993. *Justice Antonin Scalia and the Supreme Court's Conservative Moment.* Westport, Conn.: Praeger Press.

Tarrow, Sidney. 1998. *Power in Movement: Social Movements, Collective Action and Politics.* London: Cambridge University Press.

Taylor, Stuart. 1987. "Conservatives Assert Legal Presence." *New York Times* (February 1): Section 1.

Tilly, Charles. 1995. *Popular Contention in Great Britain, 1758–1834.* Cambridge: Harvard University Press.

Twiss, Benjamin. 1942. *Lawyers and the Constitution: How Laissez Faire Came to the Supreme Court.* Princeton, N.J.: Princeton University Press.

Warren, Charles. 1966. *A History of the American Bar.* New York: Howard Fetig.

Whittington, Keith E. 1999. *Constitutional Interpretation: Textual Meaning, Original Intent and Judicial Review.* Lawrence: University Press of Kansas.

Legal Cases Cited

Munn v. Illinois, 4 Otto (94 U.S.) 113 (1877).

Nollan v. California Coastal Commission, 483 U.S. 825 (1987).

Palazzolo v. Rhode Island, 533 U.S 606 (2001).

The Slaughter House Cases, 16 Wall. (83 U.S.) 36 (1873).

CHAPTER FIVE

From Cause Lawyering to Resistance

*French Communist Lawyers in the
Shadow of History (1929–1945)*

LIORA ISRAËL

L'Association Juridique Internationale (AJI) was founded at the end of the 1920s by a prominent communist lawyer, Marcel Willard. The activities of the association, which was composed of lawyers and law professors, were mainly of two types: the advocacy of communist opposition groups in various countries, and the defense of trade unionism and of worker's rights. The AJI was also a political school for young communist lawyers. It disappeared when the Communist Party was declared illegal in 1939. At that time, many members of the former AJI became the public defenders of their former political leaders, the communist representatives imprisoned after the Von Ribbentrop-Molotov Pact. The strategic dimension of their double commitment to their profession and to their party then became evident. When the party was declared illegal, being a lawyer allowed them to continue the political struggle on the basis of the traditional conception of lawyering for the defense of their clients.

But with the coming of the war and the German occupation, this commitment became more dangerous. In September 1941, the Germans killed three communist lawyers who had been taken as hostages. But even though their professional activity, as well as their political commitment, became illegitimate, some of these former communist lawyers, joined by others, continued to apply their legal skills to the political struggle. They did so by shaping the Judiciary Resistance, which was a clandestine form of opposition based on legal devices and legal practices. The question raised in this chapter centers on an undemocratic transition (i.e., from democracy to totalitarianism): What are the possibilities open to the law(yers) to check power during a war, during an occupation, when the rule of law is dismantled?

This chapter applies the "cause lawyering" approach to a sociohistorical analysis of the AJI in France during the 1930s, and the new forms of commitment of its members after 1939. This type of analysis leads us, first, on a methodological basis, to reconsider the type of empirical material that sustains most of the research on cause lawyering, based mostly on interviews. This method cannot be adopted to study an organization active 70 years ago. Moreover, it has some very concrete implications on the researcher's point of view: the use of archives leads us to focus less on motivations (that actors can no longer produce) and more on the types and contexts of action. Another important introductory point is the risk of anachronism: when using the cause lawyering approach as in this chapter, it is important to remember, among other considerations, the specificity of the communist ideology and organization of the 1930s and 1940s, the modern history of the French bar since the eighteenth century (Karpik 1995), the fact that France has a civil code, the absence of the UN or of the Universal Declaration of Human Rights at that time, and the legal or political context of France during World War II.[1] That is to say, it is important to contextualize the term cause lawyering and perhaps propose criteria that specify principles that underlie many analyses of cause lawyering.[2]

This chapter intends both to extend the validity of the cause lawyering paradigm and to specify its relevance in contexts that may not be contemporary, American, democratic, or liberal.[3] This leads to a reevaluation of issues of motivation by abandoning a definition in terms of "lawyering for the good" (Menkel-Meadow 1998). I find that definition too vague and normative and instead choose to focus on more political domains, especially the importance of the judiciary to legitimate a political struggle, in various contexts. The variation of context, central to this research that covers fifteen years, from the Third Republic to the end of the Vichy regime, is also an opportunity to focus on the question of relations between cause lawyering and democracy.

Part I: The "Association Juridique Internationale," an Organization Inspired by Lenin's Conception of Justice

(1) Origins

The AJI was created in Berlin in December 1929 during an international conference organized by the International Red Help (IRH). According to Michel Dreyfus, his biographer,[4] the communist lawyer Marcel Willard had already founded the AJI in 1925 to enter Sofia (Bulgaria), but the IRH was already famous enough to prevent him from obtaining a visa.

The international conference held in Berlin marked the (second) formal creation of the AJI, but with few public activities between 1934 and 1939, it did not really expand and develop until the late 1930s. For example, not many more than a dozen members discussed repression in Indochina in a meeting at the press center of the Palais de Justice de Paris in 1930. The official registration of the AJI as an association at the Parisian police headquarters dates from 1934.

Although its visibility was not important, the AJI's ideological program had already been defined in some internal papers of the International Communist Movement, such as quoted here from a circular (August 1928) written before the International Conference of Berlin—initially programmed for Paris in 1928:

> Struggle against bourgeois justice is one of our major aims, it would be a breach of our duty to neglect anything that could reinforce our struggle against it. But even if International Red Help organizations can not envisage the transfer of the burden—struggle against class justice in capitalist societies—to other organizations and personalities, we must anyway take into account any form of assistance that can be carried out by institutions or people sympathizing with our cause.[5]

This circular announced the AJI's ambivalent attitude toward bourgeois justice and yet, taking into account the support provided by bourgeois organizations, reveals a strategic attitude of the international communist movement, which was utilitarian and instrumental toward its allies.

The foundation for this attitude can be found in a crucial older document, Lenin's letter on defense, written in 1905 in response to members of the Social-Democratic Labor Party of Russia who had been arrested in 1904 and did not know how to prepare their defense. Lenin's answer, published in 1925, was the major reference of Marcel Willard when he organized the AJI, and later, in 1938, when he published his reflection on political defense (Willard [1938] 1955). This document can help us to reconstruct the political objectives of this organization.

According to Willard, the strategy developed by Lenin was based on two points, depending on the degree of oppression imposed by the state. First, if defense proves impossible, that is if justice is useless for political action, then it is legitimate to boycott the trial, after having exposed the reasons by an overt protest. Second, if defense, as it happens generally in democracies, is possible on a political ground, then the trial must be used as an arena where one fights with rhetorical weapons. Then, without evoking his belonging to the Communist Party, the militant must use the tribunal as a scene for his propaganda.

Lenin and Willard stress the fact that the defendant must not say a word about the organization or activities of the party, which could provide information to the adversary.

The major example for Willard was Dimitrov's self-defense during the Leipzig trial, "where he had cleverly outflanked Hermann Goering's clumsy efforts to convict him of burning the Reichstag" (Keys 2000). According to Willard, Dimitrov did not provide the police with the information required to decode the addresses and organizational papers seized during his arrest.

What is the role of the lawyer in such a conception of justice, when self-defense is said to be the best solution? Lenin and after him Willard were convinced that a lawyer, even if he is liberal, is "led by his professional training to sacrifice everything to 'his cause,' that is the verdict of not guilty or the minimal charge for its client" (Willard 1955: 26). That is why, when it came to defending grassroots militants, Lenin and then Willard preferred a revolutionary trained as a lawyer to a lawyer sensitive to revolutionary ideals. Willard stressed the fact that in most cases the lawyer had to fight against his own professional and social tendencies to be a good advocate of the political cause. In fact, the defense of the political ideals of the party before the court could entail a heavy sentence for the client; whereas a speech for the defense based on the search for extenuating circumstances, more profitable for the client, would be synonymous to a loss of the political dimension of the trial.

Concretely, Willard advised the militant to choose an honest lawyer and to ask him to confine himself to the juridical dimension of his activity and to let his client assume his own political defense; the juridical part of the defense being subordinated to the political goal. If the militant could not choose his own lawyer, according to Willard, he should rely on himself to learn and use every resource of the law, every possibility of defense, and ultimately check his lawyer's strategy.

This reminds us of the debate concerning the legitimization of the system through lawyering that Stephen Ellman analyzes on the basis of a symposium called "Lawyering in Repressive States" (Ellman 1995). There he suggests that the costs of lawyer's work (in terms of legitimization of the system) may be greater than the benefits, putting into question the lawyer's contribution to the struggle against injustice (Ellman 1995). Confronted with this dilemma, Lenin's answer, transcribed by Willard, was to refuse to be compelled by the judiciary system's demands and to use the court as an arena. The ultimate goal was to address a political message to the magistrates and, beyond them, to the masses, without taking individual risks into account.

(2) Affairs, Trials, Campaigns: The Activity of the AJI

Even if Lenin's letter, reinterpreted by Willard, set up the ideological frame-work of AJI program, this strategy was confronted with three limitations.

First, France in the 1930s was not czarist Russia or Nazi Germany (as during the Dimitrov trial). Thus, the "oppressive" nature of the state is quite different, especially on a political level, in a democracy, even "bourgeois" according to the Communist Party ideological framework, and in a dictatorship. Moreover, it is obvious that the judiciary could be used, in France, as a political arena but also as a way of solving problems such as labor issues, particularly with the new laws implemented during the Popular Front.

Second, in such a regime, the definition of political justice was not straight-forward, especially when the left was in charge of the government (notably in 1936 when the Communist Party supported the Popular Front). The question can be raised concerning the position adopted by attorney members of the AJI in trials where they could objectively gain something. This was evident in cases related to their organizational activities such as their press (Marcel Willard was the attorney of the communist newspaper *L'Humanité*), or concerning grass-roots militants such as trade unionists.

Third, a privileged ground of activity for the AJI was the international do-main, more favorable to radical strategies of opposition to power, especially in countries ruled by rightist or fascist governments. Nevertheless, even in those radical situations, the AJI's goal might have been to soften the severity of ver-dicts pronounced in cases involving labor activists. One could point out the ex-ample of Mrs. Bombard-Stodel, an attorney in Paris, who visited Albania in 1935 in the name of the AJI to appeal (successfully) for clemency on behalf of Fieri insurgents who had been sentenced to death. The public campaigns, based on the support to persecuted activists, could not follow the line indicated by Lenin and Willard. Indeed, the "court-as-an-arena" maxim would have endan-gered the situation of those militants, and would thus be contradictory to the desire to make the people aware of the cause by claiming support for the ac-tivists' release.

This example leads us to an examination of the concrete activities of the AJI, especially between 1934 and 1939. Along with the famous Dimitrov trial, inter-national campaigns were numerous, as it was reported in the association bul-letin.[6] Among others, including the Albania example, one can evoke the visits of Auguste Buisseret, a Belgian attorney, Joë Nordmann, and Renaud de Jouvenel, his French counterparts, in 1936, to Rumania and Greece to assess detention conditions in those countries. De Jouvenel later wrote an article entitled "Rumania and Greece Following Hitler's Way"[7] to denounce the situation. Besides those trips as political observers, other campaigns aimed at pressuring international institutions. The well-known attorney Ernest Charles de Moro-Giafferi from the Parisian bar took part in the defense of political refugees by representing the AJI in a delegation in favor of their interests before the Society of Nations in Geneva.

The campaigns were intended to make people conscious of what happened in those countries as well as to support grassroots militants, trade unionists, or members of oppressed minorities anywhere—except in the Soviet Union.

Some correspondents were also used, along with visits from foreign members of the AJI, to give accounts of what happened in their own country. For instance, in 1938 Margaret Fry, from the Howard League for Penal Reform, published an article in the association journal about the reform of the penitentiary regime in Great Britain. The same year, Giuseppe Gadoli produced an account of racist legislation in Italy.

Members of the AJI gave prominence to international events for many reasons. First, to make visible the presence of the AJI and its mission, to signal "violations of international laws and of principle admitted universally by civilized people."[8] This insistence on denouncing injustice enabled them to bring to the fore, as a contrast, the advancements that were, according to them, realized in the USSR. Second, they studied the consequences of these developments for French and international law. For example, Marc Jacques, attorney in Paris, wrote an article called "Repercussions of Non-intervention Policy in French Law," and A. Schlisselman wrote "Chinese-Japanese Conflict and International Law."[9] These articles presented an opportunity to make the lawyers aware of international questions through their shared interest in comparative and international law.

The struggle against fascism was the second major objective of the AJI, which grew during the second half of the 1930s. At its height, the association organized a large number of conferences more or less devoted to the rise of fascism and nazism.

Through conferences such as the two organized in 1935 and 1937 at the Sorbonne,[10] the struggle against fascism—a leitmotiv of communist organizations—was shaped into the research of juridical evolution in European countries. The law was considered here both as a tool of analysis and as a political weapon. In these conferences, sponsored and attended mostly by law professors and attorneys, the IRH's conception of capitalist justice as unjust and bourgeois was molded into a defense of substantial rights such as civil liberties and freedom of speech. In those matters, the position of AJI was very close to the ones of the famous Ligue des Droits de l'Homme (Human Rights League), founded at the time of the Dreyfus affair and well known for its republican and liberal positions since the late nineteenth century.

A third topic developed by the association was the juridical dimension of class struggle as it appeared in labor law. For example, an AJI mailing in 1937 enumerated new themes of reflection to be analyzed: "the right to strike—sit-in strikes in the workplace and their consequences—the law on collective conventions—the law on compulsory arbitration—law on taking-in and taking-off—new measures concerning juvenile delinquency—a new bill about immigration." This juridical study of social problems linked two types of concerns. On the one hand, especially during the Popular Front, they developed a doctrinal reflection on political questions that was classical for this period (e.g., they reprinted an article published in *L'Oeuvre* by Gaëtan Piriou about "L'aspect juridique des occupations d'usine" [Juridical dimensions of sit-in strikes in the workplace]). On the other hand, they focused on new bills that could offer new resources of action to labor movements (and to their attorneys) through jurisprudence.

(3) Were AJI Members Efficient?

Sensitive to social problems as well as to the rise of fascism in European countries, members of the AJI were recruited among leftist, including noncommunist, lawyers. An internal report about recruitment in southern France in June 1937[11] illustrates this point by focusing on the creation of local branches. The report's author evokes the creation of branches in Poitiers, Bordeaux, Toulouse, and Montpellier, where prospective members, former communist militants as well as established lawyers, exemplified the interest of the organization in local networks of the bourgeoisie. At the same time, young communist lawyers underwent political training with Marcel Willard. Pierre Kaldor insists that the AJI was a political school for them.[12] Those young lawyers (Kaldor, Joë Nordmann, Jérôme Ferrucci, and Paul Vienney) assumed the defense of militants in court as well as in the propaganda, writing a bulletin or translating pamphlets (Kaldor, for example, translated Dimitrov's correspondence). This activity was essentially unpaid. In fact, Nordmann worked for the socialist attorney Vincent Auriol (the future French president) and Kaldor gave lessons before leaving the bar in 1938 to work for an insurance company.

Based on a presumption of common interests and reasoning among leftist lawyers, the AJI distinguished itself by its linkage with the IRH as well as by its recruitment among lawyers. But it is difficult to estimate *a posteriori* the impact of such an organization whose influence diminished rapidly at the eve of World

War II and disappeared with the Nazi-Soviet pact. At least, as stated above, the association was important for a minority of lawyers who received political training through participation in its activities. More generally, it played a role in the communist strategy, especially in the public-awareness campaign against fascism among intellectuals in the 1930s.

The first conclusion related to the AJI in the 1930s that we may draw is that law played a major role in this association, both as a resource for political action (communist militants needed to be defended and it helped to unify their defense in the practical sense) and as a basis for propaganda, thanks to the lawyers' predilection for doctrine and jurisprudence. This sensibility was used to make the lawyers conscious of legal evolutions that were described as related to political ones, some being criticized (influence of fascism), others being praised (labor laws implemented by Popular Front governments).

Conclusion to Part I: Were They Cause Lawyers?

Those lawyers certainly struggled for a cause—the cause of communism, or at least that of liberal rights in international contexts—through its various, and sometimes contradictory, forms, alliances, and strategies, from the late 1920s until the eve of the World War II.

Among the members of the AJI, we must specify two types of militants. The first was a small group of young attorneys surrounding Marcel Willard who were members of the Communist Party. In their journal as well as in courts around the world, they defended the cause of militants or figures designated by the international communist movement. They embodied a solution to Lenin and Willard's dilemma: as communist lawyers, they knew that they were supposed to fight for the cause of their party, rather than the client's specific charge. Despite the fact that many of them were socially rooted in the bourgeoisie (Willard, Nordmann), those lawyers were devoted to political involvement in favor of communism. The existence of such lawyers contradicts Karpik's analysis of the classical political lawyer, defined by his political liberalism and his rejection of extremism (Karpik 1995). Karpik considers broadly that cause lawyering is defined by being outside the scope of political lawyering (Halliday and Karpik 2001).[13] This distinction is questionable on the grounds of the historical complexity of the AJI, combining the vocabulary of liberal rights with the strategy of the IRH. Indeed, those lawyers based on the very core of their juridical competence the possibility to defend and legitimate communism in the courts as well as in public opinion. Moreover, as Karpik acknowledges it, his articulation of cause lawyering and political lawyering is contradictory to the definition of the concept by Austin Sarat and Stuart Scheingold, and more particularly with the definition of cause lawyering as a continuum from politi-cal liberalism to extremism (Bloom and Scheingold 1998). This indirect con-troversy with Karpik refers to a double debate. First, the definition of classical lawyering by Karpik is based on an idea that Richard Abel (1998) describes as an ideological position, that is, the assumption that the lawyers rise is associated with political liberalism (and vice versa). This assumption leads to some conse-quences: first, the accent on liberalism instead of power,[14] and second, the de-piction of a golden age of the profession, associated with liberalism, which is contrasted with the new profession submitted to the logic of markets. Is there a place for cause lawyering, associated neither with political liberalism nor with big law firms, in this representation of the profession? The second dimension of the problem is related to the definition of political liberalism, based on the de-fense of individual liberties notably during the Third Republic, associated with center-left or right-moderate ideas in France, whereas its contemporary Anglo-Saxon definition is different. This could explain both the contradictions be-tween the different contributions to Halliday and Karpik's (1997) book picked up by Abel, as well as his anachronistic remark concerning Karpik's use of the term "liberalism": "Is it helpful to call a politics that represses and excludes workers (and women, and racial, religious and ethnic minorities) liberal?" (Abel 1998).

This controversy concerning definition is not relevant to our analysis, since we refer to the classical definition of cause lawyering (professional, radical, highly political). But on a factual ground, this analysis of the AJI suggests other articulations between lawyering and politics in the French context than Karpik's analysis.

This complexity appeared also in the sociodemographic patterns of the AJI concerning the second type of militants we studied. The majority of the AJI members, especially the members of its honor committee (law professors at the Sorbonne, deputies, famous attorneys of the Parisian Bar), were lawyers sensi-tive to radical ideals or to the defense of civil liberties and often tied to the rad-ical or socialist party.[15] Characterized by their professional position or notabil-ity, they represented the "bourgeois" supporters targeted by the strategy already detailed in the secret note of 1928 of the AJI to the IRH. The support of mem-bers of the elite was important to legitimate political struggles encountered by the Communist Party in cases where they took the form of defense of civil lib-erties. Even so, this in fact was contradictory to the radical opposition to capi-talist justice that represented the core of communist doctrine, as expressed by Lenin and later by Willard.

This paradoxical definition of justice between communist strategies and liberal values, as well as the heterogeneity of the members of the association (a few devoted to a cause, a majority associated to various struggles), leads me to insist on the strategic and ambiguous function of lawyers in radical political mobilizations. Although the idea that law is gaining in importance in social life is so important today in the social sciences (the idea of *juridicisation* in French [Commaille et al. 1999]), it is noteworthy that the international communist movement already had a strategy in the late 1920s and 1930s that took into account the role of law in the political struggle. Their consciousness of the legitimacy entailed by the use of legal arguments, as well as their profound mistrust of capitalist justice as intrinsically unjust, reminds us of patterns of action concerning contemporary left-activist lawyers. When it came to their attitude in courts, Lenin and Willard's analysis of lawyering is close to the one described by Stuart Scheingold: "in their willingness to help make the courtroom into a political forum for their clients, Seattle's left-activists have found themselves in conflict with more conventional lawyers for whom 'the lawsuit is the main event' and 'victory in the court' room the essential objective" (1998: 128). This conclusion may lead us to relativize the novelty of this phenomenon.

I distinguished two types of lawyer members of the AJI: attorneys who were devoted to the cause, and others who provided their legitimacy and their talent but were just sympathetic to specific struggles. Which ones were the most efficient for the cause in a democratic society? The question is still open.

Part 2: From Democracy to War and Occupation: The Necessity of Inventing New Forms of Action for Communist Lawyers

(1) The "44's" Trial

From 1939 to 1945, two major periods framed the situation of communist members, including lawyers: the "phony" war (September 1939–June 1940) and the German occupation and the Vichy regime (June 1940–summer 1944).

First, between the Molotov-Ribbentrop Pact in August 1939 and the Franco-German Armistice in June 1940, France was still under the Third Republic regime, but the Communist Party had been suppressed and dismantled for treason, on the basis of its support of the pact of nonbelligerence between the Soviet Union and Germany. This new situation involved major developments in the Communist Party. Among rank and file militants, it entailed for some a sense of disillusion, since the party had been at the core of the antifascist mobilization during the previous five years. For others, accordance to this new line of action was accepted and portrayed as pacifist. This paradoxical situation was even worse for communist members of the parliament. As communist leaders, they had to justify and support openly this new line of action, but, as MPs, they were confronted with a harsh contradiction between their function, representing the French nation, and their commitment to a party accused of national betrayal.

Confronted with the dissolution of their party, declared by decree on September 26, 1939 (after the declaration of war against Germany), most of the communist representatives decided to form a new group at the Assembly, called Groupe Ouvrier et Paysan Français (French Peasants and Workers' Group). There, they signed a common declaration in support of the so-called Russian initiative for peace. Some communist representatives did not join this initiative, but, they, as well as others, were nonetheless accused of treason, arrested, and appeared before a military tribunal in March 1940 (Azema et al. 1986). This historical detour leads us to the questions: Who defended them? How? Could it be described as cause lawyering?

Jean Fonteyne gave an interesting report of the trial in the book, *The 44's Trial*, published clandestinely in the Netherlands in September 1940 (supposedly by a printer whose firm had been destroyed). Fonteyne himself was a lawyer, a communist, and a former member of the AJI, but he was Belgian. He nevertheless defended one of the French MPs (Florimond Bonte) in this trial. His description of this event is both a good illustration of this arena and an insider point of view on the communist use of this trial.

Not all of the lawyers were communists. If some were members of the party, such as Marcel Willard, accompanied by young lawyers who had surrounded him during the interwar period (Robert Foissin, Maurice Boitel), others were representing what Karpik calls "l'avocat politique," that is, the political lawyer. Alexandre Zévaès, who defended some of the MPs, was one of them, and among the most famous. He was a well-known *chroniqueur* (columnist) of Parisian life and more specifically of the Court of Paris, including political pieces on individuals such as Jean Jaurès. He had also been part of famous trials in defense of socialist members. Four lawyers defended the three MPs who did not sign the letter, and their defense was primarily separate. To be more precise, we will focus mostly on three lawyers and their strategy: Marcel Willard, the major communist lawyer, Jean Fonteyne (the narrator), and Alexandre Zévaès, the liberal.

The first political issue at stake in the trial was the question of publicity: the debate was centered on the need of imposing the closure of the trial to the public and the press. Confronted with this eventuality, lawyers focused on the question from a double perspective before the court. According to Fonteyne, Zévaès stressed the fact that French political history contained only one example of a closed political trial: the Dreyfus Affair. By mentioning this event, he included this trial in the liberal tradition of fighting against discrimination and unfairness that had been the basis of the French main association for the defense of human rights, the Human Rights League. Hence, with the reference to the Dreyfus Affair, he inscribed this trial implicitly in a genealogy, associated to the defense of liberty, and could then accuse the court of asking for the closure on the grounds that the military judges would publicly be unable to justify their position. Communist lawyers also accused the authorities of hiding the truth and of preventing the court from being an arena. They mentioned another historical precedent, such as the trial of Babeuf during the French Revolution (referred by Marcel Willard) in order to insist on the fact that the defender of the forty-four deputies did not address himself only to a court but also to the people in its entirety.

Nevertheless, the military judges decided in favor of the closed trial. During the trial, again according to Fonteyne, all the defenders finally joined in a global advocacy of their clients; and thus the lawyers divided their work by function of their political and professional profile instead by clients. This new organization provoked a functional division of labor among lawyers, whereas usually they tried to distinguish one from another in a sort of competition. They divided the work during the audience as following: Zévaès insisted on the fact that the MPs were treated as normal prisoners and not as political detainees. Then he presented a history of the relations between socialism and war. Some other lawyers (liberal) pointed out the constitutional issue of parliamentary immunity. Fonteyne focused on the philosophical question of communism and peace. Then the question of political repression of communism in France was developed and Willard concluded, defensively, stressing three main ideas: "the French people want peace, USRR is a major factor of peace, the political position of the Communist Party is fair."

Willard also accused the French government of being more repressive than the one "from the other side of the Rhine," on the basis of its censorship of communist (then called "nonconformist") newspapers or books, and on the fact that French ministers did not show up at this trial; whereas Goering came to the bar to accuse the communist Dimitrov of being the incendiary of the Reichstag in Berlin.

Finally, all of the MPs were condemned to various sentences, depending on their individual pasts and positions toward the Nazi-Soviet pact. This trial is interesting for us because it constitutes a transition between the interwar period and the occupation years, on a chronological basis as well as concerning the analysis of cause lawyering. Indeed, what we can see in the 44's trial is both:

(a) The continuation—after the forced dissolution of AJI—of the defense of communism as an ideology on the basis of liberal rights such as freedom of expression. This combination appeared in the common work of liberal and communist lawyers: the first group focused on French political culture and rights as being contrary to such a trial, the second group was more violent toward the French regime (especially Willard), focusing on the content of communism itself as an ideology associated with peace and fairness.

(b) The premonition of defense under a repressive regime. This trial happened before the Vichy regime, but it was at the very end of the Third Republic, when the government had special powers. Furthermore, France had declared war on Germany, and the Communist Party, which had represented 1.5 million voters in the 1936 elections, had been banned. The nature of the regime was then affected by some restrictions, as illustrated by the fact that this trial was closed to both the public and the press. This closure was especially important for the lawyers who defended the communist MPs: it meant the disappearance of the only remaining arena where they could address and justify the political choice of their clients. Their defense, especially of communist ideology, was then useless in front of the military tribunal, although the book that Jean Fonteyne published a few months later was read by some people, albeit in the new context of Nazi occupation.

During the phony war, when communist deputies were accused of treason after the act of nonbelligerence between the Soviet Union and Nazi Germany, Marcel Willard and others defended them in front of the military tribunal. Other members of the AJI, such as Paul Vienney, defended rank-and-file militants. Regaining their role as defenders of communist interests, the AJI lawyers could come to the bar benefiting from the preserved legitimacy of their profession. This annoyed the authorities of the late Third Republic, as is evident in a police report about Marcel Willard (1939): "As an attorney, Mr. Willard was in charge of the defense of communist militants till the dissolution of the French Communist Party. He continues doing it, unofficially, entrenching himself behind his professional duties. . . . To put it in a nutshell, Mr. Willard devotes himself to the defense of those who forget voluntarily to obey our laws."[16]

Thus appeared the strategic dimension of the double commitment of those attorneys, on the one hand to their profession and on the other to their party. As a matter of fact, when the party was declared illegal, their professional occupation allowed them to go on battling, no longer in the name of ideology, but with reference to the tradition of defense embodied in their profession. Then, beyond any possible reproach on judicial grounds, even if they were under the control of the police, those lawyers ideologically trained through support and defense of communist causes, became the defenders of their former leaders, communist representatives imprisoned and politically muted by the Nazi-Soviet pact. They were still associated with liberal lawyers who were not communists but sensitive to their cause, even though this common commitment coming from the AJI period disappeared a few weeks later with the beginning of Vichy regime and Nazi occupation. This was notably the end of the republican regime and its rights and the beginning of the radicalization of the anticommunist repression.

(2) Under the Vichy Regime and German Occupation: Secret and Invention

I focused on the 44's trial because it was paradigmatic of many of the trials between September 1939 and June 1940 where communist activists were accused of treason and defended mostly by communist lawyers, especially in Paris where the AJI had been implanted. The insistence on this particular trial is justified by the fact that it exemplifies the transition between democracy and nondemocracy, especially reflecting the transition from the existence of a public space to its disappearance, which is of particular relevance for this chapter. Indeed, the example of the 44's trial symbolizes an intermediary situation: the Communist Party was forbidden, but the communist lawyers could continue to practice; the judicial arena still existed, including the rights of defense, but the closed trials prevented it from being echoed more largely through the press and in the public opinion. This dimension of publicity appears to be essential to cause lawyering analysis, especially in such situations where victory in court cannot be obtained, and where the success of lawyering for the cause is essentially an affair of publicity.

I cannot continue with the same precision over the four years of German occupation, which would be outside the scope of this chapter (but see Israël 2001, 2003). However, the purpose in this part is to specify two major dimensions of the activity of former communist cause lawyers under the authoritarian regime that prevailed in France between 1940 and 1944.

Indeed, during the first month of French occupation, the situation was ambivalent toward communist members: in the occupied zone, communist leaders, including the former member of the AJI Robert Foissin, a lawyer, tried to

obtain from the Nazis the right to again publish the communist newspaper
L'Humanité (Peschanski 1980). In the name of their fidelity to the German-So-
viet pact, they tried to regain legitimacy from the new power in the occupied
zone, whereas in southern nonoccupied France, the Vichy regime continued the
fight against communism with the laws of 1939. However, communists did not
regain the right to publish their newspaper, and the Germans kept on applying
their traditional anticommunist policy, despite the pact. The situation was clarified significantly after June 1941: even if communist Resistance had already begun, especially among intellectuals with the publication of *L'Université Libre*
(Free University) in November 1940, the invasion of the USSR by Nazi Germany simplified drastically the quite ambiguous situation of communist members. The situation for lawyers also evolved, when on June 25, 1941, the Nazis arrested five communist lawyers, all former members of the AJI and lawyers of
communist militants. Three of them, Antoine Hajje, Georges Pitard, and
Michael Rolnikas, were shot by the Germans as hostages after the murder of a
Nazi officer in Paris. Other members of the AJI had already "disappeared," for
example Marcel Willard left Paris in April 1940. Many others were still in the
army in June 1940 and could not return to Paris immediately, like Joë Nordmann who tried to escape via Spain and was arrested. Moreover, the anti-Jew-
ish statutes of October 1940 and June 1941 forbade some of them from continuing to practice their profession: Willard and Nordmann were expelled from
the bar. This could be the end of our story: by 1941, communism was banned
from political life, communist lawyers had been especially targeted by the Nazi
occupation forces, and most of the Jewish communist lawyers had been expelled from the profession. However, one can study the reconfiguration created
by this new situation to trace the heritage of the original form of cause lawyering we observe in the 1930s.

Resistance, defined as an act of transgression against the power perpetrated
consciously with a political aim (Laborie 1997), was the major commitment of
former communist lawyers in the name of their ideals. The main movement to
be analyzed in this perspective is the Front National des Juristes, which was part
of a bigger movement called the Front National[17] that developed among a variety of professions (Virieux 1996) under the direction of the Clandestine Communist Party. Among lawyers, due to the repression already discussed, this
movement was especially slow to develop. The first action that gathered
lawyers, whether formerly committed or not to communism, to a form of re-
sistant political activity embedded in their professional practice, was the defense of jailed communist members. In that, their traditional activity of defense
was influenced by the parallel activities they could have in favor of the Com-

munist Party, their access to the detainees being politically useful as well as a source of comfort for the families. This practical dimension of the profession had a very important role during the war in the connection between the professional practice of lawyers and the political objectives of the Resistance movement: the lawyers and the judges were in many cases the only ones in contact with detainees. They also had access to the judicial files, and that meant they could give information about the procedures or even modify them, for example, by destroying pieces of evidence. Moreover, they had access to the courts, including the numerous closed sessions, during the period of development of exceptional courts derogatory to juridical principles. The observation, during those trials, of the attitudes of lawyers and judges in courts could lead observers to send letters to make them feel the Resistance noticed them and considered them too repressive (some judges were even murdered by members of the Resistance). On the contrary, it could also make members of the Resistance aware of the courage of other lawyers, and sometimes they were asked to join them. The concrete dimensions of professional practice then took a peculiar political stature that certainly was not visible previously, when freedom of speech and other rights were guaranteed.

This political redefinition of routine, through the changes in the signification of visits to clients, access to judicial files, or attendance at trials, was not the only means of professional and political involvement for lawyers. Their political involvement in the Resistance movement was also intellectual. In fact, lawyers (including law professors, judges, and high-ranking civil servants) had a role to play in the construction of the legitimacy of the Resistance as an alternative to the Vichy regime. Lawyers used their specialized knowledge, their competence in law, to demonstrate that even if it appeared so, the Vichy regime was not legal. For example, members of the Front National des Juristes (FNJ) wrote an act of accusation against Pierre Pucheu (Virieux 1996: 445), former minister of Internal Affairs of Vichy, who was arrested, judged, condemned, and then executed by the French government in exile in Algiers. On the contrary, they helped to establish the legal right to resist (for example, against work deportation in Germany[18]) as well as the legitimacy of the Gaullist government from a constitutionalist and international point of view. The expertise of communist lawyers was then part of a larger involvement of jurists in the war, the communist part of it being particularly mobilized in the clandestine press and through the communist representatives in London and Algiers. On the other side, members of FNJ belonged to the larger network of communist Resistance, notable on the question of humanitarian assistance to prisoners.

The question of publicity, central in the definition of the political arena,[19] and in the analysis of cause lawyering, apparently disappeared with the establishment of an authoritarian government, strengthened by the growing power of Nazi occupation forces over public policies. Communist lawyers were part of the clandestine movement that developed in this context, through their embeddedness in "law in action," whether it was the fight against repression in metropolitan France or the legal debate in the Resistance movement, in France or while in exile. They demonstrated again the accuracy of their position by using their commitment to the major organized forces of Resistance in France after 1942–1943, the clandestine Communist Party, and their intellectual and professional competence in the debate over France's future institutions in the perspective of victory. Though those communist lawyers were still not numerous (indeed, some of them had been killed, which afforded prestige to their struggle), and though they participated in a larger fight of which they were only a part, their long experience of repression (since 1939) and their preexisting political culture made them central to the judiciary Resistance as well as in the secret debate concerning the reorganization of French institutions.

This certainly explains why on the liberation of Paris the interim Ministry of Justice, chosen by the members of French provisional institutions in exile, was Marcel Willard, assisted by Joë Nordmann.

Conclusion to Part II

The peculiar position of communist lawyers (and their new allies who they met during World War II) was a combination of political determination sustained by communist slogans, along with the credibility won through their practical involvement in the fight for liberty. They used the tradition of their profession, the defense, as synonymous with their Resistance. This cross-legitimacy of a profession through its political effectiveness, and of an ideology as a tool in the use of law, exemplifies the changes in the definition of cause lawyering involved in a transition to a context where the definition of law itself was not evident (Vichy laws? Republican laws? Natural law?), and where the public sphere, destroyed by the authoritarian regime, tried to survive clandestinely. The use of the courts as a political arena, which had been the basis of the communist utilization of justice, was then of no use, except on a virtual basis, that is, on the prefiguration of judicial purges after the liberation. Lawyers who still had the right or the possibility to play their role of defenders could try to protect their clients, in court and eventually outside the court, through the various actions we defined. However, political defense, openly based on values such as communism and even liberalism, was dangerous both for the lawyers and their clients. The only possibility was, therefore, to protect, deny, and excuse.

This example may be an incentive to enlarge the scope from an analysis of cause lawyering focusing on courts and affairs, to the consideration of broader competences of lawyers as political actors, through their practical and intellectual capacities, and to questions such as the definition of the political legitimacy, which is mostly determined by law and crucial in nondemocratic contexts.

Conclusion

This chapter addresses a threefold question to the paradigm of cause lawyering. The first question is methodological. Is "cause lawyering" a proper analytical tool to analyze a period when the term did not exist, and when lawyers of that time have been described through a framework, Lucien Karpik's political lawyer ideal-type, which supposedly excludes the cause lawyering approach? The first answer to this question is factual: cause lawyering as an analytic frame of analysis conciliating a professional and a political approach is indeed successful in the analysis of the cross-legitimization of legal competence and political commitment embodied by the communist lawyers we studied. The second answer is more ambiguous. The use of archives, synonymous with historical distance, leads us to adopt a less empathic and comprehensive approach than in many other cause lawyering pieces. This distance, entailed by time, involved a focus on historical depiction instead of normative conclusions; compared with other chapters that directly address the question of the best sort of lawyering.

The second question to the cause lawyering paradigm is partially redundant with the title of Part 4 of *Cause Lawyering* (vol. 1) titled "The Possibilities of Cause Lawyering beyond Liberal Legalism." In fact, the transition from the Third Republic to the Vichy regime reveals the alterations of cause lawyering entailed by an undemocratic evolution, characterized notably by a brutal shrinkage of the public space. Hence, the crucial dimension of publicity to cause lawyering underlines the strength of the relation between the Habermasian definition of the modern society as a society of communication and cause lawyering. It would also lead to reinserting cause lawyering among other possibilities of political mobilization (Kahn-Zemans 1983).

By contrast, the examination of cause lawyers in various historical contexts brings to light how legal competence could be used in clandestine and dangerous situations, when the defense of a cause could require its denial in front of the court.

The third question to the cause lawyering approach is then to decide whether the focus is mostly on cause lawyers, and thus on the various forms of their practice among diverse settings, or on cause lawyering as a form of practice, mostly associated with a democratic public space.

Notes

1. Among the numerous publications devoted to the study of the Vichy regime, the classical book by Robert Paxton (1972) is still a very good introduction to the period.

2. The same operation of contextualization to a different sociopolitical environment is realized by R. Michalowski (1998) concerning Cuba.

3. It has already been done in Part 4 of *Cause Lawyering* (Sarat and Scheingold 1998), titled "The Possibilities of Cause Lawyering beyond Liberal Legalism."

4. In the *Historical Dictionary of French Labour Movement* ("Le Maitron"), Ed. de L'Atelier, Paris.

5. Circular quoted in a police report, 1939, Archives Nationales BB 30 1887, AJI file. All translations are mine.

6. Some of them are available at the Bibliothèque Nationale de France.

7. Bulletin de l'AJI no. 14, December 1936, p. 17.

8. I quote from the introduction of an article in the AJI's bulletin, 1935.

9. *Bulletin de l'Association Juridique Internationale*, 1937.

10. Concerning those two conferences at the Sorbonne, the first one (30 November–1 December 1935) was entitled "Le droit national socialiste" (National-socialist law) and the second (10–11 July 1937), "Régression des principes de liberté dans les réformes constitutionnelles de certains pays démocratiques" (On the decline of freedom principles in the constitutional reforms of some democratic countries).

11. Joë Nordmann private archives, Institut d'Histoire du Temps Présent Library, Cachan, France.

12. Interview with Pierre Kaldor, June 17, 1999.

13. The exact quotation in French for this distinction is: "alors que les avocats politiques se définissent, dans le passé comme aujourd'hui, par la défense du noyau central du libéralisme politique (les libertés individuelles et la modération de l'État), les avocats des causes se définissent par toutes les formes de conflit et de défense qui sont extérieures au domaine d'action des avocats politiques" (p. 69).

14. This lack of attention to the question of symbolic as well as material power is apparent in the fact that Karpik accepts at face value lawyer's pretention to "disinterest." Abel (1998).

15. The Radical Party of the Third Republic was not radical in the modern sense of the term, but mostly defined by its center-left republicanism.

16. Archives Nationales, BB 30 1887.

17. Jean-Marie Le Pen's Front National adopted the same name many years later to benefit from the symbolic and national dimension of this reference. But the ideas defended by this party are at odds with the ideals of the French Resistance.

18. Leaflet edited by the Front National des Juristes, "Les déportations devant le droit".

19. For example Habermas or Arendt.

References

Abel, Richard. 1998. "Lawyers for Liberalism: Axiom, Oxymoron or Accident ?" Review of *Lawyers and the Rise of Western Political Liberalism,* ed. Terence Halliday and Lucien Karpik (New York: Oxford University Press, 1998). Review published on "JURIST: The law professor network." http://jurist.law.pitt.edu/lawbooks/revnov98.htm#Abel.

Azema, Jean-Pierre, Jean-Pierre Rioux, and Antoine Prost, eds. 1986. *Le Parti Communiste des Années Sombres (1938–1941).* Paris: Seuil.

Bloom, Ann, and Stuart Scheingold. 1998. "Transgressive Cause Lawyering: Practice Sites and the Politicization of the Professional." *International Journal of the Legal Profession* 5: 209–53.

Commaille, Jacques, Laurence Dumoulin, and Cécile Robert, eds. 1999. *La juridicisation du politique.* Collection Droit et Société. Paris: LGDJ.

Ellman, Stephen. 1995. "Struggle and Legitimation." Editor's introduction to the symposium "Lawyering in Repressive States." *Law and Social Inquiry* 20 (2): 339–48.

Fonteyne, Jean. 1940. *Le procès des quarante-quatre* [The 44's Trial]. Anvers: Regenboog.

Halliday, Terence C., and Lucien Karpik, eds. 1998. *Lawyers and the Rise of Western Political Liberalism. Europe and North America from the Eighteenth to Twentieth Centuries.* Oxford: Clarendon Press; New York: Oxford University Press.

Halliday, Terence C., and Lucien Karpik. 2001. "'Avocats des causes' et avocats politiques: deux formes d'engagement de la défense," in *Justices,* Hors Série (December), dossier "La défense engagée": 68–70.

Israël, Liora. 2001. "La Résistance dans les milieux judiciaires. Action collective et identités professionnelles en temps de guerre." *Genèses* n 45 (December): 45–68.

Israël, Liora. 2003. "Robes noires, années sombres. La résistance dans les milieux judiciaires. Sociologie historique d'une mobilisation politique." Ph.D. dissertation, Ecole Normale Supérieure de Cachan.

Kahn Zemans, Frances. 1983. "Legal Mobilization: The Neglected Role of the Law in the Political System." *American Political Science Review* 77, no. 3 (September): 690–703.

Karpik, Lucien. 1995. *Les avocats. Entre l'Etat, le public, le marché. XIIIème-XXème siècle,* Gallimard, Paris, 1995. [Translation: *French Lawyers: A Study in Collective Action, 1274 to 1994.* Translated by Nora Scott. Oxford: Clarendon Press; New York: Oxford University Press, 1999.]

Keys, Barbara. 2000. Review for "H-Russia" of *Dimitrov and Staline, 1934–1943, Letters from the Soviet Archives,* ed. A. Dallin and F. I. Firsov. New Have, Conn.: Yale University Press.

Laborie, Pierre. 1997. "L'idée de Résistance, entre définition et sens: retour sur un questionnement," in "La Résistance et les Français. Nouvelles approches." *Cahier de l'Institut d'Histoire du Temps Présent* n 37 (December).

Menkel-Meadow, Carrie. 1998. "The Causes of Cause Lawyering: Towards an Understanding of the Motivation and Commitment of Social Justice Lawyers," in *Cause Lawyering: Political Commitments and Professional Responsibilities,* ed. A. Sarat and S. Scheingold. New York: Oxford University Press.

Michalowski, Raymond. 1998. "All or Nothing. An Inquiry into the (Im)possibility of Cause Lawyering under Cuban Socialism," in *Cause Lawyering: Political Commitments and Professional Responsibilities,* ed. A. Sarat and S. Scheingold. New York: Oxford University Press.

Paxton, Robert. 1972. *Vichy France, Old Guard and New Order, 1940–1944.* New York: Knopf.

Peschanski, Denis. 1980. "La demande de parution légale de l'Humanité (17 juin–27 août 1940)." *Le mouvement social* 113 (October–December): 67–90.

Sarat, Austin, and Stuart Scheingold, eds. 1998. *Cause Lawyering: Political Commitments and Professional Responsibilities.* New York: Oxford University Press.

Sarat, Austin, and Stuart Scheingold, eds. 2001. *Cause Lawyering and the State in a Global Era.* New York: Oxford University Press.

Scheingold, Stuart. 1998. "The Struggle to Politicize Legal Practice: A Case Study of Left-Activist Lawyering in Seattle," in *Cause Lawyering: Political Commitments and Professional Responsibilities,* ed. A. Sarat and S. Scheingold. New York: Oxford University Press.

Virieux, Daniel. 1996. "Le Front National de lutte pour la liberté et l'indépendance de la France, Un mouvement de résistance. Période clandestine (mai 1941-août 1944)." Ph.D. dissertation, Université Paris VIII.

Willard, Marcel. 1938. *La defense accuse.* Paris: Éditions Sociales. [reprint 1955].

Making a Practice

Balancing Professionalism and Activism

Supporting a Cause, Developing a Movement, and Consolidating a Practice

Cause Lawyers and
Sexual Orientation Litigation in Vermont

SCOTT BARCLAY AND ANNA-MARIA MARSHALL

On November 18, 2003, the Massachusetts Supreme Judicial Court ruled that the state constitution prohibited denying same-sex couples the right to marriage. Shortly after that Court's decision, spontaneous actions in support of same-sex marriage occurred among an unprecedented number of city, county, and state government officials outside of Massachusetts. Initially, Gavin Newsom, the then newly elected mayor, authorized the San Francisco city clerk to begin issuing marriage licenses to qualified same-sex couples. The mayor of New Paltz in New York state and county commissioners in Sandoval County in New Mexico and Multnomah County in Oregon authorized city and county clerks, respectively, to follow suit. The mayor of Chicago expressed support for permitting similar action in his city, and elected officials in several states requested city and town councils to investigate the legal steps required to allow their town or city to similarly issue marriage certificates to same-sex couples.[1] New York state's attorney general, relying upon a legal opinion by the New York state solicitor general (Halligan 2004), publicly acknowledged that New York State would formally recognize as marriages for all legal purposes same-sex marriages that were celebrated in other states and jurisdictions, including Massachusetts. Moreover, he openly questioned the constitutionality of the existing Department of Health regulation that prohibited such marriages from being performed in New York State.

These milestones in the public campaign to legally recognize same-sex unions have also met with some legislative and gubernatorial resistance. Before the first Massachusetts marriage could be performed, the Massachusetts legislature began the initial steps in the long and complex process to amend its state constitution in order to prohibit gay marriage. Legislatures in thirteen states began the same process, notwithstanding existing legal restrictions upon recognizing or performing same-sex marriages in those same states. President George W. Bush proposed amending the United States Constitution to incorporate the proscription of same-sex marriage. There is little question that same-sex marriage is currently high on the nation's legal and political agenda at all levels of government.

In the midst of this tumultuous political debate, many activists and policymakers on both sides of the political spectrum turned their attention back to Vermont, which in 2000 was the first state to successfully pass into law the equivalent of same-sex marriage. Although Vermont's Civil Union Law withheld from lesbian and gay couples the popular social status accorded the use of the term "marriage," it nevertheless authorized the legal recognition of civil unions for same-sex couples and extended to civil union partners "all the same benefits, protections and responsibilities under law, whether they derive from statute, administrative or court rule, policy, common law or any other source of civil law, as are granted to spouses in a marriage." Interestingly, as in Massachusetts, the impetus for the change of the Vermont law was a state court decision. In *Baker v. State* (1999), the Vermont Supreme Court ruled that depriving same-sex couples of the benefits of marriage violated the Common Benefits Clause of the state constitution.

The fundamental redefinition of the existing legal order represented by the actions of the Vermont Supreme Court and the subsequent actions of the Vermont legislature reflected changes in national and local attitudes toward sexuality and sexual orientation wrought through long and bitter struggles by an emerging lesbian, gay, and bisexual rights movement over the course of decades. But the actions in Vermont were also directly in response to successful legal challenges and the effective incorporation of new legal definitions of lesbian and gay rights that were actively constructed in part by two attorneys in private practice. Susan Murray and Beth Robinson of the law firm of Langrock, Sperry and Wool (LSW) in Middlebury, Vermont, handled pivotal gay and lesbian rights litigation, including *Baker v. State* (1999). But in addition to their work on this groundbreaking litigation, they also simultaneously developed a statewide grassroots campaign in support of same-sex marriage and coordinated much of the legislative lobbying that preceded and followed the decision in *Baker v. State*. Murray and Robinson acted to initiate and facilitate a change in the legal and social status accorded to gay, lesbian, and bisexual Vermonters.

Further, they helped to reenergize the national lesbian and gay rights movement that was reeling from the rejection of same-sex marriage court decisions in Hawaii and Alaska through popular amendments of their respective constitutions. In doing so, Murray and Robinson challenged the traditional model of cause lawyers who are engaged exclusively in private practices.

In developing the litigation that became *Baker v. State* as well as their involvement in the social movement for same-sex marriage, Robinson and Murray embody the idea that cause lawyers fabricate new legal orders in an attempt to eliminate existing inequality and injury. Laws constrain the everyday world in ways that often make inequality and injury natural and unquestioned by many. In response, social movements attempt to reinvent the established political, economic, cultural, or social world in a manner that seeks to recognize, highlight, and hopefully eradicate discrimination and mistreatment. For their part, cause lawyers are required to generate the legal means to realize the world imagined by social movements.

For cause lawyers involved in sexual orientation litigation, they must reimagine accepted legal notions associated with romantic love, sex, sexuality, and the family. They must create legal claims that promote these new legal definitions as part of the transformative process of simultaneously problematizing and denaturalizing existing laws and norms while fabricating a new legal order for constituting their ideal everyday world. Working with groups who have been marginalized by existing social constraints, cause lawyers related to sexual orientation are forced to describe the invisible world that existing inequality imposes upon this community. They do so in the public forum afforded them by their legal challenge as part of their attempt to fabricate through legal imagining an environment free of these existing inequalities. Cause lawyers craft their legal challenges to make real their legal imaginings and hence render visible these marginalized communities.

Although cause lawyers for gay and lesbian rights interest groups, such as Gay and Lesbian Advocates and Defenders (GLAD) and the LAMBDA Legal Defense and Education Fund Inc. (LAMBDA), have been the focus in the creation of new national and local public policies concerning sexual orientation, less attention has been paid to cause lawyers operating outside of these public interest organizations (cf. Trubek and Kransberger 1998, Shamir and Chinski 1998). Yet, as the Vermont example demonstrates, such lawyers pursuing a litigation strategy based on both their political beliefs and their existing private practices can be an important force for legal change.

In the growing body of literature about cause lawyers, the category named "cause lawyers" is narrower than the group of attorneys who engage in cause lawyering. The definition of cause lawyering is broad, encompassing a variety of tactics and strategies and emphasizing the transformative goals and motivations of the attorneys engaged in the work. Studies of cause lawyering are also attentive to the social and political struggles in which the lawyering is situated. Yet when studies try to identify the characteristics of cause lawyers, particularly those in private practice, they focus almost exclusively on "rebellious lawyers" who have organized their practices in ways that reflect their political beliefs. In this chapter, we argue that this contraction of our understanding of cause lawyers may ignore the important cause lawyering of attorneys in traditional legal settings, which, in turn, diminishes our ability to understand the larger political struggles behind the legal tactics.

This chapter suggests that studies of cause lawyers should begin to emphasize the "cause" over the "lawyer." By focusing on the category of "cause lawyers," we may unduly restrict the attorneys and legal practices we count as cause lawyering, excluding lawyers who fail to demonstrate sufficient ideological commitment or who are well paid for "doing good." On the other hand, by focusing on the cause, we can identify all the lawyers who labor for political goals regardless of their practice settings or their client lists. Analyzing the activities of these lawyers provides a more complex picture of the variety of legal strategies a movement might use to advance its goals, uncovering possibly obscure but potentially powerful transformative tactics. Moreover, these lawyers can point out the tensions and struggles within movements themselves regarding what issues are most important, how those issues should be framed, and what strategies to pursue. Thus, we use the current case to both challenge and extend the existing definitions of cause lawyers.

Parameters of Cause Lawyering

Because cause lawyers construct politics, most definitions of cause lawyering emphasize the lawyer's political goals and ideological commitments. For example, Sarat and Scheingold (1998: 7) argue, "cause lawyers tend to be distinguished primarily by a willingness to undertake controversial and politically charged activities and/or by a sense of commitment to particular ideals." Impact litigation is one common method cause lawyers use to construct politics out of legal argument (Scheingold 1974; Kilwein 1998; McCann 1994; Olson 1984). Test cases and planned litigation often seek favorable judicial precedent or judicial orders requiring changes to political or social institutions that redress inequality or relieve marginalized groups from oppressive burdens (Kilwein 1998). Impact litigation can also serve broader purposes for the social and political struggles in which it is situated (McCann 1994; Olson 1984). Social movements use litigation to gain leverage in bargaining with powerful elites and to publicize their causes. Lawsuits tell stories about how real individuals have suffered at the hands of more powerful actors. These stories, then, become effective tools for winning support from the public (McCann 1994; Olson 1984). Impact litigation, then, can reveal the often reciprocal relationship between law and politics.

But impact litigation, and cause lawyering more generally, have critics among academics and activists alike because the politics they create is elitist and ineffective. Litigation is expensive and time-consuming. Victory is uncertain, and even if the lawsuit is successful, the rights created provide inadequate remedies that are rarely self-enforcing (Menkel-Meadow 1998; Bell 1976; Scheingold 1974). In the struggle for gay rights, in particular, going to court has been a risky proposition, often producing damaging precedent (Eskridge 1999; Murdoch and Price 2001; Leonard 2000). In addition, litigation translates conflict into rarefied and unfamiliar jargon that must be managed and negotiated by legal professionals, such as lawyers and judges. Thus, it displaces ownership of the conflict from ordinary people, who are potential activists, and places it in the hands of elites who are often remote and distant from the struggle itself (Menkel-Meadow 1998; White 1987).

This critique of litigation has led some cause lawyers to expand their activities by engaging in political mobilization, for example, where they move beyond their roles as skilled legal technicians and become community activists. Recognizing that few social problems are cured with legal solutions alone, these lawyers often include grassroots organizing and political mobilization in their tactics (Kilwein 1998; Trubek and Kransberger 1998; Menkel-Meadow 1998). In adopting these strategies, cause lawyers are in a better position to give voice to their clients and to members of marginalized groups (Alfieri 1991).

Yet these broad definitions of cause lawyering are not completely settled. For example, one contested dimension in the cause lawyer is ideological commitment (Israël, this volume; Maiman, this volume; Willemez, this volume). Cause lawyers are often motivated by social values seeking greater equality for subordinated and marginalized groups. Yet not all lawyers involved in causes exhibit the same level of political or ideological consciousness. Indeed, some cause lawyers have relatively conventional goals, such as making a living or developing a reputation (Maiman, this volume). For example, employment discrimination lawyers can generate novel theories, such as sexual harassment, even as they collect statutory attorneys' fees (Marshall 2001). In this volume, Richard Maiman shows that in the wake of 1998 Human Rights Act, human rights cases have become profitable in England, leading some cause lawyers to worry about ideological dilution in this type of practice, while others pursued the "cause" but shied away from defining themselves in terms of ideological definitions. Shamir and Chinski (1998) have even argued that ideological commitment is a resource that gets depleted, where more conventional attorneys have more stamina to undertake the arduous work associated with long-term struggles.

The definitions of cause lawyering also mask the tension that cause lawyers are often thought to feel between their commitment to the cause and their commitment to their individual clients (Trubek and Kransberger 1998). Conventional attorneys owe their clients the obligation of zealous advocacy and must avoid any commitments that could interfere with that obligation. Pursuing a broader social agenda may be an example of such interference. Compromising an individual client's interests for the sake of a movement would be unacceptable according to prevailing professional norms and ethical standards. On the other hand, cause lawyers are zealous advocates on behalf of the movement and seek to have a social impact above and beyond the results of any individual client (Scheingold and Sarat 1998). However, this service-impact distinction assumes a dichotomy between client and movement that might be sharper in theory than in practice.

Finally, recent studies of cause lawyering have revealed the many different practice settings in which they operate, including legal services offices (Lawrence 1992) and public interest organizations (Olson 1984; Scheingold 1974; Handler 1978). Recently, these studies have increasingly focused on cause lawyers who work in private practice (Kilwein 1998; Trubek and Kransberger 1998; Porter 1998; Shamir and Chinski 1998; Scheingold 1998). Because of cuts in funding, opportunities for traditional public interest legal jobs are disappearing (Trubek and Kransberger 1998). Attorneys in private practice have stepped into this void by supplying legal services to the poor and disenfranchised as well as by assuming responsibility for some impact litigation.

Yet the studies of private practices are relatively limited to attorneys who have organized their practices in politically self-conscious ways. For example, many cause lawyers in private practice work in small, nonhierarchical law firms with a few lawyers and staff members who enjoy relative equality in firm decision making (Trubek and Kransberger 1998). These firms finance their political work by taking on paying clients whose legal work neither advances nor undermines the firm's broader political agenda. Such firms often choose neighborhood locations populated by the poor and subordinated groups that make up their constituencies (Trubek and Kransberger 1998; Kilwein 1998). Yet these po-

Murray and Robinson first started representing gays and lesbians through LSW's family law practice. In 1989, Murray heard a story on the radio about a guardianship dispute over the child of lesbian couple. After the child's mother was tragically killed in a car crash, her partner fought to retain guardianship of the child (as specified in an existing will) that the couple had been co-parenting since his birth. The day Murray heard the story, she persuaded her senior partner Peter Langrock that, based on her experience in family law and the firm's greater resources, she should offer assistance to the smaller law firm that had been handling the case. This case—*In re Hamilton* (1989)—received a great deal of publicity in the *Burlington Free Press*, the highest circulation newspaper in Vermont, and in regional gay and lesbian media outlets, such as *Out in the Mountains*. According to Murray, her success in this case created positive word-of-mouth that encouraged other potential lesbian and gay clients to seek her help with legal issues, thus increasing the percentage of time that she worked on gay and lesbian family rights issues.

Part of Murray's expanding practice included pursuing adoption rights on behalf of gay and lesbian parents. In 1991, Murray won the first Vermont probate court decision recognizing second parent adoption by a lesbian couple. Vermont's adoption statute restricted a biological parent's rights when the child was adopted, except when the adoptive parent was a stepparent. But Judge Chester Ketchum in *In re Adoption of R.C.* (1991) expanded the exception to include the same-sex partners of the biological parent. The Vermont Supreme Court upheld this view in a different case, *Adoption of B.L.V.B. and E.L.V.B.* (1993), where it held "a woman who was co-parenting the two children of her same-sex partner could adopt the children without terminating the natural mother's parental rights" (as reported in *Baker v. State* 1999: 200).[3] Murray filed one of the two *amicus curiae* briefs in this case; the other was filed by LAMBDA Legal Defense Fund, a national gay and lesbian rights group.[4] The Vermont legislature subsequently embodied these same-sex parents' adoption rights in a statute in 1995 (15A V.S.A. § 1–102(b)).

Murray and Robinson and 'Baker v. State'

For Murray and Robinson, their gay-friendly legal practice exposed them to serious inequalities that were in direct conflict with their general ideological commitment to equality for all. As they handled complex estate planning, custody disputes, and adoption proceedings on behalf of their gay, lesbian, and bisexual clients, they began to see the way that existing legal institutions contributed to the second-class citizenship of members of the gay and lesbian community. In addition, as early as 1995, individual clients directly asked them to take on a same-sex marriage case (Robinson 2001: 241). They did not pursue such a case at that time because they did not believe that the political and social environment would yield the requisite endorsement *by the legislature* of such a case if and when they were to win the legal case in the courts. "Judges don't live in a vacuum, and every judicial decision is subject to some sort of political response, whether it be statutory, executive, or constitutional" (Robinson 2001: 241).

When they decided to pursue a case to establish a right to same-sex marriage, Murray and Robinson fully understood the political dimensions of the litigation. First, there was very little legal support for such a right. In 1995 when Murray and Robinson first considered the lawsuit, only the 1993 Hawaii Supreme Court's ruling in *Baehr v. Lewin* questioned the legality of denying marital privileges to same-sex partners. Contrary decisions had been rendered in a number of state courts starting in 1971, including in New York (*Anonymous v. Anonymous*), Minnesota (*Baker v. Nelson* 1971), Kentucky (*Jones v. Hallahan* 1973), and Washington (*Singer v. Hara* 1974). As late as January 1995, the District of Columbia Court of Appeals rejected the proposition that the District's refusal to permit same-sex marriage represented discrimination in any form (*Dean v. District of Columbia* 1995).

In light of this unsympathetic legal environment, Murray and Robinson emphasized legislative success over litigation strategies. Despite discouraging results in same-sex marriage cases in other state courts, they were relatively optimistic about their chances before the Vermont Supreme Court. Instead, they believed that the possibility of legislative reversal was the greatest potential barrier to success in such cases—a view that anticipated the legislative and constitutional reversal of judicial decisions in Hawaii and Alaska. This skeptical view of the Vermont policymakers was somewhat surprising in light of their prior positive legislation and gubernatorial action on sexual orientation issues.[5] But it was this skeptical view that led Murray and Robinson to commit resources to an active public relations campaign targeted at both legislators and the public at large to protect any victories in the courts from legislative reversal.[6]

On July 22, 1997, Murray and Robinson filed suit in Chittenden Superior Court on behalf of three couples—Holly Puterbaugh and Lois Farnham, Nina Beck and Stacy Jolles, and Peter Harrigan and Stan Baker—to whom town clerks had refused to issue marriage licenses in April and May 1997. Mary Bonauto, of the Boston-based Gay and Lesbian Advocates and Defenders (GLAD), was also an attorney of record on the case. In December 1997, the Chittenden Superior Court dismissed the case against the state and the town clerks. Murray, Robinson, and Bonauto, who expected to lose at the trial court level, appealed to the Vermont Supreme Court. Oral arguments in the appeal of *Baker v. State* were heard before that court on November 18, 1998.

In their briefs and oral argument before the Vermont Supreme Court, Murray, Robinson, and Bonauto asserted that "civil marriage, recognized by the State, gives rise to a broad panoply of legal, economic and social protections and supports for married couples and their families, and imposes legal responsibilities on married couples in addition to the moral obligations they have assumed by virtue of their mutual commitment" (Bonauto, Murray, and Robinson 1999: 415). At oral argument, Robinson suggested there were over a thousand such rights and obligations associated with marriage buried within the Vermont laws. Moreover, the state accorded other important benefits to married couples, including the improved social status that traditionally accompanied marriage in most communities. They argued that their clients were denied the benefits of these rights and obligations by being legally proscribed from access to the institution of marriage, which conferred these rights. More important, this denial was based only on the gender and sexual orientation of their clients, whom met all other criteria (including age, sanguinity, residency, and other requirements) established by the state for marriage.

Unlike many of the key prior same-sex marriage cases,[7] Murray, Robinson, and Bonauto did not rely upon the U.S. Constitution. Instead, they invoked the Common Benefits Clause, an antiprivilege provision that had been a fundamental component of the Vermont constitution since its ratification in 1777. They argued that the Common Benefits Clause restricted state action that, without sufficient justification, offered privileges to only a limited section of the population. Further, paralleling Justice Hill's argument, they proposed that the Vermont constitution was more expansive in its protection of rights than the U.S. Constitution.

During oral argument, Robinson compared the state's justification for differential treatment of same-sex couples seeking to marry to the arguments used in 1948 by the state of California to justify a California law against interracial marriage. She also challenged the Vermont Supreme Court to follow the pathbreaking approach adopted by the California Supreme Court in *Perez v. Sharp* (1948) that rejected these arguments as insufficient to maintain a ban on interracial marriage. Thus, Robinson explicitly equated current restrictions based on sexual orientation with earlier restrictions based on race that had since been socially and legally repudiated.

The case attracted enormous attention nationwide, not just from the gay and lesbian legal rights community, but also from civil rights organizations, medical professionals, and communities of faith. In total, nineteen legal briefs were filed in the case, including seven *amicus curiae* briefs in support of the plaintiffs by LAMBDA Legal Defense Fund, American Civil Liberties Union, National Organization for Women, Vermont Psychiatric Association, as well as briefs from law professors and religious groups.

It took almost a year for the Vermont Supreme Court to reach its decision. In December 1999, Chief Justice Jeffrey Amestoy, writing for the majority, observed that marriage provides a multitude of legal and social benefits that can only be accessed by married couples but that the current legal definition of marriage in Vermont precluded marriage by same-sex couples. Given that the marriage laws singled out the lesbian and gay community for negative treatment, the Court considered the constitutional validity of the justifications offered by the state in light of the requirements of the Common Benefits Clause of the Vermont constitution.

The Court rejected the state's arguments linking marriage and procreation because many married couples do not have children (by choice or physical limitation), nor did the state require different-sex couples applying to marry to prove that they could and would bear children. Similarly, the plaintiffs showed that gay and lesbian couples had an interest in procreation which they fulfilled through the same variety of means that many nongay couples utilize, including IVF and adoption. This latter point, and the earlier judicial and legislative support by the state for gay adoption, challenged the state's argument that equated marriage and the state's interest in childrearing. Nor did the Court accept the state's argument that tradition dictated such requirements, especially given the variation in age and consanguinity requirements among states (e.g., first cousin marriage was acceptable in Vermont but in very few other states). Finally, while the Court recognized that public opinion and the actions of other states indicated a reticence to move on this issue in most other states, they were unwilling to be bound by such reticence. Thus, because the state failed to justify, under the Common Benefits Clause of the Vermont constitution, denying gays and lesbians the benefits accorded by the state through marriage, the Vermont Supreme Court held that all of legal benefits and obligations associated with marriage must be extended to same-sex couples.

Although it required Vermont to provide benefits equivalent to marriage, the Vermont Supreme Court stopped short of extending marriage to same-sex couples. In doing so, the Court rejected Robinson's argument in oral argument that the social status accorded marriage by the community was itself a key benefit offered by the state. In fact, Robinson (interview 2002) notes that in the "nineteen briefs in this case, there wasn't any suggestion in any of the briefs on either side of the case that the concept of the legal status of being married could somehow be severed from the concept of the benefits that accompany the legal status of marriage." But once the two concepts—benefits and marriage—were severed, no single remedy was mandated. Consequently, over the arguments of two justices, the Vermont Supreme Court withheld ordering a remedy for the constitutional violation. Instead, the chief justice directed that the legislature be permitted time to ascertain an acceptable method for ensuring that such benefits were equally accorded to such couples either through marriage or through other means. Thus, notwithstanding Murray and Robinson's earlier promises to Vermont legislators that they would not be forced to act on same-sex marriage, the Court's decision placed the fate of same-sex marriage in the hands of the legislature.

In the wake of the Supreme Court's decision, Murray and Robinson became key figures during the legislative debate, both at the committee level and subsequently in the Vermont House and Senate. By January 3, 2000, Susan Murray had testified before the House Judiciary Committee after having made the "mental transition from court to legislature" (Robinson interview 2002). Their role was as intermediaries between the plaintiffs (who still had an active court case),[8] an active social movement, and a legislature that was not initially expecting to resolve this issue by statute. Robinson (interview 2002) noted that neither she nor Murray "was in the office more than one day, one or two days a week for the next six weeks" as the legislature debated this issue. They remained active in the legislature as it settled on the notion of civil unions—a state-sanctioned status identical to marriage in every way including all benefits and obligations, but restricted only to same-sex parties who were still to be precluded from marriage. Further, they had to reconcile both their clients and other members of the social movement to the important distinction in nomenclature (and subsequently, in social status) that the legislature eventually introduced in Act 91 of 1999 on April 25, 2000. Governor Howard Dean, who had strongly pushed for civil unions, signed the Civil Union Law on April 26, 2000, and it took effect on July 1, 2000.

From July 1, 2000, until December 31, 2001, over 3,471 civil unions (and one civil union dissolution) involving parties from forty-eight different U.S. states and several foreign countries were issued by the state of Vermont (Vermont Civil Union Review Committee Report, 2002). Murray and Robinson continued to be active in the electoral battles fought in the 2000 election around Act 91 and they continued to be involved, as does Mary Bonauto, around legislative debates and commission hearing on the issue of civil unions.[9]

Coming Out on Gay and Lesbian Rights:
The Process of Cause Lawyering

Baker v. State was a straightforward piece of lawyering for a political purpose. When Murray and Robinson filed the lawsuit, they were both seeking a
change in Vermont's marriage laws and pursuing broader social and political
goals of challenging the inequality suffered by lesbians and gays as a group. The
plaintiffs they represented became the human face of oppression and their stories were the backdrop of a wider campaign designed to convince the public to
support same-sex marriage. And even though they were private practitioners
and might be expected to prefer legal strategies, they nevertheless deployed
many tactics—including grassroots activism discussed below—to achieve that
goal of greater equality for gays and lesbians. As we demonstrate in this section,
Murray and Robinson's work on *Baker v. State* vividly illustrates a process of
cause lawyering that embraces activities both inside and out of a courtroom.

The Political Significance of the 'Baker v. State' Litigation

The law has been an important means of regulating sexuality (Foucault
1990). Through the exercise of the law, homosexuality has been denigrated in
an attempt to eliminate it, and gays, lesbians, and bisexuals have been rendered
invisible in the social and political arena. As Justice William Brennan once
noted: "[b]ecause of the immediate and severe opprobrium often manifested
against homosexuals once so identified publicly, members of this group are
particularly powerless to pursue their rights openly in the political arena. Moreover, homosexuals have historically been the object of pernicious and sustained
hostility" (*Rowland v. Mad River Local School District* 1985: 1014).

Legal claims, like those advanced by Murray and Robinson, can force the law
to recognize homosexuality in a form that literally requires the state to justify
its ongoing marginalization of the acts and lives of lesbians, gays, and bisexuals.
Such legal claims challenge the existing power structures by denaturalizing the
accepted state of affairs (Sarat and Scheingold 1998). Marginalized groups often
situate their grievances in legal categories that most closely parallel existing social categories, and by doing so, expand the meaning of the legal category in a
way that renders the group visible and its claims routine. By advancing co-parenting adoption rights for gays and lesbians and same-sex marriage rights,
Murray and Robinson transformed those initially controversial claims into the
legal world of the mundane, reconstituting untraditional relationships into the
existing frameworks of the legally familiar, in this case, family law and consti-

tutional rights. Existing legal categories are expanded to embrace definitions of sexuality other than the imposed mores of heterosexuality.[10]

Moreover, Murray and Robinson's litigation strategies provided a particularly salient way of depicting the struggles of marginalized groups to wider public audiences. The plaintiffs became the faces of the lawsuit, and the circumstances of their lives were vivid illustrations of the burdens of being a member of an oppressed minority. In lawsuits, individuals are rendered visible for the first time: real people were produced in public through the court documents and surrounding publicity. But unlike race and gender claims, gay and lesbian rights cases make special demands on the plaintiffs. Being rendered visible in these cases requires one to publicly identify one's sexual orientation—to literally "out" oneself publicly. For many such plaintiffs, the lawsuit "outed" them to co-workers, families, and friends as well as the larger world. Thus, as Robinson (2001: 243) recognized, the litigation told "real stories about real people and the reality of our lives."

Murray and Robinson had several goals in their pursuit of the *Baker* case. One was to change the marriage laws to provide gay and lesbian couples the wide array of benefits available to heterosexual couples who get married. The legal protections guaranteed to married heterosexual couples are largely taken for granted. Gay and lesbian couples do not enjoy routine access to each other's pension or insurance benefits; they cannot be sure of access to emergency rooms if their partners suffer life-threatening injuries; they face financial burdens when they try to share property with their partners (Robinson 2001). The lawsuit's effort to allow same-sex couples to marry sought to redress the exclusion of gays and lesbians from these benefits, exclusions that Murray and Robinson noted in the course of their private practice (Robinson 2001).

But there was a broader social and political agenda behind Murray and Robinson's work on *Baker*, an agenda that became increasingly important to them as the case progressed. They grew to see their lawsuit as a challenge to the legal structures that supported the marginalization of gays, lesbians, and bisexuals. In this view, law was an important source of legitimacy and validation. Withholding such validation helped reify that marginalization. In an article reflecting on *Baker*, Robinson (2001: 240–42) wrote:

> But the law does more than simply delineate rights and obligations, or distribute benefits and burdens. The law also tells a story. It's a story about who we are as a community, how we view ourselves, and how we view one another. And it's a dynamic process; on the one hand, the law reflects our values and assumptions, and at the same time the law helps shape our values and assumptions.... This story told by the laws—that our relationships don't exist, or have no value—... touches every gay,

lesbian or bisexual person, regardless of whether we are partnered, and regardless of whether we have any desire to ever avail ourselves of the legal protections and obligations of marriage.

The lawsuit directly challenged this story told by Vermont's laws by demanding that the state explain why it marginalized gays, lesbians, and bisexuals in denying them the benefits of marriage. When the Supreme Court rejected the state's justifications as being insufficient, it partly dismantled some of these legal barriers to equality.

In addition, as Robinson had noted, the law can "tell stories" about the value of social arrangements. The court's opinion is *Baker* provides a legal redefinition of the social status of gays and lesbians. The opinion both praises existing gay families for their love and support for their children and recognizes committed gay and lesbian couples in romantic relationships. Murray and Robinson successfully fought to have these ideas incorporated into the preamble of the Vermont Civil Union Law, which states:

> Despite long-standing social and economic discrimination, many gay and lesbian Vermonters have formed lasting, committed, caring and faithful relationships with persons of their same sex. These couples live together, participate in their communities together, and some raise children and care for family members together, just as do couples who are married under Vermont law. (Preamble to Vermont Civil Union Law, §1(9)).

But by withholding marriage, the Civil Union Law still undermined, in Murray and Robinson's view, the potential for transforming the social status of gays, lesbians, and bisexuals in the state. As Robinson (interview 2002) noted:

> [The law] of civil unions tells a story of separation. It's still a dramatically different story. If you look at the preamble to the law . . . , there's some really unusual language about the state recognizing that same-sex couples form families, . . . and that those families have value, and that the state has an interest in promoting stable and lasting relationships with partners of the same sex. . . . So there has been a shift in the story. It's just not the full shift we ought to have.

Through their law practice, Murray and Robinson noticed an opportunity to bring a suit that would advance their clients' interests in obtaining the benefits of marriage. Their work on the case, and the underlying political action, however, strengthened their ideological commitment to the cause. Their goal was more than the challenge to the distribution of existing legal benefits. They used the law to accomplish the transgressive political goal of introducing gays, lesbians, and bisexuals into the society as equal citizens accorded social and legal status appropriate to their existing roles as citizens.

Grassroots Organizing Around 'Baker'

The process of cause lawyering has increasingly come to include grassroots organizing, media campaigns, and other work that takes cause lawyers out of the courtroom. But in the cause lawyering literature, there are conflicting accounts of the relationship between the attorneys and the communities they serve. Cause lawyers are either remote elites, disengaged from the groups whose interests they are trying to promote (Bell 1976; Scheingold 1974; Handler 1978), or they are "rebellious lawyers," living and working among the disenfranchised people they represent (Trubek and Kransberger 1998; Porter 1998). Murray and Robinson are closer to the latter category of cause lawyers. They were deeply embedded in Vermont's gay, lesbian, and bisexual community by virtue of their gay-friendly legal practice, handling co-parent adoption cases, and performing the legal work needed to simulate marriage—wills, trusts, and powers of attorney. Their contact with this community led them to help found the Vermont Freedom to Marry Task Force ("Task Force"), a grassroots movement that became the political vanguard for same-sex marriage in Vermont. Thus, Murray and Robinson helped to create a political movement to support their legal work.

From the beginning of their effort to establish marriage for same-sex partners, Murray and Robinson knew that community action was a vital part of the legal strategy in *Baker*. Writing about her experience with the *Baker* litigation, Robinson has observed: "We can craft the best arguments in the world in court, but if we're not also standing in booths at the local county fair, or speaking to a nearby church congregation on a Wednesday night, we risk losing in the court of public opinion our well-deserved gains in the court of law" (Robinson 2001: 243). In their understanding of the political nature of the litigation campaign that they were beginning, Murray and Robinson sought to lay the groundwork with a massive public education campaign that required extensive mobilization of volunteers. They began that mobilization by founding the Task Force.[11]

The Task Force consists of individuals and organizations from many different walks of life in Vermont, all of whom share a commitment to "full and equal legal rights for gay and lesbian Vermonters including, in particular, the legal right to marry" (www.vtfreetomarry.org in 2002). Its primary goal has been to raise public consciousness about the value of marriage. To pursue this goal, the Task Force mounted a massive effort to reach out to as many Vermont citizens as possible. Murray (interview 2002) described the three different audiences that the Task Force had to reach:

We always talked about having the population broken up into thirds: a third who are always going to be in favor; a third who are always going to be against; and a third in the middle who haven't really thought about it. And we wanted to talk to the people who haven't really thought about it and get them to start thinking about it, and if they're fair-minded people, they would get it. But they need to be educated about it, so a lot of what we were doing was not organizing so much as really educating, saying "Did you know that these are the benefits that gay people can't have because they can't get married?"

Murray and Robinson's organizing efforts began with organizations and groups they expected to be most sympathetic—gay and lesbian organizations, women's groups, and the ACLU, for example. In these early stages, the Task Force placed special emphasis on mobilizing the support of religious communities, particularly the Unitarian Universalist Church which had a long tradition of progressive community activism in Vermont. Task Force members made many presentations to not just Unitarians but also other congregations and groups of clergy and networked with religion-based organizations supportive of their cause, such as the Vermont Organization for Weddings of the Same Gender (VOWS). According to Robinson (interview 2002):

The key allies that made this happen in Vermont were communities of faith. Clergy were incredibly active, and I saw that as the first stage in building those bridges and developing the alliances that ultimately proved to be vital for what we've accomplished. So [we weren't] so much worried that they were going to hurt us but actually wanting to enlist them as partners in this effort.

Upon rallying their core supporters, Task Force members continued their public education campaign, targeting the "middle third" audience who had not yet thought about marriage for same-sex partners. They conducted presentations before community organizations, including Rotary Clubs, college campuses, and open public discussions. The Task Force also sponsored booths at county fairs and harvest festivals. The booths contained wedding photographs of same-sex couples and literature about the benefits of marriage denied to these families. In these different locations, according to Murray, they were "actually able to have some pretty good conversations [where] people felt comfortable asking questions that may have seemed awkward or may have seemed homophobic . . . but at least they felt comfortable asking, and they got answers, and that helped a lot" (Murray interview 2002).

To conduct this public education campaign, the Task Force recruited and trained dozens of volunteers. Murray and Robinson developed training manuals to teach people to speak to the media and to engage in constructive debate on the marriage issue. These training manuals "developed a specific 'speaking

style' to dialogue with members of the straight community in a thoughtful, in-
formational, and non-confrontational way" (www.vtfreetomarry.org in 2002).
In addition to personal outreach to different groups and organizations, the Task
Force mounted a sophisticated media campaign to reach a broader audience.
Task Force members spoke to the press, local television talk shows, and radio
call-in programs. They produced a video entitled *A Freedom to Marry: A Green
Mountain View* that they provided to public access television stations around
Vermont. They developed extensive contacts with Vermont newspapers. Robinson and Murray, in particular, were frequently quoted as experts in press reports. In addition, Task Force members wrote many letters to the editor en-
dorsing marriage for same-sex couples. Finally, the Task Force developed an
extensive Web site making the case for marriage for same-sex partners.

Murray and Robinson's involvement with Vermont Freedom to Marry Task
Force facilitated their interaction with "people who had gotten involved in the
organization because they wanted to get married, a lot of them" (Robinson interview 2002). Interest in the issue was so high that when Robinson and Murray organized the first marriage workshop at the 1996 Queer Town Meeting
(based on Vermont's Town Meeting political system), approximately eighty
people attended (Eskridge 2002). It was through Task Force efforts that the
plaintiffs in *Baker* came forward. The six plaintiffs attended Task Force work-
shops and engaged in other activities on behalf of the movement before the litigation began. Lois Farnham and Holly Puterbaugh first met Murray and
Robinson when they attended a Queer Town Meeting and heard about Task
Force efforts to promote marriage for same-sex couples. Stan Baker lent his
voice to the Task Force's videotape about the movement. Nina Beck and Stacy
Jolles had a son and moved to Vermont in part so that they could have a legal
relationship with him.

In the aftermath of the Vermont Supreme Court's decision in *Baker* (1999),
the Task Force strategy moved to the state legislature. Murray and Robinson
helped to form a new organization to engage in lobbying, Vermonters for Civil
Union Legislative Defense Fund, but the volunteers remained essentially the
same. During the legislative debate about civil unions, members from all parts
of the state contacted their state representatives and senators. Vermont legislators reported that where controversial issues in the past resulted in three or four
letters or phone calls, this issue attracted dozens of contacts, not just from constituents but from all over the world. In addition, Task Force members gave testimony before Vermont legislative communities about the problems confronted
by same-sex couples denied the ability to marry.

In their work surrounding *Baker v. State* (1999), Murray and Robinson challenged the image of a cause lawyer as an erudite professional, committed exclusively to legal strategies and uninterested in the grassroots movement she represents. First, they realized that legal strategies alone would not provide lasting results and that they needed to create a supportive political environment before undertaking the litigation. Second, to generate this political environment, they engaged in grassroots organizing in the gay and lesbian community—a community whose problems they already understood through their private legal practice. Finally, they reached out to other social movements and public-spirited organizations, including civil rights groups and church groups, for their support in this public education campaign. Thus, Murray and Robinson demonstrated sophisticated skills at grassroots organizing, perhaps surprising in light of their positions as private practitioners in a private law firm.

When Is a Cause Lawyer Not a Cause Lawyer?
Challenging the Typology

Using a definition of cause lawyering that emphasizes the attorneys' goals, motives, and activities on behalf of a movement, Murray and Robinson are clearly cause lawyers. Not only did they take on a controversial and politically charged lawsuit, but they did so on behalf of a socially and politically marginalized group of people. Moreover, they moved beyond litigation by helping to develop a social movement around same-sex marriage and by acting as legislative lobbyists. Their cause lawyering activities have helped to redefine gay and lesbian rights in Vermont and in the United States more broadly.

Yet Murray and Robinson do not fit comfortably in the model of cause lawyering that emphasizes the structure of their practice setting. In contrast to many cause lawyers in private practice, Murray and Robinson do not operate within a "rebellious" law firm (Trubek and Kransberger 1998: 203). Instead, they practice as partners in a large and well-established full-service law firm with a traditional structure (cf. Shamir and Chinski 1998: 230–31). They engage in traditional billing practices for their clients; their selection of clients is governed by the legal needs of the residents in their region, market forces and their own legal interest. Moreover, their pursuit of landmark gay and lesbian rights cases throughout the 1990s, including *Baker*, arose largely as an extension of the goals of existing clients. Thus, Murray and Robinson did not experience the tension between their clients' interests and the broader goals of the social movement—a tension often experienced by cause lawyers.

In the following sections, we explore these apparent contradictions between the existing understandings of cause lawyers and the social, legal, and practice environment of Murray and Robinson. We highlight two areas of incongruence: the traditional structuring of their law firm, Langrock, Sperry and Wool (LSW); and the relationship between the pursuit of causes and the goals of their clients. Obviously, both areas are interrelated and together they capture a general approach to cause lawyering that Murray and Robinson encapsulate—politically sophisticated private practitioners working in the public interest.

Langrock, Sperry and Wool: Private Practice and Public Interest

One of the most prominent law firms in Vermont, LSW consisted in 2002 of twenty-three lawyers in Middlebury and Burlington. Most of the attorneys graduated from the leading law schools in the United States, including Harvard University, New York University, and the University of Chicago. In addition, many of them held prestigious clerkships with judges before coming to LSW. The firm's practice combines "small town" lawyering with a sophisticated commercial practice. LSW represents many different kinds of clients, ranging from corporations and businesses, educational institutions, and municipalities to farmers, persons accused of crimes, and men and women seeking divorces. The firm's practice areas include everything from complex commercial and environmental litigation to drafting wills and representing defendants in DUI cases.[12] In fact, consistent with the image of themselves as a "small town law firm," the lawyers of LSW pride themselves on providing a full range of services to each of their clients: As Murray notes of LSW founder Peter Langrock: "Peter would represent the farmer [buying] the outlying property. On the first day they might have a car accident and second day he might want to buy or sell his car and the third day his kid's got a DWI and fourth day he's getting divorced, you know, and the fifth day who knows" (Murray interview 2002).

The firm balances its fee-generating work with a strong commitment to public service. Most of the attorneys in the firm serve in some public capacity in their own communities. Robinson observed: "I'm amazed how many partners in this firm are on their school board or are on their town select board or are on boards of important organizations doing important community work— heading up recreation programs in their town or things like that" (interview 2002). Peter Langrock, one of the name partners at LSW, fosters this public service orientation. Langrock is himself a prominent attorney in Vermont, having taken on significant free speech and civil rights cases. Under his leadership, the firm has also sponsored impact litigation in such areas as school funding, school choice, and prisoner rights. According to Murray and Robinson, Langrock has always encouraged his partners to take on hard cases in the public interest:

Peter describes us as the best firm in the cosmos. He never speaks in hyperboles, but . . . he believes that you take on a case when it's fun. You know, obviously, this is a business, and you have to—in order to do cases that are fun or are good for the community—you have to stay in business. But with that caveat, you don't turn down a case if you want to pursue it just because it won't pay.

In addition to the lawyers' sense of public spirit, some of LSW's fee-generating work also serves the public interest. For example, LSW attorneys handle environmental tort litigation where they represent the parties demanding that polluters clean up rivers and streams. In addition, they represent members of marginalized groups in their civil rights and employment discrimination practice. Even their representation of some personal injury plaintiffs has political ramifications that lead them out of the courtroom and into the realm of legislative activity. As a spokesperson for the Vermont Trial Lawyers' Association, for example, Beth Robinson recently announced the association's opposition to a bill that would provide ski resorts with greater immunity from lawsuits brought by individuals injured on the slopes. Thus, the law firm makes money from representing individuals who have been harmed by more powerful social forces.

The attorneys at LSW often pursue cases in the public interest long after the client is able to pay. In such cases, Peter Langrock's admonition to take on "fun" cases even when the firm cannot collect a fee is particularly salient. LSW attorneys have taken cases to the Supreme Court in such areas as worker's compensation, DUI, and adoption, not necessarily because there was a client paying the bill, but because there was an opportunity to have an impact in an area of law. Thus, many of the firm's *pro bono* cases emerge from its paying clientele.

LSW's domestic relations practice is a particularly clear example of a fee-generating enterprise with enormous transformative potential. On the one hand, LSW's domestic relations practice mirrors similar practices in completely traditional law firms. LSW attorneys represent both men and women with no clear ideological agenda driving their choice of clients. A great deal of the work in this area of the firm's practice is rather routine. Murray's description of her practice sounds much like that of family lawyers in any other firm: "I do family law in its broadest sense, which includes a lot of divorce work. It includes adoption work, both straight and gay. I do a lot of what I call planning for death and disability. Sounds morbid. Some people may use the phrase estate planning but more than just trusts and wills, you know, helping people figure out nursing home issues and power of attorney, health care matters" (Murray interview 2002). On the other hand, some of LSW's clients have sufficient assets to make the negotiations and litigation surrounding a divorce extremely complicated. Murray describes this aspect of her practice: "What I end up doing is representing people that have significant assets who need expert witnesses, accountants. . . . So there's really a component of commercial litigation embedded in the divorce practice" (Murray interview 2002). LSW also represents both men and women in these kinds of divorce actions.

Yet LSW is also a gay-friendly law practice, particularly in the area of estate planning and domestic relations. Susan Murray, for example, specialized in drafting the legal instruments that helped gay and lesbian couples re-create the legal rights and obligations traditionally ensured by marriage, such as wills, trusts, and durable powers of attorney. In addition, Murray represented gays and lesbians in adoption cases and custody disputes. This gay-friendly law practice has been transformative. They provided services to a group of people officially excluded from most legal protections; they pursued litigation on behalf of clients who would set precedents in the Vermont Supreme Court. But in addition to its transformative potential, some of this legal work also generated fees for the firm.

Although LSW has egalitarian qualities, it is not necessarily a "rebellious" law practice. All but one of the attorneys are partners in the firm and the partners enjoy friendly, informal relations. For example, all the lawyers have lunch together whenever they are in the office (Robinson interview 2002). Yet LSW is not really a "collective." There is no cooperative decision-making process in which the lawyers come together to collectively endorse and pursue their social justice values. Instead, when taking on *pro bono* cases, the attorneys make relatively independent decisions. For example, when Murray and Robinson took on *Baker*, they simply informed the rest of the firm. Indeed, their colleagues offered unconditional support although it represented a financial sacrifice for all the members. Still, most of the members of the firm did not participate in the decision to take the case (Murray and Robinson interview 2002).

Murray, Robinson, and their partners work in an unusually egalitarian and public-spirited law firm, but it is not a "rebellious" legal practice. Although the firm is serious about its public interest work, the attorneys also take seriously their traditional practice billing corporate, organizational, and individual clients. Undertaking *Baker* meant a financial sacrifice by the partners in the law firm, a sacrifice they were prepared to make in the struggle for gay and lesbian rights. However, neither the firm nor Murray and Robinson would identify themselves as strictly gay rights attorneys. Thus, they show that ideological commitment may be a resource for cause lawyers, but that such commitment can emerge from other obligations found among traditional lawyers, including the attorney's duty to zealously represent his or her client and to engage in public service.

Reconciling the Service-Impact Distinction

In their representation of the plaintiffs in *Baker v. State*, Murray and Robinson did not feel tension between the movement and their clients, a tension often emphasized in the cause lawyering literature. First, there was a close relationship between the movement, as embodied in the Vermont Freedom to Marry Task Force, and the plaintiffs. The cause for marriage for same-sex partners emerged from the everyday needs of gay and lesbian people in Vermont. This overlap between client interests and the cause made the service-impact distinction less pronounced, even in the context of a private practice. Second, Murray and Robinson had a relatively narrow view of the movement to which they were responsible—gay, lesbian, and bisexual people in Vermont who sought same-sex marriage rights. They paid little attention to the views of gay rights organizations outside of Vermont or broader debates in the gay community that were critical of the pursuit of same-sex marriage rights.

The plaintiffs in the case agreed to be plaintiffs because they already seemed married—they were three couples in committed relationships; they were financially secure; they were respected members of their communities "living quiet lives," as Robinson (interview 2002) noted. In addition, they were willing to come forward and talk publicly about their own lives and their reasons for wanting to be married. All the plaintiffs articulated very practical, everyday problems that led them to want to participate in the litigation. For example, Stan Baker argued that marriage would ease decision making in medical emergencies.

> If Peter were sick, and I needed to be with him in the hospital, I wouldn't have to show legal papers and go through all of this stuff that some couples have had to go through, or be denied access to each other. I want to be seen as his next of kin, as the person who knows him the best, and has the most intimate connection with him, and I want that to be legally recognized so I don't have to stand on my head in hospital situations . . . for people to see him as my next of kin, as my spouse. (*Out in the Mountains* 1997b)

Similarly, Nina Beck and Stacy Jolles signed on to the lawsuit because of their late son, Noah. Beck was Noah's biological mother, and Jolles adopted him shortly after they moved to Vermont in 1996. So while they both had a legal relationship with their son, they did not have a recognized relationship with each other. To Beck and Jolles, marriage was a key component of establishing families in the gay and lesbian community. Beck observed:

> I told Stacy we had to get married before we had kids; and part of that was joking around, but part of it was real. The part of it that was very real was that if I could avoid it, I wanted to ensure in as many ways that I could that I didn't become a sin-

gle parent. . . . It's another way that society has of asking people to make a public commitment to each other. It does ensure that it is a little more difficult to just pick up and leave. (*Out in the Mountains* 1997a)

These everyday issues implicated broader concerns revolving around social and cultural acceptance for gay and lesbian couples and families. Legal recognition of their relationships would be one way of achieving that acceptance. Thus, for the plaintiffs, their everyday concerns with property ownership, finances, medical care, pensions, and childrearing implicated the more symbolic issues of equality—the very issues at stake in a broader social movement to establish and protect the rights of the gay, lesbian, and bisexual community to form families. Beck gave an example of this relationship to an interviewer in 1997:

> We were traveling back from Europe. In Amsterdam airport [they ask you some questions before you can get on the plane]. . . . The security agent came, and I had Noah, and Stacy was standing next to me. She said, "Are you two traveling together?" And we said yes. She said, "Are you a family?" And we said yes. And so she took all three of us to her podium and asked us the same questions at the same time. And I almost cried because I felt so seen, so validated and so ordinary in that moment. It was everything I was looking for. It's like that is why I want to be married. I want that feeling in my life on a regular basis. (*Out in the Mountains* 1997a).

These client concerns for both the practical benefits of marriage as well as the acceptance that legal recognition would entail were mirrored in the legal arguments made during the litigation. During the course of the *Baker* lawsuit and the surrounding publicity, Murray and Robinson worked closely with the plaintiffs crafting the arguments they would all make to the press. In fact, in many of their interviews with the press, the plaintiffs compared the struggle for gay and lesbian marriage to the civil rights struggle to decriminalize interracial marriage—one of the central legal arguments in the case. Moreover, according to Robinson (interview 2002), there were few strategic decisions that needed to be made in the course of the litigation. As a result, Murray and Robinson were able to represent the plaintiffs without compromising the cause of marriage for same-sex couples.

The service-impact conflict did emerge in the context of the debate over civil unions in the Vermont legislature. Once the issue reached the legislature and marriage was no longer a realistic possibility, Murray, Robinson, the plaintiffs, and active members of the Task Force found that they had to make a series of compromises, settling for something less than marriage. Although Murray and Robinson felt tension from time to time in their roles as attorneys and as representatives in the legislative cause, they generally tried to proceed on a consensus basis (Murray and Robinson interview 2002).

Murray and Robinson's unified commitment to cause and client was made possible by their relative insulation from the broader debates in the gay, lesbian, and bisexual community about the merit of pursuing same-sex marriage. They did not have extensive contacts with the gay rights legal establishment, apart from their working relationship with Mary Bonauto of GLAD, who among other things, reassured the lawyers at LAMBDA that they were competent to handle such an important case (Robinson interview 2002). In fact, they used their standing as attorneys at one of Vermont's most prominent law firms as a badge of legitimacy with their Vermont constituents who worried that they might be too attentive to national gay rights organizations. In an interview with *Out in the Mountains* (1998), Robinson explicitly rejected the notion that her law firm was "acting as puppets" of LAMBDA and noted that LSW was "investing a lot of money and people in this case, because everyone at the firm believes strongly in the rights of all Vermonters."

Moreover, Murray and Robinson largely dismissed the qualms about same-sex marriage as "academic," and not reflecting the needs or concerns of real people. Robinson (interview 2002) argued:

> Some people look at the work that we've been doing and see it as profoundly conservative because of the extent to which it seeks to plug in gays and lesbians into existing social structures. And then for every one of those there's somebody who sees us as radical because we're transforming the deeply imbedded social structures of gender relations as codified in marriage into something completely different and I don't think we're radicals in either direction but I think it's true that there's a real element of traditionalism to what we've been advocating and there's also an element of the real paradigm shift.

Their standing as private practitioners gave them influence in Vermont's legal and political arenas. Further, it allowed them to build sufficient credibility among a significant section of the gay and lesbian community in Vermont in order to pursue the goal of same-sex marriage without public dissent from within Vermont's gay and lesbian community. Thus, they could use their social standing in Vermont as a powerful source of legitimacy in extending their legal claim in *Baker*. For this reason, Robinson and Murray were explicit in rejecting any connection beyond their law firm and its clients.

Private practitioners are supposedly compromised when they engage in cause lawyering. They must choose between their ethical duty to their individual client and their commitment to the cause when the interests of the client and the movement diverge. The *Baker* case suggests that in some cases, where social movements emerge from the everyday concerns of individuals, this tension may not present a serious problem. In these cases, private practitioners will not be confronted by the stark choice between serving a client and serving a cause.

Conclusion

Cause lawyering is an important component of many contemporary social movements. Through legal strategies, cause lawyers construct new rights and challenge institutionalized oppression on behalf of disadvantaged groups. Over time, cause lawyers have also engaged in political mobilization and grassroots organization, in recognition of the limits of litigation's transformative potential. Studies of lawyers engaged in these activities have focused on those employed in social movement organizations or public interest law firms to understand the motivation and nature of cause lawyering.

In the case described in this chapter, Susan Murray and Beth Robinson have most certainly engaged in cause lawyering. They were politically committed to dismantling legal barriers to equality faced by the gay, lesbian, and bisexual community, and self-consciously pursued this case as a strategy for achieving that goal. They handled a piece of litigation, *Baker v. State*, which declared it unconstitutional in Vermont to deprive gays, lesbians, and bisexuals of the benefits of marriage. They used this litigation for political purposes. The case put a human face on the legal project of redefining the social status of gay, lesbian, and bisexual Vermonters. But it also allowed them to define their clients as ordinary people challenging a routine law that impacted upon their daily lives and whom had sought conventional lawyers to resolve this complaint—a position that allowed more empathy to those who watched the case in Vermont. Murray and Robinson managed a lobbying campaign in the Vermont legislature that created a new institution, civil unions, to provide the benefits of marriage to same-sex partners. They developed a grassroots organization of activists to develop a political environment supportive of these new rights and institutions and to protect their judicial and legislative achievements.

Yet in meaningful ways, Murray and Robinson do not fit the definition of cause lawyers. They are private attorneys in a large profitable law practice that, although public-spirited and committed to law reform, is hardly "rebellious." And as private attorneys, with no history of activism, they were unusual in their ability and their willingness to engage in grassroots mobilization of Vermont citizens. Moreover, the *Baker* case was not a *pro bono* case, divorced from the routine practice of the law firm. Rather, *Baker* represented an extension of the legal work Murray and Robinson were already doing on behalf of paying gay, lesbian, and bisexual clients who needed legal documents to protect their families. This relationship between the problems, struggles, and aspirations of their clients and the underlying movement helped ease the tension other private practitioners might feel between the broader goals of the movement and the individual client.

We argue that the study of cause lawyers must be expansive enough to embrace attorneys like Murray and Robinson. Specifically, we suggest that studies of cause lawyering should emphasize the "cause" over the "lawyer." Researchers should examine social movements on behalf of marginalized groups and identify the varied roles that different lawyers play in the movement (Shamir, this volume). This struggle-centered approach would have several advantages. First, it would not automatically exclude the sometimes significant contributions of private practitioners who make money at the same time that they serve a movement. As resources for legal services and rights-based organizations dwindle, private practitioners may be able to provide assistance to social movements. Moreover, as this case shows, prominent law firms may lend other kinds of resources to a struggle, such as the firm's stature or local legitimacy.

Second, emphasizing the cause over the lawyers offers the possibility of developing a complex picture of the social movement itself. Social movement organizations and public interest law firms may develop planned litigation campaigns that reflect their own elite views of the political priorities of marginalized groups. Yet such organizations may not necessarily represent the views or needs of their constituents who may have no means to hold these organizations accountable. Ironically, private practitioners who serve paying clients may be closer and more responsive to the individual needs and problems of marginalized groups. Thus, including the work of private attorneys can help reveal the tensions in struggles over rights and raise interesting questions about democracy and legitimacy in social movements.

Murray, Robinson, and their work in Vermont allow us to witness cause lawyers purposely operating in an environment that goes beyond the traditional site of much cause lawyering. More important, the Vermont example demonstrates that private practice emerges as a potentially strong tool in the hands of some cause lawyers. As such, it is certainly worthy of fuller consideration in understanding the motivation and nature of cause lawyering.

Notes

1. For example, the towns of Cohoes and Olive in New York each pursued such action and their separate inquiries were the basis of the response by the New York State solicitor general regarding the legality of same-sex marriage in New York State (Halligan 2004).

2. Hill argued that the Vermont constitution, which dated from 1777 when Vermont was a republic, allowed state constitutional rights to be interpreted consistent with the state's extensive legal history rather than bound to simply follow federal parameters. Hill's opinion in State v. Badger in 1982 outlining this point formed an important part of

Chief Justice Amestoy's subsequent reasoning for relying upon the Vermont constitution in *Baker v. State*—the same-sex marriage case in 1999—rather than the Fourteenth Amendment of the U.S. Constitution as state courts had in Washington (in *Singer v. Hara* 1974) and Hawaii (in *Baehr v. Lewin* 1993).

3. Julie Frame and David Curtis, two private practice lawyers who had been associated with the Vermont Coalition for Lesbian and Gay Rights (Eskridge 2002: 45), litigated the *B.L.V.B.* case. Julie Frame would later represent one of the parties in another important Vermont sexual orientation case, *Titchenal v. Dexter* (1997). David Curtis was the former defender general of the state of Vermont and from 1997 until his death in 1999, he was chair of the Vermont State Democratic Party.

4. Paula Ettelbrick, who was then legal director of LAMBDA, filed LAMBDA's separate brief. Interestingly Ettelbrick would later emerge as one of the more outspoken opponents of same-sex marriage (Ettelbrick 1997).

5. In addition to codifying judicial decisions recognizing adoption rights for same-sex partners, the Vermont legislature had produced extensive legislation protecting various gay and lesbian rights. In 1989, Vermont included sexual orientation in groups protected from hate crimes (13 V.S.A. §1455). In 1991, Howard Dean, then the Vermont governor, introduced domestic partnership benefits for state employees through collective bargaining. In 1992, Vermont passed the Human Rights Law that introduced sexual orientation into the categories of classes explicitly protected from discrimination in terms of housing (9 V.S.A. §4502), public accommodation (9 V.S.A. §4503), private employment (21 V.S.A. §495), state employment (3 V.S.A. §961), union membership (3 V.S.A. §963), financial transactions (8 V.S.A. §1211), and education (16 V.S.A. §11).

6. See "Grassroots Organizing Around *Baker*" below for a discussion of Murray and Robinson's activities on behalf of the Vermont Freedom to Marry Task Force.

7. Examples include cases in Minnesota (*Baker v. Nelson* 1971), Washington (*Singer v. Hara* 1974), and Hawaii (*Baehr v. Lewin* 1993).

8. The Supreme Court retained jurisdiction over the case so that it could confirm that the legislative action met the parameters of an appropriate remedy in the case.

9. For example, Mary Bonauto, of GLAD, was an expert witness for the Vermont Civil Union Review Committee. Further, in 2001, she filed suit in Massachusetts on behalf of seven gay and lesbian couples seeking the right to marry in the case of *Goodridge v. Department of Public Health* (2003).

10. Unlike many of the other forms of legal and moral approbation that is brought to bear against lesbians, gays, and bisexuals, litigation on same-sex marriage and co-parent adoption occurs in part because "the demands—for same sex marriage—could easily be expressed in terms of constitutional rights" (Eskridge 2002: 5). For this reason, same-sex marriage claims have a legal history that extends back to 1971, but same-sex marriage has also consistently been a fundamental demand of gay and lesbian rights groups since the late 1960s (see Eskridge 1996: 73–74, 2002: 6–7).

11. The Task Force grew out of an established social movement organization, the Vermont Coalition for Lesbian and Gay Rights (VCLGR). VCLGR engaged in public education and supported such initiatives as Vermont's hate crime legislation and laws prohibiting discrimination on the basis of sexual orientation (Eskridge 2002: 45). In addi-

tion, VCLGR sponsored public events in the gay and lesbian community, including annual Queer Town Meetings. In the aftermath of *Baehr v. Levin* (1993) in Hawaii, VCLGR sponsored a committee on the question of marriage for same-sex partners. As members of the committee, Murray and Robinson presented a workshop on the subject at one of the VCLGR town meetings in 1995. That particular workshop attracted widespread attendance. Eventually, the committee evolved into the Task Force, becoming a separate organization in 1996 (Robinson interview 2002; Eskridge 2002).

12.   The firm's "Statement of Practice" in Martindale Hubbell lists the following practice areas: Civil and Criminal Trials in all State and Federal Courts. Administrative, Agricultural, Antitrust, Bankruptcy, Civil Rights, Commercial Litigation and Transactions, Construction, Corporate, Discrimination, Education, Employment, Environmental, Family, Insurance Coverage Disputes, Labor Relations, Land Use, Municipal, Pensions and Profit Sharing, Personal Injury, Probate, Product Liability, Professional Negligence, Public Utility, Real Estate, Ski Injury Litigation, Taxation, Workers Compensation, and Wrongful Death.

References

Books and Articles

Alfieri, Anthony V. 1991. "Reconstructive Poverty Law Practice: Learning the Lessons of Client Narrative." *Yale Law Journal* 100: 2107–47.

Bell, Derrick. 1976. "Serving Two Masters: Integration Ideals and Client Interests in School Desegregation Litigation." *Yale Law Journal* 85: 470–516.

Bloom, Anne. 2001. "Taking on Goliath: Why Personal Injury Litigation May Represent the Future of Transnational Cause Lawyering," in *Cause Lawyering and the State in a Global Era,* ed. Austin Sarat and Stuart Scheingold. New York: Oxford University Press.

Bonauto, Mary, Susan M. Murray, and Beth Robinson. 1999. "The Freedom to Marry for Same-Sex Couples: The Opening Appellate Brief of Plaintiffs Stan Baker et al. in *Baker et al. v. State of Vermont.*" *Michigan Journal of Gender and Law* 5, no. 2: 409–75.

Eskridge, William N. Jr. 1999. *Gaylaw: Challenging the Apartheid of the Closet.* Cambridge: Harvard University Press.

————. 2002. *Equality Practice: Civil Unions and the Future of Gay Rights.* New York: Routledge.

Ettelbrick, Paula. 1997. "Since When is Marriage a Path to Liberation." In *Same-Sex Marriage: The Legal and Moral Debate*, edited by Robert M. Baird and Stuart E. Rosenbaum. New York: Prometheus Books.

Foucault, Michel. 1990. *The History of Sexuality: An Introduction.* New York: Vintage Books.

Halligan, Caitlin. 2004. "Opinion of the New York State Solicitor General on the Legality of Same Sex Marriages in New York State." Issued by the New York State Attorney General's Office, March 3, 2004.

Handler, Joel F. 1978. *Social Movements and the Legal System: A Theory of Law Reform and Social Change.* New York: Academic Press.

Kilwein, John. 1998. "Still Trying: Cause Lawyering for the Poor and Disadvantaged in Pittsburgh, Pennsylvania," in *Cause Lawyering: Political Commitments and Professional Responsibilities*, ed. Austin Sarat and Stuart Scheingold. New York: Oxford University Press.

Lawrence, Susan E. 1992. *The Poor in Court: The Legal Services Program and Supreme Court Decision-Making*. Princeton, N.J.: Princeton University Press.

Leonard, Arthur S. 2000. "From *Bowers v. Hardwick* to *Romer v. Evans*: Lesbian and Gay Rights in the U.S. Supreme Court," in *Creating Change: Sexuality, Public Policy and Civil Rights*, ed. John D'Emilio, William B. Turner, and Urvashi Vaid. New York: St. Martin's Press.

Marshall, Anna-Maria. 2001. "A Spectrum in Oppositional Consciousness: Sexual Harassment Plaintiffs and Their Lawyers," in *Oppositional Consciousness: The Subjective Roots of Social Protest*, ed. Jane Mansbridge and Aldon Morris. Chicago: University of Chicago Press.

McCann, Michael W. 1994. *Rights at Work: Pay Equity Reform and the Politics of Legal Mobilization*. Chicago: University of Chicago Press.

Menkel-Meadow, Carrie. 1998. "The Causes of Cause Lawyering: Toward an Understanding of the Motivation and Commitment of Social Justice Lawyers," in *Cause Lawyering: Political Commitments and Professional Responsibilities*, ed. Austin Sarat and Stuart Scheingold. New York: Oxford University Press.

Murdoch, Joyce, and Deb Price. 2001. *Courting Justice: Gay Men and Lesbians v. the Supreme Court*. New York: Basic Books.

Olson, Susan M. 1984. *Clients and Lawyers: Securing the Rights of Disabled Persons*. Westport, Conn.: Greenwood Press.

Out in the Mountains. 1997a, September. "Courtside Seats: A Conversation with Vermont's Most Famous Plaintiffs." By Chris Tebbets—Part One of Three Part Series.

Out in the Mountains. 1997b, December. "Courtside Seats: A Conversation with Vermont's Most Famous Plaintiffs." By Chris Tebbets—Part Three of Three Part Series.

Out in the Mountains. 1998, March. "Freedom to Marry: The Right Strike Back."

Porter, Aaron. 1998. "Norris, Schmidt, Green, Harris, Higginbotham and Associates: The Sociolegal Import of Philadelphia Cause Lawyers," in *Cause Lawyering: Political Commitments and Professional Responsibilities*, ed. Austin Sarat and Stuart Scheingold. New York: Oxford University Press.

Robinson, Beth. 2001. "The Road to Inclusion for Same-Sex Couples: Lessons from Vermont." *Seton Hall Constitutional Law Journal* 11 no. 2: 237–57.

Sarat, Austin, and Stuart Scheingold. 1998. "Cause Lawyering and the Reproduction of Professional Authority: An Introduction," in *Cause Lawyering: Political Commitments and Professional Responsibilities*, ed. Austin Sarat and Stuart Scheingold. New York: Oxford University Press.

Scheingold, Stuart. 1974. *The Politics of Rights: Lawyers, Public Policy and Political Change*. New Haven, Conn.: Yale University Press.

———. 1998. "The Struggle to Politicize Legal Practice: A Case Study of Left-Activist Lawyering in Seattle," in *Cause Lawyering: Political Commitments and Professional Responsibilities*, ed. Austin Sarat and Stuart Scheingold. New York: Oxford University Press.

tivists. Lawyers will vary in their involvement with causes and movements, and this study explores the ways in which professional identity may or may not be relevant to causes.

Similarly, sociolegal researchers concern themselves with cause lawyers as a subset of the legal profession, rather than considering the possibility that they step outside their professional roles and obligations and act as ordinary activists. This body of research is limited by the broad assumption that lawyering and cause work are at odds. It becomes interesting, then, to explore the conditions under which lawyers either step out of their professional role to become activists or manage their professional role by blending it with their personal, activist role or identity.

Moving beyond assumptions from past research, this study of cause lawyers provides an alternate way of considering lawyers involved with movements: (1) cause lawyers may or may not hold salient their professional identity; thus, they may act in movements beyond a legalistic capacity; (2) cause lawyers take on collective identities in the same way as other activists; and (3) cause lawyers vary in the degree to which they feel tensions between being a lawyer and working for the cause. Underlying my research is the question how lawyers, as activists, reconcile their professional and activist roles and identities. Specifically, I explore the ways in which lawyers fabricate their identities in the face of institutional constraints, providing one illustration of the processes of identity correspondence (Snow and McAdam 2000) and identity work (Snow and Anderson 1987).

Social movement research does provide an important conceptual foundation for cause lawyering research by viewing activism and collective identity as *processual,* such that varied careers in activism and varied commitment to causes and to collective identities can be explained. Applied to cause lawyers, these identity processes are illustrated in varied social contexts, thus illuminating the variation among cause lawyers, whether they experience tensions between their work and cause, and whether their professional identity as lawyers determines their actions with movements. I draw upon rich interview data with a sample of thirty-seven cause lawyers in Arizona to demonstrate the conditions under which various cause lawyers work and how these conditions impact the personal and collective identity processes associated with activism. Using the movement concept of identity correspondence, I illustrate differences among cause lawyers in their approach to their work, the cause, and their identity as activists. I propose a typology of lawyers as "core" or "marginal" to a broader cause lawyering community that examines cause lawyers as activists—the greater their engagement as core, the more likely their avoidance of identity conflicts.[1]

Before discussing the varied self-definitions held by cause lawyers, I first introduce some other definitional concerns. Lawyers involved with political and social movements have been called "radical" lawyers, "movement" lawyers, "cause" lawyers, "progressive" lawyers, "transgressive" lawyers, or "political" lawyers, all of which refer to the political nature of their role.[2] Typically these terms are associated with the politics on the left in this country. However, cause lawyering could involve representing conservative interests on the right wing of the political spectrum (e.g., lawyers actively supporting pro-life interests in the abortion conflict). It should also be noted that the above definitions of cause lawyering fit the United States, often defined in contrast to the "traditional" business or corporate law. In other countries, cause lawyering may be the traditional form of practice.[3] In this research I focus on individual lawyers who work in or for a variety of organizations (legal and movement), with a primary focus on lawyering on the left.[4]

Implied in the above question about reconciling professional and activist identities is an assumption that some conflict is inherent to these roles or identities. Cause lawyering can be seen as a challenge to the traditional norms of the legal profession since lawyers are expected to advocate clients' interests while remaining neutral (Sarat and Scheingold 1998b; Simon 1978; Scheingold and Bloom 1998). The examination of how lawyers reconcile their causes and their work also assumes that cause lawyers identify with the profession in the same way as other lawyers, and assumes that cause lawyers' advocacy for causes somehow conflicts with advocacy for clients. It is important to explore the conditions under which cause lawyers work because it may be that the cause and the client advocacy are not in conflict. Similarly, if cause lawyers identify primarily as activists instead of lawyers, then the norms and professional obligations may be less important in governing their daily work. Individuals may avoid identity conflicts as identities of activist and cause lawyer correspond. If cause lawyers do in fact identify with the traditional professional norms and obligations, the question then becomes how this distinguishes their work and behaviors from cause lawyers who do not so identify. Clearly the identity processes of cause lawyers need further exploration.

Although lawyers may not be explicitly defined in social movement theory, lawyers might be viewed as state actors, or an "arm of the law," acting in ways that either constrain or facilitate movement strategies and goals (della Porta 1996; McAdam, McCarthy, and Zald 1996; Tilly 1978). Further extensions of social movement theory would view lawyers as elites who co-opt movement strategies and goals in line with their own interests (McCarthy and Zald 1973, 1987; McCarthy et al. 1991). Lawyers have also been discussed in terms of tactics or strategies in movement, but again this discussion is narrowly defined in

terms of the professional role of lawyers: inclined to think of litigation apart
from other political tactics or broad movement goals (Scheingold 1974; Mc-
Cann 1986; Weisbrod, Handler, and Komesar 1978). This can be problematic for
movements as resources are diverted to litigation strategies at the expense of
other, potentially effective strategies (Rosenberg 1991; McCann and Silverstein
1998). Movement researchers also argued that elite patronage and organizing
serve to "professionalize" social movement organizations (SMOs) and channel
them toward more moderate goals (Jenkins and Eckert 1986; McAdam 1982;
Piven and Cloward 1977). It has been argued that mass disruption, the one
power that otherwise resource-poor groups had, was removed by the involvement of professionals and elites (Haines 1984; Piven and Cloward 1977). More
recent scholarship has challenged the moderating influence of external sponsors by specifying the conditions under which benefactors appeared to help
movements without removing the potential for radical action (Cress and Snow
1996). Again, it becomes important to understand how lawyers involve themselves with movements and within the cause lawyering community in order to
better explain whether they change a movement. Cause lawyers will likely vary
in their awareness of their role or intention in causes, and this should be illustrated as the context of their work and identities are defined.

In addition to further attempts to define the conditions under which one
type of professional becomes involved with movements, I also question
whether they are, in fact, professionals or outsiders. Cause lawyering should be
different for those lawyers participating as outsiders (according to a narrow
professional role) and those participating as insiders or ordinary activists. It is
important to understand whether, and under what conditions, lawyers are able
to achieve correspondence between their professional and personal role identities.

Analytic Strategy

Because I am interested in the identity processes of cause lawyers and
whether they act as lawyers or activists, I chose to focus on the lawyers across
many different movements or causes rather than focusing on one organization
and its structures and goals. Previous research on lawyers within one setting
served as a starting point for defining roles that lawyers might play, but this research also demonstrated the utility of studying the "pool" of cause lawyers
(McCann and Silverstein 1998). Other research has indicated the importance of
setting in explaining cause lawyers (Scheingold and Bloom 1998), and my study
extends this work by further demonstrating how practice setting matters—in

terms of structural support or constraint for various identities. In order to capture the widest range of cause lawyering, and since I did not want to impose my
own definitions onto the lawyers, I defined the pool quite broadly to include
lawyers in many contexts and "degrees of activism." This included lawyers in
government positions, private practice, public interest centers, and professors.
Through conversations with lawyers and activists, as well as professional listings
of public interest lawyers, I composed a list of potential interviewees.[5] Through
snowball sampling, a total of thirty-seven lawyers were contacted and interviewed; the interviews averaged about one-and-a-half to two hours in length.

The research setting of Arizona becomes important in comparing the demographics of the sample to the profession at large, and also in considering the
structural and political constraints that may be placed on the practice of cause
lawyering. Initial perceptions of Arizona are: (1) it is politically conservative and
has a long history of being so, and therefore (2) the lawyers in Arizona may be

TABLE 7.1

Demographic Summary of Legal Profession and Cause Lawyer Sample

	U.S. lawyer population	Sample	
	(%)	%	n
Gender (% female)	25.0[a]	52.9	18
Race (% nonwhite)	5.8[b,c]	17.6	6
Legal education			
Elite (%)	n/a	23.5	8
Nonelite (%)	n/a	76.5	26
Setting of legal practice			
Law school/Education	1.0	35.3	12
Public interest organization	0.5	17.6	6
Legal aid	1.1	14.7	5
Government	8.2	11.8	4
SMO	n/a	2.9	1
Small firm	16.0	8.8	3
Other firm	56.8	5.8	2
Judiciary	2.6	0	
Industry	9.5	0	
Other	4.5	2.9	1

SOURCE: Information on U.S. Lawyer Population comes from American Bar Association
(ABA) reports (1995a and 1995b), including the following sources: the American Bar
Foundation, the annual Martindale-Hubbell Directories, the U.S. Bureau of the Census and
the Bureau of Labor Statistics, and the National Association for Law Placement. Some figures
are estimates for the current population. Sample does not include the three non-active
lawyers.

[a] Class of 1995 43.0 percent.

[b] Arizona only.

[c] Class of 1995 17.0 percent.

more representative of traditional lawyers who focus on business and economic law (i.e., represent corporations and conservative, "wealthy" interests), where public interest lawyers would be few and far between. Exactly because of these perceptions, however, I decided that Arizona lawyers would be a valuable source of information about activist lawyering. There are regional variations in the opportunities for public interest law or cause lawyering. The National Association for Law Placement (NALP) study of the class of 1996 indicates that 51 percent of law graduates in Arizona took jobs in private practice, 9.9 percent in business, 14.6 percent as judicial clerks, 18.6 percent in government, and 3.1 percent in public interest (see Table 7.1). Although one class does not define the entire population of public interest lawyers in Arizona, it does show that the numbers compare favorably nationally (i.e., that Arizona is not a state with a lower than average proportion of such lawyers).

Of the lawyers I interviewed, eighteen were men and nineteen were women. They ranged in age from twenty-five to one semiretired person at seventy-two. Just six were nonwhite (one African American, five Hispanic), and thirty-one were white. Although I did not ask about religious background, five brought up in the course of the interview that they were Jewish. These demographic variables are listed for informational purposes; in the study they did not appear to correlate with identity processes. Data analysis suggests another important pattern among this sample of cause lawyers.

Constructing the "Core" and "Marginal" Cause Lawyer Community

My analysis of the interviews suggests a group of "core" cause lawyers, a group of more "marginal" cause lawyers, and three that ultimately are not engaged in cause lawyering. This typology of cause lawyers and the work they do is grounded in their own experiences in the legal profession and social movements, though the terms are strictly for analytic purposes. I define "core" cause lawyers to be those who define activism as their primary identity and work, are involved in multiple movements and causes, and are seen by others (activists and lawyers) as the center of cause lawyering in the community. "Marginal" cause lawyers are those who straddle lawyering and activism in a way that does not give precedence to one or the other, do not define themselves primarily to be activists, and limit their activities to primarily legal representation or advocacy. Marginal cause lawyers also were likely to downplay or deemphasize their activist contributions. This is an important form of identity work: although the actual impact of their activism is not marginal, these lawyers were quick to suggest that other lawyers were "much more involved in that." By comparing themselves to such an "other," these lawyers are both defining themselves and the category of core cause lawyers. I characterize seven lawyers as currently at the core, twenty-seven as currently marginal, and three nonactive.

For "core" and "marginal" activists, I coded in terms of the number of others who identified them as cause lawyers, as well as through an analysis of actual behaviors. The majority (nearly all) of the other lawyers in the sample named the "core" activists as those who are cause lawyers. The behavior of core and marginal cause lawyers vary mainly in terms of frequency and degree. Marginal lawyers often engaged in similar behaviors as the core, just less frequently or less extremely when it comes to activism, that is, they used more institutional political means such as letter writing than extrainstitutional (demonstrating) means. "Core" cause lawyers are characterized by their commitment to and involvement in a range of causes and social movements, their definition of themselves as activists, and their range of activist behaviors beyond institutional means, including protests, sit-ins, and representation of activists who had been arrested. Their location at the core of cause lawyering is also defined by their overlapping ties: many of the core have multiple and overlapping ties to each other as they sit on each other's boards and serve together in local activist and community organizations. Table 7.2 compares core and marginal cause lawyers.

TABLE 7.2

A Typology of Core and Marginal Cause Lawyers (CLs)

	Core Cause Lawyer (n = 7)	Marginal Cause Lawyer (n = 27)
Other-identified as CL	nearly all in sample identified them as CL	1–3 others identified them as CL
Self-identify	activist first, lawyer second; or not identify self as lawyer at all	lawyer who does activism or just lawyer
Current activities	includes full range of extra-institutional and legal; wide range of activities	mostly institutional; only "moderate" extra-institutional
Organizations	alternate professional; many; political	fewer; some political; some community
Network	densely and tightly connected to other CLs; multiple and overlapping ties; strong ties to activist community	frayed; weakly tied to other CLs; weak or absent ties to activist community
Movements/causes	multiple; central to almost all local movement activities	one or two issues or case by case
Frequency of cause work	participate almost daily; much overlap with work	participate regularly, but not daily; less overlap with work

NOTE: The author originally developed this typology as part of a larger project. See Jones (1999, 2001), both of which laid the groundwork for the current usage of these ideas. Also, the three non-active lawyers are not included in this table.

It is important to recognize that past or future biographical, structural, or political circumstances might "relocate" these lawyers from core to marginal, or marginal to core. These are not fixed categories or identities, but rather a positioning in the cause lawyering community and activist community that can and does change over time. For instance, success in achieving the goals of a cause may lead to a more marginal status for a lawyer for that cause; however, the lawyer may change to another issue depending on other ties. Also, the terms do not refer to greater commitment to cause by core lawyers, or weaker commitment by marginal lawyers. Both core and marginal cause lawyers demonstrate strong commitment and significant impact work. Rather, the terms refer in large part to the perceived support for (or barriers to) cause work and positive negotiation of cause lawyer identities. Those defined as "core" have settled the issue of tensions between the cause and the profession, and the data will illustrate that this has much to do with their positioning in networks of other activists and other cause lawyers. Those defined as "marginal" have more tenuous ties or supports for their work as cause lawyers; thus, they face more daily struggles and fit the old assumption that the cause and the lawyering may be at odds. The barriers to successful correspondence of activist and lawyer identities will be discussed later.

Other research studies have defined "hired guns" and "technical experts" to be the lawyers who come into a movement somewhat briefly and act primarily according to their professional role (Scheingold 1998). This last type may be the only one that has the channeling impact on movements described above. I do not have "hired guns" included in this sample. This typology of core and marginal demonstrates that cause lawyers are not always acting in movements according to their professional role or identity, thus the impact on social movements cannot be assumed to be "legalistic" or deradicalizing. For example, those at the core who identify as activists typically put the cause above all else. The examination of correspondence between activism and lawyering is contextualized in the work and experiences of cause lawyers.

Formal Work Setting of Sample Cause Lawyers

The cause lawyers in this study are currently located across a range of work settings. Cause lawyers often move between work settings, and the reasons and motivations for working in particular settings are abundant and diverse: politics or cause, financial reasons, structural supports, or constraints. The remainder of this chapter examines some of these issues. For now, it is important to note that each lawyer has his or her own career path, moving in and out of dif-

TABLE 7.3

Current Work Setting of Cause Lawyers

Location/Type of position	No. of core	No. of marginal	No. of nonactive
Public interest law center	4	2	
Law school clinic	3	1	
Law school/Other professor		6	
Legal aid		7	
Law school dean		2	
Public defender/Government		3	1
Social movement organization		2	
Large firm		1	1
Small firm		3	
Social work			1

ferent work settings and causes, and in and out of core and marginal cause lawyering. So, the definition here of the current work setting should not be viewed as a permanent location, just as being core or marginal can change. The structural and identity issues that are discussed later in the chapter suggest how and why location of work may change or remain the same as identities and network ties support and constrain the work of cause lawyers. The work setting should not be viewed as prohibitive of cause lawyering because there were active cause lawyers in similar settings. The difference appears to be other network supports and obligations. Similarly, work setting does not *determine* strategy or tactics, but some work settings do allow for more flexibility and freedom to do the range of cause work (see Table 7.3).

Both the core and marginal cause lawyers were found across a range of settings, but the core seem to be more narrowly concentrated in two types of settings: law school clinics (four) and small public interest law centers (three). The core are not located in legal aid, public defender offices, larger firms, or as nonclinic professors at the law school. All of those at the core described their work settings as a necessity in that they specifically chose to work in those places that best allow them to practice their cause work. They also begin to talk about their positioning in terms of identity: for example, those working as professors in law school clinics described their work with clinics as central to being professors and that they couldn't imagine being "ordinary" professors. Here, the work is structured to avoid a traditional teaching role and to allow for "community impact," as one explained. Another left his position at legal aid and started his own public interest law center in order to maintain his strategy of class action lawsuits. Throughout the Reagan era, and continuing with the Republican Congress of 1994, the government imposed a set of restrictions on the Legal Services Corporation, and class action lawsuits were no longer possible through legal aid programs. This lawyer, in order to pursue his cause strategy, was forced to relocate, and he is now well known as "the guy" or "the place" for class action work. His identification by others as *the* center of class action work in the community offers a continued support for his core status.

The marginal cause lawyers varied significantly in their work settings and can be found in all types of legal settings as well as movement or other nonlegal organizations. Specifically, they are located in law school clinics, as professors and deans, in government positions, public interest centers, large and small firms, and movement organizations (see Table 7.3). Their work settings do not alone explain their cause lawyering or their marginality, but work setting can be seen as one circumstance that can both constrain and enable their cause work. For example, one clinic professor explains how he was "once an activist who demonstrated all the time," and that he might be again someday, so he is keeping himself "near" that possibility. His use of the term "near" indicates his awareness that locating his work in certain places can either pull him away from causes or keep him close. He describes his current marginality to be due to financial and family constraints: "I have two daughters in college, and I just cannot afford to work for a public interest salary." Obviously an easy way to fund a college education would be to take a highly paid position in a firm, but he ignores that option and structures his work to balance both cause lawyering (albeit marginal) and traditional professional rewards (professors are paid more than those with a public interest position).

Another marginal cause lawyer describes how her work setting and position as a public defender keep her from being more active, or core. She describes herself as an activist, but she argues that she is less politically active than others because "being a public defender just kills you physically, emotionally, psychologically. I did twenty-eight felony trials last year!" The work hours of her job are not as flexible as those of other cause lawyers, and this creates constraints. Of the thirty-seven lawyers interviewed, the three nonactive were located in a social work organization, a large firm, and as a government lawyer (public defender). The accounts of why they were inactive varied, but most focused on time and how their current work was just "too busy to allow for any time for causes." Additional constraints will be discussed later.

Occupational setting may enable or constrain opportunities to work, or provide certain kinds of network ties and support (either in favor of or against cause lawyering). However, simply knowing the occupational position or setting is not enough to explain the difference between core and marginal cause lawyering, or the movement between core/marginal and types of positions over time. The next sections of this chapter will further examine the relationship between work setting and cause lawyering with a theoretical and empirical analysis of identity.

Role and Identity among Cause Lawyers

Legal scholars have taken on issues of identity, but not necessarily with consideration of cause lawyers. Legal discourse analysis points out the varied ways in which individuals and groups are constructed in the law and by players in legal institutions. One recent article by Richman (2002) offers an important contribution on identity construction in child custody cases involving gay or lesbian parents. Espeland (1994) demonstrates how legal institutions can benefit a group's interests while simultaneously challenging that group's self-constructed collective identity. Sociolegal research benefits from a conceptual merging with theoretical and empirical constructs from the field of social movements.

Scholars of new social movements in the 1960s and 1970s defined the concept of *collective identity* as a necessary component of movements. For people to pursue a collective solution to their problems, they need to successfully articulate and sustain a shared definition of group (Taylor 1996). Collective identity processes occur within the context of social movement communities. Social movements work to "bridge the individual and societal levels by convincing people to interpret their problems in collective terms" (Taylor 1996: 126). Scholars of social movements examine identity by exploring how the personal or individual identities of activists and potential activists become aligned with movement organizational identities or more generalized collective identities such as "feminist." Snow and McAdam (2000) define this process of aligning identities as "identity correspondence" between individual and movement identities. For cause lawyers, the professional identity of "lawyer" and the identification with the cause might correspond in the collective identity of "cause lawyer." Or, the lawyer identity, if viewed according to previous definitions of professionals in movements, might be the barrier to such correspondence with activist or movement organization collective identities. Much of the emphasis on identity in social movements centers on the micromobilization process, or how identity factors into the conditions under which individuals and movements are linked, thus encouraging activism.

Recent movement scholars have challenged an overly deterministic (or structural) view of identity and argued for a more interactionist (or social constructionist) understanding of identity and social movements (Melucci 1989,

1996; Hunt, Benford, and Snow 1994; Hunt and Benford 1994; Snow and McAdam 2000). The current emphasis in the field is on the *process of identity construction*, which influences immediate and future mobilization and actions once mobilized. Here, personal and collective identities are products of inter-action: "they are constructed, reinforced, and transformed by the interactions between and among movement participants and outsiders" (Hunt and Benford 1994: 489). Although organizational and network affiliations are not determin-istic of identities, these ties and structures are the foundation and "guidelines" for interaction. Individuals draw on their particular structural roles or identi-ties, yet they retain a degree of agency to construct and align their personal identities with those of the organization or other collectivities, and they con-struct their own personal variations of the meaning and presentation of such identities.

The possible variation in salience and centrality of identities is also a con-cern of the social constructionists. Snow and McAdam (2000) point out that the link between individual and collective identities cannot be assumed just be-cause someone holds a certain structural role (e.g., membership in a movement organization does not tell us about variation in identity salience or commit-ment across individual members). Individuals can participate in SMOs without adopting the group's identity or ideology. Snow and McAdam (2000: 45) cau-tion against inferring identity correspondence between individual and collec-tive identities based solely on structure (membership, participation, affiliation). For cause lawyers, then, just because they are positioned in a profession does not mean that their personal identity matches their professional one (i.e., that the lawyer identity blends with personal); or it does not mean that their profes-sional identity (lawyer) is limited to the professional definition (negotiate an al-ternate definition of this professional identity). Thus, interviews with individ-uals and analysis of their "identity talk" provide insight into how the identities are negotiated and potentially constrained within such structural positions. For cause lawyers, work setting is relevant to explaining their actions, but it is the way lawyers discuss their identities within these work settings that demon-strates their identity. Also, the collective identity to which lawyers are corre-sponding may be "located" in a general cause lawyering community as opposed to a single organization (practice setting, movement organization). It is degree of correspondence with this larger cause lawyering community, as defined by core and marginal categories, that becomes important when discussing con-flicts between lawyering and the cause.

The constructionist approach to identity and social movements moves away from the deterministic assumptions and arguments that ignore the ongoing processes by which individuals and movements negotiate, interpret, construct, and maintain activist identities. Although previous work in this area has dealt with processes through which collective identities are created and maintained (Taylor and Whittier 1992), there is a need for outlining the conditions under which personal and collective identities are *aligned* (Snow and McAdam 2000). Rather than favoring interaction over structure, most scholars emphasize the importance of both sets of variables. Knowing something about organizational membership, networks, occupational or professional roles, and other structural variables provides an important foundation for the understanding of movement identities and their alignment with individual identities. However, richer data on the processes of interaction, the identity work and identity talk by movements and activists, and the salience of various identities provide information about construction that goes on within those structures (thus accounting for variation).

The data here on cause lawyers provide one illustration of the process of identity correspondence, and I use the concepts of identity work defined by Snow and McAdam (2000: 46–53). I focus on the organizational or professional roles and identities and how these correspond with activist identities. I use the more general "activist identity" because this study does not focus on one movement or a particular activist identity such as "feminist." Certainly the salience of a particular activist (or other) identity will link that person to particular movements and not others. For example, a salient environmentalist identity might link the person to an environmental movement more so than a feminist movement.

Affiliation with one or multiple organizations does not presume the salience or correspondence of particular activist identities. Rather, this information was a starting point, which later proved to be relevant as a basis for identity work. Also, I wanted to explore whether their professional identity was salient to the degree that it made activist identities incompatible, or whether the professional identity "changed" in a way that made it more compatible with activism. This last question is based on assumptions that the professional role and identity of lawyer carry certain meanings, ideologies, obligations, and ties that might be opposed to those of activists. So, how is it that the correspondence between lawyer and activist identities occurs? Is it that the two converge in some way? Are they really at odds with one another? Are there structural bases for one or the other, or both (in other words, do the profession, the organization, or the network ties support the correspondence of the identities)? Does correspondence occur even when structural "barriers" (i.e., lack of support) exist? The data here cannot answer all of these questions absolutely. However, this study does define the process by which one group of activists faces a potential role or identity conflict and negotiates correspondence between a professional identity, personal identities, and various collective identities.

Understanding identity in the context of interaction allows for the extension of the concept beyond the micromobilization stage. The continual process of shaping and reshaping individual and collective identities then tells us about the conditions under which individuals can become more or less committed to their activist roles, how they manage potential tensions among their roles and identities (in this case the lawyer and activist identities), and how the meaning of collective and personal identities changes (or does not change) over time. For activists, identities are often constructed and aligned in SMOs or more informal networks of activists (Snow and McAdam 2000). For lawyers, the range of SMOs or legal organizations and the informal networks to which they belong are varied, so the identities will also likely vary—again underscoring the importance of unpacking the concept of "professionals" in social movement research.

This research simultaneously addresses two concerns about roles and activism by professionals. First, my analysis of cause lawyers contributes to the study of role and identity in social movements. In this case, a professional identity (lawyer) and a personal identity (activist) come together in various ways. I examine the conditions under which there is correspondence between the two identities or roles. I also examine whether the two roles are compatible, whether tensions arise between the professional and activist roles, and what consequences follow from compatibility and tension. I do not assume that correspondence means that the identities blend so that they always occur simultaneously or become one. Though this is possible, I also allow for the possibility that the identities do not occur simultaneously, but that they are "correspondent" in the sense that one can move between the identities easily. If they cannot move between the identities easily, is that an indicator of noncorrespondence or conflict? Also, one may hold both identities (activist, lawyer) while performing or acting in just one role (i.e., they may not really be acting in an activist role, yet they self-identify as activists).

Second, the analysis also serves to unpack the category of professionals, and within that, it unpacks the category of lawyer. Rather than viewing lawyers who also are activists as acting in one way (typically assumed to be according to their professional role), this study explores the degree of involvement in activism by lawyers by exploring the difference between core and marginal lawyers. Not only can cause lawyers act in different ways as lawyers in movements, they also can act in ways that have little to do with their professional roles. In addition, not all public interest lawyers share identical characteristics, identities, lifestyles, ideologies, and so forth. The variation within this category of lawyers further illustrates the structural and interactionist sources of identity, salience, and commitment.

Lawyers in Movements

McCann and Silverstein (1998) discuss the common criticisms about lawyers' involvement in social movements and try to demonstrate how lawyers do not always create the problems that critics have suggested. Most of the criticisms are based on the assumption that lawyers will "overwhelm movements with this single-minded commitment to litigation as a tool for social change" and that movements often "fall under the spell of legal professionals and their legalistic biases" due to "widespread acceptance of the 'myth of rights' and deference to professional expertise in our society" (McCann and Silverstein 1998: 263; Rosenberg 1991).[6] Typically these concerns about lawyers depend on the assumption that lawyers emphasize legalistic activities. Lawyers in movements are thought to have a negative impact on movements for the reasons summarized by McCann and Silverstein (1998: 263):

1. Litigation is costly because of its sap on time, energy, and monetary resources.

2. Expenditures of resources are inefficient because inherent institutional weaknesses and constraints impede the judiciary's ability to deliver on the promise of promoting reform.

3. The legalistic propensities of lawyers tend to directly and indirectly inhibit alternative movement strategies by depleting scarce movement resources and by diverting concerns away from long-term projects such as grass-roots mobilization, alliance building, or more radical tactics such as public protest.

4. The inclination of lawyers to frame movement goals in terms of disputes among discrete parties can narrow the range of movement goals as well as undermine broad-based movement organization and alliance building.

5. The limited ideological biases of legal professionals, which privilege individual controversies to the detriment of collective struggles and goals, unconsciously narrow lawyers' conceptions of movement ends.

6. Problematic tensions between cause lawyers and their clients often develop as lawyers come to dominate movement efforts.

McCann and Silverstein (1998) take a step in the right direction and challenge the above assumptions about, and criticisms of, cause lawyering. Their study of activists in the pay equity movement and the animal rights movement includes an analysis of the role of lawyer and nonlawyer activists, and the relationship between legal and extralegal tactics. In their research, they suggest four categories of movement lawyers: (1) *staff activists* work for movement organizations and tend to function as movement leaders and organizers; (2) *staff technicians* work for movement organizations in a more traditional, professional sense of serving clients without much concern for activism; (3) *independent cause lawyers, or hired guns,* work for a fee as special counsel on particular movement cases; (4) *nonpracticing lawyers* who have stepped out of their professional roles to contribute in other ways to the cause—they were formally trained as lawyers but do not use legal credentials in their current role (McCann and Silverstein 1998).

By categorizing lawyers in this way, McCann and Silverstein (1998) address some of the criticisms of cause lawyering. For example, they suggest that the "staff technicians" are characterized by an emphasis on formal counsel and litigation as strategies. "Staff activists," on the other hand, were "the most strategically oriented, the most wary about formal legal tactics, and the most connected to activities outside the judicial realm" (280). Thus, it should not be assumed that lawyers necessarily impact movements in a negative, controlling way, as suggested by scholars of movement professionals (Staggenborg 1988; McCarthy and Zald 1973, 1987).

In contrast to McCann and Silverstein's (1998) typology of cause lawyers in a particular organizational setting (SMO), I identify *role identities* of cause lawyers as core or marginal to the larger community of cause lawyering activity. This conceptualization emphasizes the more flexible and mutable nature of the work and selves of "cause lawyer." It allows for the possibility of an activist identity situated in the context of various legal roles or types. Though McCann and Silverstein do call these "ideal types," thus allowing for an imperfect fit of a person to these roles, they limit our understanding of cause lawyers by ignoring the following: the conditions under which these roles are played, the possibility of simultaneously playing multiple roles or shifting among roles over time, and the potential for conflict between these and other roles within one person or across individuals. Although some overlap exists with the types outlined by McCann and Silverstein, this categorization covers a broader range of behaviors by cause lawyers by allowing lawyers themselves to define their work and identity as activists.

My analysis builds on the above findings by further challenging the criticisms about cause lawyering. Rather than assuming that lawyers either act as lawyers or as nonlawyers in their roles, I extend the challenge to the critics by leaving it open and looking at the lawyers themselves across multiple contexts and multiple movements. It is not just that lawyers may act as staff technicians, but that under various conditions, they may be staff technician, fundraiser, strategist, or simply rank-and file member. All of this role-playing by lawyers depends on organizational constraints, network support (both to constrain and enable), other role demands, and individual identification and ideology. In addition, the ways in which lawyers are mobilized into activism also help us understand the roles and identities involved in their cause lawyering (and the degree of activism). It is not just that "lawyers are socialized to be ABC" so they act in "XYZ ways." They, like other activists, come from varied backgrounds and socialization, have a variety of motivations, and can act in a multitude of ways in a movement(s) or SMO(s).

According to the critics of cause lawyering, "leadership roles" are exactly what lawyers should not be doing because they are viewed as "professionals," or otherwise as outsiders, who do not share the interests of the movement participants. By taking a leadership role in a movement, lawyers are thought to remove the potential for disruptive and often illegal strategies and channel a movement into costly and time-consuming litigation strategies and institutional goals. This sample of cause lawyers offers one answer found in the lawyers' accounts of the extent to which they act as a "lawyer" or "legal professional" and lead movement actions. If a lawyer does not really act as a lawyer, then the challenge to the literature on movement professionals is supported. The tensions between the multiple roles of cause lawyers will be further discussed later in this chapter.

Lawyers as Activists

Challenging the assumption that professionals who are also activists act according to their professional role obligations, this analysis suggests that being a lawyer is sometimes, but not always, part of their activism. Most of the lawyers interviewed were conscious of the perceptions of others of their profession. In other words, they understand that even if they are not acting as a lawyer, others still might view them as lawyers and react or interact with them according to expectations about them as a lawyer (rather than as an ordinary activist). In fact, many were almost amused that others reacted to them as something "more than just another activist." I made every attempt to ask the lawyers to clarify and elaborate this issue as it arose. A typical statement was "People knew I was a lawyer, but I was not involved as a lawyer."

Once involved as activists, these lawyers *do not necessarily behave or act as lawyers*. Their behavior in movements, SMOs, and the profession tells us something about the salience of their various identities in various social settings or over time in the same settings. When they do act as lawyers, it is described as "a skill" rather than as a role or identity. For example, a female disability rights lawyer described her involvement with local movements: "Not so much as a lawyer, though I certainly feel my training and experience has given me certain organizational skills, abilities to logically map out, plan out things, that are not acting as a lawyer, per se, but using some of those skills."

If lawyers emphasize the skills or technical expertise that was learned, and not a professional role, then we cannot assume there is alignment between the profession and the actual roles or identities held. Lawyers may "pick and choose" the parts that are relevant, rather than assuming a predetermined, or oversocialized, professional role. She then went on to describe how others may see her as a lawyer, and how that can be a concern for the movement in terms of "taking over where you shouldn't be."

Cause lawyers engage in a form of identity work (Snow and Anderson 1987) known as "identity talk" (Hunt and Benford 1994), in which they resist being cast as lawyers and attempt to downplay that identity in favor of the activist identity or collective identity of the particular movement. "I remember one of my friends said to me, 'I call press conferences, and people come, and they quote me. I'm saying the same stuff that I used to say as a member of the church, and a member of political organizations, but now the difference is they listen just because I'm an attorney."

At the end of the statement she highlights the typical rejection of status by these cause lawyers. They are very conscious of the fact that their professional identity carries a certain status, yet they do everything they can to reject this unless it works to the advantage of the movement.[7] So, personally, the prestige or status of the professional identity is not as meaningful. Again, this is a form of identity talk (Hunt and Benford 1994).

I will now turn to a discussion of the organizational conditions that both constrain and enable particular identities among lawyers, including the professional identity.

Aligning Organizational and Personal Identities

Organizational support for a cause lawyer collective identity

Organizational roles both constrain and enable professional identities. For lawyers, working in different organizational settings provides different guidelines for what is the appropriate "lawyer identity." Individuals may self-select into certain specialties of law or particular work settings, hoping to find organizational roles that fit with their own view of what it means to be a lawyer, or what a lawyer "should be." In addition to this self-selection, once lawyers are on the job there may be factors acting to encourage or discourage certain aspects of their various identities. Organizations may work to encourage (or discourage) certain aspects of individuals' identities by setting rules for appearance, conduct, and professional advancement. Some other aspects of the organizational culture that shape individuals' identities are more informal, such as jargon or lingo that is unique to that organization (or a department within it), social situations such as happy hours or lunches, and reactions or attitudes toward "the boss." Lawyers, for example, may be told to wear suits when in the office and when in court. They may be taught the way to speak when in court. They may be taught how to "bill hours." In addition to these profession- or work-based sources of identity, there are external influences such as family, friends, and affiliations with organizations such as churches, social clubs, recreation clubs, neighborhood groups, and other associations. The organizational roles, as well as the individual "others" who react and interpret the role lawyers play, set the stage for negotiation of identities, the norms for what is appropriate, and the salience of certain identities in personal, professional, and other public situations.

Structural positions and relationships (ties) can support activist identities and also discourage professional identities. Similarly, certain settings and personal ties might stifle any activist tendencies by lawyers, either by demanding too much in terms of time and energy for other activities or by forcing salience of particular ideologies and identities that run counter to activist ideologies. Again, assuming a particular identity just because of organizational affiliation is avoided by interviewing lawyers about these concerns. It also is not assumed that lawyers are committed activists just because they work in a public interest law setting (which might be more encouraging of activism through work and outside of work). By exploring the various work settings in which these lawyers work, as well as their own sense of the work they do and identities they hold salient, this study illuminates the ways in which organizations, both directly and indirectly, constrain and enable a professional identity that corresponds (or does not correspond) with activism (Snow and McAdam 2000). It is important to remember the agency of individuals here as well—organizations do impact the individuals' identities, but the individuals also engage in identity work (Snow and Anderson 1987). This section will focus more on the formal organizational constraints, whereas the next section on networks will address more informal supports and personal identity work.

In some ways, the kind of work or the organizational setting in which the lawyers work serves as a typology of their activism. Those who are the core activists are in the least traditional work settings, those who are marginal activists are in "mixed" settings (e.g., law clinics, in which lawyers are both professors and those who operate the clinics), and those who are the least active, or are no longer active, are in the most formal, or traditional, settings. The more traditional the work setting corresponds to the more traditional (less activist) professional identities. It is also important to note that the "role" may be more that of a lawyer, while the "identity" (self-identification) may still be activist. In other words, there are conditions under which the lawyer can still see him- or herself as an activist even though his or her work or professional role is not manifest as activism. There is a greater range of acceptable identities in the mixed or less traditional settings; in large part this seems to be due to there being fewer rules and obligations, thus allowing for much individual variation and agency. The more traditional settings have more of the imprint of the profession: rules of attire, demeanor more formal, offices more formal, and so forth. The core and marginal analytic categories offer an important insight here. Marginal cause lawyers are not prevented from aligning with the cause lawyer collective identity. Rather, they simply must *work harder* to achieve that balance or blending in personal and professional identities. Marginal cause lawyers have to rely more on self-supports and engage in more challenging identity work due to fewer or weaker external supports for this collective identity.

The work setting clearly had an impact on the personal and professional identities of these lawyers. When asked whether they identified themselves as activists, lawyers, or some combination, there were definite response patterns according to the work setting. Also, when asked whether they were "an activist who does law, or a lawyer who does activism," the responses matched the variations in the organizational environment for their work and served to define the core and marginal cause lawyers. For example, all the lawyers who worked in some kind of public interest law setting (legal aid, law centers for poverty, housing, disability, the environment—note: they rarely specialized in the title of the organization; most were called something like "Center for Public Interest Law") identified themselves as activists. Those involved with clinics who were also professors identified themselves as activists. The other professors were not as definitive in calling themselves activists: some said no, others said "sort of," still others said yes, but after some discussion. Those in administrative positions at the law school did not consider themselves activists; though the one who was a former dean did. It is important to mention that most of the lawyers in public interest law centers also could be considered administrative because they were directors or presidents (typically these offices employed just a few people, so the lawyer was often fulfilling multiple job tasks and titles simultaneously);

yet their activities and the nature of the work setting did not compare to the other administrators.

One core lawyer describes how she came to work in a particular setting, emphasizing that money, though rewarding, is not worth sacrificing what you believe in or what you really want to do:

> I certainly investigated—there were a few firms . . . that I looked into that were doing civil rights types of things. I had certain financial obligations as well. So I don't think I was tied to working for a public agency, but there were definitely certain things I didn't want to do. I would not have worked as a prosecutor. I would not have worked for a large firm doing commercial types of litigation, or representing primarily corporations against individuals.

This was typical of core activists—they balked at the "financial obligations argument" for choosing a more traditional path in law. It is important to recognize that debt is a significant barrier for many, but emphasizing debt also ignores the other variables that impact one's activist and professional career: network ties, mentors, and prior activism and work. Also, it is not likely that debt is the sole reason why others chose a legal career with a large firm. It appears, then, that the proper reference group or "location" of cause lawyers may not be the traditional legal profession, but rather an identification with and embeddedness in a community of clients. Also, this illustrates the reference group or salient identity: other lawyers or the profession provide one reference, but one lawyer also identifies with the clients and subculture in which he works and feels quite well-off.

An older lawyer, speaking about a younger lawyer whom he had mentored, described the pressures that can arise in certain work settings:

> If I had a clear choice between a good public interest job and a job in a big law firm, I would take the public interest job and I think she might, too. But if you think you're going to make a lasting impact, if you could do it through a large firm, that's fine. The pressures on her are going to be fantastic, and the choices that she'll have to make will come daily. And the great risk in those things is that she'll begin to make compromises and pretty soon there won't be a hell of a lot left.

I probed him on his description of "compromises" and he explained that she will likely abandon her principles because the pressures of the large firm are "just too great." This was a typical response by all core lawyers and most marginal lawyers about how the work setting can really hurt a person's attempts to support causes.

Many of the lawyers talked about their work in their current practice setting in the context of why they became a lawyer in the first place. One environmental lawyer described how he grew up near Lake Erie and became politicized by the local environmental issues: "One summer the lake just got dirtier and dirtier. As the years went by, it made me really angry." This politicization is an important process in becoming politically active, but it does not necessarily explain the choice to become a lawyer. I asked this lawyer to more specifically explain how he became not just an activist, but a cause lawyer: "Well, I'm not somebody who went to law school, became a lawyer, and decided to hang out his shingle and specialize in activist issues. That's not the case. I became a lawyer because I thought being a lawyer would be a way to promote social justice . . . so that's why I answered that I am an activist who does law as opposed to a lawyer." His response indicates a distancing from the profession in that his primary identification remains an activist.

Maintaining an Activist Identity

My analysis of interviews suggested that lawyers identify themselves as more or less central to the cause lawyering community. Those who are the core cause lawyers are found in either the public interest law centers or are professors involved with clinics. These are two settings in which a more flexible role and identity for "lawyer" is allowed, and even fostered. In both cases, the lawyers and the organizations are part of the core of activism in the community (and sometimes nationally). There is the most freedom from traditional professional constraints in these two settings, and thus the most freedom to be activist alongside being a lawyer. Freedom to be a cause lawyer, however, is *not* the same thing as support for being a cause lawyer. The lawyers did not really describe how their jobs impacted their identity in so many words, but there were definite patterns among the lawyers in the different categories of jobs in how they described their activism.

Core cause lawyers' interviews consisted of lengthy discussions of movements, activism, and social change. Most described their activism, or that of cause lawyers in general, as being involved in "protecting individual rights" and "social change" or "justice." One professor who runs the clinics at the law school described activist lawyers in the following way:

> Someone who cares about people. Someone who is interested in issues, causes, principles. Is not concerned or interested in any financial remuneration or compensation that they get from what they do. . . . I'm active. I mean, I'm busy, and I'm active, and I'm involved in a lot of things, so, I guess if that makes you an activist. Sometimes I do law, or sometimes I don't, but I'm *always* an activist.

This statement shows how the profession does not necessarily define the role of this individual. Rather, the activist identity is more enduring.

Another lawyer who runs one of the clinics and is also a core activist describes activism in a similar way: "[An activist is] somebody, first of all, who knows what's going on. Secondly, vocalizes their opinion on it. Either by going out to a protest, or writing a letter to their congressman. That takes time, effort, but has a huge impact. I think I am. Definitely!" This lawyer defines herself as an activist, and this was something that not all cause lawyers did. The more activist the lawyer, the more likely the self-definition as activist. Identity salience in this case may not be about one's professional role, as much as one's position in a subculture (professional or otherwise) that supports the activism and keeps it salient. These lawyers are embedded in groups of other activists and other progressive lawyers who offer continual support for their identities as cause lawyers.

One older male lawyer hinted at the difficulties in identifying oneself as an activist, particularly in a conservative state. When asked if he would characterize himself as an activist, he hesitated, laughed, and said, "Yes . . . do I have to whisper that in Arizona?" He points out an important constraint to collective identities of activists—the state's political structure. It should be noted that this particular lawyer is categorized as marginal, though earlier in his career in Arizona he was at the core of the cause lawyering community. His recognition of the political context in the state is an example of the identity talk that activists typically engage in to justify particular identities or distance themselves from others.

A core activist demonstrated how his maintenance of ties to the activist community not only fosters his cause lawyer identity, but also explains his work for causes. Because he is at the core and defines himself primarily as an activist, and because he has strong support for and correspondence of his activist identity with the professional identity, this lawyer is relatively stress-free as he flows between legal and cause work:

> I'm busy. I'm active, and I'm involved in a lot of things. So, if that makes you an activist, then I'm an activist. Sometimes I do law, and sometimes I don't. I mean, I would be an activist whether I was a lawyer, or not. Many times I enjoy being an activist and not taking the law role. And sometimes I do bring my legal skills to it. A lot of times I enjoy just being one of the people that are involved and not necessarily a lawyer.

Here, the cause lawyer has successfully negotiated his identities so that he can easily choose to emphasize the activist component. Those who are marginal, or who face structural constraints for activism and pressures to conform to a traditional professional identity, cannot so easily resolve their work and identity practices.

There are a great number of assumptions, especially in the literature on lawyering and careers, that describe the constraints against activism in terms of the prestige and status of the profession, as well as the overwhelming ideology to be conservative and work for and in the interests of those with money and power. One lawyer describes the expectations of most lawyers for their professional career:

> Transactions. Corporation law. Basically, you don't even like people. You're not even thinking about people in [activist] issues at all. I think the people end up at large law firms, make a tremendous amount of money, and that's what they want to do. They want the power and prestige of the law. In the back of their minds they thought someday I'm gonna be partner, I'm gonna be judge. They were on the fast-track of law. Big bucks, big corporation. Totally different lifestyle. . . . That's not my thing.

The correspondence between professional and personal identities is harder to imagine in relation to this traditional career path. Buying into "the power and the prestige of the law" is partly a lifestyle, partly ideological, and neither is compatible with activist concerns about uprooting the power structure or inequalities in the system in this country.

Another lawyer described how the lure of money is a hard thing to overlook: "Many want to do it [public interest law], but they're not sure how they're going to afford it. Law school is very expensive, and you graduate with a lot of debt." This is a commonly cited reason why there are not more public interest or activist lawyers: they just can't afford it. One cause lawyer directly challenged that by saying that it wasn't that they couldn't afford it because they had too much debt ("Who doesn't?!"), but because they had the opportunity to make money. He argued that most lawyers have a hard time turning down the tremendous opportunities to make money that exist in the profession. Many argue that this money issue characterizes the difference between cause lawyers and other lawyers: that cause lawyers are "willing to be poor" and that this is a necessary characteristic. The profession itself makes it hard to define oneself as a lawyer if one does not hold to the ideals of prestige, money, power, and status.

Most of the core activists reject membership in the American Bar Association (ABA), which is the traditional organizational affiliation for members of the legal profession. They begrudgingly describe it as "just a requirement" and not much of a location for networking or support. Many are members of the "alternative" professional organization, the National Lawyer's Guild (NLG). Membership in the NLG is another indicator of core cause lawyering. Most who are considered activist in the community are either current or past members of the NLG. In fact, for many, it seems that membership in the NLG during law school (the student chapter) seemed to be an important source of ties to other cause lawyers, as well as ties to activists in the community. Those who are marginal cause lawyers are typically not members of the NLG. So, although the ideological commitment may qualify someone as a cause lawyer, it is the network of support through organizational and community membership that appears to really bolster the identity and practice of cause lawyering. The informal networking, as well as the alternative professional organization, proves invaluable for activism by lawyers. In this setting, a subculture of the profession allows for the correspondence of activist and lawyer identities.

Involvement in, and ties to, this alternative legal organization seem to follow a distinct pattern. The most activist of the lawyers were heavily involved with the student chapters of the NLG during law school, and typically maintain their membership after graduation. However, the degree of involvement in the organization varies according to the current work that the lawyers do. One of the core cause lawyers in this sample is involved nationally in the NLG and is the regional chapter president. He is the most radical of the lawyers interviewed, as well as the one mentioned most by others as "the guy to talk to" about cause lawyering. Other core activists were all involved in the NLG on paper, but may not have been as involved in the organization in terms of attendance at meetings. One lawyer explained this to be a result of the nature of the work:

> Here in Arizona, there's a NLG chapter, and I joined, and was actively involved. And then I got really busy at Legal Aid, and became less and less and less involved with the NLG. And one of the things that I noticed here . . . is that there are a lot of people that are on the mailing list, but very few people go to the meetings. I think there's lots of reasons for that, but the big reason is that most of the [activist] attorneys in town are solo practitioners. Or they're in small offices. They're not working in big firms, and they're very, very busy. So it's hard to create time for outside work. Really, really hard. They're probably taking the case volunteer and they're thinking, this is my volunteer effort for the community, and I don't have time to go out and do additional work.

The issue of "solo practitioners" is not unique to cause lawyers, but it may be more of a strain because of the typically limited resources of their office. They are not solo practitioners with a huge staff of paralegals and interns. They are the only one, often with a part-time secretary or paralegal. Because of the time issue, it may be easiest for these lawyers to combine their activism with their work. For example, environmental lawyers are limited in their activism to primarily environmental issues. This does not mean, however, that their activism is limited to just their legal work. They may not be active in organizations or in leadership roles because of this; yet they are still quite committed to and involved in a range of movement activities. All of the cause lawyers in the study talked about time and role conflict, but the core activists were unique in that they rarely "removed themselves" from membership in the NLG. Even though it was a time conflict, all of the activist lawyers "found the time" to continue their involvement in the NLG. Even if they were not attending meetings on a regular basis, the core cause lawyers were in contact with each other and aware of others through the NLG membership list. So, NLG membership, while variable in terms of commitment, clearly served as an important "location" in which professional and personal identities could merge: "we identify issues . . . we usually have one big community event, like a few years ago we brought in Angela Davis to speak . . . the Guild is just part of the progressive community here, and just gets involved in most of the progressive issues." Here, the importance of community support for one's activist identity is emphasized, and the implication is that the profession does not provide these supports.

Although fostering an alternative place in the profession and rejecting much of what the mainstream profession entails, the core cause lawyers still were faced with tensions that their professional role obligations produced. Most of these lawyers talked about the importance of reputation as a professional, and this was more of an issue the more traditional the setting in which the lawyers worked. Although there may have been things they would do as an activist, such as blast the press or certain individuals, these lawyers were aware of the potential problems in doing so. Lawyers used particular strategies to get around some of the professional obligations:

> There are tensions because you, at least in my field, you need to deal with people to benefit your clients—with people you might as an activist be blasting in the press. And you can burn bridges very easily. And if you get this reputation, I mean, reputation is all-important as an attorney or a businessperson or as anything else. Scientists, for sure. So that reputation, a good part of what you bring besides your knowledge and skills, to help this client. And, so, a lot of times, if you're respected by the district counsel of INS, you can call up and say "this is what I want to do" and they'll listen to you as someone they respect. As opposed to if you've been speaking out in Human Rights Watch, or the press in a way that *made* them angry or in a way that they feel is false, or even worse lying, then that's gonna be a problem in your work. There's a balance you can establish though. But you obviously are going to have to be very careful about what risks you take, or what issues you speak out on. It doesn't mean that I wouldn't write a letter to the editor about some issue or, if I was sure about what I was saying, give information to Human Rights Watch. But, if I was going to do that, I would call up the district counsel and let her know, or try some other way first.

The profession appears to constrain activism, but only in a way that occasionally changes the form. This lawyer describes how she does not so much curtail her activism as channel it in different ways. She mentions the concern with "taking risks"—mainly this was described in terms of the risk to the movement or the future abilities as an activist lawyer, not in terms of suffering in the legal profession or career. Another lawyer also mentioned the importance of presentation of information in the press, and he noted how acting like a lawyer and using the appropriate jargon was necessary, but also how it could really signal the underlying activist meaning. For example:

> Well, sure there are tensions. For example, the rules of ethics preclude you from arguing in public about the merits of the case when it's pending in court. There's always a tension there because most of our litigation involves issues that are in the public eye, that are probably before the legislature, before Congress at the same time they're before the court. And so you get asked a question by a reporter about "do you feel that what the government is doing here is right?" As an activist, I'd like to say "Hell, no it's not right! It's an outrage! These guys ought to be thrown out of office for interpreting the law this way!" But I can't say that. I have to say, "Well, in the lawsuit, we are contending blah-de-blah-de-blah"—be very careful about how I say that.

He maintains compatibility between his professional and activist obligations by speaking out in a way that can satisfy both.

Another core activist described how being an activist was not about stepping outside the boundaries of law. Even the most radical of the activist lawyers understood the importance of professionalism, and this would only enhance the success for clients and for movements. The lawyers seem to perform identity work here—acting to meet the standards of their professional role expectations while simultaneously keeping the fire going as activists. Changing the way they speak and dress for court, or to the press, is a relatively easy way for these lawyers to "please the professional community" without changing anything in terms of their activist identity and role. One demonstrated how being a radical could help his clients, even within the rules of the profession:

> Then people say to me, "well, if you're a radical, you should use any means necessary." I don't need that shit. I'm a good lawyer. And a radical. I can win cases because of my abilities, because of the rightness of the case, because of the client's interest. I don't have to use that shit. "Well, if you're a radical, you should just not give a shit." No, I don't do that. It's my personal philosophy because we're taking the moral high ground, and I'm certainly not gonna get down in the mud like that. I mean, I'll work like crazy for my client. I've been characterized as a zealous advocate. I can be a nut, just go in there and argue like crazy and fight like crazy. And I can be a complete asshole when I need to be, but I won't do shit like that. I'm surprised how easily I've run across lawyers who will lie to the court, lie to opposing counsel. I don't do that. Don't need to. I've filed plenty of lawsuits that are *creative*. But they have a real basis in the law. I don't *have* to file frivolous lawsuits. There's too many *good* lawsuits out there to file.

Although this statement appears to illustrate a challenge to his activist identity, this lawyer argues that that was not the case. He explains how it was important for him to redefine what being a radical meant in terms of behavior and ideology. Being an activist behaviorally means knowing which strategies will work in which contexts, all the while remaining consistent with the beliefs and goals of the movement. Being an activist is not just about protesting all the time; it is about "being in for the long haul" and recognizing the big picture. Working through the tensions of one's professional position as a lawyer and tempering the outward expressions of one's radical beliefs in certain contexts are key to maintaining a positive cause lawyer identity.

> When I was first learning about politics, I thought to be a radical meant just be a nut. Just get up in the middle of a meeting and say "Fuck you!" that was to be radical. But that is the downfall of so many movements. I don't necessarily believe that. I put on a tie, put on my suit when I go to court. I go to city council meetings. I do all that shit because being a radical is that my ultimate goal is really empowering the people, and making a real drastic change of reworking the system. Someone said "you know, I've talked to a number of people about you and they say, despite your radical beliefs, you're a reasonable person." Of course! It's not like I'm insane. I can achieve a lot of positive things as a lawyer.

This lawyer demonstrates that the impression work has to be done both as an activist and as a lawyer. Others' definitions of what it means to be a radical, and how that alters their interpretation of that person as a professional, are demonstrated by the lines referring to how people say "despite your radical beliefs, you're a reasonable person." The lawyer does not see the incompatibility between the two, but he is well aware that others do see cause lawyering almost as a contradiction or impossibility.

The core activists were typical in their explanation of how those in the activist community "knew them" and supported their activist lawyering. Others talked about the ties to "specialty" networks as a source of support for their work. This support also means that the identity as a cause lawyer is reinforced by others. For example, one lawyer who is active in immigration causes explained numerous sources of support. She participated in many sessions at a recent NLG convention (much like an academic conference) and networked with others working in immigration law. The important difference from an academic conference is that here, information about legal cases and movement strategies was shared and spread. She described an affinity for other lawyers in public interest work and also in her specialty: "certainly the colleagues in private practice immigration law here, I know and mostly respect. So there is the tie that comes with being in the same, similar work." She also describes her embeddedness in the activist community for immigration issues as a strong source of information and support for her. By maintaining ties to the immigration law and activist communities, and since there is overlap between the two, she has a continual source of reinforcement for her activist lawyer identity. The professional and personal identities and roles correspond because of their links into this network. And obviously, lawyers who were activist before entering law school will likely have stronger ties to these communities than those who "begin" their activism during law school, with its pressures that oppose entering those communities.

There is less correspondence between the professional and personal identities of the more marginal activist lawyers, primarily because the activist and professional subcultures do not overlap, are not as developed, or are in conflict. For example, one lawyer, who is primarily involved in employment law and is less activist than others in this study, found it difficult to maintain her activism in law school; and once she took a job, it was in a large, traditional firm. She defines herself as a feminist and talks about her interest in activism, but she never was quite able to become an activist in spite of her desire. Does that mean her commitment or belief in the cause is less strong than others who do act? Possibly. But it is also interesting to look at the organizational pressures she faced. During law school, she joined a women's law organization—apparently on the right track to developing her interest in women's issues and the law. However, she also understood the importance of "making journal" (or law review), and worked successfully toward that goal. She did not join any public interest law organizations or become involved in the local activist community. As she became a member of the law review, she was further pulled into some of the traditional networks of the profession and came into contact with countervailing beliefs about the appropriate path for her law career. By the end of her law school career, she rarely called herself a feminist and was more likely to amuse others with the self-deprecating "lawyer jokes" that now applied to her. She had earned a prestigious clerkship with a district appeals court judge for her first year out of law school, followed by a partner-track position at an elite law firm in a large, Midwestern city. In her words, she felt that "she could best change things by working from the inside." She redefined her activism to fit with her professional role obligations. Activism was not really compatible with her new position, though she assured me that she would "definitely work on pro bono cases." For her, the tensions between the two roles were "removed" as she was pulled further into traditional networks and organizations and away from more activist or political ones. It is impossible to predict whether this lawyer will ever become an activist or what her career will entail professionally and personally, but it seems unlikely that she will easily find her way back to activism as she moves further away from its supports over time.

Typically those lawyers in legal aid, in public interest law centers, and in clinics at the law school are most able to blend their professional and activist roles and identities. Although typically suffering under tremendous time pressures, individuals in these settings are most able to express their activism outwardly and reject and criticize the system, including the legal system and their profession, without suffering any consequences professionally. In fact, it is within these work settings that activism is encouraged.

Certain organizations seek to "engulf" an individual's personal identity by fusing it with their organizational identity. Different organizations embrace people's personal identities differentially. Specifically, organizations not only differentially embrace personal identities, but also encourage or constrain activist roles, depending on the type of organization and the position within that organization. Even with the constraints placed on them professionally, there is always room for some role distancing to allow for activism. Lawyers who might be considered marginally activist demonstrate such role distancing. Those who are core activists, however, usually avoid the underlying tensions of role management and probable role conflict by working to find positions that allow the two to correspond more directly. The informal organizational supports for the activist lawyer identity will now be discussed.

Network support for lawyer identity and for activist identity

Social networks (within or external to organizations) can create tensions, reinforce, or have no effect on organizationally induced roles and identities. The effect depends on the strength of the network ties (investment individual has in it) and the content of the identities/roles in the network. Network ties were shown to have an important effect of supporting activist identities and alternative professional identities, thus making the two more compatible (fewer tensions). When one is in a network that is not as supportive of activism (or of left activism), there are more tensions as the lawyering role and activist role are more incompatible. Lawyers who feel tensions can seek out such networks, or they can distance themselves from one of them, thus distancing themselves from either activism or traditional lawyering.

One lawyer described the significance of her law school classmates as a source of alternative views of the legal profession and support for activism. This shows how the network of individuals within the larger organizational structure of the law school worked to enable the activist identity. By talking with others who supported her activist beliefs, these beliefs and identity were allowed to progress to the point of becoming a cause lawyer. The view that "everything is connected" is characteristic of those at the core, who often defined their activism in relation to "the movement"—generally opposing system inequality.

One lawyer described how his ties to other activists are an important way for him to become aware of issues and events, as well as maintain the salience of his activist identity and behavior. He describes how people may turn to him as a lawyer for help or to answer certain questions, but ultimately his involvement with other activists demonstrates to others, and to himself, that he is "just an activist":

> There's no doubt that because I'm a lawyer people will look to me for certain help, certain answers, and so on. But I try to come to it a lot of times just as another person in the movement. Not say "I'm the lawyer." I'm out there sleeping for a month at the county courthouse with the homeless people and everyone else. I wasn't there as a lawyer. I was there sleeping on the cement along with everyone else. That kind of thing.

Rather than emphasizing one's professional background, these lawyers prefer to be more anonymous in the sense of being "just another activist." And being a lawyer may never come into play, as in the case of protesting homelessness by "sleeping on the cement" like other activists and the homeless. Again, the identity work is evident in this example as the professional identity is minimized for the cause.

Sometimes there are tensions with the lawyer role and identity, and developing ties to other alternative lawyers or the subculture of activist lawyers best helps this. The core cause lawyers were least likely to describe tensions they feel professionally because most have secured a position in the subculture within the profession, in addition to other ties to the broader activist subculture. *They have not so much distanced themselves from the professional identity; rather, they have created an alternative one.* The alternative identity does share some aspects of the more traditional lawyer identity, but it blends the activist identity as well. Cause lawyers identify with other cause lawyers, with public defenders, with some government lawyers, as well as with other more traditional lawyers who work in their area or on the same issues. Core cause lawyers do not identify with the profession as a whole, with corporate lawyers, with industry lawyers, or with prosecutors.

Conclusion

My findings suggest that viewing cause lawyering as "at odds" with the traditional legal profession may be ignoring the diverse experiences of these lawyers. Not all cause lawyers feel the apparent conflict between their profession and activism because they have defined and created a positive alternative to the traditional profession of law, particularly those at the core. Considering the lawyers' own perceptions of who they are in the profession and in causes is an important analytic step in the study of cause lawyers. Cause lawyers can be viewed as a subculture within the legal profession, and their connections to an activist subculture should be emphasized as much as their connections to the profession. Core cause lawyers might also be defined as a subset of the activist community, rather than the profession. Studying the core and marginal relations of lawyers to causes and movements helps to explain where loyalties lie and how such identification may change over time. The blending of cause and career, found in the core cause lawyers, shows how identity work, as well as creating and maintaining positive supports for identities, is an important component in helping both the cause and the career of the lawyer. More marginal cause lawyers might better be able to manage the tensions and other consequences of their work and activism by linking with the core of activist lawyering, or by changing to work environments that are "less traditional" and thus provide the positive supports for activism.

The marginal activists who feel strain are those who have ties that continually challenge either the activist or the professional identity. Lawyers often seek professional settings that are more alternative and flexible as a means to their activism. The organizational constraints in more traditional legal positions work against activism both ideologically and structurally. Role conflict is evident, and lawyers have to change positions to maintain activism or alter their personal identity to stay in the position. Marginal cause lawyers are able to engage in effective cause work; it just may be more dependent on negotiating an appropriate time or set of conditions. Core cause lawyers have already specifically negotiated their work structure so that cause work is possibly on a daily basis. Lawyers who act as ordinary activists negotiate their professional careers and identities in such a way that "activist" and "lawyer" correspond and are not in conflict. Work settings, such as public interest centers, allow for network ties to activism as well as distance one from the conflict-causing traditional professional role obligations and ties. Cause lawyers follow complex paths into their careers, and scholars should turn to literature on social movement activism to better understand this process and the work of these lawyers.

Notes

1. This conceptualization builds on an earlier article by Jones (2001).

2. Carrie Menkel-Meadow (1998) discussed the difficulties in defining the goals, behaviors, and forms of cause lawyering. The variety of terms used to describe cause lawyering generally are "generic" definitions to describe lawyering as compared to ac-

tivism—with lawyers working to further the rights of the underrepresented in arenas that include, but are not limited to, legal and justice institutions. It should also be noted that similar definitional debates exist when defining "social movement," and movements and causes usually are defined by their inclusion of extra-institutional activities. "Cause lawyer" is used here as it is the dominant term used by sociolegal scholars today; see multiple articles in volumes titled *Cause Lawyering*, edited by Austin Sarat and Stuart Scheingold in 1998 and 2001. However, since this chapter is situated in social movement concepts, I do allow for "cause lawyering" to include extra-institutional activities.

3. See the numerous articles in this volume about cause lawyering in countries other than the United States, which demonstrate the varied positioning of cause lawyers in relation to the state.

4. See Hatcher's and Southworth's chapters in this volume for research on right-wing cause lawyering. In this study, initial data analysis demonstrated the importance of lawyers' own definitions of activism and cause lawyering, and most rejected the idea that right-wing lawyering is cause lawyering. Although the character of the lawyering differs from right- to left-wing lawyers, it should be noted that the identity processes might not differ.

5. Due to the processual emphasis on identity (collective identity, identity correspondence, potential identity, and role conflicts), interviews provide the voices of these lawyers as they give accounts about their work and their "selves" as lawyers and activists.

6. See Handler (1978), Katz (1982), and Scheingold (1974) on movement lawyers' tendency toward litigation. See also Rosenberg (1991) on how lawyers often waste the scarce resources of a movement in litigation while ending in nothing more than a hollow victory in court and little substantive change. Rosenberg (1991:341) argues that movement lawyers, by emphasizing courts, which "seldom produce significant reform," will steer the movement away from alternative, and perhaps more successful, political actions: "if groups advocating such reform continue to look to the courts for aid, and spend precious resources on litigation, then the courts also limit change by deflecting claims from substantive political battles, where success is possible, to harmless legal ones where it is not" (341).

7. See the chapter by Shdaimah in this volume for a different outcome—the lawyers in her study do not similarly reject their professional status.

References

American Bar Association Commission on Women in the Profession. 1995a. *Unfinished Business: Overcoming the Sisyphus Factor*. Chicago: American Bar Association.

———. 1995b. *Women in Law: A Look at the Numbers*. Chicago: American Bar Association.

Cress, Dan, and David A. Snow. 1996. "Mobilization at the Margins: Resources, Benefactors, and the Viability of Homeless Social Movement Organizations." *American Sociological Review* 61: 1089–109.

della Porta, Donatella. 1996. "Social Movements and the State: Thoughts on the Policing of Protest," in *Comparative Perspectives on Social Movements: Political Opportunities,*

Mobilizing Structures, and Cultural Framing, ed. Doug McAdam, John D. McCarthy, and Mayer N. Zald, 62–96. Cambridge/New York: Cambridge University Press.

Espeland, Wendy. 1994. "Legally Mediated Identity: The National Environmental Policy Act and the Bureaucratic Construction of Interests." *Law and Society Review* 28: 1149–78.

Haines, Herbert H. 1984. "Black Radicalization and the Funding of Civil Rights: 1957–1970." *Social Problems* 32: 331–72.

Handler, Joel. 1978. *Social Movements and the Legal System: A Theory of Law Reform and Social Change.* New York: Academic Press.

Hunt, Scott A., and Robert D. Benford. 1994. "Identity Talk in the Peace and Justice Movement." *Journal of Contemporary Ethnography* 22: 488–517.

Hunt, Scott A., Robert D. Benford, and David A. Snow. 1994. "Identity Fields: Framing Processes and the Social Construction of Movement Identities," in *New Social Movements: From Ideology to Identity*, ed. Enrique Larana, Hank Johnston, and Joseph R. Gusfield (185–208). Philadelphia: Temple University Press.

Jenkins, J. Craig, and Craig Eckert. 1986. "Elite Patronage and the Channeling of Social Protest." *American Sociological Review* 51: 812–29.

Jones, Lynn C. 1999. "Both Advocate and Activist: The Dual Careers of Cause Lawyers." Ph.D. dissertation. University of Arizona, Tucson.

———. 2001. "Career Activism by Lawyers: Consequences for the Person, the Legal Profession, and Social Movements," in *Legal Professions: Work, Structure and Organization*, ed. J. Von Hoy (181–206). New York: Elsevier Science and Technological Books.

Katz, Jack. 1982. *Poor People's Lawyers in Transition.* New Brunswick, N.J.: Rutgers University Press.

McAdam, Doug. 1982. *Political Process and the Development of Black Insurgency, 1930-1970.* Chicago: University of Chicago Press.

McAdam, Doug, John D. McCarthy, and Mayer N. Zald. 1996. *Comparative Perspectives on Social Movements: Political Opportunities, Mobilizing Structures, and Cultural Framing.* Cambridge and New York: Cambridge University Press.

McCann, Michael. 1986. *Taking Reform Seriously: Perspectives on Public Interest Liberalism.* Ithaca, N.Y.: Cornell University Press.

McCann, Michael, and Silverstein, Helena. 1998. "Rethinking Law's 'Allurements': A Relational Analysis of Social Movement Lawyers in the United States," in *Cause Lawyering: Political Commitments and Professional Responsibilities*, ed. Austin Sarat and Stuart Scheingold. New York: Oxford University Press.

McCarthy, John D., David W. Britt, and Mark Wolfson. 1991. "The Institutional Channeling of Social Movements by the State in the United States." *Research in Social Movements, Conflicts, and Change* 13: 45–76.

McCarthy, John D., and Mayer N. Zald. 1973. *The Trend of Social Movements in America: Professionalization and Resource Mobilization.* Morristown, N.J.: General Learning.

———. 1987. "The Trend of Social Movements in America: Professionalization and Resource Mobilization," in *Social Movements in and Organizational Society*, ed. Mayer N. Zald and John D. McCarthy (337–91). New Brunswick, N.J.: Transaction.

Melucci, Alberto. 1989. *Nomads of the Present: Social Movements and Individual Needs in Contemporary Society*. Philadelphia: Temple University Press.

———. 1996. *Challenging Codes*. Cambridge: Cambridge University Press.

Menkel-Meadow, Carrie. 1998. "The Causes of Cause Lawyering: Toward an Understanding of the Motivation and Commitment of Social Justice Lawyers," in *Cause Lawyering: Political Commitments and Professional Responsibilities*, ed. Austin Sarat and Stuart Scheingold (31–68). New York: Oxford University Press.

Piven, Frances Fox, and Richard Cloward. 1977. *Poor People's Movements: Why They Succeed, How They Fail*. New York: Vintage Books.

Richman, Kimberly. 2002. "Lovers, Legal Strangers, and Parents: Negotiating Parental and Sexual Identity in Family Law." *Law and Society Review* 36: 285–324.

Rosenberg, Gerald S. 1991. *The Hollow Hope: Can Courts Bring about Social Change?* Chicago: University of Chicago Press.

Sarat, Austin, and Stuart Scheingold, eds. 1998a. *Cause Lawyering: Political Commitments and Professional Responsibilities*. New York: Oxford University Press.

———. 1998b. "Cause Lawyering and the Reproduction of Professional Authority," in *Cause Lawyering: Political Commitments and Professional Responsibilities*, ed. Austin Sarat and Stuart Scheingold (3–28). New York: Oxford University Press.

———, eds. 2001. *Cause Lawyering and the State in a Global Era*. New York: Oxford University Press.

Scheingold, Stuart. 1974. *The Politics of Rights: Lawyers, Public Policy, and Political Change*. New Haven, Conn.: Yale University Press.

———. 1998. "The Struggle to Politicize Legal Practice: A Case Study of Left-Activist Lawyering in Seattle," in *Cause Lawyering: Political Commitments and Professional Responsibilities*, ed. Austin Sarat and Stuart Scheingold, 118–48. New York: Oxford University Press.

Scheingold, Stuart, and Anne Bloom. 1998. "Transgressive Cause Lawyering: Practice Sites and The Politicization of the Professional." *International Journal of the Legal Profession* 5, no. 2/3: 209–53.

Simon, William H. 1978. "The Ideology of Advocacy." *Wisconsin Law Review*, 30–144.

Snow, David, and Leon Anderson. 1987. "Identity Work among the Homeless: The Verbal Construction and Avowal of Personal Identities." *American Journal of Sociology* 92, no. 6: 1336–71.

Snow, David A., and Doug McAdam. 2000. "Identity Work Processes in the Context of Social Movements: Clarifying the Identity/Movement Nexus," in *Self, Identity, and Social Movements*, ed. Sheldon Stryker, Timothy J. Owens, and Robert W. White, 41–67. Minneapolis: University of Minnesota Press.

Staggenborg, Suzanne. 1988. "Consequences of Professionalization and Formalization in the Pro-Choice Movement." *American Sociological Review* 53: 585–605.

———. 1989. "Organizational and Environmental Influences on the Development of the Pro-Choice Movement." *Social Forces* 68, no. 1 (Sept.): 204–40.

———. 1991. *The Pro-Choice Movement: Organization and Activism in the Abortion Conflict*. New York: Oxford University Press.

Taylor, Verta. 1996. *Rock-a-By Baby: Feminism, Self-Help, and Postpartum Depression*. Routledge.

Taylor, Verta, and Nancy Whittier. 1992. "Collective Identity in Social Movement Communities: Lesbian Feminist Mobilization," in *Frontiers in Social Movement Theory*, ed. A. Morris and C. McClurg Mueller. New Haven, Conn.: Yale University Press.

Tilly, Charles. 1978. *From Mobilization to Revolution*. Boston: Addison-Wesley.

Weisbrod, Burton A., Joel F. Handler, and Neil K. Komesar. 1978. *Public Interest Law: An Economic and Institutional Analysis*. Berkeley: University of California Press.

Zald, Mayer N., and Roberta Ash. 1966. "Social Movement Organizations: Growth, Decay, and Change." *Social Forces* 44: 327–41.

CHAPTER EIGHT

Dilemmas of "Progressive" Lawyering

Empowerment and Hierarchy

COREY S. SHDAIMAH

The Helping Gesture

In 1968 Ivan Illich exhorted a group of would-be student volunteers and educators who were visiting Mexico to go home. In his view their proffered largesse was one more form of subordination, harmful to both recipients and benefactors. Illich admonished:

> If you insist on working with the poor, if this is your vocation, then at least work among the poor who can tell you to go to hell. It is incredibly unfair for you to impose yourselves on a village where you are so linguistically deaf and dumb that you don't even understand what you are doing, or what people think of you. And it is profoundly damaging to yourselves when you define something that you want to do as "good," a "sacrifice" and "help." (1990: 320)[1]

Illich's admonition raises a number of important implications. Is aid proffered by another ever devoid of paternalism? If so, should would-be do-gooders not offer aid? Should people seeking assistance be turned away for their own good? Is this really such a Hobson's choice, or is there a way to mitigate the disempowering nature of the process that allows for a middle ground? How do we assess the opinion of those who are the intended beneficiaries regarding these questions?

These questions were not new when Illich put them so sharply, nor have they disappeared. Although Illich may be extreme in his position, more tempered versions of these questions persist in a variety of contexts. They seem particularly troubling to people who profess a desire to work toward social change or social justice and for whom these amorphous and contested terms include notions of self-determination, equality, or empowerment.

Theorists have alerted us to power and the possibility of resistance and subordination in all relationships. Perhaps the most influential and controversial theorist of power is Michel Foucault, for whom power is ever changing and ubiquitous. It is a dynamic present in all relationships, intentionally or not, and it is best comprehended and challenged in its local, fragmented manifestations (Foucault [1976]1993).[2] Moreover, from a strategic perspective, searching for a central locus of power residing in any one identifiable agent or cause may be something of a red herring—impractical and a waste of precious energy in a political and social climate unresponsive to broad-scale tactics (Cruikshank 1999).[3] The client-professional relationship has drawn attention as a local manifestation of power deserving investigation (see, for example, the work of Sarat and Felstiner [1995] on divorce lawyers and clients and Chambon, Irving and Epstein [1999] on power in the social work context).[4]

Professionalism as Hierarchy

A critical examination of the sociological literature of professions reveals that a shared characteristic of professions is the creation and maintenance of boundaries.[5] Some of the concrete mechanisms distinguishing laypeople from professionals that form the basis for enactments of power and resistance in social justice work include: training in "expert" knowledge (Goode 1969); socialization through the adoption of professional lingo and inculcation into professional norms (Edelman 1977); setting boundaries and determining relevance within the context of the professional/client relationship (Rose 2000; White 1990); and the promulgation of codes, often referred to as professional ethics[6] that recommend, prescribe, and proscribe behaviors and are often accompanied by sanctions associated with their breach (Gustafson 1982; Merton 1982). The individual and cumulative effect of these attributes is to place putative professionals in a higher position than laypeople or paraprofessionals and to enhance or reinscribe the power of the professional and the profession (Edelman 1977). This can be particularly "effective" if there are additional status differentials such as level of education, gender, race, or class separating professional and client. Licensing and other gate-keeping practices help reify the distinction between the initiated and the uninitiated (Rhode 1981).

Within the legal profession, left activist lawyering (Scheingold 1998)[7] has its own body of critical literature. Using different terms such as rebellious lawyering (López 1992), client-centered lawyering (Ellman 1987), collaborative lawyering (White 1994), and facilitative lawyering (Marsico 1995) theorists and practitioners struggle with the tensions between social justice goals and the hierarchical, disempowering aspects of lawyering and the legal process. Although these carefully justified terms and the distinctions drawn between them are persuasive, it is telling that most of the lawyers in this study did not distinguish between them nor were they even familiar with them.

I refer to the collection of practices and lawyering theories as they bear on this subset of left-activist lawyers as "progressive lawyering," which through its very practice poses a challenge to dominant notions of lawyering and the social order (López 1992). This term encompasses elements shared by the other terms, and it is one of the many words that the lawyers and theorists themselves use to describe these orientations in broad strokes, even while it focuses on aspects of the client-lawyer relationship within the broader range of left activist lawyering practices. The term is also identified with those who emphasize a complex confluence of social, political, and legal forces; those who emphasize elements of inequality and oppression (Polikoff 1996);[8] and those who emphasize the dangers of working for social justice within deeply flawed systems (Freire [1970] 1999).[9]

Critical scholarship has been important in raising awareness among lawyers and academics regarding issues of power within the context of progressive lawyering. This is a particularly rich field in which to explore the client-professional role as it highlights the dilemmas of power. Progressive lawyers and clients want (and often need) lawyers to use power in order to serve their clients. However, their self-declared adherence to values of equality, empowerment, client autonomy, and social change leads them to try to enhance their clients' abilities to harness power in their encounters with others while simultaneously seeking to curb the effects of power in their own relationships with clients.

Although in serving clients progressive lawyers largely wield power vis-à-vis people and institutions outside of the immediate lawyer-client relationship, the very tools, education, and status that give lawyers power in their professional milieu come to bear within that relationship. Its presence within the lawyer-client relationship is given further weight by the relative power differentials between lawyers and clients and in the lawyers' ability to delineate the contours of the client-professional relationship, despite clients' ability to navigate within that relationship (Sarat and Felstiner 1995). These dilemmas are ever-present for legal services lawyers who choose to focus their work on direct client service and thus are embedded in relationships with clients.

Much of the existing literature on lawyer-client relationships relies on the firsthand experiences of theorists who engaged in the practice of law (Simon 1991; White 1990) or composite characters (López 1992). But few have systematically investigated the daily expectations, practices, and dilemmas of progressive lawyers engaged primarily in client representation.[10] The self-reflection in which many of these lawyers engage and the adaptations they make to reconcile their practice of law with other ideals that they embrace remain largely unexplored.[11]

There is also a dearth of studies involving clients of progressive lawyers,[12] particularly surprising because much of the literature espouses a vision of practice that recognizes client dignity and respects client autonomy and decision-making capacity. Although many of the critiques and theories are designed to foster certain qualities and achieve certain goals for and with clients (all believed to be in their best interest), clients' voices are rarely heard in formulating these visions of practice.

These lacunae leave us with theories that are incomplete and two-dimensional, failing to properly describe what happens in the settings where actual lawyers and clients negotiate their relationships. Although many theorists of progressive lawyer/client relationships purport to have an interest in revising their practice to better conform to ideals of empowerment and justice, to the extent that they fail to account for the realities and needs of actual lawyers and clients they will continue to have limited relevance to the very people they intend to influence.

This study bridges a gap between theory and practice, leading us to a revised understanding of the lawyer-client relationship that sheds light on the dilemmas of progressive lawyering outlined above. In the next section, I provide a summary of the research site and methods. In the three sections that follow, I explore three different aspects of the power dilemma that are drawn from concerns shared by theorists and practitioners: client decision-making; collaboration as a tool for client empowerment; and the centrality of the personal encounter. This chapter ends with concluding thoughts that integrate theoretical insights and the practical dilemmas faced by lawyers and clients and the ways in which they resolve them in order to continue to practice despite these dilemmas.

Research Design

This chapter relies on preliminary data collected from intensive interviews[13] with lawyers and clients of Northeast Legal Services (NELS),[14] a nonprofit legal services organization established over thirty years ago. Originally started as part of the legal services initiative with funding from the Office of Economic Opportunity and later through the Legal Services Corporation (LSC), in 1996 NELS ceased accepting federal funding due to the increasingly strict constraints placed upon recipients. I chose NELS for my interviews because although it allows lawyers to do both individual and impact work, most have a large caseload and frequent client interaction. In nearly all units, lawyers participate in the intake process and handle cases for further assistance if those clients and/or cases are eligible based upon a variety of criteria that include income and the substantive area of law involved.

Seven lawyers responded to a recruitment e-mail posted to all NELS attorneys by the director that included a brief description of the research topic and her endorsement of the study. All other lawyers were referred by individuals familiar with the study.[15] Thus all participating lawyers were either self-selected or recommended on the basis of their interest in exploring their relationships with clients. This technique of purposive sampling allowed me to seek understanding from participants whose experiences and interests were relevant to the study. All participating lawyers referred three clients who they thought would be able to shed some light on the topics discussed during the interview.[16] Follow-up interviews were conducted with lawyers upon completion of client interviews.

The data in this chapter are drawn from the thirty interviews conducted so far in this ongoing study: seven initial lawyer interviews, nineteen client interviews, and follow-up interviews with four lawyers. All lawyer interviews and three client interviews took place at NELS' offices, while the remainder of the client interviews took place in the homes of clients throughout Northeast City with the exception of one telephone interview.

All clients met NELS's income eligibility criteria of 125 percent of the federal poverty line; in other words, all NELS clients are poor. Out of nineteen clients, fourteen are African American, two are recent immigrants (one from Nigeria and the other from Indonesia), and three are white. Fifteen are women and four are men. The age range was approximately 30–80. The majority had other individuals dependent upon them, including some with adult children who were mentally or physically disabled. The issues they brought to NELS included problems with public housing, child custody, Social Security Disability Insurance benefits for mental and physical conditions, TANF benefits, consumer bankruptcy, and predatory lending.

NELS lawyers work in units specializing in particular substantive areas that are in some cases tied to the needs of specific populations such as the elderly or juveniles. The lawyers interviewed practice in the areas of public benefits, elderly law, family law, and consumer advocacy. Lawyers' work experience ranged from several months to nearly thirty years. Four of the lawyers are men, three are women; all are white. Lawyers report being overwhelmed by burdensome caseloads and inadequate resources. Most also expressed satisfaction with their work, their colleagues, and the level of professional and social interactions at NELS. Nearly all chose their careers out of a commitment to some notion of social justice or social change and are grateful to have found paying jobs that allow them to pursue these commitments full time (Thomson, this volume; Jones, this volume).

Autonomy

Most theories of progressive lawyering espouse a value of client autonomy which views clients as competent and entitled to make informed decisions. These theories also regard decision making as a tool to maximize self-reliance and empower clients. Progressive lawyers are those who facilitate rather than impede client autonomy. As Simon (1991) points out, this brand of autonomy has inherent contradictions, as in its extreme it represents a paternalistic or "best interest" view that forces even reluctant clients (for their own good) to make decisions that they might not want to make.

Nuanced discussions of client autonomy recognize the more subtle ways that lawyers influence client decision making. Lawyers in this study were troubled by what they perceived as their own ability to manipulate clients in the decision-making process. They seemed to understand manipulation in the broad sense that Ellman (1987: 277) employs, that is, to include "even well-intentioned, or seemingly modest, interferences with client decision-making." In fact, they seemed aware that even unintentionally, they manipulate their clients' decision making. When asked what about this was troubling, most lawyers responded with variations on themes of autonomy. On an ideological level, they viewed autonomy as a component of respect for clients. On a more practical level, not only did they view most clients as capable of making decisions for themselves but also as having the expertise necessary regarding their own life circumstances and complex motivations and goals to best make these decisions. In seeming contradiction to the practical reasons for their concern, lawyers also perceived most clients as reluctant to make decisions on their own.

Although clients echoed a reluctance to make decisions independently, they were less likely than the lawyers to perceive their reliance on lawyers' advice (rather than just neutral information) as undermining their own decision-making power or as a form of manipulation. This might be due to the fact that many of the clients were in situations where their previous lack of knowledge and the difficulty in obtaining information from government agencies led to the problems that brought them to NELS in the first place. In describing how she chose between options, a client of the benefits unit said she would ask her lawyer his opinion:

> And I would ask him how would he go about this? And he would tell me his point, but he would also tell me that you don't have to do this. You can go by your mind, you know, but I, and I always use my mind but I like to hear how you feel about it, so maybe I could make my decision right, but I don't want to make the wrong decisions [laughs].

Viewed in this light, reliance on lawyers' advice and assistance, even beyond the point that a progressive lawyer might feel comfortable, can increase client options. Although client autonomy may not be maximized in the context of representation, many clients feel that discussing a problem with a lawyer is a decision that increases autonomy in the broader context of their lives by helping them make what they see as better decisions.

Both lawyers and clients viewed this type of "lawyerly advice" as a luxury that paying clients demand. Mary, another client, joked that she felt comfortable talking with her lawyer about any problem that arose and that their relationship is reminiscent of the relationship that the rich people she sees on television have with their lawyers:

> It's like he's a family lawyer or something. A family friend/lawyer. Like . . . what I see on TV or something, that's what type of person he is . . . [like on] some kind of legal show or something, and this family has this lawyer, like that they're totally like coming to their gatherings, and they're friends as well as professional or something like that.

When I asked Mary how she chose between various options, she marveled at her good fortune in being able to call her lawyer:

> I always call Pete [her lawyer] and ask him. 'Cause if I'm not clear about what I'm going to do, I do! I just like call him right away. You know, like, if I feel as though I come up to a situation where I think that I have to choose and I don't know if I'm going to make the right choice or something, I'll definitely call him. I mean, that's real. It's real. 'Cause sometimes it, it's like, damn, this is like kind of too good to be true!

In our follow-up interview I questioned Mary's lawyer Pete about this type of relationship and he was more ambivalent. On the one hand, he is not a proponent of what he called the "retainer model" of legal services, although some lawyers at NELS are. He feels the retainer model is a practical impossibility due to resource constraints, and he dislikes it from an autonomy perspective in that he suspects that it promotes client dependence. Although many lawyers at NELS remain for a long time, at the time of the interview Pete had applied for another job and he wondered how the clients who have grown accustomed to calling him for advice would fare if he left. He also worries that Mary and other clients use him as a first resource before solving problems that he believes they could handle on their own. As an example, he mentioned another client in the study who turned to him for help finding an apartment:

> She went to family court and the court ordered that she could take all the possessions from his [her husband's] property, anything she wants in there she can take, whether it's hers or his. But she had to move within, I forget what it was, I think it was thirty days, it was a very short period of time. And she called me up that night stressed out. "I really need your help, can you go on-line and try to do some apartment searches for me." And I told her "No, I can't do that. Go to the library." And I actually did a couple of searches and said here's some good Web sites. And part of it was I'm not doing that for her, but part of it was also, you know, I'm trying to fight her instinct of having to turn to someone from the outside to help her get through this because she's capable of doing it.

Even in the absence of ambiguity surrounding the meaning and scope of client autonomy, lack of knowledge of the legal system limits client independence. Knowledge is a prerequisite to informed decision making and both lawyers and clients perceive lawyers as professional interpreters of the law. Many of the lawyers in this study noted that their own specialty was particularly complex in terms of navigating the legal issues or the relevant bureaucracy, thus impeding extensive client input into the handling of their cases.[17] Ben, a consumer lawyer, claimed that lawyers as a professional group tend to mystify the legal process, but that he himself was uncomfortable with the impression he received from clients that he would "do the magic." Although he did not want to further contribute to the mystification of law, at the same time he found that many clients did not understand nor want to know the detailed explanations of the legal or financial minutiae that made up much of his work when he did attempt explanations. All of the clients I interviewed said they understood their lawyers, but many did not seem to know (or care) about the legal arguments or even necessarily what stage their case was at. Most clients understandably were more interested in the bottom line or the outcome of their case: Will I get my children back? Will I be reinstated for public housing? Will my disability make me eligible for Social Security Disability benefits?

Lawyers spoke of attempting to communicate with clients in language that is clear and understandable. Several lawyers made a practice of keeping their clients abreast via written documents even if they spoke to them on the phone or in person. They did so in order for the client to have a record, but also specifically so that the clients could review the information as often as they liked and would have time to think about it, discuss it with family and friends, and formulate any questions. They tried to explain simply without "dumbing down." One public housing client said of communication with her lawyer:

> He didn't use legal language that I didn't understand . . . he explained it in such a way that anybody could understand. No, it was no big technical things that needed to be explained, you know. And if it was, he didn't put it to me that way, he put it to me in such a way that I thoroughly understood it even when he wrote the letters. . . . It's not a whole bunch of whereas and you got to break down words and whatever.

Most clients perceived their lawyers as explaining things clearly and to their satisfaction, often decoding incomprehensible documents that came to them from a variety of government agencies. Another described a notice she received in her ongoing battles with a public housing authority:

> when I don't understand I say right away "I don't understand that can you explain that a little better to me." So he [her lawyer] really explains it pretty good. He explains things where I can understand. Cause a matter of fact, I had got this paper, you know? And housing, instead of writing my paper out—that's what really made me go to them [NELS]. . . . They was trying to put me out and I didn't understand the reason because the way they'd written it only a lawyer could understand it. And it was a mess, I couldn't understand none of this stuff. . . .
>
> I was like "what is this?" What is they done? I know it got to be something but I don't understand this stuff. I took it in . . . "yeah they was trying to get you." They tried to . . . put so much stuff in there that I couldn't understand.

In this case, it is not the lawyers at NELS who are responsible for the legal smoke and mirrors, but the agencies who refuse to explain, mislead, or make things difficult for clients. If NELS lawyers were to empower their clients with knowledge, there still seems to be little that they can do to change the systems for their own clients, never mind other beneficiaries who do not enlist their help. Thus even if progressive lawyers take steps to demystify the legal process, to the extent that their practice takes place in a larger institutional context, a focus on the individual relationship can effect change only marginally, if at all.

This is not to say that the lawyers did not attempt to clarify documents and improve agency encounters for a broader group than their immediate client population. In fact, nearly all the lawyers interviewed described some project in which they attempted to produce and widely distribute informational pamphlets or conduct trainings with service providers and laypeople. Some also described successful attempts to change agency guidelines or forms substantively so they would be more simple and straightforward. In one case, an attorney working with the elderly explained how she helped to elucidate and formulate substantive criteria for state regulations and then developed a brochure to explain this to potential recipients:

> There is a federal law that requires that states try to reimburse themselves for the care that they've paid for in the nursing home. . . . The state is required to try to collect after that person's death, from any remaining assets. So this policy . . . has been misinterpreted for a very long time. And there's a lot of bad information sort of out on the street. . . . We get clients to come in and say to us . . . the person who did the assessment said that my dad's going to lose his home, even though I've been living in this home and caring for him for the last five years.
>
> There are exceptions to this estate recovery policy . . . there are ways that people can transfer their homes. If they do it far enough in advance it doesn't have any ill effect, that's the kind of information that really is important to get out to people in advance. And in fact, I wrote a brochure . . . once we produced that brochure people were saying—social workers and hospital staffs and families were saying "wow this is great, no one ever explained it to us." And the state had this brochure that was like you know "all your property belongs to the state after you die" [laugh]!

Liz went on to explain how her work on clarifying the brochure for service providers and recipients also involved substantive changes in the way the law was interpreted and implemented:

> When I first came here there weren't any state regulations about how this policy would be implemented and there is a commission . . . and I've been on that workgroup now for several years. . . . While the people who are administering the program now may have good hearts there's not a lot of guidance for people on the street to know about how they're going to be handling this process, what the exceptions are. . . . The state didn't have any published criteria. And then we found out that there was an internal unpublished criteria—but they still make exceptions even in addition to that one set of criteria. So regulations were finally published. . . . Coincidentally the brochure that we developed here actually became the model for a brochure . . . and it's being distributed statewide.

However, such projects are usually specific and in many ways seem to be a drop in the proverbial bucket. Although I do not mean to belittle the importance of the changes for those affected, most clients still had difficulty accessing, understanding, or complying with documents and procedures. In fact, nearly all clients mentioned misinformation, lack of information, or incompetence on the part of various agencies or complained that written documents they received were unintelligible, incorrect, or not sent in a timely manner that allowed them to comply with instructions.

Maximizing client knowledge is further complicated by that fact that many of the clients are also coping with other difficulties. This makes it hard for clients to focus or devote time and energy to fully comprehend a problem that they expect their lawyer to handle anyway. Poverty can both stem from and be exacerbated by a variety of other difficulties that people face, including racism, homelessness, and physical and mental health problems. Lawyers are keenly aware of this. One lawyer in the benefits unit noted that although the work that he did with a particular client was the most pressing issue *for him*, this was often not the case for the client. This was the reason he often did not ask clients to perform various tasks on their behalf but preferred to take care of the tasks himself:

> 'cause that way I know it gets done. And I don't mean that in a blame sense. 'Cause there's lots of— sometimes it's that there's blame, but most of the time it's like, yeah, of course it doesn't get done because there's six million other things going on in the client's life, and why should this be the most important thing? It's the most important thing to my relationship with the client because I'm not helping them with their eviction and their homelessness and their—all of that stuff. That's not— You know, so for me this is very important, but for some of my clients it's not critical and so when you're in crisis only that gets done which absolutely has to get done.

Many clients also come to NELS in states of extreme stress that make it difficult to process information. All the clients I interviewed (or their family members) experienced some of the problems mentioned above. In addition, many described the feelings about the problems that led them to seek assistance from NELS using palpable physical symptoms of stress such as chest pains, difficulty sleeping, headaches, and crying. A client seeking reinstatement of eligibility for public housing described nearly a year and a half of moving from house to house throughout Philadelphia with her teenage daughter while trying to keep her job (and her furniture): "It was so sad. It was sad, a lot of times I was just like, I just broke down and cried, we [she and her daughter] both cried together and I kept telling her you know, things going to be okay. . . . [Sighs] Oh, it's stress, it's really stress."

When I asked another public housing client why she sought assistance from NELS, she replied:

> I was hoping they'd get these people off my back. . . . I was really up against a wall because I was paying a awful lot of rent considering my income. . . . And when I went over there to try to help those people see that it was something wrong with the amount of rent I was paying and my income, they told me that they couldn't change anything. . . . My daughter is a schizophrenic and my son is autistic and they're adults. So I have to stay home with them, I can't work. So, it was like, you're between a rock and a hard place. And these people had me with nightmares, and they weren't going to do anything, "We just want our money."

Even when clients are able to fully comprehend their situations and articulate their goals, lawyers are not always able to assist them in carrying out such goals due to institutional and professional constraints.[18] One lawyer who works closely with a welfare rights group felt that such constraints hampered his choices and his ability to represent the group:

> An institutional constraint is we get funding. Our funders do not fund us to disrupt the Olympics. They fund us to help people on welfare who are getting their benefits cut off by the welfare system. . . . And we have much fewer institutional constraints than all those other legal services organizations that have congressional restrictions that are imposed upon them. Which they can't do some of the very things that Lucie White and Gerry López say they must do. They can't do organizing, they can't do administrative advocacy, so that's sort of institutional constraints.

This lawyer felt that his inability to represent his client as that client saw fit was a source of tension between him and the client and led the client to question his commitment to her cause. It underscored that this lawyer was an outsider, one whose assistance and choices are circumscribed by his professional and institutional identity. As Polikoff (1996) notes, the lawyer's professional role is a double-edged sword. In order to provide ongoing legal assistance through NELS that his client deemed of critical importance, such as representation in benefits hearings for client, this lawyer refused to engage in other types of representation and political activities that might jeopardize his role as a lawyer. Although he considers himself committed to his clients' cause, he nevertheless feels compelled to maintain a certain professional distance to be effective in the ways that his profession allows.

Collaboration

Collaborative lawyering models see lawyers and clients as "co-eminent problem solvers" (López 1992). They are rooted in a belief that both lawyers and clients can and should contribute knowledge and skills to the relationship. Clients and lawyers are equals, and collaborative practices seek to mitigate the hierarchical aspects of the professional client relationship. Although lawyers may have formal training and greater access, clients are experts in their own lives and possess knowledge and problem-solving skills that are at least as important to the "success" of the lawyering relationship. Collaborative lawyers also seek to engage clients as much as possible in the representation so they can learn from the process and develop tools to advocate for themselves or others, perhaps obviating the need for a lawyer in the future.

Lawyers' decisions as to how much to involve clients and in what aspects of the representation were often framed as a cost/benefit analysis within a discussion of time constraints. Investing the time to educate some clients would necessarily mean serving fewer clients. One factor lawyers weigh in determining how much to involve clients is the perceived efficacy of involving the client, both for the case at hand and for the client's future encounters with government bureaucracies. One benefits lawyer specializing in Social Security Disability Insurance said the process of determining and proving disability status was very complicated and thus he tended not to involve the client in those details. Furthermore, he was aware that these encounters were not likely to repeat. Once a client's disability status is established, it is not likely to be revisited nor was this process, in the eyes of the lawyer, similar to any other process the client might encounter. Therefore, he saw little point in having the client understand the process so as to be able to replicate it at a later time on his or her own.

Another lawyer who viewed collaboration as a value found it inefficient and thus a luxury that was simply too resource intensive:

> We have a ton of work to do. I mean it's absurd. And how few of us there are relative to the nature of the problem and we set up all these artificial ways to safeguard us from clients like having nine hours of intake a week. But still, even with that, the time—the workload is unbelievable. And then that creates this problem of having to cut corners basically and not do educational or empowering work. There's a strain of the collaborative lawyering stuff that I think theorizes that it could be more efficient to do collaborative lawyering because you're garnering the strengths and the skills and abilities of the client also, who then are going to do work on their case. I don't believe that that's usually true. I think from my experience it's usually less efficient. There has to be a certain level of collaboration 'cause there's certain things that the client has to provide to you but in most cases it's more efficient to just assume all the responsibilities and do it yourself.

Where lawyers did see an important and productive venue for more collaborative work is not in the legal context but in solving practical problems, such as obtaining documents or trying to strategize with clients about the practical ramifications that would facilitate or impede decisions or settlements.

> I like to talk to my clients about what I perceive to be the weakness in your case, because frequently they can problem-solve on how to resolve that weakness much better than I can. A good example was we had a client who is wheelchair-bound. He lives in a subsidized Section VIII unit, he'd been there for a long time but the place wasn't being kept clean. And most judges would say to that particular person you got to figure out a way to get somebody in to clean your unit. . . . So I talked to him about that. I said, listen, you know, if you can find somebody to clean your unit on a regular basis, and they're willing to come into court and say that they're going to do it, then I think you can succeed. Well, he went out and found somebody. I was not aware of

any service that I could get for him to do that, but he did it. So the kind of talking to your clients about the weaknesses in the cases helps move things along.

Collaborative lawyering models assume that clients desire participation in the legal process. But is this what clients want? And if not, would respect for client autonomy in the strictest sense mandate that lawyers take this into consideration? Many clients do not express a desire to understand the legal process or achieve future self-sufficiency but instead seek to share, or in some cases to unload, one of the many burdens they experience. They seek lawyers as professionals who can resolve problems through use of professional tools and as providers of information who "know the ropes." This is often lost on progressive lawyering proponents. As Southworth (1994) points out in a critique of López's rebellious lawyering that could easily be applied more broadly, the call for greater client involvement in the legal process too often downplays the contributions that lawyers can make. Clients are less inclined to seek collaboration and many rationally and prudently perceive such skills and experience as necessary to successfully navigate the legal system or the relevant agency. One client, speaking of legal services, told me: "Services like that *are* needed and are necessary. Because our society's a legal society. You may not like it . . . but you can't live without [lawyers]. Not in our world anyway."

Most clients do not feel competent to handle legal proceedings on their own. I asked Dara, a client who had been through consumer bankruptcy proceedings, whether she could handle a similar proceeding on her own in the future.

> Dara: No. No. No, it's no way because the deal is that there is some things—I mean you can't. If you look at the paperwork you need to be—there's some things that you need to be able to observe, and you need to know, you need to know professionally what it is you're looking for.
> Corey: So it's not something that lay people . . .
> Dara: No, not at all. Not at all, not at all.
> Corey: Is it the language on the forms . . . or it's just legal/technical?
> Dara: It's the process. I mean, it's a process that's not a familiar process for most people. And it's something that a professional should handle. There's no way in this world I would go and file any legal proceedings and not know what I'm doing.

Dara's assessment of legal processes as requiring professional skills is one echoed by many clients. Another client explained by example, telling me that just as she would not provide medical care to herself, neither would she take charge of her legal affairs, given the choice of receiving competent legal assistance.

Clients feel that lawyers are important not just for their professional skills, but also because they are more likely to be listened to. Claire, a client of the consumer advocacy unit, consistently referred to her lawyer (Marjorie) as a "mediator," and said that without Marjorie neither the agency she was challenging nor the court would listen to her. After Claire explained to me how she had been a conscientious client by fulfilling her responsibilities, such as following instructions, procuring documents, and appearing in court on time, I asked her if she thought that she and Marjorie had worked as a team:

> Well naturally she did it all. I wouldn't have known, . . . what do you call it? The chain of command. You know I couldn't go to the judge and say "please judge your honor could you do this for me." The chain of command was my representative, my lawyer, my mediator. So she did a lot of work too as well. And found out things where she can get information through, "Hello my name is Marjorie Donald, esquire." Like they wasn't going to talk to me.

In this client's case, even were she to acquire the knowledge and take the actions learned from her lawyer, she suspected that the agency and the court system she dealt with would not likely respond to her because she is not a lawyer. Clients unequivocally stated the importance of a good lawyer in a system that some viewed as arbitrary and others viewed as responsive only to those with competent representation.

Using a narrow definition of collaboration, the data presented here would seem to indicate that clients do not want or are unable to collaborate. However, it would be incorrect to conclude that clients are passive, do not work with their lawyers, or do not learn. Instead, we need to look for other forms of collaboration in the context of clients' lives. For many clients, initiating and maintaining the lawyer-client relationship is in itself a demonstration of will and resourcefulness. The difficulties that childcare, disability, transportation, and/or the need to hold on to poverty-wage jobs that entail hours of commuting complicate even the simplest tasks. Although some clients reach NELS only after being shepherded by helping professionals, other clients displayed persistence and exertion of significant efforts in finding NELS and following through on their cases. One client only heard of NELS after she went to her city council representatives' office. Another client told of tapping into any organization that she could think of, explaining that she was not sure that NELS could help but that she was not going to give up until she had tried everything.

On an even more basic level, the clients who initiated contact with NELS showed an understanding that their problems might be legal problems, although for some this was a "shot in the dark." Felstiner, Abel, and Sarat (1981) refer to the transformation of troubles into a legal problem as "naming, blaming and claiming," a socially constructed process that is far from obvious or inevitable. To use their terms, it is usually only clients who have already "named" ("perceived an injurious experience") and "blamed" ("attributed responsibility for that grievance") who went to NELS to assist them with "claiming" ("voic[ing] that grievance to the person or entity believed to be responsible and ask[ing] for a remedy") (635–36). Many of the clients in fact told of friends or family members who experienced similar problems but who did not take any steps to respond to the problems, despite their urging, and as a result "allowed themselves" to lose a home or eligibility for desperately needed benefits.

The transformation of troubles into legal problems presents an opportunity for client-lawyer collaboration. Even though most clients initiating contact with NELS have named and claimed, their claims or attribution of responsibility are often tenuous and intertwined with conflicting notions of responsibility. Their ambivalence is reflected in one client's apparently contradictory assessments of poor people like herself. At one point in the interview, JoAnn was sympathetic to people whom she saw as compelled to break the rules due to the shear impossibility of living on the paltry benefits of a stingy welfare state:

> Well when you're poor you know what? You kind of know you have to find a way to make ends meet. You have to find a way to get your needs met. And you tend to be one of these survivors. One, usually when you're on public assistance, 90 percent of people on public assistance have been low-income their whole life. So they learn to manage a budget real close and know how to fight the system to get everything and anything. And sometimes the fight is hard. And sometimes you literally have to lie to get your needs met. Be really resourceful, we will find a way to get what we need. And it's sad that we have to go to the extremes sometimes. But it's good to know that people are still willing to fight for everything they need.

In a seemingly contradictory vein, JoAnn gave a harsher judgment of beneficiaries whom she had earlier admitted were compelled by their circumstances to be rule-breakers in order to survive. She was at first hesitant to speak to her lawyer about what to do with the proceeds from the possible sale of her home because she was afraid that he would see her as "one of those people" trying to "get over on" the system. Despite her fears she consulted with him, largely because she trusted him as someone who would not prejudge or be suspicious. Her narrative reveals her attempts to distance herself from other people who cheat the system.

> I just decided that he was open enough and honest enough and very caring with me that he would see me as who I was and that my fears weren't really rational. That he would see me as somebody trying to mess with the system. Because a lot of people do. You know, they do. I have friends that are still getting over on the system and I'm like "you're the reason I'm still fighting so hard" [laughs]. But I don't say that to people's face, I'm not—but at the same time I do get mad at the abusers of the system be-

cause they have made it difficult for me to get what I need. And I blame that for the reason that I've had to fight so hard to keep my medical benefits. It's that there's so many people out there abusing the system that there's not enough services for those who truly need them.

Some of this ambiguity can of course be attributed to clients' assessment of a variety of people, some rule breakers and some (like themselves) deserving claimants.[19] The frequency with which clients explained to me that they were in fact "deserving" or "faultless" (and that their lawyers saw them this way, too) and the ambivalence reflected in their attitudes toward others goes well beyond this explanation. In large part it may be attributed to the stigma associated with poor claimants of all stripes and the messages that these people get from the bureaucracies that teach them that poor people's claims are suspect. Like JoAnn, even when clients understand themselves and others who are similarly situated as victims of an unjust or capricious system, they are careful to point out their own virtues, and in some cases, distance themselves from "trouble-makers." Many of the clients went to great pains to explain that they were "good": they were wronged and not at fault; they procured documents; they were organized; they followed their lawyers' instructions; they did not cheat the system, despite the opportunity to do so.

For the clients interviewed in this study, lawyers often shored up clients' conception that even "deserving" individuals can be wronged by institutions or agencies, and that they may have recourse. In this way, clients and lawyers collaborate to produce and shape legal claims. Lawyers reassure clients that they were indeed wronged. In cases where clients may have no legal recourse, or where the benefits they will eventually get are still paltry, lawyers commiserate with clients by agreeing that the benefits are meager, that the system is unjust, or that the rules are punitive and intrusive. In this way, lawyers can help to reinforce an emerging or fragile legal consciousness.

This dialogue may also result in clients expanding their claims to include more general indictments very much in the way Meili (this volume) describes the use of new collective legal techniques in Mexico and Argentina, respectively, even when the claims are unsuccessful. Many clients come to NELS with a problem that they believe is unique to them. Some put off seeking assistance due to embarrassment. Clients were often surprised and indignant to discover that others experienced similar difficulties. Not only did this knowledge lend support to their claims, but it also shifted their perception of the problem as individual to systemic. A client of the public housing unit did not know that her complaint against the management of the public housing unit in which she lived was one of many until she came to NELS and her lawyer told her about a number of infractions against other tenants. I asked Mrs. Nathanson about her decision to agree to be a named plaintiff in a class action suit:

> I saw the advantage of pursuing. He asked me did I mind being a part of a class action suit? I have no problem with that. Because something has to be done about where we live. And I told him it would be fine and he told me my name would appear, and that was fine with me. And like I said, he didn't make the decision for me, he asked me. You know, would I consent? It wasn't like he was bullying me or pushing me or urging me. He just laid out the facts, told me what was happening, and would I like to participate? See because I could have very well said well I got what I want, the heck with everybody else. But as it stands, what could happens, I could get the recourse that I have now, but who's to say they won't come up with something else later? Because they had a lot of infraction down there.

Lawyers and clients also work together to counteract the demeaning experiences that clients have with the bureaucracies that they enlist NELS' help to challenge. When asked about her view of the law after her experience with the Public Housing Authority (PHA), one client said:

> The law sucks as far as public housing, dealing with public housing authority, Section 8. . . . How they talk to you, how they look at you, how they look down at you. You know and I'm like, "Well why is you talking to me like that?" I said, "I'm human just like you are. You want me to respect you? You got to respect me too." I said "if we didn't come into this office you all wouldn't get paid!" . . . I just can't understand. . . . They are very nasty. The whole system is very nasty. . . . And somebody needs to be looking into how the Public Housing Authority and Section 8 run their establishment and how they treat their tenants, the clients, whatever we are to them. . . . It's not right.

Lawyers concurred with this assessment, and for many it underscored the importance of treating clients with respect and dignity:

> typically our clients' interactions with the system are negative. The people are mean to them, bureaucrats are mean to them, they always get told no and they're treated rudely and nastily. So I think it's extremely important that we show and are respectful to our clients. And I think that's incredibly important because I think what, one of the worst things I think is that happens to poor people is they're dehumanized. And if I can treat my clients respectfully, that is, not as important as winning their case, but it's pretty damn important.

Clients collaborate with lawyers not only on the abstract level of understanding and reinterpreting their experiences, but also on a more mundane level. Clients gain practical skills, such as learning when and how to use lawyers as an informational resource or for leverage. One of the public housing clients cited earlier felt that working with her lawyer has helped her cope with other problems:

I'm trying, my nerves have been so bad. It's just so bad. But it's getting stronger now, 'cause you see now I'm knowing how to deal with them. Without getting angry, you know, I do, it's just go to the source, I'll just find out what's going on, when they send me letters I keep all my documents, you understand what I'm saying? Then I go find me a legal aid lawyer. And then the lawyer will deal with that. For real. It's, I mean, it's we'll be working together, you know, I ain't going to put all the work on them, but they be doing basically the work theirselves. But I still have to do my part, you know. I don't even get upset and uptight no more like I used to, because I was like on pins. I was on pins and needles, I didn't know which way I was going or coming.

Although this type of learning may appear insignificant when compared to some ideal notion of collaboration, this client certainly perceives her experience as a significant learning experience in terms of her ability to cope, handle documents, and enlist relevant aid.

Some clients also use the information they obtain from working with their lawyers to help others. An asylee from Indonesia assists refugees from his country with knowledge that he gained from his own experiences and information from government offices and the Internet, often calling lawyers for supplemental information or steering people to legal services and *pro bono* lawyers. Although the collaborative lawyering that takes place at NELS does not obviate the need for lawyers in the future for clients and other individuals they assist, many are better able to know when and how to enlist a lawyer's services and feel more confident that with the assistance or information provided by a lawyer they can challenge recalcitrant institutions. This confidence can be of primary importance, increasing the likelihood that clients and others will enlist NELS' help. Client data suggest that clients who initiated contact with NELS already had some hope or expectation that NELS might be willing and able to assist them. This was in contrast to friends or relatives with similar problems who may have similar problems and had even "named" and "blamed" but despaired of "claiming" due to a perception that this would be fruitless.

Clients also come through their experiences feeling better able to demand and receive service. Some became more willing to challenge government offices without fear of recrimination. When I asked a client who was also active in a welfare rights organization whether she was ever nervous about appealing or challenging the decisions of the welfare office she responded:

Not actually. No, because, because I know I had him [her lawyer]. And then I know, like my organization does a lot of this, like looking this stuff up and we know our rights. So I know from the time they try to BS me, you know what I mean? I'd be like "that's BS [laughs]. I'm calling my lawyer," you know. Especially if they try to say you can't appeal.

Another client, who is the type of client Steve describes admiringly as "up-pity," contrasted her lack of knowledge in a previous situation to her confidence in making demands on the Social Security Agency after she began working with Steve:

> Well I was like, you know, this decision; I'm not satisfied with it. She didn't say well you have the right to appeal. I didn't even think about appeal at that time, I just, you know, "this isn't right, this can't be." But never did I get any paperwork that says you have the right to appeal this decision, here's how you appeal it until after Steve got in-volved. Then of course they kept everything totally legal because they had no other choice. I mean even today when I went, the woman said "oh your lawyer's not with you?" I said "no there's no need for him to be here. Unless of course you're going to try to aggravate me again" [laughs]. Yes I did, I didn't care.

I do not intend to go so far as to suggest that clients and lawyers learn to view these institutions as any less capricious or mean-spirited. In fact, one of the lawyers I interviewed hoped it did not mean this, as he viewed these insti-tutions as fundamentally inimical to the interests of poor people. This lawyer did not wish to encourage his clients to think otherwise, even if the clients were successful in working the system to obtain favorable results in a particular in-stance. As noted above, these institutions remain intimidating, incomprehensi-ble, and unresponsive to unrepresented people. Nevertheless, clients can be gal-vanized by their experience. Although most clients do not engage in large-scale political or social action, many spoke of referring others to legal services or speaking out about their problems. This meant going beyond initial feelings of embarrassment, self-judgment, or victimization to an understanding of their problem as widespread or having a broader social context, and it begins in the personal encounter.

The Centrality of the Personal Relationship

Progressive lawyering literature stresses the importance of listening to and engaging clients, and one of its underlying themes is that of respect for clients as human beings who are to be accorded dignity and viewed as equals. This can be a challenge for progressive lawyers, who both recognize the importance of the professional identity and skills and also believe that the client is not just as deserving of assistance but can be a source of knowledge, inspiration, and car-ing. What often remains unsaid but is at the heart of the personal relationship is the possibility for transformation that is embedded in encounters between people when they are open to each other.

Situated practice often forces progressive lawyers to alter abstract notions of client empowerment in light of their relationships with particular clients. Drawing on early social change workers, Jane Addams (1911) best articulated the importance of personal interactions. For Addams, it was not so much the "client" who needed changing (although he or she might need material assistance) so much as the professional. Often would-be beneficiaries had a better understanding of contextual realities than the professional and the mutual encounter and learning not only benefited the individual professional helper but also formed the basis for broader social change.

> the contact with the larger experience, not only increases her sense of social obligation but at the same time recasts her social ideals. She [the helper] is chagrined to discover that in the actual task of reducing her social scruples to action, her humble beneficiaries are far in advance of her, not in charity or singleness of purpose, but in self-sacrificing action. . . . She has socialized her virtues not only through a social aim but by a social process. (Addams 1911: 69)

Although most lawyers do not articulate the importance of the individual encounter in such terms, this is a thread that connects the different ways in which lawyers and clients describe the way they affect each other. Using this lens allows us to better understand why the lawyer-client relationship is so central to questions of power and change, and it offers a more compelling rationale for understanding why some lawyers choose direct service over policy work that involves much less client contact.

NELS is an organization that is devoted largely to direct representation, which means that the bulk of its work involves client contact. Some lawyers in this study chose to engage primarily in individual representation because they desired client contact from the outset. Others who fell into it desired to engage in some form of social justice work, and the substantive content and form of that work took shape only after they found jobs. When asked if they had any personal guidelines for working with clients, many lawyers cited small gestures, such as standing up when clients entered the room, calling them by their surname, or shaking their hands. Others used techniques such as not sitting behind a desk when meeting with clients or proffering a legal pad to use during the interview. Marcia, who described her rapport with clients as very good, said that she worked hard on putting them at ease when they come into her office:

> I try really hard, at least while they're here. I had to think about it, I mean, "won't you please take your coat off." Because sometimes we're all so busy, and I'm so busy. If I don't say okay, "now I'm going to like [takes a deep breath], you know like calm down, we're going to like focus on this person, are they comfortable? Do they have a Kleenex? Is their coat off? Do they realize they really have my undivided attention?" And they, they'll need to explain you know, how hard it was to get down here. And

sometimes the situation is so desperate that they're worrying about the fact that they don't have a token to get home. And if I can like clue in to where they are and say you know [snaps fingers], "I've got an extra token, how 'bout . . ." and then we can focus.

These gestures may seem superficial, but they are what López (1992) refers to as the "practical moments," and lawyers clearly thought about these details and intended for them to signal respect and set the tone for the encounter.

Although lawyers attempted to fashion a client-centered practice with an orientation of respect for clients, they universally lamented a variety of interrelated funding, personnel, and time constraints. Lawyers have overwhelming caseloads, organizations are understaffed, and many felt that they are unable to spend the amount of time with clients and on clients' cases that they would like, or may even be appropriate. Clients seemed to understand and appreciate the fact that they were one case of many, and that the lawyers were overwhelmed, at least in hindsight. One client described the frustration of not being able to reach her lawyer:

> And I felt as though, every time I called since we had to start going to court, they say well Mr. Butler is in court. And sometimes he wouldn't return my calls 'cause he was so busy, and he might have forgotten, you know. See, I'm realizing that now, but you know at that time I didn't want to hear nothing about he at a meeting [laughs]. You know, look I want him to report to me, to take care of me, and that was it. But that was being selfish. That was really being selfish. But I was really, I'm tell—I mean—I know a lot a people is need for service and stuff like that but I felt as though my time was limited. I didn't have but so much time.

This same client also told me that her lawyer gave her his home phone number. Her lawyer, a self-described workaholic with a high caseload, admitted that it was difficult for clients to reach him and therefore he routinely returned phone calls from his home on nights and weekends.

Despite the overwhelming time constraints, most lawyers made the greatest effort not to skimp on time in allowing the clients to tell their story. The lawyers viewed this as instrumental to understanding what the client was trying to accomplish. According to Binder and Price (1977), the technique of empathetic understanding or listening to clients in an attentive, nonjudgmental way is an important tool for communicating with clients. It makes clients more comfortable to speak honestly and at length with lawyers, increasing the likelihood that lawyers will better understand clients' goals and concerns and will obtain a maximal amount of information. But the lawyers in this study also viewed this type of listening as an essential component of client respect and as a response to a need on the part of the client to give their own narrative of events—however chronologically disjointed or "nonlegal" this understanding may be. In cases where lawyers felt compelled to "focus" a client, they related these incidents with regret, and took pains to legitimate the client's need to talk and explain why they required certain information or a particular focus even as they redirected the conversation.

Most clients found that sharing their experiences with the lawyers helped relieve them of stress. Both clients and lawyers feel that some relief begins in the first encounter. This seems to happen through talking about the problem with a lawyer who imparts a sense of caring to the client, empathizes with their experience rather than judges, and gives the client the sense that they may have some recourse.[20] As one client described at the first meeting with her lawyer:

> He introduced himself . . . he looked over some of the papers I brought, he explained to me what was going on with the other lawyers, what he could do. We sat down, he reviewed the information then he told me some of things that they had done wrong. And then he told me what he was going to try to accomplish. Which was to try to get them, you know to lower the rent or do something and we [talked for] about maybe about a half hour, hour. And he really set my mind at ease. Because, not that I thought he was going to perform a miracle, but he made me feel better about the situation I was in. That you know, I had some leeway where I could get some help.

One client who had immigrated to the United States several years earlier described her experience when she first came to see her lawyer at NELS. Initially it was difficult for her to discuss certain things with him and the NELS social worker because these were not topics usually discussed outside her community. She was overwhelmed by the problems she faced, which included coping with a high-risk pregnancy and her young daughter's severe asthma. She had recently separated from an abusive husband and was fired from her job. She and her daughter were denied various benefits because of her immigration status:

> And then I was going through a lot. I was going through a lot I didn't know, at times I cried. I would talk and he would talk and I would cry and I would stop talking. I didn't know what to do. I didn't know what to say, I didn't know how to go about explaining. I felt ashamed that I was like, you know. But he made me feel that it wasn't my fault, he explained certain things to me. And gradually I started talking to him about it.

When asked what her lawyer did or said to make her feel more comfortable, she responded:

> He said stuff. He calmed me down. He talked to me quietly in a reassuring voice. That was it. He told me that everything I said to him is going to be confidential, that he would not judge me, that he's not here to do that and he's just here to help me.

Several clients went so far as to say that they thought of their lawyer as a friend. Clients were not naive about this and did not use the term in the sense of an intimate relationship but rather to indicate that they felt that their lawyer cared about them. One client who said that she viewed her lawyer as a friend also said that this probably was not the case for the lawyer, understanding that she and the lawyer were on unequal footing. Clients are more beholden to and dependent on their lawyers than vice versa, and it is usually the case that clients reveal much more extensive and intimate information to lawyers than lawyers reveal to clients.

One lawyer whom I asked about the idea of clients as friends was gratified to hear this characterization of his relationship with his clients:

> I think it's more warmth, is what the friendship thing is. There's a mutual warmth and I think a crossing of barriers and joining of empathy and a sense of connection between the client [and lawyer] that this means something to the lawyer beyond that that's my case, that he's really there for me because he cares about me or she's really there for me because she cares about me. And I think that's what we ought to be doing.

But it is also clear that there are limits to this. Practically, lawyers do not have the ability to reach that level of intimacy with all clients. Lawyers also tend to have affinities for some clients and not for others, and lawyers expressed likes and dislikes for certain clients and certain "types" of clients, like the lawyer who admitted that he was uncomfortable working with clients with mental illness. Another lawyer worried that the relationship he developed with some clients led him to treat them preferentially.

This type of empathy goes beyond the personal to the political, and it is part of what facilitates legal consciousness described above. When lawyers convey understanding of clients' situations as legitimate grievances, this validates the clients' understanding of themselves as worthy—a very different experience from the message conveyed to them in their encounters with government agency employees who are often suspicious and rude. JoAnn explained that her understanding of health care issues was bolstered by her lawyer's concurring assessment, which he revealed to her as part of his general openness and receptivity to her as a fellow human being:

> I kind of never understood what the older people used to talk about their health care. I never truly understood that issue until I was faced with it. And I feel like them. I feel like there's not enough being done for those without medical benefits. And Steve sees it the same way I do of course. And he has let me know that I guess. He's also been very open about who he is personally, you know, his children. He's shared some of that so he has made me feel like he's not just a lawyer but he's a human being and

that has helped a lot. Most lawyers they don't have enough time to get personal. He found time to get personal. Which is a good thing. It reassures people that you're human.

Whatever the quality of the relationship, personal or face-to-face encounters bring out the greatest tensions in progressive practice. Social justice ideals and ideal professional standards must be balanced against a harsh reality of limited resources and the poverty of legal remedies.[21] NELS suffers from resource constraints. As a result, lawyers take on more individual clients than they would in an ideal situation, often at the expense of policy or other impact work. They also carry larger caseloads than they feel comfortable with, and a few said they felt as if they were bordering on malpractice, despite their efforts to triage. Most lawyers, however, find it difficult to turn away clients, particularly if they have met them or have been asked to help them by another lawyer or paralegal. This results in a high level of stress, as Steve described:

> If I'm too swamped I just stop taking cases. And that's a decision that I make. Now I am known not to do that. And I take on too many cases. And when I get way swamped then I stop. But I have too many cases, I know that. And when I get overloaded is when it gets just too crazy. When I lose things. . . . Or, you know, there are . . . signs. For example when a client calls and I don't know who they are. Or when I wake up in the middle of the night and think, oh my god I didn't file the appeal and then of course I go find the file and yeah, I filed the appeal two months ago but I have no recollection of it. Then I know that I have got too much going on. Or, I mean look at this! [He points to piles of paper on desk and all over his office]. . . . But right now I'm totally overloaded, I got too much on my plate. . . . But I just can't say no to my clients.

It is clear that the stress experienced by the lawyers is not only about limited resources, but limited resources in the face of what has been famously described as "brutal need" (*Goldberg v. Kelly* 397 U.S. 254 [1970]). Lawyers understand that individuals turned away by NELS may have no other source of assistance, although NELS refers them to other services. Even if lawyers do not have the skills or resources to assist these would-be clients, they often empathize with their plight and are frustrated by the need to employ selection criteria. A lawyer specializing in family advocacy at another legal services organization best characterized the difficulty of allocating scarce resources to people in need:

> It's just very draining, this day to day. And you'll have to say no to the clients, and sometimes I think, at least in family law, I mean we only represent probably 5 percent of the people who request assistance. It's just, we just can't, the number of attorneys we have, so were just continuously telling people "well, no, I'm sorry you're going to lose your children, but I can't do anything for you." Or, our consumer housing unit,

there aren't that many of them, so "I'm sorry you're going to lose your house today, but." And you're on the front line all the time doing stuff like that, it's really overwhelming.

It can also be difficult to be the bearer of bad news, particularly when lawyers themselves are critical of and unwilling to justify the legal situation even when they must explain it to clients. Marjorie, a consumer lawyer, tried to explain to me what it feels like to tell somebody that she cannot help him or her with a mortgage. She asked, "What can I say? Sorry, but you're too poor to afford a home in America." This lawyer halted in the middle of her explanation, saying that she was uncomfortable continuing this line of discussion.

Situated practice also forces progressive lawyers to balance abstract notions of client empowerment with compassion and understanding for particular clients. Because NELS lawyers are what Shamir and Chinski (1998: 249) refer to as "field soldiers," whom they define as lawyers who "represent people and not ideas," they are much more likely to have their ideals of social change and progressive practice challenged and altered. It is the face-to-face contact that provides them an impetus to continue to practice despite frustration with the limited efficacy of direct representation in a fight for sweeping social change.[22] This is also the basis for altering ideal-types of progressive practice in favor of modifications that they feel are required by their situated practice and their perception of client needs and desires.

On the most obvious level, practice that is situated within the lawyer-client relationship is likely to engender conflicts in lawyering for a cause when the cause takes on a life of its own, independent of the individual plaintiffs or imagined constituent populations. Derrick Bell (1976) illustrates this process with lawyer-led desegregation litigation. Initially both lawyers and constituents (actual plaintiffs and the broader group of interested players) desired desegregation as a means of providing the quality education to which underserved African American children were entitled. Civil rights lawyers continued to fight for a cause that eclipsed the people it was intended to serve; however, long after the original plaintiffs and various components of the black community questioned its utility and sought other ways to achieve their original goal.

Separation of interests can happen not only in class action litigation but in individual cases. In a stark example of this, McMunigal (1996) characterizes the attitude of Norma McCorvey's (named Roe in the lawsuit) lawyer Sarah Weddington in the landmark abortion case, Roe v. Wade (410 U.S. 113 (1973)):

> Weddington also criticizes restrictive abortion laws as treating a woman as merely a means to an end, a reproductive vehicle or "carrying case for a fetus." Yet Weddington treated McCorvey almost exclusively as a means to serve the end of changing the

law of abortion. Weddington describes McCorvey as "ancillary" to the primary focus on all women. The word ancillary, derived from the Latin word "ancilla" for a maid-servant, conveys the idea of a subordinate, instrumental role. Weddington also describes McCorvey and the other individual plaintiffs in the case as "vehicles for presenting larger issues." McCorvey, from her vantage, writes of the lawyers as "using me as their plaintiff." The picture she paints is clearly one of being simply the lawyers' "ticket" to the courtroom. (McMunigal 1996: 806–7)

This description did not resonate with the lawyer or client data from this study, perhaps because NELS is a client-oriented legal services program and thus has an organizational culture which is quite different from that of more policy-focused organizations. As both Bell and McMunigal note in their descriptions, the NAACP and Weddington, respectively, "looked" for the "right" plaintiffs to come along, and the concerns of the individual plaintiffs were secondary to the concerns for the constituents as a group. This is not to say that this calculus never comes up at NELS, which does policy work as well as legal services, but that for most of the lawyers interviewed, it was clear that serving individual clients was viewed as the primary mission.[23] Liz, a lawyer at NELS who has a degree in public policy and is very interested in policy work as well as direct representation, told me that as a summer intern she chose to work "with one of these national public interest organization because they're doing this you know public policy work, they're doing the impact litigation, they've got clients, and you know, this will be really interesting." Liz went on to say that she was unhappy with that summer placement and she "realized that it was not the kind of work I wanted to do" and I asked her why:

> The reason was because it was too distant from the client—they were too distant from the clients. Not that they weren't representing adequately or appropriately but the work that I assisted them with that summer was representing families in Alabama who were suing the state of Alabama and also, Louisiana as well for . . . poor educational system. You know trying to find hooks through the state constitution that they were not meeting, they weren't providing the quality education that they should be. I never met a client, you know?! I never even talked to a client. I was just doing research. I mean my whole summer was . . . just researching and writing a twelve- to fifteen-page memo each week and that wasn't at all what I envisioned for the kind of practice I wanted to do.

It is precisely this kind of client focus that differentiates the work of the legal services lawyers in this study from other types of cause lawyering, as characterized by Scheingold and Sarat: "Because it gives priority to political ideologies, public policy, and moral commitment, cause lawyering often attenuates the lawyer-client relationship—a cornerstone of the established conception of professional responsibility" (1999: 4).

In the case of many legal services lawyers, however, the cause itself embodies a commitment to the client. In fact, the cause ("social justice," "equal opportunities," "serving the poor," or "redistribution of resources," etc.) often remains amorphous for the lawyers in this study despite the fact that they provide concrete services. Whatever the cause, it seems to include an inseparable component of service to individuals most lawyers I interviewed considered a moral imperative, often admittedly stemming from personal predilection. For NELS lawyers, client-centeredness stems not from lack of commitment to a cause,[24] but a view that the cause is for and in the service of individuals who deserve assistance not only as members of a group or carriers of a cause but as individuals.

Because of the client orientation described above, the tensions between notions of progressive lawyering and practice with individuals that come up are generally more subtle and complex than those described in much of the progressive lawyering literature. For example, Pete was concerned about his tendency to succumb to clients' requests for assistance, despite his ambivalence that such assistance might foster dependence, something which goes against his notion of progressive lawyering:

> I have a client who came in last week who is going through a ton of different things. She's got a tremendous [amount] of anxiety and depression and we've been worried that she might also be suicidal. But she came in so wound up. . . . It was this little tiny thing that means nothing. I said . . . "You've explained this, I'm going to take care of it from here. Take this off your mind. You don't need to worry about this problem, you've got enough things to try and deal with, don't worry about this one. This is taken care off." She was completely relieved, you can tell the stress just [indicates washing away].
>
> The part where it's problematic from an empowerment perspective is you really shouldn't be saying "give it to me, I'll handle it, I'll call you when it's fixed" which I basically said in that case. But I think it was appropriate for that case.

Pete's response to his client's perceived needs and desires underscores the paternalism in progressive lawyering. This client clearly wanted (and arguably needed) for her lawyer to take control of the situation. To force her to handle it herself for empowerment purposes would be an imposition of the lawyer's notion of what was in the client's best interest. The lawyer was in fact confronted with the sometimes-competing notions of best interest—client independence; compassion; and autonomy.

Pete's ambivalence provides insight to the apparent conundrum that Southworth (1996: 1106) raises in her study of lawyers in Chicago: "Some of the lawyers who seemed most committed to deferring to clients also emphasized their obligations to advise and recommend. And many of those who said that they sought to give clients control commented on the difficulties of discerning client interests and resolving conflicts, particularly in collective projects."

The answer to this puzzle is not so mysterious—it is precisely those lawyers who open themselves up to their clients and respect their individual humanity who may be most willing to temper theoretical models of lawyering. It is in the individual encounter that lawyers are forced to strike a balance among competing values. For lawyers who are "afflicted by their clients" (Addams 1911), these are not abstract theoretical morals but ethical questions that must be answered in the context of ongoing client representation and must be resolved in the context of a concrete relationship (Toulmin 2001, Chap. 8).

Lawyers usually resolve such dilemmas based upon their subjective assessment, informed by conflicting values, of the particular client's needs and capabilities. In most cases the lawyers felt that they had made the "right decisions." However, the lawyers were sensitive to the contradictions that these decisions embodied when viewed through the lens of an abstract ideal of progressive lawyering, which they contrasted to the messy practice of lawyering with "real" clients.

Concluding Thoughts

Lawyers in this study saw progressive lawyering theories and critiques (to the extent that they were familiar with them) as helpful in orienting their work and sensitizing them to client needs and their own potential to disempower clients. Lawyers and clients also shared many of the underlying values of those critiques, particularly respect and a desire to foster autonomy. As this study makes clear, however, lawyers perceive the insights of critical literature to be of limited value because they do not adequately integrate or even appreciate overwhelming personal and situational constraints. Further, many clients seem to reject what may be considered hallmarks of autonomy and collaboration if not viewed from a client perspective.

Placing a premium on respect for clients implies an interpretivist stance focusing on participant perspectives. This would seem to obligate legal theorists and social scientists espousing these values to take greater account of lawyer and client perspectives and context. The outsider perspective of what clients want or need may be very different from the insider perspective offered by clients who tell us what they want or need. It also ignores a perception of limitations and possibilities that are very real, at least for clients and their lawyers. Greater attention to participant perspectives produces a different vision of the role and function of public interest lawyers, with an emphasis on different skills and strengths. It challenges our definitions of autonomy and collaboration. It should also make us less sanguine about the possibilities of achieving any broad vision of social justice through progressive lawyering even as it underscores how crucial and significant progressive lawyering can be for individual clients.

Simon characterizes the notion of client empowerment in the autonomy literature as "liberation from lawyers as much as obtaining leverage on the outside world" (1994: 1099–100). As my study demonstrates, these can sometimes be incompatible goals. Lawyers and clients with a limited menu of resources may only have access to what Linda Gordon (1988) calls the "powers of the weak," imperfect solutions that may bring on problems even as they are used to solve immediate concerns. The arguably disempowering elements of lawyering for social justice bespeak less of the inability or unwillingness of lawyers and clients to engage in progressive representation than the intransigence of grinding poverty and entrenched systems of dominance and stigmatization that they challenge. The dilemmas that lawyers and clients face and their attempts to reconcile them while using use the "master's tools" (Lorde 1984) are inseparable from situated lawyering with clients in a historic, political, and social context.

Notes

Thanks to Jim Baumohl, Judie McCoyd, Frank Munger and Sanford Schram as well as the participants of the Cachan Cause Lawyering conference for feedback on this chapter and beyond.

1. Although Illich implies that it may be appropriate (or at least not reprehensible) to proffer assistance if the intended recipients are able to respond to such gestures, the underlying assumption that people who ostensibly speak the same language in fact understand each other is questionable, perhaps more so in the case of professionals and clients (see, for example, La Rue [1992] and White [1990]). Furthermore, if the would-be recipients are in need of aid and have no other plausible alternatives, the tendency to tell any person offering services "to go to hell" is unlikely (Lipsky 1980). This only makes Illich's critique more powerful.

2. "Power's condition of possibility, or in any case the viewpoint which permits one to understand its exercise, even in its more 'peripheral' effects, and which also makes it possible to use its mechanisms as a grid of intelligibility of the social order, must not be sought in the primary existence of a central power, in a unique source of sovereignty from which secondary and descendent forms would emanate; it is the moving substrate of force relations which, by virtue of their inequality, constantly engender states of power, but the latter are always local and unstable" (Foucault [1976]1993: 518).

3. The localized study of power in microprocesses and individual relationships can obscure structural or systemic forces, and this chapter will highlight some of the dangers of doing so in the discussion of my findings reported below. See also Flyvbjerg (2001) on

the important potential of integrating the insights of microtheorists such as Foucault with those of macrotheorists.

4. Foucault eschewed the political implications of his work, viewing power as neither good nor bad but rather attempting to understand what power is and how it works. However, many interpretations of Foucault as well as assessments of the value of his work have focused on what the ubiquitous, elusive nature of power means for the possibilities of social change (see, for example, the exchange between Simon [1994] and Winter [1994] in the context of lawyering for social justice). One take on this is pessimistic. If power is enacted everywhere, including in personal relationships, the way we act, think, and make choices—then how do we combat oppression, how do we enter into relationships where power is not used to make others into objects, and where do we even begin? How do we resist if power is something we have ourselves internalized? A different take on Foucault's assertion is one that views this perspective as creating potential. If power is everywhere, it can be challenged everywhere. Power can be used in many ways, and each relationship holds a chance for change (Cruikshank 1999; Winter 1994).

5. Here I will not address if and to what extent some of these boundaries or rules are warranted or unwarranted in the sense that such rules arguably function merely to protect professional turf with little substantive justification. The point made here would be relevant in either case.

6. One component of most of these codes, and for Merton (1982) a hallmark of professions, is "mandated altruism" or the notion that the profession subscribes to and in some ways enforces a higher obligation to others or to an idea (the "poor," the "legal system," "knowledge"). Some have mourned the loss of higher ideals (e.g., Kronman 1993), while others are suspicious of professional altruism. Brint (1994), for example, claims that the ethical/altruistic model of professionalism has its origins in a feudal sense of duty. Although altruism may motivate individuals to act for social change, it is also an exercise of power. Viewed from this angle, there is no bright line between paternalism and altruistic professionalism, and this remains a tension inherent in public interest lawyering and other professional helping ventures.

7. Here I adopt Scheingold's (1998: 144, note 2) term of left-activist lawyering as a broad, unifying concept for the many theories and practices included therein. This work, however, focuses on a subset of left-activist lawyering, one that is primarily client- rather than issue-focused, which I will further define and narrow under the term "progressive lawyering."

8. Polikoff (1996: 443, note 1) uses the term "progressive lawyer" to describe "all those who use their legal skills to end poverty, racism, patriarchy, imperialism, and other impediments to social, economic and political justice."

9. The term "progressive lawyering" also invokes Freire's ([1970] 1999) distinction between social justice work that is "preserving" and social justice work that is "progressive."

10. Although Southworth (1996), for example, has conducted research with lawyers engaged in practices that have not been traditionally used in poverty law, such as small business clinics, this still leaves us with questions about the use of traditional methods

of lawyering, particularly litigation and representation in administrative hearings. Dis-empowering as these methods may be, to the extent that they are not fungible with other types of lawyering, it does not seem feasible to abandon these practices and so there continues to be a need to investigate the more traditional strategies.

11.   López (1996) critiques this body of literature as resorting to facile, polarized caricatures of public interest lawyers and clients rather than a more complex but more accurate depiction thereof.

12.   One notable exception is Sarat 1990.

13.   All interviews were tape-recorded and transcribed. During transcription, names and identifying information were removed or altered. The names appearing in cited text have been changed to preserve confidentiality.

14.   The name of the organization has been changed to preserve confidentiality.

15.   One of the referring lawyers was himself a participant. The other individual recommended participants at my request only after she told me that one of the study participants had informed her of her participation in the study, thus disclosing the identity of the research site. Lawyers' lack of concern for protecting their own confidentiality (at least among other left-activist lawyers) as evidenced by this was typical.

16.   Clients seemed very satisfied with their lawyers, which may be a result of the lawyer referral. One reason for this is probably the client selection process—all lawyers noted that NELS does not represent clients it feels that it cannot assist. On the other hand, NELS does not engage in "creaming" in the sense of taking "easy cases." In fact, most lawyers enjoyed the challenge of difficult cases and felt that these clients were often in greater need of legal services than clients with easy cases. Another element that probably contributes to client satisfaction is the low expectations that most clients have of "free legal aid," described below. Because most clients were so satisfied, it was often difficult for them to recall (or perceive?) possible instances of conflict or tension with their lawyers, although I did attempt to probe for this.

17.   Interestingly, two lawyers noted just the opposite—that their area of the law was particularly uncomplicated. I am exploring the significance of this in ongoing interviews.

18.   As one lawyer noted, NELS does not receive any federal funding thus leaving them less constrained in their choice of representation tactics than most other legal services programs. Because of this it is likely that these types of institutional constraints have not come up in my study to the extent that they may be present in other organizations. Their existence at NELS, despite NELS's lack of federal restrictions, underscores their persistence.

19.   Hays (2003) reports the same phenomenon among welfare beneficiaries.

20.   All clients I interviewed were satisfied with the progress or outcomes of their cases. However, I suspect that clients who are dissatisfied would reflect differently on the representation, including their perception of and the importance they attach to attorney empathy.

21.   Just like the cause lawyers studied by McCann and Silverstein (1998), NELS lawyers are aware of the limitations of the services they can offer and do their best to work with and around them creatively.

22.   It is important to note that it is precisely the high value placed on helping individual clients—rather than an acceptance of what most viewed as a fundamentally
flawed, mean-spirited system—that enables the lawyers to continue to work within that
system (even as they try to change it). In other words, with some exceptions, most of the
lawyers I interviewed are "radical" in their political or philosophical orientation even
though they do work that arguably could be described as "liberal" (see Lesnick [1991] on
this possibility). This is another area being explored in this study and deserves separate
treatment.

23.   It is not my intention to imply that policy-oriented organizations do not address
issues that arise from an aggregation of individual concerns but rather that their focus is
different and therefore their relationships with clients are different. There are many examples in which public interest lawyers in Northeast City from policy-oriented and legal services programs worked, each drawing on the others' strengths.

24.   Contrast this, too, with another type of cause lawyering that emerged from representation of individuals in a more traditional setting that was far less ideology-driven
as described in Barclay and Marshall in this volume.

References

Addams, Jane. 1911. *Democracy and Social Ethics.* New York: Macmillan.

Bell, Derrick A. Jr. 1976. "Serving Two Masters: Integration Ideals and Client Interests
    in School Desegregation Litigation." *Yale Law Journal* 85: 470–516.

Binder, David A., and Susan C. Price. 1977. *Legal Interviewing and Counseling: A Client-
    Centered Approach.* St. Paul: West Publishing.

Brint, Steven. 1994. *In an Age of Experts: The Changing Role of Professionals in Politics and
    Public Life.* Princeton, N.J.: Princeton University Press.

Chambon, Adrienne S., Allan Irving, and Laura Epstein, eds. 1999. *Reading Foucault for
    Social Work.* New York: Columbia University Press.

Cruikshank, Barbara. 1999. *The Will to Empower: Democratic Citizens and Other Subjects.*
    Ithaca, N.Y.: Cornell University Press.

Edelman, Murray. 1977. *Political Language: Words that Succeed and Policies that Fail.* New
    York: Academic Press.

Ellmann, Stephen. 1987. "Symposium: Clinical Education: Lawyers and Clients." *UCLA
    Law Review* 34: 717–78.

Felstiner, William L. F., Richard L. Abel, and Austin Sarat. 1981. "The Emergence and
    Transformation of Disputes: Naming, Blaming, Claiming." *Law and Society Review*
    15: 631–59.

Flyvbjerg, Bent. 2001. *Making Social Science Matter: Why Social Inquiry Fails and How It
    Can Succeed Again.* Cambridge: Cambridge University Press.

Foucault, M. [1976]1993. "Power as Knowledge." in *Social Theory: The Multicultural &
    Classic Readings*, ed. C. Lemert. Boulder, Colo.: Westview.

Freire, P. [1970]1999. *Pedagogy of the Oppressed.* 20th ed. New York: Continuum.

Goode, W. J. 1969. "The Theoretical Limits of Professionalization," in *The Semi-Profes-*

sions and Their Organization: Teachers, Nurses, Social Workers, ed. A. Etzioni. New York: Free Press.

Gordon, Linda. 1988. *Heroes of Their Own Lives: The Politics and History of Family Violence*. New York: Penguin Books.

Gustafson, Joseph M. 1982. "Professions as 'Callings.'" *Social Service Review* 56: 501–15.

Hays, Sharon. 2003. *Flat Broke with Children: Women in the Age of Welfare Reform*. New York: Oxford University Press.

Illich, I. 1990. "To Hell with Good Intentions," in *Combining Service and Learning, Volume 1*, ed. J. C. Kendall (314–20). Raleigh, N.C.: National Society for Internships and Experiential Education.

Kronman, Anthony T. 1993. *The Lost Lawyer: Failing Ideals of the Legal Profession*. Cambridge, Mass.: Belknap Press of Harvard University Press.

La Rue, Homer C. 1992. "Theoretics of Practice: The Integration of Progressive Thought and Action: Developing an Identity of Responsible Lawyering Through Experiential Learning." *Hastings Law Journal* 43: 1147–157.

Lesnick, Howard. 1991. "The Wellsprings of Legal Responses to Inequality: A Perspective on Perspectives." *Duke Law Journal* 41: 413–54.

Lipsky, Michael. 1980. *Street-Level Bureaucracy: Dilemmas of the Individual in Public Services*. New York: Russell Sage Foundation.

López, Gerald. 1992. *Rebellious Lawyering*. Boulder, Colo.: Westview.

———. 1996. "An Aversion to Clients: Loving Humanity and Hating Human Beings." *Harvard Civil Rights-Civil Liberties Law Review* 31: 315–23.

Lorde, Audre. 1984. "The Master's Tools Will Never Dismantle the Master's House," in *Sister Outsider*. Trumansburg, N.Y.: Crossing Press.

Marsico, Richard. 1995. "Working for Social Change and Preserving Client Autonomy: Is There a Role for 'Facilitative' Lawyering." *Clinical Law Review* 1: 639–63.

McCann, Michael, and Helena Silverstein. 1998. "Rethinking Law's Allurement: A Relational Analysis of Social Movement Lawyers in the United States," in *Cause Lawyering: Political Commitments and Professional Responsibilities*, ed. A. Sarat and S. Scheingold. New York: Oxford University Press.

McMunigal, Kevin C. 1996. "Of Causes and Clients: Two Tales of *Roe v. Wade*." *Hastings Law Journal* 47: 779–819.

Merton, Robert K., with Thomas F. Gieryn. 1982. "Institutionalized Altruism: The Case of the Professions," in *Social Research and the Practicing Professions*, ed. R. Merton. Cambridge, Mass.: ABT Books.

Polikoff, Nancy D. 1996. "Am I My Client?: The Role Confusion of a Lawyer Activist." *Harvard Civil Rights-Civil Liberties Law Review* 31: 443–71.

Rhode, Deborah. 1981. "Policing the Professional Monopoly: A Constitutional and Empirical Analysis of Unauthorized Practice and Prohibitions." *Stanford Law Review* 34: 64–99.

Roe v. Wade 410 U.S. 113 (1973)

Rose, S. M. 2000. "Reflections of an Empowerment-Based Practice." *Social Work* 45, no. 5: 403–5.

Sarat, Austin. 1990. "'The Law Is All Over': Power, Resistance and the Legal Consciousness of the Welfare Poor." *Yale Journal of Law and the Humanities* 2: 343–79.

Sarat, Austin, and William L. F. Felstiner. 1995. *Divorce Lawyers and Their Clients: Power and Meaning in the Legal Process.* New York: Oxford University Press.

Scheingold, Stuart. 1998. "The Struggle to Politicize Legal Practice: A Case Study of Left-Activist Lawyering in Seattle," in *Cause Lawyering: Political Commitments and Professional Responsibilities,* ed. A Sarat and S. Scheingold. New York: Oxford University Press.

Scheingold, Stuart, and Austin Sarat. 1998. "Cause Lawyering and the Reproduction of Professional Authority," in *Cause Lawyering: Political Commitments and Professional Responsibilities,* ed. A Sarat and S. Scheingold. New York: Oxford University Press.

Shamir, Ronen, and Sara Chinski. 1998. "Destruction of Houses and Construction of a Cause: Lawyers and Bedoins in the Israeli Courts," in *Cause Lawyering: Political Commitments and Professional Responsibilities*, ed. A. Sarat and S. Scheingold. New York: Oxford University Press.

Simon, William H. 1991. "Lawyer Advice and Client Autonomy: Mrs. Jones's Case." *Maryland Law Review* 50: 213–26.

———. 1994. "The Dark Secret of Progressive Lawyering: A Comment on Poverty Law Scholarship in the Post-Modern, Post-Reagan Era." *University of Miami Law Review* 48: 1099–114.

Southworth, Ann. 1994. "Review Essay: Taking the Lawyer Out of Progressive Lawyering." *Stanford Law Review* 46: 213–34.

———. 1996. "Business Planning for the Destitute? Lawyers as Facilitators in Civil Rights and Poverty Practice." 1996 *Wisconsin Law Review* : 1121–69.

Toulmin, Stephen. 2001. *Return to Reason.* Cambridge, MA.: Harvard University Press.

White, Lucie E. 1990. "Subordination, Rhetorical Skills, and Sunday Shoes: Notes on the Hearing of Mrs. G." *Buffalo Law Review* 38: 1–58.

———. 1994. "Collaborative Lawyering." *Clinical Law Review* 1: 157.

Winter, Steven. L. 1994. "Cursing the Darkness." *University of Miami Law Review* 48: 1114–31.

CHAPTER NINE

Negotiating Cause Lawyering Potential in the Early Years of Corporate Practice

DOUGLAS THOMSON

The political economy of legal education and the legal profession in the United States of America channels most new attorneys with public interest law commitments into initial practice in corporate (large, commercial) firms. This career strategy meets the young associates' needs for substantial salaries to pay imposing educational debts and for developing legal practice skills while maintaining the dominance of the firms, the law schools that supply them, and the corporations they serve and maintain. Yet the professional socialization literature in general, and concerning law in particular, suggests that the experience will divert young attorneys from their public interest law commitments. Thus, it constitutes one more impediment to the development of effective cause lawyering and associated social justice movements. At the microlevel, the strategy carries the high risk of cooptation into long-term commitment to lucrative corporate practice and diversion away from significant involvement in social justice or cause lawyering practice. Interviews with attorneys taking this path explore how they negotiate the competing practice appeals, construct and reconstruct their career prospects, respond to intermediate options such as pro bono work and civic involvements, engage networks of support, and remain a problematic resource for cause lawyering. Interviews with peers pursuing the early career public interest path offer a contrasting perspective. The discussion focuses on implications for macrolevel issues of the articulation of public interest and cause lawyering boundaries and democratization. The observations of recent U.S. social movements offered here suggest opportunities and difficulties in linking cause lawyering capacity with social justice need.

The essence of legality lies not in the exercise of power and control, but in the predictable restraint on those using that power.
                                        —Selznick 1961, cited in Kidder 1983
Law is a conspiracy against human values, an implement to frustrate the natural tendency of people to act justly.
                                        —Zinn 1971, cited in Kidder 1983

Somewhere between Selznick and Zinn lies cause lawyering. As a special form of knowledge-power (Foucault 1977), cause lawyering suggests the tantalizing prospect of a prototypically bourgeois resource serving the pursuit of social and economic justice even as it instructively reveals the structures of power that legal practice supports and reproduces. Cause lawyering seeks the democratically responsive and constitutive aspirations of law.

As the first two volumes (Sarat and Scheingold 1998, 2001) in this cause lawyering project make abundantly clear, conceptions of cause lawyering and its kin vary greatly. In this chapter, public interest law refers to the broad continuum of practice that contrasts with conventional, client advocacy legal practice. On that continuum, cause lawyering occupies the place of honor as that which offers the greatest promise for social justice because it infuses collective effort—contrary to the individualistic hegemony of mainstream legal practice (and of the market and psychology).

Public interest law seeks the common good (in a variety of ways), while cause lawyering seeks the common good by working as part of a social movement (that is, a cause). Thus, cause lawyering offers special appeal since law only achieves much in terms of social justice, that is, more equitable distribution of wealth, power, and privilege, when it functions as part of a social movement (Kairys 1998; Handler 1978; Kilwein 1998; Morag-Levine 2001; McCann and Silverstein 1998; Meili 1998). Public interest legal consciousness provides a small part of the explanation of the emergence and efficacy of cause lawyering at any particular time and place.

During the past few years, I have been studying public interest legal education and practice. The first phase of this project involved observing in several law schools and interviewing advanced students (second- or third-year or recent graduates) . As reported in previous Law and Society Association papers (Thomson 1999, 2001), that study focused on the relatively small number of law students persisting in their public interest commitment despite the powerful socialization forces undermining it. It highlighted institutional and cultural sources for such persistence, for example, legal clinic, associated centers and conferences, practicum, professors, counter-culture, and cautionary, even subversive, lessons learned in law firm summer placements. Such persistence offers the promise, however remote, however tenuous, of eventually augmenting pop-

ulist resistance (Merry and Milner 1993) against concentrated power and oppression. It thus can serve as another way of understanding and advancing the
deviant case of law serving social justice (Turk 1976).

In a continuing search for contextual antecedents of cause lawyering, the
current study explores the experiences of young attorneys who left law school
with strong public interest law commitments. Employing a retrospective longitudinal approach, it asks how well their strategies for pursuing public interest
work presently and long-term have served them, how they have negotiated the
problems faced, and how they have altered their expectations and plans. Although concentrating on those who have chosen corporate law practice to begin their careers, this analysis also references the experiences and perceptions of
their peers who have found the more scarce positions in public interest to initiate their legal careers. How all of this might eventually lead to cause lawyering,
and what that might mean for social justice aspirations—more equitably dis-
tributing wealth, power, and privilege, and building the good society—remain
as ultimate issues guiding this inquiry.

Where Do Cause Lawyers Come From?

Cause lawyering presupposes public interest commitment (Abel 1998;
Trubek and Kransberger 1998). Most attorneys with such a commitment do not
become cause lawyers (Fox 1995; Sarat and Scheingold 1998). They instead work
in legal aid programs, in smaller firms devoted to public interest practice, or do
pro bono work in corporate firms (Scheingold and Bloom 1998). Nevertheless,
such a commitment serves as a necessary condition for cause lawyering
(Menkel-Meadow 1998). Yet the existence of cause lawyering depends not only
on public interest law consciousness, but on the coalescence of personal troubles, the sparking of sociological imagination, the community organizing, the
social activism, and the historical accidents that unexpectedly, painfully, slowly,
and abruptly rapidly spawn social movements.

As part of this ongoing, long-term individual project on public interest legal
education and practice, the current study examines the viability of public interest commitment during the early years of legal practice. In particular, it explores the several practice paths that new attorneys take in pursuing a public interest career and aspiring toward cause lawyering impact.

Recent, as well as older, scholarship has tended to focus either on the fate of
public interest (or cause lawyering) idealism during law school (Granfield 1992;
Stover 1989; Guinier 1997) or on the dimensions and impact of cause lawyering
practice (Sarat and Scheingold 1998, 2001). Much remains missing in the large

area in between. In particular, the research literature appears to provide little with regard to either public interest law transitions from law school to practice or the eventual development of cause lawyering careers. Other emerging cause lawyering research (e.g., Jones, this volume; Shdaimah, this volume) promises to help fill this void. Drawing especially on a useful analytic framework provided by Scheingold and Bloom and on a variety of complementary studies in Sarat and Scheingold, this chapter uses recent interviews and observations to examine the first issue (fate of public interest law commitments during the early years of practice) especially with regard to implications for the second (how cause lawyering practice and careers eventually emerge).

Methodology

This chapter draws on focused interviews with fifteen young lawyers (i.e., recent graduates, no more than three years in practice). I had previously interviewed nine of these attorneys when they were law students and reported findings. Eleven of the fifteen recent interviews took place in person and were tape-recorded; I conducted four by telephone (including three of the nine re-interviews). The analysis that follows focuses on these fifteen interviews, especially as represented in transcriptions and notes, with some integrative reference to my previous paper (Thomson 2001) and its foundational interviews and observations about public interest legal education. The current analysis makes substantial use of quotations, especially extended ones. In doing so, I try to avoid exampling to make a point (Glaser and Strauss 1967; Lofland and Lofland 1983) in favor of a more representational grounding in the voiced experiences of these public interest law persisters (Strauss and Corbin 1998; Engel and Munger 1996). In the interests of protecting their confidentiality, the analysis shields their actual identities in various ways, including camouflaging personal characteristics. For taped and transcribed interviews, the numbering system denotes interview number and page number (e.g., 8-3); otherwise, it indicates only interview number (e.g., 9).

Public Interest Law Persisters

These resilient young men and women have pursued a variety of paths in their long-term pursuit of public interest practice. We can group these paths in various productive ways. Thus, eight associates work in large corporate or commercial firms (employing 200 or more attorneys each), four work in medium-sized or small corporate or commercial firms (each employing fewer than 100 attorneys), and three took the public interest early path. The last route involves clerkships, legal assistance, or public interest advocacy. Along another significant analytic dimension, ten are litigators with five focusing on transactional work. The fifteen consist of nine women and six men. All but two come from European American/Anglo ethnic backgrounds. All received their undergraduate degrees in the early or middle 1990s. Almost all received their undergraduate and legal education from elite institutions. In that sense, the forces leading to "the reproduction of hierarchy" (Kennedy 1983) pose formidable cultural and political obstacles to these public interest persisters actually finding their way to cause lawyering.

Although their study focuses on attorneys more advanced in their careers, that is, those who have established reputations as cause lawyers (unlike the new attorneys interviewed for this study), Scheingold and Bloom (1998) provide a useful analytic framework for discussing varieties of cause lawyering (or public interest) commitment and practice. They pose a continuum of cause lawyering in which they array practitioners in terms of transgressiveness, that is, the extent of divergence from conventional legal practice. Transgressiveness actually references two dimensions—the professional and the political. Despite some complications arising from some incongruities between these two dimensions, Scheingold and Bloom rank types of public interest (or cause lawyering) practice as follows from a conventional pole to a transgressive pole: unmet needs; civil liberties; civil rights; public policy; radical/critical.

Their analysis highlights a strong relationship between transgressiveness and practice site. One prominent feature includes the low level of transgressiveness found in corporate law firms. Like other research in this and related areas, however, Scheingold and Bloom's cross-sectional study does not identify career trajectories—in this case, the extent to which transgressive cause lawyers in more hospitable small firms and salaried practice sites may have begun their careers in corporate firms. It is to this question that the current line of longitudinal research attends.

Themes and Nuances

I. Persistence Persists

Almost without exception, public interest law persisters from law school maintain their self-identification during the early years of practice, regardless of the setting. This central finding holds particular significance in light of the power of the socialization experience, continuing from law school into practice.

A litigator in corporate practice who has found ways to pursue a relatively high degree of public interest work explains its continuing lure:

> I certainly don't dislike it [commercial practice], but I guess I would say that I've noticed the motivation and the feeling that I get when I'm working on a clemency petition for my death row client is very different than the feeling you get writing a motion to compel for your insurance clients. (9-3: 111)

Some mild dissent from the theme of continued persistence appears too. Significantly perhaps, it comes especially from those who did not hold as strong an original public interest commitment in law school. Thus, one reports diminished respect for government attorneys as the opinion of private firm associates grows amid great personal satisfaction working at this firm:

> although I know that there are people in government who work hard too, it seems that there are too many people in government who have stopped growing as attorneys, who do not view it as a challenge anymore, whereas, in contrast, the attorneys here keep getting better because they are pushed in this competitive environment. They are driven; they are on the cutting edge of the profession. Hence, I respect every one here. (5-1)

Another associate with a more ambiguous commitment in law school, and who also much enjoys working in a large firm environment, perceives little opportunity for public interest work in his field of practice (health care transactional work) and no longer self-identifies as a public interest law persister (12). As a second-year law student when first interviewed, however, he had a much more ambiguous commitment to a public interest career than did most of that cohort's persisters (Thomson 2001).

Another recasting of the meaning of public interest practice relative to political ideology comes from a persister nevertheless quite satisfied with large firm commercial practice:

> the things that appealed to me about legal work, which is the intellectual challenge and the intellectual rigor of it, you still have in this kind of work. And there's a lot of cases where I just have the sense that people are being disingenuous or dishonest or something about their claim or about what happened, and it's an opportunity to ensure that the truth prevails for lack of a better term. Which is something that drove me to the Clinic when I was in law school and about that work that continues to drive me here. So it's some of the same feelings, even though there isn't a sense that you'd do . . . not typically think of as someone needing a champion or anything; they're [that is, corporate clients] doing just fine. And if they were to lose their cases, they would lose some money and nothing bad is going to happen to them. It's not the kind of calling where you feel like, wow, you're really making a difference but

there's still the challenge of the work and trying to make sure that what's supposed to happen happens. (8-3: 169)

A. *Avoiding Cooptation, Modifying Career Planning*

While thus avoiding cooptation or erosion of commitment with varying degrees of success, young associates (as well as their counterparts and former classmates in public interest settings) have modified their public interest career planning based on lessons learned during these early years of practice. As the ensuing quotations suggest, modifications take instrumental form such as extending the time line devoted to corporate practice, recalculating debt repayment, and rethinking the meaning of financial compensation.

> I guess as expectations go, my expectation originally was that by now I'd be working someplace else. And that hasn't happened. I think that my original plan was to stay here for two years and then begin looking at other options. . . . So far I've been reasonably happy here with the work that I've had and the people that I work with. . . . I've had opportunity to do pro bono work the whole time that I've been here. (8-2: 090)

> And so at the same time that I was feeling discouraged about the lack of opportunity that I felt were barriers to doing pro bono work, I was also realizing on a purely personal level that I would probably have to work in a private law firm for longer than I had originally anticipated due to family circumstances. I just think it was unrealistic to think that I could work here for a year and then move to the not-for-profit sector because now that I have [a child] . . . our expectation is that my [partner] won't go back to work until . . . [the child reaches] kindergarten age. That's [some] more years from now. And I've already been here for [a few] years. So that my horizon for leaving the private sector is looking more like five to seven years of practice rather than one to three years of practice. (4-5: 330)

> Well, I guess at the time, I saw working here as a very short-term kind of thing, and eventually I would leave for public interest practice. . . . [I] have changed my perception . . . have had some good experience here and enjoy the people that I work with and have gotten a lot of good substantive experience on the cases that I am working on even though they are civil cases. . . . I don't have the same burning desire to leave and try to do something else . . . right now. I['m] just kind of I guess content to hang out and learn something before I move on. I don't have a date anymore. My date was . . . 2002. Because my first couple of months were pretty bad; so that was the date that I put out there to comfort myself and say, stick it out to then and then go and do something else. And then when that date came and went, it was fine here and I don't have any need to uproot and go on to anything else. I haven't really set a new date. I guess the outer date I've set is to come at the end of 2009. . . . Which isn't really that bad. A lot of people are on thirty-year plans, and I'm on a ten-year plan. . . . And then the ten-year plan is kind of impressive with pretty large payments to make to pay off in that period of time. (8-3: 135)

The financial realities are very stark, much starker than what I had envisioned when I was in school and thinking about what I would do. I mean the funny thing is I had applied for and was prepared to take jobs paying thirty thousand, thirty-five thousand dollars a year to start at either state's attorney's or public defender's offices. And I sent resumes out, and I would have taken those jobs if they would have offered them to me. I would have turned this job down and taken one of those in a second, but no offers came. And so I started working here, and after the loan payments started—which on the ten-year plan are on the order of fourteen hundred dollars a month right now—I think how in the world could I have managed that if I was making what I would have been making then. I definitely would have had to have gone on a long-term student loan payment plan, thirty years, and I don't even know if I could have made the minimum payments then in that situation. And we don't even have children yet. That's something that's starting to come along soon, and that certainly is expensive. So I think that what it does is, if one of those jobs that I had applied for, a state's attorney's or a public defender's office, were to come open offering thirty-five, or forty, thousand dollars, I don't think that I would . . . be in position to take it. I just don't think that I could, practically speaking. (8-7: 360)

Modification also pertains to identity and strategies for presenting or concealing it. Thus, some choose to hide their public interest identity either at the recruitment and hiring stage or as an ongoing form of self-presentation throughout their early career. Other persisters, perhaps due to working in settings somewhat more conducive to public interest practice, do not find such commitment hiding necessary.

Hiding of public interest identity begins early as part of a game-like strategy that law students learn as part of anticipatory socialization. One associate, self-described in law school as "a Clinic geek" and with a powerful public interest commitment then and now, responds as follows when asked to reflect back on recruitment conversations regarding public interest law practice possibilities:

Honestly? This is a game. I played it. It's a matter of impressions. I never asked about public interest possibilities because I knew what my resume looked like. Basically I had to live that down, play down that identity. It worked. (3)

Another associate also expresses skepticism, extending the analysis:

Also, if you're interviewing at a law firm, it's probably not advisable to ask about public interest opportunities because, after all, they're interested in making money. . . . it's still not a good idea to broadcast your commitment to public interest law [after hiring]. To the firm, you're an investment. They hate to see an investment leave. This is a business. (6-2)

In addition to a perceived need for such carefulness regarding public interest commitment and plans, a myth of meritocracy attaches to megacorporate practice. How much of this comes from each of various socialization sites (elite

schools, colleges and law schools, the large firms themselves, more diffuse stratification imagery) or from empirical observation remains unknown. The power
of the mythology continues. One of the most energetically and productively engaged public interest persisters states this view:

> It's a tough call in terms of the training. Because the larger firms can send you to
> NITA [National Institute for Trial Advocacy], they can send you to seminars which is
> great, which is one component of it. But it's also just that there are really smart peo-
> ple at big firms. There's a reason why it's very hard to get jobs there. And I think the
> quality of the lawyering there is excellent, the way the strategizing, and the quality of
> the writing, and the quality of the research, and the standards that they hold their at-
> torneys to is very high. It's high for a reason, and they bill high rates for a reason. Not
> that everyone at those firms is really intelligent, but there are a lot of really good
> lawyers there. (7-6: 322)

B. Skill Development and Transferability

Interpretation of skill development and of its transferability and salience for
public interest practice varies significantly among the three major early career
paths toward public interest practice, and it serves as a key comfort for those
taking the corporate route. They, as well as their peers already in public interest
practice, tend to find merit in the view learned in law school that corporate resources translate into superior supervision and ongoing training. As always,
this view varies and comes with qualifications as subsequent extended quotes
illustrate.

Those who have experienced, in one form or another, both commercial and
public interest practice bring a nuanced view to their reflections on the Hobson's choices involved. Listen to this young litigator:

> Yeah, I think it's also a tough call in terms of if I would have gone to [a large corpo-
> rate firm] for a couple of years with the theory I'll pay back my debt and I'll get some
> good experience, I don't know how that would have worked out. I don't regret at all
> my experience [in a public interest setting]. I think I learned more doing that than I
> would anywhere. But I guess if I applied that theory to going to a . . . bigger firm, I
> don't know if I would have been doing document review for two years. . . . I have a
> friend with a larger firm, and she billed 2,000 hours two years in a row to one client.
> And she left. And so, it's not that she didn't get great experience, but she also spent a
> lot of time doing some really boring work. And so it's a trade-off here not in terms of
> substance but in terms of my responsibility. I get good responsibility; I don't get great
> supervision. But if somewhere else I wasn't getting great responsibility, but I was get-
> ting great supervision it wouldn't matter! So it's such a fine line to walk. (7-5, 6: 300)

Another litigator offers a similar balancing of benefits:

> But I don't necessarily see myself in private practice long-term. I mean there's a lot of benefits to it. For one thing, you can pay off a whole bunch of loans as a practical matter.... Another thing you get some good experience in private practice, especially as far as writing. You probably get better experience in the courtroom in the public interest sector.... There's a lot of good writers here and ... at the big firms, and people who can really help you fine-tune your writing. (9-2: 101)

This associate had moved from a large firm to a small firm to gain more trial experience. This fit in with her public interest long-term objectives, and illustrates the perceived transferable potential of firm-based litigation experience.

Another young litigator captures the interplay of personal contingencies and professional reformulations, all against the background of the privileging of corporate practice:

> Regarding my future, I don't know how long I'll stay here. There are other things going on in my life that are considerations besides my feelings about this firm and this work. So I don't know what my next move will be, but I am thinking about something in real estate [law] though. I've had a chance to get into that by way of my environmental work. Eventually, I would like to get back to public interest work, but this firm is making me a much better lawyer than I would have been if I just went straight into public interest out of law school. (5-1, 2)

Another highly satisfied litigator in a large firm similarly appreciates skills gained, albeit in a different practice setting and with a surer public interest long-term aspiration:

> [As you look ahead down the road, do you think the skills that you're learning here, the legal skills, will be easily transferable to a public interest setting?] Yeah, absolutely. That's another reason why I'm willing to hang out and stay for a while, is because staying here is doing nothing but benefiting me really. I take depositions all the time, I've had a trial, I'm in front of judges in courts all the time, I was dealing with clients, witnesses, and other opposing counsels—it just helps me no matter what I was going to do practically speaking. And, you know, if I change jobs and become a criminal attorney, well, sure I've got some substantive law that I need to catch up on but there's a lot of procedural transferability ... just the skills and the confidence, the interacting with people and having done this, in a little bit different setting but doing the same thing, is invaluable and is very helpful. And I feel like I'm getting that experience a lot faster than other people at other firms are who are still doing mostly just research. (8-7: 342)

Nevertheless, skill development in the well-endowed corporate firm may not always provide the expected transferability to a public interest setting. Thus, one associate reevaluated the initial expectations and recalibrated anticipated impact as follows:

This type of labor and employment law practice then seemed to offer the possibility of developing some courtroom-type skills that could transfer to public interest law settings. But, no, it has not worked out that way, at least not to the extent desired. I have seen some of this type of experience, but not much. That's like at any large law firm. None of them are going to provide that kind of experience, especially early on. This firm is so expensive—I bill at $200 an hour, a partner at $400—that no one is going to litigate; at these rates, they're going to settle. (3)

Resources also do not come in great abundance in public interest settings as contrasted with large corporate firms (7-2). Yet while public interest settings in general receive lower marks for supervision and training provided, they too show variation. An associate with experience in two such settings characterizes supervision as "amazing" at a legal assistance office in sharp contrast to a legal advocacy center for immigrants. The latter setting provides more opportunity for activist and impact work, but lacks the in-house resources found in the first setting (10-3). Another associate taking the public interest early career path finds another mix of pluses and minuses:

> The substantive stuff has been great. I have had some questions about whether I made the right decision in the sense that the training and supervision and feedback at a smaller place, or any place that is focused on public interest type work or social justice issues is bound to be understaffed. It's obviously a little bit of a different situation. . . . So I've wondered if I am getting the best training I could be getting. But it's a trade-off because I'm doing exactly the kind of work I want to be doing. So I'm still not sure about it. The jury is definitely still out. I don't know how long I'll stay. (7-1: 050)

For this litigator, lack of supervision and role models, more than lack of resources, represent the major drawbacks of pursuing the early public interest practice path. Even here, however, exceptions appear, most notably in terms of at least some clerkships.

II. Varieties of Dissatisfaction

Those in firms vary widely in degree of dissatisfaction with corporate practice, with implications for public interest career planning. As already indicated, those persisters who begin their careers in corporate/commercial practice exhibit a wide range of evaluations of that experience after two to three years. Reactions basically run the gamut from something like "I've got to get out of this place!" through "I can deal with it, I'm developing some useful skills" to "This isn't so bad, actually this is pretty good." This range may constitute a continuum of anticipatory cooptation.

An associate doing transactional work in a large firm values the experience of becoming a lawyer:

> Yeah, not all of it, but most of it is very challenging and very interesting. Very interesting might be an overstatement. Much of it is challenging and interesting. And particularly in my first two years, the learning curve was extremely steep. And if you can say that, then that's really saying something. It has flattened over the past six months. But particularly over the first two years, even though I wasn't doing the kind of work that would be my first choice, I just feel like I was learning so much and that's just terrific. . . . I know that I now can actually provide sound legal advice on certain subjects to certain people . . . about certain things that I definitely would not have been equipped to do upon graduating from law school. . . . there's so much more to being a lawyer than just knowing what the law is in certain circumstances. And I realize now that it would have been foolish for me just to have gone immediately from law school into the public sector. It would not have really been of any benefit to me, and I think that if I spent five years practicing law and then leave and go do something else, I will be forever . . . a better thinker, a better analyzer, and just more effective in anything that I do because of the work that I've done here. I don't even mean just in my ability to analyze the law or be a lawyer, but in anything that I do. So in that sense, yeah. People say a law degree will be good, we go back to the beginning; why do you go to law school, oh, a law degree will take you anywhere. I don't think a law degree does that. I think being a lawyer and having legal skills does that. And a law degree is a necessary prerequisite, so. (4-11, 12: 853)

In other firm settings, however, a more vigorous and apparently more genuine commitment to pro bono work serves as an important source of high satisfaction. A litigator working in a small firm with explicit public interest commitments recognizes this:

> But as far as the support, one thing is, like most law firms, we have a billable hours target requirement. Pro bono hours we bill counts toward that requirement one-for-one as if it's a . . . (paying client). . . . There's no cap on the hours you can bill the pro bono case. Obviously, you know, if I was taking on a case that was going to take up a thousand hours of my time a year, I would probably want to talk with someone about that first. . . . So that's a lot of support right there, to say that we're going to give you the freedom to do this, you know, certainly not like other firms where they say, yeah, you can do it but it's on your own time essentially. You can use our paper clips. I mean that's a different sort of support. That's pretty big. Obviously, all the support of just the office and the resources and the research materials and all that, of course, you have access to. (9-4: 155)

A litigator who appreciates her large firm's lack of red tape, its energetic and talented senior attorneys, and collegial atmosphere finds satisfaction too in unusual and substantial public interest opportunities:

> I love it here too, because with [the] economy in a slump (after September 11th), my firm, which is strongly pro bono, has let me spend half-time on pro bono work! I

have worked with Habitat for Humanity—which I really like a lot—and the Lawyers Committee on Civil Rights. I have two pro bono cases now, and have been working on predatory lending. They do encourage us to keep our billable hours up. So, as the economy improves and we have more billable work again, I don't expect it [this heightened degree of pro bono emphasis] to last when we get busy again. (5-1)

Another litigator in a large firm enjoys the benefits of a more stable feature of its structure:

[Is it also a matter of sort of having the best of both worlds: the small unit within the large firm?] Absolutely. I really, really like that atmosphere because there are about twelve attorneys in my department and those are the people that I work with. I don't work with anybody else in the firm. So I feel like I have a firm of about twelve attorneys. . . . There is the potential for it to be bad I wouldn't have anyplace to hide from them! But I feel like I know everyone here, and everyone knows me. It isn't like making yourself known or worrying about laboring in anonymity or anything like that. Everybody that I work for knows me and really appreciates my work, and it's a good feeling. Yeah, that atmosphere is a key part of why I've stayed. (8-6: 276)

Financial realities remain a major background consideration for these young professionals. The need to deal with large educational debts can exacerbate dissatisfaction with the work itself (1-2). Even persisters who enjoy their corporate practice experience voice instrumental reasons for leaving eventually, after paying down debt:

[Plan to stay here?] Not forever, no. I'm still certain about that. That when I've achieved a bit more of a sense of financial independence, that I'll probably be looking around, not just because that there's other public interest work or criminal work that is more reasonable in terms of the hours and not so much of a drag. . . . And I anticipate if I go into that that I wouldn't go into it with the idea that I can just work forty hours a week and go home, but I still anticipate that it would be less hectic than my current work schedule is. (8-4, 5: 211)

A more telling theme emerges of unhappiness about the loss of a sense of fighting for what is right. A more technical sense of law imbues corporate practice, privileging skills disconnected from stark adversarial conceptions of justice. Persisters laboring in commercial firm settings struggle with this loss. They construct nuanced understandings and preferences from the available work, as indicated by this associate:

Employment [law], I try to stay away from. It's too personal; I identify with the plaintiff. I feel like I'm representing the evil company or evil management. I don't want to do it. My liberal part of me won't let me do it. And insurance coverage, it's companies suing insurance companies for something they did like polluting the environment or something. So at least you feel better to that extent you're on the right side. That still matters to me. (1-3: 177)

Thus, we see this persister devising and pursuing a strategy of resocialization providing the degree of resistance permissible within the setting.

In contrast to Heumann's (1977) newcomers to criminal court (prosecutors, defense attorneys, and judges), these public interest law persisters do not enter private corporate practice naive about their new environment (Kennedy 1981). At the same time, however, the actual experience proves to be more intense and more disappointing than realistic but abstract or secondhand expectations.

"School's Over Now!"

Some complaints about commercial practice have more prosaic origins. Early career dissatisfaction requires an interpretation with reference to behavior and identity adjustments, having nothing to do with the type of work. Thus, one associate came to view disillusionment during the early months on the job as a function of lack of work experience in general:

> a job is a job all over the place. And working, all jobs are going to have drawbacks to them, and are going to have aspects to them that you aren't really going to care for. And it was a very big adjustment coming out of school and having to start working. If I hadn't been in school my whole life—I didn't work between college and law school, or between high school and college—so it was a very big adjustment. When you're making that adjustment, it's easy to think, well, I just need to change jobs and then it won't be so bad if I change jobs. But then the longer you do it, and you see other people coming from the job that you think you would like to do who weren't happy with it either, you think maybe it's just the fact that I'm a grownup now and I have to work all the time and that's going to be the case no matter what. (8-6: 316)

The Public Interest Contrast

The three young attorneys who have pursued the public interest early path continue in their enthusiasm for this type of work even as they express some dissatisfaction and disappointment with what they have found thus far. This mostly involves issues regarding supervision and training. Yet they appreciate and value what they have taken as a given: its relatively modest financial compensation. One notes moving to current employment because it looked like "kind of my dream job" (10: 3).

This associate has found that expectation largely met. The setting comes close to the activist/advocacy/impact ideal of social change for social justice. Our young associate deals primarily with landlord-tenant disputes, employment benefits claims, consumer complaints, and government benefits issues. The firm also has major practices regarding immigration and family law.

Those pursuing the public interest early practice path also learn valuable lessons about areas of this work that do not satisfy them. One affirms a continuing strong commitment as follows: "I'm not exactly sure what I want to do after this. I know it's going to be public interest work. There's no question about that." Yet this associate has discovered that policy advocacy does not suit him:

> But I think that I'm also learning that this sort of policy advocacy is not necessarily a good fit for me because I feel removed from the issues. There's not enough of a connection there on a day-to-day basis. A lot of what we're doing is looking at what other people are doing. . . . We're looking at [the agency's] plan for transformation of [a public good] and constantly chiming in on what they're not doing right or what they're not doing well. We're not doing the work ourselves. And it's . . . really an important role to play; it's watchdog. But I think for me, I'm slowly learning that while I acknowledge the importance of that role, it may not be the right fit for me. And so now I'm kind of struggling with what the right fit is. . . . So I've been frustrated. At the same time, I'm learning a lot. It's really valuable for me to know too what's not a fit for me in terms of the public interest scene. . . . I've never done policy work before. It always has been this very abstract thing to me that sounded somewhat sexy, you know, in past litigations. . . . But [this firm] actually litigates very, very infrequently, and more often than not just uses the threat of litigation as a tool to get [movement] in certain directions. But it's been a somewhat frustrating experience for me, but a good learning experience trying to take the value from the experience that I can. (11-1, 2: 113)

The ambiguity of this particular challenge in this type of public interest work contrasts with more programmed work at the firms.

A. Contrasting Litigation with Transactional Practice

Some of this reported variation in levels of dissatisfaction with corporate practice reflects marked differences between litigation and transactional practice and their differential amenability to transfer to public interest settings. The following quotes—the first two from litigators, the third from a transactional specialist—suggest the range of concern:

> Here, the litigators do the bulk of the pro bono work. We have those skills to give. (5-3)

> So I think to the extent you're a litigator, it's probably more transferable than anything. Because if you're writing briefs and getting great supervision on your writing style and your organization, you can write briefs about something else. So I think in terms of general commercial lit, it probably is somewhat transferable. (7-6: 348)

> I've actually done a significant amount of pro bono work. Not as much as some litigators that I know. See, litigators have this unusual circumstance, . . . that they can, particularly when they're more junior they can work on a case, a pro bono case, a

murder trial for example, and do a significant amount of pro bono work. Hundreds and hundreds of hours even, and that is often accepted and perceived as beneficial to that associate's development. [Because of experience in the courtroom?] Yes, that they wouldn't get otherwise. It's a lot harder for transactional attorneys to get access to pro bono, to good pro bono work. And this is, I think, an endemic problem to law firms. And it's not because the legal work isn't there. It seems that the structure for linking needy organizations or low-income individuals with lawyers who have those skills is not as well established as the framework for linking litigators with indigent clients. And I'm not sure why that is. It may simply be that there are legal requirements for, or constitutional guarantees for representation for criminal defendants, and so there's just been a long-standing guarantee or a long-standing system where lawyers represent indigent clients free of charge. But that hasn't carried over to the transactional and business context. Certainly in part because there's no requirement, there's no guarantee for people to have free transactional or business legal services. So it makes things harder for someone in my position to find work to do. Also because, I mentioned before, you have, it's easier to do pro bono work if the partners that are giving work to associates, and because there aren't a lot of partners doing transactional pro bono work, there isn't as much work of that nature trickling down to associates. (4-5: 362)

Larger issues loom here. They include how we structure attending to needs and the desirability of an economic bill of rights. We return to them in the final section.

Litigation covers a variety of types for these persisters, including personal injury work, such as automobile accidents and construction site accidents (2), as well as criminal defense and various commercial areas. One associate (2), with a long-term aim of transferring his litigation experience to public interest practice, chose a small firm environment to gain that experience. He notes that "everything he heard in law school in public interest settings, whether with other students or faculty, communicated the value of acquiring litigation skills which everyone told" him would transfer to public interest practice. The small firm environment has provided "lots of hands-on experience" including an appellate case and taking depositions. With multiple defendants in many cases and the firm working on the defense side, he has had opportunities to sit in on depositions and thus ease into cases.

B. The Puzzle of Public Interest Career Prospects

Associates largely labor in the dark about public interest career prospects. Questions abound as to how their corporate/commercial experience will play in the public interest arena, how long they should stay and when they should move, the transferability of their experience, and the type of positions and type of work available.

[Your strategy . . . as [a] new lawyer with pretty strong public interest law commitment, [is] to develop legal skills and experience to make self more attractive to public interest organizations who tend not to hire people right out of law school anyway?] Yes. And then also, I wanted to build up my savings so that I would be able to make a move like that and feel comfortable. [Did you have debts to pay down too?] Yeah. They do have loan forgiveness programs, but then again I couldn't find anything. And now that I'm looking again, I realize why I've stayed at the firm for so long; it's hard to find one of these [public interest] jobs. (1-8: 585)

I think that's right, I mean I think if you were talking to potential employers in the public interest, I think you would find some who would look very favorably upon someone who has several years of experience . . . and probably others who would say, well, I question that person's commitment to public interest because they didn't do it. (9-3: 125)

Even when associates actively pursue public interest possibilities during the early years of practice in a corporate firm, they continue to encounter the kind of obstacles to public interest commitment experienced in law school. Thus, a persister at a mid-sized commercial firm traces this career trajectory as she has and is experiencing it:

Policy organizations and the public interest jobs weren't very abundant. It was very difficult to find them first of all. The Internet wasn't as developed as it is now. So it was hard to find them and then hard to get them. So I liked the Clinic, and I thought, well, it's just so easy to get a law firm job, it was just too easy. You didn't have to write cover letters, you just signed up for the program and got an offer with this place, the people seemed nice, and I thought I could do this for a couple years. And then I quickly learned after a couple of weeks that it's harder than I thought to do a job that you don't feel passionate about. But then I stayed for a long time. [Three years] (057) I've tried to leave though, I've tried to look for other options. And last month and this month, I've been going like full-force. So I have more to tell you about searching for public interest jobs. First of all, it's easier now in terms of the Internet. A lot of these places have Web sites now. The law school, the Clinic, provides some links to them. So just even finding out about the organizations are easier. They [the Clinic] have a Web site with a listing of jobs. So that's great. And it's very focused toward public interest, actually because law firms don't really post jobs. They use recruiters and stuff like that. So that has been nice, except a lot of those positions either aren't in Chicago or once they're posted, they are filled. . . . So my experience has been, I've stopped looking at salaries. All right, I've got money saved now after three years here, I've suffered enough, I'm gonna just go do something I want to do. So now I'm experiencing more of a structural impediment of one position open and two hundred lawyers who think it's great and would be willing to take a pay cut. So that's the run-in I'm having now. And the frustration is, it seems that it's very difficult to even get a rejection letter back saying that the position's been filled. (1-1, 2)

III. Loss of Public Interest Law Counterculture

The loss of a supportive public interest counterculture marks the transition from law school to practice, although some have succeeded in cobbling together functional equivalents. Especially those working in settings more conducive to public interest work find opportunities to stay in touch with PILPs (Public Interest Law Persisters) from law school, or to seek out colleagues currently doing similar kinds of public interest litigation, as part of a "natural support network" that productively substitutes for a law school's public interest counterculture (7-5: 250).

> And, yeah, I was like on the board of the public interest law group at the school. And you knew who were the public interest people. Not really, not in the same way. You know, there are people that you know are interested in pro bono work. But maybe that would be a really good thing. There's no group or support network. There's a pro bono committee, but as an associate I have no interaction with pro bono committee except for the time that I asked for their approval for a project. Yeah, there's no real network. Which I guess is frustrating. (4-10: 725)

In part, this apparently represents the transition from school to work as suggested by this associate's observation of the phenomenon:

> [I] definitely miss the collaborative nature of working in the Clinic which is something that you see a lot less in private practice just due to the realities of people's lives and cost constraints and what not. (9-6: 255)

Lack of information about public interest prospects gets mirrored by commercial firm associates who wonder about the experiences of their old classmates, thus revealing another dimension of the loss of the law school public interest counterculture:

> I'd be interested in finding out what those working in public interest law jobs now assess their experience, whether the poor pay is wearing them down. (3)

IV. Hegemonic Segregation Fostered by Firms

Firm employment works as a powerful socialization process, producing a hegemonic segregation of young attorneys with similar interests from one another and instead channeling them into a view of practice defined by and identified with the firm. Billable hours function as a potent commodification of law (Balbus 1977). The structure of pro bono practice within the firms ties associates to the firm and separates them from colleagues with public interest commitments in other firms.

... it quickly became apparent that my primary responsibility was to provide services to our paying clients. The idea was, the partners have enough connections that they're not looking to me, and the clients aren't looking to me to offer those connections. I'm being looked at do the work, and not to bring in business—because it's a large firm—but more just to do the work for our existing clients. . . . Rather than having public interest work, pro bono work, community service, be an integral part of my day-to-day practice as I expected, it ended up being a sideline that I had to squeeze in between, or more accurately after, the work that I had to do for our paying clients. This was very disappointing for me because the expectations of billable hours are very, very high, here, I mean at law firms all over, but particularly in a large firm like this. . . . My required number—client-chargable billable hours—is [about 2,000]. And there's this ongoing debate whether pro bono hours count, you know quote count unquote, toward our billable hour requirements. I don't want to get too technical, but it's an important distinction that there are two ways of counting hours. One is real billable hours, and then there's what we have, called creditable hours. And the billable hours are only hours that are billed to paying clients whereas creditable hours include other things like pro bono work, training, etc. And there is a pretense given to evaluating attorneys on the basis of their creditable hours, but the reality is, in my experience, the overwhelming attention is focused on billable hours. And the requirement, at least in my group, is to do at least [about 2,000] billable hours. . . . So rather than finding that pro bono work would fit in naturally with the other work that I was doing, I found that pro bono work—if I was going to do it—would have to be done on top of the . . . hours that I was already required to bill. And that's hard to do because that's a lot of hours to put in, and I'm married and [have children]. (4-3, 4: 205)

... after working here for two and a half years, I haven't really gotten closer to the idea that I want to make a career of this, and a lot of it has to do with the fact, the bottom line here is that we do work for paying clients. It's a business. Part of the reason that I haven't been vocal on these issues is that I recognize that reality. I can't make this place into something that it's not. I can't make this place into a pro bono law firm. I can't make this place abandon its primary mission to make a profit. Early on, people said to me—and this was something I was very displeased with—that you should be careful about how much pro bono work you do. But I think that in reality, nobody cares how much pro bono work I do. I can do as much pro bono work as I want to, on pretty much anything I want to as long as it doesn't interfere with my billable hours. And the only thing that's really frustrating to me is that firms, they sell themselves as not distinguishing between pro bono work and client-chargeable work. I don't have any problem with a firm saying, we expect you to do client-chargeable work. What I do have a problem with is that they try to claim that their associates are encouraged, and certainly not discouraged from, doing pro bono work. And they tout all of these things. . . . In reality, there's a lot of work that associates have to do on their own; there's more hurdles than the firms would like to admit to. (4-10, 11: 790)

In one city, several large firms support a voluntary legal services consortium. The firms allow, and to some extent encourage, associates to use it as a vehicle to provide pro bono services in community settings to indigent clients. Yet each firm often has its own community site. This means that the firm's associates participating in this community outreach *pro bono* effort tend to encounter only other attorneys working for their firm. This presumably reinforces the firm's influence as dominant professional reference group. It also segregates public interest law persisters from one another, and thus inhibits the development of more organized efforts and of an identifiable culture. In the long run, it likely increases the long-shot that cause lawyering already is. Scheingold and Bloom (1998: 222) report that Seattle-King County Bar Association's free neighborhood legal clinics operated in a similar way in counteracting prospects for anything transformative (structurally) resulting from a similar corporate, collaborative pro bono outreach effort.

A. Pro Bono Benefits for Firms

Firms benefit in turn from the special skill development that pro bono work provides, as they benefit more generally in terms of attorney preparation and the firm's image in the profession and to the public.

> Basically, public interest at these firms is all show. It's about looking good in the community and about recruiting. I take it all with a grain of salt. (3)

> Yes, it is true that the pro bono work is a way for the firm to give younger associates some experience that they would not get from the paying work. (5-2)

> But yes, the firm does view the pro bono work as a way for associates to get experience, absolutely. So it is encouraged. With regard to your question about the level of oversight and supervision provided on pro bono work by partners, I have not had trouble finding people when I have questions. Obviously, they don't want you to commit malpractice! (6-3)

> . . . law firms always profess to providing the same level of quality and attention to pro bono clients that they do to paying clients. But in my experience, that's not always the case. And where I've seen that is in the attention and oversight given to associates who are working on pro bono matters from their partners/supervisors. For paying clients generally, the partners are very involved in the work that the associates do. They review their work, they direct them, and largely manage their interactions with the clients as well. And that diminishes certainly as associates get more senior. But for pro bono work, associates are given much more free rein to do work on their own, and partners seem to devote less attention to directing and supervising, checking the work. And that can be very liberating in some ways, but alternatively it can result in the work that is done for the pro bono clients not being of the highest quality, particularly when it's younger associates that are doing it that don't have so much ex-

perience. And one of the reasons that the firms claim that they want their associates to do pro bono work is to get experience. I recognize that, but you know throwing somebody into a project that they don't have any experience in and not giving them guidance does not seem to me to be the best way to train the associate and certainly not the best way to provide service to the client. So what end's up happening is associates, it seems to me, end up feeling isolated in doing their pro bono work, particularly if it is work that they initiate as opposed to work that they are given by a partner. And that happens sometimes. Partners will have pro bono projects that they engage associates in to assist. But I've done some pro bono work that I initiated, and definitely felt somewhat isolated because not only was I doing the work at night after I had finished my work for paying clients, I didn't feel that I had the interest or attention of partners to advise me and assist me in doing that work. (4-4: 300)

A litigator reports a different experience, albeit with an important qualification:

No, I'd say that the pro bono cases get the same oversight and supervision from partners as do the normal cases. That's probably less of a problem here because ours is a small practice group within this large firm. It's nice that way. In fact, the only times that I have [the] opportunity of working with the managing partner in real estate was actually on pro bono cases. (5-2)

In other instances, the support for pro bono work carries even more weight. We return to the smaller firm where a "a critical mass" of the associates have strong public interest commitment:

a few partners who always will be around to read briefs and bounce ideas off you. Just the other day, I was talking to our pro bono director about the clemency hearing . . . and he said, oh, you know, great, we'll put a panel together here of people if you want to like moot it for you. Which is a lot of support because it takes people's time, and a lot of law firms probably would look and say, okay, well, if we have five or six attorneys in the room for two hours, that's X number of dollars. That doesn't seem to really be the case here. (9-4: 167)

Yet even this quality of authenticity serves the interests of such firms as they compete in the recruitment of law students. Apparently, public interest appeal survives among a sufficient number of law students that firms realize the value of a pro bono commitment in recruiting.

more and more important to law firms, I think, maybe partially for altruistic reasons but also because it's very important to candidates . . . some places had good ones, and some places had none at all. They said, well, you can do it. You know, what does that mean? Well, you can do it. You know. [We won't shoot you!] Yeah, yeah, exactly! But there's no support in contract hours, you know. And you need that support. (9-4: 177)

Thus, while the liberal legalism biases Scheingold and Bloom aptly identify in corporate practice (*"Corporate attorneys* who engage in cause lawyering are overwhelmingly without transgressive aspirations of any kind" [1998: 245]) do undercut prospects for efficacious cause lawyering to emerge, the firms continue to play a potential role in making the possible imaginable. Where else can large numbers of young public interest-inclined, cause lawyer-potential, attorneys go to get legal experience and supervision? Where have cause lawyers in the United States generally developed practice skills in the first years out of law school?

B. Public Interest Operationalized as Pro Bono

In the context of the firms, public interest almost always becomes operationalized as pro bono work. This phenomenon represents and extends the more general and overwhelming tendency of legal practice and reasoning in the United States to proceed on a case-by-case basis and for public interest work to manifest as service activities rather than as impact litigation or social structural change activism.

Even pro bono, such a mild type of public interest work, demands affirmative devotion by the young associate. Personal commitment comes to the fore in the following narrative:

> You know, I just got to the point where I said that if I'm going to be happy, I need to do this stuff. And what I'm trying to do is, while sometimes it's hard to be in a big place like this and do this kind of work, I really want to take advantage of what this place has to offer. Not just the coffee and the rooms, but the fact that I'm in this huge building that has all these people, the fact that we have a marketing department that can produce these nice posters, the fact that we have the resources to help them put together brochures, you know, all of these things. The fact that we have the resources to bring in intellectual property attorneys and real estate attorneys. In these ways, it has allowed me to really provide great service to the organization that I wouldn't have otherwise been able to do. So there's good and bad to working in a place like this. And I guess one of the things it seems to me that people need to do if they're going to do pro bono work, particularly transactional pro bono work in a place like this, is try to recognize what the place has to offer, you know, what support there is for them to do the pro bono work they're doing. You know, while there are certainly hurdles that have to be overcome, it can be done. But I just don't see anything other than making a personal commitment to it as the way to accomplish the goal. The only way you accomplish your goal of doing pro bono while you're working in a private law firm is to be personally committed to doing it. Because it's too hard to do it any other way. (4-9: 667)

C. Civic Involvement

Although some young lawyers have been able to work in a bit of civic involvement, the structure of corporate practice subverts wider involvement. The small, personal injury firm provides an instructive contrast. Here an associate (2) who has not received many pro bono opportunities during his first two years of employment notes nevertheless that its size and the relatively relaxed work demands (as contrasted with large corporate firm practice) actually create the potential for pursuing pro bono or public interest commitments outside of the office. Whether this actually occurs depends also on the intensity of involvement in one's personal life and whether the political commitment level generates sufficient energy.

D. Fine-Tuning Corporate Self-Presentation

The firms use current technologies, especially Web sites, together with the interests of PILPs to advance their corporate self-presentation as committed to public interest, using various strategies. Large firms can sign the American Bar Association/Public Interest Law Initiative pro bono pledge, assign a partner full time to coordinate pro bono activities, designate an associate to do so as one responsibility, publish a newsletter on the subject, formalize collaboration with a law school clinic, or partner with a legal advocacy center.

> Actually, [this law firm] has a good reputation in terms of its commitment to pro bono work. In fact, we even have an attorney who's basically in charge of handing out public interest work. If I have the time available, I take on that pro bono work. Typically, it's not criminal work, but more often involves contracts or negotiations or a dispute with an insurance company or debt collection. It mostly all concerns individuals rather than organizations. Since I'm in antitrust work, what I get in terms of pro bono cases, focuses more on litigation rather than transactional work. We don't even get pure transactional work, as far as I can tell. (6-1, 2)

> The mission of the organization is very simple and appealing. And so, it makes a good story, it makes a good sound bite. And so, you know, I guess you could say that his choice to promote this reflects the firm's general choice to portray itself to the larger community as being committed to doing pro bono work . . . it would be extremely unusual or unlikely for a partner to come to an associate and say, "you're doing a great work and your hours are very good, but we're a little disappointed that you haven't done more pro bono work." . . . I think that when people get considered for partnership, they're not just considered for the number of hours that they've put in; they're considered for business development potential. And when people do high profile pro bono work, it raises their stature, it gives them connections, and eventually it results in enhancing their ability to bring in business. Now I don't want to make it sound too cold and calculating, and that it's all about the money but I just

think that people who do pro bono work, it's primarily done on the side and on their own initiative and based on their own personal commitment and not because the firm encourages them to do it. (4-9: 718)

Firms vary in the extent to which they value and reward pro bono. Yet, as one associate notes, a rationalization of pro bono work appears under way, perhaps merely an adjunct to the hyperbureaucratization of the megafirms:

I don't know if the commitment is increasing, but it's becoming more organized and easier to do. I mean the policy as it is now has been the same as far as I know since I started which is that pro bono work is treated exactly the same as regular billable work. As far as evaluations are made about how much work you're doing, how many hours you're billing, and how much money you're bringing in for the firm, they don't treat pro bono work any differently. So I don't know if the commitment is changing at all, but they're doing a better job making it available and accessible to attorneys, easily accessible to attorneys . . . give each attorney a list of options and say all you have to do is pick something from numerous different programs, find one thing . . . picking up one of these cases. (8-9: 470)

V. The Public Interest/Cause Lawyering Continuum, Community Organizing, and Democratization

My recent and previous (participative) observations of community organizing and social action reinforce a major finding from this project regarding democratization: "the closing of the universe of political discourse" (Marcuse 1963). Regarding social justice and the subject of this chapter, this means, among other things, the complicit exclusion of attorneys from social movement development. This concluding section addresses this issue in the context of the public interest/cause lawyering continuum and contemporary community organizing with regard to implications for democratization and social justice.

A new attorney's recollection of the law school environment highlights Marcuse's point:

I think that it is true that the students who worked at the Clinic, and had a stronger public interest law commitment, did have a different mindset from many of the other students at the school. Those of us working at the Clinic realized that money is not all there is, that if you can help, maybe you should help. But the other students would ask why I was wasting my time on the Clinic work, asking how it would advance me in corporate legal work. (6-1)

Thus, the extreme conservatism of a dominant reference group makes problematic even mildly liberal public interest work, let alone any more aggressive or structural social justice activism.

> But I think there's sort of an inherent conflict a lot of times from being an attorney and being an activist. . . . If I had to choose between the two, I would go with attorney. . . . Not that you can't be both; it's just sometimes those things really conflict. I've noticed it a lot in this work that we've been doing on this . . . that client when you've got a great deal, but it precludes all of this evidence from coming out which would help the other client. (9-3: 139)

As one law professor who read my previous paper (Thomson 2001) notes, examples of public interest legal services predominate in my research over efforts directed toward more wide-sweeping advocacy, activism, and structural impact. That reflects in large part the reality of public interest work when construed broadly and when studied from the vantage point of legal education and the early years of practice. Hence, we need a more vigorous search to find the structural impact variety—or that which, in Scheingold and Bloom's rendition, reaches beyond meeting unmet needs. The experience of the associate whose early public interest practice path led to an immigrant legal advocacy center provides an instructive and promising example (10). Its employment practice work presents difficult obstacles in going after "devious" contractors who exploit immigrants, often undocumented, as a "cheap source of labor" that often receives no compensation after weeks or even months of work. The center has begun working with some private firms to seek "the big money" awards that presumably may have more of an impact on pattern and practice. Such collaborations may lead to impact litigation such as class action suits (10-2).

At the same time, the center does outreach work in rural areas where many immigrants find work at meatpacking plants. These efforts include working with social service agencies and collaborating in getting more accurate information out about rights. Yet the center has such opportunities due largely to the prohibition on legal aid working with undocumented immigrants. As a result, this small center in effect serves as "the only agency in town" and must turn away many persons with legal needs. Its social justice promise thus reflects the "repressive tolerance" (Marcuse 1963) of a legal system that prohibits others (legal services) from engaging in such work (Shamir and Ziv 2001).

Partnering with private firms with resources holds out the prospect of going from merely providing a "band aid to litigation" (10-3). Even here, however, an observer suspects decidedly mixed motives. There is "money to be made" with the number of immigrants "growing enormously." Consequently, "the firms want to tap into the market; they want to help out but create business too." Thus, personal injury, "horrible brutality," and police brutality cases provide the opportunity to "do good but get publicity." In short, the motivation looks like the "altruistic plus good business reasons." The challenge of "transforming cases into causes" (Shamir and Chinsky 1998) persists.

Where Have All the Lawyers Gone?

As suggested at various points in this chapter, one struggles to find cause lawyering when beginning the search at legal education and early legal practice. More likely sites appear in community organizing efforts, yet they present their own difficulties especially if they are not grounded in an effective social movement[1] (McCann and Silverstein 1998; Morag-Levine 2001).

The interviews with young public interest committed lawyers reveal a large gap between the availability of legal talent and commitment and the needs of social service agencies and not-for-profit organizations. It constitutes another form of the very stark segregation between the legal world and the social service world and the small world of social action. We can analyze the disconnects in terms of problems in information flow, noting the absurdity of talent over here seeking good use and over there the needs that they could meet (Thomson and Dubow 1993). But they also share the same structural, institutional, and cultural sources as the invisibility of cause lawyering in law schools and among progressive associates in law firms and in legal assistance offices. Appropriately then, and with a breath of promise, we find interest in closing this gap and a modest strategy for doing so suggested by one of the public interest law persisters. In classic Millsian fashion, she demonstrates some sociological imagination in linking personal career concerns with social issues:

> Well, I think generally I'm not really big on policy advocacy, but also, gaining more of an understanding from what it actually means in practice, I'm realizing that it's too removed for me, its just too far from the day-to-day issues, you know, it's a great tool for maintaining a broad impact, but, I think that I'm probably more interested in more community organizations that are providing a direct service and now having the tools to be able to plug into issues and to advocate for, you know, policy, whether it's a policy within an organization or a policy of the city . . . or something even broader than that. Having the tools to be able to step in and do that or form coalitions among direct service organizations that have similar issues, . . . but that I would rather my day-to-day work be closer to the actual organizations providing direct services. (11-2: 155)

This young attorney seeks to do more than meet unmet needs but to assist and mobilize community organizations in doing so and in shaping public policy. Such a community organizing and legal education approach suggests one way for addressing contemporary challenges (Scheingold 1998) while learning from progress achieved (Meili 1998; Ellman 1998).

More broadly, discussion of some of the difficulties of realizing cause lawyering potential to advance nascent social justice movements in the contemporary political culture in the United States reflects differences and conflicts between radical lawyering and critical lawyering (Scheingold and Bloom 1998, especially p. 243; Trubek and Kransberger 1998; Scheingold 1998). Yet we can exaggerate such differences and ignore commonalities. No inexorable disjunction between the two need exist. Critical and radical lawyering instead should complement one another. Especially when viewing the trajectory of social movement development, one sees this as a possibility.

Complaints from veteran cause lawyers (Scheingold and Bloom 1998: 241) about the lack of a contemporary social movement to appreciate and benefit from political legal practice, often hearkening back to the 1960s and 1970s, remind us of a major constraint and need. But where are these cause lawyers (or their younger counterparts) as new movements—the aforementioned neo-Alinsky metropolitan initiatives and such, but potentially community mediation (Merry and Milner 1993), restorative justice (Sullivan and Tifft 2001), Students Against Sweatshops, anticorporate globalization movements in general—begin to emerge and grow (Scheingold and Bloom 1998: 243)? Opportunities emerge, even though the social movements and cause lawyering practice may take different forms than in the past.

The death penalty abolition movement and death penalty lawyering (Sarat 1999, 2001) offer instructive experience. Death penalty appellate lawyering has persisted even in the face of overwhelming cultural and political opposition. Recent experience in this area illustrates the need to be ready for the possibility of renaissance as a coalescence of circumstances, organizations, and professionals/activists have led to a moratorium and possible rollback in Illinois. The role of attorneys initially trained in firms requires illumination.

Notes

I greatly appreciate the support and guidance of various readers and listeners in responding to earlier papers and previous drafts of this chapter, including the other contributors to this volume, especially Austin Sarat, Steven Meili, Peter Fitzpatrick, and particularly, Stuart Scheingold. The anonymous law students and young lawyers interviewed contributed generously of their time and insight as did several of their professors. Thanks also, for various contributions, go to Marc Cooper, Noah Leavitt, Karen Thomson, Meridel Thomson, and Wade Thomson.

1. My informal observations during the past several years of a neo-Alinsky approach to broad-based citizen organizing in the United States find attorneys nearly invisible. Some do give their time, energy, and talents as community volunteers, but distance themselves from their professional identity. They seem to find their legal capabilities and resources largely irrelevant. Such preliminary and anecdotal findings, however, may reflect choices of strategy that do not provide opportunities for cause lawyering to emerge. On the other hand, why has available legal talent not made the case for what it can provide within and to this movement?

References

Abel, Richard. 1998. "Speaking Law to Power: Occasions for Cause Lawyering," in *Cause Lawyering: Political Commitments and Professional Responsibilities*, ed. A. Sarat and S. Scheingold. New York: Oxford University Press.

Balbus, Isaac. 1977. "Commodity Form and Legal Form: An Essay on the 'Relative Autonomy' of the Law." *Law and Society Review* 11: 571–88.

Ellman, Stephen. 1998. "Cause Lawyering in the Third World," in *Cause Lawyering: Political Commitments and Professional Responsibilities*, ed. A. Sarat and S. Scheingold. New York: Oxford University Press.

Engel, David, and Frank Munger. 1996. "Rights, Remembrance, and the Reconciliation of Difference." *Law and Society Review* 30, no. 1: 7–53.

Foucault, Michel. 1977. *Discipline and Punish: The Birth of the Prison*. New York: Vintage.

Fox, Ronald. 1995. *Lawful Pursuit: Careers in Public Interest Law*, ed. William Henslee and Sara Vlajcic. Chicago: American Bar Association.

Glaser, Barney, and Anselm Strauss. 1967. *The Discovery of Grounded Theory*. New York: Aldine.

Granfield, Robert. 1992. *Making Elite Lawyers: Visions of Law at Harvard and Beyond*. New York: Routledge.

Guinier, Lani. 1997. *Becoming Gentlemen: Women, Law School, and Institutional Change*. Boston: Beacon.

Handler, Joel. 1978. *Social Movements and the Legal System: A Theory of Law Reform and Social Change*. New York: Academic.

Heumann, Milton. 1977. *Plea Bargaining*. Chicago: University of Chicago Press.

Kairys, David, ed. 1998. *The Politics of Law: A Progressive Critique*. 3rd ed. New York: Basic.

Kennedy, Duncan. 1981. "Rebels from Principle: Changing the Corporate Law Firm From Within." *Harvard Law School Bulletin* (Fall): 38–49.

———. 1983. *Legal Education and the Reproduction of Hierarchy: A Polemic Against the System*. Cambridge, Mass.: Afar.

Kidder, Robert. 1983. *Connecting Law and Society: An Introduction to Research and Theory*. Englewood Cliffs, N.J.: Prentice-Hall.

Kilwein, John. 1998. "Still Trying: Cause Lawyering for the Poor and Disadvantaged in Pittsburgh, Pennsylvania," in *Cause Lawyering: Political Commitments and Professional Responsibilities*, ed. A Sarat and S. Scheingold. New York: Oxford University Press.

Lofland, John, and Lyn Lofland. 1983. *Analyzing Social Settings: A Guide to Qualitative Observation and Analysis*. 2nd ed. Belmont, Calif.: Wadsworth.

Marcuse, Herbert. 1963. *One-Dimensional Man*. Boston: Beacon.

McCann, Michael, and Helena Silverstein. 1998. "Rethinking Law's 'Allurements': A Relational Analysis of Social Movement Lawyers in the United States," in *Cause Lawyering: Political Commitments and Professional Responsibilities*, ed. A. Sarat and S. Scheingold. New York: Oxford University Press.

Meili, Steven. 1998. "Cause Lawyers and Social Movements: A Comparative Perspective on Democratic Change in Argentina and Brazil," in *Cause Lawyering: Political Com-*

mitments and Professional Responsibilities, ed. A. Sarat and S. Scheingold. New York: Oxford University Press.

Menkel-Meadow, Carrie. 1998. "The Causes of Cause Lawyering: Toward an Understanding of the Motivation and Commitment of Social Justice Lawyers," in *Cause Lawyering: Political Commitments and Professional Responsibilities,* ed. A. Sarat and S. Scheingold.

Merry, Sally, and Neal Milner, eds. 1993. *The Possibility of Popular Justice: A Case Study of Community Mediation in the United States.* Ann Arbor: University of Michigan Press.

Morag-Levine, Noga. 2001. "The Politics of Imported Rights: Transplantation and Transformation in an Israeli Environmental Cause-Lawyering Organization," in *Cause Lawyering and the State in a Global Era*, ed. A Sarat and S. Scheingold. New York: Oxford University Press.

Sarat, Austin, ed. 1999. *The Killing State : Capital Punishment in Law, Politics, and Culture.* New York: Oxford University Press.

Sarat, Austin. 2001. *When the State Kills : Capital Punishment and the American Condition.* Princeton, N.J. : Princeton University Press.

Sarat, Austin, and Stuart Scheingold, eds. 1998. *Cause Lawyering: Political Commitments and Professional Responsibilities.* New York: Oxford University Press.

————, eds. 2001. *Cause Lawyering and the State in a Global Era.* New York: Oxford University Press.

Scheingold, Stuart. 1998. "The Struggle to Politicize Legal Practice: A Case Study of Left-Activist Lawyering in Seattle," in *Cause Lawyering: Political Commitments and Professional Responsibilities*, ed. A. Sarat and S. Scheingold. New York: Oxford University Press.

Scheingold, Stuart, and Anne Bloom. 1998. "Transgressive Cause Lawyering: Practice Sites and the Politicization of the Professional." *International Journal of the Legal Profession* 5, nos. 2/3: 209–53.

Selznick, Philip. 1961. "Sociology and Natural Law." *Natural Law Forum* 6: 84.

Shamir, Ronen, and Sara Chinsky. 1998. "Destruction of Houses and Construction of a Cause: Lawyers and Bedouins in the Israeli Courts," in *Cause Lawyering: Political Commitments and Professional Responsibilities*, ed. A. Sarat and S. Scheingold. New York: Oxford University Press.

Shamir, Ronen, and Neta Ziv. 2001. "State-Oriented and Community-Oriented Lawyering for a Cause: A Tale of Two Strategies," in *Cause Lawyering and the State in a Global Era*, ed. A. Sarat and S. Scheingold. New York: Oxford University Press.

Stover, Robert. 1989. *Making It and Breaking It: The Fate of Public Interest Commitment During Law School.* Howard Erlanger, ed. Urbana: University of Illinois Press.

Strauss, Anselm, and Jill Corbin. 1998. *Basics of Qualitative Research: Techniques and Procedures for Developing Grounded Theory.* 2nd ed. Thousand Oaks, Calif.: Sage.

Sullivan, Dennis, and Larry Tifft. 2001. *Restorative Justice: Healing the Foundations of Our Everyday Lives.* Monsey, NY: Willow Tree Press.

Thomson, Douglas. 1999. "Beyond Public Interest? Searching for a Social Justice Path in Contemporary Legal Education." Paper presented at the Law and Society Association annual meeting in Chicago.

———. 2001. "Defending Public Interest Identity Throughout Law School." Paper presented at the Law and Society Association annual meeting in Budapest, Hungary.

Thomson, Douglas, and Fredric Dubow. 1993. "Organizing for Community Mediation: the Legacy of Community Boards of San Francisco as a Social-Movement Organization," in *The Possibility of Popular Justice: A Case Study of Community Mediation in the United States*, ed. S. Merry and N. Milner (169–99). Ann Arbor: University of Michigan Press.

Trubek, Louise, and M. Elizabeth Kransberger. 1998. "Critical Lawyers: Social Justice and the Structures of Private Practice," in *Cause Lawyering: Political Commitments and Professional Responsibilities*, ed. A. Sarat and S. Scheingold. New York: Oxford University Press.

Turk, Austin. 1976. "Law as a Weapon in Social Conflict." *Social Problems* 23: 276–91.

Zinn, Howard. 1971. "The Conspiracy of Law," in *The Rule of Law*, ed. R. P. Wolff. New York: Simon and Schuster.

Strategy and Social Capital

Cause Lawyers and Judicial Community in Israel

Legal Change in a Diffuse, Normative Community

PATRICIA J. WOODS

In 1969, the Israel High Court of Justice (HCJ) made the stunning decision that the Jewish law (*Halakhah*) for defining "Who is a Jew" had no place in the laws of the modern state of Israel (*Shalit* 1969). In a country in which religious authorities had an official position within the state, this decision was seen by many as an attack on both religious authorities and the Jewishness of the Jewish state. Within three weeks of its decision, the HCJ received a severe blow to its own institutional autonomy; the Knesset, Israel's parliament, in essence overturned the HCJ decision by enshrining the Halakhic definition of Jewishness as the law binding on all Israeli citizens.[1] For the next eighteen years, the HCJ avoided challenging religious authorities, even while it became increasingly proactive on other issues of rights (Hofnung 1996; Edelman 1994).[2] A few cases in the 1980s displeased religious authorities but did not challenge their power directly. Suddenly, in a move that undermined the autonomy of religious institutions within the state, the HCJ decided that religious authorities did not have the right to determine who would sit on local religious councils (*Shakdiel* 1988), or voting bodies for municipal rabbis (*Poraz* 1988). These last two cases initiated what I call the religious law conflict, a conflict between religious and secular forces within the state—and reflected in the wider society—that amounts to nothing less than a culture war.

Why was the HCJ able to enter the conflict when it did? I argue that cause lawyers for left-leaning social movements in Israel were critical to the onset of this conflict. Key cause lawyers, by the late 1980s, had become part of the "judicial community," the socioprofessional community in which HCJ justices, legal scholars, government lawyers, clerks, interns, and many cause lawyers participated through both informal and formal interactions. Far from being outsiders to the state, as has until recently been theorized in the cause lawyering literature (see Southworth and Hatcher, both in this volume; and Dotan 1998), these cause lawyers lived, worked, and thought about the law in close contact with the supreme judicial authority within the state: HCJ justices. Through interaction at legal and other academic conferences, public talks, court cases, and social events, key cause lawyers were part of this diffuse community that was, above all, a locus of legal norms-generation for the HCJ. The content or specific norms of this normative community changed over time, and key cause lawyers, while also subject to those changes, were important agents of change. Moreover, change occurred through conflict, not consensus; conflict over the norms of this particular legal community in Israel continues today. Challengers of the judicial community within the legal field in the 1990s coalesced around the Israel Bar. One of the most outspoken sets of nonlegal challengers was seen, perhaps not surprisingly, within the ultra-orthodox and some orthodox communities that shared primary control over the religious establishment within the state.

Theoretically, the story of the religious law conflict in Israel has important implications for a question that has concerned scholars of law and society for many years. Can courts bring about meaningful political change? Some have argued that law and legal systems act to constrain courts (Rosenberg 1991), control society (Shapiro 1981), and seek to control lawyers themselves through the setting of professional norms (Sarat and Scheingold 1998). As a result of these constraints, such scholars are skeptical of the possibility for meaningful court-directed change. Meanwhile, others have pointed out the ways in which laws and courts may be used to contribute to social and political change, however indirect or limited (Epp 1998; McCann 1994; Epstein and Kobylka 1992). Israeli work on law and courts has engaged the question of courts as a tool for meaningful change as well. Some works have suggested not only that the HCJ may act to uphold the existing political or economic elites (Shamir 1990; Hirschl 1998), but that the legal profession itself is active in executing sanctions against lawyers who do not conform to the norms of the profession, as defined by certain legal elites (in this case, the community surrounding the Israel Bar). Shamir and Chinski (1998) have shown that private Israeli lawyers who litigate for causes, as well as cause lawyers, are highly constrained by the norms of the legal profession. The Israel Bar has been at the forefront of defining and enforcing those norms of professional conduct, including sometimes severe professional self-regulation of even the sorts of legal rights arguments that should be made before the HCJ (see Israel Bar disciplinary tribunal against Ron Lev) (233). On the other hand, some analysts of Israeli law have pointed out that many cases brought to the court have achieved political change (Lahav 1997; Dotan 1999; Zamir 1996), even when those scholars question the wisdom of the court's entry into politically charged issues (Hofnung 1999, 1996; Kretzmer 1990; Barzilai 1998; Halpern-Kaddari 1997), or offer their wholesale disapproval of court-driven political changes (Gavison 1998). Taken together, these two seemingly opposing arguments beg the questions: Under what conditions can cause lawyers use the law and courts for meaningful political change, and under what conditions can they not? This chapter examines the conditions under which cause lawyers may use law and courts to initiate meaningful political change through the courts.

I will use a definition of meaningful change that draws from the insight of the possibilities for indirect change (McCann 1994), while at the same time claiming more than that in positive terms. For my purposes, meaningful court-initiated change *may* include aggregate-level, society-wide changes in political attitudes that result from court cases or other types of judicial decisions. However, it also includes two other important indicators, the second of which will be developed in this chapter: (1) changes in concrete, individual-level practices; and (2) the setting of norms, rules, and/or agendas (for more on agenda setting, see Haltom and McCann 2004).

To define the first indicator through a brief example, while *Roe v. Wade* did not broadly change society's views of abortion in either direction, it did, nonetheless, change the lives of many individual women around the United States who no longer had to get potentially dangerous abortions through the black market (including the twenty-seven cases pending before the Supreme Court between 1968–1973, see Epstein and Kobylka 1992: 162, 164–66). Although these changes were not society-wide, they were significant in the lives of many individuals. Both the legal options available to individual women and the concrete practices of many individual women changed as a result of *Roe*. In proposing attention to individual practices, I am suggesting that the relative political salience of many types of court decisions can be measured, without regard for impact on the wider political system, as a function of the number of lives (scope) affected across a society. Political salience may also take into consideration impact on the wider political system, as, for example, when a court decision has a disproportionate impact on a segment of society that has some influence in setting policy. Comparing these two measures would likely provide the most illuminating observations. In short, I would argue, changing political attitudes in a society will tell us less about the effects of courts than changes in concrete, observable practices. This should be even more the case with the most controversial issues, in which there is not infrequent dissonance between what an individual *believes* and what he or she is willing to *do*.

Throughout the late 1980s and 1990s, the challenges that the HCJ mounted changed the opportunities and everyday practices of many individuals—often women—running for office in religious councils, conducting divorce cases, dividing property settlements, and negotiating rights to pray at national holy places. By 2000, the HCJ upheld the rights of two lesbian women registered as mothers of the same child overseas (one adoptive and one birth-mother) to both be registered as mothers in the population registry (*Berner-Kadish* 2000), and, in 2002, it began to support long-standing cases on non-orthodox conversion of adopted children.[3] In 2004 and 2005, the HCJ went further to grant certain economic rights to gay and lesbian couples, such as inheritance, and it allowed lesbian mothers in Israel to adopt one another's children.[4] Admittedly, many of these changes have been contested by countervailing forces within ultra-orthodox and some orthodox communities, sometimes even violently (Mazie and Woods 2003; Lahav 1997). Nonetheless, even as those changes were contested and sometimes undermined, they resulted in real change for real women engaged in the activities in question. And, critically for the purposes of this chapter, the court decisions culminated in changes in the agenda of certain religious constituencies as well as the national political agenda, placing on the national agenda both religion and the state, and the appropriate role of the judiciary in a democracy for over a decade.

Indeed, this chapter will focus on such court-initiated changes in legal norms, rules, and agenda setting. These sorts of changes may be more easily visible at the national level than individual-level practices. If the HCJ in Israel is successful in establishing precedents that allow it to enter into new political areas, it has succeeded in rules-setting. If it succeeds in establishing norms for judicial interpretation, or other legal norms that are accepted at least on the HCJ, it may grant (or limit) power to judicial institutions. It may also affect the political agenda of major segments of society (or of the state). The extent and ferocity of religious challengers to the judicial community discussed later in the chapter suggests that the HCJ, in entering into conflict with religious authorities, did just that.

In the following pages, I outline the parameters of the judicial community. I argue that the norms of the judicial community have changed over time, and membership in that community has expanded from a small set of elites to a much wider group involved in similar social and professional circles. I identify critical interactions among social movement cause lawyers, state institutions, and the judicial community; knowledge of and participation in changing norms, and reputation appear to be the most important benefits of interaction to members. I outline some of the formal and informal alliances among social movements, which developed legal and political strategies together in their effort to encourage the HCJ to change (and undermine) existing loci of religious authority within the state. And I present several critiques of the judicial community on the part of legal scholars and social actors who see this community as a small, elite group making constitutional decisions of which the public at large does not approve.

Critiques such as these, as well as on-going social movement legal efforts, suggest that the norms of the judicial community continue to be contested. Indeed, if I am correct, the norms of the judicial community will continue to be contested and should change through such arguments and debates. However, I also argue, as presented in sections one and two below, that the judicial community is a broader group than suggested by these critiques, including cause lawyers not widely known outside this community who have also been important in the development of the community's norms. Thus, it is not quite the "closed box" that a few of these critics have suggested.

As a methodological note, I use a collection of articles from the orthodox and Haredi (ultra-orthodox) media, the intellectual newspaper in Israel, *Haaretz*, as well as personal interviews (in Hebrew and English)[5] with members of the legal community to build my argument. It should not be too surprising that, in speaking about the tight-knit judicial community, several interviewees preferred to remain anonymous. This work includes five anonymous sources within the judicial community: one former HCJ clerk for Aharon Barak (whom I have given the fictional initials, CA), one HCJ clerk (whom I have given the fictional initials CB), two sources in the Ministry of Justice (fictional initials, JA and JB), and one legal scholar (fictional initials, LS). These interviewees all lived and worked deep inside the judicial community, either at the time of the interview or at a period in the past within the time frame of this study. I have done my best to protect their anonymity.

I. What Is the Judicial Community?
Who Is the Judicial Community?

By 1999, Israel's population was 6,200,000.[6] The legal profession in the same year remained quite small—there were approximately 20,000 lawyers registered with the Israel Bar Association.[7] The legal profession in Israel was comprised of two generally separated groups, in terms of legal practice: commercial and criminal lawyers, and a group associated with constitutional law debates that form what I call the judicial community. Commercial and criminal lawyers have tended to be highly involved in the Israel Bar Association, which represents all lawyers in Israel.[8] The relationship between the Israel Bar and the judicial community has changed over time. It represented norms closer to those of the HCJ of the 1950s and 1960s—a strict interpretation of written law/legal positivism, as discussed below. The Israel Bar was not a powerful actor during this period, in contrast to the court justices and their immediate (then narrow) community. However, by the 1980s and 1990s, the HCJ as an institution (rather than as individual justices) began to reflect more activist norms. Critics seemed to coalesce around the Israel Bar, which by the 1990s continued to advocate something closer to legal positivism.

Although the judicial community was initially a group almost exclusively composed of political and social elites, it grew between the 1970s and 1990s to include the HCJ justices, legal scholars, government lawyers, cause lawyers for major social movement organizations, clerks and interns for various government bodies, including the HCJ and the Ministry of Justice.[9] A select group of cause lawyers were part of the inner circle of the HCJ justices. They met not only at wider social events of the broader judicial community but had dinner together, went to the same parties, and even met each other's children, as one legal scholar mentions in an interview below. Most people who were part of this inner circle were legal scholars rather than cause lawyers; those cause lawyers who did inhabit this social-professional space were most likely to be legal scholars as well, or perhaps senior lawyers for the most elite (yet not broadly popular) rights organizations, such as the Association for Civil Rights in Israel (ACRI). These cause lawyers were usually scholars who could invite a justice to a conference and expect that he or she would actually attend.

By the 1990s, more cause lawyers, although still relatively few, did have closer social ties with justices and other influential members of the community. However, their contacts with the justices were more distant in the 1980s, when key cause lawyers were arguing the first cases in the religious law conflict. And they decidedly did not always convince the justices that their position was correct, even with closer friendships in the 1990s. Nonetheless, they participated in larger conversations not only in private but through debates at conferences, in law reviews, and through court cases that shaped the changing norms of this community. Closer contact may, indeed, have privileged certain lawyers in the 1990s. However, the interactions that were important to the HCJ challenge of religious institutions in the 1980s were more diffuse rather than characteristic of close ties.

Indeed, cause lawyers for major social movement organizations have more often inhabited the more distant outer circle, a broader social-professional space than what I posit is a normative community (for example, key lawyers, all repeat players, in the 1990s for the Israel Women's Network [IWN], the Israel Movement for Progressive Judaism, the International Coalition of Augnah Rights [ICAR], and lower ranking lawyers for ACRI). Members knew one another by reputation, knew about general trends in legal thinking in the community and in the courts, were bound by an expansive notion of the rule of law, and, in most cases, acted in a manner seeking to expand or strengthen the rule of law in Israel. Included in this outer circle were cause lawyers from major organizations who were located in cities relatively distant from Jerusalem, the heart of the judicial community, such as Tel Aviv, Haifa, and Akko. Some attorneys from smaller, more recent organizations may have been a part of the judicial community as well, although those considered fringe groups that bothered the court with irresponsible claims decidedly were not.[10] The number of these organizations grew dramatically in the 1980s and 1990s; the newer and smaller they were, the less likely their lawyers were to be involved in this community.

Most of these lawyers were not elites except by virtue of access to this particular legal community. They had little societal recognition outside of this community. They were not of Israeli "nobility," the sons and daughters of Ben Gurion (first prime minister of Israel) and his ilk. Their entry into the judicial community was relatively "rational," in Weberian terms, although not wholly so. It came through education and professional interest, in addition to personal ties and friendships that also developed largely through education and professional interests. The work of C. Wright Mills is extremely useful in defining the role of cause lawyers in the judicial community. In his terms, one could call these lawyers elites in that they made decisions of consequence for the wider society (1956: 4). However, it is more accurate to say that they *contributed* to decisions of consequence through a diffuse process of interaction. Their power in contributing to these decisions of consequence did inhere in their relationship to the institution of the HCJ, a point that is critical for Mills. Mills argues that institutions are more important in determining the roles that elites play than are the elites themselves. Interesting for my case, he also argues that elites may question those institutions and structures and raise new ones in their place, opening new opportunities for themselves (Mills 1956: 24). Such new opportunities were characteristic of the normative changes in the judicial community, which supported a strengthened judiciary and elevated notion of the rule of law. However, critically, cause lawyers in the judicial community did not retain the wider power and prestige in the larger society that is seen in his power elite (Mills 1956: 9, 71–72). Their prestige was recognized almost exclusively within the narrow confines of the judicial community (where their reputation was important, as discussed below). Cause lawyers in the judicial community thus came closer to Mills's conception of the advisors and thinkers surrounding his power elite. However, I am suggesting that they were more autonomous than mere "advisors." They contributed to the development of the norms of the judicial community—through informal and formal interactions—from which justices drew many of their decisions in the religious law conflict.

Mills's insights into elite communities also shed light on the process of interaction within this broader and diffuse judicial community. Mills's power elite, who are involved in the upper echelons of state, the military, or the largest corporations, comprise a community that "throughout their lives . . . maintain a network of informal connections," "tend to work and think if not together at least alike," and "in making decisions, take one another into account" (Mills 1956: 11–12). Cause lawyers in the judicial community did not rise to the level of major players in the upper echelons of state, the military, or the largest corporations, nor did they incur the corollary power and prestige that Mills suggests comes with these positions. However, his description of how the elite community interacts is similar to the argument I make in the case of the judicial community. Cause lawyers (and, indeed, legal scholars and justices) who became part of the judicial community did so most often through ties made in law school, then maintained through professional contacts and beyond. And as in Mills's schema, their interactions were often informal and not reflective of conspiratorial decision making. The key difference is that, more than making decisions that took members of the power elite into account, trends in normative commitments changed over time through diffuse, informal, and formal legal interaction, debate, and conflict.

Cause lawyers' success in advocating for their social movements and their causes was highly dependent, in the case of the religious law conflict, on participation in and access to this judicial community. Access meant, in particular, knowledge of changing thinking in the community and on the court and thus knowledge of legal arguments that might be (newly) acceptable to the court. This knowledge, together with a positive reputation in the eyes of justices, allowed lawyers to push the envelope and test the willingness of justices to support certain rights issues. Lack of access to this diffuse, informal community seems to have been a hindrance for lawyers working for Bedouins, Palestinians, and others (Shamir and Chinski 1998; Bisharat 1998; Sharfman 1993). However, the significance of this community is not only a function of access; rather, nonelite participants in this community have helped to shape the (changing) norms of the community through their participation in it.

Indeed, membership in the judicial community is mutually transformative (Migdal 2001). Rather than cause lawyers either being directed by their commitment to the system (Blumberg 1967), or directing judicial decision making in some way, the judicial community is shaped and constituted by its (admittedly unequal) members. It is through debates during conferences, court battles, parties, and in classrooms that the norms of this community were constituted (and changed over time).

II. Historical Changes in the Judicial Community

The professional and political norms of the judicial community and the community surrounding the Israel Bar have become increasingly disparate since the 1970s and 1980s. The Israel Bar continues to advocate an approach to law based on formal, positive law and a constrained notion of the role of courts in shaping law. The judicial community, by contrast, has increasingly become dominated by a notion of "natural justice" (Zamir and Zysblat 1996)[11] that requires a strong judiciary prepared to defend civil and human rights. Through HCJ precedent, two rules of natural justice have been included as part of administrative legality, the principle that defines and limits the legal parameters of any state administrative body's action: "The administrative authority is bound to observe two rules of natural justice that have been developed by case law: the rule against bias and the rule concerning the right to a hearing. Originally, these rules applied only to judicial (or quasi-judicial) acts. The High Court has, however, extended their application, and they now also apply to purely administrative acts" (Zamir 1996: 28).

This expansion has meant an increasing application of principles of rights to the actions of state institutions through a de facto judicial review established through the *Bergman* decision in 1969, and legislatively enshrined judicial review through new basic laws passed in 1992.[12] The two communities increasingly clashed over these opposing principles throughout the 1990s, with some movement between them as a result. There has always, of course, been an overlap between the two communities; the Israel Bar does, after all, represent all attorneys in the country, and the HCJ maintains close contact with the Israel Bar. Nonetheless, there was increasing tension between them in the 1990s.[13] Cause lawyers involved in the religious law conflict gravitated toward the judicial community. Those skeptical of judicial activism gravitate toward the Israel Bar. The judicial community was more successful at bringing to action its normative positions, mainly through judicial decisions.

With an eye to the comparative context, it is important to note that Israel does not appear to be exceptional in the significance of cause lawyers in the development of legal norms. Even in the most extreme cases of an executive-dominated judiciary, cause lawyers may be important in influencing judicial norms. In the case of Cuba, for example, all lawyers who provide direct legal services to individuals must, by law, work in state-run legal collectives (Michaelowski 1998). These legal collectives are dominated by a wider political ideology that informs the entire state, that of a socially progressive but also centralized socialism. Moreover, the central bureaucratic organization uniting the legal collectives, the National Organization of Collective Law Offices (ONBC), was closely integrated with the Ministry of Justice, the Office of the Attorney General, and other state councils. Cause lawyers in Cuba were constrained by the political system as well as by the pervading norms of the legal community. Nonetheless, even under those circumstances, Michaelowski's work suggests that, while these prevailing norms have a strong constraining effect on a lawyer's legal choices and strategies at a given time, lawyers in the ONBC were at the same time able "to shape both the laws *and the ethic* governing legal practices in ways which gave them greater scope to defend their clients than was the case in the Soviet Union or other Eastern European socialist states" (Michaelowski 1998: 533, emphasis added). That is to say, the norms of the legal community and a highly centralized and controlled political context limited lawyers' choices; however, lawyers had some sway in the development of those norms over time through influence over legislation as well as acceptable legal practice (Michaelowski 1998: 533–35).

The Israeli legal profession maintained a high degree of institutional independence from the state in the last decades of the twentieth century. Although Israel is a well-functioning, proportional representation system, one in which citizens have extraordinarily easy access to representatives by U.S. standards, many recognize strains on the Israeli democracy—strains that some critics consider major flaws. These strains are evident particularly in legal rights and responsibilities that are defined differently by ethnic and religious affiliation (Shafir and Peled 2002; Peled 1992; Smooha 1978); in certain legal areas, by gender (Raday 1995; Shifman 1990); and in which rights have been suspended for some citizens during extended states of emergency (Kaufman 1997). An entire literature on citizenship versus (full national) membership has grown around the ethnic cleavages in Israel (Kook 1995; see also Peled and Shafir 1996; Peled

1992). And compelling criticisms of both state and HCJ treatment of noncitizen Palestinians abound (Sharfman 1993; Shamir 1990; see also Dotan 1999).

However, for the purposes of understanding the influence of the political system on the legal profession, while my interviews suggest that HCJ justices are deeply sensitive to the needs of the executive branch (as well as the public and, in some cases, their international reputations), institutionally, the Israeli judiciary was highly independent and dominated by the legal profession in the 1990s. Justices continue to be chosen by a professional committee composed of the Minister of Justice, who formally chairs the committee; the president of the High Court, who in practice has dominated the committee; two other High Court justices; two Knesset members; and two representatives of the Israel Bar Association. Thus, both in practice and in law, the judicial appointment process has been strongly directed by the legal profession, with a high degree of influence granted, in practice, to the president of the High Court. Together, the Israel Bar and the HCJ had a high degree of freedom in setting the norms of the legal profession.

The norms of the judicial community were not always dominated by a notion of an extremely strong judiciary whose reason for being was the protection of rights. And, indeed, the Israeli judiciary was not always as independent (particularly from the executive branch) as it has been in recent decades. The HCJ was founded in August 1948. It was only five years later, in 1953, that the Knesset passed the Judge's Law granting the HCJ independence and status as an official branch of the state. In the early 1950s, and even in the years after passage of the Judge's Law, it was unclear what kind of role the judiciary would play in the state of Israel. The government structure was dominated by a combination of legislative supremacy, which emphasized the will of the majority (Barzilai 1998; Gavison 1998; Edelman 1994; Zemach 1976; Cohn 1974), and an etatist ideology, which bestowed, often through Knesset legislation, power to a relatively centralized executive (Lahav 1997: 92). The notion of legislative supremacy was in keeping with many civil law countries in Europe, such as France, which had a tradition of distrust of a strong judiciary or "gouvernement des juges" (Merryman 1985: 28). The relatively centralized executive has been traced by some to "the Eastern European background of czarism, Bolshevism, and authoritarianism that shaped the consciousness of Israel's ruling elite and contributed to the rise of etatism (*mamlakhtiyut*) in the early 1950s" (Lahav 1997: 100). Drawing immigrants from around the world, Israel was a melting pot of legal and political traditions as well as people. In addition, it maintained a mixed institutional legacy from the British Mandate (common), Ottoman law (civil), as well as Halakhic (Jewish religious) law (arguably a civil law tradition).

Uncertain of its role, longevity, or the permanence even of judicial seats, the early HCJ followed a strict line of legal positivism. Although the Judge's Law was passed in 1953, granting a certain amount of autonomy to the judiciary, it was only in 1984 that a Basic Law was passed regarding the judiciary. The Basic Law: The Judiciary firmly established into law what had come to exist in practice, including judicial independence and justice tenure until compulsory retirement (age seventy) or disciplinary action. However, in the 1950s, the role of the HCJ had yet to be established. Before 1953, the justices were extremely cautious in their decision making due to this concern about the stability of the court and uncertainty of its role in the government. After 1953, they were still somewhat cautious. Moreover, it appears that most of the judges believed strongly in a restrained court that would function strictly within the confines of written law, the very definition of legal positivism.

This tradition of positivism, and in particular its extreme version, formalism, appears to have informed the manner in which justices who supported a more activist court advocated their positions in the 1950s and early 1960s. This prevailing paradigm was always challenged and tested by some, such as the late president of the Supreme Court, Simon Agranat, who wrote formative decisions during that period enshrining important rights and defining equality for the purposes of legal interpretation for decades to come (Lahav 1997). "Occasionally, of course, the Court did protect individuals, but only by confining its reasoning to the narrow boundaries of black-letter law." By contrast, "the potential for future activism, which Agranat realized a few years after he had joined the Court, remained unknown to the majority of Israel's judiciary" (92).

In the early 1970s, Haim Cohn (justice 1960s–1981) and Meir Shamgar (justice 1977–1995) began to publish articles in legal journals advocating foundational constitutional principles (in the absence of a constitution!) and the development of a written constitution, respectively (Cohn 1974; Shamgar 1974). Both articles reflected a view of law and courts that included acute attention to both human and civil rights. These articles signaled, to anyone who was listening or reading, that some justices were willing not only to entertain discourses on rights, but also to enforce them more actively. It is unlikely that these writings alone, on the part of one lone justice and another future justice, could have changed the dominant norms of the other justices or the existing judicial community as a whole. However, these writings, and others that followed from a few justices throughout the 1970s and 1980s, provided signals to any lawyer who was listening that a contest was brewing over what would be the prevailing norms of the HCJ.

Lawyers, such as Frances Raday, who became a key cause lawyer in the reli-

gious law conflict in the 1980s, heard the call and began pushing the HCJ on issues of women's rights in labor and then religious issues. She brought cases on
women's rights due to an a priori commitment to those rights issues and to the
use of the judiciary in answering such questions. As such, justices did not
change her position on rights issues, nor did they cause her to view courts, suddenly, as the appropriate venue to make decisions regarding such concerns.
Rather, like many other lawyers in Israel, she was inspired by the successes of
the civil rights movements in the United States and elsewhere. As a lawyer in the
1970s, she believed that the courts were the appropriate and even the ideal forum through which to assert and protect the rights of the few against the many.
Justices' writings, together with increasingly positive, from her perspective,
rights decisions, signaled to her and to others that a few justices on the HCJ
might be open to cases on some rights issues.[14] As a result of these signals, cause
lawyers like Raday began to push the HCJ, often faster than it wanted to move
on issues such as sexual harassment and women's rights in the spheres of labor
and religious institutions. Young organizations like the ACRI pressured the
court with petitions on a wide range of issues. By 1986, Raday opened the Legal
Department of the Israel Women's Network, which, under her tutelage, developed

> A policy linking litigation and legislation, using the cases to promote legislation, and
> . . . using the legislation to promote cases. It was actually a good strategy. . . . We did
> have to work hard on it, but things went through fairly easily on all the economic is-
> sues. On labor and on the family, and on amending the rape laws, on a whole series
> of issues [both cases and legislation were successful]. The reforms went through
> quite easily. We got very good decisions on the Supreme Court on equality for
> women.[15]

III. Cause Lawyers and the State: Interactions
within the Judicial Community

Most lawyers and scholars who became involved in the judicial community
by the 1980s knew each other through interaction in the HCJ, through their
university education (many went to the same law school in Jerusalem), through
academic work including legal conferences, and through the development of
strong social ties in these contexts. Dotan has shown, for example, that professional and social relations between ACRI lawyers and government attorneys
have been closely connected and symbiotic:

> These patterns of cooperation on the professional level are combined with social af-
> filiations between these two groups of lawyers. The members of both groups live in

the same relatively small community of lawyers in the same city (Jerusalem). Most of them graduated from the same law school and have often known each other since they were law students. The two groups of lawyers meet on an almost daily basis for professional purposes (either in or out of court), and they also meet quite often at social events. (Dotan 1998: 200)

Through informal ties within the judicial community, cause lawyers conduct their work and have contributed to the strengthening of the judiciary through a common support of the rule of law and by bringing cases to the HCJ. Social movement lawyers took advantage of signals from the HCJ that it was willing to hear arguments on rights, turning to the HCJ to make a decision in their cases and, in a feedback loop, contributing to the increased political salience of the HCJ by allowing it to make political decisions. This interaction evokes the dependence of courts on social movements and support structure as argued by Epp (1998); the increased salience given to courts when groups and individuals bring politicized cases to them (Hendley 1996); and perhaps most strongly reflects the opportunities that courts and social movements provide one another as highlighted in McCann's work (1994).

Just as I do not argue that cause lawyers were directed by the justices, I expressly do not argue that justices make decisions in coordination with this community. To the contrary, many of the justices are renown for their personal, intellectual independence. Rather, cause lawyers who brought key cases to the HCJ, for example, on women's rights under religious authorities, were aware of a broad change in thinking in the HCJ in favor of rights through their membership in this community. The judicial community has acted as a diffuse and indirect normative environment; members are aware of broad changes in that environment. It is tight-knit in the sense that members see one another through professional work, mutual social movement activities, academic and other conferences, and social engagements on a regular basis, and most live in the same area of the country. It is diffuse in the sense that members may not know one another personally, but they tend to know one another by reputation. They exchange ideas in the diffuse manner of acquaintances in fora such as conferences, professional work, and the like (Granovetter 1983). In the words of legal critic and renowned Israeli legal scholar Ruth Gavison, while the HCJ is somewhat "inbred" with people from the Ministry of Justice and academia, "Justices do not talk [with these colleagues] about cases before they are decided. *There is a more general and diffuse continuity between legal organizations and the court*" (emphasis added).[16]

Dotan suggests that there is important mobility between the ostensibly opposing groups—cause lawyers and government lawyers—who are bound by a common commitment to the rule of law (Dotan 1998, 194). Dotan cites three cases, two in which ACRI lawyers moved from their positions in this prestigious civil rights organization to even more prestigious positions in the Ministry of Justice, where they argued the opposing side of similar issues in court. Another lawyer who had argued several cases against Palestinians charged with crimes against the Israeli military moved to become a litigator for the ACRI and then a more radical human rights organization. Dotan argues that crossover government lawyers may see themselves as ideologically engaged in their work, and thus we should not unilaterally define them as something other than cause lawyers.

> The truth is, and I really believe this, that I see a close similarity between my views and feelings—as a civil rights advocate—of what the role of lawyers should be, and the views and feelings of my counterparts at the Office of the Attorney General. This is particularly true in the criminal law field. The public prosecutor strives to further the public interest and to safeguard the rights of the accused and the rules of due process. (Dotan 1998: 197)

The ideological cause that binds these lawyers across the lines of cause lawyer and state is a deep commitment to the rule of law. (This is a term understood quite differently in the "opposing" legal community, that of the Israel Bar.) Dotan argues that these lawyers are part of a tight-knit judicial community in which they are deeply involved in their causes, but what is most important is a common "ambitious (if not wholly extravagant) concept as to the role of law in society" in which the law is entirely autonomous (Dotan 1998: 201). The respect for the rule of law is the basis for protecting the rights involved in all other more particular legal issues. It is just this common ideological basis that leads to heated debate in Israel over the appropriate role of the judiciary. In the words of one lawyer whom Dotan interviewed: "The lawyer in the public service is committed, above all, to the rule of law, and to similar values, and not necessarily to what the client wants at a given moment. [We are committed] to long-term values and to public norms" (Dotan 1998: 197).

One government lawyer defined the rule of law to me as the protection of everyone against everyone under the law:

> My understanding of the rule of law is that law is the custom of everyone. . . . I think it is the third definition [all the public must abide by the law, which should protect citizens from one another], except not in the sense of citizens against citizens, but everyone against everyone. I am also prepared to accept the definition of the rule of law as usually meaning the protection of citizens from the authorities.[17]

This commitment to the rule of law leads many cause lawyers in Israel, even those who disapprove of crossing the line between cause and state, to seek close

bers of the judicial community, have noted the significance of the withdrawal of the Knesset from decision making on "sacred cow" issues such as religion and the state in the onset of social movement legal mobilization. In the words of one HCJ clerk:

> If the Knesset categorically does not function and does not legislate in certain areas, due to any number of political or electoral considerations, a man will come along who is injured by this behavior and he will petition the HCJ. Then the HCJ has to decide whether it will enter this vacuum that was created or not. . . .
>
> The fact that politicians bring cases to the HCJ does not mean that there is a social consensus [about the appropriate role of the judiciary]. Everyone in this game has his own interests. Sometimes it is in the interests of politicians to avoid the bureaucracy of the Knesset and to move directly to the top of the heap—to the HCJ. . . .
>
> The fact that the HCJ plays some sort of political role results in part from politicians using the court. . . .
>
> The Knesset is also an important part [of the judicial world] in as much as it does nothing whatsoever and thus people do not turn to it.[24]

The decreasing efficacy of the Knesset since the 1977 elections has been the subject of much study in Israel. Barzilai (1998) makes the argument that increasing HCJ intervention in religious issues is directly related to a decreasing ability of the Knesset even to address these issues after the 1977 election, which resulted in a split leadership, a highly fractured parliament, and increasing power of small parties that could then act as veto players. My own survey of Knesset discussions of new laws relating to religious authorities (particularly marriage, divorce, and conversion) supports his findings, showing an increase in the number of bills submitted on certain issues after 1977, but a decrease in the progress each bill made through the debate process (Woods forthcoming).

In addition to knowledge and participation in the development of new norms, and exchange of ideas within the judicial community, reputation is an important factor in the interaction between cause lawyers and justices on the HCJ. Just as cause lawyers know about broad changes in thinking on the court, justices know the reputations of cause lawyers, professional, intellectual, and personal. Reputation has a significant impact on the justices' first impressions of a case.

> A: Some groups he [Barak] has a lot of respect for and some groups he has no respect for. So it depends on which groups and individuals bring the case. . . . Frances Raday is one [social movement lawyer] he would have respect for because she's a professor at the Hebrew University. She's known to be intelligent, and she brings in very few cases. So, I certainly think it is relevant who brings the case.
>
> Q: More so than the issue itself?

A: No, both. I think it depends. I mean, I think if there's a movement—for example, the Association for Civil Rights in Israel. It's a very highly regarded body. It's also highly regarded by him [Barak]. So, if the Association for Civil Rights in Israel brings in a petition, it's taken more seriously than if some loony, a left-wing loony brings in a petition.

Q: Like the X [I name a group that is considered by many leftist groups in Israel to be a left-wing fringe group]?

A: Yes, exactly. If X would go and hang themselves from the trees in the cause of something, so he's [Barak's] not going to take it very seriously. Or if it's a foreign movement or observer, he couldn't care less. But if I it's a serious matter . . . I mean . . . no, I take back what I said about a foreigner. For example, if there were a serious lobby from the States on religious issues under the umbrella of Yale or Harvard University, some place that matters to him, he would take it a lot more seriously than if there were some lobby from, you know, some group he's never heard of that call themselves—I don't know—Action Freedom, or something. It really does matter.

Q: Do you think that is true of other justices as well?

A: I think it's true of every justice in every country in the world, to a certain extent.[25]

Another clerk at the HCJ confirmed at least part of this analysis. It is significant who brings the case. The justices take some petitions more seriously than others based upon the litigators and the movements involved. This is a critical factor to be highlighted about the community of the justices: the justices know the lawyers.

> The way cases are received has a lot to do with the lawyers who bring the cases. If the lawyers are perceived as serious, the case will be taken more seriously. If no one knows who these people are bringing the case, it won't be treated seriously. . . . Someone like Frances Raday is known well by the justices as a very serious lawyer, as an excellent lawyer and scholar. Everyone knows her. And when someone like Raday comes in with a case for equality of women to be representatives on local religious councils, the court will listen to her arguments. It makes a big difference.[26]

However, the significance of reputation is not that of direct contact, lobbying, or social pressure between members of this community and the justices. As Uri Regev, a rabbi and key cause lawyer for the Israel Religious Action Center of the Reform Movement in Israel, put it: "Well, you don't lobby with judges. Not in Israel, in any case."[27]

Indeed, as mentioned above, no one in the judicial community whom I interviewed, even legal critics, suggested that the justices are open to direct influence because of their social and professional ties in this judicial community. Said one HCJ clerk: "Justice Barak is typical of the most independent of the justices, known for doing much of the writing of his decisions rather than having clerks write them."[28]

All insisted that the justices did not discuss the issues of standing cases with friends in this community. Rather, a source in the Ministry of Justice, who spoke on condition of anonymity, said that the ideological proclivities of the justices on broad issues are disseminated very quickly in the small, coherent judicial community in Israel. If you have justices who are willing to turn from a more formal legal reading of law, as seen in the 1950s and much of the 1960s in Israel, that fact quickly becomes "public" knowledge within the judicial community. However, the justices are not the end of the story. I argue that cause lawyers have pressured the court on issues of religion often faster than it wanted to move (Woods forthcoming). For example, cases on reform and conservative conversion have been heard for nearly twenty years and have only recently been successful in the HCJ.

IV. Social Movement Alliances, Formal and Informal

Major social movement organization cause lawyers worked within the judicial community, developing arguments that might push the HCJ in the direction that some justices indicated they wanted the court to move: toward an expansive notion of the rule of law and a high level of judicial power. To this end, cause lawyers for these social movements also worked in close contact with one another across social movements. The women's movement, civil rights movement, and religious pluralism movement all brought important cases to the HCJ making controversial arguments challenging religious authorities in the state in the mid- to late 1980s. Cases challenging religious authorities had been brought to the HCJ before, as mentioned above. However, the mid- and late 1980s saw a change in the number of cases, in the type of argument made, and in a coalition—both formal and informal—among the three social movements. The women's movement (represented by the IWN and Naamat), the civil rights movement (represented in the main by the ACRI), and the religious pluralism movement (represented by the Movement for Progressive Judaism and the Masorti Movement in Israel) worked together, bringing some cases together, consulting informally and privately, and strategizing on specific legal questions as well as the overall approach to what would become the religious law conflict. Significantly, I have argued elsewhere that one particular argument was successful in the early years of the religious law conflict and throughout the 1990s (Woods forthcoming). That argument, first used by women's movement and ACRI attorneys, led to high rates of success regardless of which movement used it. The key to success: the women's equality argument.

In a number of landmark cases,[29] the social movement attorneys were in contact with one another, either formally or informally. The attorneys consulted with one another formally and behind the scenes. An argument relating to equality under state administration was developed first in *Nevo* and *Shakdiel*, then was used later in a series of landmark cases in which existing religious authority was undermined. Among the three movements that brought cases challenging religious authority, it was not important which movement made the argument; the lawyers in each were part of the judicial community and considered reputable. When the women's equality argument was used with regard to *administrative* equality, the argument was successful.[30] When any argument was made, including the women's equality argument, in conjunction with an appeal for "freedom of" or "freedom from" religion (as a constitutional principle), the argument was unsuccessful. That the movements were able to make an argument that could be supported in terms of the principle of administrative legality was critical because it allowed the HCJ to assert basic rights in terms of formal law rather than appeal to a constitutional principle. Such appeals remained highly unpopular in the country throughout the 1990s. Cause lawyers for these social movements developed this strategy working in close concert with one another.

All of the social movement organizations mentioned received a significant portion of their regular funding through the New Israel Fund (NIF). The NIF lists as its reason for being the promotion of the principles of freedom, justice, peace, and equality enshrined in the Israel Declaration of Independence. The opening page of its Web site states: "Since 1979, the New Israel Fund has been at the forefront of efforts to strengthen democracy and social justice in Israel."[31] As an introduction to its activities, the NIF explains:

> When the State of Israel was founded in 1948, it committed itself to the values of freedom, justice, equality, and peace as envisaged by the prophets of Israel. In struggling to maintain those values throughout decades of military conflict and massive immigration, Israel has faced unique and complex challenges. From the outset, it has had to balance the needs of diverse religious, ethnic, and political groups—Jewish and Arab, Ashkenazi and Mizrahi, religious and secular—and is still evolving its own norms for addressing potentially divisive issues.
>
> Against this backdrop, the New Israel Fund works to strengthen Israeli democracy and promote social justice. Established in 1979, the Fund is a non-partisan philanthropic partnership of North Americans, Israelis, and Europeans. It supports a network of non-government organizations in Israel that safeguard civil and human rights, promote Jewish-Arab equality and coexistence, advance the status of women, foster tolerance and pluralism, bridge social and economic gaps, pursue environ-

mental justice, and encourage government accountability. The Fund provides grants and technical assistance to Israeli public-interest groups, and also conducts public education in North America, Israel, and Great Britain about the challenges to Israeli democracy.[32]

In 1998, the NIF supported thirty-five women's organizations, including the IWN and Naamat. It supported twenty-one rights organizations (including ACRI) and twenty-nine religious pluralism organizations (including IRAC, Hemdat, discussed below, and the Masorti Conservative Movement in Israel). All NIF funding recipients are strongly encouraged to work together in a "network" in order to stretch scarce resources, both human and monetary.

Contacts among these organizations have occurred at many levels, including through membership in related organizations. Hemdat, for example, is a coalition of groups advocating religious pluralism. It was established in 1983 by none other than Justice Haim Cohn, together with law professor Yigal Yadin. Included among its organizational members are ACRI, the Movement for Progressive Judaism, and the Masorti Movement. On the other hand, the leading attorney for the Movement for Progressive Judaism has for many years been Rabbi Uri Regev. Rabbi Regev is on the board of ACRI. Raday, the lead attorney in the *Nevo* and *Hoffman* (Women of the Wall) cases, founded the IWN's legal center in 1986, has been a member of ACRI, and was the chair of the Law Department at Hebrew University in Jerusalem as of 2000. Several of her colleagues in that department and in other departments are also members of ACRI, including the current president of ACRI, Eyal Benvenisti, professor of law. Hebrew University law professor Ruth Gavison, whose critiques of the HCJ will be mentioned below, was herself president of ACRI for many years. Other fellow law faculty were affiliated to varying extents with the IWN. The IWN's lead attorney for religious law cases in 1997, Esther Sivan, was a member of ACRI, the IWN, and the International Coalition for Agunah Rights (also known as ICAR), housed in part in the IWN offices.[33]

Even without the encouragement of their funding agencies, the formal and informal coalitions of these like-minded organizations developed through organic contacts among individual lawyers who frequently had ties going back to law school or earlier. Most of these attorneys went to the law school at the Hebrew University of Jerusalem. They went to the same conferences. They belonged to the same organizations. At the very least, there was a large amount of crossover between individual memberships in the varying social movement organizations.

In the case of *Nevo*, the coalition was formal. The Nevo case was brought to the HCJ by IWN attorney Raday, and ACRI attorney Avigdor Feldman. This case, which began in 1985, was a critical turning point for the women's equality argument. In this case, Raday argued that women cannot be forced to retire before men, even in the presence of a labor agreement asserting an earlier retirement age. Raday had presented the similar reasoning—that women's equality was an inherent part of the principle of equality that the HCJ otherwise championed—to labor courts in previous harassment cases and then again to the HCJ in *Shakdiel*, for which deliberations began in 1986. It was in *Nevo* that the women's equality argument was first presented to the HCJ in full form. The *Shakdiel* and *Poraz* cases were decided in 1988, two years before Nevo. In all three cases, the HCJ brought back unanimous decisions that, indeed, women cannot be discriminated against *by virtue of being women* without the establishment of a just rationale for different treatment under the law. In *Poraz*, too, Naamat and ACRI worked together formally. Also at the formal level, the IWN, Movement for Progressive Judaism, ICAR, and ACRI all worked together throughout the early 1990s to develop a new Family Court, which was established in 1995 to allow the financial parts of a divorce case to be heard in secular court.[34] In addition, they all worked on what has become known as the Sanctions Law (also 1995), through which a rabbinical court may apply economic and other sanctions against a husband who refuses to grant a divorce paper (the *get*) to his wife when the rabbinical court finds that she has cause.[35] According to IWN representatives, the IWN and ACRI consult with one another on an ongoing basis regarding lobbying efforts.[36] "In many areas, we work in coalition with other organizations. There is, for example, the law of freedom of information, the law of the right to membership in organizations [freedom of association], housing. On large issues, like Knesset elections, municipal elections, we make an effort to organize it so that all the organizations take a piece. That is organized by the political coordinator [of each organization]."[37]

"All the organizations" refers to all related rights organizations, depending on the issue. Any NIF-funded organization can get a complete list of NIF-funded organizations and is encouraged to do so for the purposes of establishing strong working networks. The IWN and ACRI worked together, formally and informally, to a great extent. The Movement for Progressive Judaism maintained close contact with ACRI through its lead attorney, Rabbi Uri Regev. The Movement for Progressive Judaism also maintained close contact with the IWN and other women's advocacy organizations, including Naamat. These organizations worked together closely enough to establish a division of labor on issues and activities among organizations. The Movement for Progressive Judaism, for example, actively avoided those issues in which it was believed that the Movement might hurt women's causes. For instance, in the area of representing women in rabbinical court proceedings, Regev noted: "Naamat deals with representation. The reason why we don't deal with it is that we feel that us taking on representation of women in the rabbinical courts, which is where it takes place, may not serve them [the women] well."[38]

The establishment of a division of labor indicates a high level of interaction among these organizations beyond the formal interactions available through court records.

V. Contesting Norms of the Judicial Community

The persistent interaction among members of the judicial community has become a source of contentious debate in Israel over the appropriate role of the legal profession and the judiciary. Although it is difficult to pinpoint the informal membership of legal critics, one can identify in the controversy principles that have pitted the Israel Bar community and the judicial community against one another. Moreover, the contest over norms of the judicial community has become a widespread public controversy. Likewise, the public debate is a long-standing one that has not passed with a specific court case or special commission report, as has usually been the case with earlier controversies involving the HCJ. Although the interaction among members of the judicial community is, by most accounts, diffuse rather than the stuff of conspiratorial decision making, some critics within religious communities in particular have accused these judicial "elites" of being involved in something more insidious aimed at an all-powerful judiciary. The interaction has led to several shared critiques among legal critics of the HCJ and certain religious constituencies. Legal critics have tended to suggest a model of a more restrained court that follows positive law, whereas many religious critics have sought a wholesale weakening of the judiciary.

Legal critics in Israel have reprimanded the HCJ publicly for making decisions within an "elite" community that is out of touch with the people (Gavison as cited in Shavit 1999), and within academic circles for making decisions on political cases that may endanger the public's trust in the independence of the judiciary (Hofnung 1996, 1999), or, more generally, deciding cases in a way that reinforces existing social and economic power relations rather than being socially transformative (Shamir 1990; Hirschl 1998). In the critiques of both the "elites" argument and those regarding public trust, cause lawyers are implicated, either as part of the community or as unwise litigants. Most of these legal critics have upheld less extravagant notions of the rule of law than those seen in the judicial community. They advocated limitations on the judiciary's activity on political issues and transparency in certain legal processes.

By contrast, religious constituencies that engage in public criticism of the judiciary have sought, ultimately, to decrease dramatically the role of the judiciary in the political system. In some cases, these critics prefer a theocracy to a democracy; in a theocracy, a secular notion of the rule of law would be obsolete. Only God's law, as interpreted by current religious authorities, would rule. Other religious critics do not specify the need for a theocracy but seek a severely truncated court that is, in addition, limited entirely to positive law. In both of these cases, religious critics prefer that issues of political salience to them be argued in the political arena of the parliament, where they can be veto players in a fractured coalition system. Although legal critics and religious critics of the judiciary share some of the same criticisms of HCJ activism and the tight-knit nature of the judicial community, they tend to be aware that their ultimate goals are in decided contrast to one another. Below, I mention some of the criticisms they share in common, focusing on the most extreme critiques, which have come from religious communities. All of these critiques share two qualities: they suggest that the norms of the judicial community continue to be an issue of contest and debate; and they accuse the judicial community (which they identify as the community around the justices) of being comprised of a small, elite set that is out of touch with the people.

Critics of the HCJ cite what they call the insularity of the HCJ and a closed set of lawyers and legal scholars. They argue that the insularity of this group makes the judiciary in Israel a fundamentally undemocratic institution. Legal scholars and parts of the popular press in Israel have provided harsh criticism of the High Court precisely for what they see as too much activism on behalf of natural rights, even against the will of the general society (Shavit 1999; Gavison 1998). Many critics in the popular press, and especially the orthodox and ultraorthodox press, have traced this activism to the incumbency of the president of the HCJ, Aharon Barak. The criticism of Barak seems to be related to a larger concern that the judicial community in Israel, directed by Barak, is too insular and comprised of "elites" who make decisions behind doors closed to the public, who themselves appoint judges and justices and who, in general, have far too much control over the judiciary in Israel. The judiciary is seen by some as a "judicial ideological collectivity" (Gavison as cited in Shavit 1999).

One renowned legal scholar in Israel—who has been part of the inner circle of the judicial community—has become a vocal and public critic of the HCJ and the judiciary. Ruth Gavison has criticized the HCJ on a number of levels, particularly its insularity. She argues that the judiciary is *too* independent, too separate from any public recourse, too insulated from criticism.

> The result is a situation in which one court, which effectively appoints itself, creates the constitution by means of its interpretation of the basic laws. And this occurs without any of the control mechanisms that exist in the United States. So from this point of view our situation is quite distinctive. The combination of judicial criticism of Knesset legislation, in a state where there is as yet no crystallized constitution, by a court whose justices are not elected but are appointed for life by the judicial system itself, creates a very problematic situation, in my opinion.[39]

This independence is accompanied, according to Gavison, by a paternalism that closes the public off from the decision-making process where judicial and constitutional issues arise. This lack of recourse is significant in a situation in which there is no standing constitution to override public or state whim. Rather, the public should be involved, she argues, in the development of constitutional principles. To her, it is a simple matter of democracy.

> I will go further: sometimes people tell me I am naive. That it is impossible to advance certain processes without a degree of paternalism. That the nation by itself will not be able to arrive, from within itself, at an enlightened, liberal state-constitutional format. And therefore, these people argue, a hush-hush policy is both legitimate and necessary. Up to a point I am willing to accept that argument. But I think that we have now reached a situation in which this enlightened paternalism is dangerous, because it is being used to play down moves that need to be raised for open public discussion.[40]

Here Gavison is criticizing selective prosecution among the police and judiciary, particularly of crimes in the political arena, as well as the "Or Commission," which was set up to investigate questions of how to reform the structure of the judicial system. That commission was, indeed, conducted very much away from the public eye. Gavison also criticizes High Court President Barak directly:

> This is the first time we have had a Supreme Court president who is one of the central writers in both the professional literature and the journalistic literature. He does his work by writing judgments, by closely managing the system of judges, by very closely managing the entire public judicial system, and by maintaining ramified connections with other authorities and with professional elites in Israel and internationally.[41]

Despite these problems, Gavison maintains, "One thing, which is agreed upon and essential, is to bolster human rights and proper administration."[42] However, the definition of human rights and proper administration, as well as their implementation, is at the heart of the conflict. Almost all of the critics, secular and religious, claim to be supporters of rights. What each means by rights varies dramatically. Moreover, what is meant by rights seems to vary along secular/nonsecular and pro-Western/non-pro-Western lines. In Gavison's words: "The second thing, which is played down and controversial, is the attempt to impose Western-secular-Jewish values on a society that has ceased to be a secular-Western society."[43] In other words, the content of the norms of the judicial community was a matter of the most fundamental ideological but also cultural contest.

The most severe criticism has been found in orthodox and ultra-orthodox presses. These condemnations affirm the claim of an elite community out of touch with the people as well as the conflict between secular—and religious— Jewish values, but take the attacks much further. Due to the HCJ's connection with this tight-knit community, the justices have been called, among other names, "our new Bolsheviks,"[44] "the real enemy of the religious public,"[45] "classist,"[46] "disconnected from the People,"[47] and "*goyim*" (plural of "*goy*," or non-Jews).[48] All of these epithets indicate that the justices are seen as foreign, separate, insulated, and, above all, against the interests of those who do not approve of extreme secularism in government or in society.

Haredi (ultra-orthodox) criticism of the HCJ, from both Ashkenazi and Mizrahi circles, became very strong in the early 1990s, in the aftermath of the 1987 *Shas* case (in which the Shas party lost its battle to bar reform and conservative converts who had converted outside of Israel from the Right of Return),[49] and the 1988 *Shakdiel* and *Poraz* cases (in which the HCJ affirmed, for the first time, women's right to sit on religious councils and even voting councils to elect municipal rabbis).[50] It also corresponds to a marked increase in the social and political power of Shas as a party.[51] However, the real uproar between Haredi and secular communities over the HCJ can be said to have begun, somewhat arbitrarily, with the publication of an article in *Yated Neeman*, a Jerusalem based ultra-orthodox (Ashkenazi) newspaper, in August 1996. In it, *Yated Neeman* began by attacking the HCJ and specifically its president:

> A simple glance at events of the past weeks speaks to a dangerous enemy who has raised himself against the religious public. . . .
> This dangerous enemy is called Aharon Barak.
> He is more powerful than the entire government administration; with force he overshadows the police, the legislature, as well as the executive. With one decision he can remove a Minister from his post, a political party from its ability to run in elections. The era of democracy is over; the era of government by the people is over.[52]

The article continues: "A man, estranged and patronizing, disconnected but supposedly raised up by the people, conducts a one-man revolution, which he calls 'judicial activism.'" As will be discussed further below, legal scholars who criticize the HCJ agree that the judicial activism of which *Yated* speaks was not the brainchild of, nor is it limited to, Barak. However, what is important in the *Yated* piece is the treatment of Barak, who represents for *Yated* the whole of judicial activism in Israel, as estranged, completely disconnected, and patronizing to "the people," which in this context means "the Jewish People." In other words, Barak is disconnected from the Jewish community—which *Yated* presents as that community he is supposed to serve—and is placed outside the boundaries of the community.[53] In as much as the judicial community believes in Barak's cause, it, too, is outside "the Jewish People." The use of Barak as the purveyor of judicial activism may have reflected the real belief of the author or may have been an attempt to avoid a wholesale attack on the judiciary writ large. In either case, the alienation from the principles behind "Barak's" judicial activism clearly sets the community of "the People" apart from the community around Barak.

Other religious critics of the HCJ, including Religious Zionist journalist and commentator Yair Sheleg, have argued that it is shortsighted to hold Barak alone responsible for the antireligious bent of the HCJ. Sheleg is the author of an important book delineating the boundaries among, and characteristics of, the various religious Jewish groups in Israel.[54] He argues that the ideological support of natural law as opposed to religious principles has been visible to anyone who would look at the past thirty years of HCJ decisions.

> I argue that the High Court is no more secular or liberal than . . . [it] was in the past. Its ideology today is the same ideology. In past cases, it was possible to see this [same ideology]; when there were debates, the decisions almost always came out in the favor of the seculars. For example, in the case of using televisions on Sabbath; the High Court decided in 1968 that it was permitted to use television on Sabbath. In the 1968 case [sic] . . . of Shalit, he brought up the question, "Who is a Jew." . . . The High Court declared, "do it" [register Shalit's son as Jewish, against the religious legal definition of Jewishness].[55]

According to Sheleg, the ideological proclivity of the High Court in favor of rights issues is visible at least going back to the *Shalit* case. Moreover, it was clear to any group wanting to make arguments on the basis of rights that it had a sympathetic court after the publication of the *Shalit* decision in 1969.[56]

After the *Yated* piece in August 1996, Haredi critics did not limit themselves to Barak alone. In *Yated Neeman*, again, in October 1996, P. Horev argued that the HCJ and the judicial community at large set themselves up as opposed to the "ignoramuses" who criticized them.

Justice Aharon Barak called the Legal Committee of the Knesset to meeting this week and said, in passing, that the attacks on the High Court of Justice "are based on a lack of understanding of the judicial process and the ways through which it is implemented." A simple lack of understanding. If only we were a little more of sound mind, we would have no criticism. It is only because we are so without understanding that we feel that someone is running wild.

In reality, it is not Barak who puts forth this explanation. It is an argument that is heard over and over in different variations. Legal thinkers regularly say that attacks on the High Court come from ignoramuses. In the absence of more a convincing interpretation, the "ignoramus" thesis is by far the most classist of all arguments.[57]

Horev explicitly draws attention to a community of legal thinkers, of whom Barak is a part, who are responsible for this "most classist of all arguments." He explicitly presents these legal thinkers as the enemies of "us," religious Jews who criticize the court. In his piece, we see both an explicit identification of (an oppressive) judicial community, and a highlighting of the conflict between communities. The (intra-)communal nature of this conflict, between communities in Israel and, more broadly, within the larger Jewish world, becomes clearer.

Others have attacked the HCJ in a manner that evokes an intracommunal conflict. Rabbi David Yossef is the son of Ovadia Yossef, the spiritual leader of Shas. In April 1997, David Yossef equated the High Court of Justice at large with *Haman*, a biblical enemy of the Ancient Israelites in the Esther story: "'HCJ' in the Gematria equals 'Haman,'" he said. Gematria is a numerology system associated with Jewish mysticism that dates as far back as the seventh to eleventh centuries.[58] Yossef argued that the Hebrew acronym for HCJ had the same numerological value as "Haman," 5–50–40, thus verifying the HCJ as "the real enemy of the religious public."[59] By appealing to religious sources to equate the HCJ with one of the archenemies of the Ancient Israelites in the Bible, Yossef marks the HCJ as a demon. The HCJ is equated with an evil figure and, even more significant for my analysis, the HCJ is identified with a figure presented in the Bible as outside the Israelite community and explicitly out to persecute it. The biblical and mystical references heighten the critique to a cosmic battle of good versus evil. Then returning to present Israel, D. Yossef continued: "The HCJ is controlling the state of Israel in a manner that is against the law,"[60] and he called on the religious public to overthrow the illegitimate rule of the HCJ.

Jonathan Rosenblum, an American-born journalist and Haredi activist, has also presented the HCJ as the enemy of the religious public. He has even more explicitly defined the HCJ and a narrow band of like-minded secularists in the Israeli society, on the one hand, and the religious communities, on the other hand, as two major communities with entirely opposing worldviews and interests: "It is the religious/chareidi [Haredi] community that finds itself most threatened by our new Bolsheviks in yuppie disguise. For the elites that dominate the media and judicial system correctly recognize the values of the religious community as the greatest challenge to their own, and religious Jews as the group least capable of being assimilated into the uniform society for which they yearn."[61]

Rosenblum referred to Gavison's interview with Ari Shavit in describing the judicial system as a "closed, insular society of like-minded people":[62]

> The appointment power vested in the Court President has led to a situation in which the justices of the Supreme Court bear an uncanny resemblance to one another both ideologically and sociologically. Israel's Supreme Court is effectively a Court of one: the Court President and fourteen clones. . . .
>
> That uniformity is continuous over time. With no input from the elected branches of government, there is no possibility of the shifts in judicial approach that regularly occur on the United States Supreme Court. . . .
>
> Like most cults, never exposed to opposing ideas, the Court is marked by a singular lack of humility.[63]

For Rosenblum, the closed, insular, communal or, as he put it, "cult" like nature of the HCJ-and-community is one of the most egregious challenges to democracy. However, in an interview, Rosenblum also made clear that his opinions on democracy must be foregrounded with the acknowledgment that he does not favor democracy as the ideal form of state.

> Well, I define democracy—if you ask me what I'd like to see here, first of all, it has to be very clear that democracy is not, for Orthodox Jews, an ideal state of government. I mean, we're not, nowhere do you find the term democracy. It's not a Torah term. But I don't view Israel as a Torah state either. I think democracy is the best system for allowing people of divergent beliefs to live together, so I have a small bias in favor of representative democracy where the basic law making authority resides in the elected branches of the government, where a constitutional framework is more directed toward setting the rules of the game rather than the ends of life.[64]

The judiciary is thus relegated to protecting constitutions (Israel has no constitution). The "ends" to which Rosenblum refers include many areas that some associated with rights (such as the right to pray in a certain way in public, to marry individuals in a certain group of people), but which many religious communities view as opposed to divine laws. If the judiciary does set the "ends of life," it is outside the bounds of real democracy: "When you enunciate enough goals, you can end up with a one party state. And it will be called, you know, the Soviet Socialist Republics. It will be called in the name of democracy or republican government, but [it will be done] by defining democracy in terms of goals and delegitimizing those who don't share those ultimate ends."[65]

The role of social movement lawyers is addressed directly in some of this criticism of the judicial community. Rosenblum, for example, cites the Association for Civil Rights in Israel, the Meretz Party, "civil libertarians" in general, and specific officials connected to the judicial community as involved in litigation, writing of laws, and other activities used to the benefit of an HCJ that has overstepped the bounds of democratic legality.[66] These tight connections between elites, including activist (or cause) lawyers are presented as a critical part of the problem. Others have directed their criticism at other social movements, such as the Movement for Progressive Judaism (the Reform Movement in Israel, which is also a social movement), and the Conservative Movement in Israel.[67]

As mentioned above, some commentators—usually critics—argue that the judicial activism of the HCJ is new. Many who make that argument trace it to the incumbency of the president of the HCJ, Aharon Barak, rather than a wider judicial community. Barak joined the HCJ in 1979. He rose steadily in the HCJ ranks to become deputy and then president of the HCJ both in 1995. Because Barak joined the HCJ in 1979, he postdated the beginning of the trend in the Israeli HCJ toward an increasing openness to rights issues, mentioned above. Furthermore, he became president of the HCJ only in 1995, thus postdating by a significant margin the onset of the HCJ challenge of rabbinical authorities in the late 1980s, for which he is often given credit by religious critics and others. Thus, the argument that Barak is the causal agent in the activism of the HCJ, reflected by its broad, rhetorical appeals to natural justice, does not stand up to the test of timing. However, what is important and has been demonstrated in this section is that critics of the court—whether attacking the HCJ at large or Barak in particular—highlight the communal nature of the HCJ and its supporters in the judicial community as a "closed" set, a "cult," "estranged and patronizing," against the Jewish People, and even an "ideological collectivity."

Moreover, this frenzied local and national media debate reflected both a change in the agenda of these religious communities, and a fundamental shift in the political agenda of the nation. Suddenly, the issues of religion and state, and even more acutely, the legitimacy of the judiciary, were at the center of media debates across the country. The controversy has continued unabated since. Ironically, this challenge regarding the place of the judiciary in a democracy emerged in large part in response to a set of HCJ decisions that undermined the institutional autonomy of state religious officials, although some subsequent decisions in other legal areas have added fuel to the fire. The important point for my analysis is that it is court decisions that drove the furious charges of these religious communities and the corresponding nationwide debate regarding the appropriate place of the judiciary in the Israeli polity.

VI. Conclusions

I have argued, by contrast to the critics mentioned above, that changes in the HCJ toward broad support of principles of rights have emerged through a process of interaction among members of an informal, diffuse judicial community. Since the 1970s, that community has increasingly included *non*elites, who nonetheless gain substantial professional power (although not wider social power) by virtue of membership in this community. More important, nonelite cause lawyers from major social movement organizations have been influential in the development of changing norms within that community. Indeed, I have argued that the norms of this community have changed over time through a process of conflict and debate in both formal legal processes (court cases and hearings) and informal processes (conferences, parties, classrooms). The wider society has joined these debates, as seen in the harsh criticism of the HCJ and its "elite" community.

By taking politicized cases to the HCJ, cause lawyers contributed to increasing that institution's political salience, as predicted by the work of Hendley (1996). Indeed, cause lawyers and the HCJ worked within a diffuse judicial community in which major shifts in legal thinking on the HCJ became "public" communal knowledge. Major shifts in legal thinking across the community were influential on all members in as much as they lived, worked, socialized, and thought about law in conversation with that community. Moreover, through participation in the diffuse, outer circle of the judicial community, HCJ justices and cause lawyers knew one another at least by reputation. A good reputation in the eyes of justices had a strong impact on justices' initial impressions of a case and their willingness to take it seriously.

It is the wider, more diffuse "outer" circle of the judicial community that is most relevant for the diffuse, normative interaction I have identified. Cause lawyers did not direct HCJ policy, although they might influence it indirectly. Some interviews presented above suggest that changes in thinking on the HCJ had a strong impact on cause lawyers' litigation strategies. This impact was especially pronounced in (strategic) decisions to turn to litigation and in choices of legal arguments presented to the HCJ. However, justices did not direct the a priori commitment of cause lawyers to the use of litigation as an important and legitimate means of achieving rights for individuals. To the contrary, by increasingly taking political cases to the HCJ, cause lawyers pushed the court in that direction and increased the standing of those on the court who had been advocating these changes.

The story of cause lawyers in Israel suggests an important area of inquiry, namely, links between cause lawyers and the state,[68] and particularly judicial communities in small countries such as Israel. Indeed, in any country of similar size with a small population, limited number of law schools, one to several major cities, and active high court, the existence and role of a judicial community surrounding that court should be investigated. Cause lawyers' roles in that community may be critical, as has been the case in Israel, to their success or failure at achieving their judicial and political goals. As has been demonstrated in other work, it is important to note that cause lawyer and social movement goals in litigating may be a positive judicial outcome or the use of litigation for publicity, consciousness raising, membership mobilization, and the like (McCann 1994). However, judicial decision making (particularly the reasoning given for a decision) is one of the critical factors in the legal as well as the larger political outcome; a negative decision with reasoning that supports the cause may be quite useful politically, whereas the reverse may have a negative outcome for the cause. Trends in judicial decision making, far from being an outmoded line of inquiry, are of deep concern for cause lawyers, who seek specific outcomes for ideological reasons.

Cause lawyers in some places may be more closely connected than had been assumed—and, indeed, fruitfully connected—with social and professional circles linking them with members of the state judiciary, government lawyers, and others. The close connections of a judicial community may be relevant to judicial trends in certain local contexts of larger countries as well (at both upper- and lower-level courts), where lawyers and judges may have attended the same schools and may well participate in relatively small professional and social circles that constitute the same sort of diffuse normative environment seen in Israel. To put it in the terms of the question presented at the outset of this chapter, cause lawyers' ability to use courts and law to engender meaningful political change should be increased dramatically when they are able to participate in a judicial community. Through this participation they should have access to information about legal trends and reputation of justices and judges, and they should be able to engage in the formal and informal debates through which legal norms develop. Indeed, the most critical implication of my argument, if it is correct, is that cause lawyer participation in such diffuse, normative communities will allow them access to the debates through which the norms of those communities develop and change. Such participation, then, offers cause lawyers no less than a place at the table at which one dominant set of rules of the game is decided, debated, and changed.

Do these debates matter for meaningful court-initiated political change? I argue that they do. At the beginning of this chapter, I suggested a definition of meaningful court-initiated political change that included the *possibility* of society-wide attitudinal changes. However, more important (and likely), I posited, would be changes in concrete individual-level practices, and successful norm-, rules- or agenda-setting brought about by courts. Although I believe that deeply important changes in individual-level practices resulted for many women, especially, as a result of the HCJ's entry into the religious law conflict, I have not demonstrated those here. What I have demonstrated is a fundamental shift in the norms of the judicial community, as it newly incorporated nonelites into its ranks, including key cause lawyers. This shift included a gravitation toward an elevated notion of the rule of law, a strong regard for "natural justice" (Zamir 1996), and a move from legal formalism to a far more activist court. Through these normative changes, the HCJ made decisions that changed the rules for many actors, in this case, religious authorities within the state. Moreover, as demonstrated in section five, a concerted new flood of criticism of the normative changes in the judicial community marked an important political focus within ultra-orthodox and some orthodox communities. To say that these criticisms were heated is the height of understatement. Attacks on the HCJ in the press resulted in Knesset hearings on whether such attacks should be allowed and they were followed by death threats to the president of the HCJ and included at least one demonstration of at least 200,000 ultra-orthodox men, who descended upon the HCJ building en masse in February 1999 to criticize the tyranny of (HCJ president) Barak. In an ironic sense, these critiques are an indicator of HCJ agenda-setting: the HCJ challenged the autonomy of state religious institutions and authorities, and those authorities (or their supporters) fought back, attacking the HCJ, the judiciary, and at times, the secular legal system at large. It is almost certainly not the agenda the HCJ, or the judicial community, had in mind. However, court actions did lead to meaningful political change, setting the domestic national agenda to focus on religious-secular conflict and the legitimacy of the judiciary throughout the 1990s.

Notes

This chapter emerges from a larger research project and, therefore, I am indebted to many organizations for their support: the National Science Foundation (SES 9906136, Migdal PI, Woods CO-PI); the Social Science Research Council National Dissertation

Fellowship Program; the Social Science Research Council Near and Middle East Research and Training Program; the Dorot Foundation; the Near Eastern Languages and Civilizations Department, University of Washington; the Department of Political Science, Hebrew University in Jerusalem, especially Menachem Hofnung; and the Department of Sociology and Anthropology, Tel Aviv University, especially Ronen Shamir. The Department of Political Science and Center for Jewish Studies at the University of Florida provided research leave during which major portions of this chapter were written, and the Center for Middle Eastern Studies at Harvard University provided a stimulating working environment during that leave period. I am grateful for the generously critical comments of the following scholars: Scott Barclay, Peter Fitzpatrick, Jay Krishnan, Michael McCann, Steve Meili, Joel Migdal, Austin Sarat, Stuart Scheingold, Ben Smith, members of the Cause Lawyering III Workshop in Cachan, France, October 2002, and the members of the University of Florida Department of Political Science colloquium series. Errors are, of course, my responsibility alone.

1. That law was altered through precedent by a later HCJ decision, published in 1989, allowing for new immigrants, converted in a nonorthodox process before arriving in Israel, to be considered Jewish for the purposes of the Ministry of Interior's registry of one's religion: H.C. 264/87 *Shas v. Office of Population Registry*. 43 (2) 727 (1987) (Hebrew).

2. The HCJ was not uniformly an advocate of rights. Indeed, it has been criticized on both sides, for being too activist (see, for example, Gavison 1998) and for being not consistent enough on rights, particularly on issues of security or Palestinian rights (see, for example, Shamir 1990; Dotan 1999).

3. Three cases were heard together: H.C. 5070/95 The Masorti (Conservative) Movement of Israel v. Ministry of the Interior; H.C. 2901/97 World Union of Progressive Judaism v. Ministry of the Interior; and H.C. 392/99 Ministry of the Interior v. District Court of Jerusalem.

4. Dan Izenberg, "Court Allows Gay Man to Inherit Partner's Estate" in *The Jerusalem Post*, November 15, 2004, p. 4; Dan Izenberg, "Supreme Court Gives Lesbian Couple Right to Adopt Each Other's Children" in *The Jerusalem Post*, January 11, 2005, p. 1.

5. All translations from Hebrew are my own.

6. Israel Central Bureau of Statistics 1999. Also available on line: http://www.cbs.gov.il/israel_in_figures/mainmenu-e.htm.

7. This figure comes from a discussion with legal scholars and lawyers in Israel, who approximated based on the number of lawyers listed in the Israel Bar directory (available to members).

8. The schema of a division between commercial and criminal lawyers, who tend to be associated with the Israel Bar, and constitutionally oriented lawyers, who tend to be associated with the HCJ, comes through interviews with Israeli legal scholars, including especially Yoav Dotan, November 1999, Jerusalem.

9. By major social movements, I refer to long-standing organizations that have become known to the HCJ through the consistent use of litigation over the past decade or two. Cause lawyers' involvement in the judicial community worked at two levels.

10. Personal interview, CA, Jerusalem, April 2000.

11.   Zamir seems to define natural justice, for the Israeli case, as referring to basic principles that do not require legislation but provide the groundwork for a broad range of legal questions. He associates the rule of law with natural justice, particularly as it requires that the actions of the government remain within the confines of the law, and that the official decisions of public servants not be subject to conflict of interests (Zamir 1996: 8, 28; Zamir and Zysblat 1996, citing Aharon Barak in a 1980 HCJ decision, 172, 174–76).

12.   Basic Law: Human Dignity and Freedom; and Basic Law: Freedom of Occupation.

13.   Personal communication, Ruth Gavison, Jerusalem, April 2000.

14.   Personal interview, Frances Raday, Jerusalem, June 1997.

15.   Ibid.

16.   Personal communication, Ruth Gavison, April 2000, Jerusalem.

17.   Personal interview, JA, July 2000, Israel (Hebrew).

18.   Personal interview, LS, July 2000, Israel (Hebrew).

19.   Personal interview, CB, April 2000, Israel (Hebrew).

20.   Ibid.

21.   Personal interview, Frances Raday, June 1997, Jerusalem.

22.   Ibid.

23.   Personal interview, Frances Raday, June 1997, Jerusalem.

24.   Personal interview, CB, April 2000, Israel (Hebrew).

25.   Interview, CA, April 2000, Israel.

26.   Personal interview, CB, February 2000, Israel (Hebrew).

27.   Personal interview, Rabbi Uri Regev, director and attorney for the Israel Religious Action Center of the Movement for Progressive Judaism in Israel (Reform Movement), August 1997, Jerusalem.

28.   Personal interview, CB, February 2000, Israel (Hebrew).

29.   H.C. 104/87 Nevo v. The Jewish Agency et al. P.D. 44(4) 749 (1990); H.C. 262/62 Peretz v. Local Council of Kfar Shmaryahu 16 (3) P.D. 2101 (1962); H.C. 257/89 Hoffman et al. v. The Guardian of the Western Wall P.D. 48 (2) 263 (1994); H.C. 3358/95 Hoffman et al. v. The Guardian of the Western Wall. Transcript of the decision is available in Hebrew at the Israel High Court of Justice Web site, http://www.court.gov.il; H.C. 953/87 The Labor Party, Tel Aviv Branch Office, et al. v. The Tel-Aviv-Yaffo Municipal Council, et al. P.D. 42 (1988) (Poraz); H.C. 153/87 Shakdiel v. The Minister of Religion, et al. P.D. 42(2) 309 (1988).

30.   H.C. 104/87 Nevo v. The Jewish Agency et al. P.D. 44(4) 749 (1990) (Hebrew); H.C. 153/87 Shakdiel v. The Minister of Religion, et al. P.D. 42(2) 309 (1988) (Hebrew); H.C. 953/87 The Labor Party, Tel Aviv Branch Office, et al. v. The Tel-Aviv-Yaffo Municipal Council, et al. P.D. 42 (1988) (Hebrew) (Poraz); H.C. 2301/86 Shoshana Miller v. Minister of the Interior et al. (1986); H.C. 1003/92 Haia Bavli v. The Rabbinical Court of Tel Aviv-Yaffo.

31.   NIF Web site, http://www.nif.org, as of June 2001.

32.   NIF Web site: http://www.nif.org/contact/intro.html., as of June 2001.

33.   Personal interview, Esther Sivan, IWN Law Center, June 1997, Jerusalem.

34. The establishment of this court has led to what is called a "race for jurisdiction." In a divorce, whichever party files first gets to choose which court will hear the financial and custodial parts of the case, the secular Family Court or the Rabbinical Court. Typically, men prefer the Rabbinical Court while women prefer the Family Court, as the perception is that men are treated better in the former, women in the latter. Thus, the race to file first is quite literally a race.

35. Sanctions include closing bank accounts, rescinding driver's licenses, barring exit from the country, jail, and the like. Although these are stringent measures, they have rarely been applied. According to IWN documents, rabbinical courts have only applied sanctions (including jail, which was allowed before the 1995 law) a total of eighteen times, with Haifa accounting for half of those. (The Haifa Rabbinical Court is known for being fairly liberal.)

36. Personal interview, Daniela Valensi, IWN Knesset lobbyist and IWN representative for informal seat on the Knesset Committee on the Status of Women, Israel Women's Network, July 1997, Jerusalem.

37. Ibid.

38. Personal interview, Rabbi Uri Regev, IRAC, Jerusalem, 1997.

39. Gavison in interview with Shavit 1999.

40. Ibid.

41. Ibid.

42. Gavison cited in Shavit 1999.

43. Ibid.

44. Rosenblum 1999. Rosenblum writes from an Ashkenazi, ultra-orthodox (Haredi) perspective. He runs a social organization in Jerusalem called "One People" or "One Nation," which advocates for understanding of the Haredi community in the English language world, particularly in Israel, England, and the United States.

45. Eilan 1997.

46. Referring to much of the judiciary, not only the HCJ: Horev, "Disguisers of the Judicial Process." *Yated HaShavua* is an ultra-orthodox paper published in Jerusalem.

47. Eilan and Elon 1996.

48. Eilan 1996: 3a.

49. H.C. 264/87 Shas v. Office of Population Registry. 43 (2) 727 (1987) (Hebrew).

50. H.C. 153/87 Shakdiel v. The Minister of Religion, et al. P.D. 42(2) 309 (1988) (Hebrew); H.C. 953/87 The Labor Party, Tel Aviv Branch Office, et al. v. The Tel-Aviv-Yaffo Municipal Council, et al. P.D. 42 (1988) (Hebrew).

51. Personal interview, CB, April 2000 (Hebrew); personal interview, JA, July 2000 (Hebrew). Shas is a religious political party that claims to represent the Mizrahi community in Israel.

52. Velder 1996.

53. The fact that *Yated* views the Jewish community as the one that the HCJ is suppose to serve is significant. It sets *Yated* apart from human rights and civil rights advocates who argue that the HCJ should serve the entirety of Israeli citizens, including Palestinians and other non-Jews (Espanioly 1994), as well as the human rights principles of the international legal community, particularly via-à-vis Palestinians in the Occupied Terri-

tories (Shamir 1990). *Yated*'s position on the questions of citizenship and membership, debated at length in Israeli scholarship, is made clear in assigning the community to whom the HCJ is ultimately responsible (Peled 1992; Kook 1995; Peled and Shafir 1996).

54. Sheleg 2000.

55. Personal interview, Yair Sheleg, Jerusalem, June 2000 (Hebrew).

56. Ibid.

57. Horev 1996: 2.

58. Holtz 1984: 21. During this period, gematria was used as a sometimes-fanciful method of interpreting the biblical texts. In later years, it became associated with various mystical methods of attaining knowledge of or closeness to the Divine.

59. Eilan 1997.

60. Ibid.

61. Rosenblum 1999: 6.

62. Ibid., 9.

63. Ibid., 10.

64. Personal interview, Jonathan Rosenblum, May 2000, Jerusalem.

65. Personal interview, Jonathan Rosenblum, May 2000, Jerusalem.

66. Rosenblum 1998.

67. "Strong Reactions Against Large Numbers of Shabbat Desecrations and Foothold Given Reform Jews in the Aftermath of an HCJ Decision" 1996; see also Rosenblum 1997.

68. See also Hatcher, and Southworth in this volume.

References

Barzilai, Gad. 1998. "Courts as Hegemonic Institutions and Social Change." *Politika* 3: 31–51.

Bisharat, George. 1998. "Attorneys for the People, Attorneys for the Land: The Emergence of Cause Lawyering in the Israeli-Occupied Territories," in *Cause Lawyering: Political Commitments and Professional Responsibilities*, ed. Austin Sarat and Stuart Scheingold. New York and Oxford: Oxford University Press.

Blumberg, Abraham S. 1967. "The Practice of Law as a Confidence Game: Organizational Cooptation of a Profession." *Law and Society Review* 1, no. 2: 15–39.

Cohn, Chaim. 1974. "The Spirit of Israel Law." *Israel Law Review* 9, no. 4: 456–62.

Dotan, Yoav. 1998. "Cause Lawyers Crossing the Lines: Patterns of Fragmentation and Cooperation between State and Civil Rights Lawyers in Israel." *International Journal of the Legal Profession* 5, no. 2/3: 193–208.

———. 1999. "Judicial Rhetoric, Government Lawyers, and Human Rights: The Case of the Israeli High Court of Justice during the *Intifada*." *Law and Society Review* 33, no. 2: 319–63.

Edelman, Martin. 1994. "The Judicialization of Politics in Israel." *International Political Science Review* 15, no 2: 177–86.

Epp, Charles R. 1998. *The Rights Revolution: Lawyers, Activists, and Supreme Courts in Comparative Perspective*. Chicago: University of Chicago Press.

Epstein, Lee, and Joseph F. Kobylka. 1992. *The Supreme Court and Legal Change: Abortion and the Death Penalty*. Chapel Hill: University of North Carolina Press.

Espanioly, Nabila. 1994. "Palestinian Women in Israel: Identity in Light of the Occupation," in *Women and the Israeli Occupation: The Politics of Change*, ed. Tamer Mayer. New York: Routledge.

Gavison, Ruth. 1998. *The Constitutional Revolution: A Reality or Self-Fulfilling Prophecy?* Jerusalem: Israel Democracy Institute (Hebrew).

Granovetter, Mark. 1983. "The Strength of Weak Ties: A Network Theory Revisited." *Sociological Theory* 1: 201–33.

Halperin-Kaddari, Ruth. 1997. "Thinking Legal Pluralism in Israel: The Interaction Between the High Court of Justice and Rabbinical Courts." *I'unei Mishpat* 11, no. 3: 683–747 (Hebrew).

Haltom, William and Michael McCann. 2004. *Distorting the Law: Politics, Media, and the Litigation Crisis*. Chicago: University of Chicago Press.

Hendley, Kathryn. 1996. *Trying to Make Law Matter: Legal Reform and Labor Law in the Soviet Union*. Ann Arbor: University of Michigan.

Hirschl, Ran. 1998. "Israel's 'Constitutional Revolution': The Legal Interpretation of Entrenched Civil Liberties in an Emerging Neo-Liberal Economic Order." *American Journal of Comparative Law* 46 (Summer): 427.

Hofnung, Menachem. 1996. "The Unintended Consequences of Unplanned Legislative Reform: Constitutional Politics in Israel." *American Journal of Comparative Law*.

———. 1999. "Israeli Constitutional Politics: The Fragility of Impartiality." *Israel Affairs* 5, no. 2/3.

Holtz, Barry W. 1984. *Back to the Sources: Reading the Classic Jewish Texts*. New York: Summit Books.

Kaufman, Ilana. 1997. *Arab National Communism in the Jewish State*. Gainesville, FL: University Press of Florida, 1997.

Kook, Rebecca. 1995. "Dilemmas of Ethnic Minorities in Democracies: The Effect of Peace on the Palestinians in Israel." *Politics and Society* 23, no. 3: 309–36.

Kretzmer, David. 1990. "Forty Years of Public Law." *Israel Law Review* 24, no. 3: 341–67.

Lahav, Pnina. 2000. "Up Against the Wall: Women's Legal Struggle to Pray at the Western Wall in Jerusalem" in *Israel Studies Bulletin* 16, no. 19: 19–22.

———. 1997. *Judgement in Jerusalem: Chief Justice Simon Agranat and the Zionist Century*. Berkeley, Calif.: University of California Press.

Mazie, Steven V., and Patricia J. Woods. 2003. "Religion, Contentious Politics, and the Women of the Wall: The Benefits of Collaboration in Participant Observation at Intense, Multi-Focal Events." *Field Methods* 15, no. 1 (February): 25–50.

McCann, Michael W. 1994. *Rights at Work: Pay Equity Reform and the Politics of Legal Mobilization*. Chicago: University of Chicago Press.

McCann, Michael W., and Helena Silverstein. 1998. "Rethinking Law's 'Allurements': A

————. 1999. "The Arrogance of Israel's Elites." *Jewish Observer,* December: 6–15.

"Strong Reactions Against Large Numbers of Shabbat Desecrations and Foothold Given Reform Jews in the Aftermath of an HCJ Decision." 1996. *HaMotzia,* November 24.

Velder, Haim. 1996. "The Sheen Dims" (a play on words, Barak's name also meaning lightning or sheen) in his column, "Before the Mirror." *Yated Neeman,* August 25 (Hebrew).

CHAPTER ELEVEN

Transgressive Cause Lawyering in the Developing World

The Case of India

JAYANTH K. KRISHNAN

I. Introduction

One long-held convention of the legal profession has been that a lawyer needs to maintain what Max Weber might call a rational distance from the client—whereby the lawyer is careful not to step outside the sphere of neutrality that embodies her role as a professional advocate. This "legal professionalism norm"[1] was discussed nearly thirty years ago by William Simon (1978), who then noted that although the lawyer is charged with zealously defending her client's interests, at the same time principles of professional conduct recommend retaining a detached, impartial stance toward the larger scale implications of this advocacy. The argument was that if this legal professionalism norm is violated and lawyers start to become identified particularly with their less popular clients, the negative image associated with such clients might damage the name of the representing lawyer, not to mention the rest of the members of the bar.

In the 1990s, Professors Stuart Scheingold and Anne Bloom (1998) began to identify a set of lawyers in the United States whom they found intentionally disregarding, or "transgressing," this "generally accepted . . . [norm] of legal practice" (212). As Scheingold and Bloom found, these "cause lawyers" challenged the legal professionalism norm by viewing clients as instrumental for pursuing larger social and political goals, and by attempting to embody the causes that they represented (see also Kennedy 1987). However, as Scheingold and Bloom importantly discovered, the degree of transgression varied among their cause lawyers. Whether and how much cause lawyers engaged in transgressing the legal professionalism norm was affected by personal motivations,[2] the political ethos, the market for legal services, *and* primarily the practice site—or the professional office environment in which the lawyer worked (Scheingold and Bloom 1998: 210). Scheingold and Bloom's systematic data supporting their "mid-level theory" (209) is impressive, but one question that emerges is how generalizable their findings are to cause lawyers in other countries.

In this chapter, I shall argue that with some modifications and additions, Scheingold and Bloom's thesis indeed applies to cause lawyers in a rather unlikely setting—India. I use the word "unlikely" because as we shall see, in critical ways the Indian and American legal environments are very different. Unlike in the United States, in India most lawyers are solo practitioners who work as courtroom litigators. Furthermore, because they lack the ability, time, and resources most Indian lawyers refrain from transgressing the legal professionalism norm. But with this said there are those that exhibit differing degrees of cause lawyering behavior. In fact, Scheingold and Bloom's framework provides conceptual utility for studying cause lawyers in India; only some adaptations are required in the specific independent variables they identify.

For example, in India it is primarily the *practice arena* together with professional prestige, motivations, political climate, and market forces that interact to influence the actions of cause lawyers. By practice arena, I mean the actual, physical court in which the Indian cause lawyer works. Upon graduation from law school, an Indian lawyer interested in practicing usually will take up an apprenticeship with an experienced lawyer who practices in one of three arenas: a lower level district court; a state High Court; or the Supreme Court of India. Where that law graduate starts will depend on several factors, including law school performance, geographic location, personal ambition, "connections," and the like. And it is common that the court where the law graduate apprentices will be the court in which she or he practices as a lawyer until retirement.

Most practicing lawyers are also members of a national lawyers' association known as the Bar Council of India (BCI). The BCI has codified within its rules of professional responsibility a regulation paralleling the legal professionalism norm discussed above (see Part VI, *Bar Council of India Rules*[3]). But in India, how closely a lawyer adheres to the legal professionalism norm depends upon whether she or he is practicing at the district court level, the state High Court level, or in the Supreme Court. Generally, the higher the court in which an Indian lawyer practices, the more likely this practitioner will be actively transgressing the legal professionalism norm. In fact, highly transgressive behavior itself has become arguably a type of norm within the Indian Supreme Court, challenging the traditional legal professionalism norm advocated by the BCI. Conversely at the other end, practitioners at the district court level tend not to stray from the traditional legal professionalism norm. (The level of transgressiveness of practitioners in the state High Courts tends to fall in between.)

What accounts for why there is more transgression in the upper judiciary than the lower courts? For one thing, the Indian courts are extremely stratified in terms of reputation. For example, because of the power it wields and the legitimacy it holds, the Supreme Court is the most highly thought-of court in the country by the legal profession (see, e.g., Sathe 2002; Baxi 2001; Austin 2000).[4] In stark contrast, because they are under-funded, poorly maintained, gridlocked, and inefficient, the district courts are loathed by not only politicians and the public, but by many within the legal community (Galanter and Krishnan 2004). Perhaps not surprisingly, lawyers who practice in the Supreme Court, and to a lesser extent in the state High Courts, benefit, prestige-wise, from working within these respective institutions. These lawyers are generally accorded a high level of respect or status—or professional prestige—from their colleagues within the legal profession. On the other hand, lawyers who practice at the district court level tend to have lower levels of such professional prestige.

Given their positions within the profession, one might reasonably think that upper court lawyers—because they have more to lose—might be reluctant to act in ways that jeopardize their privileged standing. By the same token, lower court lawyers might be the most likely risk-takers, given that they seemingly have little to lose. As we shall find, however, upper court lawyers in India actually tend to act much more trangressively than their lower court counterparts. The courts in which these upper court lawyers practice, unlike where lower court lawyers work, provide them with more prestige, which they then use as an important resource to challenge or transgress the legal professionalism norm.

This professional prestige, as we shall also see, is not static, and within a particular practice arena it can be diminished or enhanced. That professional prestige might matter to lawyers is not a novel point, but in India this concept deserves accentuation. Some scholars have traced this almost obsession with professional status to the historic influence of caste on social relations (see, e.g., Chatterjee 1989, 1993; Srinivas 1996; Beteille 1996, 1997). For centuries individuals were classified on the basis of both the caste into which they were born and their family profession. One's professional prestige was often determined by one's caste membership (Srinivas 1966). Yet professional prestige was not necessarily fixed; acquiring a better job and more money, gaining greater education, moving within more elite social circles, adopting particular normative behavioral patterns, and fostering trusting relationships with higher-ups were just some ways of increasing one's status (see Srinivas 1966; Dumont 1980 [1966]; Galanter 1984; Quigley 1993).[5] Furthermore, one's professional prestige was, and continues to be, important for many Indians because of how it relates to the concept of karma. Traditionally, the idea was that by building up goodwill, trust, and other positive attributes, one could move up the status-oriented, caste-based, professional ladder—either within this life or alternatively in the next. Although these ancient customs arguably are no longer as strictly believed in or as adhered to today, as discussed below the effects of this tradition continue to play out in various ways (see also, e.g., Nandy 1992; Menski 2003).

This chapter, then, shall proceed in the following manner. In section two, I give a more detailed overview of the Scheingold-Bloom argument. I further explain what they mean by "transgressiveness," summarize their theoretical position, and discuss their findings. In section three, I describe why at first blush it would seem implausible that the Scheingold-Bloom model could apply to the legal setting in India. As detailed accounts correctly suggest, the Indian and American legal environments, typically speaking, are incomparable. But despite these seemingly irreconcilable differences, as I show in section four, there is a subset of lawyers whose behavior exhibits similar types of variation as the American cause lawyers described by Scheingold and Bloom. Accordingly in this section, I draw upon their model to theorize why certain Indian cause lawyers engage in transgressive activism while others are more cautious. In section five, I offer preliminary evidence supporting my argument, and in section six I conclude by proposing that elements of my model combined with that of Scheingold and Bloom's move us closer to capturing a more comprehensive explanation of why cause lawyers do what they do.

II. The Scheingold and Bloom Argument

Scheingold and Bloom strive to explain what factors affect how transgressively cause lawyers will behave. For these two scholars, transgressiveness has a very specific meaning; it is that the "professional standards of legal practice" (212)—especially the standard emphasizing the "professional" role the lawyer is to play vis-à-vis her or his client—are pushed to their limits and beyond by the cause lawyer. Yet transgressive cause lawyering has different gradations, and as Scheingold and Bloom note, its manifestation "varies widely among cause lawyers" (213). They contend that a transgressive continuum is present; at one end cause lawyers act very much like conventional lawyers. Such cause lawyers tend to work in corporate law firms and offer limited, basic unmet legal needs. It is rare for these lawyers to become deeply engaged in the causes on which they are working. Because of the structure of their work environment, these corporate cause lawyers are constrained to work on issues that do not jeopardize firm profits or conflict with wealthy client interests. While some incentives may exist for cause lawyers in corporate settings to pursue *pro bono* initiatives (such as receiving positive publicity for their efforts), Scheingold and Bloom conclude that, for the most part, "the more transgressive one's aspirations the less" (229) rewarding corporate practice will be.

In moving along the continuum, away from the corporate category, Scheingold and Bloom identify another set of cause lawyers who are likely to act in a more transgressive manner. This group consists of salaried attorneys who typically work in public agencies or for nongovernmental organizations. These individuals are best viewed as moderates. By not having to worry about generating fees from clients, salaried lawyers can focus on working for causes in which they believe (i.e., women's rights, legal aid, and labor initiatives). Also, in comparison with the grueling hours many corporate types are required to bill, salaried lawyers work "normal" hours which allows them to engage in politically transgressive activities away from the job (Scheingold and Bloom 1998: 235–36). But even with this relative flexibility, salaried lawyers are constrained by several factors, including: their own personal politics that sometimes conflict with their required duties; institutional rules within their job setting that limit their options; and the availability of outside resources that fund their employment positions.

If corporate cause lawyers are at one end and salaried cause lawyers are in the middle, then at the other end of the continuum are cause lawyers who work in small firms. Scheingold and Bloom discovered that among the various types of lawyers in their study, those who worked in small firms were able to act in the most transgressive fashion. Of course, given the competition within the legal market, these small firm lawyers are required at times to take on less redeemable, yet lucrative, clients in order to "pay the bills." Prioritizing economic considerations, on occasion, also means having to decline more open-ended, riskier cases that the small firm lawyer may believe are socially worthy or politically exciting (Scheingold and Bloom 1998: 246). For many small firm lawyers who enter this career with hopes of transforming the legal system, such dreams confront the economic, political, and emotional hardships that accompany this type of practice. Ambitions of making widespread change are replaced by goals of helping those on an individual, case-by-case level. Even with these constraints, though, Scheingold and Bloom document how such a work environment offers important opportunities for the transgressively oriented lawyer to succeed. Usually, the workplace atmosphere is encouraging and lawyers share the same ideological commitment toward transgressive legal aid. Financial pressures, while an issue, are not nearly as intense as in corporate settings. Taken together, such a situation allows small firm lawyers to engage in relatively more transgressive behavior than their counterparts.

Scheingold and Bloom support their assertion that practice site along with lawyer motivations affects transgressiveness with a rich set of data. The authors are sensitive to show that within each of these work areas variation occurs. Not all small firm cause lawyers act in a highly transgressive manner; likewise not all corporate cause lawyers are shackled to the norms that govern their practices. Furthermore, they emphasize that their model is not static, nor is their classification scheme mutually exclusive. Their continuum simply illustrates general patterns that they hope move us toward a more comprehensive theory of cause lawyering behavior. The question I address throughout the rest of this chapter is whether this continuum is applicable outside of the American context. In the next section, I describe the legal environment within India. At first glance, it might seem that there is no comparison between the two countries. But as we shall shortly discover, there indeed is room for a version of the Scheingold-Bloom model to apply to cause lawyers in India.

III. The Legal Environment in India—
A Seemingly Distinctive Setting

In the West, and particularly in the United States, many commentators accuse cause lawyers of hindering the issues they set out to champion.[6] A common refrain is that cause lawyers are too eager to steer causes toward litigation, while ignoring other possible avenues of influence (Handler 1978; Olson 1984). Cause lawyers, as the argument goes, are preoccupied with self-aggrandizement and thus narrowly construct their strategies to fit with their own expertise (see Katz 1982). Such elites often take social justice issues hostage (see O'Neill 1985). They frame issues, structure the discourse, and organize campaigns mainly through legal means, and consequently, they divert important resources away from tactics that have more significant long-term effects (Scheingold 1974; Gabel and Kennedy 1984; Tushnet 1984; Rosenberg 1991; see also McCann and Silverstein 1998: 262–64).

As is well known, the works of McCann (1994) and McCann and Silverstein (1998) place this critique into serious question. Cause lawyers, at least in the United States, do not solely operate off of "personal political beliefs and abstract programmatic commitments" (McCann and Silverstein 1998: 262). Documented evidence from these studies shows that cause lawyers can be multidimensional actors depending upon: their professional and political background; their role in shaping the cause; the organizational structure of social movement allies; and the overarching political and societal attitudes toward the cause. In optimal circumstances, cause lawyers are instrumental in combining legal strategies with mass-based tactics when pursuing a cause. Also, given the right conditions, these experts can help to create a legal and political consciousness and promote a shared rights discourse (see Kidder and Miyazawa 1993; McCann and Silverstein 1998).

In India, most lawyers—conventional and cause-oriented alike—possess few, if any, of the characteristics described by McCann and Silverstein. Marc Galanter's observation from years back still remains generally true: "Among the prominent features of Indian lawyers are their orientation to courts to the exclusion of other legal settings; the orientation to litigation rather than advising, negotiating or planning; their conceptualism and orientation to rules; their individualism; and their lack of specialization" (1989: 282; see also Epp 1998; Krishnan 2001).

Most Indian lawyers are rarely involved in noncourtroom activities, let alone mobilizing or nurturing social movements. Negotiating, strategizing, fostering a shared understanding of the law, advising, and participating in political activism are tasks left to others (Galanter 1989; Epp 1998; Krishnan 2001). Indian cause lawyers, in particular, tend to become involved in causes late in the game, and their ties to clients and activists are fleeting. Moreover, Indian cause lawyers, like conventional lawyers, are conditioned to think in narrow terms, focusing their efforts on litigation strategies. Most are atomistic actors who deal with clients, cases, and causes in a discrete, isolated fashion. Rarely are there long-term objectives vis-à-vis clients, nor do cause lawyers have the incentive (or specialization) to perform anything but the most basic of services (Epp 1998; Krishnan 2001). Furthermore, because individuals and groups interested in cause-oriented issues tend to be resource-poor and disorganized, they generally do not provide a market for cause lawyers who may wish to help but, given their own constraints, are unable to do so.

Another problem is that the institutional structure of the courts is more conducive to abuse than to cause lawyering. Procedural laws allow lawyers of clients who oppose cause lawyering petitions to submit endless interlocutory appeals. This results in massive delays in judgments and vast backlogs in cases (Galanter and Krishnan 2003, 2004).[7] Because these opposition lawyers are traditionally paid per court appearance, they have little incentive to resolve cases with cause lawyers in a timely fashion. Opposition lawyers become masters in the art of perpetuation and manipulate the civil and criminal codes to force cases to remain in the system for decades.[8] The conditions thus seem far from ripe for cause lawyering to exist on any scale in India. Since most Indian cause lawyers do not focus on long-term strategies, engage in diverse mobilization tactics, think of causes beyond individual clients, and work with other lawyers and nonlawyers on larger cause-oriented goals, the outlook is bleak for those relying on cause lawyers to make social change.

Therefore, applying the Scheingold-Bloom model to the Indian case might seem pointless. But despite these unfavorable conditions, in certain situations Indian lawyers have been able to act in a cause-oriented manner. My recent research confirms this point and shows that within this mired legal environment a subset of lawyers has demonstrated similar behavior to the cause lawyers described in the Scheingold and Bloom study. In the next section, I draw upon Scheingold and Bloom's work to develop a modest model regarding the variations of these Indian cause lawyers. Following this discussion I then provide preliminary evidence supporting this model.

IV. Cause Lawyer Transgression in India— The Beginnings of a Conceptual Model

A. Lower Court Cause Lawyers and Their Limited Transgressiveness

Despite the treacherous lower courts, some lawyers have been able to focus their attention on broader social causes. Evidence is also present which shows that in the upper level courts, lawyers have worked on a variety of causes with some degree of flexibility (Baar 1990; Epp 1998; Galanter and Krishnan 2004). And perhaps this is the main distinction between the situation in India and how Scheingold and Bloom describe the setting for cause lawyers in the United States. Rather than the type of office where a cause lawyer works, in India it is more about in which court a cause lawyer practices that determines her or his transgressiveness. (Recall that almost all Indian lawyers work as solo practitioners.)

As stated, the lower courts in India are hopelessly grid-locked. In fact, there is little incentive for the lower court lawyer to work on causes that require investing great amounts of time, money, or other resources. Furthermore, most of these individuals lack high levels of professional prestige. Judges, lawyers who practice at higher level courts, and much of the public tend to view lower court lawyers with disdain (Galanter and Krishnan 2004). In addition, most lower court lawyers are far from wealthy. Typically, they do not come from prosperous backgrounds, and many are the first in their family to have attended college. In terms of their business, lower court lawyers characteristically have an *ad hoc*, financially modest client base, and consequently, they struggle to keep their practice afloat. The ties most lower court lawyers have with either established or informal professional networks are not deep; thus they tend not to develop strong, collegial relationships with one another (ibid.).

Of course, there will be those who eventually gain some modicum of success, name-recognition, and professional prestige. Usually, this is done by expending valuable energy learning how to maneuver within the lower court system. Once such skill is acquired, the lower court lawyer can then more easily develop client-contacts, social networks, and personal connections to enhance her or his position as a lawyer. But building professional status takes time, and the lower court lawyer is reluctant to waste this resource on causes that are not directly related to furthering her or his career. Causes that conflict with the immediate goal of earning quick payments are mostly ignored. As such, because lower court lawyers generally lack the wealth, elite education, and trusting ties with others in their field—along with the fact that they work within such a difficult practice environment to begin with—engaging very transgressively on causes is neither economically viable nor professionally an option. Not surprisingly then, this is not a setting where one easily finds lawyers contemplating how best to initiate mass-scale, cause-based movements.

Still, although the above constraints certainly exist, minimal transgressive cause lawyering can take place. Some lower court cause lawyers may allot time to offer free legal consultation to poorer clients. Alternatively, other lower court cause lawyers may serve the "unmet legal needs"[9] of those, for example, who need legal advice in police interrogation quarters or who wish to make a charitable contribution of some sort. There may be overlapping incentives that prompt this type of cause lawyering. Some may hope for future business that is financially promising. Others may not wish to damage their standing among referral sources. Then there are those who may have political ambitions, or who may seek to improve their status among the bar, or who may simply wish to do "good" work; such cause lawyering can allow these goals to be realized. And still others may have family, caste, community, or religious ties to certain clients, and thus these lawyers may feel an obligation to provide this (limited) assistance. Ultimately, however, the structural constraints of day-to-day practice in the lower courts preclude most cause lawyers from engaging in anything more than episodic, narrower forms of legal aid. In sum, lawyers who work in lower courts have fewer opportunities to pursue causes in a highly transgressive fashion.

B. State High Court/Supreme Cause Court Lawyers
and Their Moderate Transgressiveness

In general, the Indian legal profession is stratified at three levels. We just discussed cause lawyers who work in the lower courts; in this section we focus on those who work in the upper courts, primarily at the state High Court level and on some occasions in the Supreme Court. These state High Court/Supreme Court (HC/SC) cause lawyers face many of the same constraints as their lower court counterparts. They tend to work mostly as solo practitioners within a system that allows for massive delays. Their work is geared toward litigation, and the manner in which they visualize causes tends to be in terms of strict legal rules and procedures. At their core, HC/SC cause lawyers are litigators; typically they are not skilled negotiators, long-term planners, or movement builders. For them, the law is viewed in terms of winning or losing in court.

These are of course general characterizations. In fact, those who wish to engage in transgressive cause lawyering and who practice mainly at the state High Court level have relatively more flexibility than lower court cause lawyers. There are several reasons why HC/SC cause lawyers are able to act in a more transgressive fashion. For one thing, the state High Courts and Supreme Court are perceived to be more open than the lower courts. Claims may be filed directly in the state High Court where the state government is accused of violating a statutorily or constitutionally protected right (Baxi 1985; Sathe 2002). Similarly, where the central government is charged with infringing upon the "fundamental rights" of an individual, claims may be filed directly in the Supreme Court (Dhavan 1994).[10] Such accessibility has allowed those highly skilled lawyers who have been trained to frame legal briefs in a manner amenable to the upper courts to pursue what are known in India as "PILs," or public interest litigation claims (Cunningham 1987; Peiris 1991; Sathe 1998, 2002). These types of claims include litigating causes involving civil rights, civil liberties, the environment, women's rights, and the like.

The opportunity to work on public interest litigation claims provides HC/SC cause lawyers with a larger market of potential clients. Not only do these lawyers receive work from individual claimants, but public interest, nongovernmental organizations (NGOs) also are a part of their clientele (Krishnan 2003). The upper courts are often viewed by NGOs—who frequently have complaints against the state—as one avenue in which to advocate their respective causes (Epp 1998; Krishnan and den Dulk 2002). Hiring and developing relationships with sympathetic HC/SC cause lawyers is seen as necessary if NGOs wish to succeed in court. In turn, HC/SC cause lawyers look at NGOs as a key source of "repeat" (Galanter 1974) business. These lawyers are willing to devote time, energy, and other resources to NGO causes because they know that most of these public interest organizations have multiple agendas and require ongoing legal services.

Along with adding client diversity, NGOs give HC/SC cause lawyers another stream of income. This source of revenue, along with the regular fees collected from their traditional clients, provides HC/SC cause lawyers with comparatively higher salaries. By having greater financial security, a more diverse network of clients, and the opportunity to work within a respected judicial arena, HC/SC cause lawyers tend to have greater professional prestige than their lower court counterparts. As we shall see, this enables the HC/SC cause lawyer to work in more transgressive ways, such as litigating public interest cases or helping NGOs devise longer-term strategies for changing the law (see Sathe 2002; Sheth and Sethi 1991).

But HC/SC cause lawyers face several constraints. For one thing, as previously noted, professional prestige is not static. HC/SC cause lawyers need to consider how their behavior affects other actors, and what impact this might have on their professional prestige. For example, will the public interest issue they are litigating conflict with a more traditional client's interest? Are members of the bar, who may wield influence over future career opportunities, likely to look askance at work done on behalf of particular public interest causes? Could these HC/SC cause lawyers suffer political consequences by taking on the claims of, say, more controversial NGOs? There also is the issue of reaction by donors of NGOs to the types of strategies the HC/SC cause lawyer undertakes. The degree to which these funders influence what the cause lawyer does may work as an additional constraint. Each of these factors, then, can affect the HC/SC cause lawyer's overall ability to act transgressively.

Finally, HC/SC lawyers themselves are not homogenous. There are two types of HC/SC lawyers: advocates and senior advocates. The former file cases, take pleadings, and administratively shepherd cases through the legal process. Senior advocates, on the other hand, are lawyers who have practiced at least ten years and who have been formally recognized by their state High Court as one of the most able in the field. These lawyers almost exclusively argue cases in front of the justices. (We will discuss next how a similar distinction between Supreme Court advocates exists as well.) As we shall see, how an HC/SC lawyer is categorized certainly can affect what that individual accomplishes as a cause activist. But overall those working in the upper courts have more flexibility to act in a transgressive legal manner than lower court cause lawyers. One who aspires to provide more than just basic "unmet legal needs" will find some satisfaction and more opportunities by working as an HC/SC lawyer.

C. Supreme Court Cause Lawyers and Their
Relatively High Transgressiveness

Whereas cause lawyers who practice mainly in state High Courts can act more trangressively than those in the lower courts, Supreme Court cause lawyers tend to be the most active of the group. In terms of the Scheingold-Bloom model, these Supreme Court cause lawyers would fall on the opposite end of the continuum from lower court cause lawyers. Many Supreme Court cause lawyers see their profession as a tool integral to changing the present political and social structure. They have "transformative interests and values" (Scheingold and Bloom 1998: 215) and are well versed in the discourse of liberal democracy, feminism, environmentalism, and civil rights. Many reject the notion that lawyers must remain above the political fray and instead believe in being directly involved in the struggle against what they perceive as the corrupt and oppressive status quo.

Like HC/SC lawyers, Supreme Court cause lawyers have similar advantages that allow them to work transgressively. For one thing, the practice arena in which they conduct their business—the Supreme Court—is arguably the most respected governmental institution in the country (Verma and Kusum 2000). Despite the occasional flak it receives for some of its more controversial rulings, the Court, overall, is viewed by the public as legitimate, democratic, and accessible (Jacobsohn 1996; Verma and Kusum 2000; Kirpal et al. 2000, Sathe 2002). It was the Court, for example, that loosened the restrictions on standing, and at various times throughout its history, the Court has been on the side of minority rights and those most disadvantaged in society (see, e.g., Austin 1966, 2000; Galanter 1984; Sathe 2002). The high reputation of the Supreme Court invariably rubs off on cause lawyers who bring these cases to this arena, but by the same token, the lawyers are also recognized as playing a key role in facilitating reform.

The acclaim that many Supreme Court cause lawyers possess results in demand for their services by an array of clients. Individual claimants, NGOs, and corporations form a strong clientele for these attorneys. Having such a client base enables the Supreme Court cause lawyer to engage in other activities, aside from just worrying about how to recruit clients and how to "pay the bills."[11] Those who have aspirations for aggressively championing causes oftentimes participate in politics, help draft legislation, fund and organize grassroots movements, and write books, articles, and op-ed newspaper columns.

By practicing in the most respected institution in India, having a diverse clientele, and working with people at all levels of society, Supreme Court cause lawyers generally are held, professionally, in very high regard. For the very transgressively oriented lawyer, this professional prestige gives her leverage to work on issues that might not otherwise garner her attention. Because of the respect she has, people listen to her. The media, policymakers, members of the bar, and others take note when she supports a cause. The Supreme Court lawyer thus is in a position to shape the discourse and lend legitimacy to a cause that in many cases might be ignored.

But just as lower court and HC/SC cause lawyers face various constraints, so too do Supreme Court cause lawyers. Typically those who wish to practice in the Supreme Court, upon graduation from law school,[12] will first seek to serve as an assistant to an already established Supreme Court lawyer. The length of this apprenticeship will vary, but many of these aspiring Supreme Court advocates will work in this manner for years, all the while trying to develop contacts to start their own individual practice.[13] At some point, these "junior advocates" will have to pass a rigorous exam if they wish to file cases on their own in the Supreme Court. Assuming one passes, that person will then be certified as an "advocate on record," but she/he must complete at least ten years of practice before asking the justices of the Supreme Court to designate her/him as a "senior Supreme Court advocate." (The decision of the justices is discretionary.) These senior Supreme Court advocates, of which there are approximately 100 at any given time, enjoy more opportunities and benefits (and face fewer constraints) than advocates on record. These include: having a wider client base, greater incomes, an overall stronger reputation in the field, and the sole power to argue cases in front of the Supreme Court. (Advocates on record can only file cases in the Supreme Court; they must defer to the senior Supreme Court advocate to perform the oral arguments.[14]) We will explore the ramifications of the differences between these two types of Supreme Court advocates in more detail shortly.

In addition to this hierarchical divide serving as a potential constraint on certain Supreme Court lawyers, there are other factors that can affect what these lawyers do. For example, Supreme Court cause lawyers come from various backgrounds; those from privileged upbringing have connections and social networks that are more extensive than those coming from modest means. Also, Supreme Court cause lawyers constantly need to consider how their transgressive actions may affect the interests of their more traditional clients. As well, the governing political climate and the attitudes of their colleagues in the bar can influence the level of transgressiveness. Even the most powerful Supreme Court cause lawyer knows that while she possesses certain advantages, her public position in society inevitably places her under immense scrutiny. The

Supreme Court cause lawyer's actions are watched and her missteps are emphasized. For this reason, she is acutely aware of the need to contemplate each of her cause lawyering decisions in a thoughtful and serious manner.

We, therefore, have a complex web of factors that interact to determine how transgressive a cause lawyer will be in India. As we shall see from the preliminary evidence below, courtroom environment, along with personal aspirations and the amount of professional prestige that a cause lawyer possesses combine to affect the nature of the lawyering that takes place. Whereas for Scheingold and Bloom, office environment ultimately was the main variable affecting lawyer-transgression, in India it is the court in which the lawyer is based that proves most significant. One point, however, needs mention before proceeding. The above descriptions made of the cause lawyers who practice in the lower courts, the state High Courts, and the Supreme Court are not isolated characterizations. Legal life in India can be more fluid than the construct detailed above. Although most lawyers who practice in the lower courts begin and end their careers in this arena, as already stated, on occasion cause lawyers who practice mainly in the state High Courts will petition the Supreme Court, and vice versa. Furthermore, among each set of lawyers, as we shall discover, variation occurs. And these different lawyers occasionally may work with one another in certain complex cases.[15] Nevertheless, the general distinctions made help to shed light on some of the more noticeable behavioral patterns of Indian cause lawyers.

In the next section, I discuss my work on cause lawyers in New Delhi, Bombay, and Hyderabad. I chose New Delhi because it is the hub for political activity within the country, and because the vast majority of full-time Supreme Court cause lawyers reside in this city. Bombay was selected because it has been historically viewed as the most diverse legal market in India. And Hyderabad was picked because it, and the state in which it is located, Andhra Pradesh, is seen as among the most progressive legal environments in the country. Between 1998 and 2003, I made repeated visits to these cities in an effort to compile a list of cause lawyers. Because no one comprehensive directory exists, I have relied on assistance from lawyers, activists, academics, politicians, and media accounts. Thus far I have conducted in-depth interviews with forty-one separate cause lawyers. The information gathered during the interviews provides a sense of what goes on behind the scenes. However, I should note that several attorneys were hesitant to speak on the record about what they considered to be confidential decision-making strategies. (In fact, unless otherwise stated, the names of the attorneys discussed below are pseudonyms used to protect their identities and privacy.) The evidence I present below, then, can at best be only a snapshot of the nuances involved in the tactical decision-making process. Yet the data marshaled move us one step closer to further explaining what affects cause lawyering behavior in India.

V. Cause Lawyering at Three Different Levels

A. *Lower Court Cause Lawyers*

Given the number of constraints placed on lower court lawyers as a whole, it seems unlikely that any of them would desire, or even be in a position, to take on cases that are not associated directly with their practice. The daily grind of life as a lower court lawyer takes its toll, and when they themselves are struggling to make ends meet, understandably, advocating for causes beyond immediate client demands is hardly a priority. But diversity exists among lower court lawyers. Some, in fact, do turn to cause lawyering as a way of escaping the drudgery of their normal routine. Others feel a real desire to help in whatever little way they can. And then there are those who see cause lawyering as a publicity tool, with the hope that future (more profitable) business will be the result.

One person who holds a combination of these sentiments is a lower court cause lawyer that I interviewed in New Delhi. This individual is a general practitioner, although the bulk of his cases involve pay equity issues, domestic violence, and divorce. His work over the years on these matters has prompted him to take up some transgressive cause lawyering. He expressed to me that because few "everyday lawyers" have his experience, it is crucial that women who need legal help know who he is (first interview with lawyer November 25, 1998; follow-up interview August 20, 2002). For this reason, he provides free consultation to women in abuse shelters and circulates literature on women's rights issues to local NGOs. Offering these services helps meet the legal needs of at least some women, and it satisfies the lawyer's own personal aspirations. (In addition, he stated that while he feels guilty about it, he performs these public service actions in hopes of gaining profitable business opportunities down the road.)

But existing constraints prevent him from conducting services that stray far from his normal practice. For example, he mentioned that his current practice barely enables him to maintain a middle-class lifestyle. Consequently, "it just costs too much to get involved in other types of good-Samaritan activities" (follow-up interview with lawyer, August 20, 2002). His precarious financial situation leaves little time for him to take clients on a *pro bono* basis, particularly if their cases are open-ended with little sight of quick resolution. Furthermore, his standing within the profession is not noteworthy. Granted, he has managed to gain some respect as a lawyer by networking with clients, NGOs, and members of the bar. But these contacts are limited, and for the most part he does not have many other meaningful professional relationships. Although he claims to have strong beliefs in the causes for which he works, he refuses to jeopardize the relationships he does have by engaging in potentially high transgressive activities that might adversely impact his already limited amount of professional prestige. As he stated, he is always "deeply concerned how . . . [his] name will be affected."

Therefore, the degree to which this lower court lawyer acts transgressively seems to depend upon where he practices, his financial success, his personal motivations, and his prestige within the profession. One factor thus far not discussed is the role that the existing political climate plays in cause lawyer transgressiveness. One lawyer who highlighted this point to me was Sanjay Shah. As has been repeatedly stated, in India most attorneys are solo practitioners. Particularly in Delhi it is customary that many of these lawyers work under small tents right outside the district courts.[16] Literally hundreds of such tents sit next to each other; the picture is one of a massive bazaar (see Geertz 1963) where lawyers stand outside their individual quarters waiting for clients to enter. Most of these "offices" have no library, no staff, and no computers; if they are lucky they have a wooden desk, an operational typewriter, and a few statutory books to which they can refer. In addition, these lawyers frequently have to compete with unlicensed brokers, better known as *touts*, who troll around the courtyard offering potential clients the ability to resolve their legal disputes for nearly half the costs.

Such is the environment in which Sanjay practices. Sanjay is a middle-aged man who has been practicing law for nearly thirty years. He is a general practitioner who works on both civil and criminal matters. His longevity as a practitioner, the various networks and relationships he has developed with colleagues, clients, and judges, and the financial success he has enjoyed has enabled Sanjay to earn a good amount of professional respect. As such, Sanjay has been able to devote his energies to working for causes that include promoting human rights, protecting civil liberties, and advocating for political accountability. He has attended, and sometimes even organized, rallies, demonstrations, and protests over the past twenty years. And unlike the first lower court lawyer we discussed, Sanjay serves as *pro bono* counsel for various needy clients.

In my meeting with Sanjay I asked him pointedly why he undertakes such extracurricular activities, especially given the fact that he is in such intense competition with other lawyers to attract clients and earn a living. He admitted that his cause lawyering services consumed massive amounts of time. He is required to work on weekends, holidays, and many hours into the night. Yet he remains devoted to assisting organizations with their causes, because, as he repeatedly said, "without people like me, where would these groups go?"

Sanjay believes that he has a responsibility to ensure that the causes he has long fought for continue. He recalled the days during the Emergency Rule (1975–1977) when he and others sought to promote rights-awareness among the public; the difficulty he faced in establishing organized support was immense. He has never forgotten the oppressive times of the mid-1970s and has maintained a personal pledge to use his standing within the profession to help represent ideological allies who depend on his involvement. The more favorable political climate today, along with his talent, financial position, and professional prestige, allows him to pursue more options than the first lawyer we examined.

However, while Sanjay is freer to engage in an array of transgressive activities, he still faces several of the constraints experienced by most lower court lawyers. His client base, while larger than our first lawyer, remains mainly "one-shotters" (Galanter 1974) who rarely yield lucrative repeat business. He, therefore, needs to allot considerable energies toward recruiting clients—in particular financially sound clients—who make it possible for him to spend as much time as he does on social causes. But such recruiting efforts take away time he could otherwise spend on cause lawyering activities. Furthermore, Sanjay has to carefully manage his professional prestige. On the one hand, he knows that by being too aggressive in pursuing his ideological commitments, he may alienate colleagues, state officials, and others who could adversely affect his career. On the other hand, by scaling back his activities, he not only compromises his own principles, but he jeopardizes his relationship with ideological partners to whom he feels closest. These partners, he worries, may look elsewhere for support if they do not believe he is demonstrating enough of a commitment.

But even with these constraints, Sanjay is able to function more transgressively than our first cause lawyer, and both attorneys are in a much better position than our last lower court cause lawyer, Ravi Verma. Ravi works in the city of Hyderabad. In 2002 I observed his practice and met different clients he represents (August 17, 2002). For Ravi, the paramount concern is to make a living. He practices in a typical, chaotic, lower court environment, where he struggles to attract clients and is further hindered by his lack of legal experience. Perhaps not surprisingly, Ravi has very little interest in working on cause lawyering matters. He is so caught up in trying to make ends meet, that he often "wonder[s] why . . . [he] got involved in this life in the first place." In essence, he has no time, nor any real interest, in becoming bogged down with matters that may divert his attention from making money.

However, Ravi is savvy enough to recognize that the Indian legal profession remains both stratified and status-driven. Although he especially despises this aspect of his job, he mentioned that to improve his professional standing it is necessary to have friends and personal connections in important places. The problem for Ravi, though, is figuring out a way to have colleagues, judges, and politicians notice him. He stated that if he were a High Court or Supreme Court lawyer, he would be more widely respected by the powers-that-be. He would have to worry less about finding clients and supporting himself, and life, overall, would be much easier. One way Ravi has sought to enhance his reputation over the past year is by serving as an advocate for the poor in alternative dispute resolution (ADR) forums, known as *Lok Adalats*. These ADR centers are heavily promoted by the same people Ravi seeks to impress. Therefore, this seemingly transgressive action is done not just to help the needy, but for an ulterior motive—to acquire the respect from those operating within an elite network who have the power to improve his career opportunities.[17] Whether this tactic alone will result in improving his professional position is something that is simply unknown to Ravi at this point.

In sum, these three examples highlight the variations that can occur among lower court lawyers. However, even someone like Sanjay remains seriously constrained by this practice arena. The struggle for resources, the daily hardships of life, and the limited number of options available to lower court cause lawyers preclude most of them from acting in too transgressive a fashion.

B. High Court/Supreme Court Cause Lawyers

The advantages of the practice arena where HC/SC cause lawyers work— mainly at the state High Court level and on occasion in the Supreme Court— offer these individuals the opportunity to engage in more transgressive behavior than their lower court counterparts. Recall that High Courts have original jurisdiction in cases where a state is accused of violating either a statutorily or constitutionally protected right. (The Supreme Court is the forum of first instance where the central government is charged with violating the latter.) Even though a backlog of cases exists in both settings, these upper courts are still perceived as relatively more accessible and are more highly thought of by the legal profession, politicians, and the general public than the lower courts. Given this well-reputed environment in which they practice, HC/SC cause lawyers tend to attract a wider range of clients. More clients seeking legal assistance contribute to more business; as such HC/SC lawyers are not required to spend as much time as lower court lawyers actively recruiting clients. The time that is saved can be used instead on issues that really matter to the HC/SC lawyer. Moreover, those who are especially good at their jobs develop greater professional prestige, which, depending upon one's personal aspirations, can help in promoting causes in a very transgressive fashion.

One HC/SC cause lawyer who believes that her position enables her to work in a highly transgressive manner is Kiran Patel. Kiran noted that she routinely receives requests from public interest organizations to serve as their legal counsel. These NGOs know that the upper courts by law have to hear complaints made against the state. Because Kiran has a history of supporting women's rights issues (both legally and politically), she is often asked to represent NGOs that focus on these matters. The NGOs recognize that in order to succeed at the upper court level they need a lawyer who knows how to frame issues and present claims in an effective manner. Kiran, in turn, sees NGO requests as a potential source of repeat business. In fact, for several years she has been "of counsel" for one of the country's leading women's organizations. With Kiran as its lawyer, the group has made important strides for women in the areas of employment law and family law, and as a result, the group keeps returning to her for its ongoing legal work.

One significant consequence of having repeat business from NGOs is that the HC/SC cause lawyer receives a second stream of income. Priya Singh, another attorney who benefits from the business of different women's organizations, noted that the extra money frees up time that she otherwise would have to devote to recruiting clients. She is able to use this extra time to work in alternative ways to promote women's rights. For example, because she believes that "the law is not just about using litigation" (interview December 4, 1998), she spends countless hours educating disadvantaged women in rural north India about the rights they are afforded under the law. "Legal literacy is the first step in making these women recognize that they are really equal" (ibid.). Kiran and Priya thus have made full use of their opportunities and have worked hard to develop a strong name within the legal community and among grassroots activists. They have legitimacy, and so when they challenge the status quo— whether by lawsuit or by other political means—they are not dismissed (by the powers that be) but rather treated with a great deal of professional respect.

That professional respect, work environment, and resources matter was also reflected in the sentiments of a renowned HC/SC cause lawyer, Manish Kaur. Kaur gained popularity during the 1980s while working on the Bhopal chemical disaster case. Today, Kaur is a wealthy lawyer who spends much of his time championing against the proliferation of toxic waste and air, water, and noise pollution. He writes legislative proposals, helps mobilize grassroots constituents, publishes articles, and serves as legal counsel for a prominent environmental organization in the country. He self-assuredly remarked that because of who he is, people take note when he becomes involved in a cause. The combination of his success as a practitioner in the upper courts with his elite background and diverse set of contacts has allowed Kaur to develop enormous legitimacy, which has enabled him to represent riskier causes, support unpopular initiatives, and back more radical policies. Although he may offend some and shock others by his level of transgressiveness, because of who he is within the profession, he is able, as he stated, "to get away" with such behavior.

Kiran, Priya, and Manish Kaur all are examples of lawyers who have reaped the benefits of working within the upper courts. But these individuals also have faced various constraints. These HC/SC cause lawyers "are certainly not free agents and remain subject to the funding and policy decisions imposed by their" work environments (Scheingold and Bloom 1998: 232). For example, the leader of the environmental NGO that provides Kaur with lucrative business opportunities told me that her financial donors have a good deal of input as to how resources are spent. One year, in fact, the board decided to reduce the budget for litigation, and this had a direct effect in cutting Kaur's workload and ultimately in his ability to shape environmental legal policy (interview with NGO leader, November 25, 1998). A fourth HC/SC cause lawyer explained that a recent reduction in the budget of a woman's organization that she assists has constrained her tactical flexibility. Whereas before the budget cuts, she could afford to engage in complex public interest litigation, since the funding has been slashed, she can only provide free legal advice to women on family law matters and help to sponsor educational seminars.

HC/SC cause lawyers are constrained as well by the fact that their professional prestige can be adversely affected. For instance, certain lawyers who perform legal work for the People's Union for Democratic Rights (PUDR) noted that if they had their way, litigation would be a tactic more frequently used to advance the issues of civil liberties and civil rights that the group promotes. However, these lawyers refused to risk damaging their professional prestige fighting over this issue, mainly because the PUDR's constituents strongly believe that the organization needs to fill primarily a political/lobbying function and have repeatedly objected to making "legal leveraging" (McCann 1994) a primary tactic (interview with two PUDR lawyers, October 25, 1998; December 5, 1998; follow-up interview with separate PUDR official, July 25, 2003).

One's professional prestige can be affected in other ways—for example, it is vulnerable to pressures exerted by judges. Priya, our HC/SC cause lawyer introduced above, remarked that when she was a junior level lawyer she was highly sensitive about how her name and reputation were viewed. Early in her career she had an opportunity to work on several controversial, high-profile cases involving the rights of Muslim women in divorce proceedings. However, she referred these cases to senior lawyers, not because she thought the work was too difficult, but rather because she feared potential backlash from judges (as well as politicians) whom she perceived as having power over her future. Similarly, a famous, now retired HC/SC cause lawyer told me: "At one time [early in my career] I used to consider myself a strong believer in the principles of Marx. I even wanted to be public about it. But in this state, I knew that I would get into trouble if I kept that 'nonsense' up. So I just let it go and concentrated on my practice" (August 20, 2002).

Yet even with these obstacles, HC/SC cause lawyers, overall, exhibit more transgressiveness than lower court cause lawyers. As a result of working in the upper courts, HC/SC cause lawyers generally benefit from a diverse clientele, greater financial resources, and higher professional status. As we shall see in the next section, these advantages are even further accentuated for cause lawyers who work primarily in the Supreme Court.

C. Supreme Court Cause Lawyers

In general, Supreme Court lawyers in India have the best opportunities to pursue causes in the most transgressive of fashions. It is worth repeating that while these lawyers conduct the vast majority of their work in the Supreme Court, it is not uncommon for them also to take on cases in various state High Courts. In many ways, Supreme Court cause lawyers share a number of advantages with HC/SC cause lawyers. The former work within the most respected institution in the country; they have a diverse client base; and they are typically from privileged backgrounds. These factors help to explain why they are held in such high regard. How then are they different from HC/SC lawyers? The main distinction is more in degree than in kind; in general, for everything HC/SC cause lawyers have, Supreme Court cause lawyers tend to possess more.

For example, M. C. Mehta is arguably the leading environmental cause lawyer in India.[18] He regularly petitions the Supreme Court, frequently accusing the central government of failing to protect the country's ecosystem. Among some of Mehta's more prominent legal victories include:

— forcing the government to require that cars, trucks, and autorickshaws use low-leaded fuel;

from a diverse clientele to greater resources to higher professional prestige—enable them to become involved in a range of activities that are beyond the reach of most lawyers in India.

VI. Conclusion

Although conditions might predict otherwise, a small segment of the Indian legal environment indeed has engaged in varying degrees of cause lawyering. By drawing on a theoretical model developed by two American scholars, Stuart Scheingold and Anne Bloom, this chapter has shown that within India cause lawyering activity depends on the interaction of several variables, primary among them, the arena, or court, in which the cause lawyer practices. In India, lawyers who practice in the lower courts and who have cause lawyering aspirations, unfortunately, are limited in what they can do. A hypercompetitive atmosphere and a financially modest client base force the lower court lawyer to concentrate almost exclusively on making ends meet, rather than strategizing about causes. In addition, lower court lawyers are generally weak political and legal leaders; they have neither the ambition nor professional prestige to make substantive changes in public policy.

But as we have seen, variation does exist among some of these lower court lawyers. For those with cause lawyering aspirations, if they are able to acquire some financial security and professional respect—and can work within a politically favorable climate—then they may be able to engage in limited legal services, such as offering free legal advice, occasionally representing a claimant on a *pro bono* basis, or speaking on behalf of the disaffected. In fact, in December 2002 certain lower court lawyers led a national one-day lawyers' strike to protest legislation barring claimants from appealing decisions rendered in government-sponsored dispute resolution forums (Venkatesan 2002).[22] Despite a Supreme Court ruling prohibiting any work stoppage, these organizers defied the order and proceeded with the strike. However, this type of transgressive behavior is more the exception than the rule. More often than not, the constraints of this practice arena are too great for most cause-inclined lawyers to overcome.

In comparison to lower court lawyers, HC/SC lawyers have the capacity to act in a more transgressive fashion. The courts where HC/SC lawyers work are relatively open and accessible. Although lower court lawyers struggle to recruit clients, HC/SC lawyers tend to have more affluent practices and do not need to worry as much about finding business. By having this extra time and money, as well as more developed professional networks, HC/SC lawyers are better able to become involved in different types of causes and engage in actions that most lower court lawyers would not contemplate. For these reasons, HC/SC lawyers have been more transgressive in their strategies, undertaking, for example, complex public interest litigation cases and efforts to mobilize grassroots constituents.

Nevertheless, HC/SC lawyers are not unconstrained actors. Recall our discussion of Priya, the HC/SC cause lawyer who refused to take controversial cases for fear of professional reprisal from powerful judges. Then there were other, junior HC/SC cause lawyers who mentioned that their actions are sometimes constrained by a lack of financial resources. Yet the constraints that HC/SC lawyers face pale in comparison to those that burden lower court lawyers. As we have seen, overall, the arena in which HC/SC lawyers practice is geared toward a much more transgressive form of cause lawyering.

For the fortunate who work primarily in the Supreme Court, this professional lifestyle provides the best opportunity to be highly transgressive. Supreme Court lawyers share many of the same advantages as HC/SC lawyers, except that these advantages are more pronounced. Supreme Court lawyers work in the most respected institution in India; they are the most elite with the most professional prestige. Senior Supreme Court advocates, in particular, tend to be the wealthiest lawyers with the most diverse client base. And for those with the necessary aspirations, they can be the most transgressive of all cause lawyers in the country. But even this group encounters various hurdles. Consider our example of the prominent Supreme Court cause lawyer whose highly transgressive legal style was curtailed by conservative legislation passed by the government; a reduction in resources; and a diminution of professional prestige due to personal charges made against him. Although those who practice at this level are in the best position to serve as extremely transgressive cause lawyers, external forces still can affect their tactical decision making.

Ultimately, then, the ability of lawyers in India to act transgressively toward causes depends on a combination of factors. We have seen that while the Scheingold and Bloom model prioritizes office environment as a leading variable that influences transgressiveness, in India it is the court in which the lawyer practices and professional prestige that seem to make the most difference. Of course, in both the United States and in India political climate, lawyer motivation, and market forces have an impact on what cause lawyers do. But perhaps the most intriguing difference, aside from the ones mentioned, is that Scheingold and Bloom end their study by noting that the office environment where their interviewees practice "best suited . . . their cause lawyering aspirations" (1998: 247). Whether the same can be said about Indian cause lawyers is less certain. The interview data suggest that some lower court cause lawyers are especially frustrated that they are unable to satisfy their aspirations within their practice arena.[23]

Finally, there are other issues that the findings from this study raise. For example, we have noted that the higher the court in which the lawyer practices, the more likely it is that the lawyer will have greater prestige within the profession, and thereby potentially be able to act more transgressively. From our discussion, however, we also know that professional prestige is not constant—it can be diminished or enhanced—and that variation occurs within a practice environment. One question that emerges though is whether it is ever possible for someone who practices in the lower court to be as transgressive a cause lawyer as someone who practices in the Supreme Court. What prevents someone like our first lower court lawyer, who has minimal professional standing but still a self-proclaimed commitment to public interest causes, from thinking that he has nothing to lose by acting as transgressively as possible? Will the constraints on him and the other lower court lawyers discussed above always limit transgressive behavior at this level?

Another question is how exactly do we best measure professional prestige, and how can we determine its impact on transgressive cause lawyering vis-à-vis the other seemingly affecting variables?[24] The structure of this preliminary study makes it difficult to answer these important questions. Indeed we do see the beginnings of identifiable patterns that illustrate how cause lawyering activity can emerge as a result of factors that include practice setting, resources, personal motivations, political climate, and professional prestige. But the hope is that the findings from this research will spur further inquiry, which then might lead to an even more detailed picture of cause lawyering in India.

Notes

The author expresses gratitude to Austin Sarat, Stuart Scheingold, Peter Fitzpatrick, and the participants at the Cause Lawyering Conference in Cachan, France, October 2002. Special thanks to Rick Tange, Russ Pannier, and Anne Bloom for their comments, as well as to Marc Galanter, Upendra Baxi, and S. P. Sathe for their insights on the importance of legal environment and reputation for Indian lawyers. Finally, I am grateful to the lawyers, judges, and activists in India who have patiently spent the last few years educating me about the Indian legal profession.

1. This is the term I assign to this norm; although to be sure it draws on Weber and Simon's discussion.

2. That motivations affect how cause lawyers behave has been observed elsewhere (see, e.g., Handler et al. 1978; Sarat 1998; Menkel-Meadow 1998; Shamir and Chinski 1998). Research by den Dulk (2001) highlights how motivations and ideology shape

strategies not just of traditionally studied (more liberal) cause lawyers, but of right-wing, religious lawyers as well (see also Southworth, this volume).

3. Part VI of the *Bar Council of India Rules* is a long, detailed section that focuses on the "standards of professional conduct and etiquette" for Indian lawyers. The preamble states: "An advocate shall, at all times, comport himself in a manner befitting his status as an officer of the Court, a privileged member of the community, and a gentleman, bearing in mind that what may be lawful and moral for a person who is not a member of the Bar, or for a member of the Bar in his non-professional capacity may still be improper for an advocate. Without prejudice to the generality of the foregoing obligation, an advocate shall fearlessly uphold the interests of his client and in his conduct conform to the rules hereinafter mentioned both in letter and in spirit. The rules hereinafter mentioned contain canons of conduct and etiquette adopted as general guides; yet the specific mention thereof shall not be construed as a denial of the existence of others equally imperative though not specifically mentioned." To review the entire Part VI section of the *Bar Council Rules*, see: http: //lawmin.nic.in/la/subord/bcipart6.htm#chapter2.

4. In fact, as the authors cited note, the Indian Supreme Court is arguably the most reputable institution in the entire country to the public, politicians, as well as the legal profession. These scholars and others (see, e.g., Kohli 1990, 2001; Khilnani 1998) have noted that while the central and state governments have been plagued by accusations of corruption and inefficiency, the Supreme Court has been able to maintain its reputation as an independent and fair body for most of the past fifty years. (Although, see S. P. Sathe (2002), critiquing the Court during the dictatorial, Emergency Period of Indira Gandhi from 1975–1977.)

5. To some, my use of professional prestige may resemble what some scholars have characterized as "social capital" (Bourdieu 1986; also see Jacobs 1961; Loury 1977). Although the term social capital itself remains highly contested (Fine 2001), theorists who are often at odds overlap in defining this concept. Glenn Loury (1977, 1987), for example, has viewed social capital as a noneconomic "good" that is produced by one's social context and which can directly affect one's economic livelihood. James Coleman (1988) has referred to social capital as a product that develops out of relationships individuals have with their family, their community, or society at large. Robert Putnam (1993, 2000) has argued that social capital can develop among individuals who participate in various civic organizations within a society. According to Putnam, the reason is that civic organizations create networks that allow people the chance to build meaningful, trusting relationships with one another. As he notes, "networks of civic engagement foster sturdy norms of generalized reciprocity and encourage the emergence of social trust. Such networks facilitate coordination and communication, amplify reputations," and thus provide opportunities for individuals to accumulate social capital from those around them (Putnam 1995: 67). But perhaps the way I use professional prestige may, to some, be most closely aligned with how Pierre Bourdieu uses this concept. For Bourdieu, social capital is a resource that can be defined in terms of power, respectability, status, and legitimacy. Kay and Hagan (1999: 527) remark that Bourdieu's social capital "identifies the importance of concrete personal relations and networks of relations in generating trust, in es-

tablishing expectations, and in creating and enforcing norms." For Bourdieu, as well as others (e.g., Coleman 1988, 1990) these "networks of relations" yield greater social capital when they are denser in nature. Where network-members are in constant interaction, norms are reinforced and intensified and the mutuality of trust among these members is further deepened (also see Bian 1995; Lin 1999). In these situations, individuals have greater opportunities to use these networks as vehicles for accessing not just monetary but also nonmonetary resources—the latter of which, for Bourdieu, includes such commodities as increased prestige and a more positively viewed reputation (Bourdieu 1984, 1985; also see Portes 1995, 1998).

6. The criticism has been nicely summarized by McCann (1994) and McCann and Silverstein (1998).

7. In 2002, the Indian Civil Procedure Code was overhauled, with the intent being to reduce the number of these types of appeals. Whether such a change will make a difference remains to be seen.

8. See R. Dev Raj (2001), "India: Consumer Courts Slow Down" (noting that "civil litigation [is] delayed indefinitely thanks to backlogs and to smart lawyers who wear out litigants through adjournments"), see http://www.oneworld.org/ips2/oct/india.html. A well-known story told in the *New York Times* a few years back highlighted how a relatively simple property law dispute between two neighbors that began in 1961 ended only after thirty-nine years of prolonged litigation. Apparently a milkman had built a wall with two drains that leaked into the meatcutter's yard. The meatcutter had won a judgment in 1961 that declared the drains illegal, but because of the inordinate number of appeals allowed by the Indian legal process the case remained open for thirty-nine years— long after both parties were dead! See Barry Bearak, "In India, the Wheels of Justice Hardly Move."

9. This phrase comes from Scheingold and Bloom's discussion of the type of activities corporate cause lawyers perform.

10. The fundamental rights guaranteed in the Constitution are found in Articles 12–35. They include such provisions as: the right to equality; the right to freedom of movement; the right to freedom of speech and expression; the right to freedom of religion, and the like. For relevant case law, see S. P. Gupta v. Union of India, Air 1982 SC 149; D. C. Wadhwa v. State of Bihar, Air 1987 SC 579; Ratlam Municipal Council v. Vardhichand, Air 1980 SC 1622; Fertilizer Corporation v. Union of India, Air 1981 SC 344; People's Union for Democratic Rights v. Union of India, Air 1982 SC 1473. To facilitate the use of these rights the upper courts accept epistle petitions (letters that state a legal claim). This form of litigation has two advantages—it is simple and inexpensive. Upper courts also have lenient standing rules. Issues in front of these courts do not need to be "ripe," nor is there a sense that upper courts may involve themselves only in actual cases and controversies.

11. A leading Supreme Court cause lawyer told me that he charges 100,000 rupees per court appearance. Given that a middle-class family of four earns this amount per year, it is not surprising why such a lawyer is viewed as wealthy.

12. Recall that many factors may affect how a law graduate gets to a particular court as an apprentice. See the introductory remarks.

13. This is generally the same type of path that exists for those pursuing a career as an HC/SC lawyer. Also for those who choose a career as a lower court lawyer, apprenticeships occur there too, with more experienced lower court lawyers taking on "juniors" as their assistants.

14. It is not exactly clear why only senior Supreme Court advocates may orally argue cases in the Supreme Court, aside from it being a status-oriented perk that accompanies this position. Interestingly, once one becomes a senior advocate, she or he loses her or his "advocate on record" categorization—thus the senior advocate may not file cases in the Supreme Court, but may only orally argue them. Why this is the case also is unclear, although again one can speculate that the idea is that senior advocates should not have to be bothered with such administrative issues; such matters should be instead handled by junior advocates who are thought to need the experience.

15. One finds that the different types of lawyers also will sometimes work with one another in what are called legal tribunals—specialized, more administrative-type courts that each handle disputes over issues such as income tax collection, government employment, consumer-oriented matters, and debt recovery. Legal tribunals emerged as a response to the overwhelming number of cases that clog the traditional judiciary. The idea was that each tribunal would exclusively handle a separate category of cases. To date a formal, comprehensive account of how these forums function has yet to be completed.

16. In Delhi there are three district courts: Patiala House District Court; Tiz Hazari District Court; Karamunda District Court (Noida).

17. I spent a Saturday afternoon witnessing how he handles these ADR cases, and the experience was both sad and troubling. In this forum, Ravi represented dozens of passenger-victims who had been injured while riding on a public bus. The victims, most of whom were uneducated, rural villagers, accused the bus driver of gross negligence and were seeking damages from the bus company. On one side of the table were several bus company officials and their lawyer; on the other side were Ravi and a line of victims who one-by-one told the presiding three-judge panel of their injuries. Each individual case took Ravi about fifteen seconds to two minutes to resolve. The bus company would propose a figure, Ravi would half-heartedly counter, then the bus company would state another figure, and more times than not, Ravi would accept—often without even consulting the client. I questioned Ravi about the assembly-line manner in which he handled these cases, and he frankly confessed that state officials judge his productivity (and that of the *Lok Adalat*) on the basis of how many cases are disposed. For a serious critique of *Lok Adalats*, see Galanter and Krishnan (2004).

18. Mehta did not mind having his real name used for this study.

19. This term comes from an inscription noted on the Ramon Magsaysay Award for Public Service, given to M. C. Mehta in July 1997.

20. In 2004, the BJP-led coalition was defeated, and a new Congress-led coalition came to power. As one of its first initiatives, the new coalition government pushed through the repealing of this anti-terrorism law. For more on this, see Krishnan (2004).

21. The charges came from staff members working within the organization.

22. This particular strike related to the central government's attempt to streamline what it referred to as small claims cases into alternative dispute forums—known as *Lok*

Adalats—in order to alleviate the vast backlog in the district courts. Under the new legislation and subsequent changes to the Indian Civil Procedure Code, judges now can transfer cases to these forums, when they believe a settlement is likely. Once in the *Lok Adalat*, the alternative forum panel can force a settlement that would then be nonappealable. Lower court lawyers protested this as denying claimants not only their right in court, but also their right to appeal what might be an unfair settlement. However, critics charged lower court lawyers with opposing this "reform" because it would be cutting into the lawyers' practice. For a full discussion of this strike, and the overall issue of *Lok Adalats*, see Galanter and Krishnan (2004).

23. For years, there have been calls on the state to reform the morass-like lower court system, but whether such efforts would substantively change the cause lawyering dynamics in India is as yet unknown.

24. Of course it might be possible to quantify professional prestige, at least to some extent. For example, the quantity of a particular cause lawyer's professional prestige might be a numerical function of: 1. the number of lawyers who recognize the cause lawyer's name; 2. the number of noncause lawyers who recognize the cause lawyer's name; 3. the number of lawyers who refer prospective clients to the cause lawyer; 4. the annual frequency with which each of those lawyers does so; 5. the number of nonlawyers who refer prospective clients to the cause lawyer; and 6. the annual frequency with which each of those nonlawyers does so. (There are probably many other factors that might be considered as well.) The point is that given any set of professional prestige numbers for a set of cause lawyers, those numbers could somehow be translated into a standardized percentage system which might allow for meaningful comparisons.

References

Austin, Granville. 1966. *The Indian Constitution: Cornerstone of a Nation*. Oxford: Clarendon Press.

———. 2000. *Working a Democratic Constitution*. New Delhi: Oxford University Press.

Baar, Carl. 1990. "Social Action Litigation in India: The Operations and Limitations on the World's Most Active Judiciary." *Policy Studies Journal* 19: 140–50.

Bar Council of India Rules, see http: //lawmin.nic.in/la/subord/bci_index.htm.

Baxi, Upendra. 1985. "Taking Suffering Seriously," in *Judges and the Judicial Power*, ed. Rajeev Dhavan, R. Sudarshan, and Salman Khurshid. Bombay: M. N. Tripathi.

———. 2001. "Saint Granville's Gospel: Reflections." *Economic and Political Weekly*, March 17.

Bearak, Barry. 2000. "In India, the Wheels of Justice Hardly Move." *New York Times*, June 1: A1.

Beteille, Andre. 1996. *Caste, Class and Power*. Delhi: Oxford University Press.

———. 1997. "Caste in Contemporary India," in *Caste Today*, ed. Chris Fuller. Delhi: Oxford University Press

Bian, Yanjie. 1995. "From Social Capital and Its Significance of the Firm." *Journal of Democracy* 6: 65–78.

Bourdieu, Pierre. 1984. *Distinction: A Social Critique of the Judgment of Taste.* Cambridge: Harvard University Press.

———. 1985. "The Market of Symbolic Goods." *Poetics* 14: 13–44.

———. 1986. "The Forms of Capital," in *Handbook of Theory and Research for the Sociology of Education,* ed. John G. Richardson. Westport, Conn.: Greenwood Press, 1986.

Chatterjee, Partha. 1989. "Caste and Subaltern Consciousness," in *Subaltern Studies 6,* ed. Ranajit Guha. Delhi: Oxford University Press.

———. 1993. *The Nation and Its Fragments: Colonial and Postcolonial Histories.* Princeton, N.J.: Princeton University Press.

Coleman, James. 1988. "Social Capital in the Creation of Human Capital." *American Journal of Sociology* 94: S95–S120.

———. 1990. *Foundations of Social Theory.* Cambridge: Harvard University Press.

Cunningham, Clark D. 1987. "Public Interest Litigation in the Indian Supreme Court." *Journal of the Indian Law Institute* 29: 494.

D. C. Wadhwa v. State of Bihar, Air 1987 SC 579.

den Dulk, Kevin. 2001. "Prophets in Caesar's Court." Ph.D. dissertation, University of Wisconsin–Madison.

Dhavan, Rajeev. 1994. "Law as Struggle: Public Interest Law in India." *Journal of the Indian Law Institute* 36, 302.

Dumont, Louis. 1980[1966]. *Homo Hierarchicus: The Caste System and Its Implications.* Chicago: University of Chicago Press.

Epp, Charles. 1998. *The Rights Revolution.* Chicago: University of Chicago Press.

Fine, Ben. 2001. *Social Capital versus Social Theory: Political Economy and Social Science at the Turn of the Millennium.* New York: Routledge.

Gabel, Peter, and Duncan Kennedy. 1984. "Roll Over Beethoven." *Stanford Law Review* 36: 1–55.

Galanter, Marc. 1974. "Why the 'Haves' Comes Out Ahead: Speculations on the Limits of Legal Change." *Law and Society Review* 9: 95–160.

———. 1984. *Competing Equalities.* Berkeley: University of California Press.

———. 1989. "New Patterns of Legal Services in India," in *Law and Society in Modern India,* ed. Rajeev Dhavan and Marc Galanter. New Delhi. Oxford University Press.

Galanter, Marc, and Jayanth K. Krishnan. 2003. "Debased Informalism: Lok Adalats and Legal Rights in India," in *Beyond Common Knowledge: Empirical Approaches to the Rule of Law,* ed. Thomas Heller and Erik Jensen. Stanford, Calif.: Stanford University Press.

———. 2004. "Bread for the Poor: Access to Justice and the Rights of the Needy in India." *Hastings Law Journal* 55: 789.

Geertz, Clifford, 1963. *Peddlers and Princes: Social Development and Economic Change in Two Indonesian Towns.* Chicago: University of Chicago Press.

Handler, Joel. 1978. *Social Movements and the Legal System: A Theory of Law Reform and Social Change.* New York: Academic Press.

Jacobs, Jane. 1961. *The Death and Life of Great American Cities.* New York: Random.

Jacobsohn, Gary J. 1996. "Three Models of Secular Constitutional Development: India, Israel, and the United States." *Studies in American Political Development* 10: 1–96.

Katz, Jack. 1982. *Poor People's Lawyers in Transition*. New Brunswick, N.J.: Rutgers University Press.

Kay, Fiona, and John Hagan. 1999. "Cultivating Clients in the Competition for Partnership: Gender and the Organizational Restructuring of Law Firms in the 1990s." *Law and Society Review* 33: 517–55.

Kennedy, Duncan. 1987. "The Responsibility of Lawyers for the Justice of Their Causes." *Texas Technical Law Review* 18: 1157.

Khilnani, Sunil. 1998. *The Idea of India*. Delhi: Penguin Press.

Kidder, Robert, and Setsuo Miyazawa. 1993. "Long-Term in Japanese Environmental Litigation." *Law and Social Inquiry* 18: 4.

Kirpal, B. N. et al. 2000. *Supreme but Not Infallible*. Delhi: Oxford University Press.

Kohli, Atul. 1990. *Democracy and Discontent: India's Growing Crisis of Governability*. Cambridge: Cambridge University Press.

———. 2001. *The Success of India's Democracy*. Cambridge: Cambridge University Press.

Krishnan, Jayanth K. 2001. "New Politics, Public Interest Groups, and Legal Strategies in the United States and Beyond." Ph.D. dissertation, University of Wisconsin–Madison.

———. 2003. "The Rights of the New Untouchables: A Constitutional Analysis of HIV Jurisprudence in India." *Human Rights Quarterly* 25: 791.

———. 2004. India's PATRIOT Act: POTA and the Impact on Civil Liberties in the World's Largest Democracy. *Law and Inequality* 22: 265.

Krishnan, Jayanth K., and Kevin den Dulk. 2002. "So Help Me God: Religious Interest Group Litigation in Comparative Perspective." *Georgia Journal of International and Comparative Law* 30: 233–75.

Lin, N. 1999. "Building a Network Theory of Social Capital." *Connections* 22: 28–51.

Loury, Glenn C. 1977. "A Dynamic Theory of Racial Income Difference," in *Women, Minorities, and Employment Discrimination*, ed. P. A. Wallace and A. Lamond. Lexington: Lexington Books.

———. 1987. "Why Should We Care About Group Inequality?" *Social Philosophy and Policy* 5, 249–71.

McCann, Michael. 1994. *Rights at Work*. Chicago: University of Chicago Press.

McCann, Michael, and Helen Silverstein. 1998. "Rethinking Law's Allurements: A Relational Analysis of Social Movement Lawyers in the United States," in *Cause Lawyering: Political Commitments and Professional Responsibilities*, ed. Austin Sarat and Stuart Scheingold. Oxford: Oxford University Press.

Menkel-Meadow, Carrie. 1998. "The Causes of Cause Lawyering: Toward an Understanding of the Motivation and Commitment of Social Justice Lawyers," in *Cause Lawyering: Political Commitments and Professional Responsibilities*, ed., Austin Sarat and Stuart Scheingold. Oxford: Oxford University Press.

Menski, Werner. 2003. *Hindu Law*. Delhi: Oxford University Press.

Nandy, Ashish. 1992. *The Intimate Enemy: Loss and Recovery of Self Under Colonialism*. Delhi: Oxford University Press.

Olson, Susan. 1984. *Clients and Lawyers: Securing the Rights of Disabled Persons*. Westport, Conn.: Greenwood Press.

O'Neill, Timothy. 1985. *Bakke and the Politics of Equality*. Middletown, Conn.: Wesleyan University Press.

Peiris, G. L. 1991. "Public Interest Litigation in the Indian Subcontinent: Current Dimensions." *International and Comparative Law Quarterly* 40: 66.

People's Union for Democratic Rights v. Union of India, Air 1982 SC 1473.

Portes, Alejandro. 1995. *The Economic Sociology of Immigration: Essays on the Networks, Ethnicity and Entrepreneurship*. New York: Russell Sage Foundation.

————. 1998. "Social Capital: Its Origins and Applications in Modern Sociology." *Annual Review of Sociology* 22: 1–24.

Putnam, Robert. 1993. *Making Democracy Work. Civic Traditions in Modern Italy*. Princeton, N.J.: Princeton University Press.

————. 1995. "Bowling Alone: America's Declining Social Capital." *Journal of Democracy* 6, no. 1: 65–78.

————. 2000. *Bowling Alone. The Collapse and Revival of American Community*. New York: Simon and Schuster.

Quigley, Declan. 1993. *The Interpretation of Caste*. Oxford: Clarendon Press.

Raj, R. Dev. 2001. "India: Consumer Courts Slow Down." *Inter-Press Service* (internet edition). http://www.oneworld.org/ips2/oct/india.html (cite no longer available—hard copy on file with author).

Ratlam Municipal Council v. Vardhichand, Air 1980 SC 1622.

Rosenberg, Gerald. 1991. *The Hollow Hope: Can Courts Bring About Social Change?* Chicago: University of Chicago Press.

Sarat, Austin. 1998. "Between (the Presence of) Violence and (the Possibility of) Justice: Lawyering against Capital Punishment," in *Cause Lawyering: Political Commitments and Professional Responsibilities*, ed. Austin Sarat and Stuart Scheingold. Oxford: Oxford University Press.

Sathe, S. P. 1998. "Judicial Activism." *Journal of Indian School of Political Economy* 10: 399.

————. 2002. *Judicial Activism in India: Transgressing Borders and Enforcing Limits*. Delhi: Oxford University Press.

Scheingold, Stuart. 1974. *The Politics of Rights: Lawyers, Public Policy and Political Change*. New Haven, Conn.: Yale University Press.

Scheingold, Stuart, and Anne Bloom. 1998. "Transgressive Cause Lawyering: Practice Sites and the Politicization of the Professional." *International Journal of the Legal Profession* 5, 209–54.

Shamir, Ronen, and Sara Chinski. 1998. "Destruction of Houses and Construction of a Cause: Lawyers and Bedouins in the Israeli Courts," in *Cause Lawyering: Political Commitments and Professional Responsibilities*, ed. Austin Sarat and Stuart Scheingold. Oxford: Oxford University Press.

Sheth, D. L., and Harsh Sethi. 1991. "The NGO Sector in India: Historical Context and Current Discourse." *Voluntas* 2: 49.

Simon, William. 1978. "The Ideology of Advocacy: Procedural Justice and Professional Ethics." *Wisconsin Law Review* 29–144.

Singh, Vir. 1997. "Guardian of the Taj." *Far Eastern Economic Review* (August 7).

S. P. Gupta v. Union of India, Air 1982 SC 149.

Srinivas, M. N. 1966. *Social Change in Modern India*. Bombay: Asia Publishing.

———. 1996. *Caste: Its Twentieth Century Avatar*. New Delhi: Viking.

Tushnet, Mark. 1984. "An Essay on Rights." *Texas Law Review* 62: 1363–1403.

Venkatesan, J. 2002. "Lawyers Defy SC, Strike Work." *The Hindu* (Internet edition; December 18). http://www.thehindu.com/2002/12/19/stories/2002121905180100.htm

Verma, S. K., and K. Kusum 2000. *Fifty Years of the Supreme Court of India: Its Grasp and Reach*. Delhi: Oxford University Press.

CHAPTER TWELVE

Cause Lawyering for Collective Justice

A Case Study of the Amparo Colectivo in Argentina

STEPHEN MEILI

Introduction

In December 2001, amid the worst economic crisis in its history, Argentina imposed severe restrictions on individual bank accounts. Under the *corralito* ("little corral"), account depositors were only permitted to withdraw 1,000 pesos (approximately $350, though the exact amount varies depending on the exchange rate) per month. The *corralito* sparked widespread popular protest and violence. Thirty people were killed during demonstrations. Two separate governments were toppled.

What the *corralito* did *not* spawn, however, was a nationwide class action of consumers of all economic stripes, led by a cadre of cause lawyers, demanding unfettered access to their bank accounts. Nor were smaller class actions filed by groups of similarly situated consumers, such as the elderly and the infirm. Instead, the courts became flooded with individual lawsuits, tens of thousands of them, mostly filed by those able to afford an attorney (which, in Argentina, is an increasingly dwindling percentage of the population). Many of those lawsuits have been successful, allowing about 4 billion pesos to be withdrawn, thus threatening the banking system with collapse. Cause lawyer Roberto Saba refers to this phenomenon as *los goteos*, or little drops of money escaping the *corralito*.[1] In July 2002, in response to the *goteos*, President Eduardo Duhalde suspended all lawsuits challenging the *corralito*. His decree was immediately challenged as unconstitutional by the national ombudsman, whose position is akin to the attorney general in the United States. The constitutionality of the decree, as well as the *corralito* itself, will be ultimately decided by the Argentine Supreme Court, all of whose members are currently facing impeachment charges because of alleged corruption and other transgressions. Every member of the Supreme Court was appointed by former President (and current presidential candidate) Carlos Menem, Duhalde's arch rival. The Supreme Court has made it clear that it might uphold Duhalde's *corralito* if Duhalde suspends the impeachment proceedings.

This anecdote offers a telling glimpse into the world of cause lawyering in modern Argentina. On one level, it demonstrates the almost comic futility of practicing *any* kind of law, including cause lawyering, within a system beset by such political intrigue and corruption at the highest levels. But on a more analytical level, the absence of a single class action challenging the *corralito*, arguably the most significant nonviolent measure limiting the rights of Argentine citizens in decades, speaks to the nature—and limitations—of cause lawyering in this postauthoritarian society.

It's not as if a mechanism for consumer class actions does not exist. As part of the Constitutional Reform of 1994, the Argentine Congress promulgated the *amparo colectivo*, which recognizes collective interests in a number of areas, including consumer protection. Indeed, cause lawyers have invoked the *amparo colectivo* to file numerous collective lawsuits against the state and private corporations over the past few years. According to Christian Courtis, a human rights lawyer and clinical law professor at the University of Buenos Aires: "Collective litigation is a whole new phenomena in Argentina, mostly because of the *amparo colectivo*. . . . Most of the interesting case law of the last five or six years is due to the employment of this legal tool. It is a true advantage in terms of the citizen's control both of the government and powerful private parties, especially after the extensive privatization process in Argentina.[2]

This chapter analyzes the *amparo colectivo* and the way it has been used by cause lawyers in Argentina over the past half decade. After a description of the history and structure of the *amparo colectivo*, the chapter presents a theoretical framework, based on class action literature in the United States, from which to view collective cause lawyering in Argentina. Next, the paper discusses the limitations and strengths of the *amparo colectivo*, using concrete cases and the practical experience of cause lawyers as examples. Finally, the chapter draws a number of conclusions that, among other things, link collective cause lawyering in Argentina to the theoretical framework outlined earlier.

Throughout this chapter, I endeavor to link Argentina's experience with the *amparo colectivo* to some of the overarching themes of this volume in the cause lawyering series; most notably that cause lawyers fabricate rights, state institutions, and their own professional lives. The important role of Argentine cause lawyers in creating, using, and interpreting the *amparo colectivo* gives them a direct stake in the evolution and preservation of the state and the rule of law in postauthoritarian society. Moreover, because cause lawyers help create and develop the state at the same time that they challenge it through lawsuits, cause lawyers occupy a unique space in the legal profession that is at once transformative and conservative. This chapter provides evidence of both of these tendencies among Argentine cause lawyers, and thus cause lawyers generally.

I. Description of the *amparo colectivo*

As noted above, the *amparo colectivo* was passed in 1994 as part of Argentina's constitutional reform. Mostly because of lobbying efforts by women's rights and environmental groups (and cause layers affiliated with those groups), the revised constitution recognized that people have "diffuse," or collective rights in the areas of environmental protection, consumer protection, discrimination, and antitrust (Sabsay 1997).[3] Thus, for the first time under Argentine law, groups of people could be joined together to collectively assert their rights within the judicial system without having to demonstrate that each individual person had suffered a specific harm.[4] The *amparo colectivo* broadened the idea of standing by permitting lawsuits from organizations devoted to the protection of interests that fall within the collective rights newly recognized by the constitution. These kinds of cases are popularly known as "collective aid."[5]

The *amparo colectivo* has relatively few procedural requirements, particularly as compared to the prerequisites for class action certification under the Federal Rules of Civil Procedure in the United States. The main criterion for approval by the court is either a showing of harm by an individual whose injury is similar to many others, or a demonstration by an organization seeking to utilize the *amparo colectivo* that one of its institutional purposes is defense of the right or assertion of the remedy at issue in that case. In making the latter determination, courts will typically look to the organization's bylaws or enabling statute. For example, an organization whose primary purpose is defense of the environment will usually have standing to initiate a lawsuit regarding pollution or other violations of environmental regulations.[6] Argentine judges focus far less on the requirements of typicality and commonality when determining the appropriateness of a collective action under the *amparo colectivo* than do U.S. judges considering class action certification. The inquiry seems to be more about the *bona fides* of the organizational plaintiff than the nature of the legal claim (or, for that matter, the adequacy of the organization's legal representation). Although it is still early to tell, this kind of emphasis could lead to vigorous courtroom battles about the legitimacy of various organizational plaintiffs. As in the United States, there is likely to be an increasing controversy in Argentina over whether a particular organization is acting within the "public interest" (Garth, Nagel, and Plager 1988).

Because the *amparo colectivo* is not a detailed statute, many questions persist regarding its implementation and impact. According to one Argentine cause lawyer, these questions include a lack of clarity about standing, management of multiple party cases, resolving contradictory claims about representation (and the adequacy thereof), and the effects of judicial decisions in cases brought pursuant to the statute.[7] Despite these lingering uncertainties, however, the *amparo colectivo* is undoubtedly one of the most significant procedural legal reforms in recent memory in Argentina. It represents perhaps the best chance for enforcing the social and economic rights in the Argentine Constitution that have amounted to little more than "hollow promises" in the past.[8]

The means by which collective rights became codified in the Argentine Constitution has had a telling impact on the cause lawyers who have litigated cases pursuant to it. First, the antecedent of the *amparo colectivo* is the traditional *amparo* or "*amparo clasico*," a judicially created procedural device that originated in the mid-twentieth century.[9] The *amparo clasico* was intended to remedy manifestly illegal or arbitrary actions or omissions, and established an expedited process for individual claims that will become moot or otherwise meaningless if they must wend their way through the notoriously slow and inefficient civil litigation system.[10] Thus, a litigant must demonstrate some type of imminent harm to be able to use the *amparo clasico*. In this way, the *amparo colectivo* is similar to the permanent injunction in the United States. The *amparo colectivo* extended the *amparo clasico*'s protection against imminent harm to collective litigation. Like the *amparo clasico*, it can only be used in emergency cases. This obviously limits its effectiveness.

Second, as a constitutional provision rather than a statute, the *amparo colectivo* lacks the procedural rules and structures which accompany legislatively created class action devices, such as Rule 23 of the Federal Rules of Civil Procedure in the United States. Many cause lawyers see this both as a necessity and as an advantage. A necessity because, according to the prevailing view among cause lawyers, the Argentine Congress would never have passed a general class action statute, given the extent to which it is influenced by powerful business interests.[11] The lack of specific procedures is also an advantage for cause lawyers, who have thus far been successful in convincing many judges to adopt broad standing requirements that might not have been approved by the legislature.[12] Many cause lawyers fear that if the legislature passed a set of detailed procedures governing class actions under the *amparo colectivo*, those procedures would limit the scope and effectiveness of such cases.[13]

Finally, because of the link between the *amparo clasico* and the *amparo colectivo*, most judges will only allow a case to proceed under the *amparo colectivo* if it can be litigated expeditiously. As a result, most cause lawyers will only use the *amparo colectivo* when a case is straightforward, that is, when the violation is clear and needs little proof, expert testimony, or other complicating evidence to establish.

The preceding description highlights the critical role of cause lawyers in engineering the way in which collective rights may now be formally asserted for the first time in Argentina's history. Much like the cause lawyers at the forefront of civil rights litigation in the United States in the 1950s and 1960s, these cause lawyers are directly responsible not only for creating rights, but also for dictating the circumstances under which those rights can be asserted (and perhaps vindicated) within a legal infrastructure. This role gives such cause lawyers a significant stake not only in the legitimacy and vitality of the rights they are championing, but also in the entire judicial system that they have entrusted to protect those rights. It is this dynamic that creates both opportunities and conflicts for Argentine cause lawyers. The next section of this chapter places these opportunities and conflicts into a historical perspective.

II. Theoretical Framework

The relationship between class actions and progressive social change has been the subject of significant scholarship in the United States (Garth, Nagel, and Plager 1988; Garth 1992; Soine and Burg 1995; Cerminara 1998; Bronstein 1977; Ellmann 1992; Chayes 1976; Mather 1982, Minow 1991, Yeazell 1989; Simon 1984; Bell 1976). Although recognized as having the potential to mobilize grassroots movements and empower traditionally underrepresented groups (Cerminara 1998; Mather 1982; Chayes 1976; Yeazell 1989), the class action has been more typically criticized in the literature for a variety of reasons, including achieving results antithetical to the purpose of the lawsuit, alienating class members from the representative plaintiff, and serving as the vehicle for plaintiffs' lawyers to advance their personal political agenda or avarice (Bell 1976; Simon 1984). Thus, it would seem that cause lawyers have a particularly problematic relationship with collective litigation: while it tantalizes them with the potential for advancing their cause on a broad scale in a single lawsuit, it can, in the end, tarnish or diminish that cause and create a rift between cause lawyers and the people they are attempting to assist.

Bryant Garth's *Power and Legal Artifice: The Federal Class Action* (1992) is particularly insightful in this regard, and serves as a useful point of reference for an analysis of the emerging class action in Argentina. Garth describes the variety of class actions populating a spectrum of potential for political mobilization and change. At one end of this spectrum are class actions initiated by lawyers where the representative plaintiff is passive, a "decorative figurehead." Such class actions, according to Garth, carry the least potential for mobilizing grassroots political involvement and, ultimately, social change. Social welfare class actions filed by legal aid lawyers who actively recruit class representatives fall into this category. So do class actions filed by entrepreneurial lawyers interested more in attorneys' fees than social movements. At the other end of the spectrum lie class actions initiated by highly motivated, organized class representatives who seek out attorneys to advocate for them in court. These representatives may or may not be part of an organized social movement at the time they retain an attorney. Class actions alleging discrimination by a private employer fit within this category.

Garth draws a number of conclusions from his study of several class actions along this spectrum, some of which are directly relevant to an analysis of Argentina's still fledgling class action experiment. On the one hand, Garth observes that regardless of where the cases in his sample fell on the spectrum outlined above, the class action attorneys he interviewed do not use the class action as an organizing tool to mobilize a social movement. As Garth notes, "This legal device as a practical matter does nothing for the lawyer as organizer" (1992: 256). Although cause lawyers may need to organize a group of individuals into a class for purposes of satisfying the requirements of class certification, those lawyers did not see class actions as mechanisms for group mobilizations.[14]

On the other hand, Garth's research suggests that the class action not be dismissed as an irrelevant weapon in the struggle for the kinds of social change in which many cause lawyers engage. First, he argues that class actions can be empowering, even if they are not the stuff of social mobilization. Class representative status can help to create an activist where none existed previously, and membership in a class can induce individuals to support one another (Garth 1992: 261). Aggregation of claims in and of itself can be empowering for a class. Thus, depending on (and sometimes in spite of) the actual results of a class action lawsuit, "the class action at least *permits* significant empowering both of individuals and of the lawyers and the classes they represent" (Garth 1992: 267).

Garth also observes that class actions provide legal scrutiny over state or corporate conduct. Class actions draw the attention of courts, attorneys, and the general public. Regardless of the result in the lawsuit, such scrutiny can bring about change. Even the threat of scrutiny can be an effective weapon, since it may deter harmful and/or unlawful behavior (Garth 1992: 268).[15]

Garth's findings thus provide a series of questions to guide a tour of the *amparo colectivo*: Do cases brought under the *amparo colectivo* align themselves evenly along the same spectrum of lawyer/client initiative that Garth found in his study, or do they favor one end of it? Do cause lawyers in Argentina view the *amparo colectivo* as an organizing tool? Has the *amparo colectivo* been empowering for cause lawyers and their clients? Has the *amparo colectivo* provided a means of greater legal scrutiny over illegal conduct by the state and private corporations? And, in a question related to one of the overarching themes of this volume, what does the experience with the *amparo colectivo* say about the way in which cause lawyers fabricate legal institutions, the state, and their professional lives?

In formulating answers to these questions, it is useful to analyze the strengths and weaknesses of the *amparo colectivo* that have emerged during the first few years of its existence.

III. Limitations

Despite its apparent promise as the means to both mobilize large numbers of people and effect social change on a grand scale, the *amparo colectivo* has fallen well short of the mark on both fronts. The reasons for this are described below. Some are particular to the *amparo colectivo*. Others are emblematic of the Argentine judicial system and legal culture. And some apply to cause lawyering generally.

1. Lack of Coordination between Judicial Decisions

One of the most significant factors limiting the potential of the *amparo colectivo* as an instrument for cause lawyering is that there is virtually no coordination among judges and judicial decisions in different parts of the country. This stems, in part, from Argentina's status as a civil law country, where precedent plays a far weaker role than in common law systems. A judge in one case or province need not feel compelled to abide by a ruling in a previous case or in a neighboring province. In addition, there is no system for consolidating similar cases filed under the *amparo colectivo* in different jurisdictions, such as under the multidistrict litigation system in the United States (Herr 2000).[16] As a result, similar cases that have been filed in different jurisdictions (sometimes intentionally, as we shall see below) have yielded completely opposite results.

One such example involved a tariff on local telephone calls imposed by the two recently privatized Argentine telephone companies. Consumer groups challenged the tariff in a lawsuit filed in Buenos Aires on the grounds that it discriminated against people who live in the provinces outside the capital.[17] Shortly after the first suit was filed, a telephone industry trade association based in the provincial city of Cordoba filed a case under the *amparo colectivo* (in Cordoba) to establish that the tariff was, in fact, constitutional (Argentine law permits parties to file lawsuits in order to preemptively establish the constitutionality of a given practice or procedure). The two courts made no attempt to consolidate the cases while they were pending. Both cases were successful for the parties that brought them, resulting in simultaneous, contradictory rulings, one upholding the tariff, the other striking it down. One of the telephone companies decided to rescind its tariff in light of the pro-consumer Buenos Aires decisions, but the other company did not, citing the Cordoba court's contrary ruling. The Supreme Court eventually settled the issue by holding that the tariff was constitutional. Several cause lawyers with whom I spoke cited this case as an example of why it is very difficult to be an effective cause lawyer while using the *amparo colectivo*, since a successful judicial decision in one part of the country can be neutralized by a counter-suit filed elsewhere.[18] Indeed, one corporate attorney is notorious for filing such counter-suits under the *amparo colectivo*.[19] Thus, the very weapon cause lawyers hoped to utilize in advancing their causes has been used by their adversaries to achieve opposite results.[20]

Inconsistent decisions can also be rendered by different judges within the same province. In one case, a consumer association filed a lawsuit in Buenos Aires under the *amparo colectivo* against the local airport management company for allowing consumers to pay the airport tax in dollars, as well as in pesos (all passengers must pay an airport tax as part of their airline tickets). Because of the recent devaluation of the peso, this policy disproportionately affects lower income consumers, who generally do not have access to dollars. The judge in the case filed by the consumer group ordered the airport company to charge pesos only. However, the airport company (represented by the same attorney who represented the telephone industry group in Cordoba) filed its own case under the *amparo colectivo* in Buenos Aires, resulting in a contradictory opinion. The airport management company did not change its policy: you can still use dollars to pay the airport tax in Buenos Aires.

Such results are obviously frustrating for cause lawyers, as they nullify successful litigation efforts and waste scarce organizational resources. They also further diminish respect for the judiciary and rule of law, since defendants are free to ignore adverse rulings as long as they can find a different judge to rule in their favor on the identical issue. It seems that this is frequently not a difficult search.

2. Procedural Limitations

There are several procedural aspects of the *amparo colectivo* that also limit its effectiveness for cause lawyers. For example, courts will generally not accept a case under the *amparo colectivo*'s expedited procedure if it involves salaries, pensions, or other monetary benefits.[21] Entitlement to such funds is not viewed as a collective or diffuse right by the courts, presumably because each person has her own claim to a particular sum. This limitation on jurisdiction is one of the principal reasons for the lack of a nationwide case challenging the *corralito* under the *amparo colectivo*. It also explains why most cases that are filed under the *amparo colectivo* are directed against the state rather than private entities: lawsuits against the government more typically seek injunctive relief rather than the redistribution or refund of money. The latter form of relief is usually sought when a group of persons sues a corporation.

The following example illustrates the futility of seeking to compel the expenditure of funds through the *amparo colectivo*: A human rights nongovernmental organization (NGO) filed a lawsuit on behalf of persons with HIV, demanding that the federal government distribute a vaccine to which it had ready access. The representative plaintiff was a law student known to the cause lawyers who represented the class. In February 2002 the court ruled in favor of the plaintiffs, ordering the state to distribute the vaccine free of charge. The state ignored the decision, forcing individuals to sue the state to obtain their vaccines. Thus, even though the case resulted in a ruling favorable to the plaintiffs, the remedy is limited to those sufficiently wealthy or well connected to hire private counsel.[22]

Another procedural obstacle to the more widespread use of the *amparo colectivo* is that judges generally permit it only when a case is not complex and the alleged legal violation is clear.[23] This relates to the requirement that the *amparo colectivo*, like the *amparo clasico*, be restricted to emergency situations: that is, the only way a case can be adjudicated expeditiously is if it is both factually and legally straightforward. As several cause lawyers noted in interviews, most cases which they would like to bring under the *amparo colectivo* are neither factually nor legally simple.[24] They typically require intensive factual investigation, expert witnesses, and previously untested legal theories. On the other hand, if judges accept more complicated cases under the *amparo colectivo* (which has happened on occasion), the result is a protracted litigation not unlike a run-of-the mill lawsuit that, as some cause lawyers note, "waters down" the underlying premise of the *amparo clasico*, a legal construct of substantial significance within Argentine law.[25]

3. Access to Justice—Attorneys Fees

The impact of the *amparo colectivo* has also been significantly limited by the law and judicial interpretations regarding attorneys' fees. For example, if the plaintiffs lose a case brought under the *amparo colectivo*, they may be required to pay the defendants' attorneys fees.[26] This is an obvious deterrent to litigating under the *amparo colectivo*, as well as another reason that some cause lawyers only file uncomplicated cases whose success is virtually assured.

Second, and more ominously, several cause lawyers noted that judges who are otherwise sympathetic to the merits of cases litigated under the *amparo colectivo* are nevertheless reluctant to award attorneys' fees to the plaintiffs.[27] The judges' reasoning seems to be that if a case is complicated, fee-shifting is unwarranted because the legal violation was not obvious to the losing defendant.[28] Thus, even though, or apparently because, the HIV vaccination case was very complicated and took two years to litigate (a very long time under traditional *amparo* principles), the judge did not award attorneys' fees to the victorious plaintiffs.[29] Since many class actions are by definition complicated, this cramped view of attorneys' fees is a significant deterrent to cause lawyers in particular, since they typically work for individuals and organizations who cannot finance large-scale litigation on their own. It is also a deterrent in cases where nonmonetary relief is sought, since there is no possibility for recovering a contingency fee as a percentage of a judgment.

The reluctance to award attorneys' fees to prevailing plaintiffs under the *amparo colectivo* extends to otherwise progressive judges. According to Mariela Puga, judges don't see fee-shifting as an access to justice issue:

> Judges don't believe in the incentive potential of the *amparo colectivo*. We write a lot about this issue in our appeals of attorneys fees decisions, but the judges don't see this as a matter of access to justice. They don't see that there is a right to fees in order to get cases into the court. . . . Judges might be more sympathetic to creating incentive for organizations to bring suits, but not to lawyers, who do not have very strong standing in society.[30]

4. Legal Culture

Several aspects of legal culture in Argentina also limit the effectiveness of the *amparo colectivo*. The Argentine judiciary has been long criticized, for example, for being nonindependent, corrupt, inefficient, and prohibitively expensive, rather than as a means to vindicate rights (Knudsen 2002; Snow and Wynia 1990; Rabossi 1993; Meili 1998). Most citizens do not even think of the court system as an option for the redress of grievances. As a result, many people, including many lawyers, are not even aware of the *amparo colectivo* and the rights it recognizes.[31] This is symptomatic of the lack of awareness that Argentines have about their rights generally.[32]

Moreover, the legal culture's emphasis on disputes between individuals renders group-based litigation anathema to many judges. Most judges prefer to rule on cases where there is a specific victim with a tangible injury, rather than a large, amorphous group that claims damage to a collective interest. As Puga notes:

> The judges need a victim who defines the violation of the right. Even though the constitution refers to collective interests, this is still new for our judiciary and in general they are reluctant to understand unless the victim exemplifies the collective interest. Under classic continental law, the judge applies the law to concrete and individual cases. Thus, public policy issues are outside of its competency. Because of this, for some to resolve collective interest cases is like moving beyond their competency. If there is a victim they feel more confident.[33]

5. Conflicts between Class Members, Organizational Plaintiffs, and Cause Lawyers

Cause lawyers who have utilized the *amparo colectivo* have learned that its usefulness is sometimes compromised by conflicts between lawyers, class representatives, and NGOs with an interest in the litigation. These conflicts have been well documented in the literature of lawyers, clients, and collective justice (see Southworth 1999). One of the most common conflicts typically arises when the idea for a lawsuit originates with the cause lawyers, who then must find a client organization to serve as the representative plaintiff. Under such circumstances, the goals of the client organization sometimes differ from those of the cause lawyers.

A vivid example of this conflict involved a lawsuit over pay phone charges. Before the case was filed, the maximum charge for a call from a pay phone was 23 centavos. However, the pay phones, which were privately owned, did not accept a 1 centavo coin. Thus, it was impossible for consumers to use exact change, and they were forced to pay at least 25 centavos for what should have been a 23 centavo call. A group of cause lawyers were aware of the problem and sought a consumer organization to act as the representative party in a lawsuit under the *amparo colectivo*. The lawyers found the NGO, but its goals and tactics were very different from the lawyers'. For example, the NGO held press conferences to discuss the case without first consulting the attorneys. These press conferences were held at times that the attorneys felt were inappropriate or counterproductive to the litigation. Moreover, once the case was settled, the NGO wanted the monetary damages directed to itself, rather than to fund other public interest initiatives supported by the cause lawyers. The *amparo colectivo* contains no procedures for allocating the proceeds of a successful lawsuit. The cause lawyers and the organization eventually negotiated a solution to the conflict (the money went to the public interest initiatives), but the dispute created an enduring rift between cause lawyer and client. It also resulted in no money being returned to any individual consumers.[34]

In a similar vein, conflicts can arise because a cause lawyer's goals in filing a lawsuit under the *amparo colectivo* typically extend beyond merely achieving a courtroom victory. According to Martin Bohmer, dean of the University of Palermo Law School in Buenos Aires, cause lawyers frequently file lawsuits for political reasons, above and beyond the facts of an individual case.[35] As Mariela Puga observes, "winning" a case does not necessarily mean obtaining a favorable judicial opinion. In many instances, the case is brought even though the lawyers know the chances of success, in the traditional meaning of that term, are slim. The purpose of such lawsuits is to attract public attention to a particular problem, not to expect the judiciary to fix it.[36] Another purpose, perhaps not stated overtly, is to allow cause lawyers to create demand for their legal services. In any event, according to the same cause lawyer, this dynamic "makes for a complex relationship with an individual client or association who is not interested in public debate but concrete results."[37] Moreover, this situation is the obverse of the case involving the pay phone charge, since in that case the cause lawyers were more interested in concrete results (prohibiting the company's practice) while the NGO client was more interested in public debate.

This conflict illustrates one of the ironies in the development and use of the *amparo colectivo*: while it is designed, in part, to permit cause lawyers to represent large numbers of people, it can actually increase—or at least highlight—the gulf that frequently separates cause lawyers and their clients. Sometimes the lawyers are unaware of what the people in an affected group need. According to Bohmer, "We listen to NGOs, but we have no idea what people are actually thinking."[38] Most cause lawyers simply do not have sufficient time or resources to become directly involved with communities and other groups in order to learn about their problems and demands firsthand. And of course if cause lawyers were to focus exclusively on the legal needs of indigent communities, they would no doubt become even more overwhelmed by the workload than, say, legal services lawyers in the United States like those chronicled by Corey Shdaimah in this volume.[39] One might conclude that cause lawyers, particularly those in developing countries like Argentina, are thus guilty of creating a demand for their services that they cannot realistically meet.

Of course, conflicts can—and do—arise even in situations where the cause lawyers are keenly aware of the needs and demands of the client organization and its members. In one example, a legal clinic at the University of Palermo represented a disability rights NGO. The NGO advocated on behalf of disabled persons who received state pensions after losing their jobs. As part of its advocacy efforts, the NGO found low-paying, public information jobs for disabled persons with other nonprofit organizations in Buenos Aires. One goal of this NGO was establishing that the disabled persons were capable of working in this way. The state sought to withdraw their pensions, alleging that they were employed. The disabled persons needed the pensions, but also did not want to concede that their public outreach tasks did not constitute work. The NGO's position made it very difficult for the cause lawyers to represent the NGO in court, since the legal remedy the NGO sought (retention of the pension) was inconsistent with its public policy goal of maintaining the jobs which afforded the disabled persons a sense of dignity. In the end, the clinic negotiated a compromise with the state under which the disabled persons were able to receive the pensions without declaring that what they were doing was not work. Although this was a welcome result for all involved (save perhaps the state), the settlement left the clinic without a judicial decision that might have furthered the cause of disability rights in subsequent disputes.

Cause lawyers can also exacerbate conflicts between an organization they represent and other groups that advocate for similar individuals or interests. For example, the Palermo Clinic sued the government of a southern province under the *amparo colectivo* on behalf of an indigenous community seeking a bilingual teacher in their school. Utilizing the clause in the Argentine Constitution that recognizes the right to a bilingual education, the clinic won the case and the community was pleased. Soon afterward, however, the cause lawyers received messages from disgruntled members of other indigenous communities who objected to the ruling and felt that the best means of defending their language and culture is by demanding that public elementary school not be mandatory and that they should receive education only in their native language and culture.[40]

A similar example of this lack of communication, with nearly disastrous results, involved the regulation of elevators by the city of Buenos Aires. The thickness of elevator doors (as mandated by city regulations) prevented wheelchairs from safely passing through them. One disability rights NGO was negotiating with the city to change the regulation. Another disability rights NGO, working with the Palermo clinic, was preparing to sue the city. The city learned of the potential suit and told the second NGO that, if sued, it would cease negotiations with the first NGO. The clinic did not file the lawsuit, but realizes that if it had not been warned by the city, it could have destroyed the chance for an amicable resolution of the situation, as well as its relationship with the first NGO. As Bohmer notes, "It's important to talk to the Board (of the NGO) so it's just not a lawyer thing. Because lawsuits can both help or hurt an NGO's political strategy."[41]

There are at least two reasons why these kinds of conflicts arise more frequently in Argentina and other Latin American countries than in the United States. One is that many cause lawyers in postauthoritarian countries like Argentina have an interest in strengthening the rule of law and democratic state institutions (including the judiciary), as well as furthering the overall public interest.[42] Since the client organization which the cause lawyers represent is less likely to have those overarching goals, and more likely to be interested in attaining immediate relief for its members, the aims of these two entities are more likely to diverge at some point during a lawsuit. In the United States, on the other hand, cause lawyers generally take the rule of law and legitimacy of democratic institutions for granted. As such, they focus their class actions lawyering on more concrete remedies (usually monetary or injunctive relief) that more typically reflect the desires of those they represent.[43]

In addition, many public interest groups in the United States, such as the National Association for the Advancement of Colored People, Sierra Club, and American Civil Liberties Union, employ their own lawyers who frequently file cases on behalf of the organization. This structure eliminates (or at least greatly reduces) conflict between members of the organization and the lawyers representing them. Staff attorneys are a luxury as yet unavailable to most public interest organizations in Argentina. Indeed, there are very few full-time cause lawyers in the entire country.[44]

IV. Strengths

Despite these limitations, the *amparo colectivo* has features that afford it the potential to be a powerful cause lawyering tool. Some of these features mirror those identified by Garth in his study of class actions in the United States.

On the most practical level, according to cause lawyer Ezequiel Nino, there have been "more wins than losses" under the *amparo colectivo*.[45] An example of a "win" was a case by the human rights group CELS (the Center for Legal and Social Studies) successfully challenging a federal election statute denying voting rights to persons arrested and detained but not yet tried. Given the delays in the Argentine criminal justice system, this was a significant victory.

In another case, and one of the first litigated under the *amparo colectivo*, the University of Palermo legal clinic filed a discrimination case against a state-run school that trains physical education teachers. The school had a policy of admitting more men than women into its program. The clinic learned about the policy after a friend of one of the law school's professors became interested in applying for the program. According to the cause lawyer who worked on the case for the clinic, the state "didn't resist the case that much," even though it is obligated by law to appeal all cases to the court of appeals. The clinic received a favorable decision from the court, after which the school instituted a new class for women. Although the clinic prevailed in this case, it is still trying to collect its court-awarded attorneys' fees.[46]

Apart from providing at least partial victories like those noted above, the most positive function of the *amparo colectivo*—at least from the cause lawyering perspective—is also one of the positive aspects of U.S. class actions identified by Garth: it has held up to public and legal scrutiny the unlawful conduct by the state and private corporations.[47] Thus, even when a case is hamstrung by counter-suits, inconsistent decisions, and judicial intransigence on attorneys' fees, and even in cases where the plaintiffs' legal claims are ultimately rejected by the court, the *amparo colectivo* nevertheless allows for a discussion of the relevant issues by the media as well as lawyers and judges.[48] Several chapters in this volume, including those by Krishnan, Shamir, and Barclay and Marshall, document a similar use of publicity by cause lawyers in furthering their goals. One example of the importance of the media to the cause lawyering agenda in Argentina concerned a recent case challenging substandard conditions on state-owned trains that frequent the poorest of Buenos Aires' suburbs. Those trains are more hazardous than those which service wealthier sectors of the city. The case was covered extensively by a national magazine. According to Nino, who worked on the case, such coverage is at least as important as any result the cause lawyers may eventually obtain in court.[49]

In a similar vein, cause lawyers believe that the *amparo colectivo* has forced the judiciary to exert at least some control over the state bureaucracy. As Nino notes:

> In Argentina we don't have a good system of controls within the public sector and the government because of corruption and bureaucracy. The institutions that are supposed to deal with these issues are ineffective. . . . When they are asked to do it,

judges react and tend to control governmental action. There are still very few public interest lawyers, but they have been very useful in controlling governmental actions. For example, the constitution contains many rights, and Congress is generous in giving rights to people. But because of the budget, corruption, and bureaucracy, these rights are not always recognized or upheld. Sometimes the violations are very clear. In these cases, public interest lawyers can be effective in getting a judge to say that rights need to be given to people. More times than not in such cases, the judges will react well.[50]

Some cause lawyers believe that it is in putting pressure on the judiciary to "react well" that the *amparo colectivo*, and public interest litigation generally, have their greatest potential for bringing about progressive social change. According to one cause lawyer, the "top-down" strategies to effect judicial reform promoted by outside foundations and some academics (e.g., seminars to encourage the judiciary to reform itself, or encouraging the executive branch to reform the judiciary) will never succeed unless judges feel pressure to promote the rule of law from the "bottom-up"; that is, by having to resolve lawsuits brought by cause lawyers.[51] Faced with such cases, judges will either "react well" or fail to do so and endure public criticism—at least from the cause lawyers and individuals affected by the adverse decision. In this way, cause lawyers use the *amparo colectivo*—and publicity generate by cases brought under it—as a means of strengthening the role of the judiciary in protecting collective rights that are now guaranteed by the constitution.

Concluding Observations

1. Theoretical Perspectives

This review of Argentine cause lawyers' experience with the *amparo colectivo* is generally consistent with Garth's observations about class actions in the United States, albeit with some notable exceptions. One difference is that the spectrum of client-generated/lawyer-generated cases in Argentina is more skewed toward the lawyer-generated end of the continuum than is the case in the United States. There are several reasons for this, all having to do with the structure of the *amparo colectivo*, as well as the legal culture in Argentina. As to the latter point, while, as Garth notes, U.S. litigants view the U.S. legal system as empowering, most Argentines have exactly the opposite view: it is an institution to be avoided (Garth 1992: 241).[52] It is not surprising, therefore, that the majority of Argentines are unaware that they now enjoy a range of collective rights under the constitution, much less the means to vindicate those rights. Few people approach lawyers with cases that might be brought under the *am-*

paro colectivo. And while NGOs are generally more aware of their rights than individuals, the long-standing aversion that many of these groups feel toward the law has kept them at arm's length from cause lawyers.[53] This is particularly true of grassroots organizations that work in and among Argentina's poorest communities. As one cause lawyer puts it:

> We are not used to working with grassroots groups. And those groups are less accustomed to working with legal groups. They don't trust the law, and rightfully so. You have to know that you have a right, that the right has been violated, and you have a process to enforce that right—that you have to get a lawyer to help navigate that process. Then you have to know how you can get that lawyer. Then you need the money to get to the lawyer, and have the time and money to obtain the lawyer. It is basically physically impossible for most poor people to get to the lawyers in downtown Buenos Aires. For example, it costs 6 pesos to get to downtown Buenos Aires, which amounts to three meals for a poor family.[54]

Thus, as noted above, it is likely that a larger percentage of collective lawsuits in Argentina are brought, in part, to educate the public about its rights. Moreover, the relaxed standing requirements of the *amparo colectivo* make it even more likely that a class action in Argentina will be driven by the lawyer, rather than client. Since Argentine law does not place restrictions on the solicitation of clients (indeed, in some cases corporations have paid people to act as representative plaintiffs in counter-suits under the *amparo colectivo*),[55] it is far easier for lawyers to devise and direct their own cases than to react to the needs of clients. Thus, in the sample of cases that I learned about in my interviews, representative plaintiffs were frequently a friend or relative of the cause lawyer, or organizations that the cause lawyers actively sought out as a plaintiff. That is to say, most were what Garth calls passive class representatives (Garth 1992: 245).

One similarity between Garth's conclusions and my findings is that in lawyer-driven cases, the class action is not a means of empowerment for class representatives or other class members (1992: 242). None of the cause lawyers I interviewed ever mentioned client empowerment as one of the benefits or strengths of the *amparo colectivo*. And while some of them mentioned the tangible benefits of a successful case (voting rights for detainees, increased enrollment for women in the physical education school), they more typically spoke of the helpful legal precedent established or the positive publicity generated. Indeed, these cases appeared to be more empowering for the cause lawyers than their clients.

This view of cause lawyer empowerment is somewhat related to Halliday and Karpik's (1997) notion of the market-based professionalism of lawyers, which assumes that there is a hierarchy of lawyers within any organized bar, and that those who litigate class actions frequently populate the top of it. They oversee large cases where significant sums of money or important principles are at stake. And particularly in an emerging democracy like Argentina, cause lawyers who utilize the *amparo colectivo* often find themselves on the cusp of cross-cutting issues of law and social policy. What is at once exciting and frustrating about being a cause lawyer in Argentina at this moment is that it is like writing on a clean slate; there is not much of a road map, although numerous foundations, law schools, and other institutions from the United States and elsewhere have endeavored to provide one. Within such an environment, traditional cause lawyering carries with it a certain degree of prestige and stature.[56] Statutes and constitutional provisions like the *amparo colectivo* enable these cause lawyers to maintain and even enhance that position while at the same time litigating against state and corporate excesses. In another similarity to Garth's (1992: 256) findings, I observed that Argentine cause lawyers do not view the class action as an organizing tool. None of the cause lawyers I interviewed mentioned community or movement mobilization as one of their goals in using the *amparo colectivo*. Indeed, in cases like the one involving bilingual instruction, the *amparo colectivo* may exacerbate divisions within a movement or community. Other cases, like the one involving pay phone overcharges, resulted in conflicts between cause lawyers and their NGO clients.

These observations are consistent with the well-documented dichotomy between generating public awareness of a particular problem and mobilizing political action to combat it (Scheingold 1974). The Argentine cause lawyers I interviewed, like those in Garth's study, tend to emphasize the former over the latter. Indeed, many Argentine cause lawyers actively eschew the role of lawyer as community or grassroots organizer.

2. Changes in Cause Lawyering Tactics Under the Amparo Colectivo

So, what has been the result, from a larger perspective, of this series of mostly lawyer-driven cases under the *amparo colectivo*? According to one cause lawyer, it is a rather haphazard style of case selection based more on happenstance than on any overarching strategic vision about the direction of cause lawyering in postauthoritarian Argentina.[57] Indeed, there seems to be a disproportionate number of cases that result from what Garth (1992: 261) describes as the serendipity that sometimes brings cause lawyers and clients together. Although the lawyers seem to have been inspired by a new legal device that provides them with the power to challenge state and corporate conduct on a scale previously unavailable, for the most part the individual clients and groups they represent don't seem to have noticed.

Still, Argentine cause lawyers have not given up on the potential of the *amparo colectivo* as a means of collective justice and grassroots mobilization. Indeed, many seem uncomfortable with the gulf that frequently exists between the cause lawyers who are dictating most everything about the collective lawsuit and the people they purport to represent. For example, several cause lawyers I interviewed were keenly aware of the need to work more closely with grassroots groups in developing litigation strategies under the *amparo colectivo*. According to one such cause lawyer, "collective lawsuits require some grassroots organizing, and could be one good way—not the only one, of course—of articulating the claims of a grassroots organization."[58] And according to Julieta Rossi of the human rights group CELS, cause lawyers in her organization make an effort to develop a relationship with the affected group, rather than to simply presume to know the nature and degree of their interests: "We try to be an echo of social demands, rather than try to build our own cases."[59] As such, Rossi suggests that a cause lawyer's legal strategy should include an educational component, so that people will learn about their rights at the same time that those rights are being litigated.[60] Alberto Binder, an Argentine criminal defense lawyer, adds that the educational function is important in creating and sustaining networks among cause lawyers, so that different advocacy groups can become aware of what others are doing and plan their own strategy and set their goals accordingly.[61]

Clinical professors at the University of Palermo have taken some of these ideas to heart in devising a way to work more closely with grassroots groups that they believe will both respond to the current economic crisis and encourage judges to uphold the rule of law.[62] One aspect of the plan deals with legal supply, another with legal demand. On the supply side, the idea is to expand the number of cause lawyers throughout Argentina. Although there is obviously little funding for cause lawyering generally (including through attorneys' fees on *amparo colectivo* cases, as noted above) the Palermo clinic is encouraging the development of public interest clinics at law schools throughout the country. In addition, the clinical professors are developing a law school curriculum that emphasizes practical legal skills rather than the traditional pedagogical model of memorization of codes and other rote learning methods. Outside the law school setting, Martin Bohmer, Palermo's dean, has been active in establishing pro bono clearinghouses to make use of attorneys in private firms who wish (and sometimes are even encouraged) to practice cause lawyering on an occasional basis. Indeed, Bohmer points out that the current economic crisis has been a boon to the pro bono effort, since most large law firms have experienced a downturn in business and would rather permit their associates to engage in a cause lawyering case than lay them off. Thus, the pro bono program in Buenos Aires has grown significantly in the last few years.

Although increasing the supply of cause lawyers may be a challenge, it is dwarfed by the task of increasing legal demand, not because of a lack of legal needs. The increase in unemployment and poverty brought on by the current economic crisis (and the *corralito*) has made the legal plight of most Argentines more intense than at any time in decades. The problem with the kind of legal demand Bohmer and others describe is overcoming the aversion to the legal system felt by many grassroots groups and poor people in general. Although some of that aversion is due to problems within the legal system itself (inefficiency, corruption, lack of independence), some is also due to the inability of cause lawyers to effectively communicate with the leaders of NGOs about their strategies.

In addition to trying to better communicate with NGOs and their leaders, the legal demand strategy being pursued by Palermo involves the legal training of members of grassroots groups. The training sessions, held at Palermo, not only allow the clinical professors to instruct the "students" in the basics of the legal system, they also provide a forum for the discussion of grievances that may have legal solutions. As Bohmer notes, "You overcome distrust of the law by getting things you want through the legal system, or getting into the newspaper."[63] And as those successful entreaties to the legal system increase, two interrelated phenomena will occur: the dispossessed will shed their loathing of the legal system, and the legal system will prove itself capable of upholding the rule of law.

This all may seem a bit idealistic, but according to Sean Arian, a Fulbright fellow from the United States assisting the Palermo clinics:

> Piqueteros [those who hold regular demonstrations throughout Argentina to protest poverty and unemployment] say they are distrustful of the law, but they like the idea of getting trained in the law. Once they start using the legal system, the system will have to react to their needs. Some judges are waiting to do the right thing. And when you encounter those who are corrupt and don't do the right thing you can expose that, you'll provide more transparency in the system.[64]

Bohmer cites a recent example of the way that this model can utilize the legal system in strengthening grassroots groups. He and other clinicians held a discussion session on domestic violence problems with the leaders of one of Buenos Aires' shanty towns (or *villas miserias* as they are known locally). The Palermo clinic does not provide direct assistance in such cases, so it referred the leaders to others who could. The clinicians then asked the leaders about consumer-oriented problems such as running water, electricity, public phones, and sewage. Contracts between the city and public service companies guarantee consumer rights in these areas, but the public is often unaware of them. At that point, according to Bohmer, "they got interested in the legal system. So people don't know about their rights in a regulatory state and how a lawyer can help them."[65]

Such efforts represent a straddling of the fence between legal advocacy and politicization. In effect, these Argentine cause lawyers are attempting to occupy a broad swath of the political-legal continuum described by Scheingold in his concluding essay to the second cause lawyering volume (Scheingold 2001: 385). Previous studies of cause lawyers suggest an inverse relationship between formal legal advocacy and politicization (Scheingold 2001; Kidder and Miyazawa 1993). Thus, for example, Japanese cause lawyers in the study by Kidder and Miyazawa (1993) opted for the latter when the former proved unsuccessful. Conversely, however, my interviews suggest that some Argentine cause lawyers are pursuing both strategies simultaneously. To these lawyers, the strategies are, in fact, complementary; that is, the way to make formal legal advocacy under the *amparo colectivo* truly effective is to consciously interact with grassroots movements in order to determine their legal needs; and the best way for cause lawyers to meet the legal needs of grassroots movements (and to encourage their confidence in the legal system) is through effective use of formal legal tools like the *amparo colectivo*.

3. Cause Lawyers as Fabricators

This chapter has suggested a number of the ways in which cause lawyers fabricate aspects of the state and their own professional lives. First, cause lawyers were involved in codifying collective rights through passage of the *amparo colectivo*. Without the efforts of cause lawyers and other activists, the nascent culture of collective rights in Argentina would not exist.

Second, by fostering public awareness of these recently promulgated collective rights through the media, as well as more direct communication with NGOs, grassroots community organizations, and local community leaders, cause lawyers fabricate demands for their services from clients who generally avoid the law whenever possible and have little or no access to lawyers.

Third, by filing collective lawsuits under the *amparo colectivo* they helped create, cause lawyers solidify the rule of law and democratic institutions. For even if a lawsuit does not result in a favorable judicial decision, the mere act of filing the case, and the publicity surrounding it, enables cause lawyers to legitimize the formal legal process.

This chapter has also suggested that each of these forms of fabrication is fraught with conflict for cause lawyers and their relationship to the causes they espouse. For example, when cause lawyers create a set of collective rights in order to advance the causes of freedom from discrimination and environmental and consumer protection, the development and preservation of the vehicle for asserting such rights (in this case the *amparo colectivo*) frequently becomes more important to the cause lawyers than the underlying cause presented by a specific case. Indeed, the creation and safeguarding of rights and the rule of law often *become* the cause. Thus, for example, the act of filing the case about disparate railroad car conditions—and the publicity surrounding it—becomes more important to the cause lawyers than the eventual result.

Similarly, when cause lawyers fabricate legal demand through public outreach and education, they foster conflict between their goals (development of the rule of law and democratic institutions) and those of the clients and organizations they hope to attract. Clients are typically interested in practical solutions to concrete problems. For them, the rule of law and democratic institutions are the means to an end; to many cause lawyers, the rule of law and democratic institutions *are* the end; the clients' causes are the means. Thus, in the case involving indigenous language, the cause lawyers may have been more interested in testing the vitality of newly created rights and the legal mechanism to enforce them than they were in determining whether a courtroom victory would deepen existing conflicts within the larger indigenous community.

Because of these conflicting roles and agendas, cause lawyers find themselves in a permanent state of contradiction, simultaneously seeking to fabricate the state (through creation/strengthening of democratic institutions and the rule of law), while challenging it through litigation and other forms of legal advocacy. This tension only underscores the somewhat counterintuitive notion that most cause lawyers are inherently conservative.

4. Back to the Coralito

Finally, we can now revisit the question presented at the start of this chapter: Why haven't Argentine cause lawyers used the *amparo colectivo* to challenge state-imposed restrictions on withdrawals from personal bank accounts? Such a lawsuit would most likely be empowering for *both* the cause lawyers and their clients in ways that Garth identifies. It would certainly be a client-driven lawsuit, with active and organized class representatives and class members. If the result were successful for the plaintiffs, it would heighten respect for the judiciary and promote the rule of law. And even if it were unsuccessful, it would increase the public's awareness of its right under the *amparo colectivo*. So why no class actions?

Part of the answer lies in the limitations of the *amparo colectivo* as an instrument of cause lawyering. Judges would be likely to reject a collective lawsuit challenging the *corralito* under the *amparo colectivo* because (1) the case would involve individual claims to money and (2) the constitutional issues on which the case hinges are complicated. Moreover, it is unclear how the proceeds from a successful challenge to the *corralito* would be distributed to the millions of class members, since the *amparo colectivo* contains no provisions for managing such payouts. Chaos—and more lawsuits—would most likely ensue, as individual investors seek a bigger slice of the bank deposit pie.

Another part of the answer lies in the priorities of Argentine cause lawyers: given the combination of few cause lawyers and massive social and economic problems facing the majority of the population, cause lawyers have chosen to focus their efforts on issues other than the *corralito*. The tens of thousands of individual lawsuits challenging the *corralito* graphically demonstrate that there is no shortage of noncause lawyers willing to take on the cause of bank depositors' rights.

A final part of the answer may have to do with the ambivalence of cause lawyers toward the state, an underlying theme of the first cause lawyering volume. For while Argentine cause lawyers are generally critical of the state and the ways its policies impact the poor, the environment, women, consumers, the disabled, persons with HIV, and indigenous communities, they also have an interest in maintaining the integrity and viability of the state and its democratic institutions. Indeed, the *corralito* experience suggests that cause lawyers may have a stronger interest in the integrity of the state and its institutions than noncause lawyers. Those noncause lawyers who chose to represent depositors in challenging the *corralito* most likely gave little thought to the impact that a victory for their client—a single *goteo*—might have on the overall economic well-being of the country. Why should they? Their duty is to their individual client. But the cause lawyers with whom I spoke, aware of the *amparo colectivo* and the potential it has for relief on a broad scale, were much more mindful of the flood that might ensue if a class action challenge to the *corralito* were successful. Despite their general feeling that the *corralito* is unconstitutional, these cause lawyers believe that the alternative is worse; the ruin of the private banking system, and all that would ensue as a result. So while cause lawyers spend much of their time and effort challenging the state, they—perhaps more so than noncause lawyers—will avoid actions that could result in the downfall of the state. Indeed, since much of their work goes into creating and legitimizing rights and state institutions, cause lawyers play a significant role in maintaining those rights and institutions over time. It seems that this role often goes unnoticed by the legal system and many cause lawyers themselves.

Notes

I am very grateful to the Tinker/Nave Research Grant program at the University of Wisconsin for its support of my field research in Argentina. I am also grateful to Jennifer Gassman-Pines for valuable research assistance and translation of documents.

1. Roberto Saba, interview conducted by author, tape recording, Buenos Aires, Argentina, August 2002.

2. Christian Courtis, interview conducted by author, via e-mail, May 2001.

3. Saba, interview; Christian Courtis, e-mail message, December 2002.

4. Public prosecutors have been able to file consumer protection lawsuits on behalf of groups of people for some time.

5. Mariela Puga, interview conducted by author, via e-mail, May 2001.

6. Courtis, interview 2001.

7. Id.

8. Holmes and Sunstein (1999).

9. Saba, interview.

10. Courtis, e-mail message, December 2002.

11. Saba, interview.

12. Mariela Puga, interview conducted by author, tape recording, Buenos Aires, Argentina, August 2002; Saba, interview.

13. There is, of course, a certain irony in Argentine cause lawyers relying on the judiciary, rather than the legislature, in creating a favorable interpretation of the *amparo colectivo*. The Argentine judiciary has long been criticized as inefficient, corrupt, and controlled by whatever civilian or military government happened to be in power at the time. Perhaps the cause lawyers' preference for judicial interpretation rather than congressional dictates concerning the *amparo colectivo* says less about the judiciary than it does about the current perceptions of the Argentine legislature.

14. Garth's view is contradicted, in part, by the research of Barclay and Marshall in this volume. Though the Vermont case involving same sex marriages was not a class action, the cause lawyers behind that case consciously organized a social movement around a lawsuit.

15. Numerous chapters in this and previous cause lawyering volumes document the importance of publicity to the work of cause lawyering. For example, see the chapters of Jayanth K. Krishnan, Ronen Shamir, and Scott Barclay and Anna-Marie Marshall in this volume. See also, Meili (2001).

16. Puga, interview 2002.

17. Saba, interview; Ezequiel Nino, interview conducted by author, tape recording, Buenos Aires, Argentina, August 2002.

18. Puga, interview 2002; Nino, interview; Saba, interview.

19. Saba, interview; Puga, interview 2002.

20. Of course, since some contributors to this volume argue that the term "cause lawyer" includes lawyers who defend private property interests (see Southworth, Hatcher chapters), one might argue that counter-suits which negate pro-consumer decisions under the *amparo colectivo* are examples of very effective cause lawyering.

21. Puga, interview 2002.

22. Nino, interview.

23. Id. Of course, this begs the question: if the violation is clear, how can two different courts reach completely opposite results when examining the identical conduct in two different cases?

24. Puga, interview 2002; Nino, interview.

25. Saba, interview; Puga, interview 2002.

26. Saba, interview.

27. Puga, interview 2002.

28. Id.

29. Puga, interview 2002.

30. Id.

31. Saba, interview.

32. Francisco Cullen, comments at the fifth seminar on Public Interest Law in South America, Buenos Aires, Argentina, November 3, 2000.

33. Puga, interview 2001.

34. Puga, interview 2001; Puga, interview 2002; Nino interview.

35. Martin Bohmer, comments at the Fifth Seminar on Public Interest Law in South America, Buenos Aires, Argentina, November 3, 2000.

36. Puga, interview 2001.

37. Id.

38. Bohmer 2000.

39. See Shdaimah, this volume.

40. Puga, interview 2001; Puga, interview 2002.

41. Martin Bohmer, interview conducted by author, tape recording, Buenos Aires, Argentina, August 2002. Bohmer 2002.

42. Mariela Puga, comments at the fifth seminar on Public Interest Law in South America, Buenos Aires, Argentina, November 3, 2000.

43. Of course, there are many instances in U.S. class actions where the attorneys' goals trump those of the class.

44. Nino, interview; Saba, interview; Meili 1998.

45. Nino, interview.

46. Id. These two cases illustrate that, as noted earlier, cases litigated under the *amparo colectivo* are more likely to succeed when they seek injunctive rather than monetary relief.

47. Saba, interview.

48. Nino, interview; Puga, interview 2002.

49. Nino, interview.

50. Id.

51. Bohmer, interview.

52. This calls to mind the famous Brazilian saying "to my friends, everything; to my enemies, the law."

53. Bohmer, interview.

54. Id.

55. Nino, interview.

56. Others have noted this prestige as one of the motivations behind cause lawyering generally (see Scheingold 2001: 391; Dezalay and Garth 2001).

57. Nino, interview.

58. Courtis, interview.

59. Julieta Rossi, comments at the fifth seminar on Public Interest Law in South America, Buenos Aires, Argentina, November 3, 2000.

60. Id.

61. Alberto Binder, comments at the fifth seminar on Public Interest Law in South America, Buenos Aires, Argentina, November 3, 2000.

62. Bohmer, interview; Sean Arian, interview conducted by author, tape recording, Buenos Aires, Argentina, August 2002.

63. Bohmer, interview.

64. Arian, interview.

65. Bohmer, interview.

References

Bell, Derrick A. 1976. "Serving Two Masters: Integration Ideals and Client Interests in School Desegregation Cases." *Yale Law Journal* 85: 470.

Bronstein, Alvin J. 1997. "Representing the Powerless: Lawyers Can Make a Difference." *Maine Law Review* 49: 1.

Cerminara, Kathy L. 1998. "The Class Action Suit as a Method of Patient Empowerment in the Managed Care Setting." *American Journal of Law and Medicine* 24: 7.

Chayes, Abram. 1976. "The Role of the Judge in Public Law Litigation." *Harvard Law Review* 89: 1281.

Dezalay, Yves, and Bryant G. Garth. 2001. "Constructing Law Out of Power: Investing in Human Rights as an Alternative Political Strategy," in *Cause Lawyering and the State in a Global Era*, ed. A. Sarat and S. Scheingold. New York: Oxford University Press.

Ellmann, Stephen. 1992. "Client-Centeredness Multiplied: Individual Autonomy and Collective Mobilization in Public Interest Lawyers' Representation of Groups." *Virginia Law Review* 78: 1103.

Garth, Bryant. 1992. "Power and Legal Artifice: The Federal Class Action." *Law & Society Review* 26, no. 2: 237.

Garth, Bryant, Ilene H. Nagel, and S. Jay Plager. 1988. "The Institution of the Private Attorney General: Perspectives from an Empirical Study of Class Action Litigation." *Southern California Law Review* 81: 353.

Halliday, Terrence, and Lucien Karpik. 1997. "Preface," in *Lawyers and the Rise of Western Political Liberalism*, ed. T. Halliday and K. Karpik. Oxford: Oxford University Press.

Herr, David F. 2000. *Annotated Manual for Complex Litigation*, 3rd ed. Minneapolis: West Publishing.

Holmes, Stephen, and Cass R. Sunstein. 1999. *The Cost of Rights: Why Liberty Depends on Taxes*. New York: W. W. Norton.

Kidder, Robert, and Setsuo Miyazawa. 1993. "Long-Term Strategies in Japanese Environmental Litigation." *Law and Social Inquiry* 18, no. 4: 605.

Knudsen, Nora. 2002. "Argentina," in *Legal Systems of the World: A Political, Social, and Cultural Encyclopedia*, ed. Herbert M. Kritzer, Bryant Garth, and C. Neal Tate. Santa Barbara, CA: ABC-CLIO.

Mather, Lynn. 1982. "Conclusion: The Mobilizing Potential of Class Actions." *Indiana Law Journal* 57: 451.

Meili, Stephen E. 1998. "Cause Lawyers and Social Movements: A Comparative Perspective on Democratic Change in Argentina and Brazil," in *Cause Lawyering: Political Commitments and Professional Responsibilities*, ed. A. Sarat and S. Scheingold. New York: Oxford University Press.

————. 2001. "Latin American Cause Lawyering Networks," in *Cause Lawyering and the State in a Global Era*, ed. A. Sarat and S. Scheingold. New York: Oxford University Press.

Minow, Martha L. 1991. "From Class Actions to Miss Saigon: The Concept of Representation in the Law." *Cleveland State Law Review* 39: 269.

Rabossi, Eduardo. 1993. "The Role of the Judiciary in the Review of Human Rights Violations in Argentina," in *Transition to Democracy in Latin America: The Role of the Judiciary*, ed. Irwin P. Stotzky. San Francisco: Westview Press.

Sabsay, Daniel Alberto. 1997. "Amparo Colectivo Created by the Constitutional Reform of 1994," in *Notebook of Judicial Analysis*, *Special Publications Series*, ed. Felipe Gonzalez Morales.

Scheingold, Stuart A. 1974. *The Politics of Rights: Lawyers, Public Policy, and Political Change*. New Haven, Conn.: Yale University Press.

————. 2001. "Cause Lawyering and Democracy in Transnational Perspective: A Postscript," in *Cause Lawyering and the State in a Global Era*, ed. A. Sarat and S. Scheingold. New York: Oxford University Press.

Simon, William H. 1984. "Visions of Practice in Legal Thought." *Stanford Law Review* 36: 469.

Snow, Peter, and Gary W. Wyna. 1990. "Argentina: Politics in a Conflict Society," in *The Civil Law Tradition: Europe, Latin America and East Asia*, ed. John Henry Merryman, David S. Clark, and John O. Haley. Charlottesville, VA: Michie.

Soine, Lynne, and Mary Ann Burg. 1995. "Combining Class Action Litigation and Social Science Research: A Case Study in Helping Homeless Women with Children." *American University Journal of Gender and the Law* 3: 159.

Southworth, Ann. 1999. "Collective Representation for the Disadvantaged: Variations in Problems of Accountability." *Fordham Law Review* 67: 2449.

Yeazell, Stephen C. 1989. "Collective Litigation as Collective Action." *University of Illinois Law Review* 42.

CHAPTER THIRTEEN

Asylum Law Practice in the United Kingdom after the Human Rights Act

RICHARD J. MAIMAN

Introduction: Incorporation of the European Convention on Human Rights in the United Kingdom

The United Kingdom historically has been a challenging setting for cause lawyering of all kinds, and particularly for legal activism on behalf of human rights. Numerous explanations have been offered for the relatively modest impact that rights-oriented litigation has had on British law. A short list of reasons might include the absence of a written constitution containing enumerated rights, the nation's historic commitment to the principle of parliamentary sovereignty, its tradition of deference to government authority and general lack of rights consciousness, and the fact that Britain's racial and ethnic minorities are poorly organized and significantly underrepresented in the national government. Those who have studied rights-based litigation in the United Kingdom have described Britain in similar ways—as a "cold climate" for cause lawyering (Boon 2001), "a highly constrained system" (Sterett 1998), and "an especially inhospitable site for the development of a judicial rights revolution" (Epp 1998).

Great Britain's formal legal regime experienced an important change with the enactment of the Human Rights Act (HRA) 1998, which went into force in Scotland in July 1999 and in England and Wales in October 2000. This law was part of an ambitious agenda of constitutional reform measures—statutory changes in basic governmental structures and processes—proposed by the Blair government after its sweeping victory in the 1997 general election. The HRA obliges public authorities in Great Britain to observe the civil and political rights enumerated in the European Convention on Human Rights (ECHR). The United Kingdom, a founding member of the Council of Europe, ratified the Convention in 1951 but did not incorporate the Convention into its domestic law. Thus, while the British government was required to observe the Convention rights of its citizens until the HRA was adopted, those rights were not enforceable in British courts. Instead, persons alleging Convention violations by the British government were obliged to seek relief through the European Court of Human Rights in Strasbourg, France.[1]

The HRA steers an intricate course between the conflicting, indeed incompatible, principles of fundamental law and popular sovereignty. On the one hand, the HRA functions as a kind of "super statute," setting a standard for all past and future legislation. However, the law does not actually "entrench" the ECHR; as an act of Parliament, it is subject to amendment or even repeal by a future Parliament. Moreover, the HRA does not go so far as to empower judges to nullify legislation that they find to conflict with Convention rights. Rather, when interpreting statutes they are directed to "take into account" the Convention and its jurisprudence in the European Court; if no reading of the law consistent with the Convention can be found, then the court may issue a "declaration of incompatibility." Parliament retains the ultimate authority to decide whether or not to remedy the incompatibility by altering or repealing the offending statute. Nothing in the HRA precludes Parliament from simply letting a law stand in spite of its declared incompatibility with the European Convention.[2]

Whatever its limitations as an instrument of fundamental law, the HRA did introduced a striking new feature into the political-legal culture of Great Britain. Since the effective consolidation of Parliament's lawmaking power in the early nineteenth century, British judges have never been nearly as active in policy-making as their counterparts in the United States, Canada, and many other democratic states. In recent decades the practice of judicial review has provided judges with a means of holding public officials accountable to the law. However, in the absence of a written constitution, judicial review has not accommodated challenges to the laws themselves. Abel's (1998: 94) general characterization of judges—that they "are adept at devising reasons for not exercising power, anxious about being attacked as political or exposed as impotent"—is a particularly apt description of the restraint traditionally exhibited by judges in the United Kingdom.[3] By making EC rights enforceable in British courts, the HRA significantly expanded the potential for judges to exercise power in relation to the executive and legislature. By extension, it also gave lawyers unprecedented opportunities to influence how that authority is used. In light of this important development, the time seems right to reexamine the status of human rights lawyering in the United Kingdom. This chapter focuses on the responses of one group of legal practitioners to what Abel (1998: 69) calls the "occasions for cause lawyering" presented by the HRA.

The Politics of Political Asylum in Great Britain

There is no field of legal practice in contemporary Britain where the adversarial lines between lawyers and government are as clearly drawn as in immigration law, particularly as it relates to the issue of political asylum. Immigration has been a highly contested political and social issue in the United Kingdom for many years. The 1951 Geneva Convention on the Status of Refugees, part of the postwar international legal response to the Nazi genocide, obliges Britain and other signatories to grant political asylum to refugees who can demonstrate a well-founded fear of persecution in their countries of origin, based on nationality, race, ethnicity, religion, political opinion, or social grouping. At the same time the Attlee government was signing the Refugee Convention, however, it was also discussing ways to slow the rising tide of immigration into Britain from throughout its colonial empire. The next Labour government, that of Harold Wilson in the 1960s, introduced the first legal restrictions on such immigration. Sterett (1998: 297) notes that while the Labour party in the 1980s and 1990s often criticized the Thatcher government's immigration policies, it was always careful to refrain from supporting more open immigration.

Labour's 1997 election manifesto included a single brief reference to asylum reform as part of its "modernizing" agenda.[4] The issue suddenly emerged from the shadows in 1999, when a sudden spike in the number of asylum applications made in the United Kingdom produced for the first time a significant backlog of unresolved cases. At the same time, notice began to be drawn to the large proportion of asylum seekers who remained in the United Kingdom after their applications were rejected. Amid mounting public concerns about its administration of asylum policy, the Blair government began articulating and aggressively pursuing the twin goals of reducing the number of applicants for political asylum in the United Kingdom and removing refugees from the country more expeditiously once their asylum claims had failed.

The 1999 Immigration and Asylum Act represented the government's first attempt to achieve what it called a "fairer, faster and firmer" process of distinguishing between ordinary economic migrants and genuine political refugees. Although the 1999 law retained some authoritarian features of earlier immigration laws, it also provided applicants with a new right of appeal from an initial rejection of their claim on human rights (that is, European Convention) grounds. This provision of the immigration law came into force with the HRA in 2000. The law also established a new agency to provide support services for the 50,000 asylum seekers who were now dispersed around the country.

As the government struggled to come to grips with the many dimensions of the asylum problem, its initial human rights orientation gave way to a much tougher approach. For example, the 2002 Nationality, Immigration and Asylum Act included a "white list" of ten "safe" countries from which asylum applications would be considered "clearly unfounded" (thus restoring a provision of the 1996 Asylum and Immigration Act that Labour had repealed in 1999). This law also codified a more restrictive interpretation of the "exceptional leave to remain" status for refugees from nations at war. In an effort to reduce asylum case backlogs, the government established a secure "fast-track" processing center where asylum applicants whose cases were considered without merit could be detained while their cases were processed. Britain also began to discuss with other European Union members and United Nations officials the possibility of developing refugee processing centers closer to refugees' home countries, a move that might have required some formal modification of the United Kingdom's commitment to the Refugee Convention. Home Secretary David Blunkett announced a new policy of refusing subsistence benefits to any refugee whose application for asylum was not made "as soon as reasonably practicable" after arrival in the United Kingdom. Blunkett argued that such a rule was needed to discourage persons from entering the country illegally and claiming asylum only after they were apprehended. Other measures included cuts in the legal aid funding available for the initial stages of some asylum cases, and the addition of seven more "safe" countries to the "white list."

The government's third major overhaul of asylum and immigration policy, the 2004 Asylum and Immigration Act, placed even greater emphasis on the persistent problem of the refusal of failed asylum seekers to return to their countries of origin. To shorten the time-consuming asylum appeal process, the law merged the two tiers of asylum appeals tribunals into one, and severely restricted judicial review of immigration tribunal decisions.

The Blair government has consistently justified its attempts to control the flow of asylum-seekers into Britain on humanitarian grounds. There are several parts to its case. The government has argued that the more reason refugees have to believe that they will never be sent home from the United Kingdom, the greater the physical risks they will be willing to take to get there. The government has also asserted that the real victims of an overburdened system are the genuine political refugees who may get crowded out by those wanting to enter the United Kingdom simply for economic reasons. The humanitarian argument shades into a more overtly political one when government officials claim that a widespread perception that the asylum system is out of control could put legal immigration itself at risk. It is no secret that since the beginning of the Blair government's second term in 2001, Labour strategists have identified immigration policy as one of the party's greatest areas of vulnerability among its core constituents. There is empirical support for this concern. In the last several years a number of European centrist parties have suffered electoral losses attributable mainly to their opponents' anti-immigration campaigns.[5] Although Britain's Conservative Party tried without success to exploit the issue in the 2001 general election, the racist British National Party did make inroads in subsequent local council elections in several northern England cities. An opinion poll in 2002 reported that nearly 40 percent of Britons are "concerned about" asylum, compared with only 5 percent in 1997 (Ahmed and Mathiason 2004); two years later, the Conservative Party was reported by another survey to be running slightly ahead of Labour in representing voters' views on immigration policy (Riddell 2004).[6]

Early in 2003 the prime minister tried to regain the political offensive on asylum policy with a dramatic pledge that his government would achieve a 50 percent reduction in the number of monthly asylum applications by September of that year. However, as the media quickly noted and often repeated, the government had chosen an artificially high monthly figure as its baseline for comparison. Thus the eventual Home Office announcement that the government had achieved its goal received little attention, much less acclaim.[7]

Asylum Practice as a Site for Cause Lawyering

Efforts by the Blair government to maintain control of the asylum issue have proceeded on the judicial front as well, with the Home Office defending itself aggressively in court against a number of HRA-based legal challenges to its asylum policies and practices. In 2002 the Home Office lost a Court of Appeal case in which the government's practice of assessing automatic 2,000 pound fines against truck drivers carrying clandestine stowaways was found "incompatible" with the fair trial guarantee under Article 6 of the European Convention.[8] Another Article 6 defeat for the government came in a 2003 Court of Appeal decision that the blanket denial of state benefits to those who made "late" asylum claims also amounted to an EC violation because of the absence of a right of appeal.[9] But in a legal challenge to one of the government's most controversial measures to reduce the backlog of asylum applications, the House of Lords held that the Home Office did not violate EC Article 5 by holding some asylum seekers in a "fast-track" detention center while their cases were being initially decided.[10]

Regardless of their outcomes, cases like these demonstrate that the HRA has had some impact in the field of asylum law, since without the new law most them would not have been in court in the first place. In addition to offering asylum seekers more grounds for resisting removal than the Refugee Convention itself, the HRA also provides a basis for substantive challenges to the asylum laws themselves. This is indeed a different situation from the one Sterett (1998: 295) described in the 1990s, when UK immigration lawyers lacked legal tools for making effective rights-based claims and had to rely instead on "arguments narrowly framed as interpretations of the existing rules." Although Britain's legal framework has changed markedly in the intervening years, the political environment has been transformed as well. With the asylum issue now representing a significant threat to its hold on power, the government has been more determined than ever to resist all challenges to its freedom of movement, including those based on human rights claims.

Under these circumstances, how useful a tool for cause lawyering is the HRA actually turning out to be? Seeking a ground-level answer to this question, I conducted interviews in 2002 and 2003 with twelve solicitors and three barristers, all specialists in immigration and asylum law practicing in the cities of London, Birmingham, and Colchester. The interviews took place at a time when asylum was arguably the most prominent domestic issue in the United Kingdom. All of the solicitors worked for small to medium-sized firms that were about evenly divided between general practices and those devoted exclusively to immigration work. Each of the three barristers was associated with medium-sized chambers whose members handled mostly immigration, employment, and social security cases. Virtually all of the respondents' asylum work was supported by legal aid. No claim is made that this is a representative sample of asylum law practitioners in the United Kingdom, and the fact that several of the respondents have been directly involved in high-profile test cases indicates pretty clearly that it is not. However, the interviews do yield useful insights into the realities of cause lawyering in a setting where legal rights are largely a gift of government, to be extended and withdrawn as political circumstances permit or dictate.

Judging the Judges

Without exception, the respondents reported that they had viewed the HRA in a positive light before its passage. Most reported having had a sense of "real anticipation" and "new possibilities" as the HRA's starting date approached. As one solicitor put it, "Prior to October 2, 2000, we thought the Human Rights Act would be the Holy Grail. We said, 'We're going to make hay with this!'" Some of the others, however, had been more measured in their expectations. A barrister who teaches part time in a law school said she "didn't expect the HRA to be that far reaching" because "it was never entrenched, it was never going to be like a constitutional piece of legislation." In her opinion, many lawyers were not well informed enough about the law to understand its limitations. "But I think from an academic point of view I was aware of that, and that's maybe where the practitioners differ somewhat from the academics."

None of these lawyers remembered having done much to prepare themselves for the HRA's arrival. Several had attended formal HRA training sessions lasting a day or less, but no one could recall ever attending a meeting to discuss potential HRA test cases with lawyers outside their own law firm or chambers. Most respondents said the daily demands of their practices left them without much time to engage in strategic, "blue skies" thinking about the HRA. However, just about all said that by the time the HRA came into force they were quite familiar with its content and at least generally aware of how the law might be used in their practices.

None of these respondents reported having any qualms about using the HRA as aggressively as possible. All said they cited its provisions frequently in support of their clients' asylum cases. There was agreement among most of the lawyers, however, about appellate judges' general lack of receptivity to HRA arguments. For example, the solicitor who had expected to "make hay" with the HRA added that he had had to quickly adjust his expectations downward as post-HRA asylum cases began to be decided. Evidently none of the lawyers had expected the HRA to make the government any more cooperative or conciliatory, but the continued resistance of adjudicators and judges to rights-based arguments came as an unpleasant surprise to some of them. "What we forgot," one respondent said, "was that the same conservative judges would be deciding HRA cases as decided Immigration Act cases overall." In fact, he had not "forgotten" who would be deciding the cases, but apparently he had either assumed or hoped that judges would respond quite differently to arguments under the HRA than they had to claims based on the Refugee Convention. Most of the respondents agreed that the HRA had not altered the fundamental hostility of immigration adjudicators and appellate judges toward asylum seekers' legal claims, and—a few respondents felt—toward asylum seekers themselves. There was general agreement that, as one respondent put it, the HRA "has delayed some removals, but in few cases has it made any substantive difference."

However, two of the respondents demurred mildly from the general perception that judges were stubbornly resisting the expansion of refugees' rights under the HRA. One solicitor reported that although he had discerned no changes among immigration adjudicators, he did believe that some appellate judges were responding to the HRA somewhat more favorably than they had to the Convention alone. Before the HRA, "judges could respond to EC-based claims or not, as they pleased," he said, but "judges now *have to* take the EC into account." The solicitor said that he now brings "lots of cases [on HRA grounds] that would fall through the cracks of the UK's immigration law, cases that would otherwise be lost because there is no specific ground." As examples he cited the Convention's Article 11 right of association, which may apply to asylum applicants who have lived for a number of years in the United Kingdom, and the Article 8 guarantee of privacy and family life. "So the Human Rights Act gives me things the Immigration Act never did. It gives you a lot more scope for arguing things, and it affects a wider range of clients. . . . The courts are being persuaded that these things can be expanded." This lawyer succinctly summarized the impact of the HRA on his work by noting that since the act's passage, "my submissions are less 'grovelly.'"

To illustrate what the HRA can add to the asylum lawyer's legal repertoire, one of the barristers described a case that she had handled prior to October 2000 involving a Colombian refugee. Although the adjudicator agreed that the applicant might face persecution in his home country, there was no Refugee Convention basis found for his asylum claim. After the HRA came into force, the barrister said, "we went back on the human rights appeal . . . and the adjudicator allowed it under human rights on the strength of the previous determination [of likely ill-treatment by government authorities]. Had the human rights been before the first adjudicator we would probably have succeeded. . . . We just went on what had gone before. The situation hadn't changed."

This barrister also reported having won a recent immigration appeal tribunal case by arguing that returning an Albanian Muslim rape victim to Kosovo would amount to a violation of her Article 8 right to respect for her private and family life. However, she noted that a Court of Appeal case with similar facts had since been decided the other way, a precedent that she worried "would certainly scupper a lot of my cases of mental health." But in any event, she said, these were both quite exceptional cases. In her experience with more conventional asylum applicants, adjudicators and judges seldom gave her clients anything more from the HRA than they had already given them from the Geneva Refugee Convention. "If you've got your bog standard, someone say from Ethiopia who is wanted because they're in the opposition party, you've got a potential reason, so your Article 3 and Convention reasons run alongside each other anyway."

All of the practitioners reported that even before the HRA became law they had routinely invoked the European Convention in their asylum cases, though usually without much success. Several of the respondents remarked that this history of EC usage might now be working against asylum lawyers, since judges who were already familiar with EC-based arguments were not inclined to re-think them now that they were being raised under the HRA. Several lawyers noted that asylum practice prior to the HRA was probably unique among legal specializations in its reliance on Convention rights. As one solicitor explained: "In immigration law, advocates have always relied on the European Conven-tion, whereas in other fields lawyers would only have used codified law. That's because if your client is facing removal to Iraq, you'll try anything. The stakes are not so high in other fields, so there's no need to push the boundaries."

"Trying anything" and "pushing the boundaries" are all in a day's work for these asylum lawyers, who appear vividly aware of the consequences in store for some of their unsuccessful clients. One solicitor compared asylum work to han-dling death penalty appeals: "You're making decisions that affect the client's life. That preys on me. Could I have done more? When *I* went to Turkey I was scared to death! That's why immigration lawyers desperately use every tactic to pre-vent clients from being sent back."

David vs. Goliath

The respondents tended to speak with a mixture of disappointment and res-ignation when they described the failure of judges to respond more positively to the HRA. However, their strongest and most negative feelings were reserved not for the judiciary, but rather for their usual adversary, the Home Office, and for the government itself. Several of the lawyers wondered out loud how the same government that had introduced the HRA could also adopt such repres-sive policies toward refugees. Virtually all of them spoke of seeing partisan pol-itics behind the government's efforts to discourage asylum seekers from com-ing to the United Kingdom. Describing "how it might have been" in asylum law, one solicitor pointed out that the HRA had had an "immediate impact" in the field of social security law. The reason, she said, was that the government had anticipated EC Article 6 "fair hearing" challenges to the long-standing proce-dure whereby welfare applicants who were turned down by a committee of the local council then appealed to another panel drawn from the same body. Even before October 2000, the Social Security Ministry had moved to establish an entirely new set of "impartial" administrative tribunals to hear such appeals. The fact that no such adjustments had been made in immigration procedures led her to conclude that the asylum issue was "too political" for the government to deal with except in a highly adversarial fashion. The government, she said, apparently regarded asylum seekers as "more expendable" than British citizens. Like several other lawyers who described their clients as "scapegoats" and "easy targets," this respondent said she felt "quite angry" at the government for what she regarded as its harsh—and politically expedient—antirefugee stance. Most of the lawyers said that they found it impossible not to sympathize with their clients, and indeed, to admire them. As one solicitor put it: "These are the kind of people you *want* in your society. They're dynamic!" Asked if he thought all of his clients were equally worthy of receiving asylum, he replied sharply, "If we get it wrong, so what? If the Home Office gets it wrong, the person goes back to be killed."

Despite these strong words, however, these lawyers seemed to think of the government less as an evil adversary than as an inordinately powerful one. Several used the metaphor of David and Goliath to capture the contrast between their resources and those of the Home Office. The government's greatest single advantage in asylum cases is its capacity to define the rules themselves. This point was nicely illustrated by one solicitor whose firm had brought an important case to the House of Lords in 2000 on the important issue of "third country removals." Under the 1996 Asylum and Immigration Act the United Kingdom was prohibited from expelling asylum-seekers if it found a substantial risk that they would face either governmental *or nongovernmental* persecution in their country of origin. However, despite having accepted this restriction on its own deportation powers, the Home Office continued to return some failed asylum-seekers to France and Germany, "third countries" that did not take nongovernmental persecution into account in deciding whether to deport individuals to their countries of origin. The House of Lords found that this practice breached the 1996 Asylum and Immigration Act.[11] The respondent's victory was short-lived, though, because a few months later Parliament amended the statute to define such removals to France and Germany as lawful. The solicitor's verdict on this outcome was: "We're smarter than the Home Office. They had to change the law to beat us."

By winning politically what it had lost in court, the government demonstrated the true extent of its power. This was neither the first nor the last time that the Home Secretary reacted to an unfavorable asylum decision by threatening, proposing, or simply announcing changes in the rules. Referring to Home Secretary Blunkett's penchant for making angry comments when his policies were dealt setbacks in court, one solicitor suggested that these outbursts might actually be calculated to call attention to the government's position, and that perhaps losing a court case might be a deliberate tactic in the government's larger campaign to strengthen its hand. "[The Home Office] seems willing to take its losses," he observed, "and then blame the judges if the public gets angry. And if the existing law isn't strict enough, the government simply offers to make new law."

Whether or not losing court cases has ever actually been part of its larger political strategy, the government does enjoy another significant advantage over individual asylum lawyers in being able to pick and choose among the cases are taken to the immigration appeals tribunal and into the courts. By settling the cases it considers weak, the Home Office avoids the risk of losing on appeal and establishing adverse judicial precedents. "We appeal everything," said one solicitor. "They appeal the odd one or two. Of course, that means you can end up in the Court of Appeal with a case you don't like." Another lawyer observed: "The Home Office has a strategy. They're choosing which cases to take and not to take. It settles all the strong cases. We can't wait for the strong case."

Several of the respondents noted that asylum practitioners rarely have the luxury of litigating strategically, of "waiting for the strong case," because their clients typically are in such desperate straits. One solicitor illustrated this problem by describing a recent case that he "didn't like" because his client, a Turkish Kurd, "simply had too many problems." Having fled Turkey to avoid the military draft, the client had first failed to gain asylum in Germany, then entered the United Kingdom illegally and made a new asylum application. Although the solicitor judged the case to be factually weak, he nevertheless felt compelled to take his client's deportation order to the Court of Appeal because it was the only hope he had of avoiding removal from the United Kingdom. Although the case predated implementation of the HRA, the Home Secretary had already adopted a policy of compliance with EC Article 3 by not deporting persons who were likely to be subjected to torture for any reason by their home governments. The case thus invited a definitive ruling on the appropriateness of *all* returns of Kurdish refugees to Turkey, a country with a reputation for harsh treatment of its ethnic minorities. After examining much confusing and conflicting evidence about the prevalence of official torture in Turkey, the court found that the Home Secretary had acted reasonably in concluding that if the applicant were sent to Turkey he probably would *not* be subjected to torture, although he would no doubt be jailed as a draft evader.[12]

The solicitor stated frankly that he regretted not having had a better case—or at least a better client—for litigating this significant issue. He could not help thinking that if the court had been confronted with a more sympathetic refugee (rather than an acknowledged draft evader and illegal entrant), it might have been inclined to reach a different conclusion about the evidence on torture. Acknowledging ruefully that many subsequent cases involving Kurdish refugees had been lost under the this precedent, the lawyer said, "We knew the government and the courts would see it as a 'floodgates' issue, since Turkey is one of the leading producers of UK asylum seekers." It also seemed to pain him to think that the outcome might have damaged his reputation within the community of asylum lawyers. In fact, this case was mentioned by several other respondents as a particularly egregious example of the dangers of litigating a weak test case.

Not all of the respondents saw an irresolvable tension between conscientiously representing asylum clients' interests and bringing the best possible test cases, however. One solicitor emphasized how seriously his firm takes its responsibility *not* to take cases forward that have little or no merit (regulations require that a legal aid case must have at least a 50 percent chance of succeeding for an appeal to be taken). "That's why [my firm] has such a good record [in asylum appeals]," he said. "We usually win *something* for our clients in the cases we take." He noted that asylum law is one area of practice where "you're spoiled for choice. You never have to worry that there won't be more cases." He expressed the strong belief that the sheer volume of asylum cases means that lawyers are morally obligated to screen out weak cases to make more room for those with a better chance of succeeding on appeal. Whether or not other solicitors observe such strict screening practices as this one does, they can never enjoy the same amount of discretion as the Home Office in choosing the cases they would like to litigate.[13]

Conclusion: Human Rights Mainstreamed, Human Rights Lawyers Marginalized?

The observations and experiences of these asylum lawyers appear to correspond closely to Abel's (1998: 103) dictum that "[c]ause lawyering is most successful when a confident government is engaged in social change and most often frustrated when a frightened government is desperately scrambling to retain power." In 1997 "a confident government . . . engaged in social change" by making good on its election pledge to incorporate the European Convention on Human Rights into Britain's domestic law. In only a few years, however, amid a widespread perception that Britain's political asylum system had broken down, "a frightened government . . . scrambling to retain power" was developing increasingly authoritarian measures to curb the influx of asylum seekers, while fighting a rear-guard action against human rights challenges to its autonomy. It was a period, then, when political conditions were shifting rapidly from those in which Abel says cause lawyering is "most successful" to those in which it is "most often frustrated." Caught in this legal-political whipsaw, asylum lawyers were struggling to use the HRA—a gift that few had expected but all were happy to receive—to improve their clients' prospects. The evident frustration of these respondents underscores some of the difficulties faced by rights lawyers working in a legal regime where rights are essentially artifacts of government policy.

Although the HRA "mainstreamed" Convention rights by making them justiciable in the British courts, it stopped well short of "entrenching" them. The essence of the British government's power—its unchallengeable capacity to make, unmake, and remake its own rules—remains unaffected by the HRA. This control, coupled with the government's capacity to decide how, when, and whether to defend its policies and practices in court, provide it with virtually everything it needs to preserve its autonomy over asylum policy. The government's ability to pass legislation virtually removing asylum appeals from the jurisdiction of the courts further illustrates the extent of its authority. With the enactment of this measure by Parliament in 2004, asylum lawyers, whose influence on policymaking was already severely limited, found themselves even more marginalized than before.

It is possible, of course, that this new provision may itself be challenged on HRA grounds in court. Since the HRA some judges have demonstrated more willingness to question some of the government's asylum initiatives, but it remains to be seen whether the courts can overcome their traditional attitude of deference to the executive, particularly on matters relating to immigration policy. An appellate court could well decide that the provision of an opportunity for human rights claims within the immigration appeal process itself fully satisfies the fair hearing requirements of the European Convention. Although such a scenario is highly speculative at this time, its very possibility reinforces the conclusion that the United Kingdom remains as problematic an environment for human rights lawyering today as it was before the HRA was adopted.

Notes

1. Through 1996, the European Court of Human Rights had found forty-one violations of the Convention by the United Kingdom, the highest figure for any Council of Europe member state. Jackson (1997).

2. Lord Irvine (2002), the former Lord Chancellor and one of the Human Rights Act's chief sponsors, has described the delicate balance struck by the law in this way: "[The Human Rights Act] retains parliament's *legal* right to enact legislation which is incompatible with the Convention. But it dramatically reduces its *political* capacity to do so."

3. The political left in Britain—traditionally deeply distrustful of the conservatism

of British judges—has never viewed judicial activism as a means of promoting progressive social change. The most influential leftist critique of judges' involvement in policy making is J. A. G. Grffith's *The Politics of the Judiciary*, published in five editions between 1977 and 1997.

4. Labour's manifesto states: "Every country must have firm control over immigration and Britain is no exception. All applications, however, should be dealt with speedily and fairly. . . . The system for dealing with asylum seekers is expensive and slow—there are many undecided cases dating back beyond 1993. We will ensure swift and fair decisions on whether someone can stay or go" (Labour Party 1997: 35).

5. The People's Party in Switzerland, the Freedom Party in Austria, and the Vlaams Bloc Party in Belgium all have been successful in national elections by campaigning on anti-immigration platforms. Home Secretary Blunkett referred explicitly to these outcomes in an article suggesting that Britain might see similar results if the public did not see Labour as having workable immigration and asylum policies. See Blunkett (2003).

6. Britain's tabloid newspaper readers have been served a steady diet of incendiary headlines and "exposes" portraying a government helpless to stop "bogus refugees" and "asylum cheats" from flooding into "soft-touch Britain." For detailed discussion of the themes of tabloid newspaper coverage of the asylum issue see Greenslade (2003).

7. The government's figures showed that 4,200 applications were received in September 2003, compared with 8,500 a year before. See Travis (2003). A few months later the Home Office announced that the number of asylum applications filed in 2004 was 41 percent lower than in 2003. See Tempest (2004).

8. *International Transport Roth GmbH and ORS v Secretary of State for the Home Department* [2002] EWCA Civ 158.

9. *R on the Application of Q and ORS v Secretary of State for the Home Department* [2003] EWCA Civ 364. When this case was initially decided against the government in the high court, it provoked an angry public reaction from Home Secretary Blunkett, who said in a radio interview that he was "fed up with having to deal with a system where parliament debates issues and the judges overturn them." His comments brought a quick response from the lord chief justice, Lord Woolf, who said, "The law now includes the Human Rights Act. By upholding the act the courts are not interfering with the will of parliament." See Dyer (2003).

10. *Saadi & ORS v Secretary of State for the Home Department* [2001] EWCA Civ 1512. When a lower court decision in this case went against the government, Home Secretary Blunkett denounced both the decision and the "human rights lobby" whose legal challenge to the detention of asylum applicants policy he said was interfering with "the effective operation of tough but fair immigration controls." See Travis (2002).

11. This case was *R v Secretary of State for the Home Department, ex parte Adan; R v. Secretary of State for the Home Department, ex parte Aitseguer* [2000] UKHL 67.

12. The solicitor was describing the case of *R v. Secretary of State for the Home Department, ex parte Abdullah Turgut* [2000] EWCA Civ 22.

13. These differences in approaches to case screening appear to be fairly closely related to the solicitor's type of practice. The respondents whose firms handle legal aid asylum cases exclusively were less inclined to emphasize stringent screening of cases on

their merits than those whose firms engage in immigration work as part of a broader practice. In the latter type of firm, the "immigration team" typically has some accountability to the rest of the organization (which may be helping subsidize its legal aid cases with its other work) for the costs and the outcomes of its asylum cases.

References

Books, Chapters, Journal Articles, and Reports

Abel, Richard. 1998. "Speaking Truth to Power: Occasions for Cause Lawyering," in *Cause Lawyering: Political Commitments and Professional Responsibilities,* ed. Austin Sarat and Stuart Scheingold, 69–117. New York: Oxford University Press.

Boon, Andrew. 2001. "Cause Lawyering in a Cold Climate: The Impact(s) of Globalization on the United Kingdom," in *Cause Lawyering and the State in a Global Era*, ed. Austin Sarat and Stuart Scheingold, eds., 143–85. New York: Oxford University Press.

Epp, Charles R. 1998. *The Rights Revolution: Lawyers, Activists, and Supreme Courts in Comparative Perspective.* Chicago: University of Chicago Press.

Grffith , J. A. G. 1997. *The Politics of the Judiciary.* 5th ed. London: Fontana Press.

Irvine of Lairg, Lord, The Lord Chancellor. 2002. "The Human Rights Act Two Years On: An Analysis." Durham University, the inaugural Irvine Human Rights Lecture, November 1.

Jackson, Donald W. 1997. *The United Kingdom Confronts the European Convention on Human Rights.* Gainesville: University of Florida Press.

Labour Party. 1997. *New Labour—Because Britain Deserves Better.* London: Labour Party.

Sterett, Susan. 1998. "Caring About Individual Cases: Immigration Lawyering in Britain," in *Cause Lawyering and the State in a Global Era*, ed. Austin Sarat and Stuart Scheingold, 293–316. New York: Oxford University Press.

Newspaper Articles

Ahmed, Kamal, and Nick Mathiason. 2004. "How Visa Scam Caught Blair in Migration Trap." *The Observer* (April 4).

Blunkett, David. 2003. "Failure to Tackle All Types of Immigration Head-On Can Open the Doors Wide to the Extreme Right." *The Observer* (December 14).

Dyer, Clare. 2003. "Woolf Defends Judge Over Rights Ruling." *The Guardian* (March 7).

Greenslade, Roy. 2003. "Lexicon of Lies." *The Guardian* (May 19).

Tempest, Matthew. 2004. "Asylum Applications Down 41 Percent." *The Guardian* (February 24).

Riddell, Peter. 2004. "Labour Setback Is Step Forward for Tories." *The Times* (May 11).

Travis, Alan. 2002. "Law Lords Clear Asylum Fast Track." *The Guardian* (November 1).

———. 2003. "More Legal Aid Cuts Planned in Asylum Cases." *The Guardian* (November 28).

CHAPTER FOURTEEN

ATLA Shrugged

Why Personal Injury Lawyers Are
Not Public Defenders of Their Own Causes

MICHAEL MCCANN AND WILLIAM HALTOM

Introduction

The post–World War II era witnessed fundamental changes in U.S. civil law, including tort law. Courts began to reduce significantly the hurdles facing civil litigants—broadening standing, trimming immunities, abandoning the privity requirement in tort disputes, liberalizing rules of procedure, amending Rule 23 to make class action suits easier—and enlarged the scope of potential awards (Galanter 2002). These legal innovations were soon followed by a variety of social reform movements that actively mobilized law to make government, corporations, and select groups of professionals (e.g., doctors) more responsive to, and responsible for, serious material injuries to middle-class consumers, minorities, women, the poor, and the environment. During the 1960s, prominent spokespersons at once exalted the promises of law for increasing civil justice in corporate America and decried the many barriers that impeded law's promises, including not least those from the legal profession. Reform leaders and cause lawyers such as Ralph Nader inspired the "public interest law" movement and "access to justice" movement, which aimed to increase the responsiveness of powerful organizations both to and through law. These developments emerged, moreover, at the same moment in the late 1960s that the number of lawyers in our nation began to increase dramatically, far beyond the rate of population growth. All in all, this era of legally focused, consumer-oriented reform politics contributed to what often is called the increasing "judicialization" of politics and regulatory policy in the United States (McCann 1986).

Specific alterations in the regime of civil law during this era were, not surprisingly, widely perceived to disadvantage substantively and substantially those
established interests who were formerly advantaged, insulated, or uninvolved.
This prompted business groups to respond in a big way, significantly revising
their traditional political strategy. E. E. Schattschneider argued forty years ago
that powerful private groups tended to keep political disputes contained and
"private," preferring insular and closed disputing processes, while less powerful
groups of citizens found advantages in "expanding the scope of conflict" to include the broader public (Schattschneider 1960). However, big business in the
1970s changed course and determined to "go public" by investing heavily in trying to shape public understandings about the growing "lawsuit crisis" (see
Smith 2000). Major goals included putting business-generated concerns and
perspectives on the public agenda, shaping public attention and "consciousness" with commonsense stories and concerns, and pushing competing concerns out of view or devaluing them (Hayden 1991). Substantively, business-
supported critics protested that the American tort law system foments litigious
and adversarial behavior, fosters rights-obsessed and individualistic relations,
and proliferates needless lawsuits to the detriment of economy, society, and
sanity (Boot 1998; Glendon 1991; Howard 1994; Olson 1991; Quayle 1991).

This effort reflected in part agenda-setting maneuvers to mobilize support
for "juridical" change through official legal reforms. Equally important, though,
the reformers have advanced their agenda of promoting "individual responsibility" as a moralistic "disciplinary" campaign directly among citizens within
society. In rhetorically bombastic tomes—including Charles Sykes's (1992) *A
Nation of Victims: The Decay of American Character*, Philip Howard's (1994) *The
Death of Common Sense: How Law Is Suffocating America*, and Walter Olson's
(1991) *The Litigation Explosion: What Happened When America Unleashed the
Lawsuit*—as well as a litany of widely disseminated "horror stories" and tall
"tort tales," conservative critics decried the loss of self-discipline and willingness of citizens to displace blame through litigation rather than take responsibility for their actions.

The most explicit targets of wrath in pop reform sermons have been plaintiffs' attorneys who, like Satans in suits, allegedly urge opportunistic claimants
on and execute their destructive, unfair, costly designs. The most obvious
charge against tort lawyers, of course, is obsessive greed, which leads attorneys
to litigate frivolous or dubious claims. "Contingency-fee law has made more
overnight millionaires than just about any business one could name," proclaims
Olson, implying by the unsubstantiated allegation an ethical line between ac-

ceptable profit motives and the excessive rapacity of attorneys (1991: 45). Moreover, personal injury lawyers have the audacity to dress up their selfishness as serving the public good and helping "the little guy" stand up against the powerful. "There is a funny thing about this brand of lawyering: the more opulent it becomes, the more cloying an odor of sanctity it becomes," he added (46). In truth, the moralists insist, lawyers mostly do damage to society. They breed dishonesty and distrust throughout society, fostering a world like Charles Dickens assailed in *Bleak House*—"a cynical, manipulative world of procedural intrigue, of lawyers manipulating court rules to guarantee, after decades of litigation, that the truth never emerges," lamented Philip Howard (1994: 85–87). Charles Sykes was even more melodramatic in his assault: "The proliferation of lawyers ... threatens to strangle the economy while further fraying our already tattered social fabric" (1992: 248). These sober assessments, typically cast in snatches of resentful assault, are like lawyer jokes without the humor, pithy lamentations about the destructive "devil's advocates" that we all bemoan around us.

The Puzzle: Where Is the Plaintiffs' Lawyers' Public Defense?

We have joined many other scholars in exposing the problematic evidence and hierarchical foundations supporting this moralistic, anecdote-based assault on attorneys, plaintiffs, and the entire system of tort law. Elsewhere we have further demonstrated a variety of factors that nevertheless have contributed to the considerable influence of the reform message about the lawsuit crisis in American culture (Haltom, McCann, and Aks 2000; Haltom, McCann, and Bloom 2001). This has, in turn, required some explanation for why the well-documented empirical challenges to tort reform rhetoric developed by sociolegal scholars have had very little practical influence in the broader culture (Haltom and McCann 2004).

Our concern in this chapter parallels and supplements this last point. In short, the focus here is the particular, even peculiar and problematic response by trial lawyers to the tort reform offensive. Trial lawyers have been galvanized by the frontal assault from critics, to be sure. Moreover, plaintiffs' attorneys have rallied massive resources behind the cause of defending the existing civil justice system and their own fundamental but often misunderstood and underappreciated role as counsel for injured consumers in that system. However, the trial lawyers have committed virtually all their resources toward a "stealth" policy of insider legislative influence to block legal reform policies, while virtually conceding the public domain of popular discourse about civil law practices to their moralistic, business-supported critics. This chapter will develop and illustrate this interpretive thesis, propose a number of interrelated factors to make sense of why trial lawyers have adopted this strategy, and conclude with some reflections regarding the implications of these strategic choices for the practices and prospects of cause lawyering in the United States.

Trial Lawyers: A Profile

The Plaintiffs' Bar

We begin with a brief sketch of the trial lawyers and their unique sector of the legal profession in the United States.[1] An influential series of studies sponsored by the American Bar Foundation (Heinz and Laumann 1982; Heinz et al. 1998) identified three general spheres of influence in the bar, each with distinct social networks, personal characteristics, and religious or political orientations: liberal politics, the corporate establishment, and trial lawyers. The last group represents injured plaintiffs in civil disputes. These attorneys perform a small part, perhaps about 6 percent, of the total legal activity of the bar (Heinz et al. 1998). In 1995, 8 percent of practicing Chicago attorneys spent one-quarter or more of their time representing plaintiffs in personal injury cases, while only 6 percent spent more than half their time on such representation (Parikh 2001).

Overall, personal injury practice has evolved in recent decades from an enterprise primarily by generalists to one of increasing specialization. The personal injury bar today features a number of well-known expert subfields: products liability, medical malpractice, workers' compensation, premise liability, auto accidents, and the like. Tort lawyers who represent *consumers* injured by various products and services are probably the most high profile of such lawyers. Moreover, many of the latter attorneys specialize quite narrowly—on hot liquids, asbestos, aviation, pharmaceuticals, and so forth. Personal injury lawyers also tend to be organized primarily in small firms or solo practices. The 1995 American Bar Foundation (ABF) study of the Chicago Bar found that 90 percent of personal injury lawyers for plaintiffs practiced in small firms or solo practice, with 29 percent as solo practitioners (Heinz et al. 1998).

Sara Parikh's (2001) well-documented study demonstrates that the personal injury bar is quite cohesive in its goals and identity but quite stratified in character. A very small high-end group of extremely profitable and affluent lawyers specializing in complex, high-stakes class action and mass tort cases receive much of the press attention, while by far the largest number of personal injury attorneys specialize in routine disputes like auto accident claims and generate relatively modest incomes. Because the overwhelming bulk of lawyers depend on contingency fees from mostly "one-shot" clients (Galanter 1974), their practices are inherently unstable, uncertain, and risky; ordinary practices oscillate insecurely between "feast and famine" (see Daniels and Martin 1999, 2000). Indeed, such attorneys must work hard to generate a routine flow of clients. Although a good reputation is arguably the more important resource for success, the pressure to "manufacture" clients in various ways, including through commercial advertising and a host of less savory methods, is common among the lower strata of the profession. It is this feature of these professionals that has provoked the most negative images of personal injury lawyers as crass "ambulance chasers," images reserved mostly for ethnic immigrants excluded from the elite corporate bar in earlier generations (Auerbach 1976). Although the anti-Semitic and other elitist residue has faded somewhat, the plaintiffs' personal injury bar remains one of the least prestigious in the legal profession (Abel 1987; Parikh 2001). The assaults on personal injury lawyers by tort reformers and in popular culture have made such practice at once more precarious and less profitable for the great majority of practitioners.

Professional Organization and Political Representation

Trial lawyers for plaintiffs in personal injury cases are represented by a variety of organizations. The largest and most important organ of representation, and hence the focus of this chapter, is the Association of Trial Lawyers of America (ATLA). ATLA grew out of an organization of attorneys who wanted to redress the lack of representation for injured workers under the developing workers' compensation system in the 1940s.[2] The organization eventually changed its name and took up the cause of personal injury lawyers, who were seriously lacking in professional respect and effective organization. The key mission of ATLA in its formative years was the dissemination of technical information about tort advocacy among plaintiffs' lawyers around the country. ATLA's membership size, identity, and power grew dramatically in response to the tort reform movement and other assaults on trial lawyers that began to percolate in the late 1970s. Today, ATLA represents 56,000 members (about 7.5 percent of the American Bar Association's 800,000 members) nationwide and boasts a substantial operating budget for advancing its causes. State-level associations of trial lawyers work both independently and in tandem with the national organization on a variety of related issues.

Liberal public interest and consumer groups with more specific political missions have allied with ATLA in defending the cause of personal injury lawyers for plaintiffs. This constellation of liberal public interest groups includes most prominently Ralph Nader and his spin-off groups such as Public Citizen and Congress Watch. Nader and his allies have been tireless opponents of the many reform proposals that undermine citizens' "rights to sue" for justice—no-fault insurance; alternative dispute resolution; tort reform; and the like. Perhaps no single person in the second half of the century was more influential than Nader in advocating a litigation-centered vision of citizen politics and judicialized democratic institutional change in the United States. Nader's staunch defense of civil justice,[3] bitter opposition to unaccountable corporate power,[4] suspicion of bureaucratic regulatory mechanisms, and personal inspiration for many trial lawyers have provided considerable ground for alliance with ATLA and the plaintiffs' bar generally (McCann 1986). However, Nader's financial resource base has always been small and depended heavily on individual trial lawyers. Moreover, Nader's prickly style has been cause for periodic tensions, and his ill-fated run for the presidency in 2000 turned many longtime admirers into bitter critics who have shunned all residue of common cause.

One significant public interest law firm that was inspired by Nader but deserves special attention here is Trial Lawyers for Public Justice (TLPJ). TLPJ is the largest public interest trial law firm in the country. It focuses on precedent setting, socially significant tort litigation and has played an important, if controversial, leadership role among trial lawyers. One of the organization's most important and contentious activities is its "Class Action Prevention Abuse Project," whereby TLPJ attorneys routinely "police" class actions in mass torts that could be considered as selling injured consumers short.

ATLA has also been joined on many occasions by a host of consumer groups in defending the civil justice system and plaintiffs' attorneys against the critics. Key organizations include Consumer Federation of America, Consumers Union, Citizen Action, National Insurance Consumer Organization, and a host of more specialized public interest and research groups. One especially important group established specifically to educate the public about the importance of civil justice and the damage done by tort reform is the Citizens for Corporate Accountability and Individual Rights (CCAIR), recently changed to the Center for Justice and Democracy (CJD), in both incarnations led by the tireless activist Joanne Doroshow. The alliance between ATLA and these groups against tort reform has been fairly strong, but there have been many points of significant discord as well, such as on no-fault insurance proposals (see Burke 2002).

Although it is recognized that these groups work together, often in a stable division of labor, it is important to emphasize that ATLA is the key organization representing plaintiffs' attorneys. That association has by far the largest and most stable constituent network of trial lawyers, the clearest motives in linking plaintiffs' lawyers' interests and principles, and the greatest resource base for taking on the business-supported forces of civil law reform.

ATLA, the Personal Injury Bar, and Cause Lawyering

But what does ATLA's representation of plaintiffs' attorneys generally have to do with cause lawyering? Personal injury lawyers for injured plaintiffs are hardly the first group of attorneys that comes to mind when one contemplates the signal concept of "cause lawyers." The unflattering images of avaricious, manipulative, self-serving parasites foisted on personal injury lawyers in our society, and especially during recent decades, no doubt have taken their toll in almost disqualifying tort lawyers from the ranks of altruistic, publicly interested, even noble champions of justice in the public mind. However, few informed observers, including critics, would agree with the veracity of these stereotypes in most cases. The popular image surely is misleading in the eyes of personal injury lawyers themselves. Indeed, if self-identification in socially recognized ethical terms, by which individual good is linked to broad social goods, is a key criterion, the plaintiffs' bar is an essential repository for the cause of civil justice in democratic society (see Menkel-Meadow 1998; Luban 1988).

Individually, scores of personal injury lawyers whom we have met, and in many cases interviewed, see themselves as lawyering for the good in both particular and general senses. Consider this quote from a lawyer who litigated a well-known case for an individual client and later was angry about simplistic, ill-founded media portrayals:

> What really drives most trial lawyers that are successful in this business, and who are winning cases, is that they really have some underlying philosophy of good—and of outrage, disgust about what's going on with corporate indifference and abuse. . . . I always had a real strong background in blue collar culture. And I was very aggravated at the way there's a lot of injustice in all phases of life. The way people abuse people. The way corporations abuse people. . . . I have always had this sense that if you really worked something real, real hard and get to the truth and win, that's the right thing to do. That's what keeps me going.

Indeed, many trial lawyers routinely define their practices as committed to representing "the little person" and "equalizing" the contest against large corporations and faceless bureaucracies. In sum, such personal injury lawyers are transparently selective about: *the clients whom they represent,* namely injured consumers and other victims, including especially women and lower income citizens; *those parties whom they tend to challenge,* namely unaccountable business corporations, professionals, and government agencies; and *the larger social values* that they aim to serve in the process, which are access to social justice, the rule of law, civil rights, and democratic accountability. As such, the model personal injury lawyer "shares and aims to share with her client responsibility for the ends she is promoting in her representation . . . stretching those ideals from the representation of individual litigants to causes" (Sarat and Scheingold 1998: 3, 7).

The organizations that represent trial lawyers for plaintiffs are even more united in articulating a vision of "wanting to do good" by working within the conventional ideology of professionalism. Consider the ATLA's strategic plan mission statement in 2003:

> ATLA is an international non-profit professional association of lawyers who preserve and protect the rights of those who have been harmed. The Association serves the public, the legal profession, and the justice system by representing lawyers and the public in the public debate of reforming the civil justice system; preserving, promoting, and improving the common law in courts and legislatures; advancing the principles of constitutional law; and providing the tools and environment for its members, to serve their clients better.

ATLA's mission in this regard appears to be barely different from that of the many liberal public interest groups with whom they regularly ally in advancing a familiar consumerist vision of the good society. This identity no doubt reflects the fact that many of the key activists and leaders in ATLA have been involved in high-profile, public interest–oriented litigation with significant policy implications. In short, the movers and shakers of ATLA tend to fit most closely the "cause lawyering" profile. Somewhat ironically, perhaps, the tort reform challenge has intensified this self-conscious identification of ATLA and its members with larger causes of justice and populist challenges to corporate power. It thus is not surprising that other scholars have included personal injury lawyers in their studies of cause lawyering (Sarat and Scheingold 1998; Bloom 2001; Boon 2001).

This is not to suggest, however, that the great majority of personal injury lawyers affiliated with ATLA fit the mold of cause lawyers as neatly as the organization's lofty rhetoric suggests. Most plaintiffs' attorneys struggle to survive or prosper through means no different, and sometimes rather more tawdry, than other lawyers or professionals. The fact that a small number of tort lawyers make an enormous amount of money, furthermore, calls into question the good they profess to achieve. Many other personal injury lawyers, like their colleagues throughout the profession, do "frequently cross and re-cross the lines between traditional and cause lawyering" (Bloom 2001: 13). But these lawyers are hardly a majority. That personal injury lawyers recognize the diversity of their ranks and the unmistakable pull of pecuniary material motives, as we shall see, arguably plays an important role in shaping their chosen political strategies for defending their professional status against political assault.

All in all, though, because many personal injury lawyers do identify themselves both collectively and often individually as cause-oriented, because these activist attorneys tend to view ATLA as their primary organizational representative, because ATLA leaders come disproportionately from this activist corps, and because ATLA has increasingly identified itself with this activist vision—we thus cautiously treat ATLA as representing lawyers with causes in this chapter. More important, ATLA's actions and inactions greatly shape the context in which cause lawyers of all types conduct their political advocacy work. That is, ATLA's success in representing plaintiffs' attorneys shapes the opportunity structures and resources available to those lawyers promoting causes of justice (McCann 1994). Finally, the dilemmas, contradictions, and difficult strategic choices faced by ATLA in representing its members are indicative of the broader challenges facing plaintiffs' attorneys generally and cause lawyers in particular. As we shall see, ATLA's representational quandaries highlight and crystallize in particular the tensions among professional responsibilities, occupational status, material reward, and political commitments—of doing law, doing good, and doing well at once—experienced by cause-oriented attorneys. Our consideration of these issues as they play out among personal injury attorneys thus will also shed light on the problematic, elusive activity of cause lawyering itself, at least in the U.S. context.

The Stealth Strategy of Inside Legislative Influence

Since its origins ATLA has pursued a very simple, clearly defined political "stealth"[5] strategy in defense of its members, the plaintiffs' bar generally, and their larger causes of legal justice. This strategy has a number of tactical components, but one commitment has dominated by far all of the others. In short, ATLA has focused the overwhelming bulk of its financial, organizational, and personal resources on cultivating support in Congress and state legislatures in order to block proposals that its members find unacceptable.

"Insider" Legislative Politics

The logic of the legislative approach was initially credited to Thomas Bendorf, a former lobbyist seasoned in California politics, in the early years of ATLA. It was developed into a "very successful formula" for several decades by the senior director of public affairs, Alan A. Parker, until the early 1990s. The approach "consistently rejected," in Parker's words, the idea that media-oriented and grassroots mobilization tactics were worthwhile for ATLA.[6] "Part of the strategy of the trial lawyers was to be quiet, to be invisible. . . . I think it was [tort reformer] Victor Schwartz who always called us 'no-see-ums.'"

There were a number of assumptions supporting the embrace of this tactic. For one thing, it removed trial lawyers from the line of fire in political disputes. "My theory always was, if the lawyers got out front, everyone beats them up," Parker proclaimed. As such, lawyers could wield influence without themselves becoming targets that diverted attention from their issues. This is a key reason we label the tactic a "stealth" approach. Moreover, by remaining largely behind the scenes, the advocates for the plaintiffs' bar could portray many conflicts as being between the corporate "special interests" and ordinary citizens, injured victims, consumers, and the like. Conversely, the "insider" strategy took advantage of the fact that trial lawyers tend to be skilled advocates who are well-connected politically, at both the state and federal levels. Given that lawyers' professional power derives from both skilled tactical maneuvering in disputing and from developed organizational contacts (Sarat and Felstiner 1995), the insider strategy thus took advantage of the lawyers' strengths to cultivate ties with legislators. Finally, the trial lawyers, and especially the elite group of high rollers in class action mass policy torts concerning asbestos and later tobacco, could raise huge amounts of money to fund their pressure tactics in legislatures.

This general strategy also fit the overall ethical, legal, and policy inclinations of ATLA leadership. In short, ATLA has been fundamentally opposed to all federal efforts to pass uniform tort reform legislation that preempts state law, and for the most part to state legislative intervention as well.[7] As the trial lawyers see it, the most reliably informed and desired changes in civil law should be initiated through the common law by judges, who are closest to the action, and of course in regular interaction with the lawyers. Courts are better situated, because the legal issues "get more seriously considered, over a longer time. The changes are incremental and the changes adapt to the exigencies of what's happening in the world. When you legislate you freeze at that millisecond whatever it is you've legislated on and you can't change it until you go back to the legislature," one leading ATLA strategist told us.[8] All in all, ATLA would prefer to take its chances with the courts on most issues of reform; if legislation must be passed, they would prefer to fight it out at the state rather than federal level.

This legislatively focused obstructionist strategy has entailed two key interrelated components. First, trial lawyers have contributed generously to campaigns by elected officials, including especially legislators, but also judges and governors or presidents. Trial lawyers have given large amounts of money to Political Action Committees (PACs) at the federal and state levels. In 1999–2000, ATLA was the second-biggest PAC contributor to federal candidates, just behind National Association of Realtors; 86 percent of the $2.661 million it contributed went to democrats. This mirrored almost exactly the same pattern the previous year. In 2001–2002, trial lawyers were the largest PAC contributor to federal candidates, although the actual amount dropped in the electoral off-year. Moreover, trial lawyers, individually and through PACs, were the seventh-largest group of contributors (over $200 apiece) overall in federal elections in 1999–2000, roughly the same as the American Medical Association and just behind the Teamsters and United Auto Workers.[9] Almost 90 percent of these contributions went to democratic candidates. Trial lawyers contribute even more aggressively at the state and local levels. For example, California trial lawyers contributed a total of $9.8 million to California candidates and another half million to political parties statewide in 1997–1998 election cycle (Civil Justice Association of California 1999). Tort lawyer contributions to electoral candidates for state judges likewise have been quite significant (Derthick 2002: 188).

These numbers can be misleading, of course. Although contributions from plaintiffs' lawyers rank high next to those of discrete industries, they are dwarfed by the aggregate of corporate groups—insurance, pharmaceuticals, manufacturers, tobacco, etc.—that they challenge. For example, lawyer groups (not just ATLA) gave $21.3 million to House members during 2002 elections in an effort to influence legislation limiting medical malpractice awards and venue shifting of class action lawsuits to federal courts, among others. This is a large amount, but it is far less than the $276.7 million that business groups as a whole contributed to House members (Salant 2003). Moreover, trial lawyers exhibit little of the structural economic power inherent in generating jobs, tax revenues, and overall productivity that renders corporations so indirectly influential in government policy making.

Second, trial lawyers have invested strategically in lobbying legislators and other elected officials. ATLA has relied on professional lobbyists, led by chief consultant Thomas Hale Boggs, Jr., of Patton, Boggs, LLP, for virtually all of their lobbying in Congress. The relationship is contracted for a fee on a quarterly basis. Comparatively, though, ATLA spends rather less on lobbying than on electoral contributions. The ATLA lobbying budget in 1999 was only $2.4 million (Burke 2002: 46), compared to nearly $200 million by the health care industry and $86 million by the insurance industry. The expenditures in the states generally parallel this same modest amount. However, the conventional focus on the amounts of money spent overlooks two important facts. One is that the trial lawyers' agenda is far narrower and more focused—namely, to stop tort reform, no-fault insurance, and the like—than that of their corporate competitors. Even more important is the fact that plaintiffs' lawyers, and especially the high-rolling elite, have labored successfully to cultivate strong personal ties to many elected officials at both the federal and state levels. Indeed, several leaders in ATLA and other organizations stressed in interviews that this was probably the most effective tactical source of influence developed by trial lawyers. Overall, a *Reader's Digest* article surely exaggerated when it claimed that ATLA was "America's Most Powerful Lobby" (Evans and Novak 1994), but trial lawyers have proved to be a potent force in legislative policy-making arenas.

These interrelated components of the trial lawyers' insider strategy are regularly urged among state-level organizations by ATLA. This coordination is facilitated by a special committee on federal/state relations and a committee of state trial lawyers' executives in the national organization, both of which share strategic political information as well as technical advocacy information on litigation with members. ATLA clearly is proud of its achievements on these matters. A former ATLA president boasted to members in his *Trial* column that they had topped the list of PACs and that *Fortune* magazine had ranked ATLA as the fifth-most influential lobbying organization in Congress (Baron 2001: 9): "We will continue to fulfill our responsibilities as the principal lobbyist for open access to justice in America." At the same time, trial lawyers have drawn periodic fire for their aggressive courting of politicians. For example, republicans during the 2000 presidential campaign effectively challenged Al Gore by publicly linking a 1995 dinner hosted by wealthy Texas trial lawyers, over $4 millions in campaign contributions that followed, and President Clinton's veto of a federal tort reform bill passed by the republican-led Congress in the following year. A Democratic Party aide purportedly wrote the script for the democratic national chairman to present to Walter Umphrey, the famously wealthy Texas trial attorney: "Sorry you missed the vice president. . . . I know [you] will give $100k when the president vetoes tort reform, but we really need it now. Please send ASAP if possible" (Van Natta and Oppel 2000).

Despite frequent criticism from opponents, it is difficult to deny the success of the general strategy. ATLA has successfully blocked federal no-fault and tort reform legislation for twenty-five years. Indeed, ATLA has been so effective at frustrating tort reform advocates that the latter's proposed bills were watered down increasingly to the point that they were almost inconsequential during the 1990s. One ATLA strategist actually considered recommending support for one bill. "It gets a lot harder to oppose it because there's not a hell of a lot left there." By supporting a toothless bill, he surmised, trial lawyers could look responsive, co-opt the corporate opposition, and yet suffer little actual impact on their practices. ATLA did not choose to do this, however, for it would violate their basic principle that the federal government should not get involved in the common law of tort at all. Trial lawyer organizations have been more uneven in their success diverting or derailing reform at the state level, but overall their obstructionist influence in the legislatures has been felt strongly in many states such as California, Ohio, Texas, and Florida.

Perhaps the ultimate compliment to this approach comes from leading tort reform advocate and American Tort Reform Association spokesperson Victor Schwartz. "I think ATLA is far more organized than the people on the other side. They are brilliant in how they spend their money. It's targeted money," he told us. At the federal level, "they can give $10,000 (in contributions) to a chairman of a committee, or a speaker, or a president. They go to the leadership, they go to the top of the bottle." Moreover, for trial lawyers "there is a very limited menu" that focuses on tort reform and related issues, whereas the business group "menu is watered down with 10 things, and they are not cohesive in focusing on liability reform. So most of the time the plaintiffs' bar wins it. They are focused" (personal interview). If the lawyers tried to pass new legislation increasing liability in courts, business interests would find it easy to mobilize as a cohesive force of opposition. However, the fact that ATLA and its allies mostly fight defensive battles to stop all affirmative legislation in tort matters gives them an advantage. Finally, in the aftermath of huge windfall returns from asbestos and tobacco litigation, trial lawyers should be able to improve their lobbying position in legislative contests long into the future (see Derthick 2002: 186–89).

Litigating to Disarm Tort Reform at the State Level

A second, parallel strategy has been developed to undo legislative reforms where they have passed in the states over trial lawyer political opposition. This strategy has enabled personal injury trial lawyers to do what they do best—to litigate against specific parts or entire packages of legislated civil justice reform. The key legal argument in nearly all these cases is that legislated tort reform violates the separation of powers principle of state constitutions by infringing on judicial discretion. As a landmark 1999 Ohio State Supreme Court stated in striking down a series of tort reform laws capping damages and modifying the collateral source rule, the latter were "openly subversive of the separation of powers and, in particular, of the judicial system."[10] As Justice Alice Robie Resnick wrote for the narrow court majority, "The general assembly has circumvented our mandates. . . . It has boldly seized the power of constitutional adjudication" that rightly belongs to the courts. Moreover, other legislation establishing statutes of repose (statute of temporal limitations) in products liability and related tort issues also have been struck down in many states as violating basic principles of due process and equal protection. Overall, between

1986 and 2000 at least ninety-one constitutional decisions were won overturn-
ing parts or all of tort reform legislation in specific states around the nation
(Smith 1999; Brakel 2000; Schwartz et al. 1997). Along with Ohio, major victories in Oregon, Illinois, Florida, and Indiana during the late 1990s demonstrated
the expansive reach of the strategy by trial lawyers in gutting tort reform. Indeed, only a handful of states had passed tort reform that was not limited by judicial rulings.

   This overall strategy of state-level constitutional litigation has been largely
guided by Robert Peck, ATLA's senior director for legal affairs and policy research. Coordination and leadership, eventually, by the late 1990s, was focused
in the Center for Constitutional Litigation, a public interest law firm designed
specifically to provide direct assistance to lawyers challenging tort reform enactments at the state level. Again the primary logic of the campaigns has been
that tort reform laws limiting damages, liability, and repose "constitute an improper legislative usurpation of judicial power, and an intrusion into the exclusive authority of the judiciary."[11] Tort reformers have vigorously challenged this
argument in court, contending that historically courts derived their common
law authority from legislatures and that the latter should act to render trial decisions consistent with general rules (Schwartz et al. 1997; Brakel 2000). But for
the most part these arguments have fared poorly (Smith 1999).

   What is most noteworthy about this litigation strategy for our concerns in
this chapter is its similarity to the primary stealth strategy of insider legislative
influence. Like the former, constitutional litigation in the states: takes place in
relatively insular official settings, largely removed from mass attention; is carefully targeted to influence elite judges rather than the general public; takes advantage of lawyers' specialized skills and professional connections; and is entirely defensive and obstructionist in character. All in all, while generally quite
effective in stopping or limiting official tort reform enactments, the strategy is
likely to have little to no effect on public perceptions of trial lawyers and the
civil litigation process. In this regard, the savvy and pervasive assaults on
lawyers projected throughout mass culture by conservative critics thus have remained relatively uncontested beyond the courts. As Carlton Carl, ATLA director of public relations in the late 1990s, related, "For years, the philosophy of
ATLA was 'don't make any noise,' even though the other side has spent billions
to change public attitudes, to change views on personal responsibility."

Public Relations: Token Efforts to Share the Load

   The fact that the two-pronged strategy outlined above has dominated ATLA
responses to tort reform assaults should not obscure the many voices in the or-

ganization advocating greater efforts on other fronts. Beginning in the mid-1980s, the insider, obstructionist strategy of ATLA was paralleled by more public advocacy-oriented strategies led by Ralph Nader, liberal public interest groups, and consumer groups at both the national and state levels to challenge tort reform. As Pam Gilbert, director of Public Citizen, put it in an interview in the early 1990s: "What we [initially] failed to do, and we're now waking up to the fact, is it's not enough to fight these defensive battles. We have to do our own campaign affirmatively expanding citizens' rights. Because there is a lot of good to say about the civil liability system . . . [we have to demonstrate that] there's a lot of flaws or problems with people being shut out." Nader not only co-authored a book, *No Contest* (1996), challenging the corporate assault on trial lawyers and the civil justice system, but he led campaigns in many states against tort reform.[12] Moreover, Nader, Gilbert, Joan Claybrook, and other public interest leaders constantly chided ATLA for not joining in the effort to shape understandings of both the general population and targeted groups—jurors, judges, politicians—around civil justice issues in the 1980s. "We wish that they [ATLA] would use their resources less in giving PAC money and more for public education," confided one high-profile activist. However, the traditional strategists and their strategy generally won out among the trial lawyers. As one former ATLA strategist put it, liberal public interest groups

> have to bring in victims and have them crawl through the halls of Congress in their wheelchairs and stuff. . . . I don't think you need that to win—or it's part of the equation, but it isn't the whole thing and not everybody should be doing that. Actually I think if Ralph [Nader] and Joan [Claybrook] would stop and think about it, the way we've done it for all this time has been a great system. You do your thing, we'll do ours, and it all adds up to we can beat 'em.

However, the argument of Nader and others, both without and within ATLA, developed momentum by the early 1990s. This resulted in and reflected a change of personnel in the public relations leadership within ATLA and the emergence of a series of presidents who placed somewhat greater emphasis on public education about trial lawyers and the civil justice system. Because "we cannot expect the public to sympathize with our positions unless they are understood and supported by strong arguments," ATLA's public education staff began to formulate initiatives during the remainder of the decade (Baron 2001: 9). This included a variety of activities.

In the first relatively uncoordinated phase, trial lawyers made some efforts to challenge the anecdotal "horror stories" and "tort tales" propagated by conservative critics. This practice had its roots in the mid-1980s, when allies of trial lawyers began to publish "counter-stories" supplying missing facts and adding positive perspectives correcting the typically apocryphal accounts of their business-supported adversaries. One early example was "The Not-So Simple Crisis" in *The American Lawyer* by editor Steven Brill and James Lyons (1986). This much-cited article set the template for future accounts. For one thing, it reflected lawyers' inherently "realist" inclinations for "getting the facts" behind the spin. "Myths about the litigation explosion that never happened shouldn't substitute for real debate." Moreover, the authors' standpoint was generally defensive in character rather than hortatory or idealistic. "What the reforms we prefer have in common . . . is that they're based on the idea that lawyers and the legal system aren't solely responsible for the 'crisis.'" Finally, the article was published in a relatively esoteric professional journal that was highly unlikely reading for anyone but a small group of lawyers and jurists.

Other essays from this period became classics among a relatively small group of trial attorneys and scholarly allies (Strasser 1987; Cox 1992). But they remained similarly reactive, defensive, and realist in their orientation, answering their critics in often defiant terms but hardly aiming at redefining the agenda of debate. Cox's article, for example, notes that tort tales are "a game that two can play. There's been time enough for the plaintiffs' bar to start collecting anecdotes of a different stripe: the wronged plaintiff." This is followed by a California lobbyist for trial lawyers who claims that "I've got a drawer full of horror stories." Across the page is a large picture of him with a large bold-letter title: "Trial Bar Aims Horror Stories at Tort Reform." A few such counter-narratives follow. Again, the article was published in a relatively esoteric professional journal with very limited mass readership.

Not surprisingly, perhaps, ATLA's efforts to challenge horror stories in the 1990s followed in pretty much the same mold. An internal ATLA memo from publicity planners in 1994 read: "We could greatly benefit from in-depth, impeccably researched, and scrupulously accurate exposes of various myths and folk tales that the tort 'reformers' have invented and propagated in order to sell judges, jurors, scholars, and legislators on the necessity for and the virtues of tort 'reforms.' The articles, could, as appropriate, put the lie to specific anecdotes."

Before long, ATLA's Web site featured a section titled "Civil Justice Facts" and subtitled "The Other Side of the Story: What They *Don't* Want You to Know." One-page accounts added little-known facts and interpretive spin about the McDonald's coffee case, Little League sports liability costs, the BMW "paint job case," and other arguably misrepresented stories that needed to be set "right." ATLA began to send such corrective accounts mirroring conservative tort tales to state organizations and journalists. At the same time, ATLA strategists prepared a litany of "fact sheets" for their members and for reporters in an effort to offset two decades of misinformation from tort "deformers."

In our view, however, such efforts were of limited value. Trial lawyers' accounts not only are reactive or defensive in character and esoteric in placement, but these "real story" materials typically lacked a compelling normative angle or political vision. Such diffuse, often complex, fact-laden accounts can hardly hope to match the simple moralistic appeal of tales told by critics or jeremiads that effectively tap common sense about cultural decline at the hands of greedy lawyers and irresponsible plaintiffs. To debunk specific tales as inaccurate or simplistic hardly does damage to the cumulative cultural logic of odes to individual responsibility and paeans to a more harmonious communal past. That such counter-narratives have not traveled far into popular culture is hardly surprising.[13]

In the mid-1990s, ATLA began to develop a more systematic, multidimensional approach to public education. The key initiative that facilitated this effort was the formation of the ATLA Endowment—a product of trial lawyer contributions used to fund research that challenges "with authority, the flawed data and unfounded conclusions foisted on the public by the organized tortfeasors. . . . Endowment funded work is under way to help refine the message that will combat our enemies' attempts to tarnish the image of trial lawyers" (Baron 2001: 9). Spearheaded by two past presidents of ATLA, Bob Habush and Larry Stewart, and taken to new levels by Fred Baron in his 2001 presidential term, the endowment was animated by the conviction that ATLA "must have a long-term strategy to combat the poisonous propaganda constantly emanating from those who seek to destroy the efficacy of the civil justice system" (9). The tax exempt endowment mobilized $16.5 million in pledges by 1998, with $5.7 million collected by early 2001, thus producing over $300,000 a year for public education.

A comprehensive Public Education Strategic Plan developed earlier in the decade outlined the multidimensional approach to education funded by the endowment. These have included:

— The Public Education Institute that is responsible for developing curricula, including mock trial exercises, for primary and high schools that imparts better information about the civil justice system to America's youth, "who will be voters and jurors" one day;
— The Law School Institute, which funds scholarship and research on the advancement of individual rights through the civil justice system;
— The Judicial Institute, which supports programs on judicial independence and provides members of the judiciary with "balanced" research;

— The Research Institute, which funds research to inform and shape public policy and dispute resolution efforts.

Special projects aligned with these working institutes included a systematic plan for developing Web-based curricula to "educate" journalists "about what lawyers do" and how the civil litigation system works as well as funding for co-ordinated focus group and mass survey studies probing how the public understands the legal system. The logic behind all of these proposals is essentially the same, according to an internal memo proposal in the mid-1990s: "enabling ATLA to develop strategic approaches—up to and including specific messages and language—to public education, which also contributes to public policy and, of course, winning back the jury pool."

In addition, ATLA has worked closely with and through the Roscoe Pound Foundation. Drawing inspiration from Judge Pound's realist philosophy of so-ciological jurisprudence, the foundation works to "facilitate positive change where outdated political abstractions have fallen short" (quoted from founda-tion pamphlet). The foundation has supported numerous outreach efforts that parallel those of ATLA in recent years, including: a Pound Fellows program that encourages dialogue about change in American jurisprudence; an annual Fo-rum for State Court Judges; publications of related writings in the *Civil Justice Digest*; annual awards to outstanding law professors and law students, in an ef-fort to offset the influx of "law and economics" support in law schools; and grants to legal scholars for research on civil justice, including to tort reform op-ponents Michael Rustad and Ken Chesebro. As should be obvious from this list, however, almost all of this funding has been directed at educating and influ-encing legal elites rather than the mass public; it is as much another expression of the targeted insider strategy as an investment in public education.

The preceding narrative and lists of new enterprises might suggest that a fundamental shift in ATLA strategy has taken place in previous years. We doubt it; the new investments are very little and very late. The present ATLA Endow-ment investment in all of its programs, after all, is only around $300,000, which is tiny relative to the sums still invested in the insider legislative and litigation strategies. Most of the institutes listed above at present are engaged in very small-scale pilot projects. Even when all the existing pledges are collected and return becomes available in a few years, the total budget for public education will be under $1 million. It is relevant here that even Fred Baron, the ATLA leader who often is credited with leading the charge for more public outreach, told us that the overall strategy of ATLA remains essentially the same as before. "ATLA has always focused on legislative policy, on a legislative strategy. We do a little bit of publicity, but what's the point? We can't even begin to match the funding by the corporations. They spend as much on a single ad as our entire public relations budget in a year."

Moreover, we again wonder whether the realist-inspired, "get out the real facts" logic of the lawyer campaigns, no matter how well funded, is likely to provide a powerful answer to the moralistic appeals of conservatives to traditional values. This is as true for individual lawyers as for the collective. We were constantly surprised to find that very few high-profile personal injury lawyers whom we interviewed actively worked to "spin" their successful cases as equally successful campaigns for social justice. "Well, I figured the jury decision to grant such an award pretty much spoke for itself," one attorney told us. Finally, tort reformers began their campaigns in earnest well over twenty years ago and have left an arguably deep mark on American popular culture. The present challenge for trial lawyers involves not just answering that message, but contending with the residue of its nearly unanswered advocacy for several decades. And this challenge is unlikely to be met by liberal public interest groups who have traditionally taken on responsibility for public relations and media communication. Given the divisive fallout over Ralph Nader's bid for the presidency in 2000, which many trial lawyers blamed as the cause of democrat Al Gore's defeat, Nader's popular authority and alliance with ATLA have been severely damaged.

The Political Context of ATLA's Strategic (Non)Investment

The preceding summary has already suggested some reasons for the trial lawyers' insider "stealth strategy" in responding to the tort reformers' assault on the existing civil justice system. This strategy has many obvious virtues. It takes advantage of trial lawyers' ample financial resources and professional connections; it targets key venues of policy change in focused ways; it requires far less funding than trying to match the massive corporate investment in public relations; and it has been quite successful in blocking or neutralizing tort reform legislation. However, this strategy has also left largely uncontested the public images of greedy trial lawyers and a civil litigation system gone awry that conservatives have circulated widely.

The aversion to public advocacy does not stem from a lack of a normative message, it would seem. Trial lawyers often boast that they have a "silver bullet" position that can win the argument with business supporters every time. For one thing, counter-stories of lawyers as the great "equalizers" who fight for the "little guy" and "underdog" against the powerful, for the "Davids versus the Goliaths," retain some currency in American culture (Speiser 1993). Moreover, as one strategist told us, "People believe their right to trial by jury is sacrosanct, just as fundamental as the First Amendment. If you tell people 'they are taking away your rights,' you can always win. . . . They've won almost every time on ballot propositions. Deep down, people agree with the position" of trial lawyers on this. But this strategist nevertheless opposed massive investment in public relations campaigns. His reasoning was grounded in the trial lawyers' common complaint that they are radically outspent by corporations. As a 2000 ATLA education committee report concluded, "Public education is all about message development, message delivery, and audience. Unfortunately, America's public opinion about the civil justice and tort law changes that would radically limit people's legal rights have been influenced by decades and billions of dollars worth of propaganda from corporate America." However, tort reform advocates can, and do, sincerely voice the same sentiments about the huge sums spent by rival trial lawyers. Although business groups do have greater financial resources, the major difference is in *how* the adversaries spend their respective funds.

Understanding why the personal injury bar has largely forfeited the struggle for public opinion, citizen understanding, and moral conviction thus invites attention to several other factors beyond those of strategy alone. We briefly suggest four additional factors that have contributed to trial lawyers' relative reticence in the face of large-scale assaults on their professional and political activities.

The Constraints of Legalized Corporate Secrecy

We begin by identifying a very important exogenous constraint of legally mandated secrecy preventing trial lawyers from publicly telling their stories about legal action to right wrongs committed by unaccountable corporate producers and professionals. This constraint is a primary subject of Ralph Nader and Wesley Smith's well-known book on corporate legal advantage, *No Contest* (1996), and many articles by members of the plaintiffs' bar (see Zitrin 1999; Zitrin and Langford 1999; Ramsey et al. 1998). The key issue at stake is the insistent efforts of corporate defense attorneys to conceal or obfuscate basic data about corporate responsibility for injuries that emerge from legal proceedings. There are three primary legal maneuvers by which corporate interests can undertake this act of concealment. The defense may: (1) obtain a protective order preventing the disclosure of discovery materials to third parties or the general public; (2) obtain a posttrial vacature of the judgment, making the case legally nonexistent; or (3) obtain a confidentiality agreement as a condition of settlement, prohibiting the plaintiff and the plaintiff's attorney from disclosing information regarding the facts of the case or the amount of the settlement. In short, from discovery through settlement, businesses and government can prevent the disclosure of information regarding harms to particular individuals, even if such harms might pose continued dangers to other citizens.

Such practices pose many problems for those who are concerned with promoting safety and democratic accountability in modern society. But most critical to our concern in this chapter are the significant restraints imposed on plaintiff's lawyers' capacities to expose corporate wrongdoing and to defend legal action that challenges such harmful practices. In other words, those attorneys who are best situated to tell powerful stories about the valuable role of cause-oriented personal injury litigation typically are forbidden to do so by law. Such proscriptions can be enforced either by fines imposed by judges or by forfeiture of monetary awards to plaintiffs—costs that in both cases target attorneys' well-defined professional obligations and reputations.

Such constraints on public disclosure of legal findings by attorneys are common. In 1988, one study reported that "the system [of court ordered secrecy] has become pervasive. In local and federal courthouses across the country, there are confidentiality orders in hundreds of cases that allege safety problems with widely used products and facilities. Every day, someone gets into a car, sees a doctor or wakes up near a toxic site that has been the subject of a confidentiality order." At that time, in the District of Columbia alone, there were twelve cases on the federal court docket that bore the designation of "Sealed v. Sealed" (Walsh and Weiser 1988). Judges have been particularly willing to seal records or otherwise prohibit disclosure where the parties have agreed, and, as noted above, there are strong incentives for plaintiffs to agree. There are powerful judicial incentives to sign broad secrecy orders, since this avoids the need for a time-consuming review of large numbers of documents to determine which are appropriately protected. A judge interviewed by the *Washington Post* reporter remarked that "I may be busy enough so that I may approve four or five or six such things before I say 'wait a minute'" (Walsh and Weiser 1988). More recent reports indicate that trial court secrecy is still fairly pervasive (Gibeat 1998).

Political and legal contests over these types of secrecy mandates have provided an important but little recognized sideshow to the larger battles over tort reform. ATLA, TLPJ, and other plaintiffs' bar allies have repeatedly argued in courts and lobbied in state legislatures for restrictions on secrecy agreements, while ATRA and business interests have supported secrecy in the name of "privacy." A few states have actually passed legislation limiting confidentiality agreements; Florida's Sunshine in Litigation Act and a parallel act in Washington are the most expansive, while at least eight other states have passed more limited acts (Ramsey et al. 1998). Several attempts to pass federal antisecrecy legislation, by contrast, have been unsuccessful. Finally, despite a good deal of appellate case law disfavoring court secrecy, courts continue to be "all over the map" on the issue. Trial courts routinely find themselves under pressure to agree to protective orders in the interest of dispatching the litigation (Gibeat 1998). Even when particular plaintiffs' lawyers do want to preach their message, they thus remain muzzled to a large extent by existing legal restrictions.

Mission Impossible: Changing the Public Image of Trial Lawyers

Trial lawyers are further constrained from publicly preaching their cause by a variety of less formal but very real endogenous factors. The first and most obvious of these reasons for reticence is the widespread skepticism that major improvement in the image of lawyers is possible. Even if the well-funded charges of conservative tort reform forces could be matched effectively in words and dollars, challenging the long-established, deeply rooted public cynicism about lawyers generally, and especially about personal injury lawyers, seems Sisyphean to many trial lawyers. That is the conventional wisdom of plaintiffs' attorneys themselves, and they may draw much support from scholars. As Robert Post wrote in the mid-1980s, just as tort reform was gaining momentum, "The most striking aspect of the image of the lawyer in popular culture is the intense hostility with which it is invested" (1987: 1). Although the topic is enormous, we review just a few relevant factors that support this perception.

For one thing, attorneys to whom we have talked echo that "lawyers have always been demonized throughout history." Legal historian Max Radin (1946) long ago identified the "ancient grudge" against lawyers that is traceable to Greek and Roman cultures. His study documented that lawyers were routinely assaulted thousands of years ago in terms similar to today—as hypocritical, rapacious, and inclined to esoteric, arcane language. The biblical invective from Luke 11:46 is also frequently recalled: "Woe unto you also, ye lawyers; for he lade men with burdens grievous to be borne." Indeed, virtually every lawyer learns as part of his or her cultural education the familiar and deep literary cuts into the legal profession, from Shakespeare's "kill all the lawyers first" to lawyer Thomas More's banishment of lawyers from his Utopia to Dickens' unflattering portrait in *Bleak House* referenced earlier (see Post 1987). Other historians have provided ample supporting evidence, such as Arthur Bryant's summary of fourteenth-century English opinion: "Of all who enforced the lord's rights, the lawyer was the most hated" (cited in Mindes and Acock 1982: 172). And American antipathy to lawyers has been a common theme from the colonial era to the present (Post 1987; Mindes and Acock 1982; Galanter 1998b). While Americans' attitudes traditionally have been ambiguous toward the legal profession, most attorneys whom we met view the dark side as most salient in our historical legacy.

Attorneys cannot, moreover, help but be overwhelmed with the negative images of their profession that surround them in contemporary popular culture. As Marc Galanter (1998b) and others (Cramton 1996) have powerfully demonstrated, the pervasive practice of telling lawyer jokes has at once expressed and deepened the profound distrust that citizens have for attorneys, and especially for trial lawyers. The fact that lawyers are among the most active tellers of such jokes only underlines the degree to which they share reservations or guilt about their own activity (Galanter 1998b). Moreover, an enormous amount of scholarly literature has documented the generally very negative images of lawyers—and especially noncriminal attorneys—in movies, in popular literature, and on television (see Chase 1986; Sherwin 2000; Asimow 1996, 2000). In fact, an entire journal—*Picturing Justice: The Online Journal of Law and Popular Culture* (http://www.usfca.edu/pj/index.html)—has been dedicated to scholarly documentation and assessment regarding the saturation of popular culture with images of attorneys and the legal system. The common conclusion in most such scholarship is that, while a relatively benign and even heroic image of lawyers balanced the dark stereotype in the 1950s and 1960s, that was a momentary blip in an otherwise continuous and increasingly negative portrayal of lawyers in American mass society.

Images of the personal injury lawyers as Satans in suits (*The Devil's Advocate*), as amoral chiselers and con-men (*The Rain-Maker*), as chronic liars (*Liar, Liar*), as apt appetizers for hungry dinosaurs (*Jurassic Park*), as elite narcissists (*A Civil Action*), or as myopic, feckless, unprincipled hacks (*Erin Brockovich*)—flood American movie and TV screens, novels, music, and other artifacts of mass culture. All in all, as law has "gone pop," much of the complexity has been eliminated and the villainous, sleazy, or greedy lawyer has become a familiar image that everyone loves to hate (Sherwin 2000).

Whatever their source, the impact of increasingly mixed, if not outright negative, images in mass culture can be measured in public opinion polls. Three widely cited summaries of national polls conducted on the subject between 1986 and 1993—two by the *National Law Journal* (Kaplan 1986; Samborn 1993) and one by the American Bar Association (Hengstler 1993; see also Galanter 1998b)—provided discouraging findings that greatly influenced trial lawyers. Although most respondents in all three polls reported that they had retained lawyers and were mostly quite satisfied with their particular performances, lawyers in the aggregate were given quite low marks. Respondents found lawyers' ethical behavior to be unimpressive, with seven times as many people rating lawyers' behavior as poor (21 percent) than as excellent (3 percent) (Galanter 1998b: 808–9). Samborn (1993) found that the ethical status of attorneys declined notably from 1986 to 1993, with those who thought lawyers were less honest than most people nearly doubling from 17 to 31 percent. He also noted that 36 percent of those polled agreed that the general image of lawyers had "gotten worse," while only 8 percent said it had "improved" (at 1). In comparative rankings of trust in the professions, lawyers also ranked very poorly; they were at the bottom of a 1991 poll, well below car salesmen and politicians, just as they were over forty years earlier (Galanter 1998b: 809).

The previous polls all confirm that the image of lawyers is still relatively mixed, with some bright as well as many dark spots. But the leading attorneys in ATLA whom we interviewed seemed only to see the dark side. After all, the plaintiffs' bar generally is regarded as at the very low end of the legal profession itself in terms of trust and respect. Hence, while tort reformers' messages may be simplistic and misleading, they are perceived to be playing with the "stacked deck" of highly negative popular images supporting them. As a 1998 ATLA memo put it, "The sad truth is not simply that these charges are false, but that they are believed by a majority of Americans, including judges, jurors, and academics." The logic of the longtime public relations director expressed the conclusion that follows this observation well. "I don't buy into that worry that we're losing the public relations battle. We've always lost the public relations battle," Alan Parker told an interviewer. "I certainly think it's a waste of time to spend millions of dollars a month trying to change the public relations image of lawyers. You might as well throw the money into the Potomac." A more recent public relations director, Carlton Carl, echoed this sentiment. It is all "very depressing, but what can we do about it, except make it worse by spending money?"

Professional Paradoxes and the Problem of Image

Many analysts relate the negative popular image of attorneys, and especially for personal injury lawyers, to the paradoxes intrinsic to their very professional status. We note two paradoxes—the first a problem for lawyers generally, and the second, a problem especially for the more cause-oriented trial lawyers.

The first paradox derives from the public's tendency to criticize lawyers as a group for doing well what individual clients most value about lawyers and what professional ethics define as the core obligation of attorneys—that is, representing clients aggressively, skillfully, and even ruthlessly. The core image of the legal professional is that of a value-neutral, technically competent "hired gun" whose competence and zealous commitment are critical to the adversary process (Luban 1988). This is what individual clients want from an attorney: zealous and skillful representation that maximizes the chances of winning a dispute, whether it goes to trial or not. Hence, it almost seems counterproductive to promote an image of lawyers that is affable, altruistic, or publicly spirited. As an ATLA leader put it, "Nobody wants a friendly, sweet, lovable, loving lawyer. They want a junkyard dog. Your lawyer you want to be tough. So I don't understand the ABA and everybody else saying 'Oh, we want everybody to love lawyers.' I don't want them to love lawyers; I don't even care. They don't have to love lawyers."

The problem is that it is just these same characteristics for which lawyers in general are distrusted and disrespected. Public opinions polls cited in the *National Law Journal* study (Kaplan 1986) suggest that the number one reason why the public dislikes lawyers is that they are "too interested in money." The contingency fee basis of compensation and increasing exposure through commercial advertising has meant that the pecuniary motives of lawyers are difficult to escape (Daniels and Martin 2000). This focus on lawyers' greed has occupied much of the internal discussion about the poor reputation of attorneys (Daniels 1986). However, such an image of financial self-interest also hardly separates tort lawyers from businesspeople, stock traders, and almost any other powerful figures in American society. The unique complaints about lawyers instead focus on two other important negative traits—that they "manipulate the legal system without any concern for right and wrong" and that they "file too many unnecessary lawsuits" (Post 1987). In short, the public assessment is contradictory; lawyers are respected and distrusted for the very same traits of aggressive client representation. As Robert Post deftly concludes in an article on this paradox, "Lawyers, it seems, can't win for trying. They are simultaneously praised and blamed for the same actions" (1987: 4; see also Galanter 1998b). And no doubt, this dilemma is exaggerated for attorneys in the plaintiffs' bar, who are among the least trusted. Like Machiavelli's prince, trial attorneys want to be both feared and loved, but the former is arguably a more reliable and realistic virtue than the latter.

Marvin Mindes and Alan Acock (1982) have argued further that an attorney's own reading of this apparent paradox makes the problem more acute. These authors contend that the public long has viewed attorneys in terms of three prevailing images. In order of salience, they are "hero," "helper," and "trickster." However, lawyers tend to reverse the order of perceived salience in the public mind. Specifically, attorneys themselves interpret the "good lawyer" as that professional who can best combine the hero and trickster traits. In short, these authors conclude that lawyers tend to embrace as critical to success that very characteristic that the public finds most problematic and troubling. If these authors are correct, then lawyers' own social constructions of their professional identity perpetuates both their negative public image and their fatalism that such an image can be improved.

Given the preceding discussion, it might seem that making the case publicly for the collective good championed by personal injury lawyers would be a productive strategy. One might think that trumpeting the "moral" commitments of many plaintiffs' attorneys to justice, accountability, and equality "puts a humane face on lawyering and provides an appealing alternative to the value-neutral, 'hired-gun' imagery that often dogs the legal profession" (Sarat and Scheingold 1998: 3). But this premise runs aground on the second fundamental paradox: as cause lawyering scholarship has demonstrated, emphasizing the moral causes that lawyers represent threatens to politicize and render partisan their actions in ways that undermine their fundamental authorizing claim to moral neutrality and technical competence. It exposes the inherent partisanship that images of legal professionalism serve to mask. As Sarat and Scheingold put it, "the result is a threat to ongoing professional projects and the political immunity of the legal profession and the legal process" (4; see Shamir 1995). Specifically, frank public advocacy of consumers' interests against corporations, of working-class people against the wealthy, of legal justice against market efficiency, and of democratic justice against corporate productivity would threaten to reduce plaintiffs' attorneys to just another political interest group, alternately pursuing partisan, divisive ideological agendas when not motivated completely by greedy self-interest.

All in all, it seems, trial lawyers for personal injury plaintiffs have concluded that they just cannot win in the public relations arena. Whatever public image they project is likely to come loaded with negative implications for their professional status. As such, it makes sense to remain off the public stage as much as possible and pursue their agendas through stealth-oriented insider politics.

Divisions among Trial Lawyers

A final factor that has weighed heavily in the political strategies of trial lawyers is their own manifold divisions among themselves. We already noted that trial lawyers are united in their opposition to tort reform but otherwise are a rather stratified and contentious group in a variety of ways. The first obvious dimension of differentiation that generates tensions is simply along the lines of differential wealth. We pointed out that ATLA includes a small stratum of extraordinarily affluent lawyers, most of whom focus on complex class actions such as mass torts; a large lower stratum of modest income attorneys who handle routine cases such as auto accidents; and a wide array of lawyers who handle divers types of cases and generate quite variable incomes (see Parikh 2001). These disparities in income and practice type not surprisingly have led to different perceptions of interest and identity, and more than a little resentment, among personal injury lawyers. Those attorneys most likely to envision their practices as within the more virtuous domains of ordinary lawyering in particular have been inclined to resentment about other types of attorneys at both the top and the bottom.

On the one hand, we have encountered many attorneys who are quite proud of their own practices but harbor some disdain for other personal injury attorneys, mostly in the lower income end, who rely on mass advertising to generate business. The former lawyers whom we interviewed or read about view advertising as a tawdry practice that both demeans those who do it and tarnishes the image of other lawyers who view themselves as motivated by ideals of justice as well as by a comfortable income. As one attorney who specializes in cases for low income plaintiffs told us:

> I think lawyer advertising is deadly. It's comical. These guys on TV with a big smile on their face holding up a check. 'I got this guy $400,000. I'll come to your hospital. I'll make house calls.' All this kind of thing. I think the average person that sees that—they don't see a caring lawyer that wants to do good. They see a lawyer out hustling business. And they see it a lot. They see it in phone books. It's on TV all day long. It's on the radio. So, you know, you go to a courtroom, what's their initial impression? Here's another one of those greedy advertising lawyers representing somebody who says they're hurt. Makes us all look like frauds.

On the other hand, many lawyers across the income spectrum seem to be offended by the ostentatious displays of wealth and power by some of the most affluent products liability attorneys. One quite affluent but humble and decidedly idealistic attorney put the sentiment in these words:

> The trial lawyers in many ways, you know, have been their own worst enemies. . . . It's hardly complicated. It's ego. It's ego and arrogance and bragging, and unfortunately lawyers have a tendency with their war stories and—ego and arrogance. For example, sometimes I just look in disbelief. You see a lawyer goes on *20/20*, goes on *60 Minutes*, and even though a high school kid would understand where they are coming from, they want to show that the lawyer lives in a mansion, and he's very rich. And the lawyer cooperates, and says "Here's my Rolls Royce" and "Here's my mansion" and "Here's my staff." What world are these guys living in? There's a lot of jealousy, there's a lot of envy out there. And this is not wonderful. If the lawyer's done well, and he's made a lot of money—if that is the focus of an interview or a program, you get the hell out of my office. I don't want to talk to you. What's the point? Where is that going? And you see a lot of that and it creates a lot of resentment. . . . You and I both

know that there are many, many lawyers who are very dedicated and who work very hard and don't make a lot of money. There's a tiny percentage of rich lawyers, but you know, this is where the focus is. And it doesn't really help when lawyers get on television and they get arrogant and they start bragging about how many cases they've won and how much money they've made.

Given that greed is the most common cited vice of lawyers in public opinion polls, this complaint is understandable.

Other divisions matter as well, especially among the top strata of lawyers who deal with complex, high-stakes litigation involving many plaintiffs—such as asbestos, diet pills, and tobacco—and who wield considerable influence in ATLA or the legal community generally. One group of such lawyers largely came up through the ranks of tort lawyers handling cases of individuals, and then began to connect divers plaintiffs who were injured by the same product. These attorneys tend to adhere to a basic "right to sue" philosophy that places a premium on individualized or specialized group cases and awards. These attorneys are often allied to some degree, at least in philosophy, with Ralph Nader, Gerry Spence, and other legal populists. The other group of attorneys in many cases developed their experience from class action litigation involving securities, consumers, and other large groups. They specialize in consolidating large numbers of complaints and developing negotiated class-wide settlements.

These two groups of lawyers have often found themselves in "rather nasty disputes," which in part are, again, "rooted in money" (Rheingold 2000). The populist lawyers take individual cases on fee contract, and thus want to maximize the recovery for each case. They often resist paying a portion of their fees to groups of lawyer "consolidators" who represent mega-classes of plaintiffs. The latter group, by contrast, tends either to amass huge amounts of billable hours for their aggregative work or take their fees—sometimes up to 25 percent—from the recoveries of plaintiffs and their individual attorneys. This clash often leads the former individualistic attorneys to take on roles as "objectors" to large class actions.

But money is not always, or necessarily, the core issue making these lawyer groups "natural born enemies, unable to cooperate effectively" (Rheingold 2000). Populist attorneys often challenge class actions as muting the diversity of facts in cases, failing to disaggregate plaintiffs into subclasses, privileging some plaintiff groups represented by the consolidators over other plaintiff groups, and selling out future plaintiffs whose harm has not yet become evident from any award for damages at all. In short, the conflicts often stem from different perceptions of fair representation, effective advocacy, and the proper means to ensure corporate accountability and just outcomes. Most dramatically, populist

trial attorneys often charge class action consolidators with willingness to negotiate pernicious deals that secure their own large incomes and the future security of corporate defendants at the expense of many or most plaintiffs, and even
the general collective interest in safety (Coffee 1995; Koniak 1995). These clashes
were especially acute in asbestos litigation, which produced two landmark
Supreme Court cases supporting the objectors' challenge to class actions.[14] One
activist lawyer was admirably branded a "traitor to his class" for his old-fashioned populist challenges that cost him both money and "the brotherhood that
had bound the plaintiffs lawyers" for decades in the "clubby asbestos bar"
(Frankel and Morris 2000). The ongoing "Stop Class Action Abuse" project led
by TLPJ and animated by the same populist vision has made this conflict
among elite personal injury attorneys an enduring feature of the plaintiffs' bar.

Finally, these latter divisions have been related, although not reducible, to
splits among leaders in ATLA over the strategy of stepping up public challenges
to tort reform critics. For one thing, some of the elite attorneys who prefer class
action approaches have actually allied with business interests to promote some
types of tort reform legislation that restrict only traditional individual actions,
most notably in Texas and Florida (Daniels and Martin 2000).[15] By contrast,
many of the high-profile populist attorneys—like Fred Baron—have become
leaders of drives to invest more heavily, widely, and creatively in challenging the
tort reform assault in law schools, among jurists, and in the mass media. After
a period of some struggle, the latter group seemed to have ascended to control
of ATLA in the 1990s, although their modest commitment to the cause hardly
produced a radical break. At the same time, we again noted earlier, this apparent emergence of populist, public interest-oriented leadership in ATLA seems
to have been seriously compromised or undermined by the traumatic split with
Ralph Nader after the 2000 election. The possibility of an outsider/insider
coalition successfully pushing for a more dramatic public challenge to business-
supporter tort reformers thus seems as meager now as in previous years.

Conclusion

We have aimed to develop three lines of argument in this chapter. First, we
have endeavored to explain and document the response of ATLA and its allies
to the pervasive public assault on personal injury lawyers and the civil legal system waged by pro-business tort reformers. Citing both the volunteered reflections by ATLA leaders and the organization's policy practices, we have charted
the stealth logic of insider influence at the core of this strategic response from
the plaintiffs' bar. The long-standing focus of this approach has been to culti-

vate support from public officials, and especially from legislators, at the federal and state level by spending large amounts of money in electoral contests and developing close personal alliances. An additional, more recent plank in the strategy has entailed the use of litigation to challenge state tort reform measures on constitutional grounds. Together, these tactics have proved quite successful in limiting the influence of tort reformers on official policy at both the state and federal levels. At the same time, organized investments in mass media and public relations to challenge the negative stories, arguments, and images of tort lawyers and tort law practice propagated by conservative critics have been minimal. Both the elected leadership and staff strategists for ATLA long have believed that staying out of the public debate was the best policy, for lawyers are more likely to hurt themselves by drawing increased attention. During the 1990s, a new wave of organizational leaders did envision much more aggressive campaigns to influence the views of targeted publics such as judges, legal scholars, and juries, but this investment so far has been very little and very late.

Our second aim has been to outline some larger contextual factors that have encouraged or rendered sensible this chosen organizational strategy by the plaintiffs' bar. Perhaps the most important factor has been the perceived success of the insider strategy itself that was inherited from early organizational leaders. If one focuses on the battle over official public policy, it is difficult to deny that ATLA's defensive insider campaign has been victorious to a large extent. Moreover, we identified four additional factors that help to explain why trial lawyers have not extended their campaign further into the arenas of public debate: the legal constraints imposed by defendants on plaintiff attorneys' capacity to reveal their knowledge about corporate harm; resignation about the deeply embedded public cynicism regarding lawyers, and especially attorneys, for injured plaintiffs; the paradoxes of professional commitment to aggressive client representation; and the substantial divisions within the plaintiffs' bar, especially among its wealthiest and most influential members. When one adds to these factors the trauma caused by Ralph Nader's presidential campaign in 2000, it seems unlikely that ATLA will become a more prominent public defender of its members, their role in the civil legal system, and their loftiest social causes in the near future.

Finally, while our goal has not been to challenge or criticize ATLA's political strategy, we have endeavored to suggest some potentially costly implications of its insider stealth tactics. For one thing, new federal campaign laws might significantly impede ATLA's traditional reliance on financial contributions to secure political influence in the future. More fundamentally, ATLA's public reticence and reluctance to answer tort reform critics—their public "shrug" to the continual barrage of attacks—have virtually ceded the public relations contest to conservatives, who already were arguably at an advantage. Indeed, we contend that this virtual silence of plaintiffs' lawyers is as important as the steady chants of tort reformers in shaping public knowledge about the civil legal system. This reticence has resulted in the fact that, as our own studies confirm, the voices of tort reformers and corporate defendants outnumber by two to one those of plaintiffs' representatives in newspaper accounts (Haltom and McCann 2004). The plaintiffs' lawyers' relative reticence has also left unchallenged media propensities for reporting conservative reformers' "horror stories" of frivolous lawsuits and, even more, for representing serious lawsuits in ways that parallel these trivialized tort tales. And this has meant as well that the individualistic logic of both dramatic media reporting and conservative moralistic spin has prevailed with hardly an articulated challenge from advocates of more complex structural accounts (Haltom, McCann, Aks 2000). Although trial lawyers have spent a bundle to make sure they won't lose the fight, the mass public has been exposed to a radical mismatch in which one side routinely refuses to raise its gloves in either defense or offense.

This relative reluctance to engage in public dialogue arguably has taken a toll at multiple different levels.[16] For one thing, opinion polls confirm that both the general public and jurors believe that there has indeed been a litigation explosion, that frivolous lawsuits have proliferated, that civil litigation favors plaintiffs over "deep pockets" defendants, that jury awards are excessive, that civil litigation is too costly, and that lawyers are greedy and untrustworthy catalysts to these tendencies.[17] As Thomas Burke concluded in his study of California contests over no-fault insurance, "The downside of ATLA's strategy . . . was that the lawyers seemed to be losing the battle of public opinion, and with it the hearts and minds of juries and judges" (2002: 49). An ATLA memo in 1992 invoked the more dramatic account of professors James Henderson and Theodore Eisenberg (1990) that the public relations battle over products liability after 1985 had become a "slaughter" (770).

These strong currents of opinion have, moreover, mattered for legal practice. Much evidence exists that these prevailing negative narratives have significantly shaped the perceptions and choices of citizens—potential plaintiffs, jurors, judges, insurance agents, corporate defendants, and the like—in their roles as legal actors responding to cause lawyers' initiatives. For example, abundant data suggest that juries not only became increasingly suspicious of plaintiffs in the last decade, but the former became much more reluctant to rule for plaintiffs and to provide high awards when they did rule favorably, relative to previous years. Professors Stephen Daniels and Joanne Martin report that almost 90 percent of plaintiffs' lawyers whom they polled in Texas said that, in their experience, juries were making lower awards than five years earlier in cases with comparable injuries. One attorney volunteered that "we start with the jury box and we start with suspicion, and it's hard to get a good verdict for a deserving victim. So very, very hard . . . [in the past] we felt a warmth in the jury box, whereas now we feel like it's a refrigerator" (cited in Daniels and Martin 2000: 31; see also Henderson and Eisenberg 1990; Hans 2000). American society arguably has become ever more like the world of Sander County, as reported by David Engel (1984), in which rights claiming for personal injuries is stigmatized as immoral, undesirable, and the sign of moral decay. These factors loom large in shaping the larger contemporary context in which cause lawyers of all types labor. There can be no doubt that the increasingly negative narratives and notions about attorneys, and especially plaintiffs' attorneys, that have come to dominate American mass culture have significantly constrained the opportunities and limited the cultural and material resources available to lawyers for diverse just causes.

At the same time, while the plaintiffs' bar has generally neutralized tort reform legislation, it has done virtually nothing to offset the tort reformers' continuous campaign to sustain concern about the litigation explosion as a core part of our broader political discourse. Indeed, ATLA's combination of public reticence and realist "counter-stories" response has enabled reformers to keep the issue very alive on the national agenda. As such, concern over the litigation explosion fed by lawyer greed has been invoked to discredit the campaigns of state attorneys general to rein in tobacco producers (Haltom and McCann 2004; Derthick 2002) and to undermine national patients' bill of rights, among other issues. Equally important, criticisms and critics of lawyers have been able to keep civil justice activists on the defensive, diverting the very possibilities of public attention to the larger issues at stake in most tort actions—the inadequacy of health insurance, especially for elderly and lower-class citizens; the paucity of provisions for facilitating care by family or friends for the injured or ill; or a lack of regulatory or remedial will in Congress to address major health hazards such as asbestos, tobacco, environmental toxins, and the like.

In this latter regard, of course, the problem is not just the reluctance of the plaintiffs' bar to aggressively voice its core political and moral vision, but the basic commitments to and interests in narrowly litigation-based approaches at the heart of that cause-oriented vision. Indeed, there is much reason to believe that even the most cause-oriented, populist-minded plaintiffs' attorneys are as antistatist, voluntaristic, and individualistic as their corporate adversaries (McCann 1986; Burke 2002).[18] All in all, there thus is little reason to think that the plaintiffs' bar is likely to be a force for either advancing new substantive policy agendas or new forms of democratic politics in contemporary U.S. society.

Notes

The authors would like to thank three people whose assistance was invaluable to this chapter. First, Anne Bloom, who generously shared with us her extensive experience as a cause-oriented personal injury lawyer, her boundless knowledge of the plaintiff's bar, and her unique access to persons and documents that we cite. Second, Thomas Burke, who provided us access to two interviews that he conducted with key figures in our account. His scholarship also was very helpful and is noted as such in various parts of the chapter. Third, Peter Hovde, a former practicing attorney, provided extremely able assistance in gathering, sorting through, and making sense of materials discussed here.

1. The dissertation by Sara Parikh (2001) was extremely helpful for developing a portrait of personal injury lawyers in this section.

2. The classic study on the evolution of the plaintiffs' bar is Stuart M. Speiser's *Lawyers and the American Dream* (1993).

3. As Congress Watch Director Pamela Gilbert put it, "Ralph Nader's very very strong view [is] that you should never cut off someone's access to the courts" (personal interview). See McCann (1986).

4. Gilbert again: "For Public Citizen that's the most important role that the civil justice system plays—the investigation and disclosure of these large institutions that have such a great effect on us and that we have little control over or ability to find out what goes on behind those closed doors."

5. By "stealth" strategy, we intend several different but related meanings offered by the *New Oxford American Dictionary*. First, the strategy is a relatively surreptitious, furtive, "behind the scenes" approach. The ATLA campaign is designed primarily to fly under the radar of popular attention and to leave its mark quietly on specific elite legislative targets. Campaign contributions, lobbying expenditures, and personal outreach to legislators all fit this strategy of focused influence that is formally public but realistically nearly invisible to the general public. Second, we want to suggest that this tactical logic, while undeniably successful in some key regards, is very cautious, cagey, and conservative in character. Third, the term's likely origins in the Middle English word "steal" are indicative of how the contemporary public tends to view such strategies of unseen "insider influence." This will be discussed in later sections of the chapter.

6. The 1994 interview with Alan Parker referred to here was conducted and graciously provided to us by Professor Thomas Burke. Every point was corroborated by at least a few other key actors whom we directly interviewed.

7. "At the national level, what tort lawyers are mainly seeking from the government . . . is inaction," notes Professor Martha Derthick (2002: 187).

8. Of course, tort reformers argue that legislatures are far more accountable and democratic in nature, that common law tort awards lack consistent, general standards, and that legislatures historically always had primary responsibility for tort principles. See Schwartz et al. (1997).

9. All figures on individual and PAC contributions as well as lobbying expenditures were taken from the Center for Responsive Government Web site: www.opensecrets.org.

10. *State ex rel. Ohio Academy of Trial Lawyers v. Sheward* (1999) 86 Ohio St.3d 451.

11.   Cited in "Constitutional Challenges: An Antidote to Tort 'Reform,'" *ATLA Advocate* 25, no. 9 (Nov. 1999): 1.

12.   Burke's study of "no-fault" in California is a classic example.

13.   Our book, *Distorting the Law: Politics, Media, and the Lawsuit Crisis* (2004), makes a similar case about the statistical studies of social scientists. The latter realist-inspired studies do effectively challenge many claims of conservative critics on an empirical level. However, they again not only tend to be highly defensive in character and placed in esoteric social science or law school publications that the mass public never reads, but they offer little coherent moral vision as an alternative to the individual responsibility ethic of conservatives. As such, both lawyers and their social science allies manage to "get good wood" on reformers' wild pitches in the dirt, but the former have repeatedly stood idle while the reformers' best pitches whiz by uncontested for call strikes.

14.   Amchem Products, Inc. v. Windsor, 521 U.S. 591 (1997); Ortiz v. Fireboard Corp. 109 S. Ct. 2295 (1999).

15.   One Public Citizen leader confided on this matter: "We fight tort reform efforts when the trial lawyers have abandoned the fight, most recently in Texas. We held a press conference accusing them of abandoning consumers because they signed off on tort reform and we would never sign off on it. We are much more hard core on protecting consumers' access to the courts than the trial lawyers ever have been."

16.   All the points in the next four and final paragraph are developed at length in our book *Distorting the Law: Politics, Media, and the Litigation Crisis* (2005).

17.   For relevant summaries of polling for the general public, see Daniels and Martin (2000: 14–18). For juror polls, see Hans (2000) and Mooney (1992).

18.   Populist attorneys tend to favor litigation as an alternative to statist regulatory and social welfare policies. This was repeatedly affirmed in our interview with ATLA leaders, including those on the "left." When asked about national health insurance, one leading populist attorney responded: "I don't think that ATLA has much stake in that." What about increased state regulation? "I used to have great faith in OSHA, EPA, all those agencies in the 1960s, but that turned out to be a really lousy deal. The same old thing, disarmed and captured by big business." The liberal "private attorney general" logic of regulatory litigation and the individual's "right to sue" thus formed his primary faith.

References

Abel, Richard L. 1982. *American Lawyers.* New York: Oxford University Press.
———. 1987. "The Real Tort Crisis—Too Few Claims." *Ohio State Law Journal* 48: 443–67.
Asimow, Michael. 1996. "When Lawyers Were Heroes." *University of South Florida Law Review.* 30: 1131.
———. 2000. "Bad Lawyers in the Movies." *Nova Law Review* 24: 533.
Auerbach, Jerold S. 1976. *Unequal Justice: Lawyers and Social Change in Modern America.* New York: Oxford University Press.

Baron, Fred. 2001. "President's Page." *Trial* (July): 9.

Bloom, Anne. 2001. "Taking on Goliath: Why Personal Injury Litigation May Represent the Future of Transnational Cause Lawyering," in *Cause Lawyering and the State in the Global Era*, ed. Austin Sarat and Stuart Scheingold. Oxford: Oxford University Press.

Boon, Andrew. 2001. "Cause Lawyers in a Cold Climate: The Impact of Globalization on the United Kingdom," in *Cause Lawyering and the State in the Global Era*, ed. Austin Sarat and Stuart Scheingold. Oxford: Oxford University Press.

Boot, Max. 1998. *Out of Order: Arrogance, Corruption, and Incompetence on the Bench.* New York: Basic Books.

Brakel, Samuel Jan. 2000. "'Besting' Tort Reform in Illinois (and Other Misnomers): A Reform Supporter's Lament." *Capital University Law Review* 28: 823–35.

Brill, Steven, and James Lyons. 1986. "The Not-So Simple Crisis." *American Lawyer* (May): 1–15.

Burke, Thomas F. 2002. *Lawyers, Lawsuits, and Legal Rights: The Battle over Litigation in American Society.* Berkeley: University of California Press.

Chase, Anthony. 1986. "Lawyers and Popular Culture: A Review of Mass Media Portrayals of American Attorneys." *American Bar Foundation Research Journal* 281–300.

Civil Justice Association of California. 1999. "Research: Campaign Contributions by California Trial Lawyers." Available at www.actr.com/research.index.hmtl.

Coffee, John C., Jr. 1995. "Class Wars: The Dilemma of the Mass Tort Class Action." *Columbia Law Review* 95: 1343–465.

Cox, Gail Diane. 1992. "Tort Tales Lash Back." *National Law Journal* (August 3): 1, 36.

Cramton, Roger C. 1996. "What Do Lawyer Jokes Tell Us About Lawyers and Lawyering?" *Cornell Legal Review* 23, no. 1: 3.

Daniels, Mitchell. 1986. "The Young Must Lead in Repair and Reform." *National Law Journal* (August 18): S-13.

Daniels, Stephen, and Joanne Martin. 1999. "'It's Darwinism—Survival of the Fittest': How Markets and Reputations Shape the Ways in Which Lawyers Obtain Clients." *Law and Policy* 21: 377–99.

———. 2000. "'The Impact that It Has Had Is Between People's Ears': Tort Reform, Mass Culture, and Plaintiffs' Lawyers." Unpublished paper.

Derthick, Martha A. 2002. *Up in Smoke: From Legislation to Litigation in Tobacco Politics.* Washington, D.C.: Congressional Quarterly.

Eisenberg, Theodore, John A. Goerdt, Brian J. Ostrom, and David B. Rottman. 1995. "Litigation Outcomes in State and Federal Court: A Statistical Portrait." Paper presented to Law and Society Association.

Evans, Rowland, and Robert Novak. 1994. "America's Most Powerful Lobby." *Reader's Digest* (April): 131–35.

Engel, David. 1984. "The Oven Bird's Song: Insiders, Outsiders and Personal Injuries in an American Community." *Law and Society Review* 18: 551–82.

Frankel, Alison, and John E. Morris. 2000. "Traitor to His Class: Watch Out World." *American Lawyer* (January): 1–9.

Galanter, Marc. 1974. "Why the 'Haves' Come Out Ahead: Speculations on the Limits of Legal Change." *Law & Society Review* 9, no. 8: 95–160.

———. 1998a. "An Oil Strike in Hell: Contemporary Legends about the Civil Justice System." *Arizona Law Review* 40: 717–52.

———. 1998b. "The Faces of Distrust: The Image of Lawyers in Public Opinion, Jokes, and Political Discourse." *U. Cin. L. Rev.* 66: 805.

———. 2002. "The Turn Against Law: The Recoil against Expanding Accountability." Paper presented at the annual meeting of the Law and Socety Association, Vancouver, B.C.

Gibeat, John. 1998. "Secret Justice." *ABA Law Journal* (April): 52.

Glendon, Mary Ann. 1991. *Rights Talk: The Impoverishment of Political Discourse*. New York: Free Press.

Haltom, William, and Michael W. McCann. 2004. *Distorting the Law: Politics, Media, and the Litigation Crisis*. Chicago: University of Chicago Press.

Haltom, William, Michael McCann, and Judith Aks. 2000. "Hegemonic Tales and Everyday News: Tort Reform, Mass Media, and the Assault on Citizen Rights." Unpublished paper.

Hans, Valerie P. 2000. *Business on Trial: The Civil Jury and Corporate Responsibility*. New Haven, Conn.: Yale University Press.

Hayden, Robert M. 1991. "The Cultural Logic of a Political Crisis: Common Sense, Hegemony, and the Great American Liability Insurance Famine of 1986," in *Studies in Law, Politics, and Society*, ed. Austin Sarat and Susan S. Silbey. Greenwich, Conn.: JAI Press.

Heinz, John P., and Edward O. Laumann. 1982. *Chicago Lawyers: The Social Structure of the Bar*. New York: Russell Sage Foundation; Chicago: American Bar Foundation.

Heinz, John P, Robert L. Nelson, Edward O. Laumann, and Ethan Michelson. 1998. "The Changing Character of Lawyers' Work: Chicago in 1975 and 1995." *Law and Society Review* 32: 751–75.

Henderson, James A., and Theodore Eisenberg. 1990. "The Quiet Revolution in Products Liability: An Empirical Study of Legal Change." *UCLA Law Review* 37: 479–553.

Hengstler, Gary. 1993. "Vox Populi: The Public Perceptions of Lawyers: ABA Poll." *American Bar Association Journal* 79: 60–65.

Howard, Philip K. 1994. *The Death of Common Sense: How Law is Suffocating America*. New York: Random House.

Kaplan, David. 1986. "What America Really Thinks about Lawyers." *National Law Journal* (August 18): S1–19.

Koniak, Susan F. 1995. "Feasting while the Widow Weeps: *Georgine v. Amchem Products, Inc.*" *Cornell Law Review* 60: 1045–168.

Luban, David. 1988. *Lawyers and Justice: An Ethical Perspective*. Princeton, N.J.: Princeton University Press.

McCann, Michael W. 1986. *Taking Reform Seriously: Critical Perspectives on Public Interest Liberalism*. Ithaca, N.Y.: Cornell University Press.

———. 1994. *Rights at Work: Pay Equity Reform and the Politics of Legal Mobilization*. Chicago: University of Chicago Press.

McCann, Michael W., William Haltom, and Anne Bloom. 2001. "Java Jive: Genealogy of a Juridical Icon." *University of Miami Law Review* 56, no. 1: 113–78.

Menkel-Meadow, Carrie. 1998. "The Causes of Cause Lawyering: Toward an Understanding of the Motivation and Commitment of Social Justice Lawyers." In *Cause Lawyering: Political Commitments and Professional Responsibilities,* ed. Austin Sarat and Stuart Scheingold (3–30). New York: Oxford University Press.

Mindes, Marvin, and Alan Acock. 1982. "Trickster, Hero, Helper: A Report on the Lawyer Image." *American Bar Foundation Research Journal* 6: 177–233.

Mooney, Sean F. 1992. *Crisis and Recovery: A Review of Business Liability Insurance in the 1980s.* New York: Insurance Information Institute.

Nader, Ralph, and Wesley J. Smith. 1996. *No Contest: Corporate Lawyers and the Perversion of Justice in America.* New York: Random House.

Olson, Walter K. 1991. *The Litigation Explosion: What Happened When America Unleashed the Lawsuit.* New York: Truman Talley Books.

Parikh, Sara. 2001. "Professionalism and Its Discontents: A Study of Social Networks in the Plaintiff's Personal Injury Bar." Sociology doctoral dissertation, University of Illinois at Chicago.

Post, Robert C. 1987. "On the Popular Image of the Lawyer: Reflections in a Dark Glass." *California Law Review* 75: 379.

Quayle, Dan. 1991. "Address to the Annual Meeting of the American Bar Association." Reprinted in Dan Quayle, *Standing Firm: A Vice-Presidential Memoir* (375–80). New York: HarperCollins.

Radin, Max. 1946. "The Ancient Grudge: A Study in the Public Relations of the Legal Profession." *Virginia Law Review* 32: 734.

Ramsey, Maja, Justine Durrell, and Timothy W. Ahearn. 1998. "Keeping Secrets with Confidentiality Agreements." *Trial* (August): 38, 40.

Rheingold, Paul D. 2000 "Analysis and Perspective: Who Are the Real Plaintiffs' Lawyers?" *Bureau of National Affairs* 1, no. 6: 216–18.

Salant, Jonathan D. 2003. "Votes in Congress mostly follow the money." Associated Press, in *The Seattle Times,* July 10, p. A.4.

Samborn, Randall. 1993. "Tracking Trends: Anti'Lawyer Attitude Up." *National Journal,* August 9, 1, 20-23.

Sarat, Austin, and William L. F. Felstiner. 1995. *Divorce Lawyers and Their Clients: Power and Meaning in the Legal Process.* New York: Oxford University Press.

Sarat, Austin, and Stuart Scheingold. 1998. "Cause Lawyering and the Reproduction of Professional Authority," in *Cause Lawyering: Political Commitments and Professional Responsibilities,* ed. Austin Sarat and Stuart Scheingold (3–30). New York: Oxford University Press.

Schattschneider, E. E. 1960. *The Semisovereign People: A Realist's View of Democracy in America.* New York: Holt, Rinehart and Winston.

Schwartz, Victor, Mark A. Behrens, and Mark D. Taylor. 1997. "Who Should Make America's Tort Law: Courts or Legislatures?" Washington Legal Foundation monograph.

Shamir, Ronen. 1995. *Managing Legal Uncertainty: Elite Lawyers in the New Deal.* Durham, N.C.: Duke University Press.

Sherwin, Richard K. 2000. *When Law Goes Pop: The Vanishing Line Between Law and Popular Culture.* Chicago: University of Chicago Press.

Smith, Mark. 2000. *American Business and Political Power: Public Opinion, Elections, and Democracy.* Chicago: University of Chicago Press.

Smith, William C. 1999. "Prying Off Tort Reform Caps." *America Bar Association Journal* (October): 29–30.

Speiser, Stuart M. 1993. *Lawyers and the American Dream.* New York: M. Evans.

Strasser, Fred. 1987. "Tort Tales: Old Stories Never Die." *National Law Journal* (February 16): 39.

Sykes, Charles J. 1992. *A Nation of Victims: The Decay of the American Character.* New York: St. Martin's Press.

Van Natta, Don Jr., and Richard Oppel Jr. 2000. "The 2000 Campaign: The Contributions; Memo Linking Political Donation and Veto Spurs Federal Inquiry." *New York Times* (September 14): A–1.

Walsh, Elsa, and Benjamin Weiser. 1988. "Court Secrecy Masks Safety Issues." *Washington Post* (October 23): A1.

Zitrin, Richard A. 1999. "The Case Against Secret Settlements (or, What You Don't Know Can Hurt You)." *Journal of the Institute for Legal Ethics* 2: 115.

Zitrin, Richard, and Carol M. Langford. 1999. "Don't Settle for Secrets." *Legal Times,* April 12, p. 22.

In the End, or the Cause of Law

PETER FITZPATRICK

> ... the *world* ... is not a "Cause."
> —Jean-Luc Nancy, *The Sense of the World*, p. 89

"It is one of the great charms of books," says Kermode charmingly, "that they have to end" (Kermode 1966: 23). What is charmed forth in the end is the combination of a containing imperative ("one cannot, of course, be denied an end") with a meaningful ability ("ends ... transfigure the events in which they are immanent") (Kermode 1966: 23, 175). Kermode's guiding instance, *Apocalypse* or the Book of Revelation, can provide our exemplar. With its evocation of an end-time or of a sacred time, as it is also called, in which the profane world is suffused with transcendent purpose or cause, *Apocalypse* is not merely an illustration but itself formative of an occidental thought of the end, the end toward which time moves linearly, purposively, finally. All that was becomes conclusively revealed in the end. Yet revelation, the very meaning of apocalypse, is uncontainable. And although *Apocalypse* concludes with a malediction against adding to it (Revelation 22:18), it also ends with the vision of "a new heaven and a new earth: for the first heaven and the first earth were passed away" (21:1). The end is a beginning. All things are made new (21:5).

In the bleak if more congenial world of Ecclesiastes, there can be found in the last chapter another end that is not an end: "of making many books there is no end: and much study is a weariness of the flesh" (12: 12). It is but a gentle distortion to see this as a premonition of reader-response theory, so-called. The book comes to existence only when it goes forth "to find the reader" (Auerbach 1953: 557). Yet if Auerbach's poignant phrase is apt, there is still something that has been brought to an end and assumed some determinate existence, something which is thence impelled searchingly into the world. The book, it may readily be granted, cannot exist apart from the practical infinity of its readership, and although that existence cannot be encompassed in any singular end, still the book does not simply dissipate in relation to its readers but remains an insistent focus for the diversity of responses to it. Yet the book, now in the world, cannot exist except in relation to its readers. That relation, in turn, will generate a variety of new determinate existences of the book, a variety of focal formations—concentrations of professional regard, for example.

So too with the law. Law is, borrowing from Blanchot, "the end," but an end not, or not just, enclosed in its own distinct existence, but an end opening onto what lies beyond that existence, what comes to and continually forms that existence (1981: 16). "Let us grant," says Blanchot, "that the law is obsessed with exteriority, by that which beleaguers it and from which it separates via the very separation that institutes it as form, in the very movement by which it formulates this exteriority as law" (1993: 434). With its always extending receptively beyond any determinate existence, law shares with the book an evanescence and a diversity of existence. Yet law has an authority that stills the importunate world and makes for some contained certainty. That very certainty, however, is only ever called for in the face of uncertainty. It is in the necessity yet impossibility of "some" certainty that law is iteratively impelled into existence. Such an operative certainty cannot endure in stasis. It has to be continuously made in law's constituent "obsess[ion] with exteriority" (Blanchot 1993: 434). To hold itself responsive to exteriority, to sustain the incipience of its becoming different to its present existence, law must refuse any primal attachment. It can, of itself, have "no material inside," as Cixous puts it (Cixous 1991: 18).

Law is then intrinsically dependent and derivative, quite lacking in any content of its own. So, as some jurisprudential traditions would require, law can only ever exist as a response to something else. Yet despite these incessant efforts to render law as society, fact, economy, and so on, it refuses being in "a world sapped by crude existence" (cf. Blanchot 1999: 395). Yet we also find that this same imperative for law to derive its contents from elsewhere resonates with a contrary jurisprudential tradition elevating law's autonomy. A persistent responsiveness, an intrinsic inability to be bound to any preexistent, would require that law always retain the ability to surpass any of its contents, modifying or rejecting them. Here law "affirms itself as law and without reference to anything higher: to it alone, pure transcendence" (Blanchot 1992: 25).

Law, then, is needful of cause to endow it with existence, even if its being must ever extend beyond the confinement of cause. And this remarkable collection amply illustrates the necessity of cause along with law's amenable responsiveness to the variety of causes, a responsiveness which extends beyond the most insistent markers of law's content, such as nation, Shamir's chapter offering perhaps the most dramatic instance of this. Nor can that responsiveness be confined to causes within a particular range of virtue, as the salutary contributions by Hatcher and Southworth serve to confirm. Nor, further, is law's need of cause a dependency on something external to it. The intimacy of law's dependence on cause is revealed most pointedly in the chapter by Woods where we see cause suffusing law and enabling it through a cohering community of law.

Given law's pervasive abjection to cause, it has to be a puzzle why the most persistent, even the predominant theme of this collection, and of the two volumes also edited by Sarat and Scheingold preceding it, comes to be, in all, the conflict between cause and profession, the profession of the law (Sarat and Scheingold 2001 and especially 1998). The puzzle is heightened in their depiction of the defining "instrumentalism" of the legal profession, the "classic, lawyer ... approach" being that of the "hired gun," a "value-neutral" self-subordination to the interests of the client (Sarat and Scheingold this volume). They would proceed to draw a contrast between the cause lawyer taking on "responsibility for the ends she is promoting" and the professional lawyers who "sell their services without regard to the ends to which their services are put" (ibid.). And if law in professional practice is unrestrainedly receptive to those ends, it follows that such law will serve overall the dominant "ends" in a society, such as "corporate wealth" (cf. Sarat and Scheingold, ibid.). Although, as Willemez reveals in his contribution, some legal professionals would more explicitly endorse such ends, the ultimate difference for Sarat and Scheingold between the cause lawyer and the mere professional is, at least by implication, that the latter is afflicted with bad faith, serving ends every bit as much as the cause lawyer but denying this by claiming to be "value-neutral" (ibid.). It would thence be imperative to distinguish professional disguise from the espoused cause with its "moral and/or political commitment" and its offering "lawyers the chance to enlist in a partisan pursuit of the good" (ibid.), a distinction cogently observed in the chapters by Thomson and by Jones.

Yet this present collection is telling also in the many instances it offers of seeming compatibilities between profession and cause. There is, for example, in Krishnan's portrayal of Indian lawyers, the correspondence so lucidly drawn between professional respectability and enterprise, even transgression, in pursuit of cause. Willemez, to take another example, acutely identifies a significant stratum of lawyers in France where professionalism fuses with commitment to cause. And this would seem to be the case with Maiman's intriguing account of

lawyers' advocacy of rights in the United Kingdom. With these and other instances in the collection dealing with situations outside the United States, it
might be tempting to locate a difference in the more instrumental filtering of
professional practice found in that country. But that this is not the whole story
is apparent from the Vermont epic recounted by Barclay and Marshall in a
chapter at once analytically incisive and moving.

There is, then, something about the legal profession which enables it to be
seen aptly as incompatible and compatible with cause. A ready resolution of
this seeming divide would be offered by the frequent identification in this volume of the legal profession with liberal values, something often compressed
elsewhere in the term "liberal profession." If such values could be made determinate, then causes lying outside of them would be incompatible with profession. Such a precipitate outcome is blocked at various points in this collection,
however. There are instances of impeccable professionals advancing causes contrary to liberal values. There is also the attribution of value-neutrality to being
professional. Most revealingly, there is Israël's essay in which Leninist advocates
would reduce legal professionalism to mere strategy only to find themselves
subsumed in a community of law generated in the Resistance—a community
reconciling cause and profession, a community both intensely existent and
passing in the contingency of war.

The existential intensity of the law itself comes from the incorporation of
what is passing within law's being. Law, thence, as we saw in Blanchot's company, must extend to what is ever different to its present existence, and to do
this, law must refuse any primal attachment and any content of its own. What
could it be, then, that one is attached to, that one is professing, in professing the
law? The answer usually advanced is that it is a professing, an avowal, of whatever the law is—again, a "value-neutral" commitment. But if this is all that is
being professed, then there is nothing to separate such a commitment from a
mere subordination to the interest, the power, or the cause that gives law its
content for the time being.

That there is more, and what that more may be, can be discerned, with Derrida's (1987) help, in the scrupulous professionalism of an exemplary cause
lawyer, Nelson Mandela in his struggle against apartheid. It would be difficult
to conceive of a situation where there was less cause for commitment to the
laws, or to conceive of a person more justified in refusing such commitment.
Yet Mandela advances a conception of "professional duty" which respects and
even admires both the law and its judicial institution even as the pervasive legal
oppressions of apartheid are being brought to bear on him (Derrida 1987: 15–16,
33–37; 35 for the quoted phrase). The law which calls forth this magnanimous

regard is the law that incipiently extends beyond its determinate existence through certain enabling qualities each of which "tends toward universality," such qualities as the generality of the law, equality, and "the independence and impartiality of . . . [the] judiciary" (Derrida 1987: 17, 20–22; Mandela, n.d. [1964]: 9).

These qualities are not ideals detached from a contrary legal reality, a reality of which Mandela was only too intimately aware, of course (see, e.g., Mandela 1995: 261, 309–10). They are qualities intrinsic to the being of law, to its integral extensiveness. So, taking the instance of equality, equality before the law, law's imperative ability to be other than its present content would ultimately dissolve and deny any set differentiation, in terms of apartheid or otherwise. But this "tending" toward equality will always be contained in the inevitable differentiation of law's determinate existence. Likewise, with law's famed generality: laws must be general but, when "applied" in the legal decision, law assumes a specific content. Yet, if the general cannot find itself in law's specific or determinate content, this does not mean that it is merely evanescent. Rather, generality remains an effective tendency within law. The inability of the specific to repeat itself exactly when combined with law's continuance creates law's operative generality. Then, to take a final instance, there is the impartiality of the judiciary. This impartiality enables law by institutionally emplacing law's lack of attachment to the existent, even if an effective partiality must supervene in the determinate act of decision. A blunt counter-example: it is exactly because the political trial is "fixed" beforehand that it is denied the character of law. And, as Shdaimah's nuanced study reveals, the quality of impartiality is intrinsic to "lawyering" generally, to being of the law.

These qualities of law in their effect within the professional setting are usually put as a matter of ethics, but that description would be quite inadequate if "ethics" is confined to its sense of some deontology brought to bear on how we are. Adequacy would be restored if ethics were seen, with Blackburn (2001), as something more intrinsic to our being, or if they were seen, with Derrida (2002: 13), as a matter of "*ethos*, of manner of being, of *habitus*." As such, this ethics would be an "actuality," something "actively produced, sifted, contained, and performatively interpreted by many hierarchizing and selective procedures" (Derrida 2002: 86). It is through such a process that law self-constitutes in its own cause, and this collection offers particularly telling instances such as that infrastructure of law which Meili so pointedly evokes, or the condign communities of law depicted by Israël and Woods, or the purposive organization of cause found in the revelatory final chapter by McCann and Haltom. In the end law must come not only to a cause without, but to its own.

References

Auerbach, Erich. 1953. *Mimesis: The Representation of Reality in Western Literature*, trans.Willard R. Trask. Princeton, N.J.: Princeton University Press.

Blackburn, Simon. 2001. *Ethics: A Very Short Introduction*. Oxford: Oxford University Press.

Blanchot, Maurice. 1981. *The Madness of the Day*, trans. Lydia Davis. New York: Station Hill Press.

———. 1992. *The Step Not Beyond*, trans. Lydia Davis. Albany, N.Y.: SUNY Press.

———. 1993. *The Infinite Conversation*, trans. Susan Hanson. Minneapolis: University of Minnesota Press.

———. 1999. "Literature and the Right to Death," trans. Lydia Davis in *The Station Hill Blanchot Reader: Fiction and Literary Essays*. Barrytown: Station Hill Press.

Cixous, Hélène. 1991. *Readings: The Poetics of Blanchot, Joyce, Kafka, Kleist, Lispector, and Tsvetayeva*, trans. Verena Andermatt Conley. Minneapolis: University of Minnesota Press.

Derrida, Jacques. 1987. "The Laws of Reflection: Nelson Mandela, in Admiration," trans. Mary Ann Caws and Isabelle Lorenz, in *For Nelson Mandela*, ed. Jacques Derrida and Mustapha Tlili. New York: Henry Holt.

———. 2002. *Negotiations: Interventions and Interviews, 1971–2001*, trans. Elizabeth Rottenberg. Stanford, Calif.: Stanford University Press.

Kermode, Frank. 1966. *The Sense of an Ending: Studies in the Theory of Fiction*. Oxford: Oxford University Press.

Mandela, Nelson. n.d. [1964]. "'I am Prepared to Die': Nelson Mandela's statement from the dock at the opening of the defense case in the Rivonia Trial Pretoria Supreme Court, 20 April 1964." Available at http://www.anc.org.za/ancdocs/history/rivonia.html.

———. 1995. *Long Walk to Freedom: The Autobiography of Nelson Mandela*. London: Abacus.

Nancy, Jean-Luc. 1997. *The Sense of the World*, trans. Geffrey S. Librett. Minneapolis: University of Minnesota Press.

Sarat, Austin, and Stuart Scheingold, eds. 1998. *Cause Lawyering: Political Commitments and Professional Responsibilities*. New York: Oxford University Press.

———, eds. 2001. *Cause Lawyering and the State in a Global Era*. New York: Oxford University Press.

Index

Index

In this index an "f" after a number indicates a separate reference on the next page, and an "ff" indicates separate references on the next two pages. A continuous discussion over two or more pages is indicated by a span of page numbers, e.g., "57–59."

ABA, *see* American Bar Association

ABCNY, *see* Association of the Bar of the City of New York

ABF, *see* American Bar Foundation

Abortion, 93f, 264–65, 309

Abraham, Spencer, 136

Academia, 95

Access, to judicial community, 314–15

Achmat, Zackie, 44, 47, 49

ACLU, *see* American Civil Liberties Union

ACRI, *see* Association for Civil Rights in Israel

Activism, activists, 63, 65, 102nn3, 4, 112, 115, 410; HIV/AIDS, 15–16, 44, 47–57; and private practice, 21–22; and professionalism, 22–23; ranges of, 83–84; conservative and libertarian, 85–86, 87–88, 138; identity as, 89, 215–17, 224–26; education and, 97–98; legal, 99, 139–40; judicial, 127, 128–29; grassroots, 184, 187–90; lawyers as, 203–4, 208–10, 219–20, 229–32; role-playing in, 218–19; work setting and, 221–22; professionalism and, 226–28, 466–67;

as risk taking, 228–29; public interest work and, 230–31; social networks and, 232–33

Addams, Jane, 259

Adoption of B.L.V.B. and E.L.V.B., 179, 199n3

Adoption of R.C, In re, 179

Adoption rights, 177, 179, 193f, 199n5, 310

ADR, *see* Alternative dispute resolution

Advocacy, 25, 58, 92, 377n14; conservative and libertarian, 93–94; organizations, 95f, 100–101; right-wing, 112–13; social movement, 314–15; environmental, 369–70; women's rights, 370–71. *See also* Activism

Affirmative action opponents, 93

Agency, 4; and structure, 5–6; professional identity and, 17–18

Agranat, Simon, 318

Agreement on Trade Related Aspects of Intellectual Property Rights (TRIPS), 40, 42, 47, 54, 55–56

Aide juridictionnelle, 67

AIDS: South African activism in, 15–16, 44, 47–57; cost of treatments, 39–40;

pharmaceutical companies and,
41–42
AIDS Consortium National Committee
(TAC), 49
AIDS Law Project (ALP), 47f
AJI, *see Association Juridique Inter-*
nationale
Alaska, 173
Albania, 151
Algerian War, 71
Alien Tort Claims Act (ATCA), 58–60
Alimony, 178
Alliances, 128; social movement, 326–30
ALP, *see* AIDS Law Project
Alternative dispute resolution (ADR),
366
Altruism, 30, 269n6, 298
Amazon Watch, 59
American Bar Association (ABA), 226
American Bar Foundation (ABF), 428
American Civil Liberties Union (ACLU),
99, 122, 182
American Consumer Project Technology,
52
American Pharmaceutical Manufacturers
Association (PharMA), 42
American Steel Workers Union, 59
Amicus briefs, 125, 128, 182
Amparo clasico, 386
Amparo colectivo, 27–28, 384; description
of, 385–87; judicial decisions in,
389–91; procedural limitations in,
391–92; legal culture in, 392–93; orga-
nizational plaintiffs and, 393–96;
strength of, 396–98; use of, 398–99;
cause lawyer empowerment and,
399–400; legal tactics under, 400–403;
legal process and, 403–4
Andhra Pradesh, 362
Animal rights movement, 217
Antiabortion advocacy, 93f, 99–100
Anticommunism, German, 161
Antifascist mobilization, 156
Antiretroviral medicines, 41

Argentina, 388; *amparo colectivo* in, 27–28,
384–87, 396–406; *corralito* in, 383–84;
judicial decisions in, 389–91, 406n13;
procedural problems in, 391–92; legal
culture in, 392–93; organizational
plaintiffs in, 393–96
Argentine Supreme Court, 384, 390
Arian, Sean, 402
Arizona, 204, 207–8, 225, 227
Ashkenazi, 333–34, 343n44
Association for Civil Rights in Israel
(ACRI), 312, 319–20, 321, 326, 328f, 337
Association Juridique Internationale
(AJI), 19–20, 147; origins, 148–50;
activities of, 151–53; effectiveness of,
153–54; lawyers in, 154–56; and Vichy
regime, 160f
Association of the Bar of the City of New
York (ABCNY), 121–22
Association of Trial Lawyers of America
(ATLA), 445, 456, 457n5, 458n18; tort
reform and, 29–30, 437–43; personal
injury lawyers and, 429–33; politics,
433–37; public opinion and, 448f;
lawyer divisions in, 450, 453; public
relations of, 454–55
Asylum and Immigration Act (U.K.), 413,
419
Asylum seekers: in United Kingdom,
412–22, 423–24nn6, 13
ATCA, *see* Alien Tort Claims Act
ATLA, *see* Association of Trial Lawyers of
America
Attlee government, 412

Babeuf trial, 158
Baehr v. Lewin, 180
Baker, Stan, 180, 189, 194
Baker v. State, 2f, 172f, 177, 184, 193, 197,
198–99nn2, 4, 8, 9; summary of,
180–83; goals of, 185–86; grassroots
activism and, 187–90
Banking issues: in Argentina, 28, 383–84,
404–5

Barak, Aharon, 331f, 334f, 337, 340
Bar associations, 121–22, 141–42n5
Bar Council of India (BCI), 350f
Baron, Fred, 441
BCI, *see* Bar Council of India
Beck, Nina, 180, 189, 194–95
Bedouins, 314
Bendorf, Thomas, 433
Bentham, Jeremy: *Principles of the Civil Code*, 118
Benvenisti, Eyal, 328
Berlin: International Red Help and, 148f
Biozole, 49
Birmingham (England), 415
Blair government: on asylum seekers, 412, 413–15
Blunkett, David, 413, 423nn9, 10
Boggs, Thomas Hale, Jr., 435
Bohmer, Martin, 394, 396, 401f
Boitel, Maurice, 157
Bolick, Clint, 126, 128
Bombay, 362
Bonte, Florimond, 157
Bombard-Stodel, Mrs., 151
Bonauto, Mary, 180f, 183, 196, 199n9
Bork, Robert, 134
Brazil, 50
Brennan, William, 184
Brill, Steven: "The Not-So Simple Crisis," 440
British Mandate, 317
British National Party, 414
Brittan, Leon, 42
Brown v. Board of Education, 116
Buckley, William, 86
Buenos Aires, 392–93, 402
Buisseret, August, 151–52
Burlington Free Press (newspaper), 179
Burma, 59
Bush, George H., 113
Bush, George W., 53, 172
Business interests, 118, 426; lawyering for, 18, 57, 88–89, 90–91, 103–4n14
Business schools, 38

Calabresi, Guido, 134, 142n11
Calabresi, Stephen, 134, 142n11
California, 125, 181, 435, 437, 440, 455
California State Chamber of Commerce, 125
CALS, *see* Center for Applied Legal Studies
Cameron, Edwin, 47
Campaign for Access to Essential Medicines, 52
Campbell, John Archibald: *Slaughter-House Cases*, 119–20
Canadian HIV/AIDS Legal Network (CHALN), 47
Capitalism: property rights advocacy and, 116–17, 140
Career paths, 210–11, 377n13; public interest law, 277–84, 289–90
Carl, Carlton, 438, 448
Carter administration, 99
Caste: and social relations, 351
Cause lawyers, 234–35n2; core and marginal, 208–10; work settings of, 210–13
CCAIR, *see* Citizens for Corporate Accountability and Individual Rights
CELS, *see* Center for Legal and Social Studies
Center for Applied Legal Studies (CALS), 47–48
Center for Constitutional Litigation, 438
Center for Constitutional Rights, 59
Center for Justice and Democracy (CJD), 430
Center for Legal and Social Studies (CELS), 397, 401
Center for Responsive Law, 54
CFDT, *see* Confédération française et démocratique du Travail
CGT, *see* Confédération générale du Travail
CHALN, *see* Canadian HIV/AIDS Legal Network
Chesebro, Ken, 442
Chicago, 171, 428

Chicago Bar, 428

Chittenden Superior Court, 180

Christian law groups, 95

Christian Legal Society, 86

Christian right, 123

Christians, 88, 91f, 94, 98, 100, 108n99

Cilliers, Fanie, 41, 45f, 60n2

Citizen Action, 430

Citizens for Corporate Accountability
and Individual Rights (CCAIR), 430

Citizenship: gay, lesbian, and bisexual,
179–80, 186; in Israel, 316

Civil code: French, 148

Civil disobedience, 14

Civil law, 317

Civil liberties, 368, 371

Civil rights, 107n94, 118, 195, 326, 368, 371

Civil Union Law (Vt.), 172, 183, 186

Civil War Amendments, 120

CJD, see Center for Justice and Democracy

Claire, 252–53

Clandestine Communist Party, 161

"Class Action Prevention Abuse Project,"
430

Class action suits, 59, 256; in Argentina,
27–28; and social change, 387–89; in
United States, 397f. See also Amparo
colectivo

Class legislation, 118

Class struggle, 153

Claybrook, Joan, 439

Client-lawyer relationships, 23–24, 105–
6n58, 191, 270n16, 271n22, 349–50;
same-sex marriage issue, 194–96; progressive issues and, 241–42; legal services organizations, 243–44; collaboration, 250–58; personal, 258–67

Clients, 270n20; autonomy of, 144–50; respect for, 267–68; organizational,
393–96

Coca-Cola, 58f

Cohn, Haim, 318, 328

Colchester, 415

Cold War, 123

Collaboration: client-lawyer, 250–58

Collective bargaining: in France, 75

Collective identity: social movements
and, 213–14

Collective rights: in Argentina, 385–87

Colombia, 59

Commercial firms, 59, 312

Common Benefits Clause (Vt.), 172, 181f

Common law, 317

Communist Party, 71; in France, 147, 154,
156, 160, 161–63

Communists: French, 19–20, 153, 154–60,
164; European, 148–49, 151–52; militancy, 149–50; under Vichy regime,
160–63

Confédération française et démocratique
du Travail (CFDT), 74, 80n45

Confédération générale du Travail
(CGT), 74

Congress Watch, 429

Conservative Directory, 87

Conservative movement, 91, 123–24

Conservative Party (U.K.), 414

Conservatives, conservatism, 17f, 84, 89,
92, 98–99, 103n13, 138; activism, 85–86,
87, 102n4; judicial activism and,
128–29; property rights and, 129–30;
Federalist Society and, 134–35, 137,
142n7

Constitutional law, 97, 99–100, 312; property rights and, 113–14

Constitutional reform: in Argentina,
27–28, 384

Constitutional rights, 184–85, 199n10

Constitutions: U.S., 118, 138, 172; state, 171;
Vermont, 178, 181, 198–99n2; Indian,
376n10; Argentine, 386–87, 395

Consumer cases, 93

Consumer Federation of America, 430

Consumer groups: and ATLA, 429–30

Consumer Project on Technology (CPT),
50; HIV/AIDS activism, 54–56, 57

Consumers Union, 430

Contingency-fee law, 426–27
Cooley, Thomas M., 120; *A Treatise on the Constitutional Limitations which Rest Upon the Legislative Powers of the States of the American Union*, 118
Co-parenting, 179
Cordoba, 390
Core cause lawyering, 23
Corporate citizenship, 38
Corporate firms, 12, 22, 96; public interest law and, 274, 277–87, 296–98; skill development in, 282–84; hegemonic separation in, 291–95; cause lawyers in, 352–53
Corporate social responsibility (CSR), 15, 37–39, 57–59, 60, 61n24
Corporations, 60, 425, 444–46
Corralito, 28, 383–84, 404–5
Courts, 13, 385; political change and, 308, 309–10; institutional structure in India, 355–56, 377n15; Indian lower, 356–57, 363–66, 376n8, 378n23; Indian high, 358–59, 366–69; Indian Supreme, 360–63, 369–72
CPT, *see* Consumer Project on Technology
CSR, *see* Corporate social responsibility
Cuba, 316
Cultural concepts: importation of, 65–66
Cut the Cost Campaign, 53

Daniels, Stephen, 455
Dara, 252
Dean, Howard, 183
Decision-making, 13, 24
Democracy, 336–37; liberal, 13–14; in Israel, 327–38; *amparo colectivo* and, 403f
Democratic Party, 90, 99, 434, 436
Demonstrations, 14, 49f
Denmark, 50
Desegregation, 264
Désintéressement, 69
Detention: in 1930s Europe, 151–52
Diflucan, 42

Dimitrov, 150
Disabled persons: in Argentina, 395–96
District of Columbia, 180, 445
Divorce law, 178, 192–93
Dobson, James, 86
Doctors Without Borders, *see* Medicins Sans Frontiers
Domestic relations practice, 192–93
Dreyfus Affair, 158
Drug companies, *see* Pharmaceutical manufacturers
Duhalde, Eduardo, 383f
Dworkin, Ronald, 131

Earth Justice International, 59
EarthRights International, 59
Easterbrook, Judge, 136
ECHR, *see* European Convention on Human Rights
Economic crisis: in Argentina, 383–84
Economic growth: laissez-faire, 117–18; government and, 118–19
Economic liberty: restoring, 103n7, 127–28
Economics: libertarian, 119–20, 123
Ecuador, 59
Education, 395; activist lawyers and, 97–98; and corporate firms, 281–82
Elevator regulation: in Buenos Aires, 395–96
Elites: and Israeli judicial community, 313–14, 330–31
Empathy: in client-lawyer relationships, 262–63
Employment discrimination law, 177
Environmentalism, 105n45; in India, 369–70
Environmental law, 113, 223–24
Epstein, Richard, 115, 123, 128, 136, 138, 142nn9, 13; on utilitarianism, 131–33
Equal access cases, 93
Equal rights, 186
Erie, Lake, 224
Estate planning, 193
Ethics, 63, 74

Ethnicity: in Israel, 316–17

European Commission, 61n24; South African Medicines Act amendment, 42–43; Medicins Sans Frontiers pressure on, 52–53

European Commissioner for Trade, 52

European Convention on Human Rights (ECHR), 411; and British immigration law, 413, 414–15, 417f, 421–22

European Court of Human Rights, 411

European Union, 43, 52–53, 59, 413

Evangelicals: Christian, 91, 98, 100

Evans, Stanton, 86

Evarts, William M., 119ff

ExxonMobil, 58f

Families: marriage and, 194–95

Family Court: in Israel, 329, 343n34

Family law practice, 177, 179, 184–85

Farnham, Lois, 180, 189

FDA, 93

Federalist Society, 19, 86, 113, 115–16, 117, 124, 130–31, 138, 142n7; founding of, 134–35; support for, 135–36; mission of, 136–37

Federal Rules of Civil Procedure (Argentina), 385f

Feldman, Avigdor, 328f

Feminism, 98–99, 103n7

Ferrucci, Jérôme, 153

Field, J. Stephen, 120

Fieri insurgents, 151

Fifth Amendment, 113, 118, 126, 140

Finances: law careers and, 279–80

Florida, 437f, 445, 453

Fluconazole, 49, 52

FNJ, see Front National des Juristes

Foissin, Robert, 157, 160–61

Fonteyne, Jean: The 44's Trial, 157f

Formalism, 318

Foucault, Michel, 240, 269n4

Fourteenth Amendment, 118f

44's Trial, The (Fonteyne), 157ff

France, 66, 419, 465; legal system in, 16–17, 164; political movements in, 19–20; labor law in, 63–65, 67–68, 77; political engagement in, 70–71, 79n42; activism in, 71–72; unions in, 73–75; jurisprudence work in, 75–76; World War II, 147–48, 159; AJI in, 151–53, 154–55; communists in, 156–57, 159–60; military tribunal in, 157–58; Vichy regime, 160–63

Freedom to Marry: A Green Mountain Valley, A (video), 189

Freeman, Alan, 134

French Peasants and Workers' Group (Groupe Ouvrier et Paysan Français), 157

Friedman, Milton, 86

Front National des Juristes (FNJ), 161f

Fry, Margaret, 152

Fuel emissions standards, 93

Gadoli, Giuseppe, 152

Garnier, Jean-Pierre, 54

Gaullist government, 20, 162

Gavison, Ruth, 328, 336; HCJ criticism and, 331–33

Gay and Lesbian Advocates and Defenders (GLAD), 173, 180, 196

Gay, lesbian, and bisexual rights, 172–73, 186, 193, 197, 199n5, 310; second-class citizen issues, 179–80; legal claims and, 184–85; client and clause relationships, 194–96

Gay rights, 175

Geneva Convention (1951), 29

Geneva Convention on the Status of Refugees, 412, 417

Germany, 50, 147, 156, 419

Gilbert, Pam, 439

GLAD, see Gay and Lesbian Advocates and Defenders

GlaxoSmithKline, 54, 60n1, 61n11

Globalization, 3–4, 50–51, 60

Goemaere, Eric, 51

Goering, Hermann, 150

Goldwater, Barry, 86
Gore, Al: HIV/AIDS activism and, 54–56; presidential campaign of, 436, 443
Government agencies: and legal services, 245, 247
Graglia, Lino, 136
Grassroots activism, 184, 403; and *Baker v. State*, 187–90
Great Britain, *see* United Kingdom
Greece: detention in, 151–52
Groupe Ouvrier et Paysan Français (French Peasants and Workers' Group), 157

Habush, Bob, 441
Hajje, Antoine, 161
Hamilton, In re, 179
Haredi, 333–35
Harrigan, Peter, 180
Harvard Law School, 130, 136
Hawaii, 173, 180
HCJ, *see* High Court of Justice
Health care, 46; Medicins Sans Frontières and, 51–53; corporate social responsibility and, 57–58
HealthGAP Coalition of the United States, 49–50
Hebrew University, 328
Hemdat, 328
Heritage Foundation, 87
Heyward, Mark, 48–49
Hierarchy, 24, 28
High Court of Justice (HCJ) (Israel), 26, 307–8, 310, 312, 315, 317, 341nn1, 2; issues heard by, 318–19, 341nn8, 9; lawyer-state relations and, 320–26; social movements, 326–30; elites and, 330–31; criticism of, 331–38; policy of, 338–40, 343–44n53
High Courts (India), 372–73; professionalism in, 350f
Hill, William C., 178, 198–99n2
HIV: treatments for, 16, 39–40; pharma-

ceutical companies and, 41–42, 60n1, 61n11; South African activism and, 44, 47–57
Hoffman (Women of the Wall) case, 328
Homosexual rights, 21–22; same-sex marriage and, 171, 172–73; legal claims and, 184–85
Howard League for Penal Reform, 152
HRA, *see* Human Rights Act
Humanitarianism, MSF, 51–52
Humanité, L' (newspaper), 161
Human rights, 10, 59, 60n2, 158, 370, 397, 401, 423n10; access to health care and, 46, 391; in South Africa, 47–48; AJI and, 152–53; litigation in, 175–76; in United Kingdom, 410, 421–22; immigration law and, 412–15, 416–18
Human Rights Act (HRA) (U.K.), 28–29, 175–76, 410–12, 422; legal challenges using, 414–15, 416–18; expectations for, 415–16
Human Rights League (Ligue des Droits de l'Homme), 153, 158
Hyderabad, 362

ICAR, *see* International Coalition of Augnah Rights
Identity, 97, 218; professional, 17–18, 84, 88–96, 114–15; as cause lawyer, 208–10; social movement and, 213–14; social constructionism and, 214–15; activist, 215–17, 224–26; organizational roles and, 220–24; social networks in, 232–33
Ideological work, 10–11
Ideology, 12, 17, 19, 87, 174f
IJ, *see* Institute for Justice
Illich, Ivan, 239, 268n1
Illinois, 438
Immigrants, 298; to Great Britain, 412–14
Immigration and Asylum Act (U.K.), 412–13
Immigration law: networking in, 230–31;

United Kingdom, 412, 423n4. *See also*
    Political asylum; Refugees
Impact litigation, 174–75
Incentives, 10
Income: lawyer, 450–52
India, 60n1, 376n10, 377n20; social capital
    in, 26–27; lawyers in, 350–52, 375nn3, 5,
    377n13, 465; court structure in, 355–56,
    377–78n22; lower courts in, 356–57,
    363–66, 373–74, 376n8, 377n17, 378n23;
    state high courts in, 358–59, 366–69,
    372–73
Indiana, 438
Indian Council for Environmental Legal
    Action, 370
Indian Supreme Court, 375n4, 376n11,
    377n14; transgressive behavior in,
    350–51, 358–63, 372–73; cause lawyering
    in, 366–72
Individual: state and, 132
Indonesia, 59
INGOs, *see* International nongovern-
    mental organizations
Institute for Justice (IJ), 11, 19, 120; orga-
    nization and activities of, 126–30
International Coalition of Augnah Rights
    (ICAR), 313, 328f
International Communist Movement,
    149
International Conference of Berlin, 149
International Labor Rights Fund, 59
International nongovernmental organiza-
    tions (INGOs), 50. *See also* Non-
    governmental organizations
International Red Help (IRH), 148f, 152ff
Israel, 342n11, 343n34; state and religious
    powers in, 26, 307–8, 341n1; judicial
    community in, 310–19; lawyer-state
    interactions in, 319–26; social move-
    ment alliances in, 326–30; criticism of
    HCJ in, 330–38; HCJ policy and,
    338–40, 341n2
Israel Bar Association, 315, 341n8; profes-
    sional conduct regulation, 308–9;

membership in, 311–12; and judicial
    community, 330–38
Israel Declaration of Independence, 327
Israel Movement for Progressive Judaism,
    313
Israel Women's Network (IWN), 313, 319,
    323–24, 326, 328f, 343n35
Italy, 50, 152
IWN, *see* Israel Women's Network

Japan, 403
Jaurès, Jean, 157
Jewish law (*Halakhah*), 307, 317
Jewishness; definition of, 307, 341n1
JoAnn, 254–55
Jolles, Stacy, 180, 189, 194–95
Jouvenel, Renaud de, 151
Judges: activism of, 127, 128–29, 411,
    422–23n3; Federalist Society and,
    136–37; Human Rights Act and, 416–17
Judge's Law (Israel), 317
Judicial community: in Israel, 26, 308,
    310–19; lawyer-state interactions in,
    319–26; social movement alliances
    and, 326–30; Israel Bar community
    and, 330–38
Judicial Institute (ATLA), 441
Judicial system: in Argentina, 389–91
Judiciary: inconsistent decisions and,
    390–91, 406n13; legal culture in,
    392–93
Judiciary Resistance, 147
Juries, 455–56
Jurisprudence, 129, 138; Federalist Society
    and, 136–37

Kaldor, Pierre, 153
Kaur, Manish, 367–68
Ken Sero-Wiwa, 59
Kentucky, 180
Ketchum, Chester, 179
Kisch, D. M., Inc., 40–41, 45
Knesset: and High Court of Justice, 317,
    323–24

Knowledge: client, 246–48

Kurdish refugees, 420–21

Labor law, 153; in France, 16–17, 63–65, 67–68, 71

Labour government: asylum seekers and, 412, 414

Laissez-faire, 139; economic growth and, 117–18; legal system and, 118–19

LAMBDA Legal Defense and Education Fund Inc. (LAMBDA), 173, 179, 196; *Baker v. State*, 182, 199n4

Lamy, Pascal, 52

Landmark Legal Foundation, 126

Langdellian case law method, 119

Langrock, Peter, 178f, 191–92

Langrock, Sperry and Wool (LSW), 22, 178; gay, lesbian, and bisexual rights and, 172, 179, 196; structure of, 191–93, 200n12

Large firms, 94, 96; professional identity and, 89–91

Law: as political tool, 66–67; cause of, 463–67

Law and economics movement, 130–31

Law and Society Movement, 66f

Law school clinics, 211f

Law School Institute (ATLA), 441

Law schools: conservatives in, 134–35, 136

Lawyer-client relationships, 7, 102nn1, 2, 190, 241–42, 270n16, 271n22; same-sex marriage issues, 194–96; collaboration, 250–58; personal, 258–67

Lawyers: as activists, 203–4, 208–10; in Israel, 308–9, 311–12, 313–14; trial, 427–44, 453–55; public image of, 446–50; divisions among, 450–53

Left, 422n3; activism for, 85, 99, 105–6n58, 205

Left-activist lawyering, 240–41, 169n7

Legal academy: liberalism of, 137–38

Legal aid: French labor law, 67f

Legal claims: homosexual rights and, 184–85

Legality, 8–9

Legal realism, 122, 137–38

Legal reform, 453–56; calls for, 426–27; trial lawyers and, 427–33, 436–37

Legal science, 120–21

Legal services, 212, 242–43, 245–46, 293

Legal Services Corporation (LSC), 212, 243

Legal systems: French, 16–17, 164; South African, 58

Leipzig trial, 150

Lenin, V. I., 149f, 155

Liberalism, 8, 17–18, 98, 121; activism of, 88, 116; of legal academy, 137–38

Libertarians, 17f, 84, 86, 126, 137f; and conservatism, 87–88; lawyering for, 92–94, 95; economic, 119–20, 123

Liberties: defending, 97, 155; economic, 127–28

Ligue des Droits de l'Homme (Human Rights League), 153

Liz, 248, 265

Lobbying, 14; HIV/AIDS, 54–57; by ATLA, 435–36

Lochner era, 138

Lok Adalats, 366, 377–78nn17, 22

London, 415

Lost-cause lawyering, 14

Love, James: HIV/AIDS activism, 54–56, 57

LSC, *see* Legal Services Corporation

LSW, *see* Langrock, Sperry and Wool

Lyons, James: "The Not-So Simple Crisis," 440

Malloy, Robin Paul, 134

Mandela, Nelson, 466–67

Maoism, 71f

Marches: protest, 49–50

Marcia, 259–60

Marcus, Gilbert, 48f

Marginalization: of gays, lesbians, and bisexuals, 185–86

Marjorie, 253, 264

Marriage: same-sex, 171–72, 180–83, 188, 194–96, 199nn9, 10, 406n14
Martin, Joanne, 455
Mary, 245
Masorti Movement in Israel, 326, 328
Massachusetts, 171–72, 199n9
Massachusetts Environmental Law Society, 59
Massachusetts Supreme Judicial Court, 171
Mbeki, Thabo Mvuyelwa, 42, 52
McCorvey, Norma, 264–65
Medicins Sans Frontiers (MSF), 50, 54; HIV/AIDS activism, 51–53, 56
Meese, Edwin, 125, 135
Megacorporate practices: as meritocracy, 281–82
Mehta, M. C., 369–70
Mellor, William, 126, 128
Menem, Carlos, 384
Merck Inc., 41–42, 61n11
Meretz Party, 337
Meritocracy, 281–82
Mexico, 239
Militants: French, 72–73; self-defense of, 149–50; AJI lawyers as, 154–56, 161
Military tribunal: in France, 157–58
Miller, Samuel, 120
Miller v. California, 100
Mills, C. Wright, 313–14
Ministry of Justice (Israel), 316f
Minnesota, 180
Mizrahi, 333
MNC, see Multinational corporations
Mobilization, 11; political, 13–14
Momboisse, Raymond, 125, 142n8
Moral advocacy, 1, 2–3, 102
Moral harassment, 76
Moro-Giafferi, Ernest Charles de, 152
Mountain States Legal Foundation, 126
Movement for Progressive Judaism, 326, 328f, 337
Multinational corporations (MNCs), 16, 37, 59

Multnomah County (Ore.), 171
Munn v. Illinois, 120
Murray, Susan, 21–22, 172f, 178, 197f; domestic relations practice, 177, 179–80, 192–93; Baker v. State, 180–83, 187–90; gay and lesbian rights, 184–86, 195–96

NAACP, see National Association for the Advancement of Colored People
Naamat, 326, 328ff
Nader, Ralph, 425, 443, 454; HIV/AIDS activism, 50, 54–56; Association of Trial Lawyers of America and, 429–30; No Contest, 439, 444
National Association for Law Placement (NALP), 208
National Association for the Advancement of Colored People (NAACP), 103n7, 116, 122
National Coalition for Gay and Lesbian Equality (South Africa), 47f
National Highway Transportation Safety Administration, 93
National Institute for Trial Advocacy (NITA), 282
National Insurance Consumer Organization, 430
Nationality, Immigration and Asylum Act (U.K.), 413
National Lawyer's Guild (NLG), 226–27, 228
National Legal Center for the Public Interest (NLCPI), 126
National membership: Israel, 316–17
National Organization for Women, 182
National Organization of Collective Law Offices (ONBC), 316
Natural justice, 315
Natural rights, 123, 133
Nazis: occupation of France, 20, 159, 160–63
Nazi-Soviet pact, 158–59
Neighborhood legal clinics, 293
NELS, see Northeast Legal Services

Netherlands: NGOs in, 52–53
Networking, 230–31
Neuhaus, Richard John, 86
Nevo case, 328–29
New Delhi, 362f
New Israel Fund (NIF), 327–28
New Mexico, 171
New Paltz (N.Y.), 171
Newsom, Gavin, 171
New York state, 171, 180, 198n1
Ngoepe, Bernard, 45
NGOs, *see* Nongovernmental organizations
NIF, *see* New Israel Fund
Nigeria, 59
Nino, Ezequiel, 396
NITA, *see* National Institute for Trial Advocacy
NLCPI, *see* National Legal Center for the Public Interest
NLG, *see* National Lawyer's Guild
No Contest (Nader and Smith), 439, 444
Nongovernmental organizations (NGOs): in South Africa, 15f; HIV/AIDS activism, 52–57; in India, 358–59, 363–64, 367, 370f; in Argentina, 391, 393–96, 399, 402. *See also by name*
Nordmann, Joë, 151, 153f, 161, 163
Northeast Legal Services (NELS), 24, 242, 265, 270n18; operations of, 243–45; client-lawyer relationships in, 245–50, 259–67, 270n16; collaborative efforts of, 253–58
Norton, Gale, 136
"Not-So Simple Crisis, The" (Brill and Lyons), 440

Obscenity decision, 100
Office of Attorney General (Israel), 316
Office of Economic Opportunity, 243
Ohio, 437f
OI, *see* Oxfam International
ONBC, *see* National Organization of Collective Law Offices

Opposition lawyers: in India, 355–56
Oregon, 171, 438
Organizational roles: identity and, 220–24
Originalism, 137
Ottoman Law, 317
Oxfam International, 50, 53–54, 60

Pacific Law Foundation, 19
Pacific Legal Foundation (PLF), 115, 124–26, 128f, 142n10
PACs, *see* Political Action Committees
Palestinians, 314
Parker, Alan A., 433, 448
Parliament: French, 157, 158–59
Patel, Kiran, 367f
Patent rights: pharmaceutical, 40f, 42f, 55
Pay equity, 76, 217
Pay phone charges: in Argentina, 393–94
Peck, Robert, 438
People's Union for Democratic Rights (PUDR), 368
Perez v. Sharp, 181
Personal injury law, 177, 192, 447, 455–56; in United States, 428–33
Personal rights, 121
Pete, 245–46, 266–67
Pfizer Inc., 42, 49, 52
PharMA, *see* American Pharmaceutical Manufacturers Association
Pharmaceutical manufacturers, 60n1; AIDS medications and, 15–16; drug act amendments and, 39–41, 46–47, 60–61n7; social responsibility campaign, 41–42; Oxfam pressure on, 53–54
Pharmaceutical Manufacturers' Association (PMA): drug act amendments and, 40–41; and South African Medicines Act amendment case and, 43–47, 49, 57, 60–61n7
Philippines, 50
Picturing Justice: The Online Journal of Law and Popular Culture, 447

PILPs, *see* Public interest law persisters
Pitard, Georges, 161
Plessy v. Ferguson, 118
PLF, *see* Pacific Legal Foundation
PMA, *see* Pharmaceutical Manufacturers' Association
Police power, 118
Policy Activist Seminars, 126
Political Action Committees (PACs), 434–35, 436
Political asylum: in United Kingdom, 412–22, 423–24nn6, 13
Political change: courts and, 308, 309–10
Political lawyering, 14; in France, 17, 70–71, 72
Political movements: in France, 19–20
Politics, 8–9, 102nn1, 3, 116, 180, 224; engagement in, 70–71, 79n42; cause lawyering and, 86, 205, 384; professional identity and, 90–91, 224; activism and, 97–98, 112; impact litigation and, 174–75; and ATLA, 433–37
Poor: as legal services clients, 243
Popular Front, 151, 153f
Poraz case, 329, 333
Pornography cases, 93, 95, 100, 103n7
Positivism, 318
Posner, Richard, 115, 123, 134, 136ff, 142n13; *The Problems of Jurisprudence*, 133
Pound Foundation, Roscoe, 442
Poverty, 107n94, 239, 249, 269–70n10
Practices: and types of work, 21–22, 206–7
Practice site: conditions of, 11–12
Prestige: professional, 351–52, 368–69, 375–76nn5, 11, 378n24, 429
Principles of the Civil Code (Bentham), 118
Private practice, 12, 21–22; public interest cases in, 176–77, 191–96
Private property, 113, 132, 141n2, 407n20
Problems of Jurisprudence, The (Posner), 133
Pro bono programs, 12, 177, 402; at private firms, 192, 292–95; litigators and, 288–89; in India, 363f

Processing centers: refugee, 413
Profession: status within, 67–68
Professionalism, 1, 8–9, 101, 102n1; and activism, 22–23, 226–34, 466–67; and hierarchy, 24, 240–42; in French law, 69–70; in Israel, 308–9; in India, 350–51, 368–69, 375–76nn3, 5, 378n24
Progressive Era, 123
Progressive lawyering, 24, 228, 241f, 269nn8, 9
Property rights, 18–19, 99, 118, 121, 123f, 132, 376n8; intellectual, 40, 42, 55; advocacy for, 113–15, 129–30, 140–41; capitalism and, 116–17
Protests: against pharmaceutical companies, 53–54
Public Citizen, 429, 439
Public education campaign: on gay, lesbian, and bisexual rights, 187–89; ATLA, 441–42
Public Education Institute (ATLA), 441–42
Public health system: in South Africa, 41
Public housing, 247, 249, 255–56
Public Housing Authority, 256
Public interest, 129, 291, 295, 439; working in, 89, 104n17, 106n81, 107–8n95, 178, 191–92; law firms and, 191–92; activism in, 222–23, 230–31
Public interest law, 25, 122, 176, 274f, 396, 425; careers in, 226, 289–90; education in, 276–77; and corporate practices, 277–82, 284–87; skill development and, 282–84; issues in, 287–298; in India, 358–59; and Association of Trial Lawyers of America, 429–30
Public interest law centers, 211f
Public interest law persisters (PILPs), 25, 291, 296
Public opinion, 446–48
Public relations, 41; ATLA, 454–55
Public service: of Langrock, Sperry and Wool, 191–92, 193
Pucheu, Pierre, 162

PUDR, *see* People's Union for Democratic Rights
Puga, Mariela, 392f
Punitive damages cases, 89
Puterbaugh, Holly, 180, 189

Queer Town Meeting, 189

Raday, Frances, 318–19, 322–23; and *Nevo* case, 328f
Rand, Ayn, 86
Reagan, Ronald, 99, 113, 125, 134ff, 142nn8, 9
Reconstruction, 139
Refugee Convention, *see* Geneva Convention on the Status of Refugees
Refugees, 152, 257, 412–21, 423n6
Regev, Uri, 328ff
Religion, 327
Religious groups, 91, 92–94, 95, 98, 182, 188
Religious law, 315–16, 318f
Religious liberties, 93f, 107n83
Religious organizations, 95–96, 107n86
Religious pluralism movement, 326, 328
Religious powers: and state, 26, 307–8
Religious rights, 99
Repression, 150
Republican Party, 91, 436
Research Institute (ATLA), 442
Resistance movement: in France, 20, 161–63
Resnick, Alice Robie, 437
Resource mobilization theory, 203
Retainer model, 245–46
Rights consciousness raising, 10
Right-wing advocacy, 112–13, 140–41
Robinson, Beth, 21–22, 172f, 197f; domestic relations practice of, 177, 178–80, 192f; *Baker v. State*, 180–83, 187–90; gay and lesbian rights, 184–86, 195–96
Roe v. Wade, 99, 264–65, 309
Role identity, 218–19

Rolnikas, Michael, 161
Rosenblum, Jonathan, 335–36, 343n44
Rostrup, Morten, 52
Rule of law: in Israel, 321–22; in Argentina, 403f
Rumania: detention in, 151–52
Russian initiative for peace, 157
Rustad, Michael, 442

Saba, Roberto, 383
SAJHR, see South Africa Journal of Human Rights
Sanctions Law (Israel), 329
Sander County, 456
Sandoval County (N.M.), 171
San Francisco, 171
Schaeffer, Francis, 86
Schattschneider, E. E., 426
Scheingold-Bloom argument: on transgressiveness, 352–54
Schwartz, Victor, 433, 437
Seattle-King County Bar Associations, 293
Secrecy: corporate, 444–46
Self-defense, 92, 150
Self-regulation: professional, 309
Sexuality, 173, 184
Shah, Sanjay, 364–65
Shakdiel case, 329, 333
Shamgar, Meir, 318
Shas, 335
Shaskelson, Arthur, 48
Shaskelson, Matthew, 48
Shavit, Ari, 336
Sheleg, Yair, 334
Shell, 58f
Singh, Priya, 367ff, 373
Sivan, Esther, 328
Skill development: public interest law, 282–84
Slaughter-House Cases, 119–20, 127
Slavery, 120
Small firms, 12
Smith, Wesley: *No Contest*, 439, 444

Social capital, 3, 25, 74; in India, 26–27, 375–76n5

Social change, 112, 239–40, 309; class actions and, 387–89

Social constructionism: identity and, 214–15

Social Democratic Labor Party, 149

Social justice, 240, 259, 274, 298, 299–300; Israel, 327–38

Social movements, 15, 31n6, 190, 274; in France, 16–17; and practice types, 21–22; impact litigation, 174–75; lawyers in, 205–6, 217–20, 337; collective identity and, 213–14; social constructionism and, 214–15; activist identities and, 215–16; advocacy, 314–15; High Court of Justice and, 323, 326–30

Social movement theory, 203f, 205–6

Social networks: activist identities and, 232–33

Social responsibility, 57; of multinational corporations, 37–38, 41–42; defining, 38–39. See also Corporate social responsibility

Social Security Disability Insurance, 251

Social Security Ministry (U.K.), 418–19

Society of Nations, 152

Sociolegal research, 213

South Africa: HIV/AIDS activism in, 15–16, 47–57; drug act amendments in, 39–43; PMA case against, 43–47; corporate social responsibility in, 57–58

South Africa Journal of Human Rights (SAJHR), 48

South African Medicines and Related Substances Control Act No. 101: amendments to, 39–43; PMA case against, 43–47; United States policy toward, 54–55, 60–61n7

Southeastern Legal Foundation, 126

Soviet Union, 157; and Nazi Germany, 156, 158, 161

Special 301 Watch list, 42

State, 132; and religious powers, 26, 307–8

State transformation, 3–4

Status: of French workers' attorneys, 67–68. See also Prestige

Steele, Theodora, 42

Steve, 258, 263

Stewart, Larry, 441

"Stop class Action Abuse," 453

Structure, 4; and agency, 5–6

Sunshine in Litigation Act (Florida), 445

Sydney, 50

Syndicat des Avocats de France, 74

TAC, see Treatment Action Campaign

Takings: Private Property and the Power of Eminent Domain (Epstein), 131

"Talking Points on the South African Case," 41

Task Force, see Vermont Freedom to Marry Task Force

Taxation, 132

Telephone calls, 390, 393–94

Texaco, 59

Texas: trial lawyers in, 437, 453, 455–56

Thailand, 50

Thatcher, Margaret, 412

Think tanks, 95f, 107n83

Third Republic, communist suppression during, 156–57, 164

TLPJ, see Trial Lawyers for Public Justice

Torrente, Nicolas de, 53

Tort system, 132; reform of, 29–30, 89, 101, 104n17, 426–27; in United States, 428–33; ATLA and, 437–43; challenging, 453–56

Trade associations, 89

Transgressiveness, 102n3; of Indian lawyers, 350–51; Scheingold-Bloom argument on, 352–54; Indian lower courts, 356–57, 373–74; Indian High and Supreme courts, 358–63, 369–73

Treatment Action Campaign (TAC), 16, 48; and South African Medicines Act amendment case, 43–46, 47; activism in, 49–50, 53f; and Medicins Sans Frontiers, 51–52

Treatise on the Constitutional Limitations which Rest Upon the Legislative Powers of the States of the American Union, A (Cooley), 118

Trial Lawyers for Public Justice (TLPJ), 430, 445, 453

Trials: open vs. closed, 157–58; right to, 443–44

Tribe, Laurence, 136

TRIPS, *see* Agreement on Trade Related Aspects of Intellectual Property Rights

Turkey: Kurdish refugees in, 420–21

UJC-ML, *see* Union des Jeunes Communistes Marxistes-Léninistes

Ultra-orthodox Jews: criticism of High Court of Justices, 333–35

Umphrey, Walter, 436

UNAIDs, *see* United Nations Joint Project on AIDS

Union des Jeunes Communistes Marxistes-Léninistes (UJC-ML), 71

Unions, 89, 93; in France, 17, 68, 71–75, 77n7

Union Sinaltrainal, 59

Unitarian Universalist Church, 188

United Kingdom: Human Rights Act in, 28–29, 50, 53; human rights in, 176, 410–11, 466; political asylum in, 412–22, 423n6

United Nations, 413

United Nations Joint Project on Aids (UNAIDS), 47

United States, 2, 396f, 466; conservative and libertarian causes in, 17–18; property rights movement in, 18–19; tort system in, 29–30; South African Medicines Act amendment and, 42f, 60–61n7; HIV/AIDS activism in, 50, 54–56; corporate social responsibility and, 58–59; same-sex marriage issues

in, 171–72; legal reform in, 426–27; lawsuits in, 427–28; personal injury law in, 428–33

U.S. Congress: HIV/AIDS issues, 56

U.S. Department of State, 42

U.S. Role in Combating the Global HIV/AIDS Epidemic, 56

U.S. Supreme Court, 100, 119ff; *amicus* briefs, 125, 128; conservative critiques of, 135, 138

United States Trade Representatives (USTR), 42

Université Libre, L' (Free University), 161

University of Chicago School of Law, 130f, 136

University of Palermo, 397, 401

Unocal, 58–59

USTR, *see* United States Trade Representatives

Utilitarianism: Richard Epstein on, 131–33

Vancouver (B.C.), 50

Verma, Ravi, 365–66, 377n17

Vermaak, Nico, 40–41

Vermont, 180; Civil Union Law in, 172, 183; family law practice in, 177, 179; constitution of, 178, 198–99n2; gay, lesbian, and bisexual rights in, 185–86, 199nn3, 5, 8, 406n14; grassroots activism in, 187–90

Vermonters for Civil Union Legislative Defense Fund, 189

Vermont Freedom to Marry Task Force, 187–89, 194, 199–200n11

Vermont Organization for Weddings of the Same Gender (VOWS), 188

Vermont Psychiatric Association: *Baker v. State*, 182

Vermont Supreme Court, 172; same-sex marriage case in, 181–83

Vichy regime, 20; communists under, 160–63, 164

Videos, 189

Vienney, Paul, 153, 159

Volunteers: of grassroots efforts, 188–89
Von Ribbentrop-Molotov Pact, 147
VOWS, *see* Vermont Organization for
    Weddings of the Same Gender

Washington Legal Foundation, 126
Wealth maximization, 131–32
Weddington, Sarah, 264–65
Western Cape, 51
Willard, Marcel, 20, 153, 155, 159, 161, 163,
    157f; and AJI, 147, 148–49, 151, 154; on
    self-defense, 149–50
Wilson, Harold, 412
Women of the Wall, 328
Women's movement, 326, 328
Women's organizations, in Israel,
    328–30
Women's rights, 319, 330, 370–71
Workers' attorneys, 77, 78n23, 79n36;
    French law and, 67–68; professional
    views of, 69–70; political engagement,
    70–71; as career stage, 71–72; and

unions, 73–75; jurisprudence work in,
    75–76
Working Group on Research and Devel-
    opment for Drugs for Neglected Dis-
    eases, 54
Work settings; of cause lawyers, 210–13;
    core activists and, 221–22; identity
    and, 223–24
World Bank, 59
World Trade Organization (WTO), 42,
    50, 55f, 59
World War II, French communists dur-
    ing, 19–20, 147
WTO, *see* World Trade Organization

Yadin, Yigal, 328
Yale Law School, 130, 134, 136
Yossef, David, 335
Yossef, Ovadia, 335

Zévaès, Alexandre, 157–58
Zumbrun, Ronald, 125